Martin Haugh

Essays on the sacred language, writings, and religion of the parsis

Martin Haugh

Essays on the sacred language, writings, and religion of the parsis

ISBN/EAN: 9783337085773

Printed in Europe, USA, Canada, Australia, Japan

Cover: Foto ©Lupo / pixelio.de

More available books at **www.hansebooks.com**

TRÜBNER'S ORIENTAL SERIES.

"A knowledge of the commonplace, at least, of Oriental literature, philosophy, and religion is as necessary to the general reader of the present day as an acquaintance with the Latin and Greek classics was a generation or so ago. Immense strides have been made within the present century in these branches of learning; Sanskrit has been brought within the range of accurate philology, and its invaluable ancient literature thoroughly investigated; the language and sacred books of the Zoroastrians have been laid bare; Egyptian, Assyrian, and other records of the remote past have been deciphered, and a group of scholars speak of still more recondite Accadian and Hittite monuments; but the results of all the scholarship that has been devoted to these subjects have been almost inaccessible to the public because they were contained for the most part in learned or expensive works, or scattered throughout the numbers of scientific periodicals. Messrs. TRÜBNER & Co., in a spirit of enterprise which does them infinite credit, have determined to supply the constantly-increasing want, and to give in a popular, or, at least, a comprehensive form, all this mass of knowledge to the world."—*Times*.

Second Edition, post 8vo, pp. xxxii.—748, with Map, cloth, price 21s.

THE INDIAN EMPIRE :
ITS PEOPLE, HISTORY, AND PRODUCTS.

By the HON. SIR W. W. HUNTER, K.C.S.I., C.S.I., C.I.E., LL.D.,

Member of the Viceroy's Legislative Council,

Director-General of Statistics to the Government of India.

Being a Revised Edition, brought up to date, and incorporating the general results of the Census of 1881.

"It forms a volume of more than 700 pages, and is a marvellous combination of literary condensation and research. It gives a complete account of the Indian Empire, its history, peoples, and products, and forms the worthy outcome of seventeen years of labour with exceptional opportunities for rendering that labour fruitful. Nothing could be more lucid than Sir William Hunter's expositions of the economic and political condition of India at the present time, or more interesting than his scholarly history of the India of the past."—*The Times*.

THE FOLLOWING WORKS HAVE ALREADY APPEARED:—

Third Edition, post 8vo, cloth, pp. xvi.—428, price 16s.

ESSAYS ON THE SACRED LANGUAGE, WRITINGS, AND RELIGION OF THE PARSIS.

BY MARTIN HAUG, PH.D.,

Late of the Universities of Tübingen, Göttingen, and Bonn; Superintendent of Sanskrit Studies, and Professor of Sanskrit in the Poona College.

EDITED AND ENLARGED BY DR. E. W. WEST.

To which is added a Biographical Memoir of the late Dr. HAUG by Prof. E. P. EVANS.

I. History of the Researches into the Sacred Writings and Religion of the Parsis, from the Earliest Times down to the Present.
II. Languages of the Parsi Scriptures.
III. The Zend-Avesta, or the Scripture of the Parsis.
IV. The Zoroastrian Religion, as to its Origin and Development.

"'Essays on the Sacred Language, Writings, and Religion of the Parsis,' by the late Dr. Martin Haug, edited by Dr. E. W. West. The author intended, on his return from India, to expand the materials contained in this work into a comprehensive account of the Zoroastrian religion, but the design was frustrated by his untimely death. We have, however, in a concise and readable form, a history of the researches into the sacred writings and religion of the Parsis from the earliest times down to the present—a dissertation on the languages of the Parsi Scriptures, a translation of the Zend-Avesta, or the Scripture of the Parsis, and a dissertation on the Zoroastrian religion, with especial reference to its origin and development."—*Times.*

Post 8vo, cloth, pp. viii.—176, price 7s. 6d.

TEXTS FROM THE BUDDHIST CANON

COMMONLY KNOWN AS "DHAMMAPADA."

With Accompanying Narratives.

Translated from the Chinese by S. BEAL, B.A., Professor of Chinese, University College, London.

The Dhammapada, as hitherto known by the Pali Text Edition, as edited by Fausböll, by Max Müller's English, and Albrecht Weber's German translations, consists only of twenty-six chapters or sections, whilst the Chinese version, or rather recension, as now translated by Mr. Beal, consists of thirty-nine sections. The students of Pali who possess Fausböll's text, or either of the above named translations, will therefore needs want Mr. Beal's English rendering of the Chinese version; the thirteen abovenamed additional sections not being accessible to them in any other form; for, even if they understand Chinese, the Chinese original would be unobtainable by them.

"Mr. Beal's rendering of the Chinese translation is a most valuable aid to the critical study of the work. It contains authentic texts gathered from ancient canonical books, and generally connected with some incident in the history of Buddha. Their great interest, however, consists in the light which they throw upon everyday life in India at the remote period at which they were written, and upon the method of teaching adopted by the founder of the religion. The method employed was principally parable, and the simplicity of the tales and the excellence of the morals inculcated, as well as the strange hold which they have retained upon the minds of millions of people, make them a very remarkable study."—*Times.*

"Mr. Beal, by making it accessible in an English dress, has added to the great services he has already rendered to the comparative study of religions history."—*Academy.*

"Valuable as exhibiting the doctrine of the Buddhists in its purest, least adulterated form, it brings the modern reader face to face with that simple creed and rule of conduct which won its way over the minds of myriads, and which is now nominally professed by 145 millions, who have overlaid its austere simplicity with innumerable ceremonies, forgotten its maxims, perverted its teaching, and so inverted its leading principle that a religion whose founder denied a God, now worships that founder as a god himself."—*Scotsman.*

Second Edition, post 8vo, cloth, pp. xxiv.—360, price 10s. 6d.

THE HISTORY OF INDIAN LITERATURE.
By ALBRECHT WEBER.

Translated from the Second German Edition by JOHN MANN, M.A., and THÉODOR ZACHARIAE, Ph.D., with the sanction of the Author.

Dr. BUHLER, Inspector of Schools in India, writes:—"When I was Professor of Oriental Languages in Elphinstone College, I frequently felt the want of such a work to which I could refer the students."

Professor COWELL, of Cambridge, writes:—"It will be especially useful to the students in our Indian colleges and universities. I used to long for such a book when I was teaching in Calcutta. Hindu students are intensely interested in the history of Sanskrit literature, and this volume will supply them with all they want on the subject."

Professor WHITNEY, Yale College, Newhaven, Conn., U.S.A., writes:— "I was one of the class to whom the work was originally given in the form of academic lectures. At their first appearance they were by far the most learned and able treatment of their subject; and with their recent additions they still maintain decidedly the same rank."

"Is perhaps the most comprehensive and lucid survey of Sanskrit literature extant. The essays contained in the volume were originally delivered as academic lectures, and at the time of their first publication were acknowledged to be by far the most learned and able treatment of the subject. They have now been brought up to date by the addition of all the most important results of recent research."—*Times.*

Post 8vo, cloth, pp. xii.—198, accompanied by Two Language Maps, price 7s. 6d.

A SKETCH OF
THE MODERN LANGUAGES OF THE EAST INDIES.
By ROBERT N. CUST.

The Author has attempted to fill up a vacuum, the inconvenience of which pressed itself on his notice. Much had been written about the languages of the East Indies, but the extent of our present knowledge had not even been brought to a focus. It occurred to him that it might be of use to others to publish in an arranged form the notes which he had collected for his own edification.

"Supplies a deficiency which has long been felt."—*Times.*

"The book before us is then a valuable contribution to philological science. It passes under review a vast number of languages, and it gives, or professes to give, in every case the sum and substance of the opinions and judgments of the best-informed writers."—*Saturday Review.*

Second Corrected Edition, post 8vo, pp. xii.—116, cloth, price 5s.

THE BIRTH OF THE WAR-GOD.
A Poem. By KALIDASA.
Translated from the Sanskrit into English Verse by
RALPH T. H. GRIFFITH, M.A.

"A very spirited rendering of the *Kumárasambhava*, which was first published twenty-six years ago, and which we are glad to see made once more accessible."— *Times.*

"Mr. Griffith's very spirited rendering is well known to most who are at all interested in Indian literature, or enjoy the tenderness of feeling and rich creative imagination of its author."—*Indian Antiquary.*

"We are very glad to welcome a second edition of Professor Griffith's admirable translation. Few translations deserve a second edition better."—*Athenæum.*

Post 8vo. pp. 432, cloth, price 16s.
A CLASSICAL DICTIONARY OF HINDU MYTHOLOGY AND RELIGION, GEOGRAPHY, HISTORY, AND LITERATURE.
By JOHN DOWSON, M.R.A.S.,
Late Professor of Hindustani, Staff College.

"This not only forms an indispensable book of reference to students of Indian literature, but is also of great general interest, as it gives in a concise and easily accessible form all that need be known about the personages of Hindu mythology whose names are so familiar, but of whom so little is known outside the limited circle of *savants*."—*Times.*

"It is no slight gain when such subjects are treated fairly and fully in a moderate space; and we need only add that the few wants which we may hope to see supplied in new editions detract but little from the general excellence of Mr. Dowson's work."
—*Saturday Review.*

Post 8vo, with View of Mecca, pp. cxii.—172, cloth, price 9s.
SELECTIONS FROM THE KORAN.
By EDWARD WILLIAM LANE,
Translator of "The Thousand and One Nights;" &c., &c.
A New Edition, Revised and Enlarged, with an Introduction by
STANLEY LANE POOLE.

". . . Has been long esteemed in this country as the compilation of one of the greatest Arabic scholars of the time, the late Mr. Lane, the well-known translator of the 'Arabian Nights.' . . . The present editor has enhanced the value of his relative's work by divesting the text of a great deal of extraneous matter introduced by way of comment, and prefixing an introduction."—*Times.*

"Mr. Poole is both a generous and a learned biographer. . . . Mr. Poole tells us the facts . . . so far as it is possible for industry and criticism to ascertain them, and for literary skill to present them in a condensed and readable form."—*Englishman, Calcutta.*

Post 8vo, pp. vi.—368, cloth, price 14s.
MODERN INDIA AND THE INDIANS,
BEING A SERIES OF IMPRESSIONS, NOTES, AND ESSAYS.
By MONIER WILLIAMS, D.C.L.,
Hon. LL.D. of the University of Calcutta, Hon. Member of the Bombay Asiatic Society, Boden Professor of Sanskrit in the University of Oxford.
Third Edition, revised and augmented by considerable Additions, with Illustrations and a Map.

"In this volume we have the thoughtful impressions of a thoughtful man on some of the most important questions connected with our Indian Empire. . . . An enlightened observant man, travelling among an enlightened observant people, Professor Monier Williams has brought before the public in a pleasant form more of the manners and customs of the Queen's Indian subjects than we ever remember to have seen in any one work. He not only deserves the thanks of every Englishman for this able contribution to the study of Modern India—a subject with which we should be specially familiar—but he deserves the thanks of every Indian, Parsee or Hindu, Buddhist and Moslem, for his clear exposition of their manners, their creeds, and their necessities."—*Times.*

Post 8vo, pp. xliv.—376, cloth, price 14s.
METRICAL TRANSLATIONS FROM SANSKRIT WRITERS.
With an Introduction, many Prose Versions, and Parallel Passages from Classical Authors.
By J. MUIR, C.I.E., D.C.L., LL.D., Ph.D.

". . . An agreeable introduction to Hindu poetry."—*Times.*

". . . A volume which may be taken as a fair illustration alike of the religious and moral sentiments and of the legendary lore of the best Sanskrit writers."—*Edinburgh Daily Review.*

Second Edition, post 8vo, pp. xxvi.—244, cloth, price 10s. 6d.

THE GULISTAN;
OR, ROSE GARDEN OF SHEKH MUSHLIU'D-DIN SADI OF SHIRAZ.

Translated for the First Time into Prose and Verse, with an Introductory Preface, and a Life of the Author, from the Atish Kadah,

BY EDWARD B. EASTWICK, C.B., M.A., F.R.S., M.R.A.S.

"It is a very fair rendering of the original."—*Times.*

"The new edition has long been desired, and will be welcomed by all who take any interest in Oriental poetry. The *Gulistan* is a typical Persian verse-book of the highest order. Mr. Eastwick's rhymed translation . . . has long established itself in a secure position as the best version of Sadi's finest work."—*Academy.*

"It is both faithfully and gracefully executed."—*Tablet.*

In Two Volumes, post 8vo, pp. viii.—408 and viii.—348, cloth, price 28s.

MISCELLANEOUS ESSAYS RELATING TO INDIAN SUBJECTS.

BY BRIAN HOUGHTON HODGSON, ESQ., F.R.S.,

Late of the Bengal Civil Service; Corresponding Member of the Institute; Chevalier of the Legion of Honour; late British Minister at the Court of Nepal, &c., &c.

CONTENTS OF VOL. I.

SECTION I.—On the Kocch, Bódó, and Dhimál Tribes.—Part I. Vocabulary.—Part II. Grammar.—Part III. Their Origin, Location, Numbers, Creed, Customs, Character, and Condition, with a General Description of the Climate they dwell in.—Appendix.

SECTION II.—On Himalayan Ethnology.—I. Comparative Vocabulary of the Languages of the Broken Tribes of Népál.—II. Vocabulary of the Dialects of the Kiranti Language.—III. Grammatical Analysis of the Váyu Language. The Váyu Grammar.—IV. Analysis of the Báhing Dialect of the Kiranti Language. The Báhing Grammar.—V. On the Váyu or Hayu Tribe of the Central Himaláya.—VI. On the Kiranti Tribe of the Central Himaláya.

CONTENTS OF VOL. II.

SECTION III.—On the Aborigines of North-Eastern India. Comparative Vocabulary of the Tibetan, Bódó, and Gáró Tongues.

SECTION IV.—Aborigines of the North-Eastern Frontier.

SECTION V.—Aborigines of the Eastern Frontier.

SECTION VI.—The Indo-Chinese Borderers, and their connection with the Himalayans and Tibetans. Comparative Vocabulary of Indo-Chinese Borderers in Arakan. Comparative Vocabulary of Indo-Chinese Borderers in Tenasserim.

SECTION VII.—The Mongolian Affinities of the Caucasians.—Comparison and Analysis of Caucasian and Mongolian Words.

SECTION VIII.—Physical Type of Tibetans.

SECTION IX.—The Aborigines of Central India.—Comparative Vocabulary of the Aboriginal Languages of Central India.—Aborigines of the Eastern Ghats.—Vocabulary of some of the Dialects of the Hill and Wandering Tribes in the Northern Sircars.—Aborigines of the Nilgiris, with Remarks on their Affinities.—Supplement to the Nilgirian Vocabularies.—The Aborigines of Southern India and Ceylon.

SECTION X.—Route of Nepalese Mission to Pekin, with Remarks on the Water-Shed and Plateau of Tibet.

SECTION XI.—Route from Káthmándú, the Capital of Nepál, to Darjeeling in Sikim.—Memorandum relative to the Seven Cosis of Nepál.

SECTION XII.—Some Accounts of the Systems of Law and Police as recognised in the State of Nepál.

SECTION XIII.—The Native Method of making the Paper denominated Hindustán, Népálese.

SECTION XIV.—Pre-eminence of the Vernaculars; or, the Anglicists Answered; Being Letters on the Education of the People of India.

"For the study of the less-known races of India Mr. Brian Hodgson's 'Miscellaneous Essays' will be found very valuable both to the philologist and the ethnologist."

Third Edition, Two Vols., post 8vo, pp. viii.—268 and viii.—326, cloth, price 21s.

THE LIFE OR LEGEND OF GAUDAMA,

THE BUDDHA OF THE BURMESE. With Annotations.

The Ways to Neibban, and Notice on the Phongyies or Burmese Monks.

BY THE RIGHT REV. P. BIGANDET,

Bishop of Ramatha, Vicar-Apostolic of Ava and Pegu.

"The work is furnished with copious notes, which not only illustrate the subject-matter, but form a perfect encyclopædia of Buddhist lore."—*Times.*

"A work which will furnish European students of Buddhism with a most valuable help in the prosecution of their investigations."—*Edinburgh Daily Review.*

"Bishop Bigandet's invaluable work."—*Indian Antiquary.*

"Viewed in this light, its importance is sufficient to place students of the subject under a deep obligation to its author."—*Calcutta Review.*

"This work is one of the greatest authorities upon Buddhism."—*Dublin Review.*

Post 8vo, pp. xxiv.—420, cloth, price 18s.

CHINESE BUDDHISM.

A VOLUME OF SKETCHES, HISTORICAL AND CRITICAL.

BY J. EDKINS, D.D.

Author of "China's Place in Philology," "Religion in China," &c., &c.

"It contains a vast deal of important information on the subject, such as is only to be gained by long-continued study on the spot."—*Athenæum.*

"Upon the whole, we know of no work comparable to it for the extent of its original research, and the simplicity with which this complicated system of philosophy, religion, literature, and ritual is set forth."—*British Quarterly Review.*

"The whole volume is replete with learning. . . . It deserves most careful study from all interested in the history of the religions of the world, and expressly of those who are concerned in the propagation of Christianity. Dr. Edkins notices in terms of just condemnation the exaggerated praise bestowed upon Buddhism by recent English writers."—*Record.*

Post 8vo, pp. 496, cloth, price 10s. 6d.

LINGUISTIC AND ORIENTAL ESSAYS.

WRITTEN FROM THE YEAR 1846 TO 1878.

BY ROBERT NEEDHAM CUST,

Late Member of Her Majesty's Indian Civil Service; Hon. Secretary to the Royal Asiatic Society;
and Author of "The Modern Languages of the East Indies."

"We know none who has described Indian life, especially the life of the natives, with so much learning, sympathy, and literary talent."—*Academy.*

"They seem to us to be full of suggestive and original remarks."—*St. James's Gazette.*

"His book contains a vast amount of information. The result of thirty-five years of inquiry, reflection, and speculation, and that on subjects as full of fascination as of food for thought."—*Tablet.*

"Exhibit such a thorough acquaintance with the history and antiquities of India as to entitle him to speak as one having authority."—*Edinburgh Daily Review.*

"The author speaks with the authority of personal experience. . . . . It is this constant association with the country and the people which gives such a vividness to many of the pages."—*Athenæum.*

Post 8vo, pp. civ.—348, cloth, price 18s.
BUDDHIST BIRTH STORIES; or, Jataka Tales.
The Oldest Collection of Folk-lore Extant:
BEING THE JATAKATTHAVANNANA,
For the first time Edited in the original Páli.
BY V. FAUSBOLL;
And Translated by T. W. RHYS DAVIDS.
Translation. Volume I.

"These are tales supposed to have been told by the Buddha of what he had seen and heard in his previous births. They are probably the nearest representatives of the original Aryan stories from which sprang the folk-lore of Europe as well as India. The introduction contains a most interesting disquisition on the migrations of these fables, tracing their reappearance in the various groups of folk-lore legends. Among other old friends, we meet with a version of the Judgment of Solomon."—*Times*.

"It is now some years since Mr. Rhys Davids asserted his right to be heard on this subject by his able article on Buddhism in the new edition of the 'Encyclopædia Britannica.'"—*Leeds Mercury*.

"All who are interested in Buddhist literature ought to feel deeply indebted to Mr. Rhys Davids. His well-established reputation as a Páli scholar is a sufficient guarantee for the fidelity of his version, and the style of his translations is deserving of high praise."—*Academy*.

"No more competent expositor of Buddhism could be found than Mr. Rhys Davids. In the Játaka book we have, then, a priceless record of the earliest imaginative literature of our race; and . . . it presents to us a nearly complete picture of the social life and customs and popular beliefs of the common people of Aryan tribes, closely related to ourselves, just as they were passing through the first stages of civilisation."—*St. James's Gazette*.

Post 8vo, pp. xxviii.—362, cloth, price 14s.
A TALMUDIC MISCELLANY;
OR, A THOUSAND AND ONE EXTRACTS FROM THE TALMUD, THE MIDRASHIM, AND THE KABBALAH.
Compiled and Translated by PAUL ISAAC HERSHON,
Author of "Genesis According to the Talmud," &c.
With Notes and Copious Indexes.

"To obtain in so concise and handy a form as this volume a general idea of the Talmud is a boon to Christians at least."—*Times*.

"Its peculiar and popular character will make it attractive to general readers. Mr. Hershon is a very competent scholar. . . . Contains samples of the good, bad, and indifferent, and especially extracts that throw light upon the Scriptures." *British Quarterly Review*.

"Will convey to English readers a more complete and truthful notion of the Talmud than any other work that has yet appeared."—*Daily News*.

"Without overlooking in the slightest the several attractions of the previous volumes of the 'Oriental Series,' we have no hesitation in saying that this surpasses them all in interest."—*Edinburgh Daily Review*.

"Mr. Hershon has . . . thus given English readers what is, we believe, a fair set of specimens which they can test for themselves."—*The Record*.

"This book is by far the best fitted in the present state of knowledge to enable the general reader to gain a fair and unbiassed conception of the multifarious contents of the wonderful miscellany which can only be truly understood—so Jewish pride asserts—by the life-long devotion of scholars of the Chosen People."—*Inquirer*.

"The value and importance of this volume consist in the fact that scarcely a single extract is given in its pages but throws some light, direct or refracted, upon those Scriptures which are the common heritage of Jew and Christian alike."—*John Bull*.

"It is a capital specimen of Hebrew scholarship; a monument of learned, loving, light-giving labour."—*Jewish Herald*.

Post 8vo, pp. xii.—228, cloth, price 7s. 6d.
THE CLASSICAL POETRY OF THE JAPANESE.
By BASIL HALL CHAMBERLAIN,
Author of "Yeigo Heñkaku Shiran."

"A very curious volume. The author has manifestly devoted much labour to the task of studying the poetical literature of the Japanese, and rendering characteristic specimens into English verse."—*Daily News.*

"Mr. Chamberlain's volume is, so far as we are aware, the first attempt which has been made to interpret the literature of the Japanese to the Western world. It is to the classical poetry of Old Japan that we must turn for indigenous Japanese thought, and in the volume before us we have a selection from that poetry rendered into graceful English verse."—*Tablet.*

"It is undoubtedly one of the best translations of lyric literature which has appeared during the close of the last year."—*Celestial Empire.*

"Mr. Chamberlain set himself a difficult task when he undertook to reproduce Japanese poetry in an English form. But he has evidently laboured *con amore*, and his efforts are successful to a degree."—*London and China Express.*

Post 8vo, pp. xii.—164, cloth, price 10s. 6d.
THE HISTORY OF ESARHADDON (Son of Sennacherib),
KING OF ASSYRIA, B.C. 681-668.

Translated from the Cuneiform Inscriptions upon Cylinders and Tablets in the British Museum Collection; together with a Grammatical Analysis of each Word, Explanations of the Ideographs by Extracts from the Bi-Lingual Syllabaries, and List of Eponyms, &c.

By ERNEST A. BUDGE, B.A., M.R.A.S.,
Assyrian Exhibitioner, Christ's College, Cambridge.

"Students of scriptural archæology will also appreciate the 'History of Esarhaddon.'"—*Times.*

"There is much to attract the scholar in this volume. It does not pretend to popularise studies which are yet in their infancy. Its primary object is to translate, but it does not assume to be more than tentative, and it offers both to the professed Assyriologist and to the ordinary non-Assyriological Semitic scholar the means of controlling its results."—*Academy.*

"Mr. Budge's book is, of course, mainly addressed to Assyrian scholars and students. They are not, it is to be feared, a very numerous class. But the more thanks are due to him on that account for the way in which he has acquitted himself in his laborious task."—*Tablet.*

Post 8vo, pp. 448, cloth, price 21s.
THE MESNEVI
(Usually known as THE MESNEVIYI SHERIF, or HOLY MESNEVI)
OF
MEVLANA (OUR LORD) JELALU 'D-DIN MUHAMMED ER-RUMI.
Book the First.

Together with some Account of the Life and Acts of the Author, of his Ancestors, and of his Descendants.

Illustrated by a Selection of Characteristic Anecdotes, as Collected by their Historian,
MEVLANA SHEMSU-'D-DIN AHMED, EL EFLAKI, EL 'ARIFI.

Translated, and the Poetry Versified, in English,
By JAMES W. REDHOUSE, M.R.A.S., &c.

"A complete treasury of occult Oriental lore."—*Saturday Review.*

"This book will be a very valuable help to the reader ignorant of Persia, who is desirous of obtaining an insight into a very important department of the literature extant in that language."—*Tablet.*

Post 8vo, pp. xvi.—280, cloth, price 6s.
EASTERN PROVERBS AND EMBLEMS
ILLUSTRATING OLD TRUTHS.

BY REV. J. LONG,
Member of the Bengal Asiatic Society, F.R.G.S.

" We regard the book as valuable, and wish for it a wide circulation and attentive reading."—*Record.*
" Altogether, it is quite a feast of good things."—*Globe.*
" It is full of interesting matter."—*Antiquary.*

Post 8vo, pp. viii.—270, cloth, price 7s. 6d.
INDIAN POETRY;
Containing a New Edition of the "Indian Song of Songs," from the Sanscrit of the "Gita Govinda" of Jayadeva ; Two Books from "The Iliad of India" (Mahabharata), "Proverbial Wisdom" from the Shlokas of the Hitopadesa, and other Oriental Poems.

BY EDWIN ARNOLD, C.S.I., Author of "The Light of Asia."

" In this new volume of Messrs. Trübner's Oriental Series, Mr. Edwin Arnold does good service by illustrating, through the medium of his musical English melodies, the power of Indian poetry to stir European emotions. The 'Indian Song of Songs' is not unknown to scholars. Mr. Arnold will have introduced it among popular English poems. Nothing could be more graceful and delicate than the shades by which Krishna is portrayed in the gradual process of being weaned by the love of

' Beautiful Radha, jasmine-bosomed Radha,'

from the allurements of the forest nymphs, in whom the five senses are typified."—*Times.*
" No other English poet has ever thrown his genius and his art so thoroughly into the work of translating Eastern ideas as Mr. Arnold has done in his splendid paraphrases of language contained in those mighty epics."—*Daily Telegraph.*
" The poem abounds with imagery of Eastern luxuriousness and sensuousness; the air seems laden with the spicy odours of the tropics, and the verse has a richness and a melody sufficient to captivate the senses of the dullest."—*Standard.*
" The translator, while producing a very enjoyable poem, has adhered with tolerable fidelity to the original text."—*Overland Mail.*
" We certainly wish Mr. Arnold success in his attempt 'to popularise Indian classics,' that being, as his preface tells us, the goal towards which he bends his efforts."—*Allen's Indian Mail.*

Post 8vo, pp. xvi.—296, cloth, price 10s. 6d.
THE MIND OF MENCIUS;
OR, POLITICAL ECONOMY FOUNDED UPON MORAL PHILOSOPHY.

A SYSTEMATIC DIGEST OF THE DOCTRINES OF THE CHINESE PHILOSOPHER MENCIUS.

Translated from the Original Text and Classified, with Comments and Explanations,

By the REV. ERNST FABER, Rhenish Mission Society.

Translated from the German, with Additional Notes,

By the REV. A. B. HUTCHINSON, C.M.S., Church Mission, Hong Kong.

" Mr. Faber is already well known in the field of Chinese studies by his digest of the doctrines of Confucius. The value of this work will be perceived when it is remembered that at no time since relations commenced between China and the West has the former been so powerful—we had almost said aggressive—as now. For those who will give it careful study, Mr. Faber's work is one of the most valuable of the excellent series to which it belongs."—*Nature.*

A 2

Post 8vo, pp. 336, cloth, price 16s.

THE RELIGIONS OF INDIA.

By A. BARTH.

Translated from the French with the authority and assistance of the Author.

The author has, at the request of the publishers, considerably enlarged the work for the translator, and has added the literature of the subject to date; the translation may, therefore, be looked upon as an equivalent of a new and improved edition of the original.

"Is not only a valuable manual of the religions of India, which marks a distinct step in the treatment of the subject, but also a useful work of reference."—*Academy.*

"This volume is a reproduction, with corrections and additions, of an article contributed by the learned author two years ago to the 'Encyclopédie des Sciences Religieuses.' It attracted much notice when it first appeared, and is generally admitted to present the best summary extant of the vast subject with which it deals."—*Tablet.*

"This is not only on the whole the best but the only manual of the religions of India, apart from Buddhism, which we have in English. The present work ... shows not only great knowledge of the facts and power of clear exposition, but also great insight into the inner history and the deeper meaning of the great religion, for it is in reality only one, which it proposes to describe."—*Modern Review.*

"The merit of the work has been emphatically recognised by the most authoritative Orientalists, both in this country and on the continent of Europe. But probably there are few Indianists (if we may use the word) who would not derive a good deal of information from it, and especially from the extensive bibliography provided in the notes."—*Dublin Review.*

"Such a sketch M. Barth has drawn with a master-hand."—*Critic (New York).*

Post 8vo, pp. viii.—152, cloth, price 6s.

HINDU PHILOSOPHY.

The SĀNKHYA KĀRIKĀ of IS'WARA KRISHNA.

An Exposition of the System of Kapila, with an Appendix on the Nyāya and Vais'eshika Systems.

By JOHN DAVIES, M.A. (Cantab.), M.R.A.S.

The system of Kapila contains nearly all that India has produced in the department of pure philosophy.

"The non Orientalist ... finds in Mr. Davies a patient and learned guide who leads him into the intricacies of the philosophy of India, and supplies him with a clue, that he may not be lost in them. In the preface he states that the system of Kapila is the 'earliest attempt on record to give an answer, from reason alone, to the mysterious questions which arise in every thoughtful mind about the origin of the world, the nature and relations of man and his future destiny,' and in his learned and able notes he exhibits 'the connection of the Sankhya system with the philosophy of Spinoza,' and 'the connection of the system of Kapila with that of Schopenhauer and Von Hartmann.'"—*Foreign Church Chronicle.*

"Mr. Davies's volume on Hindu Philosophy is an undoubted gain to all students of the development of thought. The system of Kapila, which is here given in a translation from the Sānkhya Kārikā, is the only contribution of India to pure philosophy. ... Presents many points of deep interest to the student of comparative philosophy, and without Mr. Davies's lucid interpretation it would be difficult to appreciate these points in any adequate manner."—*Saturday Review.*

"We welcome Mr. Davies's book as a valuable addition to our philosophical library."—*Notes and Queries.*

Second Edition. Post 8vo, pp. x.—130, cloth, price 6s.

A MANUAL OF HINDU PANTHEISM. VEDÂNTASÂRA.

Translated, with copious Annotations,

By MAJOR G. A. JACOB,

Bombay Staff Corps ; Inspector of Army Schools.

The design of this little work is to provide for missionaries, and for others who, like them, have little leisure for original research, an accurate summary of the doctrines of the Vedânta.

"The modest title of Major Jacob's work conveys but an inadequate idea of the vast amount of research embodied in his notes to the text of the Vedantasara. So copious, indeed, are these, and so much collateral matter do they bring to bear on the subject, that the diligent student will rise from their perusal with a fairly adequate view of Hindû philosophy generally. His work . . . is one of the best of its kind that we have seen."—*Calcutta Review.*

Post 8vo, pp. xii.—154, cloth, price 7s. 6d.

TSUNI—||GOAM:

THE SUPREME BEING OF THE KHOI-KHOI.

By THEOPHILUS HAHN, Ph.D.,

Custodian of the Grey Collection, Cape Town ; Corresponding Member of the Geogr. Society, Dresden ; Corresponding Member of the Anthropological Society, Vienna, &c., &c.

"The first instalment of Dr. Hahn's labours will be of interest, not at the Cape only, but in every University of Europe. It is, in fact, in most valuable contribution to the comparative study of religion and mythology. Accounts of their religion and mythology were scattered about in various books; these have been carefully collected by Dr. Hahn and printed in his second chapter, enriched and improved by what he has been able to collect himself."—*Prof. Max Müller in the Nineteenth Century.*

"It is full of good things."—*St. James's Gazette.*

In Four Volumes. Post 8vo, Vol. I., pp. xii.—392, cloth, price 12s. 6d., Vol. II., pp. vi.—408, cloth, price 12s. 6d., Vol. III., pp. viii.—414, cloth, price 12s. 6d., Vol. IV., pp. viii.—340, cloth, price 10s. 6d.

A COMPREHENSIVE COMMENTARY TO THE QURAN.

TO WHICH IS PREFIXED SALE'S PRELIMINARY DISCOURSE, WITH ADDITIONAL NOTES AND EMENDATIONS.

Together with a Complete Index to the Text, Preliminary Discourse, and Notes.

By Rev. E. M. WHERRY, M.A., Lodiana.

"As Mr. Wherry's book is intended for missionaries in India, it is no doubt well that they should be prepared to meet, if they can, the ordinary arguments and interpretations, and for this purpose Mr. Wherry's additions will prove useful."—*Saturday Review.*

Second Edition. Post 8vo, pp. vi.—208, cloth, price 8s. 6d.

THE BHAGAVAD-GÎTÂ.

Translated, with Introduction and Notes.

By JOHN DAVIES, M.A. (Cantab.)

"Let us add that his translation of the Bhagavad Gîtâ is, as we judge, the best that has as yet appeared in English, and that his Philological Notes are of quite peculiar value."—*Dublin Review.*

Post 8vo, pp. 96, cloth, price 5s.

THE QUATRAINS OF OMAR KHAYYAM.

Translated by E. H. WHINFIELD, M.A.,

Barrister-at-Law, late H.M. Bengal Civil Service.

Post 8vo, pp. xxxii.—336, cloth, price 10s. 6d.

THE QUATRAINS OF OMAR KHAYYAM.

The Persian Text, with an English Verse Translation.

By E. H. WHINFIELD, late of the Bengal Civil Service.

"Mr. Whinfield has executed a difficult task with considerable success, and his version contains much that will be new to those who only know Mr. Fitzgerald's delightful selection."—*Academy.*

"The most prominent features in the Quatrains are their profound agnosticism, combined with a fatalism based more on philosophical than religious grounds, their Epicureanism and the spirit of universal tolerance and charity which animates them."—*Calcutta Review.*

Post 8vo, pp. xxiv.—268, cloth, price 9s.

THE PHILOSOPHY OF THE UPANISHADS AND ANCIENT INDIAN METAPHYSICS.

As exhibited in a series of Articles contributed to the *Calcutta Review.*

By ARCHIBALD EDWARD GOUGH, M.A., Lincoln College, Oxford; Principal of the Calcutta Madrasa.

"For practical purposes this is perhaps the most important of the works that have thus far appeared in 'Trübner's Oriental Series.' . . . We cannot doubt that for all who may take it up the work must be one of profound interest."—*Saturday Review.*

In Two Volumes. Vol. I., post 8vo, pp. xxiv.—230, cloth, price 7s. 6d.

A COMPARATIVE HISTORY OF THE EGYPTIAN AND MESOPOTAMIAN RELIGIONS.

By Dr. C. P. TIELE.

Vol. I.—HISTORY OF THE EGYPTIAN RELIGION.

Translated from the Dutch with the Assistance of the Author.

By JAMES BALLINGAL.

"It places in the hands of the English readers a history of Egyptian Religion which is very complete, which is based on the best materials, and which has been illustrated by the latest results of research. In this volume there is a great deal of information, as well as independent investigation, for the trustworthiness of which Dr. Tiele's name is in itself a guarantee; and the description of the successive religions under the Old Kingdom, the Middle Kingdom, and the New Kingdom, is given in a manner which is scholarly and minute."—*Scotsman.*

Post 8vo, pp. xii.—302, cloth, price 8s. 6d.

YUSUF AND ZULAIKHA.

A POEM BY JAMI.

Translated from the Persian into English Verse.

BY RALPH T. H. GRIFFITH.

"Mr. Griffith, who has done already good service as translator into verse from the Sanskrit, has done further good work in this translation from the Persian, and he has evidently shown not a little skill in his rendering the quaint and very oriental style of his author into our more prosaic, less figurative, language. . . . The work, besides its intrinsic merits, is of importance as being one of the most popular and famous poems of Persia, and that which is read in all the independent native schools of India where Persian is taught."—*Scotsman.*

Post 8vo, pp. viii.—266, cloth, price 9s.

LINGUISTIC ESSAYS.

BY CARL ABEL.

"An entirely novel method of dealing with philosophical questions and impart a real human interest to the otherwise dry technicalities of the science."—*Standard.*

"Dr. Abel is an opponent from whom it is pleasant to differ, for he writes with enthusiasm and temper, and his mastery over the English language fits him to be a champion of unpopular doctrines."—*Athenæum.*

Post 8vo, pp. ix.—281, cloth, price 10s. 6d.

THE SARVA-DARSANA-SAMGRAHA;

OR, REVIEW OF THE DIFFERENT SYSTEMS OF HINDU PHILOSOPHY.

BY MADHAVA ACHARYA.

Translated by E. B. COWELL, M.A., Professor of Sanskrit in the University of Cambridge, and A. E. GOUGH, M.A., Professor of Philosophy in the Presidency College, Calcutta.

This work is an interesting specimen of Hindu critical ability. The author successively passes in review the sixteen philosophical systems current in the fourteenth century in the South of India; and he gives what appears to him to be their most important tenets.

"The translation is trustworthy throughout. A protracted sojourn in India, where there is a living tradition, has familiarised the translators with Indian thought."—*Athenæum.*

Post 8vo, pp. lxv.—368, cloth, price 14s.

TIBETAN TALES DERIVED FROM INDIAN SOURCES.

Translated from the Tibetan of the KAH-GYUR.

BY F. ANTON VON SCHIEFNER.

Done into English from the German, with an Introduction,

BY W. R. S. RALSTON, M.A.

"Mr. Ralston, whose name is so familiar to all lovers of Russian folk-lore, has supplied some interesting Western analogies and parallels, drawn, for the most part, from Slavonic sources, to the Eastern folk-tales, culled from the Kahgyur, one of the divisions of the Tibetan sacred books."—*Academy.*

"The translation . . . could scarcely have fallen into better hands. An Introduction . . . gives the leading facts in the lives of those scholars who have given their attention to gaining a knowledge of the Tibetan literature and language."—*Calcutta Review.*

"Ought to interest all who care for the East, for amusing stories, or for comparative folk-lore."—*Pall Mall Gazette.*

Post 8vo, pp. xvi.—224, cloth, price 9s.

UDÂNAVARGA.

A COLLECTION OF VERSES FROM THE BUDDHIST CANON.

Compiled by DHARMATRÂTA.

BEING THE NORTHERN BUDDHIST VERSION OF DHAMMAPADA.

Translated from the Tibetan of Bkah-hgyur, with Notes, and
Extracts from the Commentary of Pradjnavarman,

By W. WOODVILLE ROCKHILL.

"Mr. Rockhill's present work is the first from which assistance will be gained for a more accurate understanding of the Pâli text; it is, in fact, as yet the only term of comparison available to us. The 'Udanavarga,' the Thibetan version, was originally discovered by the late M. Schiefner, who published the Tibetan text, and had intended adding a translation, an intention frustrated by his death, but which has been carried out by Mr. Rockhill. . . . Mr. Rockhill may be congratulated for having well accomplished a difficult task."—*Saturday Review.*

In Two Volumes, post 8vo, pp. xxiv.—566, cloth, accompanied by a
Language Map, price 18s.

A SKETCH OF THE MODERN LANGUAGES OF AFRICA.

By ROBERT NEEDHAM CUST,

Barrister-at-Law, and late of Her Majesty's Indian Civil Service.

"Any one at all interested in African languages cannot do better than get Mr. Cust's book. It is encyclopaedic in its scope, and the reader gets a start clear away in any particular language, and is left free to add to the initial sum of knowledge there collected."—*Natal Mercury.*

"Mr. Cust has contrived to produce a work of value to linguistic students."—*Nature.*

Third Edition. Post 8vo, pp. xv.-250, cloth, price 7s. 6d.

OUTLINES OF THE HISTORY OF RELIGION TO THE SPREAD OF THE UNIVERSAL RELIGIONS.

By C. P. TIELE,

Doctor of Theology, Professor of the History of Religions in the
University of Leyden.

Translated from the Dutch by J. ESTLIN CARPENTER, M.A.

"Few books of its size contain the result of so much wide thinking, able and laborious study, or enable the reader to gain a better bird's-eye view of the latest results of investigations into the religious history of nations. As Professor Tiele modestly says, 'In this little book are outlines—pencil sketches, I might say—nothing more.' But there are some men whose sketches from a thumb-nail are of far more worth than an enormous canvas covered with the crude painting of others, and it is easy to see that these pages, full of information, these sentences, cut and perhaps also dry, short and clear, condense the fruits of long and thorough research."—*Scotsman.*

Post 8vo, pp. xii.—312, with Maps and Plan, cloth, price 14s.

A HISTORY OF BURMA.

Including Burma Proper, Pegu, Taungu, Tenasserim, and Arakan. From the Earliest Time to the End of the First War with British India.

By LIEUT.-GEN. SIR ARTHUR P. PHAYRE, G.C.M.G., K.C.S.I., and C.B., Membre Correspondant de la Société Académique Indo-Chinoise de France.

"Sir Arthur Phayre's contribution to Trübner's Oriental Series supplies a recognised want, and its appearance has been looked forward to for many years. . . . . General Phayre deserves great credit for the patience and industry which has resulted in this History of Burma."—*Saturday Review.*

Third Edition. Post 8vo, pp. 276, cloth, price 7s. 6d.

RELIGION IN CHINA.

By JOSEPH EDKINS, D.D., PEKING.

Containing a Brief Account of the Three Religions of the Chinese, with Observations on the Prospects of Christian Conversion amongst that People.

"Dr. Edkins has been most careful in noting the varied and often complex phases of opinion, so as to give an account of considerable value of the subject."—*Scotsman.*
"As a missionary, it has been part of Dr. Edkins' duty to study the existing religions in China, and his long residence in the country has enabled him to acquire an intimate knowledge of them as they at present exist."—*Saturday Review.*
"Dr. Edkins' valuable work, of which this is a second and revised edition, has, from the time that it was published, been the standard authority upon the subject of which it treats."—*Nonconformist.*
"Dr. Edkins . . . may now be fairly regarded as among the first authorities on Chinese religion and language."—*British Quarterly Review.*

Post 8vo, pp. x.-274, cloth, price 9s.

THE LIFE OF THE BUDDHA AND THE EARLY HISTORY OF HIS ORDER.

Derived from Tibetan Works in the Bkah-hgyur and Bstan-hgyur. Followed by notices on the Early History of Tibet and Khoten.

Translated by W. W. ROCKHILL, Second Secretary U.S. Legation in China.

"The volume bears testimony to the diligence and fulness with which the author has consulted and tested the ancient documents bearing upon his remarkable subject."—*Times.*
"Will be appreciated by those who devote themselves to those Buddhist studies which have of late years taken in these Western regions so remarkable a development. Its matter possesses a special interest as being derived from ancient Tibetan works, some portions of which, here analysed and translated, have not yet attracted the attention of scholars. The volume is rich in ancient stories bearing upon the world's renovation and the origin of castes, as recorded in these venerable authorities."—*Daily News.*

Third Edition. Post 8vo, pp. viii.-464, cloth, price 16s.

THE SANKHYA APHORISMS OF KAPILA,

With Illustrative Extracts from the Commentaries.

Translated by J. R. BALLANTYNE, LL.D., late Principal of the Benares College.

Edited by FITZEDWARD HALL.

The work displays a vast expenditure of labour and scholarship, for which students of Hindoo philosophy have every reason to be grateful to Dr. Hall and the publishers."—*Calcutta Review.*

In Two Volumes, post 8vo, pp. cviii.-242, and viii.-370, cloth, price 24s.
Dedicated by permission to H.R.H. the Prince of Wales.

BUDDHIST RECORDS OF THE WESTERN WORLD,

Translated from the Chinese of Hiuen Tsiang (A.D. 629).

BY SAMUEL BEAL, B.A.,

(Trin. Coll., Camb.); R.N. (Retired Chaplain and N.I.); Professor of Chinese, University College, London; Rector of Wark, Northumberland, &c.

An eminent Indian authority writes respecting this work:—"Nothing more can be done in elucidating the History of India until Mr. Beal's translation of the 'Si-yu-ki' appears."

"It is a strange freak of historical preservation that the best account of the condition of India at that ancient period has come down to us in the books of travel written by the Chinese pilgrims, of whom Hwen Thsang is the best known."—*Times*.

Post 8vo, pp. xlviii.-398, cloth, price 12s.

THE ORDINANCES OF MANU.

Translated from the Sanskrit, with an Introduction.

By the late A. C. BURNELL, Ph.D., C.I.E.

Completed and Edited by E. W. HOPKINS, Ph.D., of Columbia College, N.Y.

"This work is full of interest; while for the student of sociology and the science of religion it is full of importance. It is a great boon to get so notable a work in so accessible a form, admirably edited, and competently translated."—*Scotsman*.

"Few men were more competent than Burnell to give us a really good translation of this well-known law book, first rendered into English by Sir William Jones. Burnell was not only an independent Sanskrit scholar, but an experienced lawyer, and he joined to these two important qualifications the rare faculty of being able to express his thoughts in clear and trenchant English.... We ought to feel very grateful to Dr. Hopkins for having given us all that could be published of the translation left by Burnell."—F. MAX MÜLLER in the *Academy*.

Post 8vo, pp. xii.-234, cloth, price 9s.

THE LIFE AND WORKS OF ALEXANDER CSOMA DE KOROS,

Between 1819 and 1842. With a Short Notice of all his Published and Unpublished Works and Essays. From Original and for most part Unpublished Documents.

By THEODORE DUKA, M.D., F.R.C.S. (Eng.), Surgeon-Major H.M.'s Bengal Medical Service, Retired, &c.

"Not too soon have Messrs. Trübner added to their valuable Oriental Series a history of the life and works of one of the most gifted and devoted of Oriental students, Alexander Csoma de Koros. It is forty-three years since his death, and though an account of his career was demanded soon after his decease, it has only now appeared in the important memoir of his compatriot, Dr. Duka."—*Bookseller*.

In Two Volumes, post 8vo, pp. xii.-318 and vi.-312, cloth, price 21s.

MISCELLANEOUS PAPERS RELATING TO INDO-CHINA.

Reprinted from "Dalrymple's Oriental Repertory," "Asiatic Researches," and the "Journal of the Asiatic Society of Bengal."

CONTENTS OF VOL. I.

I.—Some Accounts of Quedah. By Michael Topping.
II.—Report made to the Chief and Council of Balambangan, by Lieut. James Barton, of his several Surveys.
III.—Substance of a Letter to the Court of Directors from Mr. John Jesse, dated July 20, 1775, at Borneo Proper.
IV.—Formation of the Establishment of Poolo Peenang.
V.—The Gold of Limong. By John Macdonald.
VI.—On Three Natural Productions of Sumatra. By John Macdonald.
VII.—On the Traces of the Hindu Language and Literature extant amongst the Malays. By William Marsden.
VIII.—Some Account of the Elastic Gum Vine of Prince-Wales Island. By James Howison.
IX.—A Botanical Description of Urceola Elastica, or Caoutchouc Vine of Sumatra and Pulo-Pinang. By William Roxburgh, M.D.
X.—An Account of the Inhabitants of the Poggy, or Nassau Islands, lying off Sumatra. By John Crisp.
XI.—Remarks on the Species of Pepper which are found on Prince-Wales Island. By William Hunter, M.D.
XII.—On the Languages and Literature of the Indo-Chinese Nations. By J. Leyden, M.D.
XIII.—Some Account of an Orang-Outang of remarkable height found on the Island of Sumatra. By Clarke Abel, M.D.
XIV.—Observations on the Geological Appearances and General Features of Portions of the Malayan Peninsula. By Captain James Low.
XV.—Short Sketch of the Geology of Pulo-Pinang and the Neighbouring Islands. By T. Ware.
XVI.—Climate of Singapore.
XVII.—Inscription on the Jetty at Singapore.
XVIII.—Extract of a Letter from Colonel J. Low.
XIX.—Inscription at Singapore.
XX.—An Account of Several Inscriptions found in Province Wellesley. By Lieut.-Col. James Low.
XXI.—Note on the Inscriptions from Singapore and Province Wellesley. By J. W. Laidlay.
XXII.—On an Inscription from Keddah. By Lieut.-Col. Low.
XXIII.—A Notice of the Alphabets of the Philippine Islands.
XXIV.—Succinct Review of the Observations of the Tides in the Indian Archipelago.
XXV.—Report on the Tin of the Province of Mergui. By Capt. G. B Tremenheere.
XXVI.—Report on the Manganese of Mergui Province. By Capt. G. B. Tremenheere.
XXVII.—Paragraphs to be added to Capt. G. B. Tremenheere's Report.
XXVIII.—Second Report on the Tin of Mergui. By Capt. G. B. Tremenheere.
XXIX.—Analysis of Iron Ores from Tavoy and Mergui, and of Limestone from Mergui. By Dr. A. Ure.
XXX.—Report of a Visit to the Pakchan River, and of some Tin Localities in the Southern Portion of the Tenasserim Provinces. By Capt. G. B. Tremenheere.
XXXI.—Report on a Route from the Mouth of the Pakchan to Krau, and thence across the Isthmus of Krau to the Gulf of Siam. By Capt. Al. Fraser and Capt. J. G. Forlong.
XXXII.—Report, &c., from Capt. G. B. Tremenheere on the Price of Mergui Tin Ore.
XXXIII.—Remarks on the Different Species of Orang-utan. By E. Blyth.
XXXIV.—Further Remarks. By E. Blyth.

MISCELLANEOUS PAPERS RELATING TO INDO-CHINA—continued.

CONTENTS OF VOL. II.

XXXV.—Catalogue of Mammalia inhabiting the Malayan Peninsula and Islands. By Theodore Cantor, M.D.
XXXVI.—On the Local and Relative Geology of Singapore. By J. R. Logan.
XXXVII.—Catalogue of Reptiles inhabiting the Malayan Peninsula and Islands. By Theodore Cantor, M.D.
XXXVIII.—Some Account of the Botanical Collection brought from the Eastward, in 1841, by Dr. Cantor. By the late W. Griffith.
XXXIX.—On the Flat-Horned Taurine Cattle of S.E. Asia. By E. Blyth.
XL.—Note, by Major-General G. B. Tremenheere.
General Index.
Index of Vernacular Terms.
Index of Zoological Genera and Sub-Genera occurring in Vol. II.

"The papers treat of almost every aspect of Indo-China—its philology, economy, geography, geology—and constitute a very material and important contribution to our accessible information regarding that country and its people."—*Contemporary Review.*

Post 8vo, pp. xii.-72, cloth, price 5s.

THE SATAKAS OF BHARTRIHARI.
Translated from the Sanskrit
By the REV. B. HALE WORTHAM, M.R.A.S.,
Rector of Eggesford, North Devon.

"A very interesting addition to Trübner's Oriental Series."—*Saturday Review.*
"Many of the Maxims in the book have a Biblical ring and beauty of expression."—*St. James' Gazette.*

Post 8vo, pp. xii.-180, cloth, price 6s.

ANCIENT PROVERBS AND MAXIMS FROM BURMESE SOURCES;
OR, THE NITI LITERATURE OF BURMA.
By JAMES GRAY,
Author of "Elements of Pali Grammar," "Translation of the Dhammapada," &c.

The Sanscrit-Pâli word Niti is equivalent to "conduct" in its abstract, and "guide" in its concrete signification. As applied to books, it is a general term for a treatise which includes maxims, pithy sayings, and didactic stories, intended as a guide to such matters of every-day life as form the character of an individual and influence him in his relations to his fellow-men. Treatises of this kind have been popular in all ages, and have served as a most effective medium of instruction.

Post 8vo, pp. xxxii. and 330, cloth, price 7s. 6d.

MASNAVI I MA' NAVI:
THE SPIRITUAL COUPLETS OF MAULANA JALALU-'D-DIN MUHAMMAD I RUMI.
Translated and Abridged by E. H. WHINFIELD, M.A.,
Late of H.M. Bengal Civil Service.

Post 8vo, pp. viii. and 346, cloth, price 10s. 6d.

MANAVA-DHARMA-CASTRA:
THE CODE OF MANU.

ORIGINAL SANSKRIT TEXT. WITH CRITICAL NOTES.
BY J. JOLLY, Ph.D.,
Professor of Sanskrit in the University of Wurzburg ; late Tagore Professor of Law in the University of Calcutta.

The date assigned by Sir William Jones to this Code—the well-known Great Law Book of the Hindus—is 1250-500 B.C., although the rules and precepts contained in it had probably existed as tradition for countless ages before. There has been no reliable edition of the Text for Students for many years past, and it is believed, therefore, that Prof. Jolly's work will supply a want long felt.

Post 8vo, pp. 215, cloth, price 7s. 6d.

LEAVES FROM MY CHINESE SCRAP-BOOK.
BY FREDERIC HENRY BALFOUR.
Author of "Waifs and Strays from the Far East," "Taoist Texts," "Idiomatic Phrases in the Peking Colloquial," &c. &c.

Post 8vo, pp. xvi.-548, with Six Maps, cloth, price 21s.

LINGUISTIC AND ORIENTAL ESSAYS.
WRITTEN FROM THE YEAR 1847 TO 1887. *Second Series.*
BY ROBERT NEEDHAM CUST, LL.D.,
Barrister-at-Law ; Honorary Secretary of the Royal Asiatic Society ; Late Member of Her Majesty's Indian Civil Service.

In Two Volumes, post 8vo, pp. x.-308 and vi.-314, cloth, price 25s.

MISCELLANEOUS PAPERS RELATING TO INDO-CHINA.
Edited by R. ROST, Ph.D., &c. &c.,
Librarian to the India Office.

SECOND SERIES.

Reprinted for the Straits Branch of the Royal Asiatic Society from the Malayan "Miscellanies," the "Transactions and Journal" of the Batavian Society, and the "Journals" of the Asiatic Society of Bengal, and the Royal Geographical and Royal Asiatic Societies.

Post 8vo, pp. xii.-512, price 16s.

FOLK-TALES OF KASHMIR.
By the REV. J. HINTON KNOWLES, F.R.G.S., M.R.A.S, &c.
(C.M.S.) Missionary to the Kashmiris.

In Two Volumes, post 8vo, pp. xii.-336 and x.-352, cloth, price 21s.
MEDIÆVAL RESEARCHES FROM EASTERN ASIATIC SOURCES.
FRAGMENTS TOWARDS THE KNOWLEDGE OF THE GEOGRAPHY AND HISTORY OF CENTRAL AND WESTERN ASIA FROM THE THIRTEENTH TO THE SEVENTEENTH CENTURY.

BY E. BRETSCHNEIDER, M.D.,
Formerly Physician of the Russian Legation at Pekin.

In Two Volumes, post 8vo, pp. l.-408 and 431, cloth, price 36s.
ALBERUNI'S INDIA:
AN ACCOUNT OF ITS RELIGION, PHILOSOPHY, LITERATURE, GEOGRAPHY, CHRONOLOGY, ASTRONOMY, CUSTOMS, LAW, AND ASTROLOGY (ABOUT A.D. 1031).
TRANSLATED INTO ENGLISH.
With Notes and Indices by Prof. EDWARD SACHAU, University of Berlin.
*** The Arabic Original, with an Index of the Sanskrit Words, Edited by Professor SACHAU, is in the press.

Post 8vo, pp. xxxvii.-218, cloth, price 10s.
THE LIFE OF HIUEN TSIANG.
BY THE SHAMANS HWUI LI AND YEN-TSUNG.
With a Preface containing an account of the Works of I-TSING.
BY SAMUEL BEAL, B.A.
(Trin. Coll., Camb.); Professor of Chinese, University College, London; Rector of Wark, Northumberland, &c.
Author of "Buddhist Records of the Western World," "The Romantic Legend of Sakya Budda," &c.

When the Pilgrim Hiuen Tsiang returned from his travels in India, he took up his abode in the Temple of "Great Benevolence;" this convent had been constructed by the Emperor in honour of the Empress, Wen-te-hau. After Hiuen Tsiang's death, his disciple, Hwui Li, composed a work which gave an account of his illustrious Master's travels; this work when he completed he buried, and refused to discover its place of concealment. But previous to his death he revealed its whereabouts to Yen-tsung, by whom it was finally revised and published. This is "The Life of Hiuen Tsiang." It is a valuable sequel to the Si-yu-ki, correcting and illustrating it in many particulars.

IN PREPARATION:—
Post 8vo.
A SKETCH OF THE MODERN LANGUAGES OF OCEANIA.
BY R. N. CUST, LL.D.
Author of "Modern Languages of the East," "Modern Languages of Africa," &c.

LONDON: TRÜBNER & CO., 57 AND 59 LUDGATE HILL.
500—11/3/89.

TRÜBNER'S
ORIENTAL SERIES.

I.

Ballantyne Press
BALLANTYNE, HANSON AND CO.
EDINBURGH AND LONDON

ESSAYS

ON

THE SACRED LANGUAGE, WRITINGS, AND RELIGION OF THE PARSIS.

BY

MARTIN HAUG, Ph.D.

LATE PROFESSOR OF SANSKRIT AND COMPARATIVE PHILOLOGY AT THE
UNIVERSITY OF MUNICH.

Third Edition.

EDITED AND ENLARGED BY

E. W. WEST, Ph.D.

TO WHICH IS ALSO ADDED,

A BIOGRAPHICAL MEMOIR OF THE LATE DR. HAUG
BY PROFESSOR E. P. EVANS.

LONDON:
TRÜBNER & CO., LUDGATE HILL.
1884.

[*All rights reserved.*]

TO

THE PARSIS OF WESTERN INDIA

THIS REVISION OF THE

FIRST ATTEMPT, IN THE ENGLISH LANGUAGE,

TO GIVE A CORRECT ACCOUNT OF THEIR

ANCIENT ZOROASTRIAN RELIGION AND LITERATURE,

𝔈𝔰 𝔈𝔫𝔰𝔠𝔯𝔦𝔟𝔢𝔡

IN MEMORY OF THE OLD TIMES

OF FRIENDLY INTERCOURSE ENJOYED

BOTH BY THE AUTHOR AND BY

THE EDITOR.

PREFACE.

THE author of these Essays intended, after his return from India, to expand them into a comprehensive work on the Zoroastrian Religion; but this design, postponed from time to time, was finally frustrated by his untimely death. That he was not spared to publish all his varied knowledge on this subject, must remain for ever a matter of regret to the student of Iranian antiquities. In other hands, the changes that could be introduced into this second edition were obviously limited to such additions and alterations as the lapse of time and the progress of Zoroastrian studies have rendered necessary.

In the first Essay, the history of the European researches has been extended to the present time; but, for the sake of brevity, several writings have been passed over unnoticed, among the more valuable of which those of Professor Hübschmann may be specially mentioned. Some account has also been given of the progress of Zoroastrian studies among the Parsis themselves.

In the second Essay additional information has been

given about the Pahlavi language and literature; but the technical portion of the Avesta Grammar has been reserved for separate publication, being better adapted for students than for the general reader.

Some additions have been made to the third Essay, with the view of bringing together, from other sources, all the author's translations from the Avesta, except those portions of the Gâthas which he did not include in the first edition, and which it would be hazardous for an editor to revise. Further details have also been given regarding the contents of the Nasks.

Several additional translations, having been found among the author's papers too late for insertion in the third Essay, have been added in an Appendix after careful revision, together with his notes descriptive of the mode of performing a few of the Zoroastrian ceremonies.

Some apology is due to Sanskrit scholars for the liberties taken with their usual systems of representing Sanskrit and Avesta sounds. These deviations from present systems have been made for the sake of the general reader, whether English or Indian, who can hardly be expected to pronounce words correctly unless they are spelt in accordance with the usual sounds of the letters in English. Probably no European language can represent Indian consonants so easily as English; but as every English vowel has more than one characteristic sound, it is necessary to look to some other European language for the best representation of Indian vowels. The system now generally adopted by Englishmen in India, and followed in these Essays, is to use the consonants to represent their usual English sounds, the vowels to represent their usual Italian sounds, and to avoid diacritical marks as much as possible, because they are always liable to omission. In applying such a system to the Aryan languages of India, Englishmen require very few arbitrary rules. They have merely to observe that *g* is always hard and *ch* always soft, that *th* and *ph* are merely aspirates of *t* and *p* (not the English and Greek *th* and *ph*), and that *a* represents the short vowel sound in the English words *utter, mother, come,* and *blood*. As this use of *a* is often repugnant to Englishmen, it may be remarked that all the other vowels have to be appropriated for other sounds, and that it is also strictly in accordance with the Sanskrit rule that when one *a* coalesces with another the resulting sound is *â*, which could not be the case unless there were a close relationship between the two sounds.

Some unfortunate representations of Indian sounds have become too inveterate to be lightly tampered with; so it is still necessary to warn the general reader that every *w* in the Avesta ought to be pronounced like an English *v*, and that every *v* in Sanskrit or the Avesta closely resembles an English *w*, unless it be followed by *i, î, e, ṛi,* or a consonant, in which case it has a sound

PREFACE.

somewhere between *v* and *h*. Again, Sanskrit has two sets of letters represented by *t, th, d, dh, n, sh;* one set is extremely dental (pronounced with the tip of the tongue touching the extremities of the teeth, or as close to them as possible in the case of *sh*), the other set is lingual (pronounced with the tip of the tongue far back upon or near the palate). The English *t, d, n, sh* are pronounced between these two extremes, but all natives of India consider the sounds of these English letters as decidedly lingual, so that they always represent them by Indian linguals when transliterating English words. Unfortunately, European scholars have been of the opposite opinion, and have represented the dental *t, th, d, dh, n* as unmodified, and the linguals as modified, either by a diacritical dot (as in this work) or by using italics. For the sake of uniformity, this practice has been here extended to *sh;* but there can be no doubt that the dentals ought to be modified and the linguals unmodified, though neither group can be exactly represented by European sounds. Further, the letters *ṛi* do not adequately represent that peculiar Sanskrit vowel as pronounced in *Maháráshṭra*, where the Brahmans have been least disturbed by foreign influences. They say there that the correct sound is *ṛu*, and the tendency in colloquial Maráṭhí is to corrupt it into *u*. The nearest European approach to this sound appears to be the English *re* in *pretty*, which word is never pronounced *petty* when the

PREFACE. xi

r is indistinctly sounded, but has a tendency to become *pootty*.

In Avesta words *th* has the same lisping sound as in English and Greek, *ṇ* and *ñ* have the sound of *ng*, *q* ought to be sounded like *khw*, *zh* bears the same relation to *sh* as *z* to *s* (that is, it has the sound of *s* in *pleasure*), and *shk* is pronounced *sh* by the Parsis. They also pronounce the other sibilants *s* and *sh* as written in this work, and there seems no sufficient reason for departing from their traditional pronunciation, which is corroborated, to a great extent, by Pahlavi and Persian words derived from the Avesta, such as *Zaratusht, âtash*, &c.

The author's principal object in publishing these Essays originally was to present, in a readable form, all the materials for judging impartially of the scriptures and religion of the Parsis. The same object has been kept in view while preparing this second edition, giving a larger quantity of such materials collected from a variety of sources, which I may now leave to the reader's impartial judgment.

E. W. WEST.

München, *February* 1878.

CONTENTS.

	PAGE
BIOGRAPHICAL SKETCH	xvii
INTRODUCTION TO THE THIRD EDITION	xxxiii

ESSAY I.

	PAGE
HISTORY OF THE RESEARCHES INTO THE SACRED WRITINGS AND RELIGION OF THE PARSIS	3
I.—THE REPORTS OF THE GREEKS, ROMANS, ARMENIANS, AND MOHAMMEDANS	3
II.—THE EUROPEAN RESEARCHES	16
III.—ZOROASTRIAN STUDIES AMONG THE PARSIS	54

ESSAY II.

LANGUAGES OF THE PARSI SCRIPTURES	65
I.—THE LANGUAGE OF THE AVESTA, ERRONEOUSLY CALLED ZEND	67
II.—THE PAHLAVI LANGUAGE AND PAZAND	78
III.—THE PAHLAVI LITERATURE EXTANT	93

ESSAY III.

THE ZEND-AVESTA, OR THE SCRIPTURE OF THE PARSIS	119
I.—THE NAME OF THE PARSI SCRIPTURES	119
II.—THE ORIGINAL EXTENT OF THE ZEND-AVESTA —THE NASKS	123
III.—THE BOOKS NOW EXTANT AND THE SUPPOSED ZOROASTRIAN AUTHORSHIP	134
IV.—YASNA	139
V.—GÂTHAS	142

		PAGE
VI.—Gâtha Ahunavaiti	. . . .	146
VII.—Gâtha Ushtavaiti	. . . .	154
VIII.—The last three Gâthas	. . .	167
IX.—Yasna Haptanhaiti and the Minor Texts of the Old Yasna	. . . . .	170
X.—The later Yasna	. . . .	174
1. Hôma yasht	. . . .	175
2. Yasna xix.	. . . .	185
3. —— lvii.	. . . .	189
XI.—Visparad	. . . . .	191
XII.—Yashts	. . . . .	194
1. Hormazd yasht	. . . .	195
2. Haptân, Ardibahisht, and Khordâd yashts	.	195
3. Abân yasht	. . . .	197
4. Khurshêd and Mâh yashts	. . .	199
5. Tîr and Gôsh yashts	. . . .	200
6. Mihir yasht	. . . .	202
7. Srôsh Hâdôkht and Rashnu yashts	. .	205
8. Fravardîn yasht	. . . .	206
9. Behrâm and Râm yashts	. . .	213
10. Dîn and Ashi yashts	. . . .	215
11. Ashtâd, Zamyâd, and Vanant yashts	.	215
12. Two fragments of the Hâdôkht nask; the Afrîn-i Paighambar Zaratusht, and Vishtâsp yasht	. . . . .	217
XIII.—Shorter Texts (Nyâyish, Afringâns, Gâhs, Sirôzah)	. . . . . .	224
XIV.—Vendidâd	. . . . .	225
1. The first fargard	. . .	227
2. The second fargard	. . .	230
3. The third fargard	. . .	235
4. The fourth fargard	. . .	237
5. The fargards v.-xvii.	. . .	240

CONTENTS. xv

PAGE

 6. The eighteenth fargard . . . 243
 7. The nineteenth fargard . . . 252
 8. The fargards xx.-xxii. . . . 257
XV.—Brief Survey of Avesta Literature . . 257

ESSAY IV.

The Zoroastrian Religion as to its Origin and Development 267
I.—The relationship between the Brahmanical and Zoroastrian religions 267
 1. Names of divine beings . . . 267
 2. Names and legends of heroes . . 276
 3. Sacrificial rites 279
 4. Religious observances, domestic rites, and cosmographical opinions . . . 285
II.—Origin of the Zoroastrian religion.—Spitama Zarathushtra and his probable age . . 286
 1. Traces of the origin to be found both in the Vedas and Zend-Avesta . . . 287
 2. Causes of the schism . . . 292
 3. Spitama Zarathushtra . . . 294
 4. The age when Spitama Zarathushtra lived . 298
III.—Spitama Zarathushtra's theology and philosophy, and their influence on the development of the Parsi religion 300
 1. Zarathushtra's monotheism . . . 301
 2. Zarathushtra's two primeval principles . 303
 3. Development of Zarathushtra's doctrines of the Supreme Being.—The two supreme councils; Srosh and Boundless Time . 305
 4. The two intellects, two lives, heaven and hell, resurrection, and palingenesis . . 310

APPENDIX.

	PAGE
I.—Translations from the Avesta	315
1. Vendidâd, fargard iii. 1-23 and 34, 35	315
2. ,, ,, iv. 44-55	319
3. ,, ,, v.	322
4. ,, ,, xix. 10-26 and 40-47	333
II.—Translations from the Pahlavi Versions	338
1. Pahlavi Yasna xxviii.	338
2. ,, ,, xxix.	341
3. ,, ,, xxx.	345
4. ,, ,, xxxi.	348
5. ,, ,, xxxii. 1	354
6. Pahlavi Vendidâd i.	355
7. ,, ,, xviii.	364
8. ,, ,, xix.	379
9. ,, ,, xx.	391
III.—Notes Descriptive of some Parsi Ceremonies	393
1. The ceremony preparatory to Ijashne	394
2. The Ijashne ceremony	403
3. The Darûn ceremony	407
4. The Afrîngân ceremony	408
Index	411

BIOGRAPHICAL SKETCH.

MARTIN HAUG was a native of Ostdorf, an obscure Würtemberg village, situated not far from the famous castle of Hohenzollern, in the picturesque and fertile region extending between the Neckar and the Danube, from the chalk-cliffs of the Swabian Alps to the fir-clad hills and romantic valleys of the Black Forest.[1] He was born January 30, 1827, the eldest of six children. His father was a simple peasant of more than average intelligence, and in quite comfortable circumstances for a person of his class, and was especially proud of being able to trace his pedigree for many generations through an unbroken line of sturdy, and, for the most part, stolid peasant ancestry. It was this feeling that caused him to deprecate the extraordinary love of study which was shown at an early age by his first-born, and which threatened to divert the youth from the hereditary agricultural occupations and obligations strictly imposed upon him by primogeniture. That the heir to a few acres of arable land should freely renounce his birthright, and wilfully refuse to spend his days in guiding the plough and swinging the ox-goad, was, to a German *Stockbauer*, a matter of no less astonishment than if a prince "apparent to the crown" should

---

[1] The events of Haug's life until the twenty-seventh year of his age, *i.e.*, until his habilitation as *privat-docent* in the University of Bonn in 1854, are narrated in his unpublished autobiography, from which source, supplemented by letters, diaries, and oral communications, the facts of this sketch are chiefly derived.

b

reject "the round and top of sovereignty" and refuse to wield the sceptre of his forefathers.

Fortunately, however, the unusual tastes and talents of the boy were appreciated by his maternal grand-uncle, the village bailiff (*Schultheiss*), a man who was remarkable for his liberal opinions, his sound judgment, and the strict rectitude and even-handed justice with which he discharged his official duties, and whom Auerbach might have taken for the prototype of "Lucifer" in the "Black Forest Village Tales." These noble qualities left upon the boy's mind an impression which was never effaced, and exerted a decisive influence upon the formation of his character by inspiring him with the unimpeachable integrity and disinterested devotion to truth for which he was distinguished.

In the sixth year of his age Martin was sent to school, and one of the teachers, observing his zeal and ability, offered, for a hundred florins (eight pounds) a year, to take the entire charge of his education and to prepare him for the schoolmaster's career. This proposal did not suit the wishes of the father, and still less those of the mother, who, with the narrow prejudices and religious concern of a pious *Bauerfrau*, expressed her solicitude lest through much learning her son should become "as great a heretic as Strauss." But the intervention of the granduncle decided the question in opposition to the parents, and in 1838 the boy became *Schulincipient*, and received the extra instruction in branches pertaining to his future calling.

When scarcely twelve years old, although physically quite delicate, his enthusiasm was such that he often studied during the greater part of the night. His father complained of this waste of oil, and, taking his lamp away, drove him to bed; but he quietly rose again and continued his studies, so far as possible, by moonlight. Even at his meals he could not divest his thoughts from his all-absorbing pursuits; his eagerness for knowledge seemed to blunt every lower appetite; he always kept a book by his plate, and was more anxious to feed his mind than his body. He was particularly desirous of learning Latin and Greek; the schoolmaster encouraged him in this purpose, but could not assist him, and he therefore applied for aid to the pastor of his native village. This clerical gentleman, who, like Pfarrer Stollbein in Heinrich Stillings Jünglings-Jahre, "loved humility in other people uncommonly," not only refused to help him, but sternly rebuked the peasant's son for his unseemly ambition, discoursed to him about the sin of arrogance, ridiculed him for trying to get out of his sphere, and, finally, insinuated with sarcastic sneer that perhaps the *Bauerbub* would "even have the presumption to think of studying theology."

It is a noteworthy and significant fact, that of the clergymen with whom Haug came in contact during his long and severe struggle to get an education, and from whom, as university men, he would naturally expect sympathy and advice, not one deigned to cheer him by a single word of encouragement or friendly counsel. The best that he can say of any of them is, that "Pastor B—— was a humane man, and did not lay many obstacles in my way." Surely no extraordinary merit attaches to a virtue so purely negative and a humanity so cold and colourless as that which animated the bosom of this exceptionally good shepherd.

Fortunately, the young student, in addition to good pluck, was endowed with a remarkably tenacious memory, and soon mastered the Latin Grammar and Dictionary, and read such texts as he could get hold of. Before he was fourteen years old, he began also to study Hebrew, his earliest instructors being Jew boys, who visited Ostdorf as rag-buyers and dealers in second-hand clothes; the *honorarium* for this tuition he paid in old linen and other scraps purloined from the family rag-bag. The mother, as a thrifty housewife, mourned over the loss of her *Lumpen*, but the father, now for the first time, showed some interest in his son's studies, since he regarded the desire to read the Holy Scriptures in the original as a thing well-pleasing to God, and accordingly bought him Gesenius' Hebrew Grammar, and permitted him to take three lessons a week in Hebrew from a candidate of theology in the neighbouring town of Bolingen. He paid six kreutzers (twopence) a lesson; and, owing to this "great expense," his father soon compelled him to reduce the number of lessons to one a week.

In May 1841 Haug passed a public examination for admission into the *Schulstand*, *i.e.*, into the class of officially recognised and certificated teachers. For two years he performed intermittingly the duties of schoolmaster in his native village, and in November 1843 was appointed assistant teacher at Unterensingen, where he had about a hundred children under his charge, and was confined to the schoolroom from five to six hours daily. In compensation for his services he received forty florins (three guineas) a year, with board and lodging. His sleeping and study room had no fireplace, and could not be heated, and he suffered severely from the cold as soon as the winter set in. The head-master was a dull pedagogue, and the village parson a coarse and arrogant person. Neither of these men had the least sympathy with Haug's nobler aims and aspirations. Indeed, the parson having received an intimation that the new assistant was engaged in reading Latin, Greek, and Hebrew, warned him to desist, and threatened him with dismissal in case of persistency. Haug gave no heed to these admonitions, and only continued his pursuit of knowledge with increased energy and stricter privacy; and as Vesalius investigated the laws of organic structure and the principles of anatomy by stealthily dissecting the human body with the constant fear of the Inquisition before his eyes, so Haug analysed Hebrew forms and phrases in secret, and cautiously kept his daily acquisitions in learning out of the sight of his pastoral and pedagogical overseers. For this purpose he took refuge in the garret of a grist-mill belonging to a distant relative, and there read Tacitus, Plato, and Isaiah, in what was anything but " the still air of delightful studies." Occasionally, too, the miller's daughters discovered him in his retreat; but these *apsarasas* had no power to turn away the young *muni* from his austere devotion to science. Only for a short time did one rustic beauty threaten to prove the fatal Menakâ capable of diverting his ardour to herself, and thus blighting by her fascinations the fruits of his past efforts, and destroying the prospect of still greater achievements in the future; but he soon saw the folly of his passion, and returned with all the fervour of undivided affection to his first love—Philologia.

At this period Haug began to take a lively interest in religion, or rather in religions, their origin and development. He even discoursed on Sunday afternoons on these topics to the inhabitants of Hardthof, a cluster of farmhouses where he was employed as schoolmaster to about thirty children. It is quite characteristic of him that, on these occasions, he was not content with Luther's translation, but read the Bible from the original text. No doubt the young preacher of sixteen had to aim very low in order not to shoot over the heads of his rustic auditors; but he spoke from the fulness of his heart, and his sermons seem to have won general approbation, although a few of his hearers, who were of a more rigidly theological and dogmatic turn of mind, or more distinctively pietistic in sentiment, complained that he was too historical, and laid too little stress on the cardinal doctrines. What more adequate exegesis of specifically Christian truth could be expected from one who had already learned to look at all sacred scriptures and traditional creeds from a comparative standpoint?

Although, in preparing for the university, he was obliged to devote special attention to classical philology, he still kept up his Oriental studies. He procured a copy of Bopp's edition of *Nala and Damayanti*, containing the Sanskrit text with a literal Latin translation. By comparing the proper names in the translation with the corresponding combinations of signs in the original, he succeeded in gradually constructing for himself the Sanskrit alphabet and acquiring a knowledge of the grammatical forms, and thus learned to read and interpret the text by the same laborious process that was used by scholars in deciphering the cuneiform inscriptions of Western Asia and restoring the lost language of Akkad. Subsequently he procured Rosen's *Radices Sanscritæ*, Bopp's *Kritische Grammatik der Sanskrita-Sprache* and Ewald's *Ausführliches Lehrbuch der Hebräischen Sprache*. The last-mentioned work, on account of its rational system and comparative method, had peculiar attractions for him; and in order to impress it more indelibly on his mind, he read it through, section by section, and wrote it out from memory. He often studied all night, bathing his head occasionally to cool his heated brain; and during the heat of summer he was accustomed to refresh his jaded nerves and ward off sleep by keeping his feet in a tub of cold water.

With impatient and almost feverish longing, Haug read each new list of lectures of the Tübingen University published semi-annually in the *Swabian Mercury*, and fixed his eyes particularly on Ewald's announcements. His highest ideal of human happiness, he tells us, was to sit at the feet of this great teacher and to learn of him. Once, in passing through Tübingen, he could not resist the temptation of dropping into one of Ewald's lectures on Hebrew antiquities. He drank in with avidity every word, and the excitement produced such a wonderful tension of his faculties and put him into such a state of intellectual exaltation, that on leaving the auditorium he could repeat the entire lecture *verbatim*. Shortly afterwards (in April 1847) he addressed a letter to Ewald, expressing his high esteem and admiration, and stating his own aims and desires. A very friendly and cheering reply, which was soon received, determined him to free himself without further delay from the galling yoke and intolerable thraldom of pedagogy. It was one of the noble traits in the character of Ewald, himself the son of a poor weaver, that he never forgot the poverty of his birth and the severe struggles of his early life, and never failed to extend his hearty sympathy and helping hand to those who were in like circumstances.

In the autumn of 1847 Haug signified to the school inspector his intention of trying for the university, whereupon that official flew into a towering rage, and upbraided him for his conceit in imagining himself to be "too good for a schoolmaster." This outburst of impotent anger, so far from deterring Haug from his purpose, only served to strengthen him in it. Fearing lest, in a moment of dejection or physical weakness, he might prove untrue to himself and return to his old servitude, he resolved to render such a relapse impossible by not only ceasing to teach, but by divesting himself also of the public character and legal status of a teacher. He felt that he had undertaken a desperate enterprise, from which he must cut off all hope of retreat by burning every bridge behind him. By this step he severed himself from a source of sure though sour bread; but he had faith and foresight to cast aside all pennywise prudence and bondage to the rule of three, and to follow the calling that was in his character and not in his circumstances. He was already Oriental enough to trust something to his star and to the power of fate, believing that with the necessity would come also the ability to work the miracle of the loaves and the fishes.

Immediately, therefore, on recovery from a dangerous illness caused by over-study, he surrendered his certificate, and laying down for ever his rod of office, the birchen sceptre, with only two florins (forty pence) in his pocket, entered, in March 1848, the Gymnasium at Stuttgart, where he also had access to the treasures of the Royal Library. He rented a small room in a garret for two florins a month, and supported himself chiefly by giving private lessons in Hebrew. In the seclusion of this poor attic he worked on with a diligence and cheerfulness which no destitution could depress, and by his earnestness and efficiency soon won the recognition of his instructors, among whom he often mentioned Professors Zeigler and Klaiber with the warmest expressions of gratitude.

In the autumn of 1848 Haug was matriculated at the University of Tübingen as candidate of philology. Ewald, to the young student's intense regret, had just accepted a call to Göttingen; but he attended the lectures of Walz, Jeuffel, and Schwegler on classical philology, and read Sanskrit, Zend, and Persian with Ewald's successor, Rudolph Roth. In the winter of 1849-50, Haug himself delivered a course of lectures on Isaiah, at the solicitation of some Prussian theological students to whom he had already given private instruction. He also won, in the following summer (August 9, 1851), the prize proposed by the Philosophical Faculty for the best essay "On the Sources used by Plutarch in his Lives" (*In fontes quibus Plutarchus in vitis conscribendis usus est inquisatur*, published in 1854). These successes contributed to his fame as well as to his finances, the state of which was soon afterwards further improved by a stipendium procured for him by Professors Schwegler and Keller. In March 1852 he took the degree of Doctor of Philosophy, and a few days later the sudden death of his father recalled him to Ostdorf.

In recognition of his merits as a scholar Haug received from the Würtemberg Government a travelling stipend of three hundred florins (twenty-four pounds), which, with his portion of the family inheritance, enabled him to go to Göttingen (April 1852), whither he was attracted by Benfey (Sanskrit), Hermann (classical philology), and especially by Ewald, who gave him private instruction in Hebrew, Arabic, Syriac, Turkish, and Armenian, and encouraged him in every way to devote his life to Oriental studies. He was also treated with the greatest kindness by Frau Ewald (a daughter of the illustrious astronomer Gauss), whom he characterises in his autobiography as " one of the most charming women he ever knew."

On November 9, 1854, Haug habilitated as *privatdocent* in Bonn with a dissertation on " The Religion of Zarathushtra according to the Ancient Hymns of the Zend-Avesta," which was printed with additional Avestan studies in *Die Zeitschrift der Deutschen Morgenländischen Gesellschaft* for 1855 (vol. ix. pp. 683 *sqq.*) Although surrounded by pleasant friends and occupied with congenial pursuits, he still found himself as an unsalaried tutor lecturing on subjects which from their very nature attracted but few pupils and produced a correspondingly small income from fees, in straitened pecuniary circumstances. From this financial stress he was relieved by an invitation from Baron von Bunsen to remove to Heidelberg as his private secretary and collaborator on his *Bibelwerk*, duties which he performed for about three years, conjointly with Dr. Kamphausen, afterwards professor of theology in Bonn. His salary of six hundred thalers (ninety pounds) a year sufficed not only to free him from present solicitude as to what he should eat and drink and wherewithal he should be clothed, but enabled him also, during the summers of 1856 and 1857, to visit Paris and London, and make use of the manuscript treasures of the *Bibliothèque Impériale* and the East India Company's Library.

Although the *Bibelwerk* claimed nearly all his time and energy, still his industry and facility and goodly store of *Sitzfleisch*, or power of sedentary endurance, enabled him to continue his researches in the Avesta and prepare the results for publication. He translated and annotated the first Fargard of the Vendidâd, which, at Bunsen's urgent request, was incorporated in the third volume of "Egypt's Place in Universal History." He also completed a still more important as well as more difficult work, entitled *Die Fünf Gâthâs, oder Sammlungen von Liedern und Sprüchen Zarathushtra's, seiner Jünger und Nachfolger* (The Five Gâthâs or Collections of the Songs and Sayings of Zarathushtra, his Disciples and Successors), which was published (vol. i. in 1858, and vol. ii. in 1860) by the German Oriental Society in Leipsic. It consists of a translation of the text, an exact Latin metaphrase, and a freer German version, to which are added copious notes, etymological, exegetical, critical, and historical.

In the spring of 1858 an unexpected and most inviting field of labour was opened to Haug by Mr. Howard, Director of Public Instruction of the Bombay Presidency, who, through Dr. Pattison, of Lincoln College, Oxford, offered him the position of superintendent of Sanskrit studies in the Government College at Puna. He resolved to accept this offer, and immediately dissolved his connection with Bunsen, and, pending further negotiations, resumed his former duties in Bonn. In June 1859 he married Sophia Speidel of Ofterdingen, to whom he had been betrothed since 1852, and in July left Bonn for England, whence he set sail for India. After a voyage of ninety-seven days he landed in Bombay early in November, and before the middle of the month was comfortably settled in his bungalow on the Muta, in the ancient capital of the Mahrattas.

Haug's object in going to India was threefold: 1. To acquaint himself with the learning of the Brahmans and Parsis, their theological dogmas and ritual observances; 2. To reform native learning by substituting for the old school of Sanskrit and Zend scholarships the freer and more fruitful methods of European science; 3. To collect manuscripts. In the first place, he wished to gather up, as far as possible, the threads of tradition, and trace them to their origin in the complicated web and weft of Brahmanical and Parsi creeds and ceremonies, and to ascertain how far they form a part of the ancient texture, or to what extent they must be regarded as later insertions. Even before leaving Europe he was not satisfied with the theory which is disposed to regard these threads as all thrums, and to discard the whole fabric of native tradition as a worthless thing of shreds and patches in which no scrap or filament of the primitive warp and woof remains. Through his intimate and cordial intercourse with Brahmans and Dasturs he succeeded in obtaining the most extended and accurate information concerning their beliefs, rites, and customs ever vouchsafed to any European.

In 1862 he published at Bombay his "Essays on the Sacred Language, Writings, and Religion of the Parsis." "It is a volume," wrote Max Müller on its first appearance, "of only three hundred and sixty-eight pages, and sells in England for one guinea. Nevertheless, to the student of Zend it is one of the cheapest books ever published." The second and third editions of this work, revised and enlarged (chiefly from the author's posthumous papers) by Dr. E. W. West, are kept by the scholarly editor fully abreast with the rapid progress of Avesta studies.

In 1863 Haug published also at Bombay the text and an English translation of the *Aitareya Bráhmanam of the Rigveda*, embodying in the introduction to the first and the foot-notes to the second volume a vast amount of rare knowledge concerning the theory of the sacrifice, the manner of its performance, and the special purpose of each rite. It implies no discredit to European Sanskritists to affirm that such a work could have been written only by a scholar who had lived in India, and who, by actual autopsy, had learned the real meaning of Brahmanical ritualism.

In his efforts to raise the standard and change the character of native scholarship Haug was untiringly assiduous and eminently successful. He inspired the younger generation of Brahmans and Parsis with an intelligent interest in their sacred writings; and on the eve of his return to Europe he received, among other testimonials and tokens of affection, an address in Sanskrit signed by his native pupils, expressing their deep regret at the departure of their *priyaguru*, and their gratitude for the entirely new light which they had derived from his instruction in ancient Sanskrit literature and comparative philosophy. It is due in no inconsiderable degree to his influence that science in India is now becoming completely secularised, and the old priestly class of pandits, who cultivated grammar as a means of grace and valued phonetics and orthoepy as passports to eternal bliss, is rapidly passing away and will soon be numbered with megatheroids and other extinct mammals.

The collection of manuscripts was an object which Haug had especially set his heart upon and never lost sight of. For this purpose he made a three months' tour in Guzerat during the winter of 1863-64. He was everywhere enthusiastically received, and frequently invited by native gentlemen to lecture on the Vedas and the Avesta. In one city the place where he sat during his discourse was marked by a marble slab with a laudatory inscription. He succeeded in procuring a large number of manuscripts, partly in the oldest extant originals, and partly in copies made under his supervision, some of them being very rare even in India, and hitherto altogether unknown in Europe. This fine collection after his death was purchased by the Royal Library of Munich.

Towards the close of the year 1865, Haug resigned his place in Puna College and prepared to return to Europe. On his arrival in India, instead of abating his ardour to suit the debilitating climate, he kept up the habits of close and continuous application to study which he had formed in Germany, not even resting in the hot season. His health had become so seriously impaired through this imprudence that he resolved to seek its restoration in the cool and invigorating air of his Swabian fatherland. Spontaneous expressions of sorrow at his departure and esteem for his labours and learning met him on every side from the native population. The Brahmans and Parsis of Puna and Bombay attested their appreciation of his services by addresses of thanks and by splendid gifts.

On his return to Germany in 1866, Haug settled for a time in Stuttgart, where he edited "An Old Zand-Pahlavi Glossary," which was published by the Government of Bombay. In 1868 he accepted a call to the newly established professorship of Sanskrit and comparative philology in the University of Munich, where he soon secured for these hitherto alien and neglected studies a warm welcome and recognition, and effected their complete academical naturalisation. In his lecture-room and library he gathered round him students from different parts of Germany, from Spain, Portugal, Italy, Greece, Russia, England, and America, and spread out before them the treasures of his learning with a fulness and freshness, a depth and keenness of insight, that fixed the attention and kindled the ambition of his hearers.

In the Sanskrit address presented to him by his Brahman pupils of Puna, his uniform kindness and affability are particularly praised in contrast with the chilling and estranging reserve usually shown by foreign professors, who "never forget the distance between the *guru* and the *chhâttra* (preceptor and pupil), and thus check the spirit of inquiry." "To our exceeding good fortune," they add, "your conduct towards us has been the very reverse of this. In your manifestations of affection and sympathy, you have realised the character of the good teacher as described in the laws of Manu." The same freedom and friendliness and singleness of heart and of purpose, the same lively interest in their progress, marked his intercourse with his pupils in Munich, and bound them to him by like ties of personal attachment. He possessed, in reality, a frank and kindly nature, although he has been sometimes censured for his over-sensitiveness. No doubt he was often too quick to resent, with

"The flash and outbreak of a fiery mind,"

stings and thrusts against which men of thicker cuticle would have remained callous. Thus he acquired among those who did not know him personally an exceedingly unenviable and wholly undeserved reputation for testiness and pugnacity. The excess of every fine quality becomes a defect. To be thin-skinned and high-mettled marks a superior organisation, but at the same time puts one at serious disadvantage in a combat with pachyderms.

The works which Haug published during the last few years of his life embraced various and disparate topics, and although small in bulk compared with the ordinary *opus* of the German *savant*, are great in the erudition they contain and in the results they produced. They consist, for the most part, of monographs, reviews, and academical dissertations, which took a decidedly critical and polemical character, originating not in any innate contentiousness or love of controversy, but in the incipient and somewhat formless and nebulous state out of which these studies are only just emerging. These publications, often only thin pamphlets, were the results of original researches, and contributed more to the advancement of science than many a ponderous tome crammed with second-hand erudition.

Coming from the close and enervating atmosphere of India, Haug found the cool and invigorating though raw air of Munich refreshing and strengthening to his relaxed nerves, and expressed his surprise that the climate should have such a bad reputation. Eventually, however, the tonic proved too harsh and irritating for his lungs and too powerful for his nerves, intensifying the excitability of his ardent temperament, and stimulating to intellectual efforts out of proportion to his physical strength. In the summer of 1875 he made a tour through the Swiss mountains, but over-taxed himself, and returned home sick and exhausted. During the following winter he was able to lecture only for a few weeks, fell into a rapid decline, and, by the advice of his physician, went to Ragatz in Switzerland, where, a few days after his arrival, he expired, June 3, 1876. There, too, he was buried, a delegation from the University of Munich attending his body to the grave, and paying him the last tribute of respect.

E. P. EVANS.

October 1883.

INTRODUCTION TO THE THIRD EDITION.

THE issue of a third edition of these Essays affords an opportunity, not only for briefly describing the recent progress of Zoroastrian studies, but also for mentioning several emendations of the text which have been suggested, and are more or less deserving of attention. For the convenience of the reader, these additions and suggested amendments are here given in the form of notes, with references to the pages of the text to which they relate, or in connection with which they should be read.

Pages 3, 4.—The existence of a chief of the Magi at the court of Nebuchadnezzar has been disputed, and the title Rab-mag is said to mean "commander of the fleet."

The recent discovery of two cuneiform inscriptions of Cyrus, in which that king seems to proclaim his faith, and that of his son Cambyses, in the Babylonian gods, has also been considered a sufficient disproof of his having professed the religion of the Magi. But it appears from hieroglyphic inscriptions that Cambyses was likewise a devoted adherent of the Egyptian divinities; and yet the flattering language used by Isaiah in speaking of Cyrus is hardly such as could be justifiably applied to an idolator. The only reasonable way of reconciling these three contradictory facts seems to be the acceptance of all of them as being true from different points of view. These kings, like all great conquerors and statesmen, compelled to govern many different races and religions, found it necessary to conciliate all their loyal subjects in turn, and thus induced the priests of each religion to applaud them as defenders and promoters of the particular faith which those priests advocated.

Page 5.—The identity of Hara, the Avesta name of the mountain supposed to encompass the earth, and Heb. *har*, "a mountain," may be disputed.

Page 53.—The last six years have been a period of considerable activity among European investigators of the Parsi scriptures; and, in some cases, new views regarding the origin of Zoroastrianism have been advocated, which are so revolutionary in their character as to require much more adaptation to long-recognised facts than they have yet received before they can be safely adopted by careful scholars. Without attempting any exhaustive enumeration or analysis of the works and essays that have been published, the following may be mentioned as best known to the writer:—

M. C. DE HARLEZ has not only completed his French translation of the Avesta, mentioned in p. 51, but has also published a second edition of the work with an extended introduction to the study of the Avesta and the Mazdian religion, which, though disfigured by numerous misprints, and capable of improvement in many of its details, is a very instructive treatise on the history, scriptures, and dogmas of Zoroastrianism. Both in this treatise and in his essay "On the Origin of Zoroastrism," published in the *Journal Asiatique*,[1] M. de Harlez expresses two opinions of some novelty, which require much more evidence to support them than he has yet been able to collect. One of these opinions is that Darius Hystaspes was not a Zoroastrian, although his cuneiform inscriptions proclaim his faith in Aûramazdâ. But, as Aûramazdâ is a compound name, traceable to the two terms Ahura and Mazda, used separately by Zarathushtra and his successors in the Gâthas, and never becoming an actual compound in any part of the Avesta, it is only reasonable to suppose that this compound must have originated at a later date than its component parts. In other words, we must continue to believe that Darius lived later than Zarathushtra, and professed the same religion as he did, unless it can be shown that faith in Aûramazdâ was something materially different from faith in

[1] *Des Origines du Zoroastrisme*, par M. C. de Harlez, extrait du *Journal Asiatique*: Paris, 1879–80.

Ahuramazda, as stated in the Gâthas, the only portion of the Avesta that can be quoted as embodying the faith of Zarathushtra himself.[1] The other novel opinion of M. de Harlez is that Zarathushtra may have come into contact with some of the captive Israelites in Media in the eighth century B.C., from whom he may have imbibed the monotheistic ideas and general tone of morality which he adapted to his former faith. In other words, M. de Harlez wishes to believe that all the good in Zoroastrianism has sprung from Hebrew ideas. We know too little of Zarathushtra's real history to form any definite opinion as to the possibility of his being in Media at the time mentioned. But it would have been strange if a people who, like the Israelites, were led into captivity on account of their idolatry, should have become such ardent teachers of monotheism as to lay the foundation for a durable form of that faith differing materially from that professed by their own priesthood.

M. de Harlez has also published useful French manuals, both of the Avesta and Pahlavi languages, containing grammars and selections for reading with the necessary glossaries.[2]

A very different view of the origin of Zoroastrianism has been adopted by M. JAMES DARMESTETER, in his English translations of the Vendidad, Sîrozah, Yashts, and Nyâyish, published in the series of "Sacred Books of the East" (vols. iv. and xxiii.) The translations themselves are of a very masterly character, giving full weight to the teachings of tradition; but they might, in many cases, have been made more literal, and, in some places, rather too much consideration has been paid to traditional renderings that are probably later than the Pahlavi versions. Notwithstanding this tendency to give an almost undue consideration to tradition in his translations, the views adopted by M. Darmesteter in his introduction as to the origin of Zoroastrianism would trace all its legends, and even the person of its founder, to a series of meteorological myths altogether inconsistent with tradition, but affording ample scope for the exercise

[1] It is usual to assume that the laws relating to ceremonial impurity, the disposal of the dead, and similar matters, are Zoroastrian; but we have no real authority for tracing them to Zarathushtra himself, and they have more the appearance of being either later sacerdotal developments or mere tolerations of older customs.

[2] *Manuel de la Langue de l'Avesta;* grammaire, anthologie, lexique: Paris, 1878. *Manuel du Pehlevi des Manuscrits;* grammaire, anthologie, lexique, légendes: Paris, 1880.

of a vivid imagination. To obtain this result, however, some valuable results of older researches have to be sacrificed. The striking fact that the gods of the Brahmans have become the demons of the Zoroastrians and *vice versa* (see p. 268), is no longer admitted as arguing some former enmity or schism between the two religions, but is assumed to be only the result of a survival of two different names for gods, one of which was accidentally selected as supreme by one religion, and the other by the other religion. Inasmuch as this assumption gives no reason for the accidental selection, it is less reasonable than the older theory of a schism, even if the latter were unsupported by further facts of a similar character.

M. Darmesteter has also published in French a valuable collection of "Iranian Studies," including a comparative grammar of the language of Persia from the time of Darius to that of Firdausi, with several essays on particular details of Iranian etymology, mythology, and legend, as well as transcripts of the original texts of some Pahlavi, Sanskrit, and Persian translations of the Yashts and Nyâyishes.[1]

Turning to the German scholars who have recently devoted their attention to the literature of the Parsis, Dr. W. GEIGER may be noticed as a judicious scholar and careful writer. To his Pahlavi version of the first chapter of the Vendidad, with German translation and commentary,[2] it has been chiefly objected that his transcript of the Pahlavi text in Hebrew characters is much less useful than one in Roman type would be, and, as Pahlavi is now known to be an Iranian language (which merely employs a limited number of Semitic words to express itself in writing), the use of a purely Semitic alphabet is likely to give students an erroneous idea of the character of the language. It is probable, however, that Dr. Geiger will abandon the use of Hebrew type, and perhaps use the original Pahlavi character, if he should hereafter continue his Pahlavi version of the Vendidad, of which this first chapter was intended merely as a specimen.

[1] *Etudes iraniennes*, par James Darmesteter; études sur la grammaire historique de la langue persane, mélanges iraniens, et traductions indigènes du Khorda Avesta: Paris, 1883.

[2] *Die Pehleriversion des ersten Capitels des Vendidâd* herausgegeben, nebst dem Versuch einer ersten Uebersetzung und Erklärung, von Dr. Wilhelm Geiger: Erlangen, 1877.

In his "Aogemadaêchâ"[1] he has published, for the first time, a short Pâzand-Sanskrit text commencing with that Avesta word, together with a German translation, commentary, and glossary. This text also occurs in Pahlavi (see pp. 99, 100), and seems to be a kind of meditation on death and the state of the soul after death. Like the Nîrangistân, it is interspersed with many Avesta passages, which constitute, more or less completely, the original text; but these have been translated and amplified by the Pahlavi commentator in the usual manner of an Avesta-Pahlavi text. There can be little doubt that we have here a fragment of one of the lost Nasks, which has not yet been identified.

Dr. Geiger has also published a very complete German "Handbook of the Avesta Language," containing a grammar, selections for reading, and the necessary glossary.[2] But his most comprehensive work is a German account of the "Civilisation of Eastern Iran in Ancient Times."[3] In this book he has not only detailed all the allusions to manners and customs, laws and superstitions, which occur in the Avesta, but has also minutely investigated the probable geography of all the places mentioned therein. This investigation carefully avoids the common error of confusing the later geographical statements of the Bundahish with the earlier ones of the Avesta, and shows how little alteration is required in the hypotheses of earlier scholars in order to bring them up to the present state of our knowledge on the subject.

Professor H. HÜBSCHMANN, who had formerly written several essays on particular portions of the Avesta, has now turned his attention chiefly to the Armenian language. But, under the title of "Iranian Studies,"[4] he has published an important German essay on the Avesta alphabet, with some remarks on the alphabetical systems of other Iranian languages. As it is utterly impossible to ascertain the *exact* pronunciation of any living language a few centuries ago, it is useless to attempt any

---

[1] *Aogemadaêcâ* ein Pârsentractat in Pâzend, Altbaktrisch und Sanskrit, herausgegeben, übersetzt, erklärt und mit Glossar versehen, von Dr. Wilhelm Geiger: Erlangen, 1878.
[2] *Handbuch der Awestasprache*; Grammatik, Chrestomathie und Glossar; von Dr. Wilhelm Geiger: Erlangen, 1879.
[3] *Ostiränische Kultur im Altertum*, von Wilhelm Geiger; mit einer Uebersichts-Karte von Ostirân: Erlangen, 1882.
[4] *Iranische Studien* (Zeitschrift für vergleichende Sprachforschung, xxiv. pp. 323-415).

great precision in expressing the sounds of a language that has been dead for a millennium. Professor Hübschmann has, therefore, been satisfied with ascertaining the general character of the sound of each letter, and pointing out its proper place in the alphabetical system. His researches will have to be carefully considered by any one who wishes to improve the usual systems of transliteration; but his own mode of transcription is more scientific than practical, being too much burdened with Greek letters and diacritical marks.

Among these younger scholars, Professor K. GELDNER is one of the chief representatives of the school which trusts to etymology and its own ingenuity, rather than accept the teachings of tradition, in studying the meaning of the Avesta. In his German work "On the Metre of the Later Avesta,"[1] he has exercised much ingenuity and perseverance in discovering metrical passages, not only where they undoubtedly exist, but also where their existence may reasonably be doubted. He shows that many passages can be made truly metrical either by the omission of certain words, which may be considered as mere glosses, or by some slight alteration of words or syllables. So that strict attention to metre may become a valuable means of amending the text. To a considerable extent his conclusions are certainly correct, but unless his method be used with extreme caution, it may easily convert the most prosaic passage into modern verse, which it would be folly to attribute to the ancient writer.

In his "Studies on the Avesta"[2] he gives many specimens of his etymological powers, which are of a very high order; but, after all, Sanskrit is not our only source of knowledge for determining the meaning of Avesta words. We have the remnants of old tradition, diluted with mediæval commentary, in the Pahlavi versions, which, however forbidding in appearance, are apt, like other rugged friends, to rise in our estimation as we become better acquainted with them. It is this tradition that Professor Geldner should carefully study before he proceeds to carry out his scheme of an improved Avesta lexicon, of the

---

[1] *Ueber die Metrik des jüngeren Avesta, nebst Uebersetzung ausgewählter Abschnitte, von Karl Geldner: Tübingen, 1877.*

[2] *Studien zum Avesta, von Karl Geldner: Strassburg, 1882.*

preliminary investigations for which these studies were intended as a specimen.

He is now actively engaged in the preparation of a new edition of Westergaard's "Avesta Texts;" and as, through the hearty co-operation of the owners of manuscripts in India, he will be able to consult all the best sources of information known to exist, it may be presumed that his edition of the Texts will contain all that can be expected, until some other family of manuscripts is discovered in Persia.

An American clergyman, the Rev. L. H. MILLS, has been studying the Gâthas for several years, and has carefully considered the writings and opinions of all scholars who have examined these ancient hymns. The result of his studies and inquiries is in the press, and will include the Avesta, Pahlavi, Sanskrit, and Persian versions of the hymns, with English translations of the first three.

The study of the Avesta has also been taken up in Italy, where Professor PIZZI has published the "Tishtar Yasht," with an Italian translation.[1]

Among the European contributions to the study of Pahlavi may be mentioned the German translation of the Kârnâmak-î Artakhshîr-î Pâpakân, by Professor NOELDEKE, who has also done much to illustrate the period of the Pahlavi writings by his German "History of the Persians and Arabs in the Time of the Sasanians," translated from the Arabic of Tabarî.[2] While Dr. ANDREAS has done good service to Pahlavi students by his edition of the Pahlavi Mainyô-i Khard, published in facsimile from the only manuscript of the original Pahlavi text known in Europe.[3] And Dr. WEST has made several Pahlavi works accessible to English readers by his translations of the Bundahish,

---

[1] *Tishtar-Yasht;* l'inno a Tistrya nell' Avesta; testo zendo con traduzione e commento; saggio del Dott. Prof. J. Pizzi (estratto dalle Memorie della Reale Accademia delle Scienze di Torino, serie ii., tom. xxxv.): Torino, 1882.

[2] *Geschichte der Perser und Araber zur Zeit der Sasaniden,* aus der arabischen Chronik des Tabarî übersetzt und mit ausführlichen Erläuterungen und Ergänzungen versehen, von Th. Nöldeke: Leyden, 1879.

[3] *The Book of the Mainyô-i-Khard,* also an old fragment of the *Bundehesh,* both in the original Pahlavi; being a facsimile of a manuscript brought from Persia by the late Professor Westergaard, and now preserved in the University Library of Copenhagen; edited by Frederic Charles Andreas: Kiel, 1882.

Bahman Yasht, Shâyast-lâ-shâyast, Dâḍistân-î Dînik, and Epistles of Mânûshchîhar, published in the series of "Sacred Books of the East" (vols. v. and xviii.)

Page 58.—The probable meaning of the Pahlavi word *vehîjakîk* or rather *veh-îchakîk*, is "*fit* for anything good, auspicious."

Page 60.—Two more volumes of Dastur Peshotanji's Dînkard have been published. The slow progress of this work appears to be due to no want of energy on the part of the editor, but to the pecuniary delays and difficulties that usually beset the publication of a long series of volumes by subscription.

Arrangements have been made for the early publication of the Pâzand, Sanskrit, and Pahlavi texts of the Shikand-gumânî, with a vocabulary, under the joint-editorship of Dastur Hoshangji and Dr. West.

Page 61.—Dastur Jamaspji has published three volumes of his Pahlavi, Gujarâti, and English Dictionary, in which he explains the meaning of more than 7000 words, but has advanced only as far as *aîvar*, following the order of the Sanskrit alphabet. His collection includes both actual words and copyists' errors, with their traditional readings and the meanings he attaches to them. So far he has discovered about twenty times as many words as have been previously glossarised, but this excess will probably diminish as the work proceeds. The meanings have evidently been carefully considered, but no one acquainted with the uncertainties of Pahlavi readings will expect any great accuracy in determining the meaning of unusual words until all the texts containing them have been satisfactorily translated.

Page 85.—The word *hûzvârish*, or, more correctly, *aûzvârish*, is a variant of *zuvârish*, "being old or worn out," an abstract noun derived from the verb *zuvârîdan*. Darmesteter prefers tracing it directly to Av. *zbar*, "to be crooked, distorted, or perverted," or to the allied form *zavvara*, borrowed by the Arabs in the sense of "he altered or corrupted " a text, with the idea that *hûzvârish* means "a disguised mode of writing." But we have no reason to suppose that *hûzvârish* was adopted for the purpose of concealment, as it was used in all Persian writing of Sasanian times. It would be better described as the use of obsolete words in writing, and the word *zuvârish*, whether it means "decay " or " antiquity," would express this idea sufficiently well.

Page 87, *note* 1.—It seems most probable that the common Hûzvârish termination -*man* is merely an altered mode of writing the single Sasanian letter whose pronunciation is uncertain. Professor Levy has suggested that it is the Semitic *h*, which has no other representative separate from *kh* in the Sasanian alphabet; but, if it were *h*, why was it not used in *hû, havînt, yehvûn*, and the prefix of Hiphil verbs? and why was it used as an equivalent of the Chaldee emphatic termination -*â* ?

Page 98.—Transcripts of the Pahlavi translations of the *Khûrshêd, Mâh*, and *Srôsh hâḍôkht yashts*, and of the *Khûrshêd nyâyish* have been published by Darmesteter in his *Études iraniennes*.

Page 99.—An independent manuscript of the *Nîrangistân*, brought from Persia a few years ago, and said to be more complete and accurate than those previously in India, is now in the possession of Mr. Tehmuras Dinshawji Anklesaria of Bombay.

Page 100.—Transcripts of the Pâzand and Sanskrit version of the *Aogemadaêcha*, with its Avesta passages, have been published, with a German translation, by Dr. Geiger, as mentioned above (p. xxxvii).

Page 102.—An independent copy of about one-fifth of the *Dînkard* has been recently discovered in a manuscript brought from Persia by the late Professor Westergaard in 1843, and now in the University Library at Copenhagen. This manuscript contains four chapters of the third book, the whole of the fifth, nearly all the sixth, and about three-tenths of the ninth book. The copy of the sixth book is dated ninety-five years earlier than the manuscript in Bombay, and is decidedly more correct.

It appears from a manuscript of the *Dâḍistân-î-Dînîk*, brought from Persia by the late Professor Westergaard in 1843, and now in the University Library at Copenhagen, that the correct date given by its author in one of his Epistles is A.Y. 250 (A.D. 881). An English translation of this work, and also of the *Epistles of Mânûshchîhar* (which are found in the same manuscripts), has been published in the eighteenth volume of the "Sacred Books of the East;" and a portion of the *Selections of Zâḍ-sparam* has likewise been translated from these manuscripts and published in the fifth volume of the same series.

Page 105.—An English translation of the *Bundahish* has been published in the fifth volume of the "Sacred Books of the East." But it is now known that the Bundahish contained in the Indian manuscripts is only a collection of extracts from a larger work of about 30,000 words, of which two complete manuscripts, brought from Persia, are now in the possession of Mr. Tehmuras Dinshawji Anklesaria of Bombay. A fragment of the last chapter of this larger Bundahish has also been found in the manuscript of Westergaard, containing the Dînkarḍ at Copenhagen, and has been published in facsimile by Dr. Andreas in his edition of the Pahlavi Minôk-î Khiraḍ.

Page 106.—The original Pahlavi text of the *Minôk-î Khiraḍ*, as contained in Westergaard's manuscript, has been published in facsimile by Dr. Andreas, as mentioned above (p. xxxix). And a more complete manuscript of the same text has been recently brought from Persia to Bombay, and is now in the possession of Mr. Tehmuras Dinshawji Anklesaria. These two manuscripts are the only copies of the original Pahlavi text yet known. They confirm the general opinion of the substantial accuracy of Neryosangh's Pâzand-Sanskrit version; while, at the same time, they show that he occasionally misunderstood the Pahlavi text, or altered it to make it more intelligible. He has also omitted two or three short passages containing names which he could not identify.

An English translation of the *Shâyast-lâ-shâyast* has been published in the fifth volume of the "Sacred Books of the East."

Page 107.—It appears from the English translation of the *Bahman yasht*, in the fifth volume of the "Sacred Books of the East," that it does not mention the Mûsalmans by name, although many of the details evidently refer to the devastations committed by them, as well as by the Turanians and Christians. Another copy of the Pahlavi text has been discovered in the manuscript of Westergaard containing the Dînkarḍ at Copenhagen, but this copy is neither so old nor so correct as the one previously known to exist in the same library.

Page 111.—A German translation of the *Kârnâmak-î Artakhshîr-î Pâpakân* has been published by Professor Nöldeke, as mentioned above (p. xxxix).

Page 112.—An English translation of the *Mâḍigân-î haft ameshâspend* has been published in the fifth volume of the

"Sacred Books of the East," as part of the appendix to the Shâyast-lâ-shâyast.

Page 113.—The supposed Pahlavi version of the *Saḍ-dar*, or *Saḍ-dar Bundahish*, has been examined and found to be merely a portion of the Shâyast-lâ-shâyast. It is doubtful whether the name of the Saḍ-dar Bundahish (which is a Persian work distinct from the Saḍ-dar) is correctly read. It is frequently quoted in the Persian Rivâyats, but the name is there written in three different modes, which can be reconciled only by reading *Saḍ-darband-i hush*.

To the Pahlavi texts already detailed must be added a fragment of an old manuscript obtained by Mr. Tehmuras Dinshawji Anklesaria from Persia a few years ago, and now in his library. This fragment consists of twenty large folios, containing about 8600 words, and is incomplete at both ends, its first folio being numbered 74. It appears to be part of a very full treatise on the laws of property, somewhat analogous to one portion of the Hûspâram Nask, as stated in the Dînkard, and it contains many quotations of the opinions of the old commentators whose names occur in the Pahlavi Vendidad; several of the later Sasanian kings are also mentioned. As Yûdân-Yim is one of the commentators whose opinions are cited, this work is probably not older than the Dâḍistan-î Dînîk, which was written by the son of a high-priest of that name.

One of the manuscripts of the larger Bundahish, belonging to Mr. Tehmuras (see p. xlii), also contains about 270 questions and answers on miscellaneous subjects, ascribed to Hêmêḍ-î Ashavahishtân, who was probably the father of the last reviser of the Dînkard. As the extent of these questions and answers is three-fourths of that occupied by the larger Bundahish, they must contain about 22,000 words.

Of the total extent of Pahlavi literature now known to be extant, which may be estimated as consisting of about 569,000 words, the texts which have been edited do not amount to more than 182,000 words. The texts translated into English contain about 158,000 words, and the German translations include about 7600 words of further texts.

Regarding the age of the Pahlavi books in their present form, some definite information has been recently obtained. The third

Epistle of Mânûshchîhar is dated A.Y. 250 (A.D. 881), so that his other work, the *Dâḍistân-î Dînîk*, and the *Selections of Zâḍ-sparam*, who was his brother, must have been also written about the latter half of the ninth century. It also appears from Bund. xxxiii. 10, 11, that the writer of that chapter, which forms part of the *larger* Bundahish, was a contemporary of Zâḍ-sparam and also of Âtûr-pâḍ, son of Hêmîḍ, who is mentioned in the Dînkarḍ as the last reviser of that extensive work. With this information we may safely refer the latest recensions of both the *Bundahish* and *Dînkarḍ* to the latter half of the ninth century, although some copyist of the last chapter of the Bundahish has added his own date, A.Y. 527 (A.D. 1158), to that chapter. We are further told by Mânûshchîhar (Ep. I. iv. 15, 17), that Nîshahpûhar, the môbad of môbads, was a councillor of King Khûsrô, son of Kavâḍ, surnamed Anôshirvân (A.D. 531–579). Now Nîshahpûhar is the name of a commentator often quoted in the *Pahlavi Vendidad* and *Nîrangistân*, and in the *Ardâ-Vîrâf nâmak* it is said to have been a title of Ardâ-Vîrâf; we are, therefore, justified in ascribing the latest recensions of these three works to some period after the sixth century, but before the ninth, when the first two were quoted by Mânûshchîhar.

The oldest Pahlavi manuscript that has been discovered consists of several fragments of papyrus found five or six years ago in the Fayûm district in Egypt. On these fragments many Pahlavi words are distinctly legible in writing of the eighth century, but the sentences are too fragmentary to admit of complete decipherment.

Page 121.—As the connection of Av. *vi* with Pahl. *avî* (written *apî*) is liable to dispute, the word *avêzak*, "pure," may be quoted as one in which it is quite certain that the Avesta *v* has taken the form of *p* in Pahlavi.

Page 174.—Chapters xix.–xxi. of the later Yasna are called the *Bakân* in some manuscripts, and, as the first three fargards of the Bakô Nask are said (in the Dînkarḍ) to have treated of the same subjects, it is probable that these chapters were taken from that Nask.

Page 217.—The star *Vanant* is called the southern leader of the stars in the Bundahish, and, as such, may be best identified with Fomalhaut.

Page 272.—It should be borne in mind by those who are opposed to the author's views as to an ancient schism between primitive Zoroastrianism and primitive Brahmanism, that he is here collecting all the facts that tend to uphold his hypothesis, but he does not mean to assert that all these facts are of equal value. It is quite possible to explain away some of these facts as accidental coincidences without sensibly weakening the argument based upon other facts that are more refractory. Thus we know too little about the personal history of the Zoroastrian demons *Indra, Sâurva,* and *Nâoṇhaithya* to enable us to judge whether the resemblance of their names to those of the Brahmanical sacred beings, *Indra, Sharva,* and *Nâsatya,* be more than an accidental coincidence. But if these coincidences be accidental, that fact does not weaken the argument based upon the words *ahura* and *daêva* being used by the Zoroastrians in an opposite sense to the *asura* and *deva* of the Brahmans, and upon the change that took place in the meaning of *asura* in the later Vedic period. The question is whether these developments of meaning in opposite directions can be better explained by any other hypothesis than that adopted by the author, and by one that is more consistent with *all* the facts of the case.

Page 296.—According to the genealogy of Zarathushtra, preserved in the Bundahish, Dînkard, and other Pahlavi books, *Haêchaḍaspa* was his great-great-grandfather.

Page 298.—With reference to the lineage of *Vîshtâspa,* it should be observed that *Aurvaḍaspa,* his father, was not a son, but a cousin, of his own predecessor, *Kava Husrava.* According to Bund. xxxi. 28, the genealogy of *Vîshtâspa* was as follows :— Kaî-Kavâḍ (*Kavi Kavâta*), Kaî-Apîvêh (*Kavi Aipi-vanghu*), Kaî-Pîsîn (*Kavi Pisanangh*), Mânûsh, Aûzâv, Lôharâsp (*Aurvaḍaspa*), Vîshtâsp. But this family lineage is quite as different from that of Darius Hystaspes as the succession of kings' names given in the text.

Page 299.—The author has mentioned (pp. 15, 136, 264) other dates that might be suggested for Zarathushtra on various grounds, and according to various modes of calculation. But in his introduction to the Zand-Pahlavi Glossary he was inclined to adopt the date (B.C. 610) mentioned in p. 15, and to this opinion he seems to have subsequently adhered. This opinion, however, depends entirely upon certain statements of Parsi and Mohammedan writers, and these are evidently based upon the identification of Vîshtâspa with the progenitor of Darius, which has been shown to be exceedingly doubtful. The Bundahish, which evidently adopts this view, makes the interval between the beginning of the reign of Vîshtâspa and that of Alexander a period of 288 years, which corresponds very well with the 280 years mentioned by Masûdî (see p. 15). But the chronological chapter of the Bundahish is a comparatively modern addition to that work, being specially headed by the words *madam shnat mar-i Tâzikân*, " on the year-reckoning of the Arabs," and cannot, therefore, be quoted as an independent authority of ancient date on this subject.

It is also necessary to observe that the language in which Zarathushtra and his early successors composed their Gâthas is closely allied to the Vedic Sanskrit. If, therefore, we place Zarathushtra in the seventh century B.C., we must be prepared to assign nearly the same date to the Vedas.

Page 317.—Darmesteter translates the reply of Ahuramazda in Vend. iii. 11 as follows:—"It is the place whereon the wife and children of one of the faithful, O Spitama Zarathushtra! are driven along the way of captivity, the dry, the dusty way, and lift up a voice of wailing." And Geiger takes the same view of the passage in his Ostirânische Kultur, p. 190.

Page 322, *note* 1.—The term *gôkard-hômand* means " brimstoned," and *saokeñtavaitîm* means "provided with burning matter, or ignitible." From the latter word comes Pers. *saugand*, "an oath," which is always said to be "eaten" when it is administered, because it formerly meant swallowing the prepared water as an ordeal.

Page 335.—The term *vohumanô*, here translated "goodminded man," is also applied to his clothing, as Darmesteter has observed; and in Vend. xix. 20-25 it appears sometimes to mean the one, and sometimes the other. The *sadarah*, or sacred shirt, is called the *vohûmanôîk vistarg*, "garment of Vohûman," in the Dâdistân-î Dînîk, xxxix. 19, xlviii. 9, because "it is needful (to be) perfectly pure white (and) single, which one fold is because Vohûman also is thus the one creature who (was) first, and afterwards from him the garment which is innermost and concealed is called in revelation" (Dd. xl. 2).

Page 346, *note* 3.—The Pahlavi equivalent of Av. *khraozh-dishtēṅg* should be read *sâkhto-sago-nihûft*, "hard-stone-covered;" referring to the old idea that the sky is formed of ruby-coloured adamant, so as to be indestructible by wear. In the Pahlavi translations *sag* is usually written for *sang*, "stone."

Page 366, § 4 (9).—Better thus: "he uses the goad of reckoning so that one groans at it [some say that one atones]." The word *mar* may be either "a miscreant" or "the account" of sin to be rendered.

Page 372, § 30 (70).—The name of the *drûj* is not Khûduk, "disgrace," but Aûḍuk (Av. *Uda*), a demon who is described in Bund. xxviii. 19, as endeavouring to make men speak at those times when they have taken a prayer inwardly and ought to be silent. By speaking at such times they are supposed to break the spell produced by the prayer, lose its protection, and commit a serious sin.

Page 374, § 44 (98*a*).—It is better to speak of the "origin" (instead of the "beginning") of a Tanâpûhar sin. The sin is supposed to take root in the sinner, and can be eradicated only by a proportional amount of good works.

Page 377, § 62 (124*a*).—Better thus: "and it is no matter to her."

Page 378, § 69 (137).—Better thus: "he should slaughter a thousand young (cattle)." The last five notes have been suggested by Darmesteter's criticism of the second edition.

Page 381, § 5 (18).—The name of the water is better read *Kyânsâi* or *Kyânsih*. It is the brackish lake and swamp now called Hâmûn, "the desert," or Zarah, "the sea," which formerly contained fresher water than it does now.

Page 385, § 23 (77).—The *vohûmanô vistarg* is the sacred shirt (see the remarks above, regarding p. 335); and "the good-minded one" (*vohûman*) of § (78) is probably the same. We ought also to read "so that those divinely-produced stars shall illumine (it);" as *rôshanînêm* is no doubt a miswriting of *rôshanînā*, there being very little difference between *ā* and *êm* in many manuscripts.

Page 388, § 31 (102a).—Better thus: "where he performs the duty of controlling those acting as household attendants (*khavag-î-mân-karâno*)." In the Dâdistân-î Dînîk, xxxi. 5, we are told that Vohûman makes the righteous souls household attendants of Aûharmazd.

E. W. WEST.

October 1883.

I.

HISTORY OF THE RESEARCHES INTO THE SACRED WRITINGS AND RELIGION OF THE PARSIS.

FROM THE EARLIEST TIMES DOWN TO THE PRESENT.

I.

HISTORY OF THE RESEARCHES INTO THE SACRED WRITINGS AND RELIGION OF THE PARSIS.

I.—THE REPORTS OF THE GREEKS, ROMANS, ARMENIANS, AND MOHAMMEDANS.

IN this Essay it is intended to give a brief outline of the gradual acquaintance of the Western nations with the Zoroastrian religion (now professed only by the small Parsi community in India, and by a very insignificant number which remain in their ancient fatherland in Persia), and to trace the history of the scientific researches of Europeans into the original records of this ancient creed, where the true doctrine of the great Zoroaster and his successors, buried for thousands of years, is to be found.

To the whole ancient world Zoroaster's lore was best known by the name of the doctrine of the Magi, which denomination was commonly applied to the priests of India, Persia, and Babylonia.

The earliest mention of them is made by the Prophet Jeremiah (xxxix. 3), who enumerated among the retinue of King Nebuchadnezzar at his entry into Jerusalem, the

"Chief of the Magi" (*rab mag* in Hebrew), from which statement we may distinctly gather, that the Magi exercised a great influence at the court of Babylonia 600 years B.C. They were, however, foreigners, and are not to be confounded with the indigenous priests. In the Old Testament no account of their religion is given, and only once (Ezekiel viii. 16, 17) it is hinted at.[1] The Persians, however, whose priests the Magi appear to have been, are never spoken of as adherents to idolatry; and the Persian kings, especially Cyrus (called *Koresh* in Hebrew, *Kurush* in the cuneiform inscriptions), favoured the Jews. In Isaiah this great king is called "the anointed (*mashiakh* in Hebrew) of the Lord" (xlv. 1), "the shepherd who carries out the Lord's decrees" (xliv. 28); he is the "eagle[2] called from the orient, the man appointed by the Lord's counsel" (xlvi. 11); he is "strengthened by the Lord to subdue the heathens" (xlv. 1).[3] From these high terms, in which King Cyrus, who professed the religion of the Magi, is spoken of, we are entitled to infer that this religion was not so diametrically opposed to the Mosaic as the other ancient religions were; that Cyrus, at all events, was no idol-worshipper; a supposition we shall find confirmed by Herodotus, and by the sacred books of the Parsis themselves. The Zoroastrian religion exhibits even a very close affinity to, or rather identity with, several important doctrines of the Mosaic religion and Christianity, such as the personality and attributes of the devil,

---

[1] The religious custom alluded to in Ezekiel undoubtedly refers to the religion of the Magi. The prophet complains that some of the Jews worship the sun, holding towards their face certain twigs. Exactly the same custom of holding a bundle of twigs in the hands is reported by Strabo (xv. 3, 14), as being observed by the Magi when engaged in prayer. It is the so-called Barsom (*Beresma* in the Avesta), still used by the Parsi priests when engaged in worship.

[2] In *Æschylus's* celebrated play "The Persians" the eagle is the symbol of the Persian empire (verses 205-10). The eagle was, as Xenophon reports (Cyropædia, vii. 1, 2), the ensign of the ancient Persians.

[3] The Hebrew word *goyim* (literally "people"), used in the plural, as it is here, denotes the heathenish nations, the idol-worshippers, in their strictest opposition to the Israelites.

and the resurrection of the dead, which are both ascribed to the religion of the Magi, and are really to be found in the present scriptures of the Parsis. It is not ascertained whether these doctrines were borrowed by the Parsis from the Jews, or by the Jews from the Parsis; very likely neither is the case, and in both these religions they seem to have sprung up independently. In the Zend-Avesta we meet with only two words [1] which can be traced to the Semitic languages, neither of them referring to religious subjects. In the later books of the Old Testament we find several Persian words and many names, but they have nothing to do with religion. The most famous of these Persian words in the Old Testament, now spread over the whole civilised world, is the word "paradise," which means originally a park, a beautiful garden fenced in.[2]

The name Magi occurs even in the New Testament. In the Gospel according to St. Matthew (ii. 1), the Magi (Greek *magoi*, translated in the English Bible by "wise men") came from the East to Jerusalem, to worship the new-born child Jesus at Bethlehem. That these Magi were priests of the Zoroastrian religion, we know from Greek writers.

The earliest account of the religion of the Magi among the Greeks is to be found in HERODOTUS, the father of history (B.C. 450). In his first book (chap. cxxxi., cxxxii.) we read the following report on the Persian religion :—

' I know that the Persians observe these customs. It ' is not customary among them to have idols made, temples

---

[1] These are *tanûra*, "an oven;" and *hara*, "a mountain," found only in the name *Harô berezaiti*, "high mountain," considered to be the chief of all mountains; preserved now-a-days in the name *Alborz*. *Tanûra* is evidently the same with the Hebrew *tanûr* (Gen. xv. 17; Isa. xxxi. 9), "an oven or furnace;" *hara* is identical with *har* in Hebrew, "a mountain."

[2] The original form of the word is *pairi-daêza* (in the Zend-Avesta), "circumvallation or enclosure;" in Hebrew we find it in the form *pardes*; in Greek as *paradeisos*. *Pairi* is *peri* in Greek; *daêza* corresponds to *deha* in Sanskrit—*i.e.*, enclosure, generally applied to the body. Of the same root is the English *thick* (very likely identical with S. *digdha*, past participle of the root *dih*, "to besmear, pollute," in a more comprehensive sense "to surround."

'built, and altars erected; they *even* upbraid with folly
'those who do so. I can account for that, only from their
'not believing that the gods are like men, as the Hellenes
'do. They are accustomed to offer sacrifices to Zeus on the
'summits of mountains; they call the whole *celestial* circle
'Zeus. They offer sacrifices to the sun, moon, earth, fire,
'water, and winds, these *elements* originally being the only
'objects of worship; but they accepted from the Assyrians
'and Arabs the worship of Aphrodite, the Queen of
'Heaven, whom the Assyrians call Mylitta, the Arabs
'Alitta, the Persians Mitra.'[1]

'The Persians offer sacrifices to the aforesaid gods in
'the following manner. They neither erect altars nor
'kindle fires when they are about to offer a sacrifice; they
'neither use libations, nor flutes, nor wreaths, nor barley;
'but when any one is willing to offer a sacrifice, he then
'carries the sacrificial beast to a pure spot, and after
'having twined round his turban a great many wreaths of
'myrtle, in preference to any other leaf, he invokes the
'deity. The sacrificer ought not to pray only for his own
'prosperity; he must also pray for the welfare of all the
'Persians, and for the king, because he is included among
'them. When he has cut the animal into pieces, he then
'boils its flesh, spreads the softest grass he can get, espe-
'cially preferring clover, and places the pieces of flesh on
'it. After having made this arrangement, one of the Magi
'who is present sings a theogony,[2] as they call the incan-

---

[1] Here Herodotus has committed a mistake; not as to the matter, but as to the name. The Persians, in later times, worshipped a great female deity, who might be compared with the Mylitta of the Babylonians (the Ashtaroth or Astarte of the Old Testament), but she was called ANAHITA (in the Zend-Avesta and cuneiform inscriptions), and was known to the Arab and Greek writers by the name of ANAITIS. She represented the beneficial influence of water. Mitra is the well-known sun-god of the Persians and a male deity.

[2] Herodotus, who exhibits throughout the whole report an intimate knowledge of the Persian sacrifices, means by theogony here, those sections of the sacred books which are called *Yashts* or invocations, containing the praises of all the feats achieved by the deity in whose honor the sacrifice is to be offered. See the third Essay.

'tation (which is used); without one of the Magi no 'sacrifice can be offered. After waiting a short time, the 'sacrificer takes off the pieces of flesh, and uses them as 'he likes.'[1]

In the 138th chapter of the same book, the father of history says: 'Lying is regarded as the most discreditable 'thing by them; next to it is the incurring of debt, 'chiefly for this reason, that the debtor is often compelled 'to tell lies. If any one of the inhabitants of a town be 'affected with leprosy, or white spots (another kind of 'leprosy), he cannot enter the town, nor have any inter- 'course with the other Persians; they believe him to have 'that disease in consequence of having sinned in one way 'or other against the sun.[2] All foreigners affected with 'these *diseases* are driven out of the country; for the same 'reason many expel even white pigeons. They neither 'make water, nor spit, nor wash their hands, in a river; 'nor will they allow any one else to do so; for they pay a 'high reverence to rivers.'

In another passage (iii. 16) Herodotus reports that the Persians believe Fire to be a god; wherefore Cambyses committed a great sin, as he says, in burning the corpse of King Amasis.

The chief Greek writers on the manners and religion of the Persians were KTESIAS (B.C. 400), the well-known physician to King Artaxerxes II., DEINON (B.C. 350), who is looked upon as a great authority in Persian matters by Cornelius Nepos (in the life of Konon), THEOPOMPOS of Chios (B.C. 300), and HERMIPPOS, the philosopher of Smyrna (B.C. 250). The books of all these writers being lost, save some fragments preserved by later authors, such

---

[1] This custom is still maintained by the Parsis. The flesh (or any other sacrifice) to be offered is first consecrated by the priest, then for a short time left near the fire, and finally taken off by the sacrificer, to be used by him; but it is never thrown into the fire.

[2] The name given to sinners against the sun is *mithrô-drukhsh*, *i.e.*, one who has belied Mithra (the sun). Such diseases were believed to be the consequence of lying.

as PLUTARCH, DIOGENES of Laerte, and PLINY, we cannot judge how far they were acquainted with the religion of the Magi. The two chief sources whence the Greeks and Romans derived information about the religion of the Magi were THEOPOMPOS's eighth book of the history of King Philip of Macedonia, which was entitled "On Miraculous Things," and specially treated of the doctrine of the Magi; and HERMIPPOS, who wrote a separate book "On the Magi." We are left without information whether or not Theopompos derived his statements on the lore of the Magi from his intercourse with the Persian priests themselves; but Hermippos, who composed, besides his work on the Zoroastrian doctrine, biographies of lawgivers, the seven sages of Greece, &c., is reported by Pliny (Historia Naturalis, xxx. 2) to have made very laborious investigations in all the Zoroastrian books, which were said to comprise two millions of verses, and to have stated the contents of each book separately. He therefore really seems to have had some knowledge of the sacred language and texts of the Magi, for which reason the loss of his work is greatly to be regretted.

It is not intended to produce all the reports on the Zoroastrian religion and customs to be met with in the ancient writers, but only to point out some of the most important.

According to Diogenes of Laerte (Pro-œmium, chap. vi.), EUDOXOS and ARISTOTLE stated that in the doctrine of the Magi there were two powers opposed to each other, one representing the good god, called ZEUS and OROMASDES (Ahuramazda, Hormazd), and the other representing the devil, whose name was HADES and AREIMANIOS (Angrômainyush, Ahriman). Of this chief doctrine of the Magi THEOPOMPOS had given a further illustration. According to Plutarch (De Iside et Osiride) and Diogenes of Laerte (Pro-œmium, chap. ix.), he reported that Oromasdes ruled for three thousand years alone, and Areimanios for three thousand more. After this period of six thousand years had elapsed they began to wage war against each other, one attempting to destroy the other; but finally (he says) Areimanios is to perish, mankind is to enjoy a blessed state of life; men will neither be any more in need of food, nor will they cast shadows; the dead are to rise again, men will be immortal, and everything is to exist in consequence of their prayers.

A brief but full account of Zoroaster's doctrine is to be found in Plutarch's book "On Isis and Osiris (chap. xlvi., xlvii.), which being in detail, seems to have been borrowed from a writer who was actually acquainted with the original texts. The philosopher Hermippos, abovementioned, being the only scholar of antiquity who can be supposed, with sufficient reason, to have had a real knowledge of the sacred language of the Zend-Avesta, we may regard him as the author of Plutarch's statements. These are as follows:—

'Oromasdes sprang out of the purest light; among all
'things perceived by the senses that element most re-
'sembles him; Areimanios sprang out of darkness, and is
'therefore of the same nature with it. Oromasdes, who
'resides as far beyond the sun as the sun is far from the
'earth, created six gods (the six *Ameshaspentas*, now
'Amshaspends, "the archangels"); the god of benevo-
'lence (*Vohu-manô*, "good-mind," now called *Bahman*);
'the god of truth (*Asha vahishta*, or *Ardibahisht*); the
'god of order (*Khshathra vairya*, or *Shahrivar*); the god
'of wisdom (*Armaiti*, or *Isfendarmad*); and the god of
'wealth and delight in beauty (*Haurvatât* and *Ameretât*,
'or *Khordâd* and *Amerdâd*). But to counterbalance him,
'Areimanios created an equal number of gods counteract-
'ing those of Oromasdes. Then Oromasdes decorated
'heaven with stars, and placed the star Sirius (*Tishtrya*,
'or *Tishtar*) at their head as a guardian. Afterwards he
'created twenty-four other gods,[1] and set them in an egg;

[1] This statement seems at the first glance to be very strange. But one may easily explain it from the Avesta texts. This writer had evidently in

'but Areimanios forthwith created an equal number of
'gods, who opened the egg; in consequence of this, evil is
'always mingled with good. Thus the good god and the
'demon are engaged in a constant war. Of plants and
'animals, some belong to the good, some to the evil spirit;
'to the good one belong dogs, birds, and crabs; to the evil
'one, water-rats. At the end, the time is to come when
'Areimanios will perish and disappear, in consequence of
'disease and famine, caused by himself. Then the earth
'will become even and equal, and there will be only one
'state and one language, and one and the same manner
'of living to the happy men who then speak only one
'language.'

STRABO the geographer (B.C. 60) has given in the 15th
book of his celebrated Geography an account of the religion
and customs of the Magi, of which some passages may be
thus translated:—'To whatever deity the Persians may
'offer sacrifice, they first invoke fire, which is fed at their
'sacred places with dried barkless pieces of wood, and is
'never to be extinguished; they put fat over it, and pour
'oil into it; if anybody happens to throw or blow into it
'anything dirty or dead, he is to die; the fire is to be
'kindled by blowing.'

In another passage (xi. 8, 4) he enumerates as Persian deities *Anaitis, Omanes*, and *Anadates* or *Anandates*.[1]

PAUSANIUS, the celebrated Greek traveller (A.D. 180), has
the following report on the fire-worship of the Magi (v.
27, 3). 'In the temples of the Persians there is a room
'where ashes of another colour than those being burnt on
'the altar are to be found.[2] To this room he first repairs,

view the thirty spirits presiding over the particular days of the month; he was informed, or he gathered it from his own reading of the texts, that there are two distinct classes of divine beings to be worshipped, six forming the higher order, twenty-four the lower; the Supreme Being, the creator Ahuramazda, was not comprised in these. In the Parsi calendar (Sirozah, thirty days) Hormazd is included in the number.

[1] *Anaitis* is *Anâhitâ*, a goddess, representing the celestial waters. *Omanes* is *Vohu-manô* or *Bahman*; *Anandates* is *Amerctât*, spirit of the trees.

[2] The two kinds of ashes men-

'puts dry wood upon the altar, puts on the tiara, and then
'sings the invocation of the god, reading it from a book,
'in a language utterly unintelligible to the Greeks. The
'wood is to be ignited on the ashes, without fire, and to
'flame up into a bright blaze.'

Passing over DIO CHRYSOSTOMOS (A.D. 130), who has left to us, in his sermons, some remarks on the theological ideas of the Magi, as to their comparing the universe to a chariot in continual motion, drawn by four horses; we may notice an important passage of the historian AGATHIAS (A.D. 500) respecting Zoroaster. He says (ii. 24):
'The present Persians almost entirely neglect their former
'customs, and have even changed them, and observe some
'strange and spurious usages, professing the doctrines of
'Zoroaster, the son of Ormasdes.[1] The time when this
'Zoroaster or Zarades (he is called by both these names)
'flourished and gave his laws, is not to be ascertained.
'The Persians now-a-days simply say that he lived at
'the time of Hystaspes; but it is very doubtful, and the
'doubt cannot be solved whether this Hystaspes was the
'father of Darius, or another Hystaspes. At whatever
'time he may have lived, he was at all events their pro-
'phet, and the master of the Magic rites. After having
'changed the ancient form of worship, he introduced
'manifold and strange doctrines. For they (the Per-
'sians) formerly worshipped Zeus and Kronos, and all
'other gods celebrated by the Greeks, only under other
·names, as for example they call Zeus, *Bel*, Heracles,
· *Sandes*, Aphrodite, *Anaitis*,[2] and the others otherwise,

---

tioned here are those of the Dâd-gâh (*Dâityô-gâtush*), or common hearth of the temple (or any house), and of the Atash-gâh, or place for the sacred fire, which is fed with the greatest care. By 'tiara' (a turban) the Penom (*paitidâna*) is meant, a cloth used to cover the lips to prevent the sacred fire from being polluted. Pausanias well describes here the divine service as performed before the sacred fire. The observance is still maintained.

[1] Plato (Alcibiades, i. 37) says the same, calling Zoroaster a son of Ormazdes, *i.e.*, Ahuramazda, Hormazd.

[2] In this report true and false statements are mixed together. It is true that the religion of the Parsis anterior to Zoroaster was much nearer to that of the Greeks than

'as is reported by BEROSOS the Babylonian, and ATHE-
'NOKLES and SIMAKOS, who wrote on the most ancient
'history of the Assyrians and Medes.'

Before concluding this notice of the Greek records, and proceeding to those of the Armenians and Mohammedans, we may notice some passages of later Greek writers, who lived after Christ at the time of the Sasanians, on the supposed primitive principle of Zoroastrian theology, which will be treated of fully in the last Essay in this book.

The first Greek writer who alludes to it is DAMASCIUS. In his book "On Primitive Principles" (125th p. 384, ed. Kopp) he says, 'The Magi and the whole Aryan nation [1] 'consider, as Eudemos writes, some Space, and others 'Time, as the universal cause, out of which the good 'god as well as the evil spirit were separated, or, as 'others assert, light and darkness, before these *two spirits* '*arose.*'

On the same matter THEODOROS of Mopsuestia writes as follows, according to the fragment preserved by the polyhistor Photios (Biblioth. 81): 'In the first book of 'his work' (on the doctrines of the Magi), says Photios,[2] 'he propounds the nefarious doctrine of the Persians 'which Zarastrades introduced, viz., that about ZAROUAM,[3] 'whom he makes the ruler of the whole universe, and 'calls him Destiny; and who when offering sacrifices in 'order to generate Hormisdas, produced both Hormisdas 'and Satan.'

This opinion on the primitive principle of the Zoroastrian theology seems to have been current among the Christians at the time of the Sasanians, as we may learn more fully from Armenian writers of the fifth century, from

after his time; but it is not true that the Persians at that time worshipped BEL, who was the chief god of the Babylonians, and entirely unknown to the Zend-Avesta.

[1] By this name the Medes are to be understood. According to Herodotus their original name was *Arioi*.
[2] He was a Christian.
[3] He means *Zurvan akarana*, 'boundless time.'

EZNIK, who wrote a book against heretical opinions, and from ELISÆUS, who compiled a history of VARTAN, and the wars waged by the Armenians against the Persians. Eznik says, in his refutation of heresies (in the second book), containing a "refutation of the false doctrine of the Persians:"
'Before anything, heaven or earth, or creature of any
'kind whatever therein, was existing, *Zeruan* existed, whose
'name means fortune or glory.[1] He offered sacrifices for
'a thousand years in the hope of obtaining a son, ORMIZT
'by name, who was to create heaven, earth, and every-
'thing therein. After having spent a thousand years in
'sacrificing, he began to deliberate: Are these sacrifices
'of mine to produce any effect, and will a son, Ormizt by
'name, be born to me? While he was thus deliberating,
'Ormizt and Arhmen were conceived in the womb of their
'mother, Ormizt as the fruit of his sacrifices, Arhmen as
'that of his doubts. When Zeruan was aware of this
'event he said: Two sons are in the womb; he who will
'first come to me is to be made king. Ormizt, having
'perceived his father's thoughts, revealed them to Arhmen,
'saying: Zeruan, our father, intends to make him king
'who shall be born first. Having heard these words,
'Arhmen perforated the womb, and appeared before his
'father. But Zeruan, when he saw him, did not know
'who he was, and asked him: Who art thou? He told
'him: I am thy son. Zeruan answered him: My son is
'well-scented and shining, but thou art dark and ill-
'scented. While they were thus talking, Ormizt, shining
'and well-scented, appeared before Zeruan, who, seeing
'him, perceived him at once to be his son Ormizt on account
'of whom he was sacrificing. He took the rod[2] which he
'had used in sacrificing, and gave it to Ormizt, saying:
'Hitherto this has been used by myself in offering sacri-

---

[1] This interpretation is wrong. The word *zarvan* means simply "time" in the Zend-Avesta, and is preserved in the modern Persian *zamán*.

[2] This is the so-called Barsom (*Beresma*, a bundle of twigs), always used by the Parsi priests when engaged in worship.

'fices for thy sake; henceforth thou mayst sacrifice for my 'sake. When Zeruan handed over his rod to Ormizt, and 'blessed him, Arhmen approached him, saying: Hast thou 'not vowed to make that one of thy two sons king who 'should first come to thee? Zeruan, in order to avoid 'breaking his vow, replied to Arhmen: Oh thou liar and 'evil-doer! the empire is to be ceded to thee for nine 'thousand years; but I place Ormizt over thee as chief, 'and after nine thousand years, he will reign and do what 'he likes. Then Ormizt and Arhmen began the work of 'creation; everything produced by Ormizt was good and 'right, and everything wrought by Arhmen was bad and 'perverse.'

From both these Armenian writers, EZNIK and ELISAEUS, we further learn that the Zoroastrians in their times (5th century A.D.) were split into two parties, inimically opposed to each other; the one was called MOG (Magi, Maghava), the other, ZENDIK.[1]

Passing on to MOHAMMEDAN writers, who lived after the conquest of Persia by the Mohammedans A.D. 650, we may notice some interesting passages.

MASUDI, the celebrated Arabian historian and traveller (A.D. 950), has preserved to us the following notice of the sacred books of the Parsis.[2] 'The first book, made by 'ZERADUSHT, was Avesta. The Persians, not being able 'to understand it, Zeradusht made a commentary, which 'they called ZEND; further he made a commentary to this 'commentary, and called it PAZEND. After Zeradusht's 'death, the Persians made a commentary of the commen-'tary, and an explanation of all the books just mentioned, 'and called it YAZDAH.'[3]

---

[1] The Magi were chiefly spread over the West, in Media and Persia; the Zendiks over the East, in Bactria. The former seem to have acknow-ledged only the AVESTA or original texts of the sacred writings; the latter followed the traditional explanation, called ZEND.

[2] See Chwolsohn in the Zeitschrift der Deutschen Morgenländischen Ge-sellschaft, vol. vi. pp. 408, 409.

[3] He understands by it those piece which are called *Yashts*, and are un-doubtedly the latest productions in the Zend-Avesta.

In another passage, he has the following remark on the origin of the word ZENDIK, *i.e.*, heretic in Persian: 'The 'ZEND being only a commentary on what was formerly 'revealed from heaven (viz., the AVESTA), the Persians 'called any one who put forward religious opinions opposed 'to the Avesta a ZENDIK, because he held his own inter-'pretation (Zend) against that of the Avesta.'

On Zoroaster's age he remarks, that according to the Magi he lived 280 years before Alexander the Great (or about B.C. 610), that is, at the time of the Median king Cyaxares.

SHAHRASTANI, a celebrated Mohammedan writer, who died at Bagdad, A.D. 1153, has given in his highly valuable work " On Religious Sects and Creeds " (*kitâbu-l-milal wa na'hal*) an account of the religion of the Magi, of which he had a better opinion than many other Mohammedan writers. Whilst DIMISHQI (who died A.D. 1327), IBN FOZLAN, and others,[1] identify the Magi with idolators and pagans, Shahrastani brings them under the same head as JEWS, CHRISTIANS, and MUSALMANS, or those whose creed is founded on revealed books; and makes them diametrically opposed to those who follow their own imaginations and inventions (as many philosophers did), the Brahmans and Sabeans (star-worshippers). From his reports we further learn that the Magi were split into several sects, which very likely arose at the time of the Sasanians, such as the MAZDAKYAHS, who believed in the transmigration of souls, like the Brahmans and Buddhists (a doctrine which is altogether strange to the Zend-Avesta); the KAYOMARTHIYAH, who believed in a revelation made by God to the first man, called GAYOMARD by the Parsis, corresponding to ADAM of the Bible; the ZERVANITS who believed in ZARVAN AKARANA, *i.e.*, boundless time, as the supreme deity, which doctrines being altogether strange to the ancient books, were derived from other creeds.

Before taking final leave of these Mohammedan writers,

[1] See Chwolsohn, Die Sabier, i. p. 281; ii. p. 690.

we may notice a peculiar circumstance which deserves attention. In several Mohammedan writings, especially in vernacular Persian dictionaries, we find ZOROASTER, or, as he is there called, ZARADUSHT, identified with ABRAHAM, the patriarch. The Magi are said to have called their religion *Kêsh-i-Ibrâhîm*, i.e., creed of Abraham, whom they considered as their prophet and the reformer of their religion. They traced their religious books to Abraham, who was believed to have brought them from heaven. This was altogether untrue, but the Magi, or Parsi priests, invented it for the purpose of escaping the persecutions of the Mohammedans, and that they might be tolerated to a certain extent; for only those creeds were tolerated by the Mohammedans, the followers of which were able to convince them of their possession of sacred books, connected in any way with the Jewish religion, whose prophets had been acknowledged by Mohammed.

II.—THE EUROPEAN RESEARCHES.

The nations of modern Europe came into contact with the adherents of the Zoroastrian religion in the western part of India, where they had settled when they left their fatherland, Persia, to escape the persecutions of the Mohammedans. Already, in the seventeenth century, manuscripts of the sacred books of the Parsis were brought to England as mere articles of curiosity, but were sealed books to every one. The first who attempted to give a complete description of the doctrines of the Magi was the celebrated Oxford scholar, HYDE. In his very learned work, "Historia religionis veterum Persarum eorumque Magorum," the first edition of which was published in the year 1700, he displays a vast deal of information on the Parsi religion, derived from all the sources which were accessible to him; from Greek and Roman, as well as from Arabian and Persian writers; and tries his utmost to throw light on the religion of the Magi, so famous in antiquity;

but being utterly unable to read the original texts of the Zend-Avesta, though he himself was in possession of several manuscripts of them, he could not succeed in furnishing his readers with a real insight into that ancient creed. His work acted, however, as a stimulus to others to take more interest in the matter.

The first scholar who made Europeans acquainted with the contents of the sacred books of the Parsis was the celebrated Frenchman, ANQUETIL DUPERRON. His ardour and zeal are almost unparalleled in the history of scholarship. He happened once to see a facsimile of some pages written in Avesta characters, which was circulated as a mere curiosity. Actuated by the liveliest desire of earning the glory of first opening the Zend-Avesta to Europeans, he suddenly resolved upon setting out for Western India in order to purchase manuscripts of all the sacred books of the Zoroastrian religion, and to obtain a thorough knowledge of their contents, and of the religious customs of the Parsis from their priests. Being himself unable to afford the means required for carrying out his plan, he entered himself as a sailor in a ship of the French Indian Company, bound for Bombay, in the year 1754, where he safely arrived after a very protracted and dangerous voyage. All the hardships he had to suffer during his passage would have been endured in vain, and he would have ultimately failed in obtaining what he was aiming at, if the French Government had not granted him support. The Parsi priests, being full of distrust towards him, were not willing to sell him valuable manuscripts, and far less to teach him the language of their sacred books.[1] Finally, the only means of obtaining the object wished for was money. He bribed one of the most learned Dasturs, Dastur Dârâb, at Surat, to procure

[1] Since the Parsis and their priests have come more into contact with Europeans, this distrust has subsided to a great extent. The Dasturs will now readily converse about their sacred books and their religion, with any European scholar who really takes a benevolent interest in these matters; and are always willing to give him full explanations of rites and ceremonies, and even to lend him valuable and unique manuscripts, provided they are satisfied that he will not misuse the information he obtains.

him manuscripts, and to instruct him in the Avesta and Pahlavi languages. But to ascertain that he was not deceived by the Dastur, he opened an intercourse with some other priests (Kaus and Manjerj), and was very well satisfied at finding that the manuscripts he purchased first were genuine. When he thought himself proficient enough in the Avesta and Pahlavi, he set about making a French translation of the whole ZEND-AVESTA. He commenced that work in March 1759, and was engaged in it up to the time of his departure. He left for Europe in 1761, after six years' stay in different places in Western India. He had purchased about 180 manuscripts in different Oriental languages, among which were copies of the sacred books of the Parsis. When, after a long and painful passage, he arrived in Europe, he did not proceed at once to his fatherland, France, but went first to England to ascertain whether or not the Avesta manuscripts to be found there agreed with those in his own possession. Finding that they did not differ, he returned quite satisfied to France. All his manuscripts, together with the dictations of the Dasturs, were deposited in the National Library at Paris, where they may be still inspected and used by the student. Ten years after his departure from India he published (in 1771), as the fruit of his indefatigable zeal and industry, the following highly important work in French, *Zend-Avesta, the work of Zoroaster, containing the theological, physical, and moral ideas of this lawgiver, the ceremonies of the divine service which he established, and several important traits respecting the ancient history of the Persians, translated into French from the Zend original, with Notes and several Treatises for illustrating the matters contained in it.* By Anquetil Duperron. 2 vols. 4to.

This groundwork for Avesta studies in Europe created an immense sensation when it was published. A new world of ideas seemed to have been disclosed to European scholars; the veil which covered the mysteries of the famous founder of the doctrines of the Magi seemed to be lifted. But the philosophers found themselves soon greatly disappointed. KANT, the great German philosopher, said, after a careful perusal of the whole work, that throughout the whole Zend-Avesta not the slightest trace of philosophical ideas could be discovered.

The chief question, however, was the authenticity of these books. Some contested, others advocated it. In England the opinion prevailed that the books were forged, and Anquetil imposed upon by the priests. The celebrated Oriental scholar, Sir WILLIAM JONES, published in 1771 a letter in French addressed to Anquetil Duperron (W. Jones's Works, vol. x. pp. 403–99), where he tried to prove that the works translated by that scholar could not be considered as the composition of the celebrated Zoroaster. The chief reason alleged by him was, that their contents grossly contradicted common sense and all sound reasoning; the authority of these books as the chief source of information on the doctrines of Zoroaster was thus denied, and they were represented as the fictions of priestcraft brought forward as the works of Zoroaster. RICHARDSON, the celebrated Persian lexicographer, tried to prove the spuriousness of the Parsi books translated by Anquetil, mainly from philological reasons. He held the opinion (in the preface to his "Persian Dictionary") that the two languages *Zend* and *Pahlavi*, from which the learned Frenchman had translated them, were mere inventions, which had never existed in the provinces of the Persian Empire. His opinion was founded upon four reasons: (1) there is too great a number of Arabic words in both of them, which is a strong proof against their genuineness; (2) the harsh combinations of consonants are contrary to the genius of the Persian language; (3) there is no connection between them and modern Persian; (4) the contents of the books, besides, are so childish that they cannot be ascribed to the ancient Persians. All these reasons can be easily refuted in the present state of research into the Zend-Avesta; but it would be a mere waste of space and time to enter into a real discussion about the authenticity of the Avesta and Pahlavi. In these languages there are no Arabic words whatever; the Avesta is written in a purely Aryan dialect, the elder sister of Sanskrit, as can be easily seen on comparing it with the language of the Veda; in Pahlavi there are many Chaldee, but no Arabic words, and the greater part of the language has a close connection with modern Persian.

In France the authenticity of these books was not doubted, and the great merits of Anquetil were at once acknowledged. In Germany the opinions of scholars were at issue. Some, as MEINERS and TYCHSEN, acceded to the proofs alleged against the genuineness of these books; but another renowned German scholar, KLEUKER, not only admitted the authenticity of Anquetil's work, but translated the whole of it into German, and added several appendices, containing passages from ancient writers on the religion of the Magi. In advocating the authenticity of Anquetil's Zend-Avesta, he relied chiefly on the accordance of the reports of classical writers with those contained in these books.

For a long time the correctness of Anquetil's translation was not doubted by any one, for he had learned the languages from the most competent Parsi priests themselves, who were supposed to possess necessarily a thorough and profound knowledge of their sacred books. In Germany the work was thenceforth the standard authority for all researches into the ancient Persian religion, and the divines used it even for the interpretation of the Old Testament. In England it was laid aside as spurious, and not deserving any attention. The most comprehensive and best description of the Persian religion, chiefly according to the work of Anquetil, was compiled by RHODE, "The Holy Tradition of the Zend People" (1820).

Inquiries into the real nature of the Avesta and Pahlavi languages were not made until more than fifty years after Anquetil's work had appeared. The first who attempted to study this difficult subject was the great Danish scholar

Rask, who had himself been in Bombay, and had purchased many valuable Avesta and Pahlavi manuscripts, which are now deposited in the University Library at Copenhagen. He wrote in 1826 a pamphlet "On the Age and Genuineness of the Zend Language." In this little book he proved the close affinity of the language of the Zend-Avesta to Sanskrit. This proof was sufficient to remove whatever doubts might have been entertained as to the genuineness of the Avesta language. If this language was a true and genuine sister to Sanskrit, then of course it could not be a mere invention of priests, who, moreover, would have been utterly unable to invent such a well-organised language as that of the Avesta really is. Although Anquetil had deposited all the rough copies of his work, together with the dictations of his Parsi teachers (they go by the name of "les brouillons d'Anquetil"), in the National Library at Paris, for the purpose of subjecting his translation to public examination, for a long time no examiner came forward. As Anquetil possessed neither grammar nor dictionary of the Avesta language (because they did not exist), there were, in fact, no means of subjecting his work to a rigid examination. First, the grammatical structure of this ancient language, and the etymology of its words, had to be discovered; but the only means of accomplishing this were by comparing it with Sanskrit, with which highly-finished language Europeans have become acquainted since the end of last century. Anquetil himself was thinking of acquiring a knowledge of this language from the Brahmans, and translating the Vedas, but he did not succeed. The study of Sanskrit spread rapidly from England to France and Germany; everywhere the high importance of this classical language was at once acknowledged. Scholars early discovered its close affinity to Greek and Latin, and as soon as attention was directed to the Zend-Avesta, the relationship of its language to Sanskrit could not but strike the inquirer as still closer, even at the first glance. As already mentioned,

Rask first proved this close affinity, but he gave only a few hints, tending to lead men of high talents to discoveries; so that Rask himself cannot be considered as one of the founders of Avesta philology. This honour was also reserved for a Frenchman.

The first who laid the foundation of a real Avesta philology was EUGENE BURNOUF, Professor of Sanskrit at the Collége de France at Paris, one of the most gifted and talented scholars of his time, a man of whom, as their countryman, Frenchmen have just reason to be proud. Being himself exceedingly well versed in the classical Sanskrit (not in that of the Vedas)—of his mastery over which language he has left us more than sufficient specimens in his translation of the *Bhâgavata Purâṇa*, and his classical works on Buddhism—he applied his sound and critical knowledge of it to the discovery of the rudiments of Avesta grammar and etymology; and his laborious researches were crowned with success. He then first discovered the great incorrectness of Anquetil's translation, the necessary result of a total want of acquaintance with anything like the grammar of the Avesta language. In making his researches he availed himself of NERYOSANGH's Sanskrit translation of the greater part of the *Yasna*, or liturgy, but criticised it by means of comparative philology, chiefly with Sanskrit. Most of his researches he published in his excellent work entitled "Commentary on the Yasna" (1833–35), in which, starting from Neryosangh's Sanskrit translation, he gave the translation, with too copious an explanation, of only the *first* chapter out of the seventy-two which make up the present Yasna, or liturgy. In several numbers of the "Journal Asiatique" (1844–46) he published a revised text, translation, and explanation of the ninth chapter of the Yasna, containing the praise of *Homa* (corresponding to the Soma of the Brahmans). He published, besides, lithographed, the fairest copy of a *Vendidâd Sâdah* (comprising the *Vendidâd*, *Yasna*, and *Visparad*, without the Pahlavi translation) which he found among the manuscripts brought to Europe by Anquetil. This was the first edition of Avesta texts which appeared in Europe (1829–43). After that publication he relinquished his Avesta studies, and engaged himself chiefly in researches into Buddhism. In 1852 a premature death put an end to his important discoveries in several branches of Oriental antiquities.

Before proceeding to trace the further course of Avesta studies, especially in Germany, we may briefly review the merits of the two Frenchmen who have just claims to be regarded as the founders of our investigations into the Zend-Avesta.

ANQUETIL DUPERRON furnished Europe with the materials for these researches, and by his translation introduced the literary world to the chief contents of the sacred books of the Zoroastrians. His work, although utterly incorrect and inaccurate, nevertheless gives a notion of the whole of the Zoroastrian ideas. One could learn from his books the different names of the divine beings, the evil spirits, ceremonies, observances, doctrines, and the contents in general. The reader could see, for instance, that in the first chapter of the *Vendidâd* the names of sixteen countries were enumerated, which being originally good, were spoiled by the bad creations of the devil; that in its second chapter, the story of Yima (Jamshêd) was treated; that the *Yasna* contains prayers of different kinds, addressed to different objects of worship; &c. But it is in the easier parts only that he could gain even an approximate knowledge of the contents; in the more difficult ones, such as the Gâthas, he could not attain even so much, because in them nearly all was translated by Anquetil Duperron according to his own fancy and imagination. Being utterly unable to distinguish cases, tenses, moods, personal terminations, &c., he was liable to the gravest errors and mistakes, which gave rise to wrong conceptions, not only of subordinate points, but of such as were of the highest importance to those interested in the Zoroastrian religion.

To enable the reader to judge of Anquetil's way of translating, we may take his translation of one of the most celebrated passages of the Vendidad (xix. 9, edition of Westergaard), which was supposed to prove *Zarvan akarana*, "boundless time," to be the primitive being, and creator of the good and the bad spirits.

'Ahriman,[1] master of the bad law! the being absorbed 'in glory has given (created) thee, the boundless Time has 'given thee, it has given also, with magnificence, the 'Amshaspends,' &c. According to this translation Hormazd and Ahriman are not the two primitive spirits, but they themselves were created by a supreme being called *Zarvan akarana*, "boundless time." This doctrine being altogether strange to the Zend-Avesta, as we shall see hereafter, was merely interpreted into this passage by Anquetil according to the teaching of his masters, the Dasturs, in consequence of his ignorance of Avesta grammar. He translates the words *zruni akarané* as a nominative case, whilst a very superficial knowledge of Avesta and Sanskrit grammars suffices to recognise both the forms as locatives; they are therefore to be translated only, "in boundless time," the subject of the sentence being *speñtô mainyush*, "the bountiful spirit" (a name of Hormazd); were it the nominative case, and the subject of the sentence, then we should expect to find *zarva akaranem*. The right translation is as follows:—

'O evil-knowing Angrômainyush (Ahriman)! The 'bountiful spirit made (these weapons required to defeat 'the influences of the evil spirit) in boundless time,[2] the 'immortal benefactors assisted him in making *them*.'

Although we may gather from this specimen that Anquetil's translation is nowhere to be relied upon, always lacking accuracy, yet we must thankfully acknowledge how

---

[1] This verse concludes an old song, describing the devil's attacks upon Zarathushtra, and the conversation carried on between them. In the third Essay of this work the reader will find a translation of the whole.

[2] That means only, at a time unknown, at a time immemorial, or in the beginning.

much we owe to him as the founder of all researches subsequently made into the Zend-Avesta. Whilst the translation itself is utterly inaccurate and erroneous, his descriptions of ceremonies and rites are quite correct, as the author can assure the reader from his intercourse with Parsi priests.[1] He was a trustworthy man in every respect, and wrote only what he was taught by the Parsi Dasturs.[2] These high-priests of the Parsi community, who are the only preservers of the religious traditions, and their interpreters, derive all their information about their religion not from the original Avesta texts themselves, but from the Pahlavi translation made of them at the time of the Sasanians. Considering that even this translation is not quite correct, and, moreover, that it is not understood by the Dasturs in a critical and philological way, how can Anquetil be expected to have furnished us with an accurate translation? In many instances also Anquetil misunderstood the Dasturs; so that his translation was tinged with errors of three kinds, viz., those of the Pahlavi translations, those of the Dasturs, and those of his own misunderstandings. His work, therefore, cannot stand the test of close examination, and from a critical point of view it can hardly be styled a translation; it is only a summary report, in an extended form, of the contents of the Zend-Avesta. But he cannot be blamed for that; at his time it was impossible for the most learned and sagacious scholars to do more than he

---

[1] Anquetil was evidently a correct observer and an accurate describer of what he saw. His description of the cave-temples in Salsette could be read on the spot a century after his visit, as the only accurate account of them that had ever been published.

[2] The European reader will not be a little astonished to learn that Anquetil's work was regarded afterwards as a kind of authority by the Dasturs themselves. As, for instance, the late high-priest of the Parsis in Bombay, Edalji Darabji Rustamji, who passed for the most learned priest of his time in India, quotes in his Gujrati work "Mujizát-i-Zartosht" (the Miracles of Zoroaster), p. 10, Anquetil as an authority in order to countenance his strange and quite erroneous explanation of the word *stehrpaêsan-hem* (decorated with stars), as meaning *sadarah*, "the shirt" worn by the Parsis, an interpretation which contradicts the tradition as well as the contexts of the passages, and was consequently not acknowledged by other Dasturs.

actually did. From the Dasturs he learned the approximate meanings of the words, and starting from this very rudimentary knowledge, he then simply guessed the sense of each sentence.

BURNOUF, who first investigated, in a scientific way, the language of the Zend-Avesta, would never have succeeded in laying the foundation of Avesta philology without the aid of Anquetil's labours. Anquetil had left ample materials for future researches, and had furnished scholars with a summary of the contents of the Zend-Avesta. Burnouf, in making his researches, availed himself chiefly of a Sanskrit translation of the Yasna, or liturgy of the Parsis, and found on closer inquiry that this work was more reliable than Anquetil's translation. The Pahlavi translation, upon which this Sanskrit one is founded, would have better answered his purposes; but as he did not take the trouble to study this very peculiar language, it was of no use to him. Neryosangh's Sanskrit translation was then, as to grammatical forms and etymologies, rectified by Burnouf by means of comparative philology, chiefly Sanskrit. But these aids did not prevent him from committing many errors. On the one side he relied too much on Neryosangh's imperfect work; on the other, he applied too often to Sanskrit etymologies. It is true he had made extensive preparations before he commenced his researches, for he compiled for his private use a vocabulary of the Avesta words with quotations from the Zend-Avesta, where each particular word occurs. In making his laborious inquiries into the meaning of any particular word, he quoted parallel passages, the broad ground on which the whole of modern philology, now so highly developed, rests. But there being at his disposal no printed editions of the Zend-Avesta, based on different manuscripts, and pointing out the various readings, he could not peruse the whole of it so carefully as would have been requisite to guard himself against mistakes, which he was otherwise unable to avoid; he was, therefore, often obliged to forego and overlook important passages which would have guided him, in many instances, in ascertaining the exact meaning.

In his etymological proofs he was not always fortunate.[1] He lacked, to a certain extent, the skill requisite for forming sound etymologies (which is really a very difficult task), and besides, his acquaintance with the most ancient forms and words in Sanskrit, as they are to be met with only in the Vedas, was too superficial. The Iranian languages, such as Persian (the application of which requires even greater skill and knowledge than in the case of Sanskrit), were but little attended to by him. Whilst Burnouf often failed in his etymologies, he was almost always successful in determining the grammatical terminations, their affinity to those in Sanskrit being too close not to be recognised at once by a good Sanskrit scholar. And notwithstanding some undeniable defects in his researches, he was the first who gave, not a mere paraphrase or approximate statement of the contents, but a real translation of two chapters of the Yasna (1st and 9th). That was a great step taken towards a sound philological interpretation of the whole Zend-Avesta. But this great scholar seems to have become, in the course of his studies, weary of spending many years in the explanation of only a few chapters, and did not pursue his inquiries further. After having simply pointed out the way, and partially paved it, he left it for others to follow in his tracks. His results refer chiefly to

[1] Thus he says *ákhtâirya* (Yas. ix. 14, Vend. x. 11) is derived from the Vedic root *anj* (to which he ascribes the meaning "to sing"), and may be taken in the sense of "made for being sung." This is utterly wrong. The root *anj*, to which he traces the word in question, never means in the Vedas "to sing," but "to smear, anoint" (being identical with the Latin *unguo*, "to smear"). The context of the passage, where the word in question occurs, besides, requires another meaning. Had he cast a glance only at Vend. x. 3, 7, he would have recognised the word as a numeral, meaning "four times" (literally, "till the fourth time"), and being composed of the preposition *á* (up to, till, as far as), and *khtâirya*, "fourth" (comp. *quatuor* in Latin, *keturi* in Lithuanian, "four"). To the word *karafan* (he writes the crude form wrongly *karafna*, guessing it from the very frequent genitive plural, *karafnâm*), he ascribes the meaning "deaf," while it means, according to the Vedic language, a "performer of sacrifices," as we shall see in the fourth Essay.

grammatical points and the meanings of words, but very little to the general contents of the sacred books of the Zoroastrian religion, or to its origin and development. About these matters his knowledge went but little beyond that of Anquetil. He had no idea of the importance of the Gâthas; he neither knew that their language differs from the usual Avesta language of the other books, nor that they are metrical compositions, their metres agreeing with those of the Vedic hymns; so that he was unable to trace even an outline of the history of the Zoroastrian religion and its sacred writings. This task was, however, at his time, too difficult to be carried out; but he discharged his duties as the founder of the first outlines of Avesta philology with an accuracy, faithfulness, conscientiousness, and sagacity which endear him to every sincere reader, and make his premature death a matter of deep regret. He was really a master in scholarship and scientific investigations, and every page he wrote, even where he erred, bears witness to the truth of this statement.

Whilst the honor of having first opened the venerable documents of the Zoroastrian doctrines to the civilised world belongs to France, Germany and Denmark have to claim the merit of having further advanced this entirely new branch of philological and antiquarian studies.

The first German scholar who took up the study of the Zend-Avesta was JUSTUS OLSHAUSEN, Professor of Oriental Languages at Kiel. He intended to publish an edition of the Zend-Avesta according to the manuscripts extant in Europe, chiefly at Paris and Copenhagen, and to furnish the learned public with a grammar and dictionary. He commenced his edition by publishing the first four chapters of the Vendidad, or religious code of the Parsis, in the year 1829; but after this first number had appeared he stopped his edition, and relinquished this extremely difficult, and in many respects thankless, branch of studies.

This fragment, published by Olshausen, and the edition of a copy of the Vendidâd Sâdah belonging to the National

Library at Paris, by Burnouf, were the only means available for German scholars who had a desire to decipher the language and teaching of the great Zoroaster. The utter insufficiency of these, in order to make any progress in these studies, was felt by all Oriental scholars in Germany. They were, therefore, driven to content themselves with the results arrived at by Burnouf.

The first who made an extensive and useful application of them, now and then adding some remarks of his own, was FRANCIS BOPP, the celebrated compiler of the first comparative grammar of some of the chief languages of the Aryan stock. He tried to give an outline of Avesta grammar, chiefly according to the results arrived at by Burnouf, but nowhere made discoveries of so much importance in the Avesta language as that famous Frenchman had done. His sketch of Avesta grammar, scattered throughout his comparative grammar, although imperfect and incomplete as a first outline, was a valuable assistance to that increasing number of Oriental scholars who were desirous of acquiring some knowledge of the Avesta language, without taking the immense trouble of investigating the original texts themselves.

The first step to be taken by German scholars towards an advance in unravelling the mysteries of the Zend-Avesta, was to put themselves in possession of larger and better materials for their researches. There being no Avesta manuscripts of importance in any German library, students were obliged to go to Paris, Copenhagen, London, and Oxford, the only places where Avesta manuscripts of value were to be found in Europe. Among the German States the honor of having provided scholars with the necessary means to stay at these places in order to collect more ample materials belongs to BAVARIA.

The Bavarian Government granted considerable sums for these purposes to two scholars of its country, to MARC JOSEPH MÜLLER, afterwards Professor of Oriental Languages at Munich, and to FREDERIC SPIEGEL, now Professor of Oriental Languages at the Bavarian University of Erlangen. Müller went to Paris to copy the most important Avesta and Pahlavi manuscripts, and seems to have been very busy during his stay at Paris; he himself, however, made but little use of the materials collected by him. He published only two small treatises, one on the Pahlavi language (in the French Asiatic Journal 1839), treating solely of the alphabet; and one on the commencement of the Bundahish (in the Transactions of the Bavarian Academy of Sciences). Both are valuable, but chiefly based on Anquetil's papers, which the author thankfully acknowledged. Müller, very likely deterred by the enormous difficulties, like many others, then gave up this branch of study, and handed most of his materials over to his younger and more energetic countryman, FREDERIC SPIEGEL.

This scholar intended to give the learned world the first critical edition of all writings in the Avesta language, commonly called the Zend-Avesta, to be based on a careful comparison of all manuscripts then extant in Europe. The materials left to him by Müller and Olshausen not being sufficient to achieve this task, he went, munificently supported by the Bavarian Government, to Copenhagen, Paris, London, and Oxford, and copied all the manuscripts which he required for his purpose. His intention was not only to publish all the original texts, together with the ancient Pahlavi translation, but also to prepare a German translation of them with notes, and to issue both at the same time. But before he was so far advanced as to be able to publish a part of his large work, an edition of the *Vendidâd Sâdah* (comprising the *Vendidâd*, *Yasna*, and *Visparad*), in Roman characters, with an index and glossary, appeared in 1850 at Leipsic.

The author of this really very useful work, which made the original texts of the Zend-Avesta known to the learned public at large, was HERMANN BROCKHAUS, Professor of Sanskrit at the University of Leipsic. Not being in possession of such extensive materials as Spiegel, he contented himself with a transcription, in Roman characters, of Burnouf's edition of the Avesta, and pointed out in footnotes the various readings of Framji Aspendiarji's edition published at Bombay in the years 1842-43 in Gujrati characters. To facilitate the researches of students, he added an index, indicating in alphabetical order the passages where each particular word occurs. In a glossary (distinct from the index) he collected the explanations of the Avesta words, so far as they had been given by Burnouf, Bopp, Spiegel, &c. It was a rudimentary Avesta dictionary, but of course very incomplete, the author confining himself only to those words which were already explained by other scholars. Now and then he corrected errors.

This useful book contributed largely towards encouraging Avesta studies in Germany. Burnouf's edition and his commentary on the first chapter of the Yasna were too costly and comprehensive to become generally used among the students of German universities. But the work of Brockhaus formed a manual for those Sanskrit students who had a desire of making themselves acquainted with the sacred language of the Zend-Avesta. The German Sanskrit Professors began, now and then, to teach the Avesta, but their knowledge of this language being very limited, they could not succeed in training young men for this branch of study so successfully as they did in Sanskrit. The subject is really so extremely difficult, that any one who is desirous of acquiring a complete knowledge of it, is compelled to lay aside for many years nearly all other studies, and devote his time solely to the Avesta. The language could not be learned like Sanskrit, Arabic, Persian, Hebrew, Chaldee, Syriac, Æthiopic, Turkish, Chinese, &c. (all which languages are taught in German universities, but of course not always at the same place), from grammars and dictionaries; in fact, the Avesta language, before it could be learned, had first to be discovered.

But even to begin this task, a very comprehensive and accurate knowledge of several Oriental languages, as the starting-point for further inquiries, was indispensable.

In the meantime, the importance of the Avesta language for antiquarian and philological researches became more generally known, chiefly in consequence of the attempts made to read the cuneiform inscriptions found in Persia. The first language of these inscriptions (which are engraved at Persepolis and on the rock of Bisutûn in three languages) is an Aryan one, and decidedly the mother of the modern Persian. Its very close affinity to the Avesta language struck every one at the first glance; hence the great importance of this language for deciphering these inscriptions was at once acknowledged. That circumstance removed many doubts which were still entertained, especially in England, about the genuineness of the Avesta language. The first work written in English which shows any acquaintance with the original Avesta texts was the Rev. Dr. Wilson's book on the Parsi religion, published at Bombay in 1843, which, although it relies chiefly upon the results of Burnouf's researches, also contains frequent indications of independent investigation.

Whilst Spiegel was preparing his critical edition of the Zend-Avesta, WESTERGAARD, Professor at Copenhagen, announced another one also, prepared from the same materials as were at the former's disposal. This great Danish scholar had the first claims to the publication of an edition of the Avesta texts, on account of the great trouble he had taken to collect additional materials for such a work. Not satisfied with the materials extant in Europe, he left for India and Persia in order to search after new ones. During his stay in India and Persia (1841–43) he unfortunately did not succeed in obtaining manuscripts of much value. There were, indeed, some old copies of the Avesta books extant in Gujrat, and even in Bombay, but it is very difficult to purchase them. In

Persia, no books, hitherto unknown, could be discovered by Westergaard, and even of those known to the Parsis in India, he found only very few copies. We must therefore consider Western India, but more particularly Gujrat, as the only place where any books, hitherto unknown, may be discovered. In the advertisement of his edition of the Zend-Avesta, Westergaard announced the addition of a complete dictionary, with a grammar of both the Avesta dialects, an English translation of the whole, and an account of Iranian antiquities according to the Zend-Avesta.

The first fruit of Westergaard's Iranian studies was, however, not an edition of the Zend-Avesta, but one of the *Bundahish*, or " original creation," still extant in Pahlavi, but not in the Avesta. It is a compendious description of much of the Parsi religion, but is not acknowledged by the Dasturs as a canonical book, like those styled Zend-Avesta; its contents agreeing so exceedingly well with the reports of Theopompos and Hermippos, mentioned above, that we are driven to assign to the original, or its sources, a date not later than the fourth century before the Christian era. Westergaard's edition (Copenhagen, 1851) contains, however, only a lithographed version of one very old codex of the *Bundahish*, extant in the University Library at Copenhagen. He added neither translation nor notes; the only addition he made was a transcript of two inscriptions of the Sasanians, found in a cave at Hájíábád, which were copied by him during his stay in Persia. This edition was reviewed by the writer of these Essays, and the review was accompanied by a short sketch of Pahlavi Grammar.[1]

Before Spiegel issued the first number of his edition of the Avesta texts, he published a "Grammar of the Parsi Language" (Leipzig, 1851). He means by Parsi language that which is now called Pâzand by the Dasturs. It

[1] See ' Ueber die Pehlewi-Sprache und den Bundehesh,' in the ' Göttinger gelehrten Anzeigen,' 1854.

differs very little from modern Persian, except in the want of Arabic words, and is nearly identical with the language written by the great Persian poet Firdausi, A.D. 1000. We are, therefore, fully entitled to call it a somewhat obsolete form of modern Persian. Spiegel added some specimens of religious literature extant in Parsi, with a German translation. This book was also reviewed (in 1853) by the writer of these Essays, who found himself compelled to take an unfavorable view of the scholarship displayed by its author.

A short time after this grammar, the first number of his edition of the Zend-Avesta, comprising the Avesta text of about ten chapters of the Vendidad, appeared. It was printed with beautiful new type at the Imperial printing-office at Vienna (1851), and is really a masterpiece of typography. This number, containing the mere text, without either various readings or the Pahlavi translation, did not suffice to enable the reader to form a judgment of the way in which the text was edited; and the publication of the remaining portion of the Vendidad, together with the Pahlavi translation of the whole, was delayed till 1853. In the same year the first number of Westergaard's edition, printed at Copenhagen, appeared. It comprised the text of the Yasna only, chiefly based on a very old codex (written A.D. 1323),[1] but with footnotes indicating some of the more important various readings of other codices. This edition, although not printed with such beautiful type as that used by Spiegel, was very accurate, and made a much better impression upon the student than that of his rival. In this first number one could see that he had recognised the five Gâthas as metrical pieces. These first numbers of Spiegel's and Westergaard's editions, together with Spiegel's translation of the whole Vendidad, were

[1] This codex is probably the oldest Avesta manuscript in the world, and contains the Yasna alternating with its Pahlavi translation. Another copy of the same texts by the same writer, but dated twenty-two days later, is in the library of Dastur Jamaspji Minochiharji Jamaspasana in Bombay.

reviewed (1852-53) by one of the most distinguished and sagacious Sanskrit scholars in Europe, THEODOR BENFEY, Professor of Sanskrit at the University of Göttingen, in Hanover. He showed that, by a comparison with Sanskrit, which corresponds very closely with the Avesta language, one might arrive at a much better understanding of the Zend-Avesta than had been attained by Spiegel, who appeared to have relied chiefly upon the Pahlavi translation and the information supplied by Anquetil. This Pahlavi translation, made at least thirteen hundred or fourteen hundred years ago, would be a great assistance to any modern translator who understands it thoroughly,[1]

[1] That Spiegel did not understand how to avail himself of the Pahlavi translation much better than Anquetil, seems probable from many passages in his translation; but we may take the first sentences of the Vendidad as an illustration. The original Avesta text, with a literal interlinear translation, is as follows:—

Mraod̠ Ahurô Mazdâo Spitamâi Zarathushtrâi: Azem dadhãm, Spitama
Spake Ahuramazda to Spitama Zarathushtra: I created, O Spitama
Zarathushtra! asô rámô-dáitim nôid̠ kudad̠ shâitim; yêidhi
Zarathushtra! a place of pleasant formation not anywhere habitable; if
zî azem nôid̠ daidhyãm, Spitama Zarathushtra! asô rámô-
then I not should have created, O Spitama Zarathushtra! a place of plea-
dáitim nôid̠ kudad̠ shâitim, vîspô anhush astvão Airyanem
sant formation not anywhere habitable, all life existing into Iran
vaêjô fráshnvád̠.
the pure would have poured forth.

This passage is rendered in the Pahlavi translation, with explanatory phrases (here included in brackets), as follows:—' Aûharmazd said to 'Spitâmân Zaratûshtar: I created, O 'Spitâmân Zaratûshtar! a delightful 'creation of a place where no com-'fort was created [this is where man 'is, the place where he is born and 'they bring him up, seems good to 'him, that is, very excellent and 'comfortable; this I created]; for if 'I should not have created, O Spitâ-'mân Zaratûshtar! a delightful crea-'tion of a place where no comfort 'was created, there would have been 'an emigration of the whole material 'world to Airân-vêj (the earthly 'paradise), [that is, they would have 'remained in the act, while their 'going would have been impossible;

' for it is not possible to go so far as ' from region (*kêshvar*) to region, ' except with the permission of the ' yazads (angels); some say that it is ' possible to go also with that of the ' demons].'

Spiegel's translation of the same passage is as follows :—' Ahura Maz-' da said to the holy Zarathushtra : ' I created, holy Zarathushtra ! a ' place, a creation of pleasantness, ' where nowhere was created a possi-' bility (for drawing near). For if, ' holy Zarathushtra ! I had not created ' a place, a creation of pleasantness, ' where nowhere was created a possi-' bility, the whole world endowed ' with bodies would have gone to ' Airyana-vaêja.'

In this translation Spiegel differs from the Pahlavi in two notable in-as it contains much traditional information which would be vainly sought for elsewhere; but this information is given in a character and idiom not only very difficult to understand, but also particularly liable to be misunderstood. In many cases the Pahlavi translation fails to explain the original text, or evidently misinterprets it. Under these circumstances it can be safely used only as a supplementary authority, in confirmation or modification of results already obtained (after the manner of Burnouf), by a careful comparison of parallel passages, and search for Sanskrit equivalents; or, when these means fail, the Pahlavi translation may often afford valuable assistance, if used judiciously.

Before Spiegel published the second volume of his edition of the Zend-Avesta (1858), containing the Yasna and Visparad, with their Pahlavi translations, Westergaard succeeded in editing all the Avesta texts which are known as yet; and to him we owe, therefore, the first complete edition of the Zend-Avesta. The work is entitled *Zend-Avesta, or the Religious Books of the Zoroastrians, edited and translated, with a Dictionary, Grammar, &c., by N. L. Westergaard. Vol. I. The Zend Texts* (Copenh., 1852–54); but of the two remaining volumes nothing has yet appeared. Westergaard knows too well the enormous difficulties with which the study of the Zend-Avesta is beset to come forward with a hasty translation, grammar,

stances, and, unfortunately, without sufficient reason. The first deviation is with regard to the word *Spitama*, which he translates "holy," in accordance with Burnouf's explanation, which was assented to by all European scholars for a long time. But in Pahlavi it is translated by the patronymical adjective *Spîtâmân*, "the Spitaman, or descended from Spitama" who was the ancestor of Zarathushtra in the ninth generation, as recorded in the Pahlavi books. The Dasturs' tradition confirms this explanation, and the word *spitama* never occurs in any other connection with the meaning of "holy." The other deviation is with regard to the word *shâitim*, which Spiegel translates "possibility," but the Pahlavi translates more correctly by *âsânîh*, "comfort." It is derived from the root *khshi*, 'to reside,' and the meaning of the sentence in which it occurs, is that a place was made delightful which had previously been nowhere habitable. Spiegel now appears to prefer comparing *shâitim* with the Persian *shâdî*, "pleasure, joy," which is more in accordance with the Pahlavi.

and dictionary; he knows that none but he who spends many years in mere preparatory studies is able to give anything like a correct translation of even a portion of the Zend-Avesta. As a first edition of all the Avesta texts, Westergaard's work deserves much praise; he follows, in most cases, the best manuscripts; but if he finds their readings decidedly incorrect, he amends them according to sound philological principles. Compound words, so far as he could discover them, are always marked. From a careful perusal of his work, one may gather that Westergaard understood already a good deal of the texts, and had extensive collections of words, forms, various readings, &c., at his disposal. In every respect except typography, Westergaard's edition of the Avesta texts is far preferable to that of Spiegel, but he did not add the Pahlavi translations.

Passing over some small treatises by Spiegel, published occasionally in the Journal of the German Oriental Society and the Transactions of the Bavarian Academy, of which the best was his essay on the 19th Fargard of the Vendidad, we may now proceed to speak of the researches in the sacred writings of the Parsis made by the author of these Essays.

He commenced the study of the Avesta language in the autumn of 1852, shortly after the publication of the first number of Westergaard's edition of the Zend-Avesta containing the Avesta text of the Yasna. He was already acquainted with the results arrived at by Burnouf, which knowledge was chiefly due to Brockhaus's valuable compilation already noticed. But he was quite convinced, at the very outset of his studies, that, from all that had been hitherto written on the Avesta language and the Zend-Avesta, one could obtain little but merely elementary information on the subject. Actuated by mere love of these ancient records, and cherishing the hope of making some discoveries in this *terra incognita*, he set about the task of instituting inquiries into these sacred texts. He possessed no other aids than those which were accessible to all other scholars, while Spiegel and Westergaard had all the manuscripts, or copies thereof, and the Pahlavi and Sanskrit translations, at their disposal. Westergaard's edition of the Yasna enabled the author to commence this study, but it was soon apparent that unusual difficulties attended every step in this branch of philological study. He first directed his attention to the metrical portions of the Yasna, called the five Gâthas, or hymns, the explanation of which had never been attempted before by any Oriental scholar. It is true Spiegel first observed that their language is different from the usual Avesta language to be found in the Vendidad, Yashts, Visparad, and the other parts of the Yasna; but he rested satisfied with pointing out some of the most striking differences, such as the constant lengthening of final vowels, and had never undertaken to translate these hymns. The author first tried to make out the meaning of a few lines by means of Anquetil's translation, but was soon convinced of its utter insufficiency even as a guide for ascertaining the general meaning. In the Vendidad and the other books Anquetil may guide one in this respect, but not in the Gâthas. The chief reason is the peculiarity of these hymns as to language and ideas; they contain no descriptions of ceremonies and observances, like the Vendidad, nor any enumeration of the glorious feats of angels, like the Yashts, but philosophical and abstract thoughts, and they differ widely from all other pieces contained in the Zend-Avesta. As they have been unintelligible to the Parsi priests for more than two thousand years, we could not expect Anquetil to give even an approximate account of their general contents. As Anquetil's work afforded no assistance, it became necessary to take the trouble of collecting all the parallel passages throughout the Zend-Avesta, and arranging them alphabetically. The index of Brockhaus to the Vendidad, Yasna, and Visparad was a considerable aid; but it was necessary to make an index to the Yashts, which form about one-half of all the Avesta texts extant, and were for the first time published in Westergaard's edition. Being convinced, like Burnouf, that the language of the Vedas stands nearest of all Aryan dialects to the Avesta language, the author betook himself to the study of the sacred writings of the Brahmans, especially that section which is called the *Rigveda Samhitâ*, being a collection of rather more than a thousand very ancient hymns. Only one-eighth part of this large work being published at that time, it was necessary to copy out from a manuscript, kindly lent by Professor Benfey at Göttingen, the remaining seven parts. After that was done, an alphabetical index, at least to some portions of this extensive collection of hymns, had also to be made; but in this tedious work assistance was given by a friend, GOTTLOB WILHELM HERMANN (a young clergyman in Würtemberg), who possesses a remarkable knowledge of Sanskrit. Not content with these aids, the author commenced the study of Armenian (which is affiliated to the Iranian languages), and also that of Pahlavi (being already acquainted with modern Persian). The study of Pahlavi, which language resembles a mixture of Persian and Chaldee, was much facilitated by his being acquainted, to a certain extent, with all Semitic tongues, which knowledge he owed chiefly to his great teacher, Professor EWALD, at Göttingen. After these preparations, the philological operations were commenced in the following manner:— First, all the other passages were examined where the word or form to be investigated occurred, in order to ascertain its approximate meaning. But the parallels referred to being often as obscure as the passage upon which they had to throw light, it was frequently necessary first to make out their meaning also by a reference to other parallels. The approximate meaning of the word being thus arrived at, in most cases after much trouble, it was confirmed or modified by means of a sound etymology; first applying to those words and forms of the Avesta language itself which there was reason to suppose to be cognate to the word in question, and then consulting the Vedas, especially the hymns of the Rigveda. There being neither index nor glossary to these hymns, the same trouble had to be taken with them as with the Zend-Avesta, in order to ascertain from parallels the meaning of the Vedic word referred to. When no satisfactory result was obtained by these means, further search was made in modern Persian and Armenian, and now and then in Latin and Greek also. Modern Persian, especially in its older form, commonly styled Parsi, was of the highest value for such etymological researches. But an appeal to this genuine niece of the sacred language of the Zend-Avesta is in general more difficult, and subject to greater liability of error, than that to Vedic Sanskrit, which is an elder sister of the Avesta language. In modern Persian a good many Avesta words are preserved, but they have undergone such great changes as to make them hardly discernible by a somewhat inexperienced etymologist. Such corruptions of the ancient words are, however, reducible to certain rules, which, being only partially known as yet, had first to be discovered. To illustrate these remarks on the corruption of ancient words in modern Persian by some examples, we may take the Avesta *zaredaya*, "heart," which has become *dil* in modern Persian; *sareda*, "year," is *sâl*; *kerenaoiti*, "he makes," is *kunad*; *âtarsh*, "fire," is *âtash*; &c. In Sanskrit, as the elder sister, the corresponding words are much easier to recognise: thus, *zaredaya* is *hridaya*, *saredha* is *sharad*[1] (in the Vedas), *kerenaoiti* is *krinoti* (the Vedic form, altered in classical Sanskrit into *karoti*), *âtar-sh* is *athar* (preserved only in its derivative *atharvan*, "fireman, priest"), &c. Of the ancient grammatical forms, such as the distinctive terminations of cases, tenses, &c., nothing remains in modern Persian, but all are extant in Vedic Sanskrit.

---

[1] Spelt as pronounced; the letter ç, generally used by European Orientalists, misrepresents the sound of the palatal sibilant, which is that of *sh* in *sheet*, or *ss* in *assure*. The risk of leading to mispronunciation (which is by no means an imaginary evil) more than counterbalances any etymological advantage that can be gained by using *k*, *g*, and ç to represent palatal sounds.

From these remarks, it will be readily perceived that Sanskrit must be of much more use than modern Persian in deciphering the Avesta language.

The first fruit of these laborious researches was an attempt to explain the forty-fourth chapter of the Yasna (forming a part of the second Gâtha), which appeared in the Journal of the German Oriental Society (1853–54). On account of the great difficulty of the subject, and the incompleteness of the intended preparations, at that early date it was impossible to be certain of many of the interpretations proposed. But being convinced, from this first attempt, that the Gâthas contained the undoubted teaching of Zarathushtra himself, as he imparted it to his disciples, the author thought it worth the trouble to pursue these studies six years longer, and published the results of his laborious investigations in a work entitled, "The Five Gâthâs, or Collections of Songs and Sayings of Zarathushtra, his Disciples and Successors," edited, translated, and explained (2 vols., Leipzig, 1858-60). It contains the text, revised according to philological principles, and transscribed into Roman characters, a literal Latin translation, a free translation into German, and a complete critical and philological commentary, with introductions to each of the seventeen chapters, and concludes with an introduction to the whole. The basis of the whole work is the commentary, which gives, at full length, the results of a comparison of all parallel passages in the Zend-Avesta and the Veda, and the etymological researches in the Avesta and cognate languages, together with a partial review of the traditional explanations, so far as they were accessible in a bad transcript of Neryosangh's Sanskrit translation of the Gâthas. Some portions of this work, much revised, will be hereafter submitted to the reader in the third Essay.

About six months after the publication of the first part of this work, SPIEGEL published a translation of the whole Yasna (including the Gâthas), together with the Visparad. In this translation of the Yasna he appears to have relied chiefly upon Neryosangh's Sanskrit version, which, in its turn, is a mere echo of the Pahlavi translation. This is, no doubt, the traditional interpretation; but, unfortunately, the tradition goes but a short way back in the history of such ancient writings as the Gâthas, which had evidently become as unintelligible (from age or difference of dialect) in the time of the Pahlavi translators as they are to the Dasturs of the present day. Any translation based upon such imperfect tradition can claim little attention as a work to be relied on.

Spiegel had previously (in 1856) published his "Grammar of the Huzvâresh Language," a term applied to Pahlavi, and usually written *zvârish* by Persian writers; it appears, however, to mean the peculiar mode of writing adopted in Pahlavi, in which Semitic words (or other obsolete forms) could be substituted by the writer for their Iranian equivalents, and would be read by the reader just as if the Iranian words had been written. This mode of writing is by no means peculiar to Pahlavi, for even in English we often write forms which are strictly analogous to Huzvârish, such as viz., i.e., e.g., lb., %, £ s. d., Xmas, &c., which we generally read as if they were written "namely," "that is," "for example," "pound," "per cent.," "pounds, shillings, and pence," "Christmas," "et cetera." Spiegel's grammar was based upon the forms he found in the Pahlavi translations of the Avesta, and in the Bundahish; and so far as the collection and arrangement of these forms was concerned, it was very complete and useful; but he was unfortunate in his explanations of the Huzvârish forms, and so many of these explanations have since been disproved, that his grammar is practically obsolete, and likely to mislead.

In 1860 Spiegel published, as a second part of his Huzvârish grammar, a work on the traditional literature of the Parsis, illustrated by quotations from the original texts, with translations, and a glossary. This work contains many valuable notices of such Pahlavi texts as were accessible to him, especially the Bundahish, Bahman Yasht, Minokhird, and the Pahlavi translations of the Vendidad, Yasna, and Visparad; together with some allusions to the Vajarkard-i-dînî, Ardâ-Vîrâf-nâmah, Sad-dar Bundahish, Zaratûsht-nâmah, Changhraghâch-nâmah, 'Ulamâ-i-Islâm, Jâmâsp-nâmah, the Rivâyats, and a few minor writings. With some of the longest of the Pahlavi writings Spiegel was then unacquainted, and he was inclined to identify the Shâyast-nashâyast with the Sad-dar Bundahish, not being aware that it is the name applied to the Pahlavi Rivâyat by the Dasturs, and that there is also a Persian book of the same name extant.

Before proceeding to later researches, some other publications relating to the Zend-Avesta have to be mentioned. LASSEN, the well-known Sanskrit scholar, published an edition of the Avesta text of the first five chapters of the Vendidad (Bonn, 1851); but he added neither translation nor explanatory notes.

MAX DUNCKER, the author of a "History of Antiquity" which is highly valued in Germany, treated of the ancient Persian religion, its sacred books and prophets, in the second volume of his work. Although himself a mere historian, and no Oriental scholar, he succeeded in drawing a fine and correct general picture of ancient Iranian life, according to the reports of the Greeks and the modern researches in the Zend-Avesta.

WINDISCHMANN, a Roman Catholic clergyman of high position at Munich, published two valuable essays, one on the deity Anaitis worshipped by the ancient Persians, and mentioned, under the name Anâhita, in the Yashts (Munich, 1856); the other was a translation of the Mihir Yasht, with notes (Leipzig, 1857). His latest researches were published, after his premature death, under the title of "Zoroastrian Studies," edited by Spiegel (Berlin, 1863). This work contains a very useful translation of the Bundahish, with extensive explanatory notes and essays upon several of its subjects, including a translation of the first half of the Fravardin Yasht. His translations were a great improvement on those of Anquetil, being made on scientific principles. In the case of the Bundahish, he had really to rely upon the single text published by Westergaard, as previously mentioned; for Anquetil's manuscript of the text was originally copied from the same codex, now at Copenhagen.

In 1864, BLEECK published an English translation of the Avesta, at the request of Seth Muncherjee Hormusjee Cama. This was merely a translation from the German of Spiegel, but the translator referred to the original text as a guide to his choice of words in many places, and in some instances he complains of the German version being quite as unintelligible as the Avesta text itself. This translation was intended for the information of the Parsis, but it has also been useful to that portion of the English public which takes an interest in Zoroastrianism, though unprepared to face the difficulty of foreign languages. It contains, of course, all the imperfections of Spiegel's translations.

The further researches of the author of these Essays were greatly facilitated by his being appointed, in 1859, superintendent of Sanskrit studies in Poona College, near Bombay. He was thus brought into contact both with Brahmans and Parsi priests, the present possessors of all the traditional Vedic and Zoroastrian lore that has not been lost. After a short interval, employed in learning Marâthi, the vernacular language of that part of Western India, and in the further study of English, he began his observations of the native modes of study, and followed them up by close inquiries regarding their rites and ceremonies. He had, in the first place, to unlearn much that he had learnt in Europe; and to his readiness in accepting the fact that European scholarship must often stand corrected before Indian tradition was probably due his ever-increasing influence over the natives, which enabled him, in the end, to obtain fuller information regarding their ceremonies than had ever previously been given to a European.

The Parsis had gradually lost much of their reluctance to discuss religious matters with Europeans, which had been engendered or aggravated by their bitter controversy with the missionaries, some twenty years before, and which had been brought to a climax by the publication of the Rev. Dr. Wilson's book before mentioned. They felt that this book was so far one-sided as to give a false idea of their religion, and they were naturally indignant at the sarcasms it contained.[1] But the progress of time and education had dissipated this ill-feeling, and they were delighted to find a European scholar who understood so much of their religion as to appreciate its good points without dwelling too severely upon those which are doubtful or objectionable. With a feeling of growing confidence, the priests discussed their ceremonies and sacred books, and the laity were glad to receive, from a European scholar, explanations of their older scriptures which had hitherto been nearly sealed books to all. To meet this increasing demand for information, a public lecture, "On the Origin of the Parsi Religion," was delivered on the 1st March 1861; and the first edition of these Essays was published in 1862.

In the cold season of 1863–64 the author undertook a tour in Gujrat, under Government patronage, to search for Avesta, Pahlavi, and Sanskrit manuscripts. During this tour he examined most of the Parsi libraries in Surat,[2] Nâwsâri, Bhroch, and Balsâr, and succeeded in purchasing several manuscripts for the Bombay Government, including

---

[1] Any personal ill-feeling which Dr. Wilson may have occasioned by his book soon disappeared; but it was many years before his habitual kindliness, and conscientious efforts for the improvement of the natives of India, regained the confidence of the Parsis. On his death, however, in 1875, no one felt more deeply than the Dasturs themselves that they had lost one of their best friends, and that in his controversy with them he had only acted as his duty compelled him.

[2] The only Parsi priest in Surat who knew anything of Anquetil Duperron was Dastur Kai-Khusro Darab, who recollected hearing that Dastur Darab had taught Anquetil the Avesta, and shown him the sacred fire, when disguised as a Parsi.

a very old copy of the Avesta text of the Yasna, an old copy of the Vendidad with Pahlavi, and a Vendidad-sâdah written in 1626. Some other manuscripts were presented to him as tokens of personal respect on the part of their owners. Among these was a very old manuscript containing the Visparad with Pahlavi, Hâdôkht Nask, Pahlavi Rivâyat, Ardâ-Vîrâf-nâmah, Bundahish, and several minor texts, written in 1397; also copies of the Nîrangistân, Shikand-gumâni, &c. With regard to Sanskrit translations, he could find none of the Yasna extending beyond the Srôsh Yasht; and of the Vendidad, only Fargards viii. 79, 80, and ix. 1–4 (Westerg.), appear to have been ever translated into Sanskrit. He also saw a Sanskrit Sîrozah and an incomplete Avesta-Sanskrit glossary. At Nâwsâri he found two copies (one in Avesta and the other in Avesta with Pahlavi) of a book called the Vaêtha Nask, from its beginning with the word *vaêtha;* and other copies of it were seen elsewhere. Both its Avesta and Pahlavi were full of grammatical errors, and there is reason to believe that this work was fabricated by some Dastur more than a century ago, for the purpose of settling the inheritance of the children of a non-Zoroastrian wife, which it fixes at one-half the property, while the widow is to receive the other half. This is contrary to the opinion of most Parsi priests, who would consider such children not entitled to any share of the paternal property, although there appears to be nowhere, in the Avesta texts extant, any direct prohibition of intermarriages between Zoroastrians and non-Zoroastrians.

After his return to Poona, in 1864, the author recommended the Government of Bombay to employ Dastur Hoshangji Jamaspji, a younger brother of the high-priest of the Parsis at Poona, to prepare editions of several Pahlavi works for publication; and he subsequently undertook to revise these works, and see them through the press, on his return to Germany in 1866. He also delivered a lecture, " On an Original Speech of Zoroaster"

(Yasna xlv.), before an almost exclusively Parsi audience, at Bombay, on the 8th October 1864, at their special request. And in pursuance of his schemes for encouraging Parsis in the study of their religious literature, the proceeds of this lecture were appropriated as prizes for the best translations, by Parsis, of two Pahlavi works, one of which, the Pandnâmah of Adarpâd Mâraspend, was published in 1869.

Turning back to Europe, we find a young and industrious scholar, JUSTI, of Marburg, publishing a "Handbook of the Zend Language" (Leipzig, 1864), containing a dictionary (Avesta and German) of all words in the texts published by Westergaard, a grammar, and selections for reading, all printed in Roman type. This dictionary is a very useful compilation in a handy form, and, so far as arrangement is concerned, it leaves little to be desired; but having been prepared with too little study of the texts, it is often incorrect in its definitions, and is therefore likely to perplex the careful student, and mislead the unwary, unless it be used rather as a handy index than a complete dictionary. Many of these defects will probably disappear in a second edition, which ought also to include the Avesta words peculiar to the Zend-Pahlavi glossary and Nîrangistân; but the Avesta dictionary long ago promised by Westergaard would be more welcome, and be used with more confidence.

In 1868 Justi also published a translation of the Bundahish, with the Pahlavi text lithographed and transliterated into Persian characters, and a glossary, in which the Pahlavi words are printed in Persian type. From some misconception, he claims, on the title-page, to have published the Bundahish for the *first time,* whereas the lithographed text had been already published by Westergaard in 1851, and translations had been published by Anquetil in 1771, and by Windischmann in 1863. Justi had the advantage of collating another recension of the text, contained in a Pahlavi MS. at Oxford and a Pâzand

MS. in London, both of which have evidently been derived from the very old MS. written in 1397, and presented to the author of these Essays at Surat, as mentioned above. The translation is, therefore, more correct than its predecessors, though blunders are not unfrequent. Justi argues that the Bundahish is not older than the time of Firdausi, and its statement about the accession of the Arabs cannot, of course, be more than three centuries older; but many of the other signs of late date which he relies on are fallacious. It seems plausible enough to argue that the more old forms of words a MS. contains, the older it must be; but when one finds old forms substituted in a modern MS. for later forms in a MS. five hundred years old (as often happens in Pahlavi), this argument evidently fails, and we have to suspend our judgment until the period when the later forms first arose has been historically ascertained. With regard to the Bundahish, it has probably been too hastily assumed that it is a single continuous work; it may be half-a-dozen fragments, either of the same or various works, thrown together in different orders by different writers, as the MSS. vary in arrangement, and the fragments constituting Anquetil's Chapters xxviii., xxix., xxx., and xxxii., have been hitherto found only in the MS. at Copenhagen, and its two modern copies. This fragmentary condition of the book is more consistent with the supposition of its antiquity than of its later origin; it also explains how some fragments may be much older than others. However this may be, the arrangement of the fragments in the Copenhagen MS. is probably that adopted in the latest edition, as it is most consistent with the idea of a continuous text.

The author of these Essays, after his return to Germany in 1866, revised and published, for the Government of Bombay, some of the Pahlavi works prepared by Dastur Hoshangji, as mentioned above. The first of these was the "Old Zend-Pahlavi Glossary," which is found in two of the oldest Pahlavi MSS. extant. The text was printed in the original character, with an interlinear transliteration in italics, and accompanied with an introduction, English translation, and alphabetical index to the Avesta words, arranged as an Avesta glossary. The introduction treated, first, of the age and origin of Pahlavi; and, secondly, of the age and value of the glossary; and it contained the first systematic attempt to connect the Pahlavi of the Sasanian inscriptions with that of the Parsi books. This glossary was published in 1867, and was followed in 1870 by the " Old Pahlavi-Pâzand Glossary," of which the text and index had likewise been prepared by Dastur Hoshangji. The index, which was arranged as a Pahlavi-English glossary, was considerably enlarged by the addition of all the Pahlavi words in the "Zend-Pahlavi Glossary." And the work was preceded by a long and important introductory essay on the Pahlavi language, in which the nature of that language was, for the first time, fully and critically examined, and a sound basis laid for future investigations. This essay began with a history of the researches in Pahlavi literature, inscriptions, and numismatics which had been made in Europe. It then proceeded to discuss the meaning of the terms Pahlavi and Huzvârish, identifying Pahlavi with Parthian or ancient Persian, and explaining Huzvârish as the mode of writing Pahlavi with a large intermixture of foreign or obsolete words. It next deciphered several Sasanian inscriptions, and compared their language with that of the Parsi books, with the view of determining the character of Pahlavi, which it defined as a Semitic language, with an admixture of Iranian words, and a prevailing Iranian construction, if we look only to the way it is written (all the pronouns and particles, and most of the common words, being usually Semitic); or as a purely Iranian language if we consider only the way in which it is read; and to this practice, of reading the Iranian equivalents of the written Semitic words, it attributed the total disappearance of these Semitic words in modern Persian as soon as the writers began to write as they spoke. The essay concluded by discussing the origin and age of Pahlavi, and showed that traces of that language can be discovered in some short inscriptions of the fourth and seventh centuries B.C. Although this glossary was originally published by Anquetil in his Zend-Avesta in 1771, it was in such a modified form that it remained for a century practically useless.

Shortly after the publication of the first of these glossaries, the author of these Essays was appointed Professor of Sanskrit and Comparative Philology at the University of Munich, where he continued to publish, from time to time, short essays on subjects connected with Parsi literature; among them an essay " On the Present State of Zend Philology" (1868), in which he sought to correct the misapprehensions of other scholars with regard to the meanings of certain Avesta words. Also a translation of the eighteenth Fargard of the Vendidad, with a commentary (1869); and an essay on the Yathâ-ahû-vairyô, one of the most sacred formulas of the Parsis, with a translation of its commentary in Yasna xix. (1872).

The last of his works connected with the Parsi religion was the revision and publication of Dastur Hoshangji's edition of "The Book of Ardâ-Vîrâf" (1872), and its glossary (1874). In the preparation of these works, and also in the Pahlavi-Pâzand glossary, he was assisted by an English friend, E. W. West, whose attention had been first directed to Pahlavi by the discovery of inscriptions in that language at the old Buddhist caves of Kanheri, about twenty miles north of Bombay. To the Pahlavi text and transliteration of the book of Ardâ-Vîrâf were added the texts and transliterations of the tale of Gôsht-i Fryânô and the Hâdôkht Nask, with English translations of all three texts, and introductory essays describing the manuscripts used, the system of transliteration adopted, and the contents of the texts. The glossary, which was prepared by West from the original texts and from materials supplied by Dastur Hoshangji, was arranged in the alphabetical order of the Pahlavi characters, as compared with their modern Persian equivalents. It forms a complete index to the three texts, and to some Pahlavi fragments which had been published, but not glossarised, in the introductions and notes to the previous glossaries. It would be a great assistance to scholars if other Pahlavi texts were published in a similarly complete manner, but the labour of doing so, with sufficient accuracy, is alarmingly great. To the glossary was added an outline of Pahlavi grammar.

Besides assisting in the publication of Dastur Hoshangji's works, WEST had also published "The Book of the Mainyô-i-khard" (1871) which professes to give the utterances of the Spirit of Wisdom on many of the doctrines and details of the Parsi religion. In this work the Pâzand text and Neryosangh's Sanskrit translation were printed in Roman type, and accompanied by a glossary of all the Pâzand words, with an outline of Pâzand grammar.

Passing over some short essays, such as Sachau's "Contributions to the Knowledge of Parsi Literature," and also larger works of more pretension, such as Spiegel's "Iranian Antiquities," this account of European researches may be concluded by a short notice of some French works.

A new French translation of the Avesta is in the course of publication by C. DE HARLEZ, Professor at the University of Louvain, in Belgium. The first volume (1875) contains a translation of the Vendidad, with an introductory historical account of Zoroaster and the Avesta, and some details regarding Zoroastrian doctrines and ceremonies. The second volume (1876) contains translations of the Visparad, Yasna, Hâdôkht Nask, and the first ten Yashts of Westergaard's edition of the texts. These translations are based not only upon Spiegel's translations, but also upon the works of all other scholars hitherto published, which have been carefully compared with the original text by M. de Harlez, who has selected the most satisfactory explanations, or modified them in accordance with his own researches. He has endeavoured to give the meaning of the text without being slavishly literal in his translation, because the French language, in his opinion, does not tolerate strictly literal translation where the meaning is obscure. This is unfortunate, as there are many obscure passages into which it would be very hazardous to import more meaning than the original text implies. Perhaps it would be more correct to say that French writers, like Orientals, cannot tolerate that strict accuracy of translation which seems so desirable to Teutonic scholars.

With regard to the Vendidad, it may be noticed that all translators have been misled into admitting Avesta quotations, made by the Pahlavi commentator, as integral portions of the Avesta text. This mistake has arisen from the Avesta text being printed separate from the Pahlavi, instead of alternating with it as in the original manuscripts. Neither the writers of the Vendidad Sâdah, nor the European editors of the texts, have been always able to distinguish these quotations from the original text; nor is it sometimes easy to do so; but Vend. i. 4 (i. 2, Westerg.) consists of four such quotations which form part of the Pahlavi commentary.

A young French scholar, JAMES DARMESTETER, has recently engaged in the study of the Avesta texts in a strictly scientific manner, and has published several essays of considerable importance. Among these may be mentioned his "Zend Notes," and "Notes on the Avesta," in which he traces the philological relations of many Avesta words, for the purpose of fixing their meanings. His essay on "Haurvatâd and Ameretâd" (1875) traces the history of these two ideas, health and immortality, as they first became personified as archangels who oppose Tauru and Zairicha, the demons of sickness and death; secondly, as these archangels acquired the attributes of protectors of water and vegetation, and their opponents became the demons of hunger and thirst; and finally, as their names became corrupted into Khurdâd and Murdâd, when there appeared a tendency to treat them as titles of fire and the angel of death. This account of these two Ameshaspentas is ably supported, and to a great extent substantiated, by quotations from the Avesta and Veda.

His latest work is an exhaustive essay " On Ormazd and Ahriman " (1877), in which he has applied the method of comparative mythology to explain the myths, equally with that of comparative philology to explain the texts. The conclusion he arrives at is, that Mazdayasnianism was originally a dualism which taught that the universe was created by two beings, Ahuramazda, who is luminous and good, and Angra-mainyu, who is gloomy and bad; and the history of the universe is a history of their struggles for supremacy. Ahuramazda can be traced back to Asura, the supreme god of Indo-Iranian times, and is the representative of Varuna, Zeus, or Jupiter. But Angra-mainyu is a later idea of the Iranians only, although he takes the place of the Indo-Iranian serpent-demon who fought with the fire-god in storms. This dualism satisfied the popular mind, but philosophers found it necessary, in the end, to set up a First Cause, whom they called Boundless Time, or Destiny, and from whom they imagined that both the creative beings proceeded. These conclusions, so far as the primary dualism is concerned, will hardly be accepted by the Dasturs as a correct view of Zarathushtra's teachings. The Parsis are now strict monotheists, and whatever may have been the views of former philosophical writings, their one supreme deity is Ahuramazda. Their views of Angra-mainyu seem to differ in no respect from what is supposed to be the orthodox Christian view of the devil. Whether Darmesteter's conclusions regarding the dualism can be fully maintained is rather doubtful; the question depends rather upon the exact meaning of a few difficult passages in old writings, which are confessedly mere fragments, than upon the wide generalisations of comparative mythology, which may easily mislead.

III.—ZOROASTRIAN STUDIES AMONG THE PARSIS.

Before concluding this Essay, we may briefly notice the efforts of the Zoroastrians themselves to preserve and elucidate their ancient religion and literature.

The Persian cuneiform inscriptions inform us that the Achæmenian kings believed in Ahuramazda, and that their language was closely allied to that of the Avesta; in fact, the period of their rule appears to have been the Augustan age of Zoroastrian literature, when it was completed and arranged in twenty-one books, called Nasks, each indexed by one of the twenty-one words composing the sacred *Yathâ-ahû-vairyô* formula. This period is approximately mentioned in the book of Ardâ-Vîrâf, when it states that for "three hundred years the religion was in purity, and men were without doubts."

We know from classical writers that Alexander, in a drunken frolic, burnt the citadel and palace of the Achæmenian kings at Persepolis, in which one of the two complete copies of the Zoroastrian literature had been deposited; thus one copy was burnt, and the other is said to have been plundered by the Greeks. Any other copies, more or less partial, must have suffered greatly during the next 550 years, while the Zoroastrian religion received little support from either Greeks or Parthians, although the fourth book of the Dînkard mentions that Valkhash (Vologeses) the Ashkanian ordered all extant writings to be collected and preserved.

The earlier kings of the Sasanian dynasty collected and rearranged the scattered writings, and the more peaceable of the later kings encouraged literary pursuits; but the Mohammedan conquest of Persia, and the troubled times which followed, swept away nearly all these writings, notwithstanding two or three attempts of leading Zoroastrians to preserve what was still extant. Of these attempts it is recorded, at the end of the third book of the Dînkard, that

Adarpâd-i Adarfrobag-i Farukhzâdân collected all the old writings he could find; and this collection falling into decay, was again copied by Adarpâd-i Admîtân, and arranged in the form of the Dînkard, the fourth and fifth books of which appear to contain the sayings of Adarfrobag-i Farukhzâdân, and those he selected from the religious books. Of the subsequent fate of the Dinkard more will be said in the next Essay.

The Zoroastrian fugitives who settled on the western shores of India found it difficult to preserve all their religious ceremonies and literature, and frequently applied to their persecuted brethren in Persia for information during the first ten centuries after the Mohammedan conquest. Parsi writers may probably exaggerate the ignorance of their forefathers in India, as it was during these dark ages that one of their priests, the famous Neryosangh Dhaval, was able to translate several of their religious books from Pahlavi into Sanskrit. Among these books are the Shikand-gumânî, Mainyô-i-khard, and the greater part of the Yasna, the translations of which exhibit a knowledge of the original Pahlavi that is hardly yet surpassed by modern Dasturs. Neryosangh appears to have aimed at popularising the obscure Pahlavi texts by transliterating them into Pâzand; but why he should have added a Sanskrit translation is not so apparent, unless it were for the information of strangers, or as a somewhat unnecessary stepping-stone to a Gujrati version. As manuscripts of the early part of the sixteenth century are still extant, which have descended from Neryosangh's writings, it is evident that he must have lived as early as the fifteenth century; and judging from their genealogies, the present Dasturs are inclined to think that he flourished about that time.

The Parsis are also indebted, to some priests of these dark ages, for the successive copies of their sacred books which have preserved their religious writings from total destruction. The oldest of these copyists whose manuscripts still survive was Mihrâpân-i Kai-Khusro-i Mihrâpân-i Spendyâd-i[1] Mihrâpân-i Marjpân-i Bahrâm, who appears to have been a voluminous though rather careless copyist, as we find his name in many colophons dated about 550 years ago. He seems to have completed the book of Ardâ-Viuâf and Gôsht-i Fryânô (copied in K_{20} now at Copenhagen) on the 18th of the tenth month A.Y. 690; the first part of the so-called Pahlavi Shâhnâmah (now in the library of Dastur Jamaspji at Bombay) on the 11th of the sixth month A.Y. 691, and the latter part on the 19th day of another month in the same year; the Yasna with Pahlavi (now at Copenhagen) on the 27th of the tenth month A.Y. 692; another copy of the same (now in the library of Dastur Jamaspji at Bombay) on the 19th day of the eleventh month A.Y. 692; the Vendidad with Pahlavi (now at Copenhagen) on the 24th day of the fourth month A.Y. 693; the Shâyast-lâ-shâyast (copied in K_{20} now at Copenhagen) on the 9th day of the seventh month A.Y. 700; and the Hâdôkht Nask (copied in the same) on the 18th day of the ninth month A.Y. 720; also the Vendidad with Pahlavi (now in the India Office Library at London) seems to be in his handwriting, but the colophon is lost. Of these eight manuscripts, four are still extant in Mihrâpân's handwriting; three we know only from copies taken about five hundred years ago, and now contained in the manuscript K_{20} at Copenhagen; and the handwriting of the Pahlavi Shâhnâmah is so like that of K_{20}, that it may be a similar copy from Mihrâpân's manuscript. Three of his books were copied at Kambâyat from manuscripts (*yadman nipîk*) written by Rustam-i Mihrâpân-i Marjpân-i Dahishnyâr, who may have been his great-grand-uncle.

Passing on to later times, we find the arrival of the Iranian Dastur Jamasp (surnamed Wilâyati, "foreign") giving a considerable impulse to the study of religious literature among the Indian Parsis. He is reported to have left Persia on the 27th November 1720, and to have

[1] Once written Spendyâr.

given the Dasturs at Nawsari, Surat, and Bhroch much information regarding the customs and learning of the Zoroastrians in Persia. The chief Dastur at Nawsari, Jamasp Asa, became celebrated for his learning, and at his death, about 125 years ago, left a large library of manuscripts, which has become much scattered among his posterity, now in the fifth generation. The visit of Dastur Jamasp Wilâyati appears to have first called the attention of the Indian Parsis to the fact that their calendar was exactly one month behind that of their Persian brethren. This was a matter of some importance, as it would, in their opinion, destroy the efficacy of their prayers if the wrong month were mentioned, and it altered the date of all their festivals. It was not, however, till after further inquiries in Persia, and the arrival of another priest therefrom, that several Indian Parsis determined to adopt the Persian calendar, which they did on the 17th June 1745, corresponding to the 29th day of the ninth month A.Y. 1114 of the Persian reckoning, which they styled *qadîm,* "ancient," while the old Indian reckoning, which has been retained by the majority of the Parsis, is styled *rasmî,* "customary," or *shâhanshâhî,* "imperial;" the term *qadîm,* however, when found in older documents, is said to mean the old reckoning of the Indian Parsis.

This alteration in the calendar, and several small alterations in ritual in accordance with Persian usage, such as pronouncing *vohî* for *vohû,* constituted a complete schism requiring a distinct priesthood, and occasioned much controversy. The old-calendar party accounted for the difference in reckoning by supposing that the people in Persia had forgotten to insert an intercalary month which their fugitive brethren had remembered to do shortly after their flight from the Mohammedans: if this were the case, it is difficult to understand why the intercalary month was not again inserted every 120 years, according to the supposed practice. To support this theory it became necessary to prove, from the religious books, that such an intercalary (*kabísah*) month was therein enjoined, and this led to the *kabísah* controversy, in which the chief advocates for the intercalation were Dastur Aspendiarji Kâmdinji of Bhroch, who published a book on the subject in 1826, and Dastur Edalji Dârâbji of Bombay, who published the book of the Khorehe-Vêhîjak in 1828. Their chief opponent was Mullâ Fîrûz, who published the Avîjeh-Dîn, in 1830, to refute Dastur Edalji's views. Much of the controversy turns upon the meaning of one or more Pahlavi words, generally read *rêhîjakîk*, which Dastur Edalji translates as "intercalary," and Mullâ Fîrûz explains as referring to new-year's day, or the beginning. In some cases the word cited means evidently "additional," but none of the passages quoted seem to bear much on the question of an intercalary month, either one way or the other, although Dastur Edalji has mistranslated one obscure passage so as to prove his case. That there must have been some mode of keeping the calendar in accordance with the sun in former times appears evident from the Bundahish (p. 59, Westerg.), where two of the *gahanbâr* festivals are made coincident with the longest and shortest days respectively; but there seems to be no account in the Parsi books of the mode adopted for the rectification of the calendar.

The growing demand among Parsis for further information regarding the contents of their sacred books was met, to some extent, by the publication (in 1843) of the Yasna text in Gujrati characters, with a Gujrati translation, by ASPANDIARJI FRAMJI; and a similar translation of the Vendidad was made about the same time. These translations are noteworthy as being the latest Parsi works of this nature which are free from European influence, and can therefore be consulted by European scholars as the last embodiment of pure traditional information.

The foremost of the Parsi writers who represent the period of transition from confidence in old traditions to reliance on European scholars, is Dastur PESHOTANJI

PARSI WRITINGS. 59

BEHRAMJI SANJÂNÂ, the present high-priest of the Bombay Parsis of the predominant sect. In 1848 he published the Pahlavi text of the Vajarkard-i-dînî, from a modern copy of an old manuscript at Surat: this is probably the first book printed with Pahlavi type. In 1853 he published a Gujrati translation of the Pahlavi Kârnâmak-i Ardashîr-i Pâpakân, which is a fairly good specimen of correct translation. Before the publication of his "Grammar of the Pahlavi Language" (in Gujrati, 1871), Dastur Peshotanji had ample opportunity to study the views of European scholars; and his grammar, which is very complete, though rather too voluminous, is a great improvement upon the one or two Pahlavi grammars previously published by Parsi writers. He thinks that the pronunciation of the Semitic portion of the Pahlavi in Sasanian times has been correctly handed down by tradition, and that its variations from Chaldee are due to corrupt pronunciation when the words were first adopted, and not to mere misreading of the characters after the correct pronunciation was lost. This opinion, however, is not confirmed by reference to the inscriptions of Sasanian times; thus, the word traditionally pronounced *jânûn*, "become," is found inscribed *yahvûn* in unambiguous Sasanian characters, exactly as had been anticipated by European scholars, whose proposed readings of several other Huzvârish words are fully confirmed by the Sasanian inscriptions. In some cases the inscriptions have contradicted the views of European scholars, so Parsi writers exercise a wise discretion in not departing from their traditional readings too hastily.

The latest work of Dastur Peshotanji, of which the first volume appeared in 1874, is the Dînkard, in which he gives the Pahlavi text with a transliteration in Avesta letters, a Gujrati and English translation, and a glossary of some selected words. This first volume contains about one-eighteenth part of the extant portion of the Dînkard, or about one-eighth of the third book, which is the least interesting part of the work, and perhaps the most difficult to translate. Many improvements in the translation might be suggested, but it gives the meaning of the original as nearly as can be expected in a first translation of a difficult text. The second volume, published in 1876, completes the first tenth part of the extant text, and fully maintains the character of this edition of the Dînkard for accuracy.

The works of Dastur HOSHANGJI JAMASPJI have already been mentioned (p. 48–51) as having been revised by the author of these Essays, and published under his supervision. In their original state they displayed a very considerable knowledge of Pahlavi on the part of Dastur Hoshangji, who had disposed of many of the chief difficulties which might otherwise have troubled the reviser; most of the corrections required were due to additions, and to the progress of knowledge in the interval between the first preparation and the publication of the works. Dastur Hoshangji has also prepared an edition of the Pahlavi and Pâzand texts of the Shikand-gumânî, with a glossary of the Pahlavi words; and also an edition of the Avesta and Pahlavi texts of the Vendidad, with a glossary of the Pahlavi words; but neither of these works are yet published.

In 1866 a prize was offered by Seṭh Khurshedji Rustamji Kâmâ for a new Gujrati translation of the Vendidad, with a complete glossary of the words in the Avesta text. This translation was supplied, three years afterwards, by KAVASJI EDALJI KANGA, but was not published till 1874. It is based upon Westergaard's text and the best European translations which had appeared, and the writer has added, in many places, a good deal of explanatory commentary. This is likely to remain the standard translation for the use of the Parsi community, and it is to be regretted that its author has not avoided the mistake of translating Avesta quotations, made by the Pahlavi commentator, as part of the Avesta text, which has been already noticed (p. 52) as a general error of translators. In addition to the quotations admitted into the text by M. de Harlez, he has translated the five quotations which constitute Vend. ii. 6 (Westerg.), and finds considerable difficulty in adapting them to the text, as might be expected. If he had consulted a manuscript of the Vendidad with Pahlavi he would have seen at once that these five sentences are merely quoted by the Pahlavi commentator to prove the correctness of his assertions. The fact that these Avesta quotations form no part of the text is noticed by Dastur Hoshangji in his manuscript edition of the texts of the Vendidad.

In concluding these remarks upon the progress of Zoroastrian studies among the Parsis, it may be mentioned that Dastur JAMASPJI MINOCHIHARJI JAMASPASANA of Bombay has been engaged for many years in collecting materials for a Pahlavi dictionary, the first part of which is now in the press. This dictionary is likely to be exceedingly useful, being by far the largest collection of Pahlavi words hitherto made; and these are arranged in the order of the Sanskrit alphabet, which is convenient for a people speaking Gujrati. It will adhere strictly to traditional readings and interpretations, of which it ought to form a permanent record, valuable to all parties in these times of progressive transition.

Thus much had to be noticed regarding the general course of researches into the sacred writings of the Parsis. Slowly the ideas of past ages, buried for thousands of years in documents written in a language more or less unintelligible, begin to be unfolded; but many years and many laborers will be required to make this new field for antiquarian and philological research yield much fruit. The Dasturs, who are most concerned, and other younger, talented, and well-to-do members of the Parsi community, ought to consider it their duty to collect and multiply correct and unimproved copies of all the oldest manuscripts extant, and to supply themselves with all the

means (such as a knowledge of Sanskrit, Persian, Chaldee,
&c.) now required for a successful investigation of the
Avesta and Pahlavi languages, in order that they may
study the contents of their manuscripts, and learn the
foundations on which their religion rests. Let them not
be discouraged if the results be not so flattering to their
self-love as they anticipated. So far as their researches
disclose what is good and proper in their religion, they
must strengthen the belief in its divine origin; and so far
as they disclose what is bad and improper, they merely
indicate the corruptions introduced by human tradition.
Such corruptions can be neither concealed nor defended
with safety; but when discovered, they must be rejected
as mere human inventions and superstitious errors. All
religions have passed through human minds and human
hands, and are therefore likely to abound with human
errors; so that the man who believes in the infallibility
of a book is but one step removed from the superstition
of him who believes in the infallibility of a high-priest;
he merely removes the idea of verbal inspiration from the
broad daylight of the present, where its improbability
would be too obvious, into the dim obscurity of the past,
where difficulties become lost in the misty shadows of
antiquity. Whatever is true in religion will bear the
fullest investigation and most searching criticism; it is
only error that fears discussion.

II.

LANGUAGES OF THE PARSI SCRIPTURES.

II.

LANGUAGES OF THE PARSI SCRIPTURES.

THE languages of Persia, commonly called Iranian, form a separate family of the great Aryan stock of languages which comprises, besides the Iranian idioms, Sanskrit (with its daughters), Greek, Latin, Teutonic (with English), Slavonian, Letto-Lithuanian, Celtic, and all allied dialects. The Iranian idioms arrange themselves under two heads:—

1. Iranian languages properly so called.
2. Affiliated tongues.

The first division comprises the ancient, mediæval, and modern languages of Iran, which includes Persia, Media, and Bactria, those lands which are styled in the Zend-Avesta *airyâo daṅhâvô*, "Aryan countries." We may class them as follows:—

(*a.*) The East Iranian or Bactrian branch, extant only in the two dialects in which the scanty fragments of the Parsi scriptures are written. The more ancient of them may be called the "Gâtha dialect," because the most extensive and important writings preserved in this peculiar idiom are the so-called Gâthas or hymns; the later idiom, in which most of the books of the Zend-Avesta are written, may be called "ancient Bactrian," or "the classical Avesta language," which was for many centuries the spoken and written language of Bactria. The Bactrian languages seem to have been dying out in the third century B.C., and they have left no daughters.

(*b.*) The West Iranian languages, or those of Media and

Persia. These are known to us during the three periods of antiquity, middle ages, and modern times, but only in the one dialect, which has, at every period, served as the written language throughout the Iranian provinces of the Persian empire. Several dialects are mentioned by lexicographers, but we know very little about them.[1] Of the ancient Persian a few documents are still extant in the cuneiform inscriptions of the kings of the Achæmenian dynasty, found in the ruins of Persepolis, on the rock of Behistun, near Hamadan, and some other places in Persia. This language stands nearest to the two Bactrian dialects of the Zend-Avesta, but exhibits some peculiarities; for instance, we find *d* used instead of *z*, as *adam*, " I," in the Avesta *azem*; *dasta*, " hand," in the Avesta *zasta*. It is undoubtedly the mother of modern Persian, but the differences between them are nevertheless great, and in reading and interpreting the ancient Persian cuneiform inscriptions, Sanskrit and the Avesta, although they be only sister languages, have proved more useful than its daughter, the modern Persian. The chief cause of this difference between ancient and modern Persian is the loss of nearly all the grammatical inflexions of nouns and verbs, and the total disregard of gender, in modern Persian; while in the ancient Persian, as written and spoken at the time of the

[1] In Sayyid Husain Sháh Hakikat's Persian grammar, entitled *Tuḥfatu-l-'Ajam*, there are seven Iranian languages enumerated, which are classed under two heads, viz. (*a*) the obsolete or dead, and (*b*) such dialects as are still used. Of the obsolete he knows four: *Sughdí*, the language of ancient Sogdiana (*Sughdha* in the Zend-Avesta); *Zábulí* (for *Zábulí*), the dialect of Zábulistán; *Sakzí*, spoken in Sajastán (called *Sakastene* by the Greeks); and *Hiriwí*, spoken in Herat (*Haróyu* in the Zend-Avesta). As languages in use he mentions *Pársí*, which, he says, was spoken in Istakhar (Persepolis), the ancient capital of Persia; then *Darí*, or language of the court, according to this writer, spoken at Balkh, Bokhara, Marv, and in Badakhshán; and *Pahlaví*, or *Pahlavání*, the language of the so-called *Pahlav*, comprising the districts of Rai (*Ragha* in the Zend-Avesta), Ispahan, and Dínúr. *Darí* he calls the language of Firdausi, but the trifling deviations he mentions to prove the difference between *Darí* and *Pársí* (for instance, *ashkam*, "belly," used in *Darí* for *shikam*, and *abá*, "with," for *bá*), refer only to slight changes in spelling, and are utterly insufficient to induce a philologist to consider Darí an idiom different from Pársí.

Achæmenians (B.C. 500-300), we still find a great many inflexions agreeing with those of the Sanskrit, Avesta, and other ancient Aryan tongues. At what time the Persian language, like the English, became simplified, and adapted for amalgamating with foreign words, by the loss of its terminations, we cannot ascertain. But there is every reason to suppose that this dissolution and absorption of terminations, on account of their having become more or less unintelligible, began before the Christian era, because in the later inscriptions of the Achæmenians (B.C. 400), we find already some of the grammatical forms confounded, which confusion we discover also in many parts of the Zend-Avesta. No inscription in the vernacular Persian of the Arsacidans, the successors of the Achæmenians, being extant, we cannot trace the gradual dissolution of the terminations; and when we next meet with the vernacular, in the inscriptions of the first two Sasanian monarchs, it appears in the curiously mixed form of Pahlavi, which gradually changes till about A.D. 300, when it differs but little from the Pahlavi of the Parsi books, as we shall shortly see.

The second chief division of the Iranian tongues comprises the *affiliated languages*, that is to say, such as share in the chief peculiarities of this family, but differ from it in many essential particulars. To this division we must refer *Ossetic*, spoken by some small tribes in the Caucasus, but differing completely from the other Caucasian languages; also *Armenian* and *Afghanic* (*Pashtû*).

After this brief notice of the Iranian languages in general, we shall proceed to the more particular consideration of the languages of the Zend-Avesta and other religious literature of the Parsis.

I.—THE LANGUAGE OF THE AVESTA ERRONEOUSLY CALLED ZEND.

The original language of the Parsi scriptures has usually been called Zend by European scholars, but this name has never been generally admitted by Parsi scholars, although it may have been accepted by a few on European authority, which is apt to be treated with too much deference by Oriental minds. We shall see, hereafter, that this application of the term Zend is quite inconsistent with its general use in the Parsi books, and ought, therefore, to be discarded by scholars who wish to prevent the propagation of error. At present we need only observe that no name for the language of the Parsi scriptures has yet been found in the Parsi books; but whenever the word Zend (*zand*) is used alone, it is applied to some Pahlavi translation, commentary, or gloss; and whenever the word Avesta (*avistâk*) is used alone, it is applied to the Parsi scriptures in their original language. The language of the Zend, therefore, is Pahlavi, and this is a sufficient reason for not applying that term to another language, with which its connection is probably slight. For want of a better term, we may follow the example of most Parsi scholars in using the term Avesta for the language of the Avesta; and to avoid confusion, we must discard the word Zend altogether when speaking of languages; although, for reasons given hereafter, we may still use Zend-Avesta as a general term for the Parsi scriptures.

The general character of the Avesta language, in both its dialects, is that of a highly developed idiom. It is rich in inflexions, both of the verbs and nouns. In the latter, where three numbers and eight cases can be distinguished, it agrees almost completely with Vedic Sanskrit, and in the former it exhibits a greater variety of forms than the classical Sanskrit. We find, besides, a multitude of compound words of various kinds, and the sentences are joined together in an easy way, which contributes largely to a ready understanding of the general sense of passages. It is a genuine sister of Sanskrit, Greek, Latin, and Gothic; but we find her no longer in the prime of life, as she appears rather in her declining age. The forms are not always kept strictly distinct from each other, as is the case in Sanskrit, Greek, and Latin; but are now and then confounded, much less, however, in the verbs than in the nouns, where the dissolution first began. The crude form, or original uninflected state of the word, is often used instead of the original inflected forms; thus, we find *daêva*, "demon, evil spirit," which is really the crude form of the word, employed as the instrumental singular, which ought to be *daêrêna*, or at least *daêvâ*, and as the nominative plural, which ought to be *daêvâonhô* or *daêvâ*. The long vowels *â* and *î* are out of use in the nominative feminine, so that the gender is not so easily recognised from the termination alone as in Sanskrit; thus we have *daêna*, "creed, belief," instead of *daênâ*; moreover, the forms of the dative and instrumental are often confounded, especially in the plural. These deviations from the regular forms, and the confusion of terminations, are far more frequent in the classical Avesta than in the Gâtha dialect, where the grammatical forms are, in most cases, quite regular.

Notwithstanding these symptoms of decay, the relationship of the Avesta language to the most ancient Sanskrit, the so-called Vedic dialect,[1] is as close as that of the different dialects of the Greek language (Æolic, Ionic, Doric, or Attic) to each other. The languages of the sacred hymns of the Brahmans, and of those of the Parsis, are only the two dialects of two separate tribes of one and the same nation. As the Ionians, Dorians, Ætolians, &c., were different tribes of the Greek nation, whose general name was *Hellenes*, so the ancient Brahmans and Parsis were two tribes of the nation which is called *Aryas* both in the

---

[1] This is distinct from the usual Sanskrit, which alone is studied nowadays by the Brahmans. The most learned Pandits of the present Brahmanic community, who are perfectly acquainted with the classical Sanskrit language, are utterly unable to explain the more ancient portions of the Vedas, which consist chiefly of hymns, and speculations on the meaning of ceremonies, their effects, &c. They learn them parrot-like by heart, but care nothing about understanding their prayers. If they are asked to explain the meaning, they refer to a commentary made several hundred years ago by a highly celebrated Brahman (Sâyaṇa), which often fails to give a complete insight into Vedic antiquity.

Veda and Zend-Avesta; the former may be compared with the Ionians, and the latter with the Dorians. The most striking feature perceptible when comparing both Avesta dialects with Sanskrit is, that they are related closely to the Vedic form of Sanskrit, but not to the classical. In verbal forms, especially moods and tenses, the classical Sanskrit, though very rich in comparison with modern languages, is much poorer than the more primitive dialect preserved in the Vedas; thus it has lost various forms of the subjunctive mood, most tenses of all moods except the indicative (the imperative and potential moods preserving only the present tense), the manifold forms expressing the infinitive mood,[1] &c.; whereas all these forms are to be found in the Vedas, Zend-Avesta, and Homeric Greek, in the greatest completeness. The syntactical structure in Vedic Sanskrit and the Avesta is simple enough, and verbal forms are much more frequently used than in classical Sanskrit. There can be no doubt that classical Sanskrit was formed long after the separation of the Iranians from the Hindus.

The differences between Vedic Sanskrit and the Avesta language are very little in grammar, but are chiefly of a phonetical and lexicographical nature, like the differences between German and Dutch. There are certain regular changes of sounds, and other phonetic peculiarities perceptible, a knowledge of which enables the philologist to convert any Avesta word easily into a pure Sanskrit one. The most remarkable changes are as follows:—

Initial *s* in Sanskrit is changed in the Avesta into *h;* thus *soma* (the sacred juice used by the Brahmans) = *haoma ; sama,* "together, the same," = *hama ; sa,* "that, he," = *ha; sach,* "to follow," (Lat. *sequi*) = *hach.* In the middle of a word the same change takes place, as in *asu,* "life," = *aṅhu ;* except now and then in the last syllable, as in Av. *yazaêsha,* "thou shalt worship," where *sh* is pre-

---

[1] In the Vedic dialect eleven such forms can be found, which are reduced to one in classical Sanskrit.

served. At the end of a word *sh* remains unless preceded by *a*, in which case the termination *ash* is changed into *ô*, except when followed by the enclitic conjunction *cha*, when the sibilant is preserved; thus *asura-s*, "living," becomes *ahurô*, instead of *ahurash*, but we find *ahurashcha*, "and the living."

The Sanskrit *h*, when not original, but only a derived sound, never remains in the Avesta. It is generally changed into *z*, as in *zî*, "then, therefore," = S. *hi*; *zima*, "winter," = S. *hima*; *zlê* (root), "to invoke," = S. *hve*. The Avesta *z* is also sometimes equivalent to a Sanskrit *j*, as in *zan*, "to produce," (Pers. *zâdan*) = S. *jan* (Lat. *gigno*); *hizva*, "tongue," = S. *jihva*.

In comparing Avesta with Sanskrit words, we often observe a nasal in the former which is wanting in the latter; this nasal is usually followed by *h*, as in *anhu*, "life," = S. *asu*.

Instead of Sanskrit *shv* we find *sp* in the Avesta, as in *aspa*, "horse," = S. *ashva* (Lat. *equus*, Gr. *hippos*); *vîspa*, "all," = S. *vishva*; *spâ*, "dog," = S. *shvâ*.

In place of Sanskrit *rit*, besides the regular change into *aret*,[1] we find *ash* as an equivalent in the Avesta, as in *mashya*, "man," = S. *martya* (Lat. *mortalis*, Gr. *brotos*); *asha*, "right, true," = S. *rita*.

Instead of Sanskrit *sv* the Avesta has a peculiar guttural aspirate represented by *q*, and corresponding in sound probably to *qu* in Latin and *khw* in Persian, as in *qafna*, "sleep," = S. *svapna* (Lat. *somnus*, Gr. *hypnos*, Pers. *khwâb*).

These are the most remarkable phonetic differences between Sanskrit and Avesta words. By attending to them it is very easy to find the Sanskrit word corresponding to one in the Avesta, and we can thus discover a large number of words and forms similar to those in the Vedas. There are, of course, now and then (as is always the case in the

---

[1] The Sanskrit vowel *ri* is always represented by *are* or *cre*; *rit* itself is a corruption of *art*.

dialects of every language) peculiar words to be found in the Avesta, but these are always traceable to Sanskrit roots..

A comparison of the grammatical forms in the Avesta and Sanskrit can be dispensed with. They are so very similar, even when not quite identical, that they are readily recognised by any one who has a slight knowledge of Sanskrit. The strongest proof of the original identity of Sanskrit and Avesta grammatical forms is their harmony even in irregularities. Thus, for instance, the deviations of the pronominal declension from that of the nouns are the same in both languages, as *ahmâi*, "to him," = S. *asmâi; kahmâi*, "to whom," = S. *kasmâi; yaêshâm*, "of whom" (pl.), = S. *yeshâm.* Also in the declension of irregular nouns we find *span*, "dog," = S. *shvan*,* sing. nom. *spâ* = S. *shvâ*, acc. *spânem* = S. *shvânam*, dat. *sûnê* = S. *shune*, gen. *sûnô* = S. *shunas*, pl. nom. *spânô* = S. *shvânas*, gen. *sûnâm* = S. *shunâm;* likewise *pathan*, "path," = S. *pathin*, sing. nom. *pañta* = S. *panthâs*, inst. *patha* = S. *pathâ*, pl. nom. *pañtânô* = S. *panthânas*, acc. *pathô* = S. *pathas*, gen. *pathâm* = S. *pathâm.*

The extremely close affinity of the Avesta language to Vedic Sanskrit can be best seen from some forms of the present tense, in which the classical Sanskrit differs from the Vedic. Compare, for instance, Av. *kerenaomi*, "I make," with Ved. *kṛinomi* and S. *karomi;* Av. *jamaiti*, "he goes," with Ved. *gamati* and S. *gachchhati;* Av. *gerewnâmi*, "I take," with Ved. *gṛibhnâmi* and S. *gṛihnâmi.*

With regard to the differences between the two dialects of the Avesta, the language of the Gâthas and the classical or ordinary Avesta, we can here only discuss their relationship to each other in a general way. The chief question is, whether they represent the same language at two different periods of time, or whether they are two contemporary dialects, spoken in two different provinces of

---

* Spelt as pronounced, *sh* representing the palatal sibilant, and *sh* the cerebral sibilant.

the ancient Bactrian empire. Our knowledge of the dialects of the Iranian languages and the periods of their development, previous to the Christian era, is so limited, that it is extremely difficult to decide this question in a satisfactory manner.

The differences between these two dialects are both of a phonetical and grammatical nature. Were the deviations merely of the former kind, we should be fully entitled to ascribe them to two different ways of pronouncing certain vowels and consonants, as generally happens in different districts with nations speaking the same language; but should we discover in one dialect fuller and more ancient forms, and in the other evidently later and more contracted ones, then the difference between the Gâtha language and the ordinary Avesta must be ascribed to their being written at different periods.

The phonetical differences of the Gâtha language from that of the other books are, at a first glance, so considerable as to induce one to trace them to different localities of the same country, and not to different ages. But on closer inquiry we find that several of these phonetical peculiarities, such as the constant lengthening of final vowels, and the severing of one syllable into two (as of the nom. pl. n. of the relative pronoun $y\hat{a}$ into $\bar{e}c\hat{a}$), are attributable to the original chanting of the Gâthas and other shorter pieces, constituting the older Yasna, and are not to be traced to dialectical differences. These writings are the most important and holiest prayers used in the Zoroastrian divine service, and the way of chanting them was, very likely, analogous to that in which the Brahmans (originally near relations of the Parsis) used to chant the verses of the Sâmaveda at the time of solemn sacrifices, and which is kept up to this day on such occasions. On hearing a Sâmaveda priest chant some verses of this Veda, one notices that he lengthens the final vowels of the words, even when they are short. In Sanskrit, where the grammar was fixed by rules, the texts were not altered according to the mode of chanting them; while in the Avesta, where nothing regarding the grammar and pronunciation was settled, these peculiarities produced by chanting the Gâthas and some other pieces crept into the manuscripts, which were generally written from memory only, as is still often the case. Besides these phonetical changes which can be explained as the result of chanting, there are a few other changes of vowels, such as that of a final $\hat{o}$ or initial a into $\bar{e}$, as in $k\bar{e} = k\hat{o}$, "who?" and $\bar{e}mavat = amavat$, "strong;" also some changes of consonants, as that of t into s in $stavas = stavat$, "praising," and the softening of harsh consonants, as in $\hat{a}dr\bar{e}ng = \hat{a}thr\hat{a}s$ (acc. pl. of $\hat{a}tar$, "fire"). These deviations are suggestive of dialectical differences, but they are of no great importance, and no great weight can be attached to them; they are merely such differences as might exist between the idioms of neighbouring towns in the same district. That these peculiarities, notwithstanding their insignificance, have been preserved so well, and not been dissolved and changed into the current Bactrian language, which is preserved in the largest portion of the Zend-Avesta, indicates the great reverence in which these hymns were held by the Zoroastrians. Considering that the Gâthas contain the undoubted teaching of Zarathushtra himself (without adverting to other reasons), we do not hesitate to believe that the peculiar language used in the Gâthas was the dialect of his own town or district.

As to grammatical forms, the Gâtha dialect exhibits not a few deviations from the ordinary Avesta language. Most of these differences evidently represent a more primitive state of the Bactrian language, nearer to its Aryan source; but some might be considered as merely dialectical peculiarities. The genitive singular of masculine nouns in a ends, nearly throughout the Gâthas, in $ahy\hat{a}$, which corresponds exactly with the Sanskrit genitive termination $asya$, while in the ordinary Avesta we always find $ah\acute{e}$, apparently a contraction of $ahya$, thus Gâth.

daêvahya, "of a demon," = Av. *daêvahê* = S. *devasya*.
Again, the first pers. sing. imperative, expressing intention or volition, requires only the termination *â* or *âi* in the Gâthas, whereas in the ordinary Avesta the derived termination *âni* prevails, and this is also used in Sanskrit; the usual infinitive formation in the Gâthas is that in *dyâi* which is also extremely frequent in the Vedic dialect, while it is nearly unknown in the ordinary Avesta, and wholly so in classical Sanskrit. In the pronouns, especially, the language of the Gâthas exhibits more ancient forms than we find in any other part of the Zend-Avesta, as for example *maibyâ*, "to me," which ancient form, agreeing so well with Sans. *mahyam* and Lat. *mihi*, is nowhere to be found in the ordinary Avesta; observe also *mahyâ*, m. *maqyâo*, f. "of my," &c. The frequent use of the enclitic pronominal particles *î*, *îm*, *hîm*, &c. (which is a peculiar feature of the Vedic dialect, distinguishing it from classical Sanskrit), and the great freedom with which prepositions are separated from their verbs (a chief characteristic of Vedic Sanskrit and Homeric Greek), indicate a more ancient stage of language in the Gâtha dialect than we can discover in the ordinary Avesta, where these traces of a more varied and not quite settled form of expression are much fewer, and only met with, occasionally, in poetical pieces.

Judging from these peculiarities, there seems no doubt that the dialect of the Gâthas shows some traces of a higher antiquity than can be claimed for the ordinary Avesta. But the differences are not so great as between the Vedic and classical Sanskrit, or between the Greek of Homer and that of the Attic dialect, the two dialects of the Zend-Avesta being much closer to each other. They represent one and the same language, with such changes as may have been brought about within the space of one or two centuries. The Gâtha dialect is, therefore, only one or two centuries older than the ordinary Avesta language, which was the standard language of the ancient Iranian empire.

THE AVESTA LANGUAGE.

Much of the difficulty of understanding the Zend-Avesta arises, no doubt, from grammatical defects in the texts extant, owing to the want of grammatical studies among the ancient Persians and Bactrians. Had the study of grammar, as a separate science, flourished among the ancient Mobads and Dasturs, as was the case with Sanskrit grammar among the ancient Brahmans, and had Iran produced men like Pâṇini, Kâtyâyana, and Patanjali, who became lawgivers of the classical Sanskrit language, we should have less ground to complain of the bad condition of the texts, and have found fewer difficulties in explaining them than we have now to encounter. There is every reason to believe that the grammar of the Bactrian language was never fixed in any way by rules; thus the corruptions and abbreviations of forms, which gradually crept from the popular and colloquial into the written language, became unavoidable. In Sanskrit the grammarians built, by means of numerous rules, under which every regular or irregular form in that language was brought, a strong bulwark against the importation of forms from the popular and vulgar language, which was characterised by them as Prâkrit.[1] Grammar became a separate branch of study; manuscripts were then either copied or written in strict accordance with the rules of grammar, but always

[1] One must not, however, lose sight of the fact that a language is not made by grammarians, but by the common people whom they despise. The work of grammarians is merely to take the language as they find it, and try to ascertain what rules they can manufacture to account for the various forms and idioms used by the people around them. So long as such rules are laid down merely as explanations of existing facts, they will be useful to the scholar, and will not impede progress; but once let them be enunciated as inflexible laws, unalterable as those of the Medes and Persians, and then they hinder progress, ossify thought, and stop discovery. Grammar is no exception to the general rule that laws are hurtful unless subject to constant revision; for a law that cannot be altered becomes a dogma, an impediment to discussion, progress, and improvement, whether it be grammatical, medical, legal, scientific, social, or religious. Whether the stoppage of Hindu progress in knowledge beyond a certain point be not due to the excessive systematising adopted by their writers when they approached that point, is a matter worth consideration. Arrived at a certain amount of progress, they ceased to look forward, but contented themselves with surveying and arranging what they already knew.

with attention to phonetical peculiarities, especially in Vedic books, if they had any real foundation. To these grammatical studies of the Brahmans, which belong to an age long gone by, we chiefly owe the wonderfully correct and accurately grammatical state of the texts of the Vedas and other revered books of antiquity. In Iran almost all knowledge of the exact meaning of the terminations died out at the time when the ancient Iranian languages underwent the change from inflected to uninflected idioms. Books were extant, and learnt by heart for religious purposes, as is still done by the Parsi priests. But when the language of the Zoroastrian books had become dead, there were no means for the priests, who cared more for the mere mechanical recital of the sacred texts than for a real knowledge of their meaning, to prevent corruptions of the texts. Ignorant of anything like grammar, they copied them mechanically, like the monks of Europe in the middle ages, or wrote them from memory, and, of course, full of blunders and mistakes. On this account we find the copies now used by Mobads and Dasturs in a most deplorable condition as regards grammar; the terminations are often written as separate words, and vowels inserted where they ought to be omitted, in accordance with the wrong pronunciation of the writer. The best text, comparatively speaking, is to be found in the oldest copies; while in Vedic manuscripts (if written for religious purposes) there is not the slightest difference, whether they are many centuries old or copied at the present day. Westergaard has taken great trouble to give a correct text, according to the oldest manuscripts accessible to him, and his edition is, in most cases, far preferable to the manuscripts used by the priests of modern times. If older manuscripts than those used by Westergaard be known to the Dasturs, they should consider it their bounden duty to procure them for the purpose of collation with Westergaard's valuable edition, so that they may ascertain all preferable readings for their own information and that of other scholars. Why will they remain behind the Brahmans and the Jews, who have preserved their sacred writings so well, and facilitated modern researches to so great an extent? The era for a sound philological explanation of the time-hallowed fragments of the Zoroastrian writings has come, and the Dasturs, as the spiritual guides of the Parsi community, should take a chief part in it. The darkness in which much of their creed is enshrouded should be dispelled; but the only way of obtaining so desirable a result is by the diffusion of a sound and critical knowledge of the Avesta language.

II.—THE PAHLAVI LANGUAGE AND PAZAND.

It has been already noticed (p. 67) that after the five centuries of obscurity, and probable anarchy,[1] which followed the death of Alexander, when we next meet with the vernacular language of Western Iran, it has assumed the form of Pahlavi, the name generally applied to the language of the inscriptions of the Sasanian dynasty, whether on rocks or coins.

Various interpretations of the word *Pahlaví* have been proposed. Anquetil derives it from the Persian *pahlú*, "side," in which case Pahlavi would mean "the frontier language;" but although this opinion has been held by some scholars, it can hardly be correct, as it is difficult to imagine that a frontier language could have spread over a vast empire. It has also been connected with *pahlav*, "a hero," but "the hero language" is a very improbable designation. Native lexicographers have traced Pahlavi to the name *Pahlav* of a town and province; that it was not the language of a town only, is evident from Firdausi's statements that the Pahlavi traditions were preserved by the *dihgân*, "village chief;" it may have been the language

[1] 'In the Kârnâmah of Artakhshír-i 'Pâpakân it was written that after 'the death of Alexander of Rûm, 'there were 240 small rulers of the 'country of Aîrân. The warriors of 'Fârs and the borders adjacent to it 'were in the hands of a chieftain of 'Ardavân. Pâpak was governor and 'sovereign of Fârs, and was appointed 'by Ardavân.'—Kârnâmak-i A. P.

of a province, but the province of Pahlav is said to have included Ispahân, Raî, Hamadân, Nihâvand, and Adarbaîjân, and must have comprised the ancient Media, but that country is never called Pahlav by Persian and Arab historians. Quatremère was of opinion that Pahlav was identical with the province Parthia, mentioned by the Greeks; he shows, by reference to Armenian authors, that *pahlav* was a royal title of the Arsacidans. As the Parthians regarded themselves as the most warlike people of the Orient, it is not surprising that *pahlav* and *pahlavân* in Persian, and *palhav* or *pahlav*, and *pahlavig* or *palhavig* in Armenian, became appellations for a warrior; the name thus lost its national meaning altogether, and became only a title for bold champions of old. It spread beyond the frontiers of Iran eastwards to India, for we find the Pahlavâs mentioned as a mighty foreign nation in the Râmâyana, Mahâbhârata, and the Laws of Manu, and we can only understand them to have been the Persians. Regarding the origin of the word, we may compare it with *pâhlûm*, "excellent," but cannot derive it therefrom.

As the name of a nation, we can discover it only in the Parthva of the cuneiform inscriptions, which is the Parthia of the Greeks and Romans. The change of *parthva* into *pahlav* is not surprising, as *l* is not discoverable in the ancient Iranian tongues, where *r* is used instead, and *th* in the middle of an ancient Iranian word generally becomes *h* in Persian, as in Av. *mithra* = Pers. *mihir*. It may be objected that the Parthians were not Persians but probably a Scythic race, and that Pahlavi could not have been the language of the Parthians. This objection, however, will not hold good when we consider that the Parthians were the actual rulers of Persia for nearly five hundred years, and made themselves respected and famous everywhere by their fierce and successful contests with the mightiest nation of the ancient world, the Romans. It is not surprising, therefore, that the name which once struck such terror into the hearts of Roman generals and emperors was remembered in Persia, and that everything connected with antiquity, whether in history, religion, letters, writing, or language, was called *pahlaví*, or belonging to the ancient rulers of the country, the Parthians. Pahlavi thus means, in fact, nothing but "ancient Persian" in general, without restriction to any particular period or dialect. This we may see from the use made of the word by Mohammedan writers; thus, Ibn Hauqal, an Arab geographer of the tenth century, when describing the province of Fârs, the ancient Persis, states that three languages were used there, viz. (a) the Fârsî (Persian), spoken by the natives when conversing with one another, which was spread all over Persia, and understood everywhere; (b) the Pahlavî, which was the language of the ancient Persians, in which the Magi wrote their historical records, but which in the writer's time could not be understood by the inhabitants of the province without a translation; (c) the Arabic, which was used for all official documents. Of other languages spoken in Persia he notices the Khûzî, the language of Khûzistân, which he states to be quite different from Hebrew, Syriac, or Fârsî. In the Mujmilu-t-tawârîkh there is an account of "Pahlavi" inscriptions at Persepolis, but the writer evidently means those in cuneiform characters.

From all this we may clearly see that the name Pahlavi was not limited to any particular period or district. In the time of Firdausi (A.D. 1000), the cuneiform writing as well as the Sasanian inscriptions passed for Pahlavi characters; and the ancient Persian and Avesta were regarded as Pahlavi, equally with the official language of the Sasanian period, to which the term has been now restricted, since the others have become better known. The term Pahlavi was thus, in fact, never used by the Persians themselves in any other sense than that of "ancient Persian," whether they referred to the Sasanian, Arsacidan, Achæmenian, Kayanian, or Peshdadian times. Any reader of the Shâhnâmah will arrive at this conclusion. This misapplication of a more recent name to earlier historical facts is analogous to the misuse of the appellation *Arúmák*, "Roman," which the Parsi writers apply to Alexander, the Macedonian conqueror, because he entered the Persian empire from the quarter where the Roman armies appeared in later times.

However loosely the term Pahlavi may have been formerly applied, it has long been practically restricted to the written language of Persia during the Sasanian dynasty, and to the literature of that period and a short time after, of which some fragments have been preserved by the Parsis, in a character resembling that of the Avesta, but very deficient in distinct letters. These Pahlavi writings are of a very peculiar character: instead of presenting us with a pure Iranian dialect (as might be expected in the language of a period commencing with the purely Iranian ancient Persian, and ending with the nearly equally pure Iranian language of Firdausi), it exhibits a large admixture of Semitic words, which increases as we trace it further back, so that the earliest inscriptions of the Sasanian dynasty may be described as being written in a Semitic language, with some admixture of Iranian words, and a prevailing Iranian construction. Traces of the Semitic portion of the Pahlavi can be found on coins of the third and fourth century B.C., and possibly on some tablets found at Nineveh, which must be as old as the seventh century B.C.; so there is some reason to suppose that it may be derived from one of the dialects of the Assyrian language, although it differs considerably from the language of the Assyrian cuneiform inscriptions. Practically, however, our acquaintance with Pahlavi commences with the inscriptions of the first Sasanian kings on rocks and coins.

Since the Mohammedan conquest of Persia, the language has become greatly mixed with Semitic words from the Arabic, but this Semitic admixture is of a totally different character to that we find in Pahlavi. The Arabic element in modern Persian consists chiefly of substantives and adjectives, referring to religion, literature, or science; few particles or verbs have been adopted, except when whole phrases have been borrowed; in fact, the Arabic words, although very numerous, are evidently borrowed from a foreign language. The Semitic element in Pahlavi writings, on the contrary, comprises nearly all kinds of words which are not Arabic in modern Persian; almost all pronouns, prepositions, conjunctions, and common verbs, many adverbs and substantives in frequent use, the first ten numerals, but very few adjectives, are Semitic; while nearly every Arabic word in modern Persian would be represented by an Iranian one in Pahlavi writings. It is optional, however, to use Iranian equivalents for any of these Semitic words when writing Pahlavi, but these equivalents are rarely used for some of the pronouns, prepositions, and conjunctions; so rarely, indeed, that the orthography of a few of them is uncertain. Notwithstanding the Semitic appearance of the written Pahlavi, we find that all traces of Semitic inflexions have disappeared, except in a few of the earliest Sasanian inscriptions, written in a peculiar character and dialect, called Chaldæo-Pahlavi, in which the Chaldee plural suffix *în* is still often used, as in *malkîn malkâ*, "king of kings," instead of *malkân malkâ* in the ordinary Sasanian Pahlavi inscriptions of the same age, where the Iranian plural suffix *ân* is used. Besides this Iranian suffix to nouns, we find the verbs appearing in one unchangeable Semitic form, to which is added certain Iranian suffixes, except in the earliest inscriptions in Sasanian Pahlavi, where these suffixes are wanting. In addition to these indications of Iranian grammar, we also find a prevailing Iranian construction in the sentences, as much in the older inscriptions as in the later writings.

The explanation of this extraordinary compound writing, fundamentally Semitic in its words and Iranian in its construction, is that it never literally represented the spoken language of any nation. The Iranians must have inherited their writing from a Semitic people, and although they were acquainted with the separate sounds of each of the letters, they preferred transferring the Semitic words bodily, so as to represent the same ideas in their own Iranian language, and each Semitic word, so transferred, was merely an ideogram, and would be read with the sound of the corresponding Iranian word, without reference to the sounds of the letters composing it; thus the Persians wrote the old Semitic word *malkâ*, "king," but they pronounced it *shâh*. When the Semitic words had more than one grammatical form, they would, for the sake of uniformity be usually borrowed in one particular form, and probably in the form which occurred most frequently in the Semitic writings. As these ideograms were to represent an Iranian language, they would be arranged, of course, according to Iranian syntax. For certain words the writer could find no exact Semitic equivalent, especially for Iranian names and religious terms; to express them he had recourse to the alphabet, and wrote these words as they were pronounced; thus laying the foundation of the Iranian element in the Pahlavi. As the Semitic ideograms remained unchanged,[1] it was necessary to add Iranian suffixes to indicate the few grammatical forms which survived in the spoken language; these additions appear to have been only gradually made, for the sake of greater precision, as some of them are not found in the older inscriptions. In later writings we find a few other Iranian additions to Semitic words, used generally to indicate some modification of the original word; thus *abû = pid*, "father," is altered into *abîdar=pidar*; *am = mâd*, "mother," into *amîdar = mâdar*; &c. In these later writings, we also find the proportion of the Semitic element considerably reduced, being confined to the representation of some three to four hundred of the commonest words in the language, while all other words are Iranian, written as they are pronounced.

[1] The only exceptions extant seem to be a few Semitic plurals in -*în* found in the Chaldæo-Pahlavi inscriptions before mentioned (p. 82); but even these are used in phrases of Iranian construction.

As a proof that the Persians did not use the Semitic words in speaking, we may quote the statement of Ammianus Marcellinus (xix. 2, 11). When referring to the war between the Roman Emperor Constantius and Shahpûhar II., about A.D. 350, he says that the Persians used the terms *saansaan* and *pyrosen*, meaning "king of kings" and "conqueror." Both these terms are Iranian, the first being *shâhân-shâh*, and the latter *pîrûz*, "victorious," and show conclusively that the Persians of those times did not pronounce *malkân malkâ*, although they wrote those words, but they both wrote and pronounced *pîrûz*, which has no Semitic equivalent in Pahlavi. More than four centuries later, Ibn Muqaffa, a Mohammedan writer of the latter half of the eighth century, states that the Persians ' possess a ' kind of spelling which they call *zavârish;* they write by ' it the characters connected as well as separated, and it ' consists of about a thousand words (which are put toge- ' ther), in order to distinguish those which have the same ' meaning. For instance, if somebody intends to write ' *gôsht*, that is *lakhm* (meat) in Arabic, he writes *bisrâ*, but ' reads *gôsht;* and if somebody intends to write *nân*, that ' is *khubz* (bread) in Arabic, he writes *lahmâ*, but reads ' *nân*. And in this manner they treat all words that they ' intend to write. Only things which do not require such ' a change are written just as they are pronounced.' It appears from this that the Persians of the eighth century did exactly as a Parsi priest would do at the present time; when they came to a Semitic word while reading Pahlavi, they pronounced its Persian equivalent, so that their reading was entirely Persian, although the writing was an odd mixture of Semitic, Persian, and hybrid words. It was always optional to write the Persian word instead of its Semitic equivalent, and it was only necessary to make this the rule, instead of the exception, to convert the old Pahlavi into pure Persian. This final step became compulsory when the Persians adopted a new alphabet, with which the old Semitic ideograms would not amalgamate, but which facilitated the adoption of Arabic terms introduced by their Mohammedan conquerors. Hence the sudden change from Pahlavi to modern Persian was rather a change in writing than an alteration in speaking. The spoken language changed but slowly, by the gradual adoption of Arabic words and phrases, as may be seen from a comparison of the language of Firdausi with that of recent Persian writers.

Ibn Muqaffa uses the term *zavârish* for the Semitic element in Pahlavi, and this is the term usually employed in Persian, although written occasionally *azvârish* or *uzvârsh;* in Pahlavi it is written *hûzvârish* or *aûzvârishn*, but it is doubtful if the word occurs in any very old writings. Several attempts have been made to explain its etymology, but as its correct form is by no means certain, it affords very little basis for trustworthy etymology. The term Huzvârish is applied not only to the Semitic ideograms, but also to a smaller number of Iranian words written in an obsolete manner, so as to be liable to incorrect pronunciation; these obsolete Iranian written forms are used as ideograms in the same manner as the old Semitic words. The habit of not pronouncing the Huzvârish as it is written must have tended to produce forgetfulness of the original pronunciation of the words; this was to some extent obviated by the compilation of a glossary of the Huzvârish forms, with their pronunciation in Avesta characters, as well as their Iranian equivalents. When this glossary was compiled is uncertain, but as the pronunciation of some of the Huzvârish words is evidently merely guessed from the appearance of the letters, we may conclude that the true sounds of some of the words were already forgotten.

It has been already noticed (p. 68) that Pahlavi translations of the Avesta are called Zand, and we may here further observe that the Iranian equivalent of Huzvârish is called Pâzand, reserving further explanation of these terms for the third Essay. This Pâzand may be written in Pahlavi characters, as happens when single Pâzand words are substituted for their Huzvârish equivalents in a Pahlavi text; or it may be written in Avesta characters, which happens when the whole text is so transliterated, and is then called a Pâzand text; or this Pâzand text may be further transliterated into the modern Persian character, when it is still called Pâzand, and differs from the Iranian element of modern Persian only in its frequent use of obsolete words, forms, and construction. It would be convenient to call this Persian form of Pâzand by the name Pârsî, but it is not so called by the Parsis themselves, nor in their books; with them, Pârsî or Fârsî means simply modern Persian, more or less similar to Firdausi's language.

It has been mentioned above that it would be easy to forget the pronunciation of the Huzvârish words, and it is now necessary to explain how this could be. The Pahlavi alphabets, being of Semitic origin, have not only all the usual deficiencies of other Semitic alphabets, but also some defects peculiar to themselves, so that several sounds are sometimes represented by the same letter; this ambiguity is greatly increased, in Pahlavi books, by the union of two or more of these ambiguous letters into one compound character, which is sometimes precisely similar to one of the other single letters; the uncertainty of reading any word, therefore, which is not readily identified is very great. No short vowels are expressed, except initial a, but it is presumed they are to be understand where necessary, as in all Semitic alphabets.

Two or three of the earliest rock inscriptions of the Sasanian kings record the names and titles of Ardashîr-i Pâpakân and his son Shahpûhar I. (A.D. 226–270) in three languages, Greek and two dialects of Pahlavi. The Pahlavi versions are engraved in two very different characters, one called Chaldæo-Pahlavi, from some resemblances to Chaldee in letters and forms, the other called Sasanian Pahlavi, as being more generally used by the Sasanian kings in their inscriptions, both on rocks and coins. This latter character changes by degrees, on the coins of the later Sasanian kings, till it becomes nearly identical with the Pahlavi character in the manuscripts still extant; while the Chaldæo-Pahlavi appears to have gone out of use before A.D. 300. Two more inscriptions, of greater length, are engraved in both these Pahlavi dialects, but without any Greek translation; of one of these inscriptions only a few fragments are yet known, but the other is complete, and we may take it as a specimen of the Pahlavi writings of the early Sasanian times, as it refers to King Shahpûhar I. (A.D. 240–270).

This inscription is engraved on two separate tablets (one for each dialect), cut on the rock-wall at the entrance of a cave near the village of Hâjiâbâd, not far from the ruins of Persepolis. Copies of the two versions were published by Westergaard at the end (pp. 83, 84) of his lithographed edition of the text of the Bundahish. Plaster casts of the whole of the Chaldæo-Pahlavi, and of the first six lines of the Sasanian Pahlavi version, are preserved in the British Museum and elsewhere; and a photograph from one set of these casts was published by Thomas in the "Journal of the Royal Asiatic Society," new series, vol. iii. From a comparison of these copies with the photograph we obtain the following texts, the words of one version being placed immediately below those of the other for the sake of convenient comparison, and short vowels being introduced where they seem necessary.

TEXTS OF THE PAHLAVI INSCRIPTIONS AT HÂJIÂBÂD.

[SASANIAN PAHLAVI.]—*Tagaldhî zenman*[1] *lî mazdayasn bagî Shahpûharî,*
[CHALDÆO-PAHLAVI.]—Karzâvani zenman li mazdayazn alahâ Shahipûhari,
malkân malkâ Airân va Anîrân, minô-chitrî min yaztân, barman maz-
malkin malkâ Aryán va Anâryân, minô-shihar min yâztan, barî maz-

---

[1] The syllable *man* is represented by a single letter in both characters, which evidently corresponds with the common Pahlavi termination *man*, as we find it here in the common Pahlavi words *zenman* (= *denman*), *barman, ragelman, ralman, tamman, hô-* man, *lanman*, and *yadman*, as well as in the uncommon forms *gadmatman, atarman,* and *panman*. In *tamman* the syllable *man* corresponds to *mân* in Chaldee, but in other words we must suppose it to represent an original *rân, vain,* or *ân*. Thomas reads

88   THE PAHLAVI LANGUAGE.

dayasn bagî Artakhshatar, malkân malkâ Airân, minô-chitrî min yaztîn,
dayazn alahâ Artakhshatar, malkîn malkâ Aryân, minô-shîhar min yâztan,
napî   bagî Pâpakî malkâ; afan amat zenman   khitayâ shadî-
pûharî pûhar bag Pâpak malkâ;   va   amat lan zenman khireraya sha-
tun, adînan levînî shatradarân   va barbîtân   va vacharkân   va âzâtan
dît, qadmatman khshatradarîn,   barbîtân,   rabân   va âzâtan
shadîtun, afan ragelman pavan zenman dikî hankhetûn, afan khitayâ
shadît,   nagarîn   patan zenman vêm haqâîmût,   va   khireraya
lechadâ zak chîtâk barâ ramîtun, barâ valman vayâk aîk   khitayâ   ramî-
lchad [1] lchû shîtî lebarâ ramît,   bîsh   tamman   anû khireraya naflat
tun, tamman vayâk zak argûn lâ yehvân, aîk hat chîtâk chîtî hôman, adîn
lehavînd,   atarman   lâ yehût, aîk ak shîtî banît havîndê, kal
birânî patyâk   yehvân hôman; akhar lanman framât: Minô
lebarâ shadedrâ âkasî yebût havîndê; adîn   lan   aûpadisht: Minô
chîtâkî aûrundarî chîtî,   minô yadman ketab hôman, zak ragelman
shîtî panman satar banît, avat minô yadâ kedab havînt,   nagarîn
pavan zenman dikî ayû hankhetûn, va   khitayâ val zak chîtâkî ayâ
patan zenman vêm lîp haqâîmûd, va khireraya kal hû   shîtî   lîp
shadîtun, akhar minô khitayâ val zak chîtâk ramîtun; valman yadman
shadyû,   minô khireraya kal hû shîtî yûmzûd;   lehûp   yadâ
ketab.
kedab havînd.

A few words in this inscription are not quite intelligible, but by comparing one version with the other, which corresponds closely in all but two or three phrases, we can arrive at the meaning of most of the obscure passages, and translate as follows:—'

'This is an edict of me, the Mazda-worshipping divine
'being Shahpûhar, king of the kings of Iran and non-Iran,
'of spiritual origin from God; son of the Mazda-worshipping
'divine being Ardashîr, king of the kings of Iran, of spiritual
'origin from God; grandson of the divine being Pâpak, the
'king. And when this arrow[2] was shot by us, then it was
'shot by us in the presence of the satraps, grandees, mag-

the letter *t*, because it resembles *t* in some old alphabets. For a similar reason Andreas reads it *d*. Thomas points to the correspondence of *bar-man*, in one dialect of our text, with *barî* in the other. Andreas points to a similar correspondence of *yadman* with *yadâ*; he also shows that the reading *d* overcomes many etymological difficulties. We adhere to the traditional *man* on the authority of the Chaldee *tammân*, and because we do not see why there should be a second *d* in the alphabet.

[1] Andreas reads this word *lechad*, as the *h* is peculiarly formed, and may perhaps represent the letter *tsade*, or *ch* in Pahlavi.

[2] The form of the word is plural, but used probably for the singular.

'nates, and nobles; and our feet were set in this cave, and
'the arrow was shot out by us towards that target; but
'there where the arrow would have dropped was no place
'(for it), where if a target were constructed, then it (the
'arrow) would have been manifest outside; then we or-
'dered: A spirit target is constructed in front, thus a spirit
'hand has written: Set not the feet in this cave, and shoot
'not an arrow at that target, after the spirit arrow shot at
'that target; the hand has written that.'

Comparing the two versions of this inscription with the Pahlavi of the manuscripts, it will be noticed that though the Chaldæo-Pahlavi differs most, it still corresponds with the manuscripts to the extent of about one-third of the words, amongst which the preposition *kal*, "to, at," explains the manuscript *ghal*, which has been often read *ghan* or *ghû*, and is used for either *val* or *valman*. The construction of the Chaldæo-Pahlavi resembles generally that of the manuscript Pahlavi, but it does not suffix the pronoun to the initial conjunction or adverb in each phrase, which is a peculiarity of Pahlavi as compared with modern Persian. Furthermore, the Chaldæo-Pahlavi has begun to use Iranian terminations to Semitic verbs, as *t* in *haqâîmût, yehût, havînt; d* in *leharînd, haqâîmûd, yâmzûd;* and the conditional *dê* in *havîndê*. The Sasanian version has not advanced to that stage in which it adopted Iranian terminations to Semitic verbs, although they are freely used in other inscriptions some twenty or thirty years later; but in all other respects the Sasanian approaches much closer than the Chaldæo-Pahlavi to the language of the manuscripts, about two-thirds of the words being identical, and the construction of the sentences precisely the same. Thus we find the pronoun suffixed to the initial conjunction or adverb in some phrases, as in *afan* and *adînan*, only the pronominal suffix is Semitic; but in later Sasanian inscriptions we find Iranian suffixes, as in *afam* and *afash*. This inscription leaves the question of the origin of the *idhâfat*, or relative particle, very uncertain. This particle is nearly always *expressed* in Pahlavi writings,[1] and not merely *understood*, as it is generally in modern Persian. In this inscription several words, in both versions, end in *î*, but as this vowel termination cannot be the *idhâfat* in some cases, it may not be so in any. Thus in the Sasanian version the final *î* may be an idhâfat in *bagî, Shahpûharî, napî, Pâpakî, lcrînî*, and possibly in *chitrî*, but it cannot be so in *dîkî, bîrûnî*, and *chîtâkî*, and an idhâfat is wanting after *malkâ, barman, Artakhshatar*, and *lcchadû*. In the Chaldæo-Pahlavi version the final *î* may be an idhâfat in *Shahîpûharî, barî*, and *pûharî*, but it cannot be so in *shîtî* and *âkasî*, and an idhâfat is wanting after *alahâ, malkâ, Artakhshatar, pûhar, bag, Pâpak*, and *lchad*, and perhaps after *shîhar* and *qadmatman*. The omission of an idhâfat after *malkâ* is most significant, as it is a position in which it would be expressed even in modern Persian; it is, therefore, very doubtful whether any final *î* is intended as an *idhâfat*. In inscriptions a few years later we find the idhâfat in the form of the Semitic relative *zî*.

To compare with the early Sasanian Pahlavi of the inscriptions, we may take, as a specimen of the manuscript Pahlavi, a passage from the Kârnâmak-i Ardashîr Pâpakân, in which the Semitic ideograms are given in italics, and a complete Pâzand version, in Neryosangh's orthography,[2] is interlined; so that the upper line gives the text as it is written, and the lower as it is pronounced:—

[PAHLAVI].—Pâpak *amatash* nâmak *did andûhkûn ycherând, afash pavan*
[PÂZAND].—Pâpak kash nâma did andûhgin bûd, vash pa
pasukhô *val* Ardakhshîr *kard* nipisht *aîgh: Lak lâ* dânâkyîsh kard, *amat*
pasukh ô Ardashîr kard navasht ku: Thô nô dânâihâ kard, ka
paran mindaram-1 man ziyân *lâ* ajash shâyast bûdano, *lcratman* vajûrgâu
pa this-ô ke ziâ nê azhash shâyast bûdan, awâ guzurgân
stêjak *yedrûntano milayâ* drûsht-advâjyish aûbash gûft. *Kevan* bûjishn
stêzha burdan sakhun durusht-âwâzbihâ havash guft. Nuñ bôzheshn

---

[1] A few exceptions to this general rule, besides unintentional omissions, may be discovered, especially in manuscripts from Persia.

[2] Derived from other works, as no version of the Kârnâmak by Neryosangh is known.

THE PAHLAVI LANGUAGE. 91

yemalelun, pavan pêḍik-mândak[1] angâr; moman dânâkân gûft yekavîmûnêḍ
gô,   pa   pashêmânî   aûgâr;   chi   dânâgâ guft   esteḍ
aigh: Dûshman pavan dûshman zak lâ tûbân vakhdûntano mûn[2] ashô mard
ku: Dushman   pa   dushman â nê tuâ   griftan   ke   ashô mard
min kûnishn-î nafshman aûbash rasêḍ. Denmanich gûft yekavîmûnêḍ aigh:
ezh kuneshn-i qêsh   havash rasêḍ.   Iñ-cha guft   esteḍ   ku:
Min zak aîsh mûstâvarmând al yeherûnîh mûn javîḍ min valman lâ vijarêḍ.
Ezh â kas mustâvarmâd ma bâsh   ke jaḍ ezh ôi   nê guzârêḍ.
Va lak benafshman dânêḍ[3] aigh Ardavân madam li va lak va kabedân
U thô   qaḍ   dânaê ku Ardavân awar men u thô u   vasân
anshûtâ-î dên gêhân pavan tanû va khayâ va chabûn va khvâstak kâmkârtar
mardum-i añdar gêhâ   pa   tan u jân u khir u qâsta kâmkârtar
pâḍakhshâî aîto. Va keranich andarj-î li val lak denman sakhttar, aigh
pâdishâh hast. U nuñ-cha andarzh-i men ô thô   iñ   sakhttar, ku
khaḍûkânakih va farmân-bûrḍâr[4] vâdûnû nafshman-tanû varz val aûbên-
čugûnaî   u   farmâ-burdâr   kun   qêsh-tan varz ô aviu-
bûḍih al avaspâr.
bûḍi ma awaspâr.

This passage may be translated as follows:—'Pâpak,
'when he saw the letter, became anxious, and he wrote in
'reply to Ardashîr thus: Thou didst unwisely, when, to
'carry on a quarrel with the great, in a matter from which
'there need be no harm, thou spakest words fierce and
'loudly about it. Now call for release, and recount with
'sorrow; for the wise have said that an enemy is not able
'to take that, as an enemy, to which a righteous man
'attains by his own actions. This also is said: Be not an
'antagonist of that person, away from whom you depart
'not. And thou thyself knowest that Ardavân is a very
'despotic sovereign over me and thee and many men in
'the world, as to body and life, property and wealth. And
'now also my advice to thee is most strongly this, that
'thou practise conciliation thyself, and act obediently, and
'yield not to want of foresight.'

It will be noticed that many of the words in this Pahlavi

---

[1] A doubtful word, and pashêmânî is merely a guess.
[2] All MSS. have karḍano min, and no doubt some old copyist has read vâdûntano (= kardan) instead of vakhdûntano (= griftan), there being no difference between these words in Pahlavi writing.
[3] Plural used for the singular.
[4] So in all MSS., but the text is either corrupt, or the construction peculiar.

text, such as *dîḍ, karḍ, nipisht*, &c., are Pâzand, although they have Semitic or Huzvârish equivalents, such as *khadîtûnḍ, râdûnḍ, yektîlûnḍ*, &c., which might have been used. This is generally the case in Pahlavi manuscripts, as it is quite optional for the writer to use either the Huzvârish word or its Pâzand equivalent, except perhaps in the case of some of the particles and detached pronouns, which are hardly ever used in their Pâzand form in Pahlavi writings. It is necessary to observe that the proportion of Huzvârish words in a manuscript is no criterion of its age, but merely an indication of the style of its writer, for it is not unusual for a manuscript of yesterday to contain more Huzvârish than one of the same text written five hundred years ago; though sometimes the case is reversed. The reason for this uncertain use of Huzvârish is obvious; the copyist either knows the text by heart, or reads it from a manuscript, but in either case he repeats it to himself in Pâzand, so that he has nothing but frequent reference to the original to guide him in the choice between Huzvârish and Pâzand modes of writing, and for want of frequent reference he will often substitute one for the other, or even use a wrong equivalent (if he does not quite understand his text) when there are two Huzvârish forms with nearly the same Pâzand, or when he has misread a Huzvârish form which has two meanings. Thus we often find the Huzvârish *amat*, "when," confounded with *mûn*, "which," because the Pâzand of both is *ka* or *ke*; and sometimes the Huz. *aîyh*, "that," is similarly confounded, owing to its having been read *ki* instead of *ku*; on the other hand, as the Huz. *rakhdûnḍ*, "taken," cannot be distinguished from *râdûnḍ*, "done," they are both liable to be read and written either *karḍ* or *grift*, according to the knowledge or ignorance of the copyist.

III.—THE PAHLAVI LITERATURE EXTANT.

Pahlavi writings may be divided into two classes: first, translations from the Avesta; and, secondly, writings of which no Avesta original is known. The translations are always written in sentences of moderate length, alternating with those of the Avesta text; they are extremely literal, but are interspersed with short explanatory sentences, and sometimes with long digressions, serving as a commentary on the text. The Pahlavi writings without an Avesta original are nearly entirely of a religious character, though a few are devoted to historical legends. Pâzand versions of some of these writings, as well as of the translations, exist both in the Avesta and modern Persian characters. Sometimes the Pâzand, when written in the Avesta character, alternates with a Sanskrit or Gujrati translation; and when written in the modern Persian character, in which case we may call it a Pârsî version, it is usually accompanied by a Persian translation, either alternating with the Pârsî sentences or interlined; in the latter case, it is a literal translation, and in the former it is more of a paraphrase. Some writings are found only in Persian, and this is more especially the case with the Rivâyats or collections of memoranda and decisions regarding ceremonial observances and miscellaneous religious matters; these are generally very free from Arabic words, but some of them contain nearly as much Arabic as is used in Mohammedan Persian writings. These Rivâyats also contain metrical Persian versions of some of the more popular Pahlavi and Pâzand books; these distant imitations of the Shâhnâmah are generally from two hundred to three hundred and fifty years old.

Having thus taken a brief survey of the Pahlavi writings and their connection with Parsi literature generally, we may now proceed to give further details of such works as

94   THE PAHLAVI LITERATURE EXTANT.

are known to be still extant, beginning with the translations from the Avesta.

The *Pahlavi Vendidâd* is probably the most important of these translations, and extends to about 48,000 words.[1] Each sentence of the Avesta text is continuously followed by a literal translation, or attempted translation, in Pahlavi, interspersed with short explanations of unusual words, and often concluding with an alternative translation, introduced by the phrase, "There is (some one) who says." In many places the translation of a sentence winds up with a longer commentary, containing Avesta quotations, and citing the opinions of various old commentators who are named, but regarding whom very little is known. As the next sentence in the Avesta text follows without break of line, it is often difficult to distinguish it from one of the Avesta quotations before mentioned. In the translation there are probably fragments of various ages, as some of the commentaries bear traces of translation from Avesta originals, while many of the shorter explanations appear more modern, but they must have been brought together in their present form before the Mohammedan conquest. All the known extant copies of the Vendidad with Pahlavi appear to have descended from a manuscript of herbad Hômâst, from which a copy was made in Sîstân in A.Y. 554 (A.D. 1185) by Ardashîr Bahman, and taken to India by herbad Mâhyâr Mâh-mihir, who had been passing six years with the herbads of Sîstân, whither he had come from the town of Khûjak on the Indus. After the arrival of this MS. in India it was re-copied by Rûstam Mihirâpân, who has forgotten to mention the year,[2] and from his copy the oldest manuscript now extant was copied by herbad Mihirâpân Kaî-Khûsrô (who was probably his great-grand-nephew) in

---

[1] In estimating (more or less accurately) the number of words in each of the works he has examined, as the best standard of their length, the editor has not included the conjunction *va* and idhâfat *i*; and he has counted compounds as either one or two words according to the usual mode of writing them.

[2] He copied the *Ardâ-Vîrâf nâmak* in A.Y. 618 (A.D. 1249), and had visited Persia.

A.Y. 693 (A.D. 1324) in the town of Kambay. This manuscript is now in the University Library at Copenhagen, but is very defective; the first portion of the manuscript (Vend. i. 1–v. 78, Sp.) having fallen into other hands, probably on some division of property among brothers; and nearly half the remainder is so much damaged, by the ink corroding the paper, that it is almost useless. Another manuscript, which appears to be in the same handwriting, but the colophon of which is missing, is in the India Office Library in London; this is also defective, as the folios containing Vend. i. 1–iii. 48 and iv. 82–viii. 310 have fallen into other hands, and have been replaced by modern writing; the folios containing Vend. iii. 49–iv. 81, and a few others, are also damaged by the corrosive action of the ink used by Mihirâpân Kaî-Khûsrô. From a comparison of these two manuscripts, we can ascertain the state of the text 553 years ago, except with regard to Vend. i. 1–iii. 48 and a few other short defective passages, for which we must refer to other old manuscripts. One of these was formerly in the library of Dastur Jamasp Asa at Nawsari, and is said to have been transferred from Bombay to Teheran in Persia some twenty years ago. It was copied, probably from the Copenhagen MS., in A.Y. 963 (A.D. 1594), by herbad Ardashir Zivâ, in the town of Bhroch; it is rather carelessly written, and many of the later copies are descended from it.[1] Another old manuscript, now in the University Library at Bombay, was obtained at Bhroch; it corresponds very closely to the one last mentioned, and is probably about the same age, but its colophon is lost. The Pahlavi Vendidad was printed at Vienna separate from the Avesta text, and was published by Spiegel in 1853, but his text can be much improved by careful collation with the old manuscripts above mentioned. None of these MSS. contain the twelfth fargard of the Vendidad, so that the Pahlavi translation of

---

[1] The descent of manuscripts can generally be traced by their copying errors, which have been insufficiently erased; or by their misreading ill-shaped letters; but it is hazardous to argue on the authority of only one such blunder.

this fargard, which occurs in a few modern MSS., is probably the work of some Dastur in India. It is difficult to account for the omission of the twelfth fargard in the old MSS., as the fargards are all numbered, so that any accidental leap from the eleventh to the thirteenth ought to have been soon discovered; and it is unlikely that the twelfth fargard would have occupied exactly the whole of any number of folios which may have been lost from some original manuscript before it was copied.

The *Pahlavi Yasna* contains about 39,000 words, exclusive of the *kiriya* or introductory prayers. It is written alternating with its Avesta, in the same manner as the Vendidad, but the long interpolated commentaries are much less common, and fewer commentators are quoted; so it may be suspected of containing less old matter than the Pahlavi Vendidad. For the oldest manuscripts of this text we are again indebted to herbad Mihirâpân Kaî-Khûsrô, who copied at Kambay a manuscript of the Yasna with Pahlavi (now in the University Library at Copenhagen) in A.Y. 692 (A.D. 1323) from a manuscript written by Rustam Mihirâpân; in the same year he also wrote a second manuscript of the same, which is now in the library of Dastur Jamaspji Minochiharji in Bombay, and is dated only twenty-two days later than the first, but it does not mention whence it was copied. Both these manuscripts begin with a series of introductory prayers in Avesta and Pahlavi, of which the commencement is lost; some of the folios are also damaged in both by the corrosive action of the ink used by the writer; and one folio in the middle of the Bombay copy is lost, and many others are worm-eaten. Several more modern manuscripts of the Yasna with Pahlavi exist, but they are less common than those of the Vendidad. The Avesta and Pahlavi texts were printed separately at Vienna, and published by Spiegel in 1858, but his text would be improved by collation with the old manuscript in Bombay.

The *Pahlavi Visparad* contains about 3300 words, and

resembles in character the Pahlavi translation of the Yasna. Probably the oldest copy of this text extant is contained in a manuscript of miscellaneous texts brought from India by the author of these Essays; this copy was written by Pêshyôtan Râm Kâmdin at Bhroch in A.Y. 766 (A.D. 1397). The Avesta and Pahlavi texts were printed separately at Vienna, and published by Spiegel, along with the Yasna texts, in 1858.

The *Hâdôkht nask* in Pahlavi is a mere fragment, containing about 1530 words, and consisting of three fargards which were probably not consecutive in the original Nask. The first fargard details the value of reciting the *Ashem-vohu* formula under different circumstances, and is probably an extract from the first division of the Nask. The second and third fargards describe the fate of the souls of the righteous and wicked respectively during the first three days after death; but their contents do not agree very well with the description of the Nask in the Dînkard, where it is stated to have consisted of three divisions containing 13, 102, and 19 sections respectively.[1] The oldest copies of the text known to be extant are contained in the manuscript of miscellaneous texts written in A.D. 1397, which includes the Visparad, as mentioned above; also in a very similar manuscript in the University Library at Copenhagen, which must be about the same age. The Avesta and Pahlavi texts, alternating as in the manuscripts, were printed at Stuttgart, and published with the Ardâ-Vîrâf Nâmak in 1872, and a translation of the Avesta text will be found in the third Essay.

The *Vishtâsp yasht* is found with a Pahlavi translation of about 5200 words, but only one manuscript has been examined; this is in the library of Dastur Jamaspji in Bombay, and is said to have been written some thirty-five years ago. The Avesta text is probably descended from the Kirman manuscript used by Westergaard, and now at

[1] The total number of sections is given as 133; so there must be an error of one in some one of these four numbers.

Copenhagen, and the Pahlavi text has the appearance of a modern translation.

Pahlavi translations of other Yashts also exist; such as those of the *Aûharmazd yasht*, about 2000 words; the *Khûrshêd yasht* and *Mâh yasht*, each about 400 words; the *Srôsh yasht hâḍôkht*, about 700 words; the *Haptân yasht*, *Behrâm yasht*, and probably others which have not been examined. In these, as in all the other translations, the Pahlavi alternates with the Avesta; and there seems little doubt that most of these Yasht translations are old.

Among the remaining translations are the Pahlavi texts of the *Atash nyâyish*, about 1000 words; the *Khûrshêd nyâyish*, about 500 words; the *Abân nyâyish*, about 450 words; the *Afrîngân gâtha*, the *Afrîngân gahanbâr*, the *Afrîngân dahmân* (Yasna, lix. 2–15 Sp.), the last containing about 450 words; the *Afrîn myazd*, also called Afrîn Zaratusht; the *Sîrôzah* in both its forms, containing about 530 and 650 words respectively; and many short extracts from the Yasna which are much used in the Khurdah Avesta, such as the *Ashem-vohu*, *Yathâ-ahû-vairyô*, and *Yeŭhê-hâtãm* formulas; Yasna, v. 1, 2; xxxv. 4–6, 13–15; i. 65–67, Sp.; &c.

The *Chîḍak avistâk-i gâsân*, or selection from the Gâthas, is an old miscellaneous collection of short passages, sometimes merely single lines, from various parts of the Gâthas, alternating with the usual Pahlavi translation. Altogether 76 lines are quoted from the Avesta, and the Pahlavi translation of about 1100 words does not differ materially from that given in manuscripts of the Yasna. Several copies of this selection exist, but the oldest seems to be that in the manuscript of miscellaneous texts written in A.D. 1397, as mentioned above.

Intermediate between the translations and the purely Pahlavi works, there are those which contain many Avesta quotations, which are often translated, but do not in themselves form any connected text, as the bulk of the work is Pahlavi. The following three are of this class:—

The *Nîrangistân* contains about 30,000 words, including the Avesta quotations, many of which are no longer extant in the Zend-Avesta. It consists of three fargards, and treats of a great number of minute details regarding rites and ceremonies, and precautions to be adopted while performing them. Its contents correspond very closely with the description of the second section of the Hûspâram Nask, as given in the Dînkard; and the name of that section was Nîrangistân. The opinions of many of the old commentators mentioned in the Pahlavi Vendidad are also often quoted in this work. A manuscript of the Nîrangistân was brought from Persia to India by Dastur Jamasp Wilâyati, A.D. 1720; this was copied from a manuscript dated A.Y. 840 (A.D. 1471), but whether it still exists is uncertain; it was re-copied by Dastur Jamasp Asa of Nawsâri in A.Y. 1097 (A.D. 1727), and this copy is now in the library of the Khân Bahâdar Dastur Nôshirvânji Jâmâspji at Poona. Several later copies exist, but owing to the text being difficult and little known to copyists, their variations from the original are unusually numerous.

The *Farhang-i oîm khadûk*, or vocabulary of Avesta and Pahlavi, so called from its first words being *oîm khadûk*, consists of about 3300 words, including the Avesta, and contains several words and phrases which are no longer extant in the Avesta texts. Very old copies of this vocabulary exist in two manuscripts of miscellaneous Pahlavi texts, one brought from India by the author of these Essays, and written in A.D. 1397, and the other at Copenhagen, written about the same time. Dastur Hoshangji's edition of this vocabulary, printed at Stuttgart, and published in 1867 with the title of "An Old Zand-Pahlavi Glossary," could probably be improved by collation with these old copies of the text.

The *Afrîn-i dahmân*, including the *aogemadaêcha* Avesta quotations, contains about 2000 words. The first of the quotations is Yasna, vii. 60 Sp., but most of the others are no longer extant in the Avesta. They are also found with alternating Pâzand and Sanskrit translations, and without the introductory sentences of the Afrîn.

We may now proceed to notice the purely Pahlavi works, which contain but few quotations from the Avesta, and those are generally references to the proper texts to be recited on particular occasions. There is much diversity in the style of these compositions, some being merely descriptive, in which the language is easy and the construction simple; while others are more philosophical, and their language difficult and obscure.

The *Vajarkard-i dînî*, containing about 19,000 words, might almost be classed with the preceding, as the latter part of it contains several quotations from the Avesta. It is a very miscellaneous collection of injunctions and details regarding religious matters, resembling a Rivâyat, and divided into three chapters, professing to have been written by Mêdyômâh, one of the old commentators quoted in the Pahlavi translations and other works. An old manuscript of the work, written in Kirmân, A.Y. 609 (A.D. 1240), is said to have been brought to India and deposited in the library of the Mody family in Surat, where it was copied A.Y. 1123 (A.D. 1754) by an uncle of the late high-priest of the Parsis in Bombay; from this copy the text was edited by Dastur Peshotanji, and printed in Bombay in 1848, as already mentioned (p. 59). This work includes three or four of the minor texts hereafter mentioned, as will be noticed when we come to them.

The *Dînkard* is the longest Pahlavi work extant, although the first portion of it, containing the first and second books, is missing; the latter part of the work, consisting of books iii.-ix., contains about 170,000 words. The third book consists of a series of explanations of religious matters and duties, for general information and removal of doubt, concluding with a description of the solar and lunar years, and a legendary history of the Dînkard which is evidently identified with that of the Nasks generally; this book contains 73,000 words. The fourth book contains various statements selected from the religious books by Adarfrobag-i Farukhzâdân, the original editor of the Dînkard (see p. 55), extending to about 4000 words; these statements commence with the characteristics of the Ameshâspends, and in discussing those of Shatrovair, the third Ameshâspend, an account is given of the endeavours of various sovereigns, from Vishtâsp to Khûsrô-i Kavâdân (Nôshirvân), to collect and preserve the national literature. The fifth book contains the sayings of the same Adarfrobag from a book called Sîmrâ,[1] and his replies to many questions on obscure and difficult matters in history, astrology, and religious customs, extending to about 6000 words. The sixth book contains the opinions of the *pôryôdkêshân* (professors of the primeval religion of Zarathushtra) on all matters of tradition, customs, and duties, with many sayings of Adarpâd-i Mâraspendân; the whole extending to about 23,000 words. The seventh book contains an account of the wonders, or miracles, of the Mazdayasnian religion from the time of Gâyômard, the first man, to that of Sôshâns, the last of the future prophets; including many details of the life of Zaratûsht, and extending to about 16,000 words. The eighth book contains an account of the twenty-one Nasks, giving a short description of each, but going into more details of the four Nasks xv.–xviii. which constitute the majority of the seven "legal" Nasks; this book consists of about 20,000 words. The ninth book contains a much more detailed account of the contents of each fargard of the first three Nasks, concluding with some remarks upon selections from the whole Yasna, and extending to about 27,000 words. The work concludes with colophons to the extent of nearly 1000 words, which relate that this latter part of the Dînkard was copied at the place where it was found, Khûshkand in Asûristân, from an original which had been written by elders of the family of Adarpâd-i Mâraspendân, by Mâhvandâd Narimahân Behrâm Mihirâpân, and finished on the 24th day of the 4th month

[1] There are, of course, many other ways of reading this name.

A.Y. 369 (7th July A.D. 1000). From this copy others dated A.Y. 865, 1009,[1] and 1038[1] have descended, and the last appears to have been brought from Persia to Surat in A.Y. 1152 (A.D. 1783) by Mullâ Bahman, and about four years afterwards some copies of the manuscript of A.Y. 1038 (A.D. 1669) were spread among the Parsis; but before any of these copies were made, the manuscript from Persia had been lent to various parties, and more than one-sixth of the whole had been abstracted, so that all the manuscripts are now deficient to that extent; but out of 69 folios missing, 64 have been discovered, though they still remain in various hands. The manuscript itself is in the library of Dastur Sohrabji Rustamji, the high-priest of the Kadmi sect of Parsis in Bombay. Dastur Peshotanji is publishing an edition of the text, with Gujrati and English translations, as has been already mentioned (p. 59), but it will be many years before he can complete his task.

The name *Dâdistân-i-dînî* is usually confined to a work of about 30,000 words, written by Dastur Minochihar Yûdân-damân, who was high-priest of the Mazdayasnians in Fârs and Kirmân about A.Y. 350[2] (A.D. 981). It consists of 92 questions and answers about religious duties, customs, and legends; the last of these answers seems to be incomplete, so that a portion of the original work may have been lost. The oldest manuscript of this text that has been examined was written in Kirmân by Marjpân Frêdûn in A.Y. 941 (A.D. 1572); his writing was to supply the deficiencies in a still older manuscript, of which only 28 folios now remain; and his manuscript has, in its turn, had its deficiencies supplied from later copies. In this manuscript the text of the Dâdistân-i-dînî is preceded and followed by other somewhat similar writings by the same Dastur, and by Zâd-sparam-i Yûdân-damân, who appears

---

[1] These dates no longer exist in the manuscript brought from Persia, but are taken from the copies and from the account given by Mullâ Firûz in his Avijeh-Dîn.

[2] Altered to 250 in the old manuscript written by Marjpân Frêdûn, but whether the alteration was made by the original writer or not is uncertain.

to have been his brother. The first part of these extra writings contains about 23,000 words, and the last part about 30,000 words, of which 5000 are lost; if these writings be taken as part of the Dâdistân-i-dînî, the whole work contains about 78,000 words extant. The author of these Essays recommended the Parsis, twelve years ago, to have this work translated, and it is said that a translation was prepared, but has not been published. If the non-appearance of this translation be due to any of the opinions of the old Dastur of Kirmân differing from those of Parsis of the present day, it is to be regretted, as the proper course in such a case would be to publish a correct translation, and point out the probable cause of the original writer's errors in notes; this is all the more necessary as none of the Pahlavi books are free from statements which would be considered heterodox nowadays. Thus, whenever they give details regarding *khvêtûk-das*, or next-of-kin marriage, they describe it as applying to closer relationships than present customs tolerate; but whatever may have been the reasons for the establishment of this custom when the Zoroastrian faith was in power,[1] it is evident that when the faith was held merely by a persecuted remnant of the Persian people, their priests advocated the custom as a specially meritorious act, with the view of discouraging intermarriages with their Mohammedan neighbours, which would have led to the final extinction of Zoroastrianism. That the present customs of the Parsis are not quite the same as those of eight or ten centuries ago is not surprising, when we consider that it was the usual practice of all Christian sects who had sufficient power, two or three centuries ago, to put heretics and witches to death by burning or otherwise; such practices were *then* not only legal, but were considered highly meritorious; *now* they would be called judicial murders.

[1] They had probably something to do with the dislike of Eastern nations to any absolute alienation of family property; a feeling which led even the Jews to adopt stringent exceptional marriage laws, in case of a failure in direct heirs.

104 THE PAHLAVI LITERATURE EXTANT.

The *Shikand-gumâni vijâr* is a controversial work of about 18,000 words, written by Mardân-farukh-i Aûharmazd-dâd, who acknowledges the instruction he has received from the Dînkard of Adarfrobag-i Farukhzâdân, which contained a thousand chapters (*dar*), as well as from the Dînkhard[1] of Adarpâdyâvand, a work no longer known, unless it be the book of the Mainyô-i-khard, mentioned hereafter. The writer begins by answering some questions of Mihiryâr-i Mâhmâdân of Ispâhân regarding the existence and work of the evil spirit being permitted by Aûharmazd; he then proceeds to prove the existence of God, and to disprove the arguments of atheists, and of those who disbelieve in the evil spirit, and attribute both good and evil to God; and he concludes by criticising the doctrines of the Jews, Christians, and Manichæans. Most of the manuscripts of this work are incomplete, and only the first 3600 words are found in the Pahlavi character; the more complete manuscripts are in Pâzand with Neryosangh's Sanskrit translation, but there are evident indications of the Pâzand text having been originally transliterated from Pahlavi. An edition of the Pahlavi and Pâzand texts has been prepared by Dastur Hoshangji, but is not yet printed.

The *Bundahish* calls itself 'the *Zand-âkâs*[2] (zand-know-'ing, or tradition-informed), which is first about Aûhar-'mazd's original creation and the antagonism of the evil 'spirit, and afterwards about the nature of the creatures 'from the original creation till the end, which is the future 'existence, just as it is revealed by the religion of the

---

[1] The Mullâ Firûz library in Bombay contains two modern Persian manuscripts, named respectively Dinkard and Dinkhird; these were written by Mullâ Firûz to describe his voyage toPersia and the answers he obtained to seventy-eight questions proposed by the Indian Dasturs. These Persian works must not be confounded with their namesakes in Pahlavi.

[2] The word *min*, "from," with which many of the manuscripts commence, appears to be a later addition, as it is not found in the Copenhagen manuscript, and has evidently been added by a later hand in the only other manuscript of equal age mentioned in the text.

'Mazdayasnians.' The contents of this book are too well known to require further description; it contains about 13,000 words, but the manuscripts do not agree either in extent or arrangement. The most complete and best-arranged text, but not the most accurately copied, is that in the manuscript of miscellaneous Pahlavi texts at Copenhagen, which is about five hundred years old, and has lost one or more folios in the middle of the text of the Bundahish, but contains more sections (chaps. xxviii., xxix., xxx., and xxxii. of Anquetil) than are found in other independent copies. The text is found differently arranged, without those sections, but more accurately copied, in the similar manuscript of miscellaneous texts brought from India by the author of these Essays, and written in 1397. Most of the manuscripts in India seem to have been copied from the latter of these two old manuscripts, but they sometimes vary further in their arrangement. The Copenhagen text was lithographed in facsimile and published by Westergaard in 1851; a French translation was published by Anquetil in 1771, and German translations by Windischmann in 1863, and by Justi in 1868.

The *Mînôk-i*[1] *khard*, called in Pâzand *Mainyô-i khard*, or Spirit of Wisdom, consists of sixty-two answers given by the said Spirit to the inquiries of a wise man regarding the tenets, legends, and morals of the Mazdayasnian religion. It contains about 12,000 words, but the text ends abruptly, as if incomplete; and its introduction bears some resemblance to that of the Shikand-gumânî, so as to lead to the suspicion that it may be the first portion of the Dînkhard consulted by the author of that work. An old manuscript of the Pahlavi text was brought by Westergaard from

[1] This word, which is traditionally read *madônad*, has been pronounced *mînavad*, or *mainirad*, and traced to a supposed ancient Persian form, *mainirat*. Whether such a form actually existed is not known, and if it did, we should expect to find its final letter represented by $d = t$ in Pahlavi, and not by *d*. On the other hand, the Persian *mînô* must have been *mînôk* in Pahlavi; this would be liable to be written *mînôg*, and the addition of circumflexes (all the uses of which, in Pahlavi, are not thoroughly understood) changes this word into the traditional *madônad*.

Persia, but the Pahlavi versions in India are probably merely translations from the better-known Pâzand text which generally alternates with Neryosangh's Sanskrit translation; a manuscript of this Pâzand-Sanskrit text, written in A.D. 1520, is preserved in the India Office Library in London. A few fragments of the Pâzand text were published, with a German translation, by Spiegel in his "Grammar of the Parsi Language" (1851) and his "Traditional Literature of the Parsis" (1860); and the whole text, both Pâzand and Sanskrit, was published by West, with an English translation, in 1871.

The *Shâyast lâ-shâyast*, or Pahlavi Rivâyat, contains about 10,000 words, and treats of sins and good works, the proper treatment of corpses and other kinds of impurity, with the proper modes of purification, the proper use of the sacred thread and shirt, other customs and rites, with the reasons for reciting each of the Gâthas, and details of the extent of those hymns; all subjects which are generally explained in the Persian Rivâyats; but here the statements are enforced by quotations of the opinions of several of the old commentators, and by references to some of the Nasks no longer extant. The oldest extant copies of this work are contained in the two manuscripts of miscellaneous Pahlavi texts, written about five hundred years ago, which have been already mentioned. In these manuscripts the text appears in two detached portions of about 7500 and 2500 words respectively.

The *Ardâ*[1] *Vîrâf nâmak*, or book of Ardâ Vîrâf, contains about 8800 words, and describes what was seen by a chosen high-priest in a vision of the other world, where he was shown the rewards of the righteous, the punishments of the wicked, and the neutral state of stationary expectation of those who belong to neither extreme. It is stated in this work that Ardâ Vîrâf was called Nikhshâpûr

---

[1] Sometimes written *Ardât*, which should perhaps be read *Ardâk*, having been altered into *ardâg*, which is not distinguishable from *ardât*. It is no doubt merely a title meaning "righteous;" the Parsis say, however, that it is also a name.

THE PAHLAVI LITERATURE EXTANT. 107

by some; this is not only the name of a town, but is also that of one of the old commentators, sometimes quoted in the Pahlavi Vendidad, and very often in the Nirangistân; it is possible, therefore, that this commentator may have written the book of Ardâ Vîrâf. Copies of this text are found in the two old manuscripts of miscellaneous texts written about five hundred years ago, which have been already mentioned. A manuscript of a Pâzand and Sanskrit version, written A.D. 1410, was also brought from India by the author of these Essays; and Persian versions, both in prose and verse, are likewise extant. The Pahlavi text was printed at Stuttgart, and published, with an English translation, in 1872.

The *Mâdigân-i Gôsht-i Fryânô*, of about 3000 words, is a tale of the evil Akhtya of the Abân Yasht (81–83), propounding thirty-three enigmas to Yôishtô-yô-Fryananâm, to be solved on pain of death; after this is done he has to solve three enigmas in his turn, but fails and is destroyed. The enigmas are generally of a very trivial character, and nine of them seem to be omitted. This text accompanies that of the book of Ardâ Vîrâf in the two old manuscripts before mentioned, and was published with it in 1872.

The *Bahman yasht*, of about 4200 words, professes to be a revelation from Aûharmazd to Zaratûsht of the sufferings and triumphs of the Mazdayasnian religion, from his time to the end of the world, apparently in imitation of part of the Sûdkar Nask. As it mentions the Mûsalmâns, and gives many details of the sufferings occasioned by them, it must have been written a considerable time after the Mohammedan conquest. It details how the power of the Mazdayasnian religion is to be restored by the victories of Vahirâm-i Varjâvand, a prince (*kaî*) of the Kayân race, who at the age of thirty is to put himself at the head of Indian and Chinese armies, whose power will be felt as far as the banks of the Indus, which is called the country of Bambo. Foreigners should be careful not to confound this name with Bombay, which is merely a European corruption, through the Portuguese, of Mumbaî; a corruption which native writers still avoid when writing in the vernacular languages. The Pahlavi text of this work is found in the old manuscript of miscellaneous texts at Copenhagen, and its two copies, one of which is at Paris, but no other copies have been met with; a Pâzand version is, however, common in India. Spiegel has given a German translation of extracts from the Bahman Yasht in his " Traditional Literature of the Parsis."

In the same old manuscript at Copenhagen is the *Andarj-i Hûdâvar-i*[1] *dânâk*, containing about 1800 words, of which one-third have been lost, as two folios are missing. This admonition (*andarj*) is given in reply to questions asked by his disciple (*ashâkard*). No other copy of this work has been met with, but it will be found, of course, in the two copies of the Copenhagen manuscript.

In the same manuscript is also a copy of the *Mâḍigân-i gujastak Abâlish*, containing about 1200 words. The accursed Abâlish appears to have been a *zandîk* or heretic, who relied upon later corrupt traditions in preference to the true faith. In the presence of Mâmûn, the commander of the faithful (*amîr-i mûminîn*) at Baghdâd, he proposes seven questions to a Mobad, who replies to the satisfaction of Mâmûn and the confusion of Abâlish himself. The writer concludes by blessing Adarfrobag-i Farukhzâdân (the author of an old edition of the Dinkard) for having destroyed Abâlish; and he could not have written this work before A.D. 830, as Mâmûn was living at that time. Many copies of it exist in Pahlavi, Pâzand, and Persian.

The *Jâmâsp nâmak* consists of Jâmâsp's replies to King Gushtâsp's questions regarding creation, history, customs of various nations, and the future fate of the religion. The most complete manuscript examined contains about 5000 words, but seems unfinished. The Pahlavi text is rare. A very old manuscript in Dastur Peshotanji's library in

[1] This name may also be read *Khâshvar-i*, or otherwise.

Bombay contains about one-fourth of the text, but no other copy has been met with. The Pâzand and Persian versions are found in many manuscripts.

A very old manuscript in the library of Dastur Jamaspji in Bombay has been called the *Pahlavi Shâhnâmak*, as it contains several short tales connected with the kings of Persia. Its colophon states that it was finished in India, in the town of Tânak,[1] on the 19th day of some month A.Y. 691 (A.D. 1322), by Mihirâpân Kaî-Khûsrô, the copyist who wrote the oldest manuscripts of the Yasna and Vendidad that are still extant. The handwriting, however, more nearly resembles that of the old manuscript of miscellaneous texts at Copenhagen, which contains several copies of Mihirâpân's writings, with his colophons attached; so that the Pahlavi Shâhnâmak may also be a copy of his manuscript, but, like that at Copenhagen, it is certainly about five hundred years old. This manuscript is much wormeaten, but a copy of it exists at Teheran, made one hundred and ten years ago, before the original was much damaged, which will probably supply most of the deficiencies in those texts of which no other copies are known to exist.

Of the texts contained in this old manuscript and its single complete copy, the following are not known to exist elsewhere in Pahlavi:—(1.) *Yâdkâr-i Zarîrân*, of about 3000 words, containing an account of the war between King Vishtâsp and Arjâsp. (2.) *Cities of the Land of Irân*, about 880 words, giving their names and a very brief account of each. (3.) *Wonders and Prodigies of the Land of Sîstân*, in about 290 words. (4.) *Khûsrô-i Kavâdân* (Nôshirvân) *and the Slave-boy*, who replies to the king's thirteen inquiries as to what things are the most pleasant, about 1770 words. (5.) *Admonitions* to Mazdayasnians in six separate paragraphs, about 940 words. (6.) *Andarj-i*

---

[1] In another colophon, in the middle of the manuscript, this place is called Tûmûk in Jazîrak (or Gujirak) zilah, the date being the 6th day of the sixth month A.Y. 691.

Khûsrô-i Kavâdân (Nôshirvân), about 380 words, said to contain the dying injunctions of that monarch. (7.) *Sayings* of Adarfrobag-i Farukhzâdân and Bakht-âfrîd, about 320 words.

The following texts, contained in this old manuscript, are also found in Dastur Peshotanji's old manuscript, which has been already mentioned as containing part of the Jâmâsp-nâmak; but they are not known to exist elsewhere in Pahlavi:—(1.) *Mâdiyân-i sî rôz*, about 460 words, is a statement of what ought to be done on each of the thirty days of the month; at the end it is called an admonition (*andarj*) of Adarpâd-i Mâraspendân to his son, which leads one to suspect that it may be a detached por tion of his Pandnâmak. (2.) *Dirakht-i Asûrîk*, about 800 words, is a debate between a tree and a goat as to which of them is the more worthy. (3.) *Chatrang nâmak*, about 820 words, relates how a chessboard and chessmen were sent by Dêvasârm, a great king of India, to Khûsrô-i Anôshak-rûbân (Nôshirvân), with a request for an explanation of the game, which was given by Vajûrg-mihir-i Bûkhtakân, who afterwards takes the game of Nîv-Ardashîr to India, as an effectual puzzle for the Indian sages. (4.) *Injunctions* given to men of the good religion, about 800 words. (5.) The *Five Dispositions* of priests, and *Ten Admonitions*, about 250 words, which also occur in the Vajarkard-i-dînî (pp. 13–16 of Dastur Peshotanji's edition). (6.) *Dârûk-i khûrsandî*, about 120 words. (7.) *Anecdote* of King Vahirâm-i Varjâvand, about 190 words. (8.) *Advice* of a certain man (*fulân gabrâ*), about 740 words. Of the following texts contained in the two old manuscripts of Dastur Peshotanji and Dastur Jamaspji, a third copy exists in the library of the latter Dastur:—(1.) *Forms of Letters* to kings and great men, about 990 words, found also in the Vajarkard-i-dînî (pp. 102–113 of Dastur Peshotanji's edition). (2) *Form of Marriage Contract*, dated A.Y. 627 (A.D. 1258), about 400 words. (3.) *Vâchak aêchand* (some sayings) of Adarpâd-i Mâraspendân, about

1270 words. (4.) *Stâyishn-i drôn ra sipâsdârî-i myazdpân,* about 560 words.

Of the following texts contained in Dastur Jamaspji's old manuscript many copies exist:—(1.) *Pandnâmak-i Zaratûsht,* about 1430 words, contains admonitions as to man's duties. A copy of three-fourths of this text exists in the University Library at Copenhagen. (2.) *Andarj-i Adarpâd-i Mâraspendân,* about 1700 words, is sometimes called his Pandnâmak, and contains his advice to his son Zaratûsht; but the last quarter of the text is missing in the old manuscript, and the end is very abrupt in other manuscripts, which makes it probable that the next text in the old manuscript, the *Mâdîgân-i sî rôz,* may have been originally the conclusion of this, as has been already noticed. This Pahlavi text was printed in Bombay, and published, with a Gujrati translation, by Shahryârji Dadabhai in 1869; and an English version of this Gujrati translation, by the Rev. Shapurji Edalji, was published in 1870, but being a translation of a translation, it differs considerably from the meaning of the original. (3.) *Kârnâmak-i Artakhshîr-i Pâpakân,* about 5600 words, records many of the actions of King Ardashîr and his son Shahpûhar, beginning with the discovery of Sâsân, the father of the former, among the shepherds of Pâpak, and ending with Aûharmazd, the son of the latter, ascending the throne; but this is not the original work, as it begins with the phrase, 'In the Kârnâmak of Artakhshîr-i Pâpakân it was 'thus written.' A Gujrati translation of this text was published by Dastur Peshotanji in 1853. (4.) *Pandnâmak-i Vajûrg-mihir-i Bûkhtakân,* the prime minister of King Khûsrô Nôshirvân, contains about 1690 words, but seems to be merely a fragment of the work, as it ends very abruptly. This text is also called the *Ganj-i shâîgân,* because it states that it was placed in the royal treasury (*ganj-i shahakân* in the old manuscript).

The other old manuscript in Dastur Peshotanji's library, which includes some of the above-mentioned texts, likewise contains the following:—(1.) *Mâdîgân-i sî yazadân*, about 80 words, stating the one special quality of each of the thirty Yazads who give their names to the days of the month. Another similar statement, in the old manuscript of miscellaneous texts brought from India by the author of these Essays, specifies different qualities in most cases. (2.) *Mâdigân-i mâh Fravardîn rôj-i Horvadad*, about 760 words, which details all the remarkable occurrences said to have taken place, at different periods, on the sixth day of the first month of the Parsi year. A Persian version of this text is found in the Rivâyats. (3.) Another *Mâdîgân-i sî rôz*, about 1150 words, detailing the proper business and duties for each of the thirty days in the Parsi month and the five Gâtha days at the end of the Parsi year. This text is also contained in the Vajarkard-i Dînî (pp. 113-125 of Dastur Peshotanji's edition).

Copies of the remaining texts are numerous both in Pahlavi and Pâzand. The *Mâdîgân-i haft ameshâspend*, about 990 words, contains a detail of the various duties of the seven Ameshâspends, as revealed by Aûharmazd to Zaratûsht. The *Andarj-i dânâk mard*, about 520 words, details the advice of a wise man to his son.

The *Pahlavi-Pâzand farhang*, about 1300 words, is the glossary of Huzvârish and Pâzand edited by Dastur Hoshangji and published in 1870. It is called the *Mârîknâmak-i Asûrîk*, or Assyrian vocabulary, by Dastur Peshotanji in the list of Pahlavi works given in the introduction to his Pahlavi Grammar; but the origin of this name requires explanation, as it appears to be unknown to the Dasturs generally.

The *Patît-i Adarpâd-i Mâraspend*, about 1490 words, is a form of renunciation of every possible heinous sin, to be recited by the sinner. The *Patît-i khûd*, about 1000 words, is a similar form of renunciation, but somewhat abbreviated. *Avar chîm-i drôn*, about 380 words, regarding the symbolism of the ceremonial wafer-cakes, and the use of them in the *myâzd*, or sacred feast. The *Pahlavi âshirvâd*, or marriage blessing, about 460 words. The *Nâm-stâyishnî*, or praise of Aûharmazd, about 260 words. The *Afrîn-i "tû pêshgâh-i khûdâ,"* so called from its first words, about 190 words. And other benedictions and prayers which have not been examined.

A Pahlavi version of the *Saddar Bundahish* is also said to exist, but must be a modern translation, for the Sad-dar itself, although often written in Avesta characters, seems to be rather Persian than Pâzand, as it contains many Arabic words. Dastur Peshotanji mentions a few more Pahlavi texts, some of which may be included among those described above, but under different names. There are also several Persian texts, such as the book of Dâdâr bin Dâd-dukht, &c., which may have originated in Pahlavi.

From the above details we may form some idea of the probable extent of the scanty remnants of Pahlavi literature. Without making any allowance for works which remain unexamined or have escaped observation, it appears that the extant Pahlavi translations from the Avesta exceed 104,000 words, and the other Pahlavi works exceed 413,000 words, making a total of upwards of 517,000 words in all the extant Pahlavi writings which have been examined. This total is nearly eleven times the extent of the Pahlavi Vendidad, or forty times that of the Bundahish.

The Parsi community has been doing a good deal, of late years, for the preservation of the last remnants of their national literature, but it would be better if their efforts were of a more systematic character. Before much more is done for encouraging the publication of isolated texts, a systematic inquiry for manuscripts should be set on foot, for the purpose of ascertaining which are the oldest and best manuscripts, so as to avoid the error of editing texts without reference to the best materials. Influential members of the Parsi community, assisted by the Dasturs, ought to have but little difficulty in inducing all possessors of manuscripts to supply a properly organised committee with complete catalogues of their collections. Such catalogues need only be lists of the names of the works, with the names and dates of the copyists when these are recorded; but all undated manuscripts supposed to be more than a century old should be specially noted. From such lists the committee could easily prepare a statement of all extant texts and of the owners of several of the more valuable manuscripts of each text. Possessed of this information, the next step would be to obtain a copy of the oldest manuscript of each text, beginning with the rarest works, and have it collated with one or two of the next oldest manuscripts (not being copies of the first). These collated copies, if correctly made *without any attempt at emendation*, would form standard editions of the texts, and should be carefully preserved in some public institution accessible to all members of the Parsi community, such as the Mullâ Fîrûz Library.

It can hardly be expected that Westergaard's edition of the Avesta texts can be much improved from any manuscripts to be found in India; although copies from Yazd or Kirmân, in Persia, might afford valuable emendations coming from an independent source, but it is generally understood in India that there are very few such manuscripts still existing in Persia. Justi's Old-Bactrian Dictionary is a tolerably complete collection of the Avesta words, but requires to be supplemented by the addition of many words contained in the Nîrangistân, Farhang-i oîm khadûk, and Aogemadaêcha; and the meanings attached to the words want careful revision.

With regard to Pahlavi texts, it would be important to discover any Pahlavi Vendidad or Yasna descended from any other source than the manuscripts of Mihirâpân Kaî-Khûsrô, also to find the first three fargards, missing from his manuscripts in Europe, in his own handwriting. The first two books of the Dînkard, the Pahlavi text of the latter part of the Shikand-gumânî, chaps. xxviii.-xxx. of the Bundahish, and a complete Pahlavi version of the Jâmâsp-nâmak, are all desiderata regarding which some information might be obtained by a systematic inquiry for manuscripts. Hitherto the Parsis have had to rely upon Europeans for all explanations of their literature, beyond the merely traditional learning of their priesthood; they may always rely upon some European being ready to carry on such investigations, provided the materials be forthcoming; and Europeans, in their turn, ought to be able to rely on the Parsis for the discovery of all existing materials, and for rendering them accessible.

III.

THE ZEND-AVESTA;

OR,

THE SCRIPTURE OF THE PARSIS.

III.

THE ZEND-AVESTA; OR, THE SCRIPTURE OF THE PARSIS.

In this Essay it is intended to give a brief statement of the contents of the whole Zend-Avesta, together with translations of some important or interesting passages contained therein, which will enable the reader to form some judgment of the true character of the sacred books of the Parsis. After some preliminary remarks about the name, extent, and preservation of the sacred books, the separate parts of the present Parsi scriptures will be described in detail, and finally, an attempt will be made to give a short, critical, and historical sketch of this religious literature.

I.—THE NAME OF THE PARSI SCRIPTURES.

The sacred writings of the Parsis have usually been called Zend-Avesta by Europeans, but this is, without doubt, an inversion of the proper order of the words, as the Pahlavi books always style them[1] *avistâk va zand* (Avesta and Zend), and this order is confirmed by the traditional, as well as the critical and historical, explanation of both terms. In the opinion of the present Parsi priests, *Avesta* means the original text of the sacred books, and *Zend* denotes the Pahlavi translation. This view is correct to a great extent, as many passages may be quoted

[1] Only one exception has been noticed in many hundred occurrences of the phrase.

from the Pahlavi books in which *Zend* means simply "translation," or "commentary;" thus the old *Farhang-i oîm khadûk* commences (in the old manuscripts) with the words: *Madam barâ-shinâkhtano-i râj va mârîkâno-i Avistâk, aîghash Zand maman va chîgûn,* 'on fully under-'standing the words and phrases of the Avesta, that is, 'the nature and quality (lit. the what and the how) of its 'Zend.' But it is probable that the term Zend was originally applied to commentaries written in the same language as the Avesta, for in the Pahlavi translation of the Yasna, when the scriptures are mentioned, both terms, *Avistâk va Zand,* are used,[1] as if of equal authority, which would have been an instance of gross self-conceit on the part of the translator, if he meant his own translation by the term Zend. From this use of the denomination Avesta and Zend by the Pahlavi translators, we are fully entitled to conclude that the Zend they mentioned was a commentary on the Avesta already existing before they undertook their translation; and as they considered it sacred, this Zend was probably in the same language as the original Avesta. There are many traces, in the Avesta quotations and other phrases of the Pahlavi translations, of much of this old Zend having been replaced by the new Zend of the Pahlavi translators; but there are also traces of a good deal of it remaining incorporated in the present Avesta text, as will be pointed out from time to time in the translations which follow. The term Avesta and Zend, or Zend-Avesta, cannot be considered, therefore, as wholly inappropriate when applied to the Parsi scriptures in their original language, although the word Zend is improperly used when applied to that language itself, as it is much more commonly employed as a name for Pahlavi commentaries.

From the above remarks, it will be seen that the term

[1] See Yasna, xxx. 1, xxxi. 1, where the Avesta and Zend of both sayings, or both blessings, are specified in the Pahlavi translation. Neryosangh generally renders the word Zend by *artha*, "meaning," in his Sanskrit translation of the Yasna.

Avesta was originally confined to the sacred texts ascribed to Zarathushtra and his immediate disciples; but in the course of time this term has been gradually extended to all later explanations of those texts written in the same language, till at the present time it includes all writings in that language, whatever their age. All these writings, having become unintelligible to the majority of the Zoroastrians, came to be regarded as equally sacred.

The word Avesta does not occur in the sacred texts themselves with the meaning now attached to it, and it must not be confounded with the Sasanian *apistân*, engraved on gems in the phrase *apistân val yazdân*, as this phrase is also found in the Pahlavi texts, with the meaning of "prayers to God," whereas the Pahlavi *apistâk*, or *avistâk* (Avesta), is a distinct word, never used in that sense, which, indeed, would be inapplicable to nine-tenths of the Avesta. So far as the form of the Pahlavi *avistâk* is concerned, it might be best traced to *ava* + *stâ*, in the sense of "what is established," or "text," as was proposed by M. J. Müller in 1839; but such a meaning, though it might be fairly applicable to most of the Avesta now extant, would hardly describe the very miscellaneous contents of the Nasks which have been lost, and which are all said to have had both Avesta and Zend. A more satisfactory meaning can be obtained by tracing *avistâk* to *â* + *vista* (p. p. of *vid*, "to know"), with the meaning "what is known," or "knowledge,"[1] corresponding nearly with *veda*, the name of the sacred scriptures of the Brahmans. It may be objected to this etymology that the first syllable of *avistâk* is written like *ap*, and an Avesta *v* does not usually change into a Pahlavi *p;* this is only true, however, when the *p* would be initial; in other cases, such as *vi* = Pahl. *apî*, the change is common.

With regard to the term Zend, we see that its application varied at different times. Originally it meant the

---

[1] More literally, "what is announced," or "declaration;" approaching the meaning of "revelation."

commentaries made by the successors of Zarathushtra upon the sacred writings of the prophet and his immediate disciples. These commentaries must have been written in nearly the same language as the original text, and as that language gradually became unintelligible to all but the priests, the commentaries were regarded as a part of the text, and a new explanation, or Zend, was required. This new Zend was furnished by the most learned priests of the Sasanian period, in the shape of a translation into Pahlavi, the vernacular language of Persia in those days; and in later times the term Zend has been confined to this translation.

The word Zend may be traced in *âzaiñtish* (Yas. lvi. 3, 3 Sp.) and is to be referred to the root *zan*, "to know," Sans. *jnâ*, Gr. γνω, Lat. *gno* (in *agnosco* and *cognosco*), so that it has the meaning of "knowledge, science." What passages in the present Avesta may be supposed to be remnants of the old Zend will be pointed out whenever they occur in the translations we propose to give further on.

The term Pâzand, which is met with frequently in connection with Avesta and Zend, denotes a further explanation of the Zend, and is probably a corruption of *paitizañti*, which must have meant "re-explanation;" this word does actually occur (Yas. lix. 2 Sp.), but with a more general meaning. Some passages in the present Avesta will be pointed out, in the translations further on, which may be supposed to represent an old Pâzand in the Avesta language; but at present the term Pâzand (as has been already shown in the second Essay) is applied only to purely Iranian versions of Pahlavi texts, whether written in the Avesta or Persian characters, and to such parts of Pahlavi texts as are not Huzvârish.

II.—THE ORIGINAL EXTENT OF THE ZEND-AVESTA.
THE NASKS.

From the ancient classical writers, as well as from the tradition of the Parsis, we learn that the religious literature of the ancient Persians was of considerable extent, though the Zend-Avesta, in its present state, is a comparatively small book. This circumstance necessarily leads us to the conclusion, that the sacred literature of the Zoroastrians has suffered very heavy losses. Thus Pliny reports, on the authority of Hermippos, the Greek philosopher (see page 8), that Zoroaster composed two millions of verses; and an Arab historian, Abu Jafir Attavari,[1] assures us that Zoroaster's writings covered twelve hundred cowhides (parchments). These reports might appear, at the first glance, to be exaggerations, but for the enormous extent of the sacred books of other Oriental nations,[2] which affords us sufficient reason for believing that the number and extent of the books ascribed to Zoroaster by his followers may have been very considerable.

The loss of most of these writings, known to the ancient Greeks, is ascribed by the Parsis mainly to the ravages attendant upon the conquest of the Persian Empire by Alexander the Great. Thus it appears from the third book of the Dinkard, that at the time of Alexander's inroad there were only two complete copies of the sacred books (a term which the Dinkard seems to identify with itself); one of these was deposited in the royal archives at

---

[1] Hyde, De Religione Veterum Persarum, p. 318.

[2] Thus, for instance, the text of the sacred books of the southern Buddhists of Ceylon, Birma, &c., according to Turnour's computation, comprises 4500 leaves, each page being about two feet long and containing nine lines. The text being written without any spaces between the words, we may conclude that each line must contain as much as ten lines of any ordinary poetical measure. Thus, $4500 \times 2 \times 9 \times 10 = 810{,}000$ lines of ordinary measure. Again, the commentary extends to a greater length than the text, so that there must be nearly 2,000,000 lines in the whole of these sacred books.

Persepolis, which were burned by Alexander, and the other, which was deposited in another treasury, fell into the hands of the Greeks, and was translated into their language. The Ardâ-Vîrâf-nâmak mentions only the one copy of the Avesta and Zend of the religion, which was deposited in the archives at Persepolis, and burned by Alexander; but it also mentions that he killed many of the priests and nobles. Both these accounts were written ages after the events they describe, so they merely represent the tradition that had been handed down, probably in writing, or otherwise it would have been more exaggerated; but as these accounts appear to have been written before the Mohammedan conquest, they cannot have confounded Alexander's ravages with those of the Mohammedans, for details of which we may refer to the Bahman Yasht. But although these accounts must be founded upon tradition, they are singularly confirmed by the accounts given by classical writers. Thus we find from Diodorus (xvii. 72) and Curtius (v. 7), that Alexander really did burn the citadel and royal palace at Persepolis, in a drunken frolic, at the instigation of the Athenian courtesan Thais, and in revenge for the destruction of Greek temples by Xerxes. Arrian (Exped. Alex., iii. 18) also speaks of his burning the royal palace of the Persians. This act of barbarous folly was evidently the result of hasty impulse, and was probably committed at night, when the palace was full of attendants, courtiers, and priests; the last, who had special charge of the archives, would naturally attempt to save their treasures, and would certainly be opposed by the intoxicated Greeks, at the cost of many lives. The sacred books would be burned with the archives, in which they were deposited, and many Persians, priests and others, would lose their lives in the confusion. Such would be the natural consequences of the facts mentioned by the Western writers, and such are the traditional statements of the Parsis.

But besides the official copies of the sacred books, there

must have been other copies of many portions of them, which would be indispensably necessary in all cities where priests and judges had to perform their duties; and the copies of the sacred books, which the first Sasanian monarchs collected, were no doubt derived from these scattered copies. Notwithstanding the long interval of 550 years of foreign domination and domestic anarchy, which had intervened between Alexander and Ardashír Pâpakân, the Sasanian kings were able to collect a large proportion of the old writings, if we may believe the details given of the contents of the books in their days; and it is, therefore, to the later ravages and persecutions, occasioned by the Mohammedans, that we must attribute the final loss of most of the writings. No doubt the books, as restored by the Sasanians, were chiefly collections of fragments; but some portion of nearly every book seems to have been recovered by them, and the total disappearance of most of the books must be traced to recent times.

The names of all the books are, however, extant, together with short summaries of their contents. According to these reports, the whole scripture consisted of twenty-one books, called Nasks,[1] each containing Avesta and Zend, i.e., an original text with a commentary on it. The number 21 was evidently an artificial arrangement, in order to have one Nask to each of the 21 words of the most sacred formula of the Zoroastrians, which are as follows:—

> Yathâ ahû vairyô, athâ ratush, ashâḍ chîṭ hachâ,
> Vanhêush dazdâ mananhô, shkyauthnanãm anhêush mazdái,
> Khshathremchâ ahurâi â, yim dregubyô dadhaḍ vâstârem.

Each of the Nasks was, as it were, indexed under one particular word of this formula; and in the same manner

---

[1] This word occurs in the Zend-Avesta itself (Yas. ix. 73 Sp.) in the compound naskô-frasâoyhô, "studying the Nasks," that is to say, the different parts of the scripture. It seems to be of foreign origin, and is probably identical with the Assyrian nusku, and the Arabic nuskhah, pl. nusakh.

as this formula consists of three lines or verses (*gâs*), so also the Nasks were divided into three classes, according to their subjects to some extent, but not very strictly so.

Several descriptions of the contents of these Nasks are extant. The longest of these accounts forms the eighth and ninth books of the Dînkard, as has been already noticed (p. 101), and goes into many details with regard to about one-third of the Nasks, though noticing the others much more superficially. Another Pahlavi description of the Nasks is found in the Dînî-vajarkard, and this does not differ much from those given in the Rivâyats. Persian descriptions of the same are found in the Rivâyats[1] of Kâmah Bahrah, Barzû Qiyâmu-d-dîn, and Narîmân Hôshang; these differ but little, except in small details. The following statement of the contents of the Nasks is taken from the Dînî-vajarkard,[2] except where otherwise noted, but their names and the order in which they stand are corrected from the Dînkard.

1. *Sûdkar*, "conferring benefits," corresponding to the Avesta word *yathâ* in the *Yathâ ahû vairyô* formula, and called Stûdgar, or Istûdgar, in the Rivâyats and Dînî-vajarkard, consisted of 22 sections. It contained advice to mankind as to prayer and virtue, the performance of good actions and meditation, producing harmony among relations, and such-like matters. In the Rivâyats and Dînî-vajarkard this Nask is the second, as their lists begin with the twenty-first Nask, which removes all the others one step lower down; this error appears to have been occasioned by the Dînkard giving two lists, one dividing the Nasks into three classes, *gâsânîk*, *hâdak-*

---

[1] The Rivâyats are miscellaneous collections of information and decisions regarding the religion, made by various old Dasturs, chiefly in Persian, but also containing translations of passages from religious books, both in Persian verse and Pâzand.

[2] This must be a different work from the Vajarkard-i-dînî described in p. 100, but it has not been examined. The passage referring to the Nasks was extracted from a manuscript in the library of the Khân Bahâdar Dastur Nôshirvânji Jâmâspji, at Poona.

mânsarîk (or *yashtak-mânsarîk*), and *dâdîk*;[1] the other recapitulating the names in their proper order, which is preserved in the after descriptions of their contents. The first or classified list begins with the twenty-first Nask on the general list, and this may have led the writers of the Rivâyats to consider it the first Nask. That the second list in the Dînkard is correct, appears from its placing the Vendidad *nineteenth* on the list, which is confirmed by Rûstam-i Mihirâpân's colophon in the old Vendidad with Pahlavi at Copenhagen; whereas the Rivâyats and Dînî-vajarkard make it the *twentieth*.

2. *Varshtamânsar*, corresponding to Av. *ahû* in *Y. a. v.*, and called Vahisht-mânsrah (or mântar) in the Riv. and D.v., consisted of 22 sections. It contained reasons for being trustful and heedful of the Mazdayasnian religion, for attending to religion, and using the benedictions and praises of the blessed Zaratûsht; also all events before Zaratûsht which were manifestly good, and all events which are to be after Zaratûsht until the future existence; the benefits of this world, and such-like matters.

3. *Bakô*, corresponding to Av. *vairyô* in *Y. a. v.*, and called Bagh in the Riv. and D.v., consisted of 21 sections. It contained an explanation of the Mazdayasnian religion and the ideas which Aûharmazd taught to men; the exercise of reverence, heedfulness, law, and judgment; the performance of the proper duty and good actions of a magistrate; stopping the admission of the evil spirit into one's self, attaining spiritual existence for one's self, and such-like.

4. *Dâmdâd*, corresponding to Av. *athâ* in *Y. a. v.*, and called Dvâzdah-hâmâst (or homâst) in the Riv. and D.v., consisted of 32 sections. It contained an explanation of the spiritual existence and heaven, good and evil, the material existence of this world, the sky and the earth, and everything which Aûharmazd produced in water,

---

[1] The seven *gâsânîk* are Nasks 21, 1, 2, 3, 11, 20, 13; the seven *hâdak-mânsarîk* are Nasks 4-10; and the seven *dâdîk* are Nasks 15-19, 12, 14.

fire, and vegetation, men and quadrupeds, reptiles and birds, and everything which is produced from the waters, and the characteristics of all things. Secondly, the production of the resurrection and future existence; the concourse and separation at the Chinvad bridge; on the reward of the meritorious and the punishment of sinners in the future existence,[1] and such-like explanations.

5. *Nâḍar*, corresponding to Av. *ratush* in *Y. a. v.*, and called Nâḍûr in D.v., consisted of 35 sections. It contained explanations of the stars, both fixed and planetary, the good and evil (influence) of each star, the course of all the planets in the signs of the zodiac and lunar mansions. It is translated into Arabic and Persian, and they named the book Bûtâl; in Persian it is named Kapâmajân.[2]

6. *Pâjak*, or *Pâjî*, corresponding to Av. *ashâḍ* in *Y. a. v.*, and called Pâjam in the Riv. and D.v., consisted of 22 sections. It contained explanations of the slaughter of quadrupeds and sheep, and how they are to be slaughtered; which quadrupeds it is lawful to eat, and which kinds are not lawful; how he who slaughters should strike at the time the sheep is expiring.[3] The more that is spent upon a Gahanbâr,[4] so much the more

---

[1] The text appears to be *va madam vinâskârân p iḍafrâs-i ychcvânêḍ pavan tanû-i pasîn* in the Dinî-vajarkard. If the meaning be that the punishment is to endure *during* the future existence, which is not quite certain, the D.v. differs from the orthodox view; it is not, however, a book of any authority, as the text is evidently a mere translation of modern Persian.

[2] The Rivâyats are quite uncertain how to read these names, but they prefer Bawaftâl and Fawâmsubhhân, but Fawâmjasân, Fawâmîkhsân, and even Khawâsahhân, occur in different copies. The Dinkard knows nothing about the contents of the Nâḍar Nask, so that the Rivâyats must have had other sources of information.

[3] The slaughtering is performed by cutting (*peskûntano*), but the animal must be finally killed by a blow, as explained by Dastur Hoshangji.

[4] One of the six season festivals which are held on the 45th, 105th, 180th, 210th, 290th, and 365th days of the Parsi year, which commences now on the 20th of September according to Indian Parsi reckoning, or on the 21st of August according to Persian reckoning, but retrogrades one day every leap-year. These periods, which seem originally to have been the six seasons of the year, came to represent, in later times, the six periods of creation. See section xi. of this Essay.

is the reward; how much it is needful to bestow upon Dasturs, Mobads, and Herbads, and upon the unwavering doers of good works in the good religion; to every one who celebrates a Gahanbâr, and consecrates a dress[1] for a (departed) soul, what happens in the last times and in heaven, and what merit accrues to him; the giving of a dress in charity for righteous relatives, using mediation on the part of the righteous, the five greater and lesser Fravardîgân[2] days; and the performance of good works on these ten days is enjoined in this Nask; all men should read this book, with good and wise understanding, who would become fully aware of its explanations.

7. *Ratôshtâîtî*, corresponding to Av. *chîd* in *Y. a. v.*, and called Ratushtâî in the Riv. and D.v., consisted of 50 sections until the accursed Alexander burnt the Nasks, but after that only a fragment containing 13 sections came to hand, as the rest no longer existed. It contained explanations of performing service, giving orders, and remaining at the command of kings, high-priests, and judges; the means of preserving cities is declared; the commands of religion, and means of taking reptiles, birds, cattle, and fish; everything which is a creation of Aûharmazd and Ahriman; accounts of all seas, mountains, and lands; and matters similar to those mentioned.

8. *Barish*, corresponding to Av. *hachâ* in *Y. a. v.*, consisted of 60 sections at first, but after the accursed Alexander's (time only) 12 remained. It contained information as to how kings should rule, and what should be the orders and decrees of the judges of the religion; the preservation and protection of the world; making every new city flourish; accounts of false-speaking men, sinners, and such-like are given in this Nask.

---

[1] Or "a cup," the text being *va jâm-i paran rûbân yezbekhûnêd*.

[2] The last five days of the old year and the first five of the new one. During these ten days the *frôhars* (*fravashi, fravarti*), or spiritual representatives, of the deceased are believed to come to the houses; and the days are, therefore, called Fravardîgân.

I

9. *Kashkîsrôbô*, corresponding to Av. *vanhēush* in *Y. a. v.*, and called Kashkasîrah or Kashsrôb in the Riv. and D.v., consisted of 60 sections formerly, but after the accursed Alexander's (time only) 15 remained. It contained accounts of wisdom and knowledge, the cause of childbirth,[1] teaching guides to wisdom, performance of purification, speaking truth, bringing mankind from evil to good, bringing them from impurity and filth to purity; greatness and promotion are for men near kings; and in what manner men become tellers of falsehood to relatives and kings, and such-like.

10. *Vishtâsp-sâstô*, corresponding to Av. *dazdâ* in *Y. a. v.*, and called Vishtâsp-shâh or Vishtâsp in the Rivâyats, and Vishtâspâd in D.v., consisted of 60 sections, but after the accursed Alexander's (time only) 10 remained.[2] It contained an account of the reign of Gushtâsp; that Zaratûsht-i Spîtâmân brought the religion from Aûharmazd, and King Vishtâsp accepted it and made it current in the world; and such-like.

11. *Vashtî* or *Dâdak*,[3] corresponding to Av. *mananhô* in *Y. a. v.*, and called Khasht in the Rivâyats, and *Khûstô* in D.v., consisted of 22 sections originally, but after the accursed Alexander's (time only) 6 remained (called *juzwa*, "portion, bundle of folios," in the Rivâyats). The first portion was about understanding the attributes of Aûharmazd, being without doubts about the religion of Zaratûsht, all the duties and good works which are enjoined in the religion, and such-like. The second portion was about accepting service, the truth of religion, and all commands, from kings; and withholding one's hand from evil doings, so that it may be far from vice. The third portion was about debt to virtuous disputants, the advantage and merit of the last deliverance from hell, and such-like. The fourth was about the creation of the

---

[1] *Chim-i pĕḍâk-yehcvântano min amîḍar* in the original text.
[2] The Rivâyat of Barzû Qiyâmu-d-dîn says "eight."
[3] It is doubtful whether the first letter in one of the lists be part of the name, or merely the conjunction *va*.

world, the practice of agriculture, the cultivation of trees, the date-tree and all fruit-trees; whence is the chief strength of men and cattle; on the obedience of the doers of good works and the virtuous, on obedience to Dasturs, and such-like. The fifth portion was on the ranks of men; all are mentioned whose knowledge is great, as kings, judges, and the learned in religion; in the second rank are all who take care of the country and attack the enemy; in the third rank are those who are called *vâstryôshân*, "agriculturists;" the fourth rank is said to be those of great skill, market dealers of diligence and volubility to avoid loss, giving one-tenth to the Dastur and king, offering praise on their hardened knees, and whose last reward is that they obtain in heaven. The contents of the sixth portion are not stated.

12. *Chidrashtô*, corresponding to Av. *shkyaothnanãm* in Y. a. v., and called Jirasht in the Riv. and D.v., consisted of 22 sections. This Nask was sent by Aûharmazd to manifest to men what are the details of that science through which mankind is born;[1] how many individuals are still-born, and how many will live; then, how many men become kings, and how many perform the mission of prophesy and high-priesthood, how many men are very great, and how many are very small men, and how this happens; from first to last the time men are born, and all those details are in this Nask. The numbers of all the preceding Nasks, as given in the Rivâyats and Dini-vajarkard, have been one in excess of those given in the Dînkard, their order being in both cases the same; but this Nask and the next one have changed places (and so have the 16th and 17th Nasks) in the Riv. and D.v., which make this the 14th Nask.

13. *Spend*, corresponding to Av. *aŋhēush* in Y. a. v., and called Sfend in the Rivâyats, consisted of 60 sections,

---

[1] *Maman chîm zak dânishn-i mûn zerkhûnêḍ* in the original text, meau-*mardûm min ashkômbo-i mâḍo barâ* ing "midwifery."

which are valuable to great men, productive of virtuous actions, and cause attention to the great and religious. It contained accounts of Zaratûsht from his being brought forth by Dughda till his tenth year. Every Dastur and Mobad, who shall reverentially recite this Nask for several days in purity and by heart, shall obtain every wish for himself, or any favour he may request for others. This is the 13th Nask according to all authorities.

14. *Bakân-yastô*, "worship of divinities," corresponding to Av. *mazdâi* in *Y. a. v.*, and called Baghân-yasht in the Riv. and D.v., consisted of 17 sections.[1] It contained accounts of Aûharmazd the lord, the knowledge of his attributes, the service and sublimity of Aûharmazd, when is the time of every Gâh (time of prayer) till the future existence, what duty is to be performed, the offering praise for every benefit from Aûharmazd, obtaining benefits from him; the appearance (*chitar*) of the Ameshâspends, and knowing in the future existence what is such-and-such an appearance of such-and-such an Ameshâspend. This Nask, made in homage of Aûharmazd and the Ameshâspends, is very fine.

15. *Nikâdûm*, corresponding to Av. *khshathremchâ* in *Y. a. v.*, and called Niyârum[2] in the Riv. and D.v., consisted of 54 sections. It contained details about preserving wealth and placing it out, bargaining and measuring by the cubit and handful; everything the creator Aûharmazd has ordained as innocent; deliverance from hell, and how to walk in the path of reverence and worship; what is in the mind of man, and everything which is in the body of man, and similar matters to those mentioned.

16. *Dûbâsrûjd*,[3] or *Dûbâsrûd*, corresponding to Av. *ahurâi* in *Y. a. v.*, and called Dvâsrûjad, Dvâsrûnjad,

---

[1] D.v. says 18, but this is probably a copyist's error.

[2] Evidently a modern Persian blunder, as *r* and *d* are very similar in that alphabet.

[3] The Dinkard prefixes *dûbârêd* to this form of the name, but this is probably a copyist's blunder; the second form is evidently reproduced in the last Rivâyat form, which would be *drâsrût* if it were not wrongly pointed.

Dvâsrûb in different Rivâyats, and Dvâsrûzd in D.v., consisted of 65 sections. It contained accounts of *khvétûkdas* (next-of-kin marriage), forming connections among relatives, and such-like. In the Riv. and D.v. this is the 18th Nask, having changed places with the next one, as has been already noticed in the remarks on the 12th Nask.

17. *Hûspâram*, corresponding to Av. *â* in *Y. a. v.*, and called Aspâram in the Rivâyats, and Aspârûm in D.v., consisted of 64 sections according to the Rivâyats (one of them says 60), or 65 according to D.v. It contained religious matters which all people know well, the punishment suffered by sinners which they receive in their last career; everything which is innocent is allowable, and what is not innocent is not allowable; the stars which preside over the destiny of men, and such-like. This is the 17th Nask according to all authorities.

18. *Sakâdûm*, corresponding to Av. *yim* in *Y. a. v.*, and called Askâram in the Rivâyats, and Askârûm in D.v., consisted of 52 sections. About giving orders and exercising authority, practising wisdom in everything; causing the resurrection, by which every man who has passed away is made living again, and the malformations of Ahriman and the demons are destroyed; and the like.

19. *Vîk-dêv-dâd*, *Vîk-shêdâ-dâd*, or *Javîd-shêdâ-dâd*, corresponding to Av. *dregubyô* in *Y. a. v.*, and called Vandîdâd, or Jud-dêv-dâd, in the Rivâyats and D.v., consists of 22 sections. About what preserves men from evil and impurity, and will restrain them from all kinds of pollution. Of all the 21 Nasks, the Javîd-dêv-dâd has remained complete; while several remained scattered by the wretched accursed Alexander, this Vendîdâd remained in hand, and from its elucidation the Mazdayasnian religion exists now.

20. *Hâdôkhtô*, corresponding to Av. *dadad* in *Y. a. v*, and called Hâdukht in the Rivâyats, consisted of 30 sections. It contained much goodness and much gratifica-

tion. Every one who recites this Hâdôkht, drives the evil Ahriman far from him, and approaches and comes near to Aûharmazd. This is the 21st Nask according to the Rivâyats and D.v., which remove all the Nasks, except the 12th, 13th, 16th, 17th, and 21st, one step lower on the list.

21. *Stûd-yastô*, corresponding to Av. *vâstârem* in *Y. a. v.*, and called Stûd-yasht in the Riv. and D.v., consisted of 33 sections. It contained the praise and reverence of Aûharmazd and the Ameshâspends, and thanksgivings. Aûharmazd sent this Nask into the world that every one should recite it from memory; and to every Dastur who recites both the Avesta and Zend of this Nask three times accurately the Ameshâspends will come near; he knows this without doubt. This is the 1st Nask in the Rivâyats and D.v., as has been previously mentioned.

III.—THE BOOKS NOW EXTANT, AND THE SUPPOSED ZOROASTRIAN AUTHORSHIP.

Of these twenty-one Nasks, which have been enumerated, only the nineteenth, the *Vendidad*, is preserved complete; of a few of the others, such as the *Vishtâsp-sâstô* and *Hâdôkhtô*, and perhaps the *Bakô*,[1] some fragments only are extant; but by far the larger number of these ancient sacred books have been lost for ever. There are, however, in the Zend-Avesta, as used by the Parsi priests nowadays, other books extant besides the Vendidad, which are either not mentioned in the foregoing list, as the *Yasna* and *Visparad*, or not clearly indicated, as the *Yashts*. These last, as well as the shorter prayers (*Nyâyish, Afringân, Gâhs, Sîrôzah*), were very probably contained in the 14th and 21st Nasks.

---

[1] In the library of the Khân Bahâdar Dastur Nôshirvanji, at Poona, there is a small fragment said to belong to this Nask, and referring to the treatment of a dead body and the fate of the soul immediately after death; but Dastur Hoshangji is doubtful about its authenticity.

THE BOOKS NOW EXTANT. 135

As to the *Yasna* and *Visparad*, they are not to be found in any of the twenty-one Nasks, if we examine the statements of their contents. They were probably separate from them altogether, occupying in regard to the Nasks the same rank as the Vedas, in the Brahmanical literature, do in reference to the Shâstras and Purânas. That the Yasna is the most sacred book of the whole Zend-Avesta may be easily ascertained by perusing and comparing it with the other books contained in the scripture of the Parsis nowadays, where (as in the Vendidad) many verses from it are quoted as most sacred and scriptural.

The difference between the *Yasna* and the *Avesta-Zend* said to have been contained in the twenty-one Nasks is about the same as that between the five Mosaic books (Pentateuch), which were always believed by the Jews to be the most sacred part of the Old Testament,[1] and the other books of the Old Testament together with the different parts of the extensive *Talmud*.[2] There is no doubt, and the present state of the only Nask now completely extant, viz., the Vendidad, seems to prove it, that by far the larger bulk of the various contents of these books contained Zend, or the explanation of an ancient sacred text called Avesta. A good deal of the contents of these Zend books is in all probability extant in the Pahlavi literature, as yet very imperfectly known in Europe.

From the contents of the Nasks, as given above, we clearly see that they must represent the whole religious and scientific literature current throughout the ancient Persian Empire; for they treated not only of religious topics, but of medicine, astronomy, agriculture, botany, philosophy, &c. That the contents of those Zoroastrian books which were known to the Greeks and Romans,

---

[1] The Samaritan Jews acknowledge, to this day, only the five books of Moses as scripture.

[2] Some portions of this enormously large work, which may be said even to surpass the original extent of the twenty-one Nasks, especially those called *Halakah*, "rule," are as authoritative for the Jews as the Thorah (Pentateuch) itself.

were of such a various character, undoubtedly follows from the reports which have reached our time. Indexes of them, like the catalogues of the ancient literature known to Parsi priests nowadays, were extant at the time of Alexander the Great; because Hermippos (see p. 8) is said to have read and perused such a catalogue. This extensive ancient literature, which in all probability was already complete in B.C. 400 (see the last section of this Essay), shows the great activity and scientific interest exhibited by the priests of the Zoroastrian religion in olden times. So comprehensive a literature was of course the work of centuries, especially if one takes into consideration the scarcity and expense of fit writing materials,[1] the clumsiness of the ancient characters used (in all probability a kind of cuneiform), and the long time which Orientals require for original composition. The composition of the sacred literature of the Jews, from the time of Moses (B.C. 1300 to 1500) down to the close of the Talmudic literature (A.D. 960), occupied a period of about 2400 years. Were we to apply the same calculation to the Zoroastrian literature, its beginning would have to be placed as early as B.C. 2800, which would not in the least contradict the statements made by the Greeks,[2] about the age in which the founder of the Parsi religion was believed by them to have lived. At all events, this much seems to be certain, that at least a thousand years must have elapsed before a sacred literature so various and extensive could have grown up out of the seeds sown by the great founder of the Parsi creed, Spitama Zarathushtra.

[1] They used cowskins, which were prepared for the purpose. In the fragments of the ancient literature, extant in the Zend-Avesta, no word meaning "to write" is anywhere to be found. This is merely fortuitous, because systematic books on scientific matters can never be composed without the aid of writing. That the art of alphabetical writing, as practised now by European nations, was perfectly understood by the Persians in the sixth century before the Christian era, we know now from the inscriptions of the kings of the Achæmenian dynasty, such as Cyrus and Darius.

[2] See the fourth Essay.

As to the authorship of these books, they were ascribed by the ancient Greeks and Romans, and are so by the present Parsis, to Zoroaster himself. This opinion being so old as to have been known to the Greeks several centuries previous to the commencement of the Christian era, we may presume that it is not without foundation; though, on the other hand, it is impossible for a modern critic to believe that so extensive a literature as this, treating of such various topics, was the work of a single man. The Parsi tradition, it is true, gets over this difficulty by asserting that all the twenty-one Nasks were written by God Himself, and given to Zoroaster, as his prophet, to forward them to mankind. But such assertions being inadmissible in modern criticism, which tries to solve problems by appeal to reason, not to miracles of the most extraordinary character, we must dispense with them entirely, the more so as such claims to God's immediate authorship of the whole Zend-Avesta are never made in any of the books which are now extant. They lay claim to divine revelation (only the Yasna, not the Vendidad), but not in such a form as to exclude all activity on the part of the receiving prophet. As to the nature of this revelation, the reader may best learn it from the second Gâtha, of which a translation will be given in the 7th section of this Essay. He will see that the prophet was believed to have held conversations with God Himself, questioning the Supreme Being about all matters of importance, and receiving always the right answers to his questions. The prophet accordingly, after having been instructed, communicated these accounts of his conversations with God to his disciples and the public at large. Who wrote them down is quite uncertain; for in the old books no mention of this circumstance is made. The scanty texts which can be traced to the founder himself were very likely not written down by him, but learned by heart by his disciples, as was the case with the numerous Vedic hymns which for centuries were handed down orally only. To the European reader it may be somewhat astonishing to hear that such large works as the Vedas could be faithfully and accurately retained in the memory for centuries; but considering that at the present day thousands of Brahmans exist who are able to recite parrot-like with the greatest accuracy, even as to accents, the whole of one of the Vedas, we are driven to admit that the same might have been the case in those early times to which we must trace the origin of the Zoroastrian religion. As long as the language of the hymns or prayers repeated was a living one and perfectly intelligible, there was no need of committing them to writing; but as soon as it had become dead, the aid of writing was required in order to guard the sacred prayers against corruption and mutilation. That was, in all probability, the case already a thousand years before the beginning of our era.

To revert to the supposed Zoroastrian authorship of the whole Zend-Avesta, believed by the ancient Greeks as well as by the modern Parsis, the solution of the difficulty is simple, if we take the name "Zarathushtra" (Zoroaster), not as the proper name of only one individual, but as the general title of the spiritual heads of the religious community of the ancient Persians. That this was really the case the reader will see from the fourth Essay. The founder is distinguished by the name "Spitama." The high-priest of the whole Parsi community was believed to be the successor of the great founder, *Spitama Zarathushtra*, and to have inherited his spirit. His sayings and decisions, therefore, were listened to with the greatest reverence, and in the course of time believed to be as sacred and divine as those which are with reason to be ascribed to the founder alone. The meaning of the supposed Zoroastrian authorship of the whole Zend-Avesta is that the scripture is the joint work of the high-priests in the ancient Persian Empire and other priests nearest to them in rank, compiled in the course of centuries.

This circumstance throws light upon the fact, that only the Dasturs, or present high-priests, are required to understand the meaning of the Zend-Avesta, and no one who has not thoroughly studied it can be acknowledged as a real Dastur.

The texts extant now, and collected for the first time in Westergaard's valuable edition, comprise the following books :—YASNA, VISPARAD, VENDIDAD, and twenty-four sections called YASHTS, including fragments of the Hâdôkht Nask (No. 22 in Westergaard's edition) and Vishtâsp Nask (No. 24); to these are added some short prayers of different kinds, called AFRINGAN (3), NYAYISH (6), GAH (5), with some miscellaneous fragments (9), and the SIROZAH (thirty days) or calendar. We shall treat of each of them successively in detail.

IV.—YASNA.

The word *yasna*[1] corresponds exactly to the S. *yajna*, "sacrifice," and does not signify only mere prayers, like the Nyâyish, but prayers referring to sacrificial rites, and includes the performance of the latter. The solemn recital of the Yasna before the fire is always connected with ceremonies, to which several of the prayers contained in the Yasna allude. Thus they require consecrated water (*zaothra*), a kind of bread (*darctem*, "food"), butter (*gâush hudhâo*), fresh milk (*gâush jîvya*), meat (*myazda*),[2] the branches of the Homa plant together with one of the pomegranate (*hadhânaêpâta*), the juice of the Homa plant (*para-haoma*), hair of an ox (*varasa*), and a bundle of twigs (*baresma*, nowadays *barsom*) which are tied together

[1] *Yajishn* (sometimes *atjishno*) in Pahlavi, transliterated into *Ijashne* in Gujrati; the root is *yaz, yas*, "to worship by means of sacrifices and prayers;" *na* forms abstract nouns in the Avesta, and in Pahlavi *ishn* answers the same purpose.

[2] The Dasturs nowadays understand it to mean "fruit," which they use when performing the Ijashne ceremony. But originally it meant "flesh," as may be clearly seen from the cognate Armenian *mis*, "meat," (comp. Sans. *mânsa*) being identical with "meat."

by means of a reed. Without these implements, which are evidently the remnants of sacrifices agreeing to a certain extent with those of the Brahmans, as we shall see in the fourth Essay, no Ijashne can be performed by the priest. All these things must be in readiness, except the prepared Homa juice, and placed on a table of marble opposite to the fire of the *Dâdgâh*, or the common hearth of the temple (not before the sacred fires *Adarân* or *Behrâm*), before the Ijashne ceremony can be commenced.

The Yasna at the present time comprises seventy-two chapters, which number (6 times 12) is probably to represent the six *gahanbârs*, or seasons, during which Ahuramazda is said to have created the world. At all events, the extension of the several sections of the Yasna, called *Hâ* (from Av. *hâta*), to the number of seventy-two, is not accidental, but was purposely made, as we may guess easily from the fact that several chapters occur twice within the compass of those seventy-two. For instance, the 61st and 72d chapters are the same, and the 18th contains nothing but verses from the Gâtha portion of the Yasna.

On closer inquiry, we find the Yasna really consists of at least two different parts, distinguishable by considerable differences in language and contents. One part we may call "the old," the other "the later Yasna." The old Yasna is written in a peculiar dialect, styled the Gâtha dialect in the second Essay, where its chief peculiarities have been pointed out.

All parts written in this peculiar dialect [1] formed originally a separate book, which was believed to be sacred even at the time of the composition of the other books contained in the present Zend-Avesta. The original name of this collection was, in all probability, *mãthra speñta*, " bene-

---

[1] These are the five Gâthas :—Yas. xxviii.-xxxiv. ; xliii.-xlvi. ; xlvii.-l. ; li. ; liii. ; *Yasna haptaṇhaiti* (Yasna of seven chapters), xxxv.-xli., and some other smaller pieces, as Yas. iv. 26 ; xi. 9, 17, 18; xii. ; xiii. ; xiv. ; xv. 2, 3 ; xxvii. 13, 14; lvi. ; lviii. All references made to the Avesta, in this Essay, are to Westergaard's edition of the texts, unless otherwise noted.

ficent ritual" (called *Mânsarspend* in Persian writings), which is several times mentioned in the Vendidad (iv. 44) with the meaning of "Scripture." Its different parts were known by different names, as *Gâthas* or hymns, *Yasna haptaṅhaiti* or the Yasna of seven chapters, which are often quoted in the other books, as in Yas. lvii. 8 (where the angel Srosh is said to have first recited the five Gâthas of Spitama Zarathushtra), Yas. lxxi. 11, 12, 18 (where the Gâthas, the sacrificial prayers, and Yasna haptaṅhaiti, are distinguished, and a collection of all prayers is mentioned besides). In the Vendidad, especially in its tenth chapter, many sacred prayers are quoted, which are all to be found in the old Yasna, written in the peculiar Gâtha dialect.

In the first chapter of the Visparad we find a series of sacred prayers (or rather their angels[1]) invoked. This passage being of the greatest importance for the history of the Avesta literature, I shall point out here all that refers therein to this matter. As sacred prayers and sacred literature in general, the following writings are there enumerated:—1. The three most sacred short formulas, viz., *Yathâ ahû vairyô* (Yas. xxvii. 13), *ashem vohû* (Yas. xxvii. 14), and *yeṅhê hâtãm*[2] (Yas. iv. 26); 2. the *Gâtha*

[1] According to Zoroastrian ideas, everything in the good creation, whether animate or inanimate, is presided over by an angel, as the reader will learn from the 11th section of this Essay.

[2] These three formulas are very short; it is, therefore, somewhat hazardous to venture upon a translation of them. The words themselves do not offer much difficulty, but the context does. The text of the first has already been given (p. 125); it is usually called *Ahuna-vairya*, and hence the first Gâtha is called *Ahunavaiti*, as it is written in the same metre and follows this formula, which may be translated as follows: 'As a 'heavenly lord is to be chosen, so is 'an earthly master (spiritual guide),

'for the sake of righteousness, (to be) 'the giver of the good thoughts, of 'the actions of life, towards Mazda; 'and the dominion is for the lord '(Ahura) whom he (Mazda) has given 'as a protector for the poor.' The *Ashem vohû* formula, which is even more frequently used than the Ahunavairya, may be translated as follows: —'Righteousness is the best good, a 'blessing it is; a blessing be to that 'which is righteousness towards Asha- 'vahishta (perfect righteousness).' It is to be understood that "righteousness," here and elsewhere where it translates *ashem*, means "what is right or meritorious" in a ritualistic or materialistic sense, and does not necessarily imply holiness, any more than the Sans. *puṇyam* does.

ahunavaiti (Yas. xxviii.–xxxiv.); 3. *Yasna haptaṇhaiti* (Yas. xxxv.–xli.); 4. *Gâtha ushtavaiti* (Yas. xliii.–xlvi.); 5. *Gâtha speñtâ-mainyû* (Yas. xlvii.-l.); 6. *Gâtha vohukhshathra* (Yas. li.); 7. *Gâtha vahishtôishti* (Yas. liii.); 8. *Dahmi vaṇuhi* and *âfriti* (the *Dahmân Afringân,* Yas. lx., the principal prayer for deceased pious Zoroastrians, called *dahma*); 9. *Airyama ishyô* (Yas. liv., a short prayer now used at the time of the solemnisation of a marriage); 10. *Fshûshô-mãthra* (Yas. lviii., a prayer for prosperity); 11. *Berezô hadaokhdha* (perhaps Yas. xv.); 12. the conversations with and teaching of Ahuramazda, as imparted to the ruler and chief high-priest (*Zarathushtrôtemô,* "the highest Zarathushtra") of a whole country, by which a book like the Vendidad is to be understood, as we shall see afterwards.

In Vendidad xviii. 51, three classes of sacred writings are enumerated in the following order:—Gâthas, Yasna (by which very likely the Yasna haptaṇhaiti is to be understood), and a sacred tradition in a conversational form (called *paitiparshtô-sravaṇhem*), which appears to have been a work like the present Vendidad.

From these passages we may gather with certainty that the old Yasna, *i.e.,* that part of the present Yasna which is written in the peculiar Gâtha dialect, is the most ancient of the whole Zend-Avesta, being known as scripture already to the later Yasna, the Visparad, and Vendidad. All other parts of the Yasna, written in the ordinary Avesta language, are evidently of a later date; they may, therefore, be called the later Yasna. We shall first examine the contents of the chief parts of the old Yasna, the Gâthas.

V.—GATHAS.

The Gâthas, five in number, are comparatively small collections of metrical compositions, containing short prayers, songs, and hymns, which generally express philosophical and abstract thoughts about metaphysical subjects. The name "Gâtha," which is also well known in Sanskrit and Pâli literature, means "song" (especially a stanza which contains allusions to historical facts, as preserved in the mouths of the ancient bards), from the root *gai*, "to sing." That they were sung is not to be doubted, as we may learn from Greek reports (see p. 11), and from their being metrical compositions, the recital of which is always designated by a separate word: *frasrâvayêiti*.[1] At present, the priests do not make any distinction as to the way of repeating the different parts of the Zend-Avesta; they recite them equally in a singing tone. That is not to be wondered at, the different constituents of the Yasna being unknown to the present priests, which was not the case in ancient times.

As to the metres used in the Gâthas, we find them of the same nature as those which are to be found in the Vedic hymns. No rhyme is observed, only the syllables are counted, without much attention being paid to their quantity. The five collections into which the Gâthas have been brought exhibit each a different metre. Verses of the same metre were put together, irrespective of their contents. So the first Gâtha contains verses, each of which consists of forty-eight syllables; in the second, the metre is of fifty-five syllables; in the third, of forty-four, &c. The number of syllables is not always strictly observed; we find, now and then, one less or one more. To give the reader an idea of this poetry, some specimens

[1] There are three expressions used for the recital of the sacred texts, viz., *mar*, "to recite," *drêñj* (or *framru*), "to recite in a low tone," and *srâvay*, *frasrâvay*, "to recite with a loud voice and observing musical accents." The first expression conveys the most general meaning, viz., "to repeat from memory" (*mar* = S. *smar*, "to recollect"), which was very likely done in the same way as the Brahmans repeat the verses of the Rigveda, observing the accents in general. *Drêñj* means evidently a peculiar kind of recital; it is chiefly applied to spells, and may be compared to the recital of the verses of the Yajurveda, which is done with a low voice, and monotonously. *Frasrâvay* is the solemn recital in the form of a very simple tune, comparable to the way of singing the Sâmaveda by the Brahmans. This expression is pre-eminently applied to the Gâthas. Compare Yas. xix. 6, Vend. iv. 45, Yt. xiii. 20

are here quoted. In the first Gâtha (called *ahunavaiti*, from the Ahuna-vairya formula which precedes it), each verse consists of three lines, each comprising sixteen syllables, as may be seen from the following example (Yas. xxxi. 8):—

Ad	thwâ	mēñhî	paourvîm	mazdâ	yazûm	stôi	manaṇhâ
so	thee	I thought	first	Mazda	great	in creation	in mind

Vaṇhēush	ptarēm	manaṇhô	hyaḍ	thwâ	hēm	chashmaini	hēñgrabem
of the good	father	mind	therefore	thee	together	in the eye	I seized

Haithîm	ashahyâ	dâmîm	aṇhēush	ahurem	shkyaothanaēshû.[1]
true	of righteousness	creator	of life	Ahura	in actions.

In this verse the cesura is after the seventh syllable; the second half of each line comprises, therefore, nine syllables. Were the cesura after the eighth syllable, and if the whole verse comprised only thirty-two syllables, instead of forty-eight, this metre would correspond to the Sanskrit shloka, consisting of four half-verses (pâdas) each comprising eight syllables, which metre is preserved in some fragments of epic songs in the Zend-Avesta, as we shall see hereafter. It stands nearest to the Gâyatrî metre, which consists of twenty-four syllables, divisible into three pâdas, each comprising eight syllables.

In the second Gâtha (called *ushtavaiti*, from its first words, *ushtâ ahmâi*, "hail to him!") there are five lines in each stanza, each consisting of eleven syllables, for instance (Yas. xliv. 3):—

Taḍ	thwâ	peresâ	eresh	môi	vaochâ	ahurâ!
That	thee	I will ask	right	me	tell	Ahura!
Kasnâ	zâthâ	ptâ	ashahyâ			paouruyô?
What man	creator	father	of righteousness			first?
Kasnâ	qēñg	staremchâ	dâḍ			adrânem?
What man	sun	and stars	made			path?
Kē	yâ	mâo	ukhshyēitî	nerefsaitî		thwad?[2]
Who	that	the moon	increases	wanes		besides thee?
Tâchiṭ	mazdâ	vasemî	anyâchâ			vîduyē.
such things	Mazda!	I wish	and other			to know.

---

[1] See a freer translation further on.
[2] *Thwaḍ* is the ablative case, dependent on *kē (kô)*, who? The meaning "besides, else," here absolutely re-

GATHAS.

This metre is very near to the Vedic *trishtubh*, which is sacred to the god Indra, and consists of four pâdas, each comprising eleven syllables, which make forty-four in all. The Ushtavaiti Gâtha only exceeds it by one pâda of eleven syllables. In the third Gâtha, called *speñtâ-mainyû*, however, the *trishtubh* is completely represented, as each verse there comprises four pâdas, each of eleven syllables, in all forty-four, just as many as the *trishtubh* is composed of.[1] To obtain the number of syllables which is required for each pâda or foot, in the specimen quoted above (*tad thwâ peresâ*), as well as in other verses of the Gâthas, the sound *ere*, corresponding to the Sanskrit vowel *ṛi*, makes only one syllable; and the short *e* (in *vasemi*, S. *vashmi*, "I want, wish"), being a mere auxiliary vowel, and *u* in *vîduyê* (instead of *vîdyê*) being of the same nature, are not to be counted. The syllables *va* and *ya*, *yê*, are often made liquid, as is the case in the Vedic metres also, that is to say, they are pronounced as two syllables like *ua*, *ia*, *iyê*. The verse quoted above is, therefore, to be read as follows:—

> *Tad thwâ persâ ersh môi vochâ ahurâ !*
> *kasnâ zâthâ ptâ ashahyâ pouruyô ?*
> *kasnâ qêñg staremchâ dât aduânem ?*
> *kê yâ mâo ukhshiyêiti nerfsaiti thwad ?*
> *tâchit mazdâ vasmî anyâchâ vîdyê.*

In the fourth Gâtha each stanza comprises three verses,

quired for a translation into modern languages, lies implied in the context; *vîduyê* is a peculiar infinitive form of the root *vid*, "to know."

[1] To illustrate this assertion, I subjoin a specimen of this metre taken from Rigveda, i. 189, 1.

Agne	*naya*	*supathâ râye*	*asmân*
O fire god!	bring	on the good way to wealth	us,
vishvâni	*deva*	*vayunâni*	*vidvân*
all	O god!	arts	knowing!
yuyodhy	*asmaj*	*juhurânam*	*eno*
remove	from us	wrath kindled	sin,
bhûyishthâm	*te*	*nama-uktim*	*vidhema*
utmost	on thee	worship-hymn	let us bestow !

(Agni! provide us with riches through good fortune, O thou god, who knowest all arts of obtaining wealth! Remove from us all faults at which thou hast felt angry with us; let us prepare for thee a most excellent hymn for thy worship.)

K

or six pâdas or feet, each consisting of seven syllables, which make in all forty-two. In the fifth Gâtha, various metres are used.

The five Gâthas are expressly designated as the "five Gâthas of Zarathushtra" (Yas. lvii. 8), in order to distinguish them from other Gâthas or hymns, as, for instance, those devoted to the praise of Homa (Yas. x.) That they really contain the sayings and teaching of the great founder of the Parsi religion, Spitama Zarathushtra himself, cannot be doubted, as the reader will perceive from a perusal of the larger portion of them, which will be found in the following sections.

VI.—GATHA AHUNAVAITI.[1]

This Gâtha is divided into seven chapters [2] (Yas. xxviii.-xxxiv., Westerg.), which comprise 101 verses, all of them being composed in the same metre, described above (p. 144). As to its contents, it resembles more a collection of scattered verses than one continuous whole. It is even doubtful whether the author is always the same, the style being now and then different. But in consequence of one and the same spirit pervading the whole Gâtha, we must admit that it all belongs to the same age. We have in it, in all probability, the sayings and songs of Zarathushtra himself, mixed with those of his disciples *Jâmâspa*, *Vishtâspa*, and *Frashaoshtra*. Thus, for instance, the following verse (Yas. xxviii. 7) must be considered as the composition of one of the disciples of the prophet:—

'Come with the good mind, grant prosperity for life
'long, by means of thy mighty words, O thou Mazda! give
'both Zarathushtra and us thy powerful assistance to put
'down the assaults of our enemy.'

Here Zarathushtra being spoken of in the third, and the

---

[1] To the explanation of this Gâtha the whole of the first volume of the author's German work on the Gâthas (containing 246 pages) is devoted.

[2] The chapters of the Yasna are called Hâs, which is a corruption of the Avesta word *hâta*.

author in the first person, we are fully entitled to ascribe the verse to one of his followers, not to himself.

The heading of this Gâtha, 'The revealed thought, the 'revealed word, the revealed deed of the righteous Zara-'thushtra; the archangels first sang the Gâthas,'[1] is of high interest, because it does not refer to this Gâtha alone, but to all five indiscriminately. These introductory remarks are written not in the peculiar Gâtha dialect, but in the common Avesta language, which circumstance shows clearly that they proceed not from one of the authors, but from a subsequent collector of these sacred verses. We learn from them that the Gâthas were believed to contain all that has been revealed[2] to Spitama Zarathushtra; that he learnt them from the choir of the archangels, who sang them to his mental ears when, in a state of ecstasy, his mind was raised to heaven.

Translations of some parts of this Gâtha will be presented to the reader. In its second section (Yas. xxix.) it is related that the *Gēush urvâ*,[3] "the soul of the animated

---

[1] A full explanation of this heading is given in the author's German work on the Gâthas, vol. i. pp. 41–46.

[2] The term in the original is *yânîm*, which does not signify "good, happy," as the Dasturs think, but anything seen when in a state of ecstasy. This meaning is even preserved in the modern Persian word *yân*, "a reverie or a fanatic, a trance." The literal meaning is "a walk," as may be seen from its use in the Vedic Sanskrit (root *yâ*, "to go"), but applied to the gesticulations of a prophet or seer when in ecstasy, it means what he perceives with his mental eye in such an extraordinary frame of mind. The word "to see" is really used in reference to revelation in the Gâthas (see Yas. xliii. 5, xxxi. 8, xxviii. 6). This application of the word is wholly in accordance with its meaning in the Vedas, where it is stated that the sacred songs (*mantra*) have been seen by the Rishis.

[3] In the Parsi or Pâzand language, the name is corrupted into *gôshûrûn*, which is very likely preserved in the modern Persian *gawhar*, "nature." According to the tradition, it was the first animated creature, in the shape of an ox, from which, after having been killed and cut into pieces, the whole living creation is said to have sprung. The slaughterer of this primary ox, the supposed ancestor of the whole animal kingdom, is often alluded to by the name *pēush tashâ*, "cutter of the ox." Who was the killer of this ox is not stated in the Zend-Avesta, but tradition charges this murder, of course, to *Angrô-mainyush*, the devil. This legend about the origin of the animated creation apparently refers to sacrificial rites, the creation of the world being considered by several ancient nations as a sacrifice; by the Brahmans as that of Brahma himself; by the ancient Scandinavians, the people of the Edda, as that of the primary giant *Bör*.

creation," was crying aloud in consequence of attacks made upon its life, and imploring the assistance of the archangels. The murderer, frightened by this cry, asked one of the archangels, *Asha* (Ardibahisht), as to who had been appointed to protect this soul of the earth. Asha referred him to Mazda, who is "the most wise, and the giver of oracles." Mazda answered that *Gēush urvâ* was being cut into pieces for the benefit of the agriculturist. Mazda now deliberated with Asha as to who might be fit to communicate this declaration of the heavenly council to mankind. Asha answered that there was only one man who had heard the orders issued by the celestial councillors, viz., Zarathushtra Spitama; he, therefore, was to be endowed with eloquence to bring their messages to the world.

Gēush urvâ means the universal soul of earth, the cause of all life and growth. The literal meaning of the word, "soul of the cow," implies a simile; for the earth is compared to a cow.[1] By its cutting and dividing, ploughing is to be understood. The meaning of that decree, issued by Ahuramazda and the heavenly council, is that the soil is to be tilled; it, therefore, enjoins agriculture as a religious duty. Zarathushtra, when encouraging men by the order of Ahuramazda to cultivate the earth, acts as a prophet of agriculture and civilisation. In this capacity we shall also find him afterwards.

In the third section of this Gâtha (Yas. xxx.) one of the most important sections of the Gâtha literature is presented to us. It is a metrical speech, delivered by Spitama Zarathushtra himself, when standing before the sacred fire, to a numerously attended meeting of his countrymen. The chief tendency of this speech is to induce his countrymen to forsake the worship of the devas or

---

[1] *Gâus* has in Sanskrit the two meanings "cow" and "earth." In Greek *γέ*, "earth," is to be traced to this word. In the Vâmadeva hymns (fourth book of the Rigveda), the *Ribhus* (comparable to the elves of the Teutonic mythology), who represent the creative powers in nature, are said to "have cut the cow and made fertile the earth." The term evidently refers to the cultivation of the soil.

gods, *i.e.*, polytheism, to bow only before Ahuramazda, and to separate themselves entirely from the idolators. In order to gain the object wished for, he propounds the great difference which exists between the two religions, Monotheism and Polytheism, showing that whereas the former is the fountain of all prosperity both in this and the other life, the latter is utterly ruinous to mankind. He attempts further to explain the origin of both these religions, so diametrically opposed to each other, and finds it in the existence of two primeval causes, called "existence" and "non-existence." But this merely philosophical doctrine is not to be confounded with his theology, according to which he acknowledged only one God, as will be clearly seen from the second Gâtha. The following is a translation of the whole of this inaugural speech of Zarathushtra.

Yas. xxx. 1. I will now tell you who are assembled here the wise sayings of Mazda, the praises of Ahura, and the hymns of the good spirit, the sublime truth which I see arising out of these sacred flames.

2. You shall, therefore, hearken to the soul of nature [1] (*i.e.*, to plough and cultivate the earth); contemplate the beams of fire with a most pious mind! Every one, both men and women, ought to-day to choose his creed (between the Deva and the Ahura religion). Ye offspring of renowned ancestors, awake to agree with us (*i.e.*, to approve of my lore, to be delivered to you at this moment)!

(The prophet begins to deliver the words revealed to him through the sacred flames.)

3. In the beginning there was a pair of twins, two spirits, each of a peculiar activity; these are the good and the base, in thought, word, and deed. Choose one of these two spirits! Be good, not base!

4. And these two spirits united created the first (the

[1] *Gêush urvâ*, see p. 147-8. It is here evidently an allusion made to the legend mentioned above.

material things); one, the reality, the other, the non-reality. To the liars (the worshippers of the devas, *i.e.*, gods) existence will become bad, whilst the believer in the true God enjoys prosperity.

5. Of these two spirits you must choose one, either the evil, the originator of the worst actions, or the true, holy spirit. Some may wish to have the hardest lot (*i.e.*, those who will not leave the polytheistic deva-religion), others adore Ahuramazda by means of sincere actions.

6. You cannot belong to both of them (*i.e.*, you cannot be worshippers of the one true God, and of many gods at the same time). One of the devas, against whom we are fighting, might overtake you, when in deliberation (what faith you are to embrace), whispering you to choose the worst mind.[1] Then the devas flock together to assault the two lives (the life of the body and that of the soul), praised by the prophets.

7. And to succour this life (to increase it), Armaiti[2] came with wealth, the good and true mind; she, the everlasting one, created the material world; but the soul, as to time, the first cause among created beings, was with Thee.

8. But when he (the evil spirit) comes with one of these evils (to sow mistrust among the believers), then thou hast the power through the good mind of punishing them who break their promises, O righteous spirit![3]

9. Thus let us be such as help the life of the future.[4] The wise living spirits[5] are the greatest supporters of it.

---

[1] *Akem manô* (superlat. *achishtem manô*) means literally "evil mind." It is a philosophical term applied by Zarathushtra to designate his principle of non-existence, non-reality, which is the cause of all evils.

[2] She is the angel of earth, and the personification of prayers.

[3] That is to say, those who give to-day the solemn promise to leave the polytheistic religion and to follow that preached by Zarathushtra, will be punished by God should they break their promise.

[4] In this passage we have the germs of the doctrine of the resurrection of the dead; see the author's German work on the Gâthas, vol. i. pp. 109-112.

[5] These are the archangels (Amshaspends).

The prudent man wishes only to be there where wisdom is at home.

10. Wisdom is the shelter from lies, the annihilation of the destroyer (the evil spirit). All perfect things are garnered up in the splendid residence of the Good Mind (Vohu-manô), the Wise (Mazda), and the Righteous (Asha),[1] who are known as the best beings.

11. Therefore, perform ye the commandments which, pronounced by Mazda himself, have been given to mankind; for they are a nuisance and perdition to liars, but prosperity to the believer in the truth; they are the fountain of happiness.

In the fourth section of the first Gâtha (Yas. xxxi.) we have a collection of *urvâtas*, "sayings," of Ahuramazda, revealed to his prophet Zarathushtra, for the purpose of protecting the good creation from the attacks of wicked men and evil spirits. The chief means of checking evil influences is the cultivation of the soil. Some of these verses are here translated.

Yas. xxxi. 7. He (Ahuramazda) first created, through his inborn lustre,[2] the multitude of celestial bodies, and through his intellect the good creatures, governed by the inborn good mind. Thou Ahuramazda, the spirit who art everlasting, makest them (the good creatures) grow.

8. When my eyes beheld Thee, the essence of truth, the Creator of life, who manifests his life in his works, then I knew Thee to be the primeval spirit, Thou Mazda, so high in mind as to create the world, and the father of the good mind.[3]

9. In Thee was Armaiti (spirit of earth), in Thee the very wise fertiliser of the soil,[4] O Ahuramazda, Thou

---

[1] Three names of archangels.
[2] *Qâthrâ*, "by means of his own fire." Ahuramazda, as the source of light, which most resembles him, and where he appears to his prophet, is called *qâthrô*, "having his own light" (not borrowed).
[3] *Vohu-manô*. He represents the life in men and animals, the principle of vitality. If Ahuramazda is called the father of *Vohu-manô*, it means that all vital powers in the animated beings have sprung out of him, as the supreme being.
[4] Literally, "the cutter of the cow" (*gēush-tashâ*), see p. 147.

spirit! when Thou hast made her paths that she might go from the tiller of the soil to him who does not cultivate it.[1]

10. Of these two (the agriculturist and the herdsman), she chose the pious cultivator, the propagator of life, whom she blessed with the riches produced by the good mind. All that do not till her, but worship the devas (false gods), have no share in her good tidings (the fruits produced by her, and the blessings of civilisation).

11. When Thou madest the world with its bodies, and (gavest them) motions and speeches, then Thou Mazda! hast created at first through Thy mind the *gaêthas* (enclosures), and the sacred visions (*daênâo*), and intellects.[2]

18. Do not listen to the sayings and precepts of the wicked (the evil spirit), because he has given to destruction house, village, district, and province. Therefore, kill them (the wicked) with the sword.

The fifth section (Hâ) of this Gâtha (Yas. xxxii.) is one of the most difficult pieces of the whole Yasna. It depicts, in glowing colours, idolatry and its evil consequences. The prophet directs his speech against the devas, or gods, in the following manner:—

Yas. xxxii. 3. Ye devas have sprung out of the evil

---

[1] The meaning is, that Armaiti, the spirit of earth, is wandering from spot to spot to convert deserts and wildernesses into fruitful fields. She goes from the agriculturist to the shepherd, who still adheres to the ancestral nomadic life, to call upon him to cultivate the soil also.

[2] By *gaêthas*, frequently mentioned in the Zend-Avesta, the ancient settlements of the Iranian agriculturists are to be understood. Ahuramazda is constantly called their creator, which means, that these settlements belong to a very remote antiquity, and that they form the basis of the Ahura religion, or the religion of the agriculturists. The *daênas* are the revelations communicated to the prophets through visions. The root of the word is *dî*, "to see" (preserved in the modern Persian *dîdan*, "to see;" it is related to the Sanskrit root *dhyai*, "to think," thinking being considered to be a seeing by means of the mental eyes). Afterwards it passed into the more general meaning of "religion, creed," and is retained in the form *dîn* down to this day in Persian, whence it was incorporated into Arabic, like many other Iranian words, at a time anterior to Mohammed. This word is also to be found in the Lithuanian language (a link of the Aryan stock) in the form *dainô*, meaning "a song" (the mental fiction of the poet).

spirit who takes possession of you by intoxication (Shoma), teaching you manifold arts to deceive and destroy mankind, for which arts you are notorious everywhere.

4. Inspired by this evil spirit, you have invented spells, which are applied by the most wicked, pleasing the devas only, but rejected by the good spirit; but the wicked perish through the wisdom and righteousness of Ahuramazda.

5. Ye devas and thou evil spirit! ye by means of your base mind, your base words, your base actions, rob mankind of its earthly and immortal welfare by raising the wicked to power.

Of the sixth and seventh Hâs (Yas. xxxiii. xxxiv.) a few verses are here translated.

Yas. xxxiii. 2. Whoever are opposed, in their thoughts, words, and actions, to the wicked, and think of the welfare of the creation,[1] their efforts will be crowned with success through the mercy of Ahuramazda.

3. Whoever of two lords, of two yeomen, of two bondsmen,[2] behaves himself well towards a righteous man (an adherent of the Zoroastrian religion), and furthers the works of life by tilling the soil, that one will be in the fields of the righteous and good (*i.e.*, in paradise).

4. But by means of prayer I will remove from Thee (from thy community), O Mazda! irreligiousness and wickedness, the disobedience of the lord, and the falsehood of the servant belonging to him and his yeoman, and frustrate the most wicked designs plotted for destroying the fields.

14. Among the priests Zarathushtra maintains the opinion that the peculiar nature of each body (living creature) subsists through the wisdom of the good mind,

---

[1] The term in the Avesta is *asti*, "existence." It is the consequence of adherence to the good principle.

[2] These three names of the members of the ancient Iranian community are very frequently used in the Gâ- thas, but not in the other books of the Zend-Avesta. The word for lord is *qaêtu*, "owner;" that for yeoman, *airyama*, "associate, friend;" that for bondsman, *verezêna*, "workman, labourer."

through righteousness of action, and the hearing of, and keeping to, the revealed word.

Yas. xxxiv. 1. Immortality, righteousness, wealth, health, all these gifts to be granted in consequence of (pious) actions, words, and worshipping, to these (men who pray here), are plentiful in Thy possession, O Ahuramazda!

VII.—GATHA USHTAVAITI (Yas. xliii.-xlvi.)[1]

Whilst the first Gâtha appears to be a mere collection of fragments of hymns and scattered verses, made without any other plan than to transmit to posterity what was believed to be the true and genuine sayings of the prophet, in this second Gâtha we may observe a certain scheme carried out. Although its contents, with the exception of a few verses only (xlvi. 13–17), are all sayings of Zarathushtra himself, yet they have not been put together, as is the case in many other instances, irrespective of their contents, but in a certain order, with the view of presenting the followers of the prophet with a true image of the mission, activity, and teaching of their great master. In the first section of this Gâtha (Yas. xliii.), his mission, by order of Ahuramazda, is announced; in the second (Yas. xliv.), he receives instructions from the Supreme Being about the highest matters of human speculation; in the third (Yas. xlv.), he appears as a prophet before a large assembly of his countrymen, to propound to them his new doctrines; and in the fourth or last section (Yas. xlvi.) we find different verses referring to the fate of the prophet, the congregation which he established, and his most eminent friends and supporters.

As this Gâtha is the most important portion of the whole Zend-Avesta for giving an accurate knowledge of Zarathushtra's teaching and activity, a translation of the

[1] See the text, with a literal Latin translation, in the author's German work on the Gâthas, vol. ii. pp. 2-18, and the commentary on it, ibid., pp. 59-154.

whole of it is submitted to the reader in the following pages.

1. (YAS. xliii.)

1. Blessed is he, blessed is every one, to whom Ahuramazda, ruling by his own will, shall grant the two everlasting powers (health and immortality). For this very good I beseech Thee (Ahuramazda). Mayest Thou through Thy angel of piety, Armaiti, give me happiness, the good true things, and the possession of the good mind.

2. I believe Thee to be the best being of all, the source of light for the world. Every one shall choose Thee (believe in Thee) as the source of light, Thee, O Mazda, most beneficent spirit! Thou createdst all good true things by means of the power of Thy good mind at any time, and promisedst us (who believe in Thee) a long life.

3. This very man (Sraosha) may go (and lead us) to Paradise, he who used to show us the right paths of happiness both in the earthly life and in that of the soul, in the present creations, where Thy spirit dwells, the living, the faithful, the generous, the beneficent, O Mazda!

4. I will believe Thee to be the powerful benefactor, O Mazda! For Thou givest with Thy hand, filled with helps, good to the righteous man, as well as to the wicked, by means of the warmth of the fire [1] strengthening the good things. For this reason the vigour of the good mind has fallen to my lot.

5. Thus I believed in Thee, O Ahuramazda! as the furtherer (of what is good); because I beheld Thee to be the primeval cause of life in the creation, for Thou, who hast rewards for deeds and words, hast given evil to the bad and good to the good. I will believe in Thee, O Ahura! in the last (future) period of creation.

6. In whatever period of my life I believed in Thee, O Mazda, munificent spirit! in that Thou camest with

[1] The fire is supposed in the Zend-Avesta and the Vedas to be spread everywhere as the cause of all life.

wealth, and with the good mind through whose actions our settlements thrive. To these (men who are present) Armaiti[1] tells the everlasting laws, given by Thy intellect, which nobody may abolish.

7. Thus I believed in Thee, O Ahuramazda! as the furtherer (of what is good); therefore he (Sraosha) came to me and asked: Who art thou? whose son art thou? How dost thou at present think to increase and improve thy settlements and their beings (to increase the power of the good mind in all thy territories where thou appearest)?

8. I replied to him: Firstly, I am Zarathushtra. I will show myself as a destroyer to the wicked, as well as be a comforter for the righteous man. As long as I can praise and glorify Thee, O Mazda! I shall enlighten and awaken all that aspire to property (who wish to separate themselves from the nomadic tribes and become settlers in a certain country).

9. Thus I believed in Thee, O Ahuramazda! as the furtherer (of what is good); therefore he came to me with the good mind (and I asked him): To whom dost thou wish the increase of this life should be communicated? Standing at Thy fire amongst Thy worshippers who pray to Thee, I will be mindful of righteousness (to improve all good things) as long as I shall be able.

10. Thus mayest Thou grant me righteousness. Then I shall call myself, if accompanied by the angel of piety, a pious obedient man. And I will ask in behalf of both of us[2] whatever Thou mayest be asked. For the king will, as it is only allowed to mighty men, make Thee for Thy answers a mighty fire (to cause Thy glory and adoration to be spread over many countries like the splendour of a large blazing flame).

11. Thus I believed in Thee, O Ahuramazda! as the furtherer (of what is good); therefore he (Sraosha) came to

---

[1] The spirit of earth.

[2] This refers to Zarathushtra and Kava Vishtâspa, for whose welfare and renown the prophet is here praying.

me with the good mind. For since I, who am your most obedient servant amongst men, am ready to destroy the enemies first by the recital of your[1] words, so tell me the best to be done.

12. And when Thou camest to instruct me, and taughtest me righteousness; then Thou gavest me Thy command not to appear (before large assemblies as a prophet), without having received a (special) revelation, before the angel Sraosha, endowed with the sublime righteousness which may impart your righteous things to the two friction woods (by means of which the holiest fire, the source of all good in the creation, is produced) for the benefit (of all beings), shall have come to me.

13. Then I believed in Thee, O Ahuramazda! as the furtherer (of what is good); therefore he came to me with the good mind. Let me obtain the things which I wished for; grant me the gift of a long life: none of you may detain it from me for the benefit of the good creation subject to Thy dominion.

14. Therefore (Sraosha), the powerful proprietor (of all good), communicated to me, his friend, knowledge of Thy helps (Thy powers); for endowed with all the gifts granted by Thee, as to the various kinds of speech, like all other men who recite Thy prayers, I was resolved upon making my appearance (in public as a prophet).

15. Thus I believed in Thee, O Ahuramazda! as the furtherer (of what is good); therefore he came to me with the good mind. May the greatest happiness brightly blaze out of these flames! May the number of the worshippers of the liar (evil spirit) diminish! may all those (that are here present) address themselves to the priests of the holy fire!

16. Thus prays, O Ahuramazda! Zarathushtra and every holy (pure) man for all that choose (as their guide) the most beneficent spirit. May vitality and righteousness

---

[1] This refers to Ahuramazda and the archangels forming the celestial council.

(the foundations of the good creation) become predominant in the world! In every being which beholds the sun's light may Armaiti (the spirit of piety) reside! She who causes all growth by her actions through the good mind.

2. (YAS. xliv.)

1. That I shall ask Thee, tell it me right, O Ahura! whether your friend (Sraosha) be willing to recite his own hymn as prayer to my friend (Frashaoshtra or Vishtâspa), O Mazda! and whether he would come to us with the good mind, to perform for us true actions of friendship.[1]

2. That I shall ask Thee, tell it me right, O Ahura! How arose the best (present) life (this world)? By what means are the present things (the world) to be supported? That spirit, the beneficent (Vohu-manô) O righteous Mazda! is the guardian of the beings to ward off from them every evil; He is the promoter of all life.

3. That I shall ask Thee, tell it me right, O Ahura! Who was in the beginning the father and creator of righteousness? Who created the path of the sun and stars? Who causes the moon to increase and wane but Thou? This I wish (to know), O Mazda! besides what I know (already).

4. That I shall ask Thee, tell it me right, O Ahura! Who is holding the earth and the skies above it? Who made the waters and the trees of the field? Who is in the winds and storms that they so quickly run? Who is the creator of the good-minded beings, O Mazda?

5. That I shall ask Thee, tell it me right, O Ahura! Who created the lights of good effect and the darkness? Who created the sleep of good effect and the activity? Who (created) morning, noon, and night, reminding the priest always of his duties?

---

[1] The meaning is, the prophet wants to ascertain from Ahuramazda, whether or not the angel Sraosha would make communications to his (the prophet's) friend.

6. That I shall ask Thee, tell it me right, O Ahura! Whether these (verses) which I shall recite, are really thus?[1] (a) Armaiti doubles righteousness by her actions. (b) He collects wealth with the good mind. (c) For whom hast thou made the imperishable cow Rânyô-skereti?[2]

7. That I shall ask Thee, tell it me right, O Ahura! Who has prepared the Bactrian (berekhdha) home with its properties? Who fashioned, by a weaving motion, the excellent son out of the father?[3] To become acquainted with these things, I approach Thee, O Mazda, beneficent spirit! creator of all beings!

8. That I shall ask Thee, tell it me right, O Ahura! What soul (what guardian angel) may tell me good things, to perform five times (a day)[4] the duties which are enjoined by Thyself, O Mazda! and to recite those prayers which are communicated for the welfare (of all beings) by the good mind. Whatever good, intended for the increase of life, is to be had, that may come to me.

9. That I shall ask Thee, tell it me right, O Ahura! How shall I bless that creed which Thy friend (Sraosha), who protects it with a true and good mind in the assembly (of the heavenly spirits), ought to promulgate to the mighty king?

10. That I shall ask Thee, tell it me right, O Ahura! The faith which, being the best of all, may protect my possession, and may really produce the good things, by means of the words and actions of Armaiti (the spirit of earth). My heart wishes (it is my lively desire) that I may know Thee, O Mazda!

[1] Here are quoted the first phrases of three ancient prayers which are no longer known.
[2] This is a mythological name of the earth, to be found in the Gâthas only. It means "producing the two friction woods (two wooden sticks, by means of rubbing which fire was produced)." See the author's work on the Gâthas, vol. ii. pp. 91, 92.
[3] This refers to the production of fire by the friction of two wooden sticks, which was in ancient times the most sacred way of bringing into existence the fire, commonly called 'Ahuramazda's son.' See the author's work on the Gâthas, vol. ii. pp. 81, 82.
[4] The so-called five gâhs: Hâvani, from 6 to 10 A.M.; Rapithwina, 10 A.M. to 3 P.M.; Uzayêirina, from 3 to 6 P.M. (sunset); Aiwisrûthrema, from 6 to 12 P.M.; Ushahina, from 12 P.M. to 6 A.M.

11. That I shall ask Thee, tell it me right, O Ahura! How Armaiti[1] may visit those men to whom the belief in Thee, O Mazda! is preached? By those I am there acknowledged (as a prophet); but all dissenters are regarded as my enemies.

12. That I shall ask Thee, tell it me right, O Ahura! Who is the righteous man and who the impious, after whom I wish to inquire? With which of the two is the evil (spirit), and with which the good one? Is it not right to consider the impious man who attacks me or Thee to be an evil one?

13. That I shall ask Thee, tell it me right, O Ahura! How shall we drive away the destruction (destroyer) from this place to those who, full of disobedience, do not respect righteousness in keeping it, nor care about the thriving of the good mind (that it may be diffused all over the earth)?

14. That I shall ask Thee, tell it me right, O Ahura! How shall I deliver the destroyer into the hands of truth, to be annihilated by means of the hymns for Thy praise? If Thou, O Mazda! communicatest to me an efficacious spell to be applied against the impious man, then I will destroy every difficulty and every misfortune.

15. That I shall ask Thee, tell it me right, O Ahura! When or to whom of the lords givest Thou as proprietor this fat flock (of sheep), two armies being gathered for a combat in silence, by means of those sayings which Thou, O Mazda! art desirous of pronouncing?

16. That I shall ask Thee, tell it me right, O Ahura! Who killed the hostile demons of different shapes, to enable me to become acquainted with the rules established for the course of the two lives (physical and spiritual)? So may the angel Sraosha, assisted by the good mind, shine for every one towards whom Thou art propitious.

---

[1] This refers to the wanderings of Armaiti, the spirit of earth, by which is to be understood the progress of agriculture and the arts of a more civilised life.

17. That I shall ask Thee, tell it me right, O Ahura! How may I come, O Mazda! to your dwelling-place (that of God and the angels) to hear you sing? Aloud I express my wish to obtain the help of (the angel of) health, and that of immortality, by means of that hymn which is a treasure of truth.

18. That I shall ask Thee, tell it me right, O Ahura! How shall I, O Righteous! spend this gift, ten pregnant mares and a camel,[1] to obtain in future the two powers of health and immortality, in the same way as Thou hast granted them to these men (to others known to the prophets)?

19. That I shall ask Thee, tell it me right, O Ahura! How is the first intellect[2] of that man, who does not return (what he has received) to the offerer of this gift,[3] of him who does not grant anything to the speaker of truth? For the last intellect of this man (his doing) is already known to me.

20. What, O good ruler Mazda! are the Devas (evil spirits)? Thus I might ask Thee for those who attack the good existence (the good beings), by whose means the priest and prophet of the idols expose the earth (the cultivated countries) to destruction; and (I wish to know besides) what the false prophet has gained by doing so. Do not, O Righteous! grant him a field to fence it in (to make it his own property).

3. (YAS. xlv.)

1. All ye, who have come from near and far, should now listen and hearken to what I shall proclaim. Now the wise have manifested this universe as a duality. Let

---

[1] This refers to a sacrifice. Sacrifices of animals were customary in Zarathushtra's time.

The first and last intellects are notions of the Zoroastrian philosophy; see the fourth Essay. The first intellect is that which is innate in the soul, which came from heaven; the last is that one which man himself acquires by experience.

[3] That is to say, 'who is ungrateful towards God.'

not the mischief-maker destroy the second life, since he, the wicked, chose with his tongue the pernicious doctrines.

2. I will proclaim the two primeval spirits of the world, of whom the increaser thus spoke to the destroyer: Do not thoughts, do not words, do not wisdoms, nor doctrines, do not speeches, nor actions, do not meditations, do not souls follow us?

3. I will proclaim the primeval (thought) of this life which Ahuramazda, who knows it, spoke unto me; for those of you who do not carry my word into practice so as I think and speak it, the end of the life will come.

4. I will proclaim the Best in this life. Mazda knows it in truth, who created it as the father of the Good Mind who is working (in the minds); its daughter is Devotion (Armaiti) with good works. The Lord (Ahura) who is giving all (good things) cannot be deceived.

5. I will proclaim the word which the Most Beneficent (the source of all prosperity) spoke to me, which is the best for men to hear. All those who give a hearing to this my word, will be free from all defects and reach immortality. Mazda is Lord through the instrumentality of the Good Mind.

6. I will proclaim, as the greatest of all things, that one should be good, praising only righteousness. Ahuramazda will hear those who are bent on furthering[1] (all that is good). May He whose goodness is communicated by the Good Mind, instruct me in his best wisdom.

7. All that have been living, and will be living, subsist by means of His bounty only. The soul of the righteous attains to immortality, but that of the wicked man has everlasting punishment. Such is the rule of Ahuramazda, whose the creatures are.

8. Him whom I wish to extol with my praises I now behold with (my) eye, knowing him to be Ahuramazda, the reality of the good mind, deed, and word. Let us thus

[1] Literally, " who are good with the increasing (beneficent) spirit."

set down our gifts of praise in the dwelling-place of the heavenly singers (angels).[1]

9. Him I wish to adore with my good mind, Him who gives us fortune and misfortune according to His will. May Ahuramazda make our progeny (and) cattle thrive, that of the master as well as that of the servant, by producing in them the good qualities of the Good Mind.

10. Him I wish to extol with the prayers of my devotion, who calls himself Ahuramazda, that is,[2] He knows with his true and good mind, and gives to this world the freedom from defects and immortality, which are in His possession, as two permanently active powers.

11. Whoever thinks the idols and all those men besides, who think of mischief only, to be base, and distinguishes such people from those who think of the right; his friend, brother, or father is Ahuramazda. This is the beneficent revelation of the supreme fire-priest.

4. (Yas. xlvi.)

1. To what land shall I turn? whither shall I go in turning? owing to the desertion of the master (Zarathushtra) and his companion? None of the servants pay reverence to me, nor do the wicked rulers of the country. How shall I worship Thee further, O Ahuramazda?

2. I know that I am helpless. Look at me being amongst few men, for I have few men (I have lost my followers or they have left me); I implore Thee weeping, O Ahura! who grantest happiness as a friend gives (a present) to his friend. The good of the good mind is in thy own possession, O Righteous![3]

4. The wicked man enjoys the fields of the angel of truth who is protecting the earth in the district as well as

---

[1] The meaning is that our prayers, offered here, may go up to heaven, to be heard before the throne of God.
[2] What follows is an explanation of the meaning of the name Ahuramazda.
[3] These two verses (1, 2) refer evidently to Zarathushtra's persecution. The third verse, consisting of several sentences which seem not to be connected with each other, is omitted. See the author's work on the Gâthas, vol. ii. pp. 130, 131.

in the province; but by choosing evil, instead of good, he cannot succeed in his deeds. Whoever drives him out of his dominion, or out of his property, O Mazda! he is going further on the paths of good intellect.[1]

5. If in future a ruler takes hold of one who trespasses the law, or if a nobleman takes hold of one who violates the bonds of friendship, or if a righteous man, living righteously, takes hold of a wicked man: he shall then, having learned it, inform the master; into distress and utter want he shall be thrown to be unhappy.[2]

6. But whoever, although he may be able, does not go to him (the chief of the community), he may, however, follow the customs of the untruth now prevailing.[3] For he is a wicked man whom another wicked one considers to be the best, and he is a righteous man whose friend is a righteous one. Such sayings of old hast Thou revealed, O Ahura!

7. Who[4] is appointed protector of my property, O Mazda! when the wicked endeavour to hurt me? who else, if not Thy fire, and Thy mind, through whose operation Thou hast created rightful existence (good beings), O Ahura! Tell me the power necessary for upholding the religion.

8. Whoever spoils my estates, and does not choose me by bowing before my fire (the symbol of the deity), retribution may be made to him for his person in the same way. He shall be excluded from every good possession, but not from a bad one filled up with evils, O Mazda!

9. Who is that man, who whilst supporting me, made

---

[1] It is considered to be a good work to destroy the enemies of agriculture, because by laying waste the cultivated soil they cause great damage to the good creation.

[2] This and the following verses refer to the breaking of solemn promises (called *mithra*, see Vend. iv.) and apostasy.

[3] The meaning is that a man, who does not assist in punishing such crimes as apostasy and promise-breaking, is himself an infidel and no more to be recognised as a member of the Zoroastrian community.

[4] This verse is one of the most celebrated prayers used by the Parsis now-a-days. It is the so-called *Srosh báj*.

me first acquainted with thee as the most venerable being, as the beneficent righteous Lord?[1] The true sayings revealed by the maker of the earth[2] come to my hands by means of thy good mind.

10. Whatever man, or woman, O Ahuramazda! performs the best actions, known to thee, for the benefit of this (earthly) life, promoting thus the truth for the angel of truth, and spreading thy rule through the good mind, as well as gratifying all those men, who are gathered round me, to adore (the heavenly spirits): all these I will lead over the bridge of the gatherer (heavenly bridge[3] to Paradise).

11. The sway is given into the hands of the priests and prophets of idols, who by their (atrocious) actions, endeavour to destroy human life. Actuated by their own spirit and mind, they ought to avoid the bridge of the gatherer, to remain for ever in the dwelling-place of destruction (hell).

12. When after the defeat of the enemy Fryâna the true rites (fire-worship and agriculture) arose amongst the (Iranian) tribes, and their allies, thou fencedst with stakes the earth's settlements. Thus Ahuramazda, having fenced them all, assigned them to those men (his worshippers) as property.[4]

13. Whoever amongst men pays reverence zealously to Spitama Zarathushtra, such a one is fit to deliver in public his lore. To him (Zarathushtra) Ahuramazda entrusted life (the existence of all good beings to protect them); for him he established through the good mind the settlements; him we think to be your good friend (that is, of thyself and thy angels), O Righteous!

---

[1] This refers very likely to the gēush urvâ, "the soul of earth," to whose oracles the prophet was constantly listening.

[2] Lit. "the cutter of the cow," see p. 147.

[3] None can enter Paradise without having first passed the "bridge of the gatherer" (Chinvat), the passing of which can be facilitated to the deceased by prayers recited for him.

[4] Here the origin of the gaêthas, "possessions, estates," so frequently alluded to in the Zendavesta, is described. We must understand by them the original settlements of the Iranians exposed to constant attacks on the part of nomadic tribes.

14. Zarathushtra! Who is thy sincere friend (to assist in performing) the great work? Or, who will deliver it in public? The very man to do it, is Kavâ Vîshtâspa. I will worship through the words of the good mind all those whom thou hast elected at the (heavenly) meeting.

15. Ye sons of Hêchad-aspa Spitama! to you I will speak; because you distinguish right from wrong. By means of your actions, the truth, (contained) in the ancient commandments of Ahura, has been founded.

16. Venerable Frashôshtra! Go thou with those helpers whom we both have elected for the benefit of the world (the good beings), to that field where Devotion resides, attended by Righteousness, where the stores of the Good Mind may be acquired, where is the dwelling-place of Ahuramazda (*i.e.*, Paradise).

17. Where from you only blessings, not curses,[1] venerable wise Jâmâspas! are to be heard, always (protecting) the goods of the leader and performer of the sacred rites, namely of Ahuramazda himself, endowed with great intellectual power.

18. For him, who bestowed most favours on me, I collect all the best of my goods (acquired) through the Good Mind. But to their last shifts I will put all those, Mazda, O righteous! who have put us to them. I will beseech you to assist me. Such is my decision conceived according to my intellect and understanding.

19. Whoever makes this very life increase by means of righteousness, to the utmost for me, who am Zarathushtra myself, to him the first (earthly) and the other (spiritual) life will be granted as a reward, together with all goods to be had on the imperishable earth. Thou art the very owner of all these things to the greatest extent, thou who art my friend, O Mazda!

---

[1] When on earth, they used to pronounce curses as well as blessings. But in Paradise only good, no bad, words can be heard from them. They were celebrated Magi (*magavas*).

THE LAST THREE GATHAS.

VIII.—THE LAST THREE GATHAS (SPENTA-MAINYU, Yas. xlvii.–l.; VOHU-KHSHATHREM, Yas. li.; VAHISHTOISHTI, Yas. liii.)[1]

These three collections of ancient hymns are much smaller than the first two; the fourth and fifth consist only of one Hâ (chapter) each. Merely a short account of them will be given, with a translation of a few verses. The several chapters, except the last of the third Gâtha (Yas. l.), form nowhere a whole as regards composition, but are generally mere collections of detached verses, which were pronounced on different occasions, either by Zarathushtra himself, or by his disciples. While in the first two Gâthas the majority of the verses can be traced to Zarathushtra himself, in these last three Gâthas most of the verses appear to be the work of the master's disciples, such as Jâmâspa, Frashôshtra, and Vishtâspa, and some verses are perhaps the work of their pupils, as they themselves are therein spoken of (especially in Yas. li.) with great reverence.

Yas. xlvii. 1. Ahuramazda gives through the beneficent Spirit, appearing in the best thought, and in rectitude of action and speech, to this world (universe), perfection (Haurvatât) and immortality (Ameretât), wealth (Khshathra) and devotion (Armaiti).[2]

2. From his (Ahuramazda's) most beneficent spirit all good has sprung in the words which are pronounced by the tongue of the Good Mind (*Vohû manô*), and the works wrought by the hands of Armaiti (spirit of earth). By means of such knowledge Mazda himself is the father of all rectitude (in thought, word, and deed).

Yas. xlviii. 4. He who created, by means of his wisdom,

---

[1] See the author's German work, vol. ii. pp. 20–38 and 155–217.

[2] Ahuramazda is in this, and the following two verses, described as the only God and Spirit, in whom good and evil both originate. All the Ameshaspentas (archangels) of the later Parsiism are only his gifts.

the good and evil mind in thinking, words, and deeds, rewards his obedient followers with prosperity. Art Thou (Mazda!) not he, in whom the final cause of both intellects (good and evil) exists?

10. When will appear, O Mazda! the men of vigour and courage to pollute that intoxicating liquor (the Soma)? This diabolical art makes the idol-priests so overbearing, and the evil spirit, reigning in the countries, increases (this pride).[1]

Yas. xlix. 4. Those poor (wretches) who, instigated by their base minds, cause mischief and ruin to the wealthy (settlers) through the spells uttered by their tongues, who are devoid of all good works and find delight in evil doings only; such men produce the demons (*devas*) by means of their pernicious thoughts.

5. Mazda himself, and the prayers (offered by men), and every one who is a truly noble son of Armaiti, (the earth), as well as all that are in Thy dominions, O Ahura! will protect this faith (Zoroastrian religion) by means of the good (inborn) mind.

11. The spirits (of the deceased)[2] are fighting against the wicked, evil-minded, evil-speaking, evil-doing, evil-thinking, disbelievers (in the true god, Ahuramazda). Such men will go to hell!

Yas. l. 6. Zarathushtra is the prophet who, through his wisdom[3] and truth, utters in words the sacred thoughts (mantras). Through his tongue he makes known to the world, the laws given by my[4] intellect, the mysteries hidden in my mind.

---

[1] This verse refers to the Brahmanic Soma worship, which, as the cause of so much evil, was cursed by Zarathushtra. See the second section of the fourth Essay.

[2] In the original *urvânô*, "souls." In the other books the common name of the spirits of the deceased pious Zoroastrians, who are fighting against the attacks made by the hellish empire upon the kingdom of light and goodness, is *fravashi*, "guardian spirit," which name is, however, never to be met with in the Gâthas.

[3] Lit. "through *mazda*" which word is, now and then, used in the appellative sense "wisdom."

[4] The speaker in this verse, as well as in the whole 50th chapter, is the *gêush urvâ*.

10. All the luminaries with their bright appearances, all that is endowed with a radiant eye by the good mind, stars and the sun, the day's foreteller, wander (in their spheres) to Thy praise, O righteous Ahuramazda!

Yas. li. 6. Ahuramazda bestows, through His power, the best of all upon him who brings offerings to please Him; but the worst of all will fall to the lot of him who does not worship God in the last time of the world (when the good is engaged in a hard struggle against the bad).

7. Thou who hast created earth, water, and trees, give me immortality (Ameretât) and prosperity (Haurvatât), O Mazda, most beneficent spirit! Those everlasting powers I will praise with a good mind.

15. Zarathushtra assigned in times of yore, as a reward to the Magavas[1] the Paradise where first of all Mazda Himself had gone! You (O Ameshaspentas!) have in your hands through your good and true mind those two powers[2] (to obtain everlasting life).

16. Kavâ Vishtâspa obtained, through the possession of the spiritual power (*maga*), and through the verses which the good mind had revealed, that knowledge which Ahuramazda Himself, as the cause of truth, has invented.

17. Frashôshtra, the noble, wished to see my Highlands (*berekhdha kehrpa*, *i.e.*, Bactria), to propagate there the good religion. May Ahuramazda bless this undertaking! cry aloud that they may aspire after truth!

18. The wise Jâmâspas, the noble, the illustrious, who have the good mind with truth, prefer the settled

---

[1] This word is the original form of "Magi," which name was given in later times to all the Persian priests. Its form in the cuneiform inscriptions is *magush*. According to this verse it seems to have denoted the earliest followers of Zarathushtra.

[2] These are *Ameretât*, and *Haurvatât*, the last two of the seven archangels in the Parsiism of later times.

life,[1] saying: Let me have it, because I cling to Thee, O Ahuramazda!

Yas. liii. 1. It is reported that Zarathushtra Spitama possessed the best good; for Ahuramazda granted him all that may be obtained by means of a sincere worship, for ever, all that promotes the good life, and he is giving the same to all those who keep the words, and perform the actions, enjoined by the good religion.

IX.—YASNA HAPTANHAITI, AND THE MINOR TEXTS OF THE OLD YASNA.

The *Yasna haptaṇhaiti*, or as its name indicates, the Yasna of seven Hâs (comprising the sections from Yas. xxxv. to xli.), though written in the Gâtha dialect, is to be distinguished from the Gâthas. It is undoubtedly very old, but there is no sufficient evidence to trace it to Zarathushtra himself. Its contents are simple prayers, in prose, which are to be offered to Ahuramazda, the Ameshaspentas, and the Fravashis; to the fire, as the symbol of Ahuramazda who appears in its blazing flame (Yas. xxxvi. 1); to the earth and other female spirits (called *genâ*, "wife," Greek, *gyné*, see Yas. xxxviii. 1), such as the angel presiding over food (*îzhâ*, corresponding to *ilâ*, a name of the earth in the Veda), devotion, speech, &c.; to the waters, to the animating spirit of creation, and to all beings of the good creation. Compared with the Gâthas, they represent the Zoroastrian religion not in its original unaltered, but in a somewhat developed and altered state. The high philosophical ideas which are laid down in Zarathushtra's own hymns, are partially abandoned, and partially personified; and the philosophical, theological, and

---

[1] This can be understood only, if one bears in mind, that the Zoroastrian religion arose at the time of transition from pastoral life to agriculture. The kindred Brahmanical tribes, who were inimical to this new mode of life, continued to lead the pastoral life of their ancestors. Agriculture was considered as a religious duty by the ancient Zoroastrians.

moral doctrines have given way to the custom, which has lasted to the present time, of addressing prayers to all beings of a good nature, irrespective of their being mere abstract nouns (such as *Asha*, "rightfulness, truth," or *Vohûmanô*, "good thought"), or real objects (such as waters, trees, or fire). The formula, with which here and in the later Yasna (for which the *Yasna haptaṇhaiti* has undoubtedly furnished the model) the prayers begin, viz., *yazamaidê*, "we worship," is entirely strange to the Gâthas, as well as the invocation of waters, female spirits, &c.; even the name *Ameshaspenta* (except in the heading of Yas. xxviii. 1, see p. 147) as the general term for the highest angels, and the term *Fravashi*, which is so extremely frequent in the later Avesta literature, are never to be met with in those metrical compositions.

Although the *Yasna haptaṇhaiti* is more recent than the Gâthas, still it has just claims to be considered as more ancient and original than the sections of the later Yasna. A very striking proof, besides the difference of dialect, is that the objects of worship are much fewer than in the later prayers; thus, for instance, the six seasons, the five divisions of the day, the five Gâthas, Zoroaster, the sacred twigs (Barsom), the sacred drink (Homa), &c., are never mentioned in the Yasna of seven chapters. It formed originally a separate book, and was very likely composed by one of the earliest successors of Zoroaster, as it stands intermediate between the Gâthas and the later Yasna, in point of style.

The following are some extracts from it:—

Yas. xxxv. 1. We worship Ahuramazda the righteous master of righteousness. We worship the Ameshaspentas (the archangels), the possessors of good, the givers of good. We worship the whole creation of the righteous spirit, both the spiritual and earthly, all that supports (raises) the welfare of the good creation, and the spread of the good Mazdayasnian religion.

2. We praise all good thoughts, all good words, all good deeds, which are and will be (which are being done and which have been done),[1] and we likewise keep clean and pure all that is good.

3. O Ahuramazda, thou righteous happy being! we strive to think, to speak, and to do, only what of all actions may be best fitted to promote the two lives (that of the body and that of the soul).

4. We beseech the spirit of earth by means of these best works (agriculture) to grant us beautiful and fertile fields, to the believer as well as to the unbeliever, to him who has riches as well as to him who has no possession.

Yas. xxxvii. 1. Thus we worship Ahuramazda, who created the spirit of earth and righteousness, and who created the good waters and trees, and the luminaries, and the earth, and all good things.

2. Him we worship by the first prayers which were made by the spirit of earth, because of his power and greatness and good works.

3. We worship him in calling him by the Ahura names which were chosen by Mazda himself, and which are the most beneficent. We worship him with our bodies and souls. We worship him as (being united with) the spirits (Fravashis) of righteous men and women.

4. We worship righteousness, the all-good (Ashem vahishtem), all that is very excellent, beneficent, immortal, illustrious, every thing that is good.

Yasna xii. is written in the Gâtha dialect, and contains a formula, by which the ancient Iranians, who were weary of worshipping the Devas (Brahmanical gods) and of the nomadic life, were received into the new religious community established by Zarathushtra Spitama.

---

[1] The words *verezyamnanâmchâ* and *vâverezyamnanâmchâ* are evidently only an explanatory note on the rare words, *yadachâ* "(yet) now," and *anyadachâ*, "not now," *i.e.*, either in the future, or in the past.

YASNA XII.

1. I cease to be a Deva (worshipper). I profess to be a Zoroastrian Mazdayasnian (worshipper of Ahuramazda), an enemy of the Devas, and a devotee of Ahura, a praiser of the immortal benefactors (Ameshaspentas), a worshipper of the immortal benefactors. I ascribe all good things to Ahuramazda, who is good, and has good, who is righteous, brilliant, glorious, who is the originator of all the best things, of the spirit of nature (*gâush*), of righteousness, of the luminaries, and the self-shining brightness which is in the luminaries.

2. I choose (follow, profess) the beneficent Armaiti, the good; may she be mine! I abominate all fraud and injury committed on the spirit of earth, and all damage and destruction of the quarters of the Mazdayasnians.

3. I allow the good spirits, who reside on this earth in the good animals (as cows, sheep, &c.), to go and roam about free according to their pleasure. I praise, besides, all that is offered with prayer to promote the growth of life. I will cause neither damage nor destruction to the quarters of the Mazdayasnians, neither with my body nor my soul.

4. I forsake the Devas, the wicked, bad, wrongful originators of mischief, the most baneful, destructive, and basest of beings. I forsake the Devas and those like Devas, the sorcerers and those like sorcerers, and any beings whatever of such kinds. I forsake them with thoughts, words, and deeds; I forsake them hereby publicly, and declare that all lie and falsehood is to be done away with.

5. 6. In the same way as Zarathushtra, at the time when Ahuramazda was holding conversations and meetings with him, and both were conversing with each other, forsook the Devas, so do I forsake the Devas, as the righteous Zarathushtra did.

7. Of what party the waters are, of what party the trees, and the animating spirit of nature; of what party Ahuramazda is, who has created this spirit and the righteous man; of what party Zarathushtra, and Kavâ Vishtâspa,

and Frashôshtra, and Jâmâspa were; of what party all the ancient fire-priests (Sôshyañtô), the righteous spreaders of truth, were—of the same party[1] and creed (am I).

8. I am a Mazdayasnian, a Zoroastrian Mazdayasnian. I profess this religion by praising and preferring it to others (the Deva religion). I praise the thought which is good, I praise the word which is good, I praise the work which is good.

9. I praise the Mazdayasnian religion, and the righteous brotherhood which it establishes and defends against enemies, the Zoroastrian Ahuryan religion, which is the greatest, best, and most prosperous of all that are, and that will be. I ascribe all good to Ahuramazda. This shall be the praise (profession) of the Mazdayasnian religion.

X.—THE LATER YASNA.

This part of the Yasna, which is written in the common Avesta language, is of much less importance, as regards the history of the Zoroastrian religion, than the older Yasna. Its contents are, however, of various natures, and consist evidently either of fragments of other books, or of short independent writings. Thus, for instance, the chapters i.–viii. contain the preliminary prayers to the Ijashne ceremony (see p. 139); chapters ix.–xi. refer to the preparation and drinking of the Homa juice; chapter lvii. is a Yasht, or sacrificial prayer, addressed to the angel Srosh; chapters xix.–xxi. are commentaries (Zend) on the most sacred prayers, *Yathâ ahû vairyô, Ashem vohu,* and *Yéñhé hâtãm.*

Refraining from giving a full account of it, we shall notice here only some remarkable passages, and translate a few extracts.

In Yas. viii. 5–8 there is a short prayer, concluding with a benediction by the high-priest, the two last verses

---

[1] The word used is *varana, varena,* lit. "choice" (*var,* "to choose"); it is, then, applied to religion.

of which are of particular interest. The high-priest, who calls himself Zarathushtra (see p. 188), addresses all the heads of the various divisions of the Iranian empire as follows:—

7. I, who am Zarathushtra, exhort the heads[1] of houses, villages, towns, and countries to think and speak and act according to the good Zoroastrian Ahuryan religion.

8. I bless the splendour and vigour of the whole rightful creation, and I curse[2] the distress and wretchedness of the whole wrongful creation.

I.—HÔMA YASHT.

Chapters ix. and x., which compose the so-called *Hôma Yasht*, are, strictly speaking, no part of the Yasna, but belong to that extensive class of Avesta literature which is known by the name of Yashts, or sacrificial invocations of a special spiritual being, and which we shall describe hereafter. As to style, these two chapters contain no prose, but on close inquiry we find they consist of verses, and at the end (Yas. x. 19) they are even called *gâthâo*, "hymns." The metre itself is near the Sanskrit Anushṭubh (four times eight syllables, with the cesura in the middle of every half verse), which has given origin to the common Shlokas, but it is apparently often irregular. Each half verse consists of seven to nine syllables, the normal measure being limited to eight.

To give the reader an idea of this ancient metre, the commencement of this Yasht is here subjoined :[3]—

---

[1] The word used is *fratema* (S. *prathama*) "first." It is one of the Persian words which are to be found in the Old Testament. Its form there is *partemîm* (*îm* is the Hebrew plural suffix), by which the grandees of the Persian empire are meant. In the sense of "head, chief," the word *ratu* is more usual in the Avesta.

[2] For blessing and cursing one and the same word is used, *âfrînâmi*. The same peculiarity is to be observed in the old Hebrew word *bêrêk*, to give a blessing, and to curse.

[3] *ere* is to be read as a single syllable, and the short *e* does not generally constitute a separate syllable.

Hávaním	á	ratûm	á	Haomô	upáiḍ	Zarathushtrem
morning prayer	at	time	at	Homa	came	to Zarathushtra
átarem pairi		yaozhdatheñtem		gáthâoscha		srávayañtem.
(who was) fire everywhere		cleaning		and hymns		singing.
á dim	peresad	Zarathushtrô:		Kô	nare	ahi yim azem
Him	asked	Zarathushtra:		Who,	man,	art thou? whom I
vîspahê	aŋhēush	astratô		sraēshtem	dâdaresa	qahê
of the whole	life	having bodies		the best	I have seen	of his own
gayêhê	qanvatô	ameshahê ?		âaḍ	mê aêm	paiti-aokhta
body,	brilliant,	immortal?		Then	to me that one	answered
Haomô	ashava	dûraoshô:		Azem	ahmi	Zarathushtra !
Haoma	righteous	death-removing:		I	am	O Zarathushtra !
Haomô	ashava	dûraoshô;		â mâm	yâsanuha	Spitama !
Homa	righteous	death-removing;		to me	bring worship,	O Spitama !
frâ mâm	hunvanuha	qarctêê ;		avi	mâm staomaini	stûidhi,
me	squeeze out	to taste (me);		on	me in praising	praise,
yatha	mâ	aparachid		saoshyañtô		stavân.
as	me	the other all		fire-priests		praised.

The word *Homa*, which is identical with the Vedic word *Soma*, is used in two senses in the Zend-Avesta. First it means the twigs of a particular tree,[1] the juice of which is extracted and drunk before the fire; secondly, they understand by it a spirit who has poured his life and vigour into that particular plant. There were many stories current in ancient times about the miraculous effects of the drinking of the Homa juice (a panacea for all diseases), which led to the belief, that the performance of this ceremony (which is only the Soma worship of the Brahmans, very much reformed and refined) proves highly beneficial to body and soul. These stories were embodied in a hymn (preserved in Yas. ix.), which contains an enumeration of the miracles effected by Homa, composed in his honour.

The following is a translation of the first part of this Yasht:—

Yas. ix. 1. In the forenoon (Hâvan Gâh) Homa came to Zarathushtra, while he was cleaning around the fire,[2]

[1] The Dasturs obtain them from Persia in a dried state. For their preparation, see section I. 3, of the fourth Essay.

[2] Meaning, probably, that he was averting evil from the fire by feeding it around with fuel.

and chanting the Gâthas. Zarathushtra asked him: Who art thou, O man?[1] who appearest to me the finest in the whole material creation, having such a brilliant, immortal form of your own.[2]

2. Thereupon answered me Homa the righteous, who expels death: I am, O Zarathushtra! Homa the righteous, who expels death. Address prayers to me, O Spitama! and prepare me (the Hom juice) for tasting. Repeat about me the two praise hymns,[3] as all the other Soshyants repeated them.

3. Then spake Zarathushtra: Reverence to Homa! Who was the first who prepared thee, O Homa! for the material world? What blessing was bestowed upon him? What reward did he obtain?

4. Thereupon answered me Homa the righteous, who expels death: Vîvaṅhâo was the first man who prepared me for the material world; this blessing was bestowed upon him, this reward he obtained, that a son was born to him, Yima-khshaêta (Jamshêd) who had abundance of flocks, the most glorious of those born, the most sun-like of men; that he made, during his reign over her (the earth), men and cattle free from death, water and trees free from drought, and they were eating inexhaustible food

5. During the happy reign of Yima there was neither cold nor heat, neither decay nor death, nor malice produced by the demons; father and son walked forth, each fifteen years old in appearance.

---

[1] Some MSS. of the Yasna without Pahlavi insert here the phrase: *Mithrô zayâd Zarathushtrem,* " may Mithra favour Zarathushtra." This is evidently an Avesta phrase formerly existing in the Pahlavi commentary, but now translated into *Mitrôk khûpo aîto Zaratûshtar,* and the commentary implies that this was a friendly salutation proffered by Homa on his arrival. Here we have a distinct trace of a commentary, or Zend, in the Avesta language, which has been translated into Pahlavi, the usual language of the present Zend.

[2] The phrase *amereza gayêhê stâna,* "O imperishable pillar of life," concludes the commentary on this sentence, and is another fragment of the original Zend.

[3] Reading *staomaini,* instead of *staomainê.* The two hymns may be the two chapters of this Yasht (Yas. ix. and x.), or the two Homa rituals (Yas. i. to xi. and xii. to xxvii.).

6. Who was the second man who prepared thee, O Homa! for the material world? What blessing was bestowed upon him? What reward did he obtain?

7. Thereupon answered me Homa the righteous, who expels death: Athwya was the second man who prepared me for the material world; this blessing was bestowed upon him, this reward he obtained, that a son was born to him, Thraêtona (Frêdûn) of the hero tribe,[1] (8.) who smote the Serpent (*Azhi*) Daháka which had three mouths, three heads, six eyes, a thousand spies,[2] which was of enormous strength, a fiendish destroyer, an evil, a devastator of the Gaêthas[3] (settlements), a nuisance which was a destroyer of most enormous strength, and (which) Angrômainyush produced in the material world for the destruction of the settlements of righteousness.[4]

9. Who was the third man who prepared thee, O Homa! for the material world? What blessing was bestowed upon him? What reward did he obtain?

10. Thereupon answered me Homa the righteous, who expels death: Thrita the most useful (of the family) of the Sâmas was the third man who prepared me for the material world; this blessing was bestowed upon him, this reward he obtained, that two sons were born to him, Urvâkhshaya and Keresâspa; the one was a judge administering justice, the other a youthful hero who wore a sidelock[5] and carried a club, (11.) who slew the serpent Srvara[6] which devoured horses and men, which was

---

[1] This is the literal translation of *vîsô sûrayáo* which may, however, be the name of a locality. The Pahlavi translation is *afzâr-vîs*, "of a village of resources;" and it explains *afzâr-vîsth* by "his house became numerous from the continued residence of his forefathers, and was retained by the oppression of Dahâk; and his authority was that he preserved the relatives who had disappeared."

[2] In Pahlavi *hazâr vajôstâr adâǵako paran gôharako*, "a thousand inquirers unjust in disposition."

[3] Reading *gaêthâ-rayô*, in accordance with several old MSS.

[4] The Pahlavi commentary contains the imperfect Avesta phrase: *kô thrâm yim Ahurem mazdâm*, "who (worshipped) thee who art Ahuramazda?" probably.

[5] The Pahlavi translates *gaêsush* by *gêsvar* = Pers. *gîs-bar*, "ringlet-wearing." Compare the epithet *kapardin*, "wearing braided hair," applied to the Vasishthas, Rigveda, vii. 83, 8.

[6] Pronounced *Srûara*.

poisonous and yellow, over which yellow poison flowed a hand's-breadth high.[1] On which Keresâspa cooked a beverage in a caldron at the mid-day hour, and the serpent scorched, hissed, sprang forth, away from the caldron, and upset the boiling water; Keresâspa Naremanâo fled aside frightened.

12. Who was the fourth man who prepared thee, O Homa! for the material world? What blessing was bestowed upon him? What reward did he obtain?

13. Thereupon answered me Homa the righteous, who expels death: Pourushaspa was the fourth man who prepared me for the material world; this blessing was bestowed upon him, this reward he obtained, that thou wast born to him, thou O righteous Zarathushtra! of the house of Pourushaspa, (who art) opposed to the demons, and of the Ahura religion. (14.) Famous in Airyana-vaêjô thou, O Zarathushtra! first recitedst the Ahuna-vairya four times, with pauses between the verses,[2] each successive time with a louder recitation.[3] (15.) Thou madest all the demons hide themselves beneath the earth, who formerly flew about the earth in human shape, O Zarathushtra! who wert the strongest, firmest, most active, swiftest, and most triumphant of the creatures of the two spirits (Spentômainyush and Angrô-mainyush).

16. Then spake Zarathushtra: Reverence to Homa! good is Homa, well-created is Homa, rightly created, of a good nature, healing, well-shaped, well-performing, successful, golden-coloured, with hanging tendrils,[4] as the

---

[1] The Pahlavi says, "as high as a horse;" it also quotes the following Avesta phrase: *khshvaêpaya vainaiti barenush*, "the angry one(?) strikes by darting."

[2] The epithet *vî-berethwañtem* is from the root *bar* = Sans. *bhri* = *hri*, "to take." In the Brahmanical ritual *viharati* (originally *vibharati*) is a technical term for pausing after each *pada*, while reciting verses, literally taking asunder the verses. The Ahuna-vairya formula consists of three such padas, lines, or verses.

[3] This practice of gradually raising the voice with each successive recitation, is also observed in the Hotṛi ritual of the Brahmans.

[4] The Pahlavi translation has *narmtâk*, "with soft tendrils;" but *nâmyâsush* must be traced to the root *nam*, "to bend downwards."

best for eating and the most lasting provision for the soul.[1]

17. O yellow (Homa)! I keep in thee by my word [2] (thy power of giving) knowledge, strength, victory, health, healing, advancement, growth, vigour to the whole body, understanding of subjects of every kind. I keep in (thee by my word) that (power) that I might wander freely in the world, putting an end to troubles (and) annihilating the destructive powers (of the enemies of the good creation). (18.) I keep in (thee by my word) that (power) that I might put down the troubles caused by those whose very nature is to give troubles, such as the demons and (bad) men, the sorcerers and witches, the oppressors, wizards, and idol-priests, the criminals with two legs, the apostates with two legs, the wolves with four legs, of the army with a wide front, shouting and flying (in the air).[3]

19. On this first walk [4] I ask from thee, O Homa! who expellest death, the best life (paradise) of the righteous, the splendid, the all-radiant with its own brilliancy. On this second walk I ask from thee, O Homa! who expellest death, the health of this body. On this third walk I ask from thee, O Homa! who expellest death, the long life of the soul.

---

[1] The term *pâthmainya* means "remaining on the way," hence provisions for a journey.

[2] The words *nî mruyê*, "I call down," are here used technically in the sense of binding by calling together, so that none of the powers may be dissipated. In the Brahmanical Soma ritual this is done by reciting eight mantras before the juice is extracted from the Soma twigs.

[3] The term *davâithyâo* must be traced to the root *du*, "to talk (as an evil being)," and is very appropriate to this flying host of evils which is analogous to the band of Odhin among the Scandinavians, the Wodan's heer of the ancient Germans, and the host of Marutas of the Veda, sweeping through the air, who are all represented as shouting and making a noise.

[4] That the word *yânem* has here its primitive meaning of "walk" (from *yâ*, "to go") is clear from the practice of the Parsi priests who, during the Homa ceremony, walk about six times round the sacred fire with the Hom, and each time a distinct blessing seems to be asked for. Nearly the same ceremony is performed by the Brahmans, when they put the Soma twigs on a cart, and carry them round the sacrificial area in the six directions: east, west, south, north, up, and down (according to an ancient Aryan division).

20. On this fourth walk I ask from thee, O Homa! who expellest death, that I may stand forth at will, powerful (and) successful upon the earth, putting down troubles (and) annihilating the destructive powers. On this fifth walk I ask from thee, O Homa! who expellest death, that I may stand forth as victor (and) conqueror in battle upon the earth, putting down troubles (and) annihilating the destructive powers.

21. On this sixth walk I ask from thee, O Homa! who expellest death, that we may first become aware of a thief, murderer, (or) wolf; may no one else become aware (of him) sooner! may we become aware of everything first!

22. Homa grants strength and vigour to those who, mounted on white horses, wish to run over a race-course.[1] Homa gives splendid sons and righteous progeny to those who have not borne children.[2] Homa grants fame and learning to all those who are engaged in the study of books.[3]

23. Homa grants a good and rich husband to those who have long been maidens, as soon as he (Homa), the wise, is entreated.

---

[1] The verb *takhsheñti* is a desiderative form of the root *tach*, "to run;" *erendum* is explained as "a horse" by the Pahlavi translator, but this can be merely a guess; it must be traced to the root *ar* = Sans. *ri*, "to move, go, instigate," and is here taken as "a race-course."

[2] So the Pahlavi translator understands the word *azizandîtibish*, but in that case the prefix *â* must be miswritten for the privative *a*.

[3] This is the only occurrence, in the extant Avesta, of the word *naskô* which is applied, in later writings, to the twenty-one books, or divisions, of the Zoroastrian writings; here, however, it is probably used in the general sense of "book," and even nowadays Parsi writers sometimes apply the term to any Avesta writing. It has been probably borrowed by Arabic, in the forms *nuskhat*, "a copy" (pl. *nusakh*), and *naskhî*, the name of Arabic writing; for these words can have no real connection with the Arabic root *nasakha*, "he obliterated, abrogated." The application of a general term for "book" to sacred writings in particular, is common to many religions; thus the Brahmans use the word *grantha*, which denotes any literary composition, for the Vedic writings, and in Mahârâshṭra the compound *dashagranthî*, "one who knows the ten Granthas by heart," refers solely to the Vedic writings, for the ten Granthas are the Saṅhitâ, Pada, Brâhmaṇam, Araṇa (always used there for Aranyaka by the Brahmans), and the six Vedângas.

24. Homa deposed Keresâni[1] from his sovereignty, whose lust of power had so increased that he said: No âthrava's (fire-priest's) repetition of the *apãm aiwish̲tish*[2] ("approach of the waters") shall be tolerated in my empire, to make it prosper; (and) he would annihilate all that are prosperous, (and) put down all that are prosperous by destroying them.

25. Hail to thee who art of absolute authority through thy own strength, O Homa! hail to thee! thou knowest many sayings rightly spoken. Hail to thee! thou askest for no saying but one rightly spoken.

26. Mazda brought to thee the star-studded, spirit-fashioned girdle (the belt of Orion) leading the Paurvas[3] [(Pâzand) the good Mazdayasnian religion]; then thou art begirt with it, (when growing) on the summit of the mountains, to make lasting the words and long accents[4] of the sacred text (*mãthra*).

[1] It is evident, from the context, that Keresâni is the name of some enemy of the Athrava religion, and there can be little doubt that he is the Kṛishânu of the Vedic books, who appears as the guardian of the Soma in heaven (Aitareya Brâhm. iii. 26); he is represented as an archer (Rigveda ix. 77, 2; x. 64, 8; iv. 27, 3), and identified with fire (Vâjasaneyi sañhita v. 32, Shânkhâyana shrautasutras vi. 12, Raghuvañsha ii. 49). As a personage Kṛishânu appears to represent "lightning," and perhaps a particular kind of it.

[2] These words are evidently a technical name for the Atharva-veda Sañhita which commences, in some manuscripts, with the mantra: *shañ no devtṛbhish̲taya āpo bhavantu vîtaye*, in which both words occur; this mantra is omitted at the commencement of the printed edition, but is given in i. 6, 1, where it also occurs again in the manuscripts alluded to. That the Atharva-veda actually commenced with these words about 2000 years ago, is clearly shown by Patanjali's quotation of the initial words of the four Vedas, in his introduction to the Mahâbhâshya, where the words: *shañ no devtṛbhish̲taye* represent the Atharva-veda.

[3] In the word Paurva we readily recognise the Persian name of the Pleiades, which is variously written *parû, parvah, parrîn*, and *parvîz*; this *parvîz* is given as the name of the third and fourth lunar mansions in the Bundahish (p. 6, Westerg.), corresponding to the Indian Nakshatras *kṛittikâ* (Pleiades) and *rohiṇî* (Aldebaran and Hyades); the fifth Nakshatra is *mṛigashiras* (in the head of Orion), over which Soma (= Homa) is presiding deity (Taittirîya Brâhmanam iii. 1, 2, 3); hence the constellation Orion is in advance of the Paurvas on the moon's path, and the epithet "leading the Paurvas" is appropriate for Orion's belt. The idea of Homa being begirt with Orion's belt, implies that the Homa plant was supposed to be specially under the sideral influence of the constellation Orion.

[4] The term *aiwidhâiti* must be equivalent to Sans. *abhidhâna*,

27. O Homa! (thou) lord of the house, lord of the clan, lord of the tribe, lord of the country, (thou) successful physician![1] I further invoke thee for strength and prosperity for my body, and for the attainment of much pleasure.[2] (28.) Keep far from us the vexations of (our) enemies! divert the mind of (our) abusers! Whatsoever man in this house, in this clan, in this tribe, in this country, may injure (us), take strength from his feet! darken his intellect! disorder his mind!

29. May he be paralysed in the feet! may he be palsied in the hands![3] may he not see the earth with (his) eyes! may he not see nature with (his) eyes! who injures our mind, or injures our body.

30. Strike a deadly blow, O yellow Homa! at the yellow blackish[4] serpent, emitting poison for destroying the body of the righteous man.[5] Strike a deadly blow, O yellow Homa! at the murderer who has wrought mischief, who angrily inflicts wounds for destroying the body of the righteous man.

31. Strike a deadly blow, O yellow Homa! at the impious tyrant in human form, who has a darting at the head[6] for destroying the body of the righteous man. Strike

---

"name, appellation, word;" and the reading garûshcha (preferable to graûshcha) gives garu, which represents Sans. guru, " a long vowel," a very noticeable feature of the Gâthas.

[1] Literally, "master of physicians (or doctor of medicine) through beneficence;" vaêdhyâ here must be equivalent to Sans. vaidya, "a physician," or vaidyâ, "a drug."

[2] Thrima must be traced to the root tar = Sans. trî, " to pass over, attain;" and baokhshnahê is to be taken in the same sense as baoshnâoscha in Yt. iv. 1, i.e., "pleasure, enjoyment," compare Sans. bhuj, "to enjoy."

[3] More literally, "May he not be able to progress with the feet! may he not be able to work with the hands!"

[4] Sima is here taken as equivalent to Sans. shyâma, " dark-coloured," from the root shyai, some derivatives of which change shyâ into shî.

[5] The construction kehrpem nâshemnâi ashaonê is literally "for the righteous being made to lose (his) body;" compare drishe vishvâya sûryam, "that all should see the sun" (Rigveda, i. 50, 1); kehrpem is not governed by paiti, but by nâshemnâi, and is to be regarded as the accusative of the object which retains its original case when the active construction is changed to a passive one.

[6] This appears to be an allusion to Zohak and his troublesome serpents.

a deadly blow, O yellow Homa! at the body of the disturber of righteousness, the impious, who destroys the life of this (Zoroastrian) religion, by proposing thoughts and words, but not carrying them into action, for destroying the body of the righteous man.

32. Strike a deadly blow, O yellow Homa! at the body of the bewitching courtezan who causes madness, who acts as procuress, whose mind is unstable as a cloud driven by the wind, for destroying the body of the righteous man. Strike a deadly blow, O yellow Homa! at whatever serves for destroying the body of the righteous man.

Yas. x. 1. Let the water-drops fall here for the destruction of the Devas and Devîs. May the good Sraosha slay (them)! May Ashi-vaṇuhi (the spirit of fortune) take up her abode here! May Ashi-vaṇuhi grant happiness here, in this sacred abode of Homa, the transmitter of righteousness.

2. I accompany thy preparation, at the beginning each time, with words of praise, O intelligent! when he (the managing priest) takes thy twigs. I accompany thy preparation, in each successive act by which thou art killed through the strength of a man, with words of praise, O intelligent!

3. I praise the cloud and the rain which make thy body grow on the summit of the mountains. I praise the high mountains where thou hast grown, O Homa!

4. I praise the earth, the wide-stretched, the passable, the large, the unbounded, thy mother, O righteous Homa! I praise the earth that thou mayest grow, spreading fast (thy) fragrance, as thou growest on the mountain, O Homa! with the good Mazdian growth; and that thou mayest thrive on the path of the birds (*i.e.*, on high), and be, in fact, the source of righteousness.

5. Grow! through my word, in all stems, in all branches, and in all twigs.

6. Homa grows when being praised. So the man who

praises him becomes more triumphant. The least extraction of Hom-juice, the least praise, the least tasting (of it), O Homa! is (sufficient) for destroying a thousand of the Devas.

7. The defects produced (by the evil spirit) vanish from that house, as soon as one brings, as soon as one praises, the healing Homa's evident wholesomeness, healing power, and residence in that village.

8. For all other liquors are followed by evil effects,[1] but this which is the liquor of Homa is followed by elevating righteousness,[2] (when) the liquor of Homa (is in him who) is grieved.[3] Whatever man shall flatter Homa, as a young son, Homa comes to the aid of him and his children, to be (their) medicine.

9. Homa! give me (some) of the healing powers whereby thou art a physician. Homa! give me (some) of the victorious powers whereby thou art a victor. &c.

From the contents of this Homa Yasht one may clearly see, that the Homa worship was not instituted by Zarathushtra, but was known at a much earlier period. Zarathushtra is only said to have adopted it. But in the second division of the fourth Essay, we shall see that he was fighting against the Brahmanical Soma worship and trying to overthow it.

2.—YASNA xix.

This chapter, written in prose, is a kind of theological commentary on the most sacred formula, *Ahuna-vairya* (Honovar). The following is a translation of this chapter:—

1, 2. Zarathushtra asked Ahuramazda: O Ahuramazda! most munificent spirit, creator of the settlements supplied with creatures, righteous one! Which was the word, O Ahuramazda! that thou spakest unto me, (which was) before

---

[1] Literally, "by the cruel Aêshma" (Wrath, one of the demons).
[2] Literally, "by Asha who is carrying up."
[3] Or perhaps, "the liquor of Homa exhilarates."

the heavens, before the water, before the earth, before the animals, before the trees, before the fire, son of Ahuramazda, before the righteous man, before the demons and savage men (cannibals), before the whole material world, before all good things created by Mazda, that are of rightful origin?

3, 4. Then said Ahuramazda: This was the parts of the Ahuna-vairya, O Spitama Zarathushtra! which I spake unto thee, (which was) before the heavens, before the water, &c. (as before).

5. These my parts of the Ahuna-vairya, when recited without mistake (and) without mispronunciation, are equal, O Spitama Zarathushtra! to a hundred of the other principal stanzas (Gâthas), recited without mistake (and) without mispronunciation. Even recited with mistakes (and) mispronunciation (they are) equal to ten other principals.

6. And whoever, in this my world supplied with creatures, O Spitama Zarathushtra! shall recall (mentally) one part of the Ahuna-vairya, or in the course of recalling shall mutter it, or in the course of muttering shall chant it, or in the course of chanting prays to it,[1] his soul will I, who am Ahuramazda, carry all three times over the bridge to paradise (*Vahishtem ahûm*, "the best life," *Bahisht* in Pers.), [(Pâzand), to the best life, to the best righteousness, to the best luminaries.]

7. And whoever in this my world supplied with creatures, O Spitama Zarathushtra! takes off in muttering a part of the Ahuna-vairya, either a half, or a third, or a fourth, or a fifth of it, his soul will I, who am Ahuramazda, separate from paradise, to such a distance in width and breadth as the earth is, [(Pâzand) and the earth has the same width as breadth].

8. And I spake for myself this saying, about the heavenly

---

[1] Here the different ways of recital are mentioned; see p. 143. After chanting, or reciting, sacred verses one prays to them (the verse, or hymn, being considered a being) with the formula: *Yazamaidê* (we worship, pray to) *Ahunem vairîm* (the Ahuna-vairya formula).

lord (*ahu*), and earthly master (*ratu*), before the creation of the heavens, before the water, before the earth, before the trees, before the creation of the four-footed animals, before the birth of the righteous biped man, before the sun-composed matter for the creation of the archangels (Ameshaspentas).

9. The more beneficent of my two Spirits[1] has produced, by speaking it, the whole rightful creation, which is, and was, and will be, through the operation of the actions of life towards Mazda.[2]

10. And this is the highest saying of those sayings which I have spoken, and do speak, and (which) are to be spoken; for the nature of this saying is such that if the whole material world had learned it, being preserved by reciting it, it would escape liability to destruction.

11. And this our saying I proclaimed, and repeated, and counted (the repetitions), as it is for every being for the sake of the righteousness which is best.

12. As he (who recites it) has here said that he has appointed it as heavenly lord (*ahu*) and earthly master (*ratu*), so he recognises him who is Ahuramazda as prior to the creatures, the first being the Mind. As he acknowledges it as the greatest of all things, so he acknowledges the creatures are (due) to it.

13. That the good beings are (works) of Mazda he shows by reciting the third phrase (beginning with) *vaṇhēush* (" of the good "). (With the words) *dazdâ manaṇhô* ("the giver of mind") he acknowledges it (the Ahunavairya) from the first as the Mind. As (the word) *manaṇhô* thus makes it the producer for the Mind, he then makes it the heavenly lord of actions (*shkyaothnanãm ahûm*).

14. As he acknowledges it for the creatures through

---

[1] The two spirits united in Ahuramazda, as the one God, are *speñtô mainyush*, "the beneficent spirit," and *aṇrô mainyush*, "the hurtful spirit."

[2] These words (*shkyaothnanãm aṇhēush Mazdâi*) are quoted from the second line of the Ahuna-vairya formula, and are again referred to in verses 13, 14.

Mazda, so (he does) this, that the creatures are his. (The phrase) *khshathrem Ahurâi* (" the dominion is for Ahura ") acknowledges it as thy dominion, O Mazda! (The phrase) *dregubyô vâstârem* (" protector for the poor ") acknowledges, as a friend to Spitama, the five phrases, the whole recital of the saying, the complete saying of Ahuramazda.

15. The most excellent Ahuramazda proclaimed the Ahuna-vairya; the Most-excellent, the Eternal, caused it to be repeated (after him). Owing to a pause Evil originated, but he restrained the Wicked One with this interdict: Neither our thoughts, nor sayings, nor intellects, nor creeds, nor words, nor deeds, nor creative ideas, nor souls, agree.

16. And this saying, uttered by Mazda, has three verses (lines), the four classes, the five chiefs, (and) a conclusion with liberality.[1] How (arose) its verses? (Through the words) well-thought, well-spoken, well-done.[2]

17. Through what classes? The priest, warrior, agriculturist, (and) artizan, through the whole duty pertaining to the righteous man, to think rightly, to speak rightly, to act rightly, to appoint a spiritual guide, (and) to fulfil religious duties, through which works the earthly settlements advance in righteousness.

18. Which are the chiefs? (Those) of the house, of the village, of the tribe, of the province, (and) Zarathushtra as the fifth in those countries which are distinct from the Zarathushtrian Ragha.[3] The Zarathushtrian Ragha has

---

[1] This is an allusion to the words *dregubyô vâstârem*, " protector for the poor," in the last phrase of the Ahuna-vairya, which evidently imply liberality.

[2] These words, *humatem hûkhtem hvarshtem*, contain the fundamental principles of Zoroastrian morality, and are repeated habitually on many occasions.

[3] The word *Rajôiḍ* is the ablative of a crude form *Raji*. a softer form of *Rayhi*, which variant of *Ragha* seems to have been used, as we find traces of more than one form of the name in Greek writings. That one form should be used here, and the other in the next phrase, is owing, no doubt, to the next phrase being a later addition to the text. It is also possible that the regular ablative of *Ragha*, which would be *Raghayâḍ* or *Raghayaḍ*, might become *Rajôiḍ* by the change of *aya* into *aê, ê, ôi*, which change would probably occasion the softening of *yh* into *j*.

YASNA LVII.

four chiefs. Which are its chiefs? (Those) of the house, of the village, of the tribe, (and) Zarathushtra as the fourth.

19. What is "well-thought"? The righteous original Mind. What is "well-spoken"? The munificent Word. What is "well-done"? (That done) by the praising creatures, first in righteousness.

20. Mazda proclaimed. What did he proclaim? The righteous (Ahuna-vairya) both spiritual and earthly. What was he who proclaimed the recital (of the Ahuna-vairya)? The best ruler. As what (did he proclaim it)? As true perfection, but not despotic authority (*i.e.*, subject to the ruler).

3.—YASNA lvii.

This chapter is devoted to the praise of the angel Sraosha (Srosh), and is, therefore, called the Srosh Yasht. He is the personification of the whole divine worship of the Parsis. This Yasht is to be recited at the commencement of the night-time.

2. We worship (the angel) Srosh, the righteous, the beautiful, the victorious, who protects our territories, the true, the master of truth, who of Ahuramazda's creatures first worshipped Ahuramazda by means of arranging the sacred twigs (Barsom), who worshipped the Ameshaspentas (the archangels), who worshipped the two masters, the two creators [1] (*thwôreshtâra*) who create all things.

3. For his splendour and glory, for his power and victory, for his praying to the angels (in our behalf), I will worship him with an audible prayer and with the offering of consecrated water (*zaothra*). May he come to help us, he, the victorious, righteous Srosh!

6. He who first arranged the bundle of sacred twigs (Barsom), that with three, that with five, that with seven, and that with nine stalks, those which were as long as to

---

[1] These are the two spirits *spentô-mainyush* and *angrô-mainyush*, mentioned in the note to Yas. xix. 9.

go up to the knees, and those which went as far as the middle of the breast, (he arranged them) to worship, to praise, to satisfy, and to extol the archangels.

8. He who first sang the five Gâthas of the righteous Spitama Zarathushtra according to their stanzas and their sentences, distinguishing their high and low tones.

10. He who wounds after sunset with his drawn sword the cruel demon Aêshemô (*i.e.*, attack, rapine).

15–18. He who slays the demon of destruction (*devî-drukhsh*), who prevents the growth of nature, and murders its life. He who is the guardian and protector of the whole world here below.[1] He who, never slumbering, preserves by vigilance the creatures of Mazda. He who, never slumbering, protects by vigilance the creatures of Mazda. He who guards, with his sword drawn, the whole world supplied with creatures after sunset. He who never enjoyed sleep since the two spirits, the beneficent and the hurtful, created (the world); he is watching the territories of the good creation and fighting, day and night, against the Devas (demons) of Mazenderan.[2] He is never frightened nor runs away when struggling with the demons; but all the demons must flee from him and hide themselves in darkness.

21. He who has a palace with a thousand pillars erected on the highest summit of the mountain Alborz.[3] It has its own light from inside, and from outside it is decorated with stars. He whose victorious sword is the Ahuna-vairya formula, the Yasna of seven chapters (see p. 170), the victorious Fshûsha-prayer (Yas. lviii.), and all the sections of the Yasna.

24. He who walks, teaching the religion, round about

---

[1] In the original *fraróish* (see the same in Yt. x. 103), which has the same origin as the modern Persian *farû*, *farûd*, "down, downwards." The Pahlavi translators (who have *frâj*, "forth, forwards") misunderstood this rare word.

[2] In the original *mâzanya*. These Mazanian Devas, several times alluded to in the Zend-Avesta, are evidently the Divs of Mazenderan, so well known to the readers of the Shâh-nâmah.

[3] In the Avesta *harô berezaiti* "the high mountain."

the world. Ahuramazda, Vohu-manô, Ashem-vahishtem, Khshathra-vairya, Spenta-ârmaiti, Haurvatât, Ameretât,[1] the Ahuryan question, and the Ahuryan creed (*i.e.*, their respective angels) believed in this religion.

25. Protect our two lives, that of the body and that of the soul, O Srosh! against death, against the attacks of evil spirits. &c.

XI.—VISPARAD.

The name Visparad (Av. *vîspê ratavô*) means "all chiefs, or heads." By this name a collection of prayers, composed of twenty-three chapters, is understood. They are written in the usual Avesta language, and bear a great resemblance, as regards their contents, to the first part of the later Yasna (chap. i.–xxvii.). They refer to the same ceremony, as does that part of the Yasna, viz., to the preparation of the sacred water, and the consecration of certain offerings, such as the sacred bread, the twigs of Homa, with a twig of the pomegranate-tree, and the juice obtained from them (called *Parahoma*), fruits, butter, hair, fresh milk, and flesh, which are carried round about the sacred fire, and after having been shown to it, are eaten by the priest, or by the man, in whose favour the ceremony is performed. These offerings, which are nothing but a remnant of the ancient Aryan sacrifices, so carefully preserved to this day by the Brahmans (see the fourth Essay), represent a meal, given to all the heads or chiefs (called *ratus*) of both the visible and invisible world, who are all severally invoked. In the first chapter of the Yasna, there are a good many more enumerated than in the first chapter of the Visparad. In the Yasna the enumeration of "the heads" begins with Ahuramazda and the archangels, while in the Visparad the invitation[2]

---

[1] The six names after that of Ahuramazda are those of the archangels.

[2] The formula is *nivaêdhayêmi haṅkârayêmi*, "I invite and prepare for" (I prepare a meal and invite to it). With *nivaêdhayêmi* compare the *naivedya* of the Brahmans, *i.e.*, the food given to the gods. The Brahmans

commences with the heads of the spiritual (*mainyava*) and terrestrial (*gaêthya*) world, the chiefs of all that is in the water, in the sky, born out of eggs, of what is walking on its face (quadrupeds), and of water crabs.[1] In this rough division of created living beings (of the good creation only) the whole animal kingdom is comprised. The primary type of each class is its respective *ratu* or chief. After the chiefs of the animals, the six chiefs of the year, or the six seasons,[2] are enumerated, which are now called Gahanbârs. These are believed to have been instituted by Ahuramazda in commemoration of the six periods, during which, according to the Zoroastrian doctrine, the world was created, and they are strictly observed by the Parsis to this day. The names of these six seasons are:—1, *Maidhyô-zaremya* (now 3d November); 2, *Maidhyô-shema* (now 2d January); 3, *Paitish-hahya* (now 18th March); 4, *Ayâthrema* (now 17th April); 5, *Maidhyâirya* (now 6th July); 6, *Hamaspathmaêdaya* (now 19th September), the season at which great expiatory sacrifices were offered for the growth of the whole creation [3] in the two last months of the year.[4]

After the six seasons, the chiefs of all the sacred prayers

begin all their ceremonies with the words, *aham karishye*, "I shall perform a ceremony."

[1] *Chaṇraṇhâch*, "who follow (the species) *chaṇra*," Pers. *chaṇra*, "a crab." That crabs are creatures of Ahuramazda, is reported by Plutarch; see p. 10.

[2] The ancient name for "season" was the word *ratu* itself, which is preserved in the corresponding Sanskrit *ṛitu* (the six seasons, as representatives of the Creator Prajâpati or Brahma, are often mentioned in the Vedic writings). But after the employment of this word in a more general sense, *yâre* was used for "season," being evidently identical with "year."

[3] This the name implies, and also its epithet *aretô-kerethana*, "killer of enemies," by which animals of the bad creation, as frogs, lizards, serpents, are to be understood. In the Bundahish this season is said to be about the vernal equinox, while Maidhyâirya is made to correspond with midwinter, and Maidhyô-shema with midsummer; but since the disuse of intercalary months, the season-festivals have receded to the dates given in the text according to the Indian Parsi reckoning, or thirty days further back according to the Persian Parsis.

[4] In the first period heaven was created, in the second the waters, in the third the earth, in the fourth the trees, in the fifth the animals, and in the sixth man.

(which are believed to be angels), including more especially the Gâthas, are invited, together with the female spirits (*ghena*), "who give abundance of all things, and especially posterity;" also Ardvi Sûra Anâhita (the heavenly water, see the Abân Yasht), the mountains, the angels Behram, Mithra, Râma-qâstar (presiding over food), the ruler of the country, the Zarathushtrôtema (supreme highpriest or Dastûr-i-Dastûrân), &c.

After this general invitation of the spirits of all orders to come to the meal prepared for them, the water and Barsom (sacred twigs) are presented to them as a welcome (chap. ii.). Several other invocations follow (chap. iii.). The chief priest, who superintends the whole ceremony, the Zaota (called *Hota* in the Vedas), orders his subordinate priest *Rathwi* (now *Raspi*, *Adhvaryu* in the Vedas) to summon the different orders of priests, the representatives of the three castes (priests, warriors, cultivators), the heads of houses, villages, towns, and districts, the ladies of houses, other respectable women, &c. Very likely all chiefs of the Iranian society of a whole district were, if possible, obliged to be present at the time of the celebration of the Gahanbârs, for which the Visparad seems to be particularly intended, and on which occasions it must be used even now.

This whole assembly then praises all good things (chap. iv.), after which the chief priest (Zaota) says, that he is the praiser and worshipper of Ahuramazda and the archangels, and that he is worshipping them with words and ceremonies (chap. v., vi.). Then the members of the congregation invoke several spirits, as Sraosha, Mithra, &c. (chap. vii.).

After these introductory prayers, the principal parts of the meal, Homa with a branch of a pomegranate tree, butter, fresh milk, bread, fruits, and flesh, are consecrated and presented to the chiefs of the whole creation (chaps. ix.–xii.). After the whole meal has been offered in a solemn way, the ritual concludes with a series of prayers and invocations, in which, however, nothing remarkable occurs.

XII.—YASHTS.

The name Yasht (*yêshti*, "worship by prayers and sacrifices") is applied to certain collections of prayer and praise, of which there are twenty extant, which have been collected and published for the first time in Westergaard's edition of the Zend-Avesta (pp. 143–293). Their chief difference from the prayers of the Yasna and Visparad is, that each of them is devoted to the praise and worship of one divine being only, or of a certain limited class of divine beings, as Ahuramazda, the archangels (Amshaspends), the heavenly water Ardvi Sûra Anâhita, the sun (Mithra), the star Tishtrya, the Fravashis, &c., whereas in the Yasna and Visparad all these beings are invoked promiscuously. The majority of these beings are called *Yazatas*[1] (now Izads) or angels.

The devotee endeavours, by an enumeration of all the glorious feats achieved by the particular angel, and the miracles wrought by him, to induce him to come and enjoy the meal which is prepared for him, and then to bestow such a blessing upon the present worshipper, as had been bestowed by the angel upon his devotees in ancient times.

These praises are often highly poetical, and on close inquiry we find they really contain, in several cases, metrical verses. They are to be traced to the songs of the Median bards, who are mentioned by Greek historians, and were the primary sources of the legends contained in the Shâhnâmah. For the legendary history of the ancient Iranians, and especially for a critical inquiry into the celebrated Shâhnâmah, the Yashts are the most important part of the Zend-Avesta.

In the following pages a brief summary of them is given, and occasionally some extracts are translated from the more interesting parts.

---

[1] Corresponding to the Vedic *Yajata*, "a being which deserves worship." The modern Persian *Yazdân*, "God," is the plural of this word *Yazata*.

1. Hormazd Yasht.

Zarathushtra asked Ahuramazda for the most effectual spell (*māthra*) to guard against the influence of evil spirits. He was answered by the Supreme Spirit, that the utterance of the different names of Ahuramazda protects best from evil. Thereupon Zarathushtra begged Ahuramazda to communicate to him these names. Ahuramazda then enumerates twenty names. The first, for instance, is *ahmi*, " I am ;" the fourth, *asha-vahishta*, "the best righteousness" (the name of the archangel Ardibahisht); the sixth, " I am the wisdom ; " the eighth, " I am the knowledge ; " the twelfth, *ahura*, " living ; " the twentieth, " I am who I am,[1] Mazda " (*ahmi yaḍ ahmi mazdâo*). Ahuramazda says then further: " If you call me by day or at night by these names, I will come to assist and help you, the angel Srosh will then come to assist and help you, the spirits of the waters and the trees, and the spirits of deceased righteous men will come to assist you." For the utter defeat of the evil spirits, bad men, sorcerers, Paris[2] (*pairika*), &c., a series of other names of Ahuramazda are suggested to Zarathushtra, such as protector, guardian, spirit, the holiest, the best fire-priest, &c.

2. Haptân, Ardibahisht, and Khordâd Yashts.

In the *Haptân Yasht* (*i.e.*, the praise of the seven supreme spirits) Ahuramazda and the six archangels, who constitute the celestial council, are invoked. The greater part of it is of no particular interest. At the end (Yt. ii. 11) there is a short spell, such as we find now and then in the Zend-Avesta. It is composed of short verses, each consisting of six or seven syllables, in the following manner:—

---

[1] Compare the explanation of the name *Jehovah*, as given in Exod. iii. 14; *chych asher ehyeh*, " I am who I am."

[2] The Paris, *i.e.*, fairies, so well known to the readers of modern Persian poetry, are evil spirits in the Zend-Avesta, because they seduce men by their beauty.

Yátu	zi	Zarathushtra,	vanaḍ	daêvô	mashyô
may he come	then	Zarathushtra,	may he destroy the devils and bad men
Kôi	nmânahê,	bâdha	Spitama	Zarathushtra!
who (are)	in the house,	soon	Spitama	Zarathushtra!
Vispa	drukhsh	jânâitê,	vispa	drukhsh	náshâitê,
every	evil spirit	is slain,	every	evil spirit	goes away,
Yatha	haonaoiti		aêshãm	vachãm.
when	he hears		these	words.

In the *Ardibahisht Yasht*, Ahuramazda requests Zarathushtra to protect and promote the *asha vahishta* (now Ardibahisht), "the best righteousness," by praising, invoking, inviting (to sacrificial meals), worshipping, singing, &c., in order to keep up the splendour and light of the luminaries, which is indispensable for the growth of the good creation.

Zarathushtra is ready to obey the divine command, but he first wants to know the appropriate words which would have the effect proposed by Ahuramazda. The chief *mãthra* for this purpose is the *Airyēmā ishyô* prayer (Yas. liv.).[1] Some spells follow, which are intended to remove diseases and evils of every kind, like the spells found in the Atharvaveda, and those used down to the present time by wizards in Europe, as, for instance, "Go away, diseases! Go away, death! Go away, ye devils!" &c.

Then the killing of the "serpent seed" (*azhi-chithra*), i.e., all noxious creatures, such as wolves, frogs, mice, ants, snakes, &c., which are believed to be the mere disguises of evil spirits, is enjoined as meritorious, and contributing largely towards the growth of nature and preservation of light, which are both represented by the archangel Ardibahisht. The last sentences of this Yasht occur also in Vend. viii. 21.

The *Khordâd Yasht* is devoted to the archangel *Khordâd* (*Haurvatâḍ* in the Avesta), which name signifies "completeness, wholesomeness, health." Ahuramazda says to Zarathushtra: "I created the Haurvatâḍs for the righteous men, and aids so that the archangels come to help them."

[1] Addressed to *Airyama*, an angel who is a friend and assistant of pious men, and in possession of numerous resources.

As a chief means of preserving the Haurvatâd, or the same good condition in which every being of the good creation has been created by Ahuramazda, the recital of *mâthras* is recommended, together with the Barashnom ceremony (described in Vend. ix.; see section xiv. 5). The *mâthra*, which is intended to drive away the evil spirits, is hardly intelligible in a grammatical point of view; the grammar of this and the two preceding Yashts being extremely bad. At the end Zarathushtra is strictly ordered by Ahuramazda not to communicate this effective spell to any other man than to a son, or brother, or relative, or to a priest of one of the three orders (*thrâyava, i.e.*, Herbads, Mobads, and Dasturs). Such interdictions of divulging *mâthras*, or spells, are not unfrequent in the Yashts.

3. ABÂN YASHT.

This Yasht, which is of considerable length (thirty sections containing 132 verses in all), is devoted to *Ardvi Sûra Anâhita* (now called Arduisur), the mighty goddess Anaitis of the ancient Persians, corresponding to the Mylitta of the Babylonians, and the Aphrodite (Venus) of the Greeks. Her name *Anâhid* is even still preserved in modern Persian, and well known to the readers of Hafiz. In this Yasht she is always called by the three names just mentioned, which are only epithets. *Ardvi* means "high, sublime," *sûra* "strong, excellent," and *anâhita* "spotless, pure, clean," which terms refer to the celestial waters represented by her. The contents are as follows:—

i. Ahuramazda calls upon Zarathushtra to worship Anâhita, who rolls under bridges, who gives salubrity, who defeats the devils, who professes the Ahura religion, who is to be worshipped and praised in this living world. She, as the giver of fertility, purifies the seed of all males, and the wombs of all females, and provides the latter at the right time with milk. Coming from one of the summits of the mountain Alborz, she is as large as all other waters taken together, which spring out of this heavenly source. When she discharges herself into the sea *Vouru-kasha*, then all its shores are widened. This heavenly fountain has a thousand springs and a thousand canals, each of them forty days' journey long. Thence a channel goes through all the seven *kêshvars*, or regions of the earth, conveying everywhere pure celestial water. She was created by Ahuramazda himself for the benefit of the house, village, town, and country.

iii. Her chariot is drawn by four white horses, which defeat all the devils.

From the fifth section, nearly to the end, all the praises which Anâhita has received, and the rewards which she has granted to her devotees, are enumerated.

v. Ahuramazda himself is said to have worshipped her, in order to secure her assistance in inducing Zarathushtra to become his prophet. She readily granted his request.

vi. *Haoshyanha* (*Hôshang* in the Shâhnâmah) sacrificed to her a hundred horses, a thousand cows, and ten thousand young animals. She gave him strength to conquer all the demons and men, and to establish an empire.

vii. *Yima Khshaêta* (Jamshêd) asked the same blessing from her which she readily granted, while she refused (viii.) to grant *Azhi dahâka's* (Zohak, an incarnation of the devil) prayer for strength to kill all the men on the surface of the earth. (ix.) But she assisted *Thraêtaona* (Frêdûn), who had worshipped her also, to destroy this tyrant. Besides these heroes, a good many others are mentioned as worshippers of Anâhita, such as *Kava Us* (*Kai Kavus* in the Shâhnâmah), *Kava Husrava* (*Kai Khusrô*), &c. The example set by Ahuramazda himself and the great heroes and sages of Iranian antiquity, of worshipping Anâhita in order to obtain blessings from her, was followed, of course, by Zarathushtra and his royal disciple *Kava Vishtâspa* (*Kai Gushtâsp* in Sh.), who are always represented as having respected the ancient forms of worship.

In sections xxi. and xxx. two short hymns are preserved, on the recital of which Anâhita was expected to appear. The first is ascribed to Ahuramazda himself. It commences as follows :—

âidhi	paiti	ava-jasa,
come	before (me)	come down,
Ardvi-sûra		Anâhitê!
Arduisur		Anâhita!
hacha	araḍbyô	starcbyô
from	yonder	stars
avi zãm		Ahuraḍhâtãm.
on to the earth		created by Ahuramazda.
Thwãm	yazâoñtê	aurvâoṇhô
Thee	shall worship	the handy
ahurâoṇhô¹		daṅhupatayô,
lords		the rulers of countries,
puthrâoṇhô		daṅhupaitinãm.
sons		of the rulers of countries.

4. KHURSHÊD AND MÂH YASHTS.

The first of these Yashts is devoted to the sun, which is called in the Avesta *hvare khshaêta*, "sun the king" (preserved in the modern Persian *khurshêd*, "sun"); the second is devoted to the moon, called *mâoṇh* (in modern Persian *mâh*).

The prayer addressed to the sun commences as follows:—
"We worship the king sun, the immortal, brilliant. When he burns with his rays, then all the heavenly spirits rise by hundreds and by thousands to spread his splendour, to send it down to the earth, created by Ahuramazda, for protecting the cultivated fields (*gaêthâo*) and their bodies.² When the sun rises, then he purifies the earth, created by Ahuramazda, he purifies the flowing water, as well as that of springs and lakes, he purifies all the creatures of the beneficent spirit. As long as the sun has not risen, all the demons are endeavouring to spread havoc throughout the

---

¹ It is nom. pl. From this passage one may clearly see that *ahura* is not a title confined to the Supreme Being, but can be applied to men also. The same is the case with the Hebrew word *elohím*, "God," which is now and then used in the sense of "judges," Exod. xxi. 6 (according to the ancient Chaldaic translator Onkelos), and in that of "kings" (see Ps. lxxxii. 1, 6).

² In this passage, as well as in many others in the Yashts and the Vendidad, some interpolations have been made in later times to illustrate phrases which were considered hardly intelligible. Thus, for instance, *hãm-bârayêiñti* (*anbâshtan*, "to fill" in Pers.), "they carry everywhere," is explained by *nipârayêiñti*, "they make pass down (everywhere)."

seven regions of the earth, and none [1] of the heavenly spirits withstands and slays them, whilst all the living creation is drowned in sleep."

At the end the conjunction of sun and moon is particularly mentioned as the luckiest of all conjunctions. The word for "conjunction," *hakhedhrem*, is of particular interest, because it is preserved in the modern Persian *akhtar*, "star," whose original meaning "conjunction" may still be found in some phrases, such as *akhtar-i-dânish*, "Jupiter and Mercury" (literally, the conjunction foreboding wisdom).

In the Mâh Yasht the moon is invoked by the epithet *gaochithra*, which means "cow-faced." All "the immortal benefactors (archangels) rise and spread the moonlight over the surface of the earth created by Ahuramazda, then the light of the moon shines through the tops of the golden-coloured trees; and gold-like it rises from the earth (*i.e.*, it is reflected by her)." [2] The new moon and the full moon are especially alluded to.

5. Tîr and Gôsh Yashts.

The Tîr Yasht is devoted to the praise of the star *Tishtrya*, "Mercury" (*tashtar* in Parsi, *tîr* in modern Pers.). He is called the giver of wealth (*bakhta shôithrahê*); his lustre is red, and of great beauty. His most significant epithet is *afsh-chithra*, "waterfaced" (of one and the same nature with the water), because he brings the waters from the celestial ocean, Vouru-kasha, down on the earth to fertilise the soil. He discharges this duty, which is assigned to him, with the utmost quickness, being "as swift as the river Tighrish, which has the swiftness of an arrow, and is the swiftest of all Aryan (rivers) when it falls from the

---

[1] This seems to be in contradiction to the Srosh Yasht, where Srosh is said to fight at night-time against the evil spirits. But one has to bear in mind that Srosh is not one of the *Yazatas*, or angels, but of a higher order; he is the representative of the religion itself; if it were not for him the world would fall a prey to the demons during the night-time.

[2] The reflection of moonlight is called *paitiditi*, "what looks against."

Khshaotha mountain down to the *Qanrat* mountain." (Yt. viii. 6.)

He defeats and expels the fairies (*pairika* = *parî* in Pers.), who "fall as star-worms (*i.e.*, glow-worms) between earth and heaven into the sea Vouru-kasha (to prevent the waters from coming out)." But Tishtrya enters this sea in the shape of a horse, and by swelling it, makes it overflow its shores, and so carries its waters, as showers, over the "seven regions of the earth."

His worship was compulsory at the time of a drought; for unless the prayers of men were addressed to him, he was powerless to defeat the evil spirits, who kept back the waters in the sea. If men invoke him, says he, as they invoke other angels, then he proceeds from his magnificent palace to the Vouru-kasha. He steps into the sea in the shape of a red horse with yellow ears. There the Deva *Apaoshô*, in the shape of a black horse with black ears and tail, encounters him. Both fight for three days and nights; at length he is defeated by the Deva. Tishtrya then leaves the sea, crying aloud: "I am lost, the waters are lost, the trees are lost, the Mazdayasnian religion is destroyed. Men do not worship me as they worship other angels. If they would worship me, I would gain the strength of ten horses, ten camels, ten oxen, ten mountains, ten navigable rivers." When men then come to aid him by their prayers, and consequently his strength increases, he descends for a second time into the sea, attacks the Deva again, and defeats him. After having conquered him, he proclaims the victory, gained by him, to the whole good creation. He makes the waters of the sea then flow over its borders, and fertilises the soil. In the midst of the sea there is a mountain called *Hendva* (very likely the Hindu-kush range of mountains is to be understood), over which the clouds gather together. The winds carry them rapidly off, and they then discharge their watery load upon the thirsty and parched soil.

The Gôsh Yasht is devoted to a female spirit who is

called here *Drvâspa*, i.e., one who keeps horses in health. The name *Gosh*, "cow," which was given her in after times, refers to *gēush urvâ*, the universal soul by which all living beings of the good creation are animated. From the terms in which Drvâspa is spoken of in this Yasht, she was believed to preserve the life of the good animals. In heaven she represents the Milky-way, and in this respect is described as having many spies (eyes), having light of her own, having a far way, and a long constellation (*dareghô-hakhedhrayana*).

She was worshipped by the heroes of antiquity, such as *Haoshyanha Paradhâta* (Hoshang the Peshdadian in the Shâhnâmah), *Yima* (Jamshêd), *Thraêtaona* (Frêdûn), *Kava Vishtâspa*, *Zarathushtra* himself, &c., and different favours were asked of her, such as, to give strength for defeating enemies, to rid the creation from the evils of heat and cold, to propagate the good religion, &c.

6. Mihir Yasht.

In this long Yasht, which comprises thirty-five sections (146 verses in Wester.), the angel presiding over, and directing the course of the sun, who was called *Mithra*, "friend" (*mihir* in Persian), is invoked and praised. His worship was widely spread, not only in ancient Persia itself, but far beyond its frontiers in Asia Minor, and even in Greece and Rome.

In the first section of this Yasht, Ahuramazda says to Spitama Zarathushtra: "I created Mithra, who rules over large fields (*vouru-gaoyaoitish*), to be of the same rank and dignity (as far as worship is concerned) as I myself am. The wretch who belies Mithra,[1] spoils the whole country. Therefore, never break a promise, neither that contracted with a fellow-religionist, nor that with an infidel. Mithra gives those who do not belie him, swift horses; the fire,

---

[1] *Mithra* has several meanings, viz., "angel of the sun, sun, friend," and "promise, contract." Promise-breaking, or lying, or not paying debts which have been contracted, is called *Mithrô-drukhsh*, "belying Mithra."

MIHIR YASHT.

Ahuramazda's son, leads such men on the straightest way, the Frohars (Fravashis) give them children of superior qualities."

Near the end of the first section there is a short hymn by which Ahuramazda is said to call him. It consists of verses, each of about eight syllables, and commences as follows:—

ácha	nô	jamyâḍ	avaṇhê,	ácha	nô	jamyâḍ	ravaṇhê,
Hither	to us	may come	to help,	hither	to us	may come	to face (before us),

ácha	nô	jamyâḍ	rafnaṇhê, &c.
hither	to us	may come	to joy, &c.

uṇhrô	aiwithârô	yasnyô,	vahmyô,	anaiwidrukhtô,
the strong	conqueror	deserving worship,	deserving praise,	not to be belied,

vispem	â	aṇuhê	astraitê,
all	in	the life	supplied with bodies (i.e., in the creation),

Mithrô	yô	vouru-gaoyaoitish.
Mithra	who	rules over large fields.

"Mithra, who always speaks the truth, has a thousand ears, ten thousand eyes, and is always watching, without falling asleep, over the welfare of the creation" (ver. 7).

"He, first of the celestial spirits, crosses the mountain *Harô-berezaiti* (Alborz, the supposed centre of the world) on its eastern side, where the immortal sun with his swift horses is stationed; he first, covered with gold, reaches the summits of that mountain, and thence overlooks the whole of Iran. Through him the rulers build their high fortresses, through him the high mountains, with their many pasturages, produce food for the animals, through him the deep wells have abundance of waters, through him the large navigable rivers run swiftly through *Aishkata*,[1] *Pouruta* (Parthia, *Parthava* in the cuneiform inscriptions), *Mouru* (Marv), *Harôyû* (Herat), *Gau Sughdha* (Sogdiana, Samarkand), and *Qâirizem* (Khowaresmia). He brings light to all the seven regions (the whole earth); victory resounds in the ears of those who, by their know-

[1] A locality not yet identified.

ledge of the appropriate prayers and rites, continuously worship him with sacrifices." (Yt. x. 13–16).

He protects those who do not break their promises when in distress and misery; but inflicts severe punishments upon those who sin against him by lying and promise-breaking; he makes their arms and feet lame, their eyes blind, their ears deaf (ver. 23). The same idea is embodied in the short hymn which forms the 11th section (vers. 47–49). The verses consist of eight syllables, as in the following specimen :—

âaḍ	yaḍ	Mithrô	fravazaiti	avi	haêmayâo	khrvîshyêitîsh,
Then	when	Mithra		drives	in the two armies	ready for battle,
avi	hãm-yanta		rasmaoyô		añtare	dañhu-pâperetânê,
against	they encounter	in two battle lines			in order	for the country
(each other)						to fight,
athra	narãm	mithrô-drujãm		apãsh	gavô	darezayêiti,
then	of the men	who break promise		away	the hand	he binds,
	pairi	daêma		vârayêiti, &c.		
	round	the face		he covers, &c.		

i.e., at the time of a battle taking place between two hostile armies, and both being arrayed in battle lines against each other, in order to fight for a country, Mithra drives in his chariot to the battlefield, and punishes all those who were formerly sinning against him by breaking promises; he causes some to be made prisoners, and dooms others to lose their eyes, or their feet, or their ears.

The residence of this mighty angel, the punisher of rascals and scoundrels, is on the mountain *Harô-berezaiti* (Alborz), where Ahuramazda himself has built a palace for him, where is "no night, no darkness, no cold wind, nor hot, no smoke, no putrifaction, no fogs," which is the model of an Iranian paradise (ver. 50).

All the demons (*devas*) flee from him when he, as the ruler of the whole earth, drives in his chariot on her right side. On his right side he is followed by *Sraosha*, the angel ruling over the whole of the divine service, and by *Rashnu razishta* (Rashnu râst), the angel of justice, and the spirits of the waters, trees, &c. (vers. 100, 101).

In verse 104 mention is made of the eastern and western Hindus (*hiñdvô = sindhavas*, i.e., the (seven) rivers in the Vedas, the ancient name of India).

Ahuramazda paid his respects to him. He drives out from paradise (*garôdemâna*) in a splendid chariot, drawn by four white horses. He carries with him weapons of all kinds for the destruction of the Devas; among them is the *vazra*,[1] the most powerful.

7. SROSH HÂDÔKHT AND RASHNU YASHTS.

The former Yasht, which is now particularly used at the time of initiating priests (chiefly of the lower grade, the Herbads) into their office, is dedicated to the angel Sraosha, of whom we have already given an account (see p. 189). An analysis of this Yasht would, therefore, afford no particular interest.

In the Rashnu Yasht the angel *Rashnu razishta*, " the rightest righteousness," who is believed to preside over the eternal laws of nature, as well as morality (corresponding to the idea of *Themis* among the ancient Greeks), is invoked and worshipped. He is everywhere, and represents, to a certain extent, the omnipresence of the divine being. He is particularly distinguished by firmness and the greatest hatred of disorder and immorality of every kind. His devotee, in paying reverence to him, by placing various sweet fruits and oil before the sacred fire, invokes and praises him wherever he may be, whether in one of the seven regions (*karshvare*), or in different parts of the sea *Vouru-kasha* (the ocean surrounding the earth), either on the large tree, bearing all kinds of fruits at the same time, which is planted in its middle, or on its shores, or in its depths. He is further praised whether he be on the ends of the earth, or on the celestial mountain *Harô-berezaiti* (Alborz), or in one of the stars, such as

---

[1] *Gurz*, " a club, battleaxe," in Persian is identical with *vajra*, " thunderbolt," in the Vedas, where it is Indra's weapon.

Churl's Wain (Ursa major) called *Haptóiriñg*,[1] or in the water stars, or vegetation stars, or in the moon, or sun, or in the luminaries which were from the beginning (*anaghra raocháo*), or in paradise.

8. Fravardin Yasht.

This Yasht, comprising thirty-one chapters, which are divided into 158 verses, is the longest of all. It is dedicated to the praise of the Frohars, *Fravashi* in the Avesta (preserved in the name *Phraortes*, which is *Fravartish* in the ancient Persian of the cuneiform inscriptions), which means "protector." These Frohars or protectors, who are numberless, are believed to be angels, stationed everywhere by Ahuramazda for keeping the good creation in order, preserving it, and guarding it against the constant attacks of fiendish powers. Every being of the good creation, whether living, or deceased, or still unborn, has its own Fravashi or guardian angel who has existed from the beginning. Hence they are a kind of prototypes, and may be best compared to the "ideas" of Plato who supposed everything to have a double existence, first in idea, secondly in reality.[2] Originally the Fravashis represented

---

[1] In modern Persian *haftwarang*. This word is highly interesting from its identity with the ancient Vedic and Greek names of the same constellation. The original form in the Vedas is *riksha*, "a bear" (which is found only once in the hymns of the Rigveda, i. 24, 10) = Greek *arktos*. According to an account in the Shatapatha Bráhmana, ii. 1, 2, 4 (second part of the white Yajurveda) this name was changed afterwards into that of *Sapta rishayah*, "the seven Rishis," by which name the stars of Ursa major are called in the later Vedic hymns (see Rigveda x. 82, 2, Atharvaveda vi. 40, 1) and in the classical Sanskrit writings. The sounds of *riksha*, "bear," and *rishi*, "seer, prophet," were so near to one another, that at the time when they commenced to deify those great founders of Brahmanism, nothing was more natural than to assign to them a place in the sky, and make them one of the brightest and most beautiful constellations. In the Iranian languages, however, the old name "the seven bears" was faithfully preserved.

[2] The ideas are the models (paradeigmata) of everything existing; the realities (or, according to Plato, non-realities, because only the ideas have a real existence according to his doctrine) being only imitations thereof. The ideas are unborn, eternal, invisible, imperishable, but their imitations, the substances, are subject to all changes. See Parmenides, p. 132, d. Steph. Timœus., 48, c. 52 a. According to Aristotle (Metaphysics, i.

only the departed souls of ancestors, comparable to the *pitaras*, "fathers," of the Brahmans, and the *Manes* of the Romans. The following extracts are translated from the Fravardîn Yasht:—

1-7. Ahuramazda spoke to Spitama Zarathushtra: To thee alone I shall tell the power and strength, glory, usefulness, and happiness of the holy guardian-angels, the strong and victorious, O righteous Spitama Zarathushtra! how they come to help me, [(Zend) how they give me assistance]. By means of their splendour and glory I uphold the sky which is shining so beautifully, and which touches and surrounds this earth;[1] it resembles a bird which is ordered by God to stand still there; it is high as a tree, wide-stretched, iron-bodied, having its own light in the three worlds (*thrishva*); on which (the sky) Ahuramazda, together with Mithra, Rashnu, and Spenta Armaiti, puts a garment decked with stars, and made by God in such a way that nobody can see the ends of its parts.

By means of their splendour and glory, I uphold the high, strong Anâhita (the celestial water) with bridges, the salutary, who drives away the demons, who has the true faith, and is to be worshipped in the world, and to be praised in the world; the righteous who furthers life, the righteous who increases wealth, the righteous who increases property, the righteous who makes the fields thrive, the righteous who makes the countries thrive; who purifies the seed of all males, who purifies the wombs of all females to make them fit for conception, who makes all pregnant females bear fine offspring, who provides females at the right time with milk; the praised, the far-renowned, who is as large as all the waters which flow over the earth, who runs with might from the celestial heights into the sea

---

9, 2), Plato imagined as many "ideas" as there are things really existing. Such celestial, or invisible, prototypes of terrestrial things are mentioned also in the Bible; see Heb. ix. 23; Exod. xxv. 9, 40.

[1] *Bavâva* would be according to Sanskrit the first person dual, but this meaning does not agree with the structure of the sentence; it is evidently put for *bavaiti va*, "it is for both."

Vouru-kasha. All its shores are then overflowing from its very centre, when those waters fall into it, when the high, strong Anâhita pours them forth into their channels. She has a thousand springs, a thousand channels; each of these springs and each of these channels is of the circuit of a forty days' journey for a well-mounted messenger.

11. By means of their splendour and glory, I keep, O Zarathushtra! the embryos alive in the pregnant females, to be formed out of a formless inanimate mass, to obtain a living soul, bones, form, consistency, growth of the faculty of walking, and speaking.

12. If the strong guardian-angels of the righteous would not give me assistance, then cattle and men, the two best of the hundred classes of beings, would no longer exist for me; then would commence the devil's power, the devil's reign, the whole living creation would belong to the devil.

13. Between earth and heaven may the devilish spirit take up his residence! [(Zend) between earth and heaven may the devil reside!]; but he (the devil) will not be able to destroy entirely (the influence) of the beneficent spirit (Ahuramazda).

14. By means of their splendour and glory, the waters flow straight forward in inexhaustible sources; by means of their splendour and glory, trees grow out of the earth; by means of their splendour and glory, the winds blow, carrying with them vapours from inexhaustible sources.

15. By means of their splendour and glory, the females are getting with children; by means of their splendour and glory, they produce good offspring; by means of their splendour and glory, there will be descendants.

16. By means of their splendour and glory, that ingenuous man (Zarathushtra), who spoke such good words, who was the source of wisdom, who was born before Gotama[1] had such intercourse (with God, obtained revela-

---

[1] *Gaotema* (in the original) is the proper name of Buddha, the founder of Buddhism. Its Sanskrit form is *Gautama*. That Buddhism existed at Balkh is well known.

tion). By means of their splendour and glory, the sun goes on his path; by means of their splendour and glory, the moon goes on her path; by means of their splendour and glory, the stars go on their path.

17. These guardian-angels of the righteous give great assistance in great battles (to be fought against the devilish empire). The guardian-angels of the righteous among the believers in the old religion, or those of the prophets (*Saoshyañtô*) to come, for making perpetuation of life, are the strongest of all; then the guardian-angels of the living righteous men are stronger than those of the dead.

18. When a man living, who is the ruler over all the estates of a country, supports well the guardian-angels of the righteous, then each of his dominions will be well populated [(Zend) who supports well your good friend (the sun, *mithra*) with his far-extended dominions, and the probity which is protecting and sheltering estates].

19. Thus I tell thee, holy Spitama! the power, strength, glory, support, and delight of the strong, victorious guardian-angels of the righteous, as they come to assist me, [(Zend) as the strong guardian-angels of the righteous bring me assistance].

20. Ahuramazda said to Spitama Zarathushtra: When in this world, O Spitama Zarathushtra! thou hast to pass mischief-bringing, bad, baneful ways, and thy life is threatened, then shalt thou recite these words, [(Zend) then shalt thou speak these victorious words, O Zarathushtra!]:

21. I praise, invoke, and extol the good, strong, beneficent, guardian-angels of the righteous. We praise those who are in the houses, those who are in the villages, those who are in the towns, those who are in the countries, those who are in the Zoroastrian communities, those of the present, those of the past, those of the future righteous, all those invoked in countries where invocation is practised.

22. Who uphold heaven, who uphold water, who uphold earth, who uphold nature, &c.

49, 50. We worship the good, strong, beneficent, guardian-angels of the righteous, who come to the village in the season called Hamaspathmaêda. Then they roam about there during ten nights, wishing to learn what assistance they might obtain, saying : Who will praise us ? who will worship (us) ? who will adore (us) ? who will pray (to us) ? who will satisfy (us) with milk and clothes in his hand, with a prayer for righteousness? whom of us will he call here ? whose soul is to worship you ? To whom of us will he give that offering in order to enjoy imperishable food for ever and ever?

51, 52. Then the man who worships them with milk in his hand, and with clothes, and the prayer for righteousness, upon him the pleased (with this sacrifice), favourable, not-hurting, strong guardian-angels of the righteous bestow blessings. In this house (where they are worshipped in such a way) there will be abundance of cows and of men (posterity); there will be a swift horse and a well-fastened carriage ; there will be found a prudent man who will worship us (in future) with milk and clothes in his hand and with the prayer for righteousness.

82-84. We worship the good, strong, beneficent guardian-angels of the righteous, those of the immortal benefactors (Ameshaspentas), the rulers with their watchful eyes, the high, powerful, swift, living ones of everlasting truth. All seven are of the same mind, speak the same words, perform the same actions ; [(Zend) they have the same mind, the same words, the same action, and the same master and ruler, the Creator Ahuramazda]. One looks into the soul of the other, considering about good thoughts, considering about good words, considering about good deeds, considering about the best life, that the prayer may go up to their brightly shining paths.

85. We worship the good, strong, beneficent guardian-angels, that of the blazing, beneficent, penetrating fire, and that of Sraosha, the righteous, swift, self-speaking, swiftly-running, the living, and that of Nairyôsanha (the angel).

86. That of the rightest righteousness (*Rashnu razishta*),

that of Mithra with his far-extended dominions, that of the holy word (*Māthra spenta*), that of the day, that of water, that of earth, that of the trees, that of nature, that of existence, that of the two righteous worlds (visible and invisible, earthly and spiritual).

87. We worship the guardian-angel of Gayô-marathan (Gayomard, Kayomars, the Adam or Manu of the Iranians), the righteous, who first listened to Ahuramazda's thoughts and sayings; out of whose body he (Ahuramazda) formed the central mass (*nâfô*, "navel")[1] of the Aryan countries, the surface of the Aryan countries.

88-94. We worship the rule and the guardian-angel of Zarathushtra Spitama, who first thought good thoughts, who first spoke good words, who first performed good actions, who was the first priest, the first warrior, the first cultivator of the soil, the first prophet, the first who was inspired, the first who has given (to mankind) nature and truth and words, and hearing of words, and wealth and all good, created by Mazda, of rightful appearance. Who first made turning the wheel among gods and men,[2] who first was praising the rightfulness of the living creation, and destroying idolatry, who confessed the Zarathushtrian worship of Mazda, the religion of Ahura opposed to the demons. Who first spoke the word opposed to the demons,[3] being the religion of Ahura in the animated creation, who first promulgated the word opposed to the demons, being the religion of Ahura in the animated creation. Who first spoke the whole of what is given by the demons in the animated creation, and what is neither to be worshipped nor invoked (it is profane), that is the strong, blessed, old religion of the countries (the ante-Zoroastrian, Deva religion).[4] Through whom the whole true and revealed word

[1] Compare the Greek appellation of Delphi: *Omphale gês*, "navel of the earth," i.e., its centre.
[2] This is a Buddhistic expression, meaning "established and propagated the good religion."
[3] That is to say, the Vendidad.
[4] This means that Zarathushtra is the originator of all religious thoughts, both those current after, and those current before his time.

was heard, which is the life and guidance of the world, the praises of the righteousness [1] which is the greatest, best, and most excellent, and the promulgation of the best religion of those existing. Whom all Ameshaspentas, together with the Sun, worship with believing inquiry in the mind, for the duration of life, as the patron spirit and religious preceptor of the world, as praiser of the righteousness which is the greatest, best, and most excellent, and the promulgator of the best religion of those existing. Through his knowledge and speech the waters and trees become desirous of growing; through his knowledge and speech all beings, created by the beneficent Spirit, are uttering words of happiness. For our welfare the fire-priest (âthrava), Spitama Zarathushtra, was born, he offered sacrifice for us, and arranged the holy twigs. Thus comes forth from the waters (i.e., from its source) the good religion of the Mazdayasnians, spreading over all the seven regions of the earth.

95. There the friend of the waters (the sun), ruling over far-extended dominions, produced all virtues of the countries by their means, and makes them play when overflowing; there the son of waters, the strong fire, produced all virtues of countries, and appeases them when overflowing.

We worship the virtue and the guardian angel of Maidhyô-mâonha, the disposer (of the good faith), who first heard Zarathushtra's speech and sayings.

99. We worship the guardian-angel of Kavi Vîshtâspa, the bold, who speaks his own verses, the attacker of the demons, the believer in Ahura, who defiled,[2] for the benefit of the good creation, the face of the devil and the witches, [(Zend) who cleft the face of the devil and the witches, that is to say, who was the arm and support of the Zoroastrian belief in Ahura]; (100.) who carried away from the

---

[1] The "praise of righteousness" is the Pahlavi technical name of the Ashem-vohu formula.

[2] The words from yô druja, to vâs- trahêcha, contain fragments of an old epic poem in honour of Kavi Vishtâspa, with some interpolations. The metre is the Shloka.

Hunus[1] the standard [(Zend) which was tied], and deposited it in the impregnable fortress Maidhyôishâdha, shielding cattle and fields, [(Zend) favourable to cattle and fields].

104. We worship the guardian-angel of Hushkyaothna, son of Frashaoshtra, that of Qâdaêna, son of Frashaoshtra, that of Hanhaurvat, son of Jâmâspa, that of Vareshan, son of Hanhaurvat, that of Vohu-nemanh, son of Avâraoshtra, to ward off the mischief done by nightmares, by ghosts disguised as black-coloured animals, by demons, and by witches.

105. We worship the guardian-angel of Simaêzhi, the reciter of spells, the Herbad, who slew most of the Usaghanas, who polluted the bodies and disturbed righteousness, who were irreligious, acknowledging neither patron spirit nor religious preceptor, who were charmers, frustrating the help of the guardian-angels to resist the hostilities which were crushing the righteous.

129. We worship the guardian-angel of Astvad-ereta who is called the victorious Saoshyâns. He is called Saoshyâns, as he will conduce (*sâvayâḍ*) to the welfare of the whole animated creation. He is called Astvaḍ-ereta, as he is keeping up the animated creation, guarding it against destruction, especially against the destruction caused by the two-legged Drukhsh (the personification of destruction), caused by the hatred of (the demons) who annihilate rightful things.

9. BEHRÂM AND RÂM YASHTS.

The Behrâm Yasht is devoted to the angel *Behrâm*. The original form of this name is *Verethraghna*, which means "killer of enemies," *i.e.*, conqueror, and is to be identified with Indra's name *Vritrahâ* to be found in the Vedas. He is the giver of victory, and appears personally before his

---

[1] This nation is mentioned by the name of *Hûnâs* in Indian writings also. See *Vishnu Purâna*, translated by H. H. Wilson, pp. 177, 194. They were hostile to the Iranians, who seem to have often been engaged in war with them. They were the white Huns who were once the terror of Europe.

devotee in such different forms as he may choose to assume. He appears in the form of a wind, in that of a cow, in that of a horse, in that of a camel, in that of a boar (*varâzu*, Sans. *varâha*), in that of a boy aged fifteen, in that of a warrior, &c. Zarathushtra worshipped him, and was rewarded by the angel with strength in his arms and vigour in his whole body.

Zarathushtra once asking Ahuramazda in what way the angel Behrâm should be worshipped, is answered in the following manner: The Aryan countries (*i.e.*, their inhabitants, the Iranians, ancestors of the Parsis) shall consecrate water (called *zaothra*), arrange the sacred twigs called Barsom, and kill an animal of a reddish or yellowish colour, the flesh of which is to be cooked. Of this meal of Behrâm, which is prepared occasionally to this day, neither a criminal, nor a courtezan, nor an infidel who is an enemy of the Zoroastrian religion, is allowed to eat. Should that happen then the Aryan countries will be visited by plagues, and devastated by incursions of hostile armies.

The Râm Yasht is devoted to the angel Râm, who is, however, never mentioned in it by this name, but is called *vayush* [1] *uparô-kairyô*, *i.e.*, the wind whose business is above (in the sky), the celestial breath; or he is simply invoked by the names of *Apâ*, "who is far, remote," and *Bagha*,[2] "destiny." He is described as being everywhere (on all sides), and as the primary cause (*âkhshti*) of the whole universe. From these remarks we may gather that he represents that very fine and subtle substance which is called *ether*, and known to the Indian philosophers as *âkâsha*.

He was worshipped by Ahuramazda and the great heroes and sages of antiquity, such as *Haoshyanha*, *Takhma-urupa* (*Tahmûras*), *Yima*, &c. Old maids beg him to grant them husbands.

In the last (eleventh) section his manifold names are

---

[1] This name seems to be connected with the Vedic god *Vâyu*, "the wind," the original long *â* having been shortened to *a*.

[2] See the first section of the fourth Essay.

explained Vayush is there traced to the root vi, "to go, penetrate," and to va, "both," and explained by "I go to both creatures, those of the beneficent, and those of the malevolent spirit." By this and other names he is to be invoked at the time of worship. He has then the power of defeating hostile armies.

10. Dîn and Ashi Yashts.

In the Dîn Yasht the *daêna mâzdayasnish*, or the Zoroastrian religion, is invoked as an angel. She was, of course, pre-eminently worshipped by Zarathushtra. The way in which he invoked her is described in a short hymn commencing as follows:—

Yt. xvi. 2. Rise from thy place! go out from thy house! thou wisdom, created by Mazda! which is the rightest; if thou art in the front (of the house), put up with me; if thou art behind it, return to me.

Ashi is a female angel whom the Dasturs at present compare with *Lakshmi*, the Hindu goddess of wealth. But the Yasht devoted to her does not countenance this opinion. Her full name is *Ashish vanuhi* (now corrupted to Ashishang), which means "the good truth." She is called a daughter of Ahuramazda, and a sister of the Ameshaspentas or archangels. She makes the wisdom of all prophets continue, and inspires them in their turn with the heavenly (lit. original) wisdom. She comes to help all that invoke her from far and near. The ancient heroes and sages, Yima, Thraêtaona, Zarathushtra, Kavâ Vîshtâspa, &c., worshipped her, and to all she granted what they were praying for, such as wealth, victory, or children.

11. Ashtâd, Zamyâd, and Vanant Yashts.

The name *Ashtâd*, which is to be traced to the Avesta word *Arshtâd*, "height," does not occur in the Yasht bearing this name. The glory of the Aryan countries (*i.e.*, their riches and wealth in trees, cows, sheep, and all other things of the good creation, which are the most effective means for destroying the works of the demons, and for preserving everything in its original rectitude), and the *Ashi vaṇuhi berezaiti* (the good, high truth) are invoked in this Yasht. The glory (*qarenô*) being chiefly the subject of the Zamyâd Yasht, and the Ashi Vaṇuhi that of the preceding Ashi Yasht, we cannot ascribe any independent value to this Ashtâd Yasht, which is only an appendage to those two others. The name Ashtâd, by which the Dasturs understand the height of mountains, was given to this short chapter only to distinguish it by a separate name from the two other Yashts.

The name *Zamyâd* refers to the earth. She is not directly invoked in this Yasht, which is chiefly devoted to the praise of the "glory" (*qarenô*) above mentioned. Its first section, which describes the origin of all mountains out of the heart of the central and primeval mountain Alborz (*Harô berezaiti*),[1] stands separate. Several names of mountains are particularly mentioned,[2] such as *Ushidhâo* (creator of light), *Ushi-darenem* (district of light), &c. The number of all the mountains is said to be 2244.

In the following sections of this Yasht we find always invoked "the mighty glory which was peculiar to the Kavis" (the chiefs of the Iranian community in ancient times, mostly before Zoroaster). Ahuramazda produced it at the time of creating all that is good, bright, shining, and propagating life. It attached itself generally to one of the great heroes of antiquity, such as Thraêtaona, Yima, &c., and enabled him to achieve great feats. This heavenly glory is essential for causing the dead to rise at the end of the world. About this resurrection of the dead, which is a genuine Zoroastrian doctrine, we find in this Yasht two very interesting passages, which are almost identical (Yt. xix. 11, 12 and 89, 90). The following is a translation of the second passage :—

[1] Here we find the peculiar form *haraiti baresh*, in which *haraiti* is an abstract noun, meaning "mountain range," and *baresh*, *barez* (in the Vedas *brihas*) "elevated, high." Its heart (*zaredhô*) is here regarded as a separate mountain, surrounded by its vast mountain ranges.

[2] To express the word "mountain" we find here two words used: *gairi* and *paurvata*, which are both to be found also in Sanskrit (*giri* and *parvata*).

'This splendour attaches itself to the hero (who is to rise
'out of the number) of prophets (called *Saoshyantô*) and to
'his companions, in order to make life everlasting, unde-
'caying, imperishable, imputrescible, incorruptible, for ever
'existing, for ever vigorous, full of power (at the time)
'when the dead shall rise again, and imperishableness of
'life shall commence, making life lasting by itself (without
'further support). All the world will remain for eternity
'in a state of righteousness; the devil will disappear from
'all those places whence he used to attack the righteous
'man in order to kill (him); and all his brood and crea-
'tures will be doomed to destruction.'

The *Vanant Yasht* is a very short prayer addressed to
the star *Vanant* (by which the Dasturs understand the
Milky-way, or *Kâh-i-kashân* in Persian), to kill all dis-
turbers of the good creation. This constellation is said to
stand directly over hell in order to frighten the demons.[1]

12. Two Fragments of the Hâdôkht Nask; the Afrîn-i
Paighambar Zaratusht and Vishtâsp Yasht.

These four texts conclude the collection of all the Yashts
extant, in Westergaard's edition.

In the first fragment of the *Hâdôkht Nask*, the praise of
Ashem or righteousness is recommended by Ahuramazda
to Zarathushtra as one of the most meritorious works. By
this praise we can understand only the recital of the sacred
formula, *Ashem vohu*, which is called, in Pahlavi, "the praise
of righteousness." The larger or smaller amount of merit,
resulting from repeating this prayer, depends on the time
and occasion when it is done. Thus, for instance, the
merit is far greater if the praise is uttered at night than if
uttered in the day-time.

The second fragment treats of the fate of the soul immediately after death, till it reaches either heaven or hell on

---

[1] The Dasturs are of opinion, that
this constellation is the weapon
(*vazra*) which is constantly aimed by
Mithra at the head of the Devas, as
stated in the Khurshêd Yasht.

the fourth morning (inclusive of the day of death), according as its good words, or its sins, have preponderated during life. The following is a translation of these fragments :—

Yt. xxi. 1. Zarathushtra asked Ahuramazda: O Ahuramazda! most munificent spirit, creator of the settlements supplied with creatures, righteous one! in whom [1] alone is thy word, the enunciation of all good, of all that is of rightful origin!

2. Ahuramazda answered him: In the Ashem-reciter,[2] O Zarathushtra!

3. Whoever recites the Ashem, with believing inquiry (remembrance) in his mind for the continuance of life, he praises me who am Ahuramazda, he praises the water, he praises the earth, he praises the cattle, he praises the trees, he praises all good, created by Mazda, that is of rightful origin.

4. For this saying, O Zarathushtra! being recited correctly (in addition) to the saying Ahuna-vairya if outspoken, is for strength and victory in the soul and religion so benefited.

5. For one recital of the Ashem, or one eulogy of a righteous man, is worth, O Spitama Zarathushtra! a hundred sleep-(prayers), a thousand (prayers) when eating meat, a myriad (of prayers) for the conception of bodies occurring in the primary existence.

6. What is the one recital of the Ashem which is worth ten of the other recitals of the Ashem in greatness and goodness and excellence?

7. Ahuramazda answered him: That, indeed, O righteous Zarathushtra! which a man recites as the Ashem for Haurvatâd and Ameretâd when eating, praising good thoughts and good words and good deeds, renouncing evil thoughts and evil words and evil deeds.

8. What is the one recital of the Ashem which is worth

---

[1] Reading *kahmya*, which in the Avesta character is very like *kahmái* the form given in all the manuscripts.

[2] *Ashem-stâtô*, taken here as a locative, seems to be a genitive.

a hundred of the other recitals of the Ashem in greatness and goodness and excellence?

9. Ahuramazda answered him: That, indeed, O righteous Zarathushtra! which a man recites as the Ashem after swallowing of the out-squeezed Homa, praising good thoughts, &c. [as in ver. 7].

10. What is the one recital of the Ashem which is worth a thousand of the other recitals of the Ashem in greatness and goodness and excellence?

11. Ahuramazda answered him: That, indeed, O righteous Zarathushtra! which a man recites as the Ashem, starting up from sleep and going to sleep again, praising good thoughts, &c. [as in ver. 7].

12. What is the one recital of the Ashem which is worth a myriad of the other recitals of the Ashem in greatness and goodness and excellence?

13. Ahuramazda answered him: That, indeed, O righteous Zarathushtra! which a man recites as the Ashem, awaking and rising from sleep, praising good thoughts, &c. [as in ver. 7].

14. What is the one recital of the Ashem which is worth the whole region of Qaniratha, with cattle and with wealth in humankind,[1] in greatness and goodness and excellence?

15. Ahuramazda answered him: That, indeed, O righteous Zarathushtra! which a man recites as the Ashem at the extreme end of life, praising good thoughts and good words and good deeds, renouncing all evil thoughts and evil words and evil deeds.

16. What is the one recital of the Ashem which is worth all this which is in the earth and in the sky, and this earth, and those luminaries, and all good things created by Mazda (and) of rightful origin?

17. Ahuramazda answered him: That, indeed, O righteous Zarathushtra! when one forsakes evil thoughts and evil words and evil deeds.

Yt. xxii. 1. Zarathushtra asked Ahuramazda: O Ahura-

[1] Or perhaps "with chiefs among men."

mazda! most munificent spirit, creator of the settlements supplied with creatures, righteous one! when a righteous man passes away, where dwells his soul that night?

2. Then said Ahuramazda: It sits down in the vicinity of the head, chanting the Gâtha Ushtavaiti, imploring blessedness (thus): Blessed is he, blessed is every one to whom Ahuramazda, ruling by his own will, shall grant[1] (the two everlasting powers). That night the soul experiences as much of pleasure as all that which (it had) as a living existence (*i.e.*, when living in this world).

3. Where dwells his soul the second night?

4. Then said Ahuramazda: &c. [as in ver. 2]. That night, too, (the soul perceives) as much of pleasure, &c. [as in ver. 2].

5. Where dwells his soul also the third night?

6. Then said Ahuramazda: &c. [as in ver. 2]. And that night, too, (the soul perceives) as much of pleasure, &c. [as in ver. 2].

7. On the passing away of the third night, as the dawn appears, the soul of the righteous man appears, passing through plants and perfumes. To him there seems a wind blowing forth from the more southern side, from the more southern quarters, a sweet scent more sweet-scented than other winds.

8. Then, inhaling that wind with the nose, the soul of the righteous man considers: Whence blows the wind, the most sweet-scented wind which I have ever inhaled with the nostrils?

9. Advancing with this wind there appears to him what is his own religion (*i.e.*, religious merit), in the shape of a beautiful maiden, brilliant, white-armed, strong, well-grown, erect, tall, high-bosomed, graceful, noble, with a dazzling face,[2] of fifteen years, with a body as beautiful in (its) limbs (lit. growths) as the most beautiful of creatures.

---

[1] These phrases constitute the first two lines of the Gâtha Ushtavaiti. See p. 155.

[2] Or "of brilliant origin."

10. Then the soul of the righteous man spoke to her, asking: What maiden art thou whom I have thus seen as yet the most beautiful of maidens in form?

11. Then answered him his own religion: I am, O youth! thy good thoughts, good words, good deeds, (and) good religion, who (am) thy own religion in thy own self. Every one has loved thee for such greatness and goodness and beauty and perfume and triumph and resistance to foes, as thou appearest to me.

12. Thou hast loved me, O youth! the good thoughts, good words, good deeds, (and) good religion, with such greatness, &c. [as in ver. 11] as I appear to thee.

13. When thou chancedst to see another performing burning (of the dead) and idol-worship, and causing oppression, and cutting down trees, then thou wouldst sit down, chanting the Gâthas, and consecrating the good waters and the fire of Ahuramazda, and extolling the righteous man coming from near and far.

14. Then (thou madest) me being beloved, more beloved, (me) being beautiful, more beautiful, (me) being desirable, more desirable, (me) sitting in a high place thou wouldst seat in a still higher place, through this good thought, through this good word, through this good deed. Then men afterwards worship me, Ahuramazda, the long-worshipped and conversed-with.

15. The soul of the righteous man first advanced with a step he placed upon Humata (good thought); the soul of the righteous man secondly advanced with a step he placed upon Hûkhta (good word); the soul of the righteous man thirdly advanced with a step he placed upon Huvarshta (good action); the soul of the righteous man fourthly advanced with a step he placed on the eternal luminaries.[1]

16. To him spake a righteous one, previously deceased, asking: How, O righteous one! didst thou pass away? how, O righteous one! didst thou come away from the dwellings supplied with cattle, and from the procreative

[1] These four stages are the four grades in heaven.

birds? from the material life to the spiritual life? from the perishable life to the imperishable life? how long was it for thee in the blessing?[1]

17. Then said Ahuramazda: Ask not him whom thou askest, who has come along the frightful, deadly, destructive path which is the separation of the body and soul.

18. Of the nourishments brought to him (is some) of the Zaremaya oil;[2] that is the food, after decease, of a youth of good thoughts, of good words, of good deeds, of good religion; that is the food, after decease, for a woman of very good thoughts, of very good words, of very good deeds, well-instructed, ruled by a master, (and) righteous.

19. Zarathushtra asked Ahuramazda: &c. [as in ver. 1] when a wicked man dies where dwells his soul that night?

20. Then said Ahuramazda: There, indeed, O righteous Zarathushtra! in the vicinity of the head it runs about, chanting the Gâtha Kâm-nemôi-zâm, the saying: To what land shall I turn? whither shall I go in turning?[3] That night the soul experiences as much of discomfort as all that which (it had) as a living existence (*i.e.*, when living in the world).

21, 22. Where dwells his soul the second night? &c. [as in ver. 20].

23, 24. Where dwells his soul the third night? &c. [as in ver. 20].

25. On the passing away of the third night, O righteous Zarathushtra! as the dawn appears, the soul of the wicked man appears, passing through terrors and stenches. To him there seems a wind blowing forth from the more northern side, from the more northern quarters, a stench more foul-smelling than other winds.

26. Then, inhaling that wind with the nose, the soul of

[1] That is, "how long wast thou reciting the Gâtha Ushtavaiti?" See ver. 2.

[2] A cupful of this beverage is said to be given, by the archangel Vohuman, to the soul of a righteous person before it enters paradise. By drinking it the soul is supposed to become oblivious of all worldly cares and concerns, and is thus prepared for eternal happiness.

[3] These phrases constitute the first line of the fourth section (Yas. xlvi.) of the Gâtha Ushtavaiti. See p. 163.

the wicked man considers: Whence blows the wind, the most foul-smelling wind which I have ever inhaled with the nostrils?

27–33. [This passage, which must have been the converse of ver. 9–15, is omitted in all known manuscripts as far as] the soul of the wicked man fourthly advanced with a step he placed on the eternal glooms.[1]

34. To him spake a wicked one, previously dead, asking: How, O wicked one! didst thou die? how, O wicked one! didst thou come away from the dwellings supplied with cattle, and from the procreative birds? from the material life to the spiritual life? from the perishable life to the imperishable life? how long was thy distress?

35. Angrô-mainyush shouted: Ask not him whom thou askest, who has come along the frightful, deadly, destructive path which is the separation of the body and soul.

36. Of the nourishments brought to him (are some) from poison and poisonous stench; that is the food, after death, of a youth of evil thoughts, of evil words, of evil deeds, of evil religion; that is the food, after death, for a harlot of very evil thoughts, of very evil words, of very evil deeds, ill-instructed, not ruled by a master, (and) wicked.[2]

The *Afrîn-i Paighambar-Zaratusht* contains the blessing, by which the high priest (Zarathushtra) of the Iranians used to bless a governor or king. It is said to have been bestowed by Spitama Zarathushtra on his royal friend Kavi Vishtâspa. The high priest wishes the king to have children, to be as victorious as the hero Frêdun, as brilliant as Kai Kaus, as radiant as the sun, as shining as the moon, as just as the angel of justice himself, as free from disease and death as Kai Khusro; and that, hereafter, he (the blessed) may enjoy the happy life of the blessed in the

---

[1] This is the fourth and lowest grade in hell; the first three grades being *dushmata*, "evil thought," *duzhûkhta*, "evil word," and *duzhvarshta*, "evil deed."

[2] The remaining sentences, appended in Westergaard's edition, do not belong to the Hâdôkht Nask.

land of light and splendour. The blessing concludes by the words "so it shall happen[1] as I bless you."

The *Vishtâsp Yasht*, the first chapter of which is partly identical with the preceding text, is so corrupt in its grammatical forms that we may refrain from examining its contents, which, besides, do not appear to be particularly interesting. It is divided into eight chapters, of which the last is nearly identical with part of the second fragment of the Hâdôkht Nask (Yt. xxii. 1-18); but the whole composition seems to be of comparatively late date.

XIII.—SHORTER TEXTS (NYAYISH, AFRINGANS, GAHS, SIROZAH).

These writings, which are comparatively very short, contain the prayers most commonly used by the Parsis nowadays; but their contents, which are all taken from other parts of the Zend-Avesta (chiefly from the Yasna and Yashts), are of no particular interest either for the history of Avesta literature, or for that of the Parsi religion.

The five *Nyâyishes* or praises are devoted to the Sun (khurshêd), the Angel of the sun (*Mithra*, Mihir), the Moon (mâh), Waters (âbân), and Fire (âtash). The prayers addressed to the Sun and Mithra, are to be repeated thrice every day by every pious Parsi. Habitual neglect of this prevents the soul from passing the bridge *Chinvaḍ* after death. Thrice every month the praise addressed to the moon is absolutely necessary. The repetition of the praise of the waters and fire is meritorious, but not so indispensable as that of the three other Nyâyishes.

Afringâns are blessings which are to be recited over a meal consisting of wine, milk, bread, and fruits, to which an angel or the spirit of a deceased person is invited, and in whose honour the meal is prepared. After the

---

[1] *Atha jamyâḍ* in the Avesta; this phrase corresponds to our *amen* at the end of prayers and blessings.

consecration (which only a priest can perform) is over, the meal is eaten by those who are present.

The performance of these Afringâns is required of every pious Parsi at certain fixed times during the year. These are the six Gahanbârs, each lasting for five days (at the six original seasons of the year), for which the *Afringân-Gahanbâr* is intended; the five Gâtha days (the five last days of the year), during which the *Afringân Gâtha* must be used; and lastly, the third day (Ardibahisht) of the first month (Fravardin) in the year, at which the performance of *Afringân Rapithwin*, devoted to the spirit presiding over the southern quarter (who is the guardian of the path to paradise), is enjoined to every Parsi whose soul wants to pass the great bridge Chinvaḍ after death.

The *five Gâhs* are the prayers which are devoted to the several angels who preside over the five watches, into which the day and night are divided (as detailed above in the note on p. 159). These prayers must be recited every day at their respective times.

The *Sîrozah*, referring to the thirty days, is extant in two forms. It is nothing but a calendar enumerating the names and attributes of the thirty spiritual beings, each of whom is supposed to preside over one of the thirty days of the month, and by whose names the days are called. It is chiefly recited on the thirtieth day after a man's death.

XIV.—VENDIDÂD.

The Vendidâd,[1] which is the code of the religious, civil, and criminal laws of the ancient Iranians, consists, in its present state, of twenty-two chapters, commonly called *fargards* (exactly corresponding to the word *pericope*), *i.e.*, sections. The style of its constituent parts is too varied to admit of ascribing it to a single author. Some parts are

---

[1] This name is a corruption of *vî-daêvô-dâtem*, " what is given against the demons," *i.e.*, to guard against their influence. In Pahlavi it is usually translated literally by *javiḍ-shêdâ-dâḍ*.

evidently very old, and might be traced to the first centuries subsequent to the prophet; but the greater bulk of the work contains (like the Talmud) too minute a description of certain ceremonies and observances to allow a modern critic to trace it to the prophet, or even to one of his disciples. The Vendidâd as a whole (some of its parts seem to be lost, especially those containing the original texts, or the Avesta, of the old laws) is apparently the joint work of the Zarathushtras, or high-priests, of the ancient Iranians during the period of several centuries. They started with old sayings and laws (Avesta), which must partially have descended from the prophet himself,[1] and interpreted them in various ways, often contradicting each other. These interpretations, the so-called Zend, became in the course of time as authoritative as the Avesta, or the original text, of the scripture itself, and in many cases, seem to have superseded it. This Zend was then capable of further explanation, which was less authoritative and went by the name "Pâzand." That we can actually discover these three different stages in the present Vendidâd, the attentive reader will learn from a perusal of the following pages, where they will be separated from each other as much as possible.

The Vendidâd may, as to its contents, be divided into three parts. The first (fargard i.–iii.) is only introductory, and formed very likely part of a very ancient historical or legendary work of a similar kind to the Shâhnâmah. It contains an enumeration of sixteen Aryan countries, over which the Zoroastrian religion was spread (farg. i.), the legends of King Yima (farg. ii.), and strong recommendations of agriculture as the most useful and meritorious work (farg. iii.). The second part (farg. iv.–xvii.), forming the groundwork of the Vendidâd, treats of laws, ceremonies, and observances, without keeping to any strict order. The third part (farg. xviii.–xxii.) is apparently an appendix treating of various subjects. Several extracts from this

[1] Compare for instance Vend. iv. with Yas. xlvi. 5 (see p. 164).

text are here translated, and a summary is given of the contents of the remainder.

1. THE FIRST FARGARD OF THE VENDIDÂD.

The First Sixteen Settlements of the Iranians.

Avesta.

1. Ahuramazda said to Spitama Zarathushtra : I created, O Spitama Zarathushtra ! a delightful spot (which had been previously) nowhere habitable; for if I had not created, O Spitama Zarathushtra ! a delightful spot (which had been previously) nowhere habitable, all earthly life would have poured forth towards Airyana-vaêjô (the earthly paradise).[1]

3. As the first best of regions and countries, I, who am Ahuramazda, produced Airyana-vaêjô of good capability. Thereupon, as an opposition to it, Angrô-mainyush, the deadly, formed a mighty serpent and frost caused by the Devas.

Zend.

4. Ten months of winter are there, two of summer;[2] and these (the latter) are cold as to water, cold as to earth, cold as to plants;[3] then, as the snow falls around, then is the direst disaster.

Avesta.

5. As the second best of regions[4] and countries, I, who am Ahuramazda, produced Gâu, in which Sughdha is

---

[1] The disconnected phrases which constitute ver. 2 are evidently fragments of an old Avesta commentary, either quoted by the Pahlavi translator, or left untranslated by him, and must be read as portions of the commentary, not as part of the text. The Pahlavi commentary, which contains these Avesta phrases, is rather obscure, but evidently refers to the general arrangement of the after part of the fargard, as well as to the details of the first sentence.

[2] The Pahlavi translator adds:

"and afterwards also *hapta hêñti hāminô mâoṇhá, pañcha zayana* (seven are the summer months, five the winter) is declared."

[3] The phrase *adha zimahê maidhîm, adha zimahê zaredhaêm* (then is midwinter, then is the heart of winter), not being translated by the Pahlavi commentator, appears to be merely quoted by him from some older Avesta commentary.

[4] That is, "second of the best regions."

situated. Thereupon, as an opposition to it, Angrômainyush, the deadly, formed a pestilence [1] which is fatal to cattle great and small.

6. As the third best of regions and countries, I, who am Ahuramazda, produced Môuru (Marv), the strong, the righteous. Thereupon, as an opposition to it, Angrômainyush, the deadly, formed war and pillage.

7. As the fourth best of regions and countries, I, who am Ahuramazda, produced fortunate Bâkhdhi (Bactria), with the lofty banner. Thereupon, as an opposition to it, Angrô-mainyush, the deadly, formed buzzing insects and poisonous plants.

8. As the fifth best of regions and countries, I, who am Ahuramazda, produced Nisâi (Nisæa), [(Zend) which is between Môuru and Bâkhdhi]. Thereupon, as an opposition to it, Angrô-mainyush, the deadly, formed the curse of unbelief.

9. As the sixth best of regions and countries, I, who am Ahuramazda, produced Harôyu (Herat), the water-diffusing.[2] Thereupon, as an opposition to it, Angrômainyush, the deadly, formed hail and poverty.

10. As the seventh best of regions and countries, I, who am Ahuramazda, produced Vaêkereta,[3] in which Duzhaka is situated. Thereupon, as an opposition to it, Angrômainyush, the deadly, formed the witch (*pairika*, " malevolent fairy ") Khnâthaiti, who attached herself to Keresâspa.

11. As the eighth best of regions and countries, I, who am Ahuramazda, produced Urvâ,[4] abounding in pasture. Thereupon, as an opposition to it, Angrô-mainyush, the deadly, formed the curse of devastation.[5]

---

[1] The Pahlavi translation has *kûrako mêg*, " a swarm of locusts."

[2] The Pahlavi translator calls it "the village-deserting; and its village-desertion is this, where we keep the periods of nine nights and a month, they desert the house as evil, and go away:" that is, they deserted polluted houses altogether, and did not believe in their becoming purified after a certain lapse of time. Herat is called Hariva in the cuneiform inscriptions.

[3] Probably Sajastân; though the Pahlavi translator identifies it with Kabul.

[4] Perhaps Kabul.

[5] Perhaps "evil invasions."

12. As the ninth best of regions and countries, I, who am Ahuramazda, produced Khneūta,[1] in which Vehrkâna is situated. Thereupon, as an opposition to it, Angrô-mainyush, the deadly, formed the evil, inexpiable deeds of pæderastism.

13. As the tenth best of regions and countries, I, who am Ahuramazda, produced the fortunate Haraqaiti.[2] Thereupon, as an opposition to it, Angrô-mainyush, the deadly, formed the evil, inexpiable deeds of burying the dead.

14. As the eleventh best of regions and countries, I, who am Ahuramazda, produced Haêtumat,[3] the brilliant, the glorious. Thereupon, as an opposition to it, Angrô-mainyush, the deadly, formed evil sorceries.

Zend.

15. And this was its essential token, this (its) essential appearance; as wherever they attained the sorcery of incantation, then are the worst sorceries, then those even arise which are for murder and wounding the heart; they are capable of any blights and potions.[4]

Avesta.

16. As the twelfth best of regions and countries, I, who am Ahuramazda, produced Ragha with the three races.[5] Thereupon, as an opposition to it, Angrô-mainyush, the deadly, formed the curse of over-scepticism.

17. As the thirteenth best of regions and countries, I,

---

[1] Possibly Kandahar.
[2] The Harauvati of the cuneiform inscriptions, and Arachosia of the classics.
[3] The modern Hilmand, and Etymander of the classics.
[4] These phrases are evidently the remains of an old Zend in the Avesta language, the first portion of which is given by the Pahlavi translator only in Pahlavi, while he gives these phrases in both languages. This old Zend, or commentary, as translated into Pahlavi, states that 'sorcery is 'this, that although they desire it 'not, yet it happens, and then it is 'said that it is in a way not allow-'able;' &c. [as in ver. 15 in the text].
[5] The Pahlavi explains the three races as the three original classes of the community: the priests, warriors, and husbandmen. The extra phrase *vaêdhanhô nôid uzôish* is to be taken probably in connection with the end of the Pahlavi commentary.

who am Ahuramazda, produced Chakhra, the strong, the righteous. Thereupon, as an opposition to it, Angrômainyush, the deadly, formed the evil, inexpiable deeds of burning the dead.

18. As the fourteenth best of regions and countries, I, who am Ahuramazda, produced Varena, which is four-cornered;[1] at which was born Thraêtaona (Frêdûn), the slayer of the destructive serpent (Azhi-Dahâk). Thereupon, as an opposition to it, Angrô-mainyush, the deadly, formed untimely menstruations, and non-Aryan plagues of the country.[2]

19. As the fifteenth best of regions and countries, I, who am Ahuramazda, produced (the land) of the seven rivers (India).[3] Thereupon, as an opposition to it, Angrô-mainyush, the deadly, formed untimely menstruations, and irregular fever.

20. As the sixteenth best of regions and countries, I, who am Ahuramazda, produced those who dwell without ramparts on the sea-coast. Thereupon, as an opposition to it, Angrô-mainyush, the deadly, formed frost caused by the Devas, and hoar-frost as a covering of the land.

Zend.

21. There are also other fortunate regions and countries, valleys and hills, and extensive plains.

2. The Second Fargard.

(*Yima, or Jamshêd, the King of the Golden Age.*)

Avesta.

1. Zarathushtra asked Ahuramazda: O Ahuramazda!

---

[1] Varena is probably Ghîlân; but the Pahlavi translator states that some say it is Kirmân, and that it was called four-cornered because it had either four roads, or four gates.

[2] Perhaps "non-Aryan invasions of the country."

[3] Hapta Hindu is the *sapta-sind-havas* of the Vedas, a name of the Indus country, or India. The additional phrase: *hacha ushastara Hiñdva avi daoshatarem Hiñdum*, "from the eastern (lit. more morning) Hindu to the western (lit. more evening) Hindu," is merely an Avesta phrase quoted by the Pahlavi translator.

most munificent Spirit, creator of the settlements supplied with creatures, righteous one! with what man didst thou, who art Ahuramazda, first converse, besides me, who am Zarathushtra (*i.e.*, before me)? [(Pâzand) to whom didst thou teach the Ahuryan, Zoroastrian faith?]

2. Then said Ahuramazda: With Yima, the fortunate, the rich in flocks, O righteous Zarathushtra! with him I, who am Ahuramazda, conversed first among men, besides thee (*i.e.*, before thee), who art Zarathushtra. [(Pâzand) to him I taught the Ahuryan, Zoroastrian faith.]

3. Then I said to him, O Zarathushtra! I, who am Ahuramazda: Become, O fortunate Yima Vîvanghana! my promulgator and bearer of the faith (the Zoroastrian religion). Then he, the fortunate Yima, answered me, O Zarathushtra! Neither am I fit, nor known, as promulgator and bearer of the faith.

4. Then I said to him, O Zarathushtra! I, who am Ahuramazda: If thou, O Yima! wilt not become my promulgator and bearer of the faith, then enclose my settlements; then thou shalt become the conservator and the herdsman and the protector of my settlements.

5. Then he, the fortunate Yima, answered me, O Zarathushtra! I will enclose[1] thy settlements; I will become the conservator and the herdsman and the protector of thy settlements; in my empire there shall be no cold wind nor hot, no fog, no death.[2]

7. Then I, who am Ahuramazda, brought forth his implements, a golden sword[3] and a goad decorated with gold. Yima is to bear the royal dignity.

8. Then the sway was given to Yima for three hundred winters (*i.e.*, years). Then his earth was to be filled with

---

[1] Or "enlarge, extend."
[2] The phrases which constitute ver. 6 are merely Avesta passages quoted by the Pahlavi commentator in support of his statements, and form no part of the text.
[3] In Pahlavi *sûlâk-hômand*, "having holes, a sieve," which supports the view that *sufra*=Sans. *shûrpa*, "winnowing tray." A ploughshare would be *sâlak* (not *sûlâk*) in Pahlavi.

cattle, oxen, men, dogs, birds, and red blazing fires. They found no room therein, the cattle, oxen, and men.

9. Then I made known to Yima: O fortunate Yima Vîvanghana! the earth is to be filled with the assemblage of cattle, oxen, men, dogs, birds, and red blazing fires. They find no room therein, the cattle, oxen, and men.

10. Then Yima went forth towards the stars on the sun's noonday path;[1] he touched this earth with the golden sword, he pierced into it with the goad, speaking thus: Extend, O bounteous Armaiti! enlarge and spread, O bearer of cattle and oxen and men!

11. Then Yima made the earth expand herself by one-third larger than she was before; there the cattle and oxen and men walk according to their own will and pleasure, [(Pâzand) just as it is their pleasure].

Zend.

12–15. Then the sway was given to Yima for six hundred winters, &c. [as in ver. 8–11, but substituting "two-thirds" for "one-third"].

16–19. Then the sway was given to Yima for nine hundred winters, &c. [as in ver. 8–11, but substituting "to three-thirds" for "by one-third"].[2]

Avesta.

21. An assembly was held with the heavenly angels by Ahuramazda, the creator, the renowned in Airyana-vaêjô of good qualities.

Zend.

An assembly was held, with the best men, by Yima, the king, rich in flocks, the renowned in Airyana-vaêjô of good qualities. To this assembly, with the heavenly angels, came Ahuramazda, the creator, the renowned in Airyana-vaêjô of good qualities.

---

[1] That is, towards the south; *rapithwa* means the time called *gâh rapithwan*, lasting from 10 A.M. to 3 P.M.

[2] The phrases constituting ver. 20 are merely Avesta passages quoted by the Pahlavi commentator, and form no part of the text.

Avesta.

To this assembly, with the best men, came Yima, the king, rich in flocks, the renowned in Airyana-vaêjô of good qualities.

22. Then spake Ahuramazda to Yima: O fortunate Yima Vîvanghana! unto the material world the evil of winter will come, and consequently a strong, deadly frost.

Zend.

Unto the material world the evil of winter will come; consequently much driving snow will fall on the highest mountains, on the summits of the heights.

23. From three places, O Yima! the cows should go away, when they are in the most baneful of places (deserts), and when they are on the tops of the mountains, and when in the gorges of the valleys, into the well-fastened cottages.

Avesta.

24. Before the winter the produce of this country was pasturage; the water used before to overflow it, and afterwards the melting of the snow, and pools would occur there, O Yima! in the material world, where the footprints of cattle and their young would appear.

25. Then make that enclosure the length of a riding-ground on each of the four sides; bring thither the seeds of cattle, oxen, men, dogs, birds, and red blazing fires.

Zend.

Then make that enclosure the length of a riding-ground on each of the four sides, for a dwelling-place of men; the length of a riding-ground on each of the four sides, as a field for cows (a cattle-run).

Avesta.

26. There collect the water into a channel the size of a Hâthra;[1] there fix land-marks on a gold-coloured spot

[1] A measure equivalent to a Farsang of one thousand footsteps of two feet; see Bund. p. 63.

(provided) with imperishable food; there erect houses (composed of) mats and poles and roofs and walls.

Zend.

27. Thither bring the seeds of all men and women who are the greatest and best and finest on this earth. Thither bring the seeds of all kinds of cattle which are the greatest and best and finest on this earth.

28. Thither bring the seeds of all plants which are the tallest and most odoriferous on this earth. Thither bring the seeds of all foods which are the most eatable and most odoriferous on this earth. Make pairs of them unceasingly, in order that these men may exist in the enclosures.

Avesta.

29. There shall be no overbearing, no low-spiritedness, no stupidity, no violence, no poverty, no deceit, no dwarfishness, no deformity, no monstrous teeth, no leprosy overspreading the body, nor any of the other signs which are the badge of Angrô-mainyush, and are laid upon men.

30. In the uppermost part of the country make nine bridges, in the middle six, in the lowermost three. To the bridges in the uppermost part bring the seeds of a thousand men and women, to those of the middle part six hundred, to those of the lowermost part three hundred; and compass them in the enclosures with the golden sword,[1] and furnish a door to the enclosure, (and) a self-lighting window from the inside.

31. Then Yima considered: How shall I make the enclosure as Ahuramazda told me? Then Ahuramazda spoke to Yima: O fortunate Yima Vîvanghana! distend this earth with the heels, rend it with the hands, like as men now separate the earth in cultivating.

32. Then Yima did so as Ahuramazda desired; he dis-

---

[1] If this implement be a plough it would surround them with a furrow, but this would not be a very effectual enclosure. If the implement be a winnowing-tray, they are to be covered over with it.

tended this earth with the heels, he rent it with the hands, like as men now separate the earth in cultivating.[1]

33-38. Then Yima made the enclosure, &c. [corresponding to ver. 25-30].

Zend.

39. Creator of the settlements supplied with creatures, righteous one! Which then are those lights, O righteous Ahuramazda! which shine there in those enclosures which Yima made?

40. Then spake Ahuramazda: Self-created lights and created ones. [(Pâzand) All the eternal lights shine up above, all created lights shine below from inside.] Once (a year) one sees there the stars and moon and sun rising and setting.

41. And they think that a day which is a year. Every forty years two human beings are born from two human beings, [(Pâzand) a pair, female and male]. So also with those which are of the cattle species. Those men enjoy the greatest happiness in these enclosures which Yima made.

42. Creator of the settlements supplied with creatures, righteous one! Who propagated there the Mazdayasnian religion in these enclosures which Yima made? Then spake Ahuramazda: The bird Karshipta, O Spitama Zarathushtra!

43. Creator of the settlements supplied with creatures, righteous one! Who is their heavenly lord and earthly master? Then said Ahuramazda: Urvatad-narô, O Zarathushtra! and thou who art Zarathushtra.

3. THE THIRD FARGARD.

(*The Holiness of Agriculture,* Vend. iii. 24-33.)

Avesta.

24. For this earth is not a place which is to lie long un-

[1] This verse is found only in the Vendidâd Sâdah, and is probably an addition made by the Zendist.

cultivated. She is to be ploughed by the ploughman, that she may be for them (men) a habitation of a good (kind). Then the beautiful woman (the earth), who long goes childless, so (produces) for them male progeny (bulls) of a good (kind).

Zend.

25. Whoever cultivates this earth, O Spitama Zarathushtra! with the left arm and the right, with the right arm and the left, unto him she bears fruit; in like manner as a loving man does to (his) beloved, she stretched on the connubial couch [(Pâzand) lying on a place [1]] brings forth to him a son [(Pâzand) or fruit].

26. Whoever cultivates this earth, O Spitama Zarathushtra! with the left arm and the right, with the right arm and the left, then speaks the earth to him: O man! who cultivatest me with the left arm and the right, with the right arm and the left, (27) I will, indeed, prosper the countries here, I will, indeed, come to bear all nourishments here; [(Pâzand) may they (the fields) yield a full crop besides barley].

28. Whoever does not cultivate this earth, O Spitama Zarathustra! with the left arm and the right, with the right arm and the left, then speaks the earth to him: O man! who dost not cultivate me with the left arm and the right, with the right arm and the left, (29) here thou standest, indeed, at another's door obtaining victuals [(Pâzand) among the beggars], and victuals are brought to thee, sitting outside, indeed, in driblets. [(Pâzand) They are brought to thee by those who have abundance of goods.]

30. Creator, &c., [as in ii. 39]: What causes the growth of the Mazdayasnian religion? Then said Ahuramazda: Whatever is efficacious in the cultivation of barley, O Spitama Zarathushtra!

---

[1] The words *gâtush sayamnô* are an explanation of the older phrase *rañtavê starcta; gâtush,* "place," explaining *rañtavê,* and *starcta,* "stretched," corresponding to *say-* *amnô. Vañtu* evidently appertains to *rañta,* which is defined as "a virtuous woman" in the Farhang-i Oim-khadûk.

VENDIDAD, FARGARD III. 237

31. Whoever cultivates barley, he cultivates righteousness, [(Pâzand) he promotes the Mazdayasnian religion], he extends this Mazdayasnian religion as by a hundred resistances (against the demons), a thousand offerings, ten thousand prayer-readings.[1]

Avesta.

32. When barley occurs,[2] then the demons hiss;
When thrashing occurs, then the demons whine;
When grinding occurs, then the demons roar;
When flour occurs, then the demons flee.

Zend.

So the demons are driven out from the place [(Pâzand] in the house for this flour]; they shall burn their jaws, whereby it happens that the greater number are fellow-fugitives when barley becomes plentiful.

33. Then may he (the cultivator), therefore, recite the text:

Avesta.

There is no strength in those who do not eat,
Neither for vigorous righteousness,
Nor for vigorous husbandry,
Nor for vigorous begetting of sons.
[(Pâzand) For by eating all living beings exist; without eating they must die.]

4. THE FOURTH FARGARD.

(*Civil and Criminal Laws.*)

Avesta.

1. Whoever does not return property to the owner of the property, becomes a thief of the property, taking it by

[1] Cultivation of barley, or wheat, is equivalent, so far as the destruction of the bad creation (the duty of every Zoroastrian) is concerned, to 100, 1000, and 10,000 other meritorious works.

[2] The original is in metrical verses, which contain even rhymes.

force,[1] if he seize for his own out of anything of theirs agreed upon, whether by day or by night.

Zend.

2. Creator of the settlements supplied with creatures, righteous one! how many such agreements (*mithra*) are thine, who art Ahuramazda? Then said Ahuramazda: Six, O righteous Zarathushtra! The first by words, the second by offering the hand, the third by (depositing) the value of a sheep, the fourth by (depositing) the value of an ox, the fifth by (depositing) the value of a man (slave), the sixth by (depositing) the value of a district [(Pâzand) of a well-thriving, fenced-in, walled-in, well-arranged, prosperous district].

3, 4. The word makes the first agreement (promise). After that, the offering of the hand is marked, [(Pâzand) the offering of the hand takes place after that among friends]; after that, that of a sheep's value is marked, [(Pâzand) that of a sheep's value takes place among friends]; after that, that of an ox's value is marked, [(Pâzand) that of an ox's value takes place among friends]; after that, that of a man's value is marked, [(Pâzand) that of a man's value takes place among friends]; after that, that of a district's value is marked, [(Pâzand) that of a district's value takes place among friends].

5. Creator of the settlements supplied with creatures, righteous one! What punishment has the breaker of an agreement, made by words, to undergo? Then said Ahuramazda: He has to pay a fine of 300 pieces to the next kinsmen (of the defrauded one).

(The fine varies from 300 to 1000 pieces; the breaking of the second class of agreement is fined by 600, that of the third by 700, that of the fourth by 800, that of the fifth by 900, and that of the sixth by 1000 pieces of atonement money.)

---

[1] The phrase *yad nâ kasvikâmchana* translator, and forms no part of the is merely quoted by the Pahlavi text.

Pâzand.

11. Creator of the settlements supplied with creatures, righteous one! Whoever violates an agreement made by words, what is his punishment? Then said Ahuramazda: One may give him three hundred blows with a horse-goad [(later Pâzand) three hundred with a whip].

(According to this Pâzand the number of blows varies from three hundred to one thousand, exactly in the same order as in the Zend above.)

Avesta.

17. When a man's weapon rises, that is his attempt (*âgereptem*); when it assails, that is his assault (*avaoirishtem*); when it penetrates any one with evil intention, that is his perpetration (of manslaughter, *aredush*); at the fifth perpetration the man forfeits himself (his life).

What follows (ver. 18–42) is Pâzand, which, as to its character, is completely in accordance with the Pâzand in ver. 11–16. The Zend or old explanation of this criminal law is lost, but from this Pâzand it may be seen that the distinctions regarding the degree of guilt in attempted or accomplished murder, have become in course of time much more numerous. In the old text or Avesta, as quoted above (ver. 17), there are only three degrees distinguished, namely, *âgereptem*, or attempt; *avaoirishtem*, or assault; and *aredush*, or perpetration. In its Zend or commentary there were probably more distinctions made, and different degrees of punishment mentioned, as we may infer from the Zend following ver. 1. In this Avesta capital punishment is ordered only when *aredush* has been committed five times. In the Pâzand or sub-commentary there is a detailed list of punishments, consisting of blows with a horse-goad or whip, varying from five to two hundred in number.

Towards the end of the fourth Fargard (ver. 44–54), we have only Avesta without Zend or commentary. This

Avesta, which is certainly very old, and refers apparently to various subjects, is so very obscure in style as to be the most difficult passage of the whole Vendidad. In its beginning there is an ancient law, enjoining the greatest friendship and equality among the members of the Zoroastrian community. It runs as follows: 'And when men 'of the same (Mazdayasnian) religion should come here, 'either brothers or friends, seeking a field, or seeking a 'wife, or seeking wisdom, if they should come seeking a 'field, they may acquire their field here, if they should come 'seeking a wife, you may make some of the women marry; 'if they should come seeking wisdom, you may recite the 'beneficent texts.'

5. THE FARGARDS V.-XVII.

From the fifth to the eighth Fargard, we find very minute and detailed precepts for the treatment of a dead body, the construction of Dakhmas or "towers of silence," and the purification of men or things brought into contact with a corpse. The idea pervading the whole is the utter impurity of a dead body, and the extreme purity and sacredness of earth, fire, and water. No impure thing can, therefore, be thrown upon any one of these elements, because it would spoil the good creation by increasing the power and influence of the *daévas* or demons, who take possession of the body as soon as a man is dead. The corpse is, therefore, to be carried on to the barren top of a mountain or hill, and to be placed on stones (or iron plates), and exposed to dogs and vultures, so as to benefit in this way the animals of the good creation. A man who touches a dead body, the contagious impurity of which has not been previously checked by holding towards the corpse a peculiar kind of dog,[1] is said to be at once visited by a

---

[1] Which is called "the four-eyed dog," a yellow spot on each of its eyelids being considered an additional eye. He has yellow ears, and the colour of the rest of his body varies from yellow to white. To his eyes a kind of magnetic influence is ascribed.

spectre, representing death itself. This is called *drukhsh nasush*, "the destructive corruption." To get rid of this annoyance he is to be sprinkled with water on the different parts of his body, as described with the greatest minuteness in the eighth Fargard.

In the same Fargard (vers. 73–96) the preparation of the sacred fire is described. Fires from sixteen different places are required, which, after having been purified by praying over them, must be brought to one and the same hearth (called *dâityô-gâtush*, now *Dâdgâh*). The fire in which a dead body is being burnt is indispensable; although it be the most impure of all,[1] it is believed to have absorbed the fire (heat or electricity) which was in the animal body. It is called *nasupâka*, and its obtainment and purification by putting it into a certain number of holes called *hañdarcza* (Persian *andâzah*, "a measure"), which requires much trouble, are more minutely described than the acquisition of the other fires (those of dyers, potters, glassworkers, blacksmiths, bricklayers, &c.). The collective fire obtained in this way represents the essence of nature, the fluid pervading the whole earth, the cause of all growth, vigour, and splendour, and it is, therefore, regarded with great reverence by the Parsis.

In the ninth Fargard there is a very detailed description of the great purification ceremony, called the "Barashnom of nine nights," which lasts for nine days (or rather nights). It is intended for the removal of any impurity whatever, and is practised chiefly by priests. The person who has to undergo the ceremony must drink the urine of a cow, sit on stones within the compass of certain magic circles, and while moving from one heap of stones to another he must rub his body with cow's urine, then with sand, and lastly wash it with water. This custom has descended from the most ancient times, when a purifying and healing influence

---

[1] To burn a dead body is, according to the spirit of the Zoroastrian law, one of the greatest crimes.

was ascribed to the urine proceeding from so sacred an animal as the cow was to the ancient Aryans.[1]

In the tenth and eleventh Fargards prayers are enumerated, which were believed to have the power of removing the impurity caused by contact with a dead body. All these prayers are to be found in the older part of the Yasna.

The twelfth Fargard treats of the duration of mourning for the death of the head of a family, and of relations in different degrees. For those who die as righteous men by the law of nature (who are called *dahmas*) only half as much time of mourning is required as for those who die by their own hands, or are executed (who are called *tanu-perethas*).

The thirteenth and fourteenth Fargards treat of dogs and water-dogs (*udra*, "otter"), which are not to be badly treated, wounded, mutilated, starved, or killed. Should a man be found guilty of such charges, he is to be severely punished. The killing of an otter is especially regarded as a horrible crime, since this animal is believed to contain the souls of a thousand male and a thousand female dogs. A man who commits this crime has to receive ten thousand lashes with a horsewhip, according to the later interpretation; or he must kill ten thousand animals of the bad creation, such as snakes, mice, lizards, frogs, &c., and carry ten thousand loads of wood to the fire, &c.

In the fifteenth Fargard various topics are treated, such as the sins called *peshô-tanu* (*i.e.*, such actions as are not of themselves considered specially hurtful or injurious, but which may under certain circumstances cause damage or injury), the crime of procuring abortion in the case of an illegitimate child,[2] and the treatment of pregnant dogs.

The whole sixteenth Fargard is devoted to the treatment of women at the time of their menstruation.

---

[1] Cow's urine was probably a metaphorical name for "rain-water" originally—the clouds being cows metaphorically.

[2] This is strictly prohibited, and if it be committed, the seducer, the girl, and the nurse, are equally guilty of the murder.

In the seventeenth Fargard precepts are given how to treat hair and nails which have been cut. The demons must be prevented from using the cuttings for doing injury to the good creation.

6.—THE EIGHTEENTH FARGARD.

The commencement of this Fargard is probably lost, as it appears to begin now in the middle of a subject; and its contents are of a very miscellaneous character, as may be seen from the following translation:—

1. For many a man—so said Ahuramazda: O righteous Zarathushtra! wears another mouth-veil[1] (penôm, though) unclothed with religion; falsely he is termed a fire-priest; thou shouldst not call him a fire-priest,—so said Ahuramazda: O righteous Zarathushtra![2]

2. He carries another vermin-killer[3] (khrafstraghna, though) unclothed with religion; falsely he is termed a fire-priest; thou shouldst not call him a fire-priest,—so said Ahuramazda: O righteous Zarathushtra![4]

3. He carries another plant[5] (as barsom, though) unclothed with religion; falsely he is termed a fire-priest; thou shouldst not call him a fire-priest,—so said Ahuramazda: O righteous Zarathushtra!

4. He wields the deadly poniard (for sacrificing, though) unclothed with religion; falsely he is termed a fire-priest;

---

[1] That is, not the kind of mouth-veil used by priests. The paitidâna, "a putting-on, a mouth-veil" (Pahl. padâm, Pâz. penôm), consists of two pieces of white cotton cloth, hanging loosely from the bridge of the nose to at least two inches below the mouth, and tied with two strings at the back of the head. It must be worn by a priest whenever he approaches the sacred fire, so as to prevent his breath from contaminating the fire. On certain occasions a layman has to use a substitute for the penôm by screening his mouth and nose with a portion of his muslin shirt.

[2] The extra words baê-crezu-frathaŋhem, "two fingers' breadth," are merely an Avesta quotation, made by the Pahlavi translator, with reference to the extent of the Penôm.

[3] That is, not the kind used by priests. The krafstraghna was some implement that has now gone out of use.

[4] The two additional phrases are quoted by the Pahlavi translator.

[5] This seems to refer to the use of twigs of any improper plant for the sacred barsom.

thou shouldst not call him a fire-priest,—so said Ahuramazda: O righteous Zarathushtra!

5. Whoever lies the whole night through without praying, without reciting (the Gâthas), without repeating (the short prayers), without performing (any ceremony), without studying, without teaching,[1] in order to acquire a soul fit for the Chinvaḍ (bridge),[2] falsely he is termed a fire-priest; thou shouldst not call him a fire-priest,—so said Ahuramazda: O righteous Zarathushtra!

6. Thou shouldst call him the fire-priest—so said Ahuramazda: O righteous Zarathushtra!—who, the whole night through, would interrogate a righteous understanding, free from anxiety (or defect), fit for the widening (and) gratifying[3] Chinvaḍ bridge, (and) obtaining the life, righteousness, and perfection of the best life (paradise).

7. Inquire, O just one! of me who am the Creator, the most munificent, the wisest, and the readiest replier to questions; so will it be better for thee, so wilt thou be more beneficent, if thou wilt inquire of me.

8. Zarathushtra asked Ahuramazda: O Ahuramazda! most munificent spirit, creator of the settlements supplied with creatures, righteous one! through what is one a criminal worthy of death?

9, 10. Then said Ahuramazda: By teaching an evil religion, O Spitama Zarathushtra! Whoever, during three spring seasons, does not put on the sacred thread-girdle (*kustî*),[4] does not recite the Gâthas, does not reverence the good waters, and whoever sets this man,[5] delivered into my custody, again at large, thereby performs no better

---

[1] Or, perhaps, "without studying the accents, and without intoning them:" comp. Sans. *shikshâ*.

[2] That is, a soul so good that it will find the Chinvaḍ bridge wide enough to allow it to pass over it to heaven. If the soul be wicked it is said to find the bridge too narrow for it to pass over.

[3] Or, perhaps, "assisting," "serviceable."

[4] The Parsis wear the *kustî* as an indispensable symbol of their religion; it is formed of seventy-two fine woollen threads twisted together.

[5] Who neglects his duties as before stated, and so incurs punishment or tribulation.

work than if he should cut the extent of the skin off his head.¹

11. For the prayer of one heretical, evil, unrighteous (man) lengthens the chin; (that) of two lengthens the tongue; of three there is no (such prayer) whatever; four invoke themselves.²

12. Whoever gives of the out-squeezed Hom-juice, or of the consecrated meats, to one heretical, evil, unrighteous (man), thereby performs no better work than if he should lead a troop of a thousand horse into the Mazdayasnian villages, should slay the men, and should drive away the cattle as booty.

13. Inquire, O just one! &c. [as in ver. 7].

14. Zarathushtra asked, &c. [as in ver. 8, to] righteous one! who is the dutiful attendant (*sraoshâvareza*) of Srosh the righteous, the mighty, the embodiment of the sacred word, the impetuous runner?

15-17. Then said Ahuramazda: The bird named Parô-darsh, O Spitama Zarathushtra! which evil-speaking men call by the name Kahrkatâs.³ Moreover, this bird raises (its) voice at the approach of dawn⁴ (thus): Arise ye men! praise the righteousness which is most perfect; repulsed are the demons; this one oppresses you, Bûshyâsta⁵ the long-handed, she lulls to sleep the whole living creation after it is awakened by the light (saying): Sleep long, O man! it befits thee not (to rise); trouble not about the three best things, the well-considered thought, the well-spoken word, and the well-done action; (but) trouble about the three worst things, the ill-considered thought, the ill-spoken word, and the ill-done action.

18, 19. Moreover, for the first third of the night, my fire

---

¹ That is, should scalp him.
² The meaning of this verse is very obscure, and the text may be defective.
³ A nickname of the domestic cock.
⁴ The term *ushâm sûrâm* is given as a name for the third quarter of the night in the Farhang-i Oîm-khadûk.
⁵ The demoness personifying unseasonable sleep and lethargy.

of Ahuramazda [1] entreats the master of the house (saying): Arise to help, O master of the house! put on thy clothes, wash thy hands, fetch firewood, bring it to me, with washed hands make me blaze again by means of purified firewood; the demon-formed Azi (covetousness) may get at me, he seems clinging around (my) life.

20, 21. Then for the second third of the night, my fire of Ahuramazda entreats the husbandman (saying): Arise to help, O husbandman! put on thy clothes, &c. [as in ver. 19].

22. Then for the third third of the night, my fire of Ahuramazda entreats Srosh the righteous (saying): Arise to help, O righteous, handsome Srosh! does one bring to me any of the purified firewoods of the material world with washed hands? the demon-formed Azi may get at me, he seems clinging around (my) life.

23–25. Then he, Srosh the righteous, wakes the bird named Parô-darsh, &c. [as in vers. 15–17].

26. Then speaks each of two companions lying on a bed: Do thou arise! he (the cock) drives me away; whichever of the two rises first will attain to the best life (paradise); whichever of the two brings to the fire of Ahuramazda (some) of the purified firewoods with washed hands, him will the fire, pleased (and) unharmed, bless in the following manner:

27. May a herd of cattle accompany thee! (and so) may a multitude of men (sons)! may an active mind and an active life attend thee! mayst thou subsist with an existence of the nature of (this) blessing, so many nights as thou shalt live! This is the blessing of the fire for him who brings dry firewood, selected for burning, (and) purified by the utterance of the Ashem (-vohu formula).

28. And whoever had given away, with perfect rectitude, these my birds, O Spitama Zarathushtra! in a pair, male and female, to a righteous man, may consider his

---

[1] That is, my sacred fire, often called the son, or offspring, of Ahuramazda.

gift a mansion with a hundred columns, a thousand girders, ten thousand rooms,[1] (and) ten thousand windows.

29. And whoever had given a morsel [2] of flesh to this my bird Parô-darsh, I who am Ahuramazda shall never be asking him a second word, forth I will depart to the best life (paradise).

30. The righteous Srosh, with lowered club, asked the Drukhsh: O Drukhsh, inglorious (and) inactive! dost thou then alone of all the living creation engender without cohabitation?

31, 32. Thereupon, she who is the fiendish Drukhsh answered him: O righteous, handsome Srosh! I do not alone of all the living creation engender without cohabitation: indeed I have even four paramours; they cohabit with me just as any other males cohabit with females for progeny.

33. The righteous Srosh, with lowered club, asked the Drukhsh: O Drukhsh, inglorious (and) inactive! who is the first of these thy paramours?

34, 35. Thereupon, she who is the fiendish Drukhsh answered him: O righteous, handsome Srosh! that, indeed, is the first of these my paramours, when a man gives not the merest trifle of unused clothes to a righteous man (when they are) begged for with perfect rectitude, he cohabits with me just as, &c. [as in ver. 32].

36. The righteous Srosh, with lowered club, asked the Drukhsh: O Drukhsh, inglorious (and) inactive! what is the extermination of (the result of) this?

37, 38. Thereupon, she who is the fiendish Drukhsh answered him: O righteous, handsome Srosh! this is the extermination of it, when the man gives even a trifle of unused clothes to a righteous man (when they) are not begged for with perfect rectitude, he destroys my concep-

---

[1] The exact meaning of the words translated "rooms" and "windows" is very uncertain.
[2] The words *tanu mazô* may be otherwise translated, but hardly so as to make sense out of all parts of the sentence. The flesh would pollute the cock if he ate it.

tions just as a four-legged wolf would utterly tear a child out of the womb.

39. The righteous Srosh, with lowered club, asked the Drukhsh: O Drukhsh, inglorious (and) inactive! who is the second of these thy paramours?

40, 41. Thereupon, she who is the fiendish Drukhsh answered him: O righteous, handsome Srosh! that, indeed, is the second of these my paramours, when a man makes water an instep's length beyond the toes;[1] he cohabits with me just as, &c. [as in ver. 32].

42. The righteous Srosh, &c. [as in ver. 36].

43, 44. Thereupon, she who is the fiendish Drukhsh answered him: O righteous, handsome Srosh! this is the extermination of it, when the man, after he shall stand up,[2] shall repeat, three steps off, the Ashem (-vohu formula) thrice, the Humatanām (Yas. xxxv. 2) twice, the Hukhshathrôtemâi (Yas. xxxv. 5) thrice, shall then recite the Ahuna-vairya (Yas. xxvii. 13) four times, (and) shall pray Yênhê-hâtām (Yas. vii. 27); he destroys my conceptions, &c. [as in ver. 38].

45. The righteous Srosh, with lowered club, asked the Drukhsh: O Drukhsh, inglorious (and) inactive! who is the third of these thy paramours?

46, 47. Thereupon, she who is the fiendish Drukhsh answered him: O righteous, handsome Srosh! that, indeed, is the third of these my paramours, when a man asleep emits semen; he cohabits with me just as, &c. [as in ver. 32].

48. The righteous Srosh, &c. [as in ver. 36].

49-52. Thereupon, she who is the fiendish Drukhsh answered him: O righteous, handsome Srosh! this is the extermination of it, when the man, after waking from sleep, shall repeat the Ashem (-vohu formula) thrice, &c.

---

[1] Literally: 'the length of the 'fore-part of the foot beyond the 'fore-part of the foot;' *frabda* (Sans. *prapada*), "the fore-part of the foot," is understood to be a measure equivalent to a hand's-breadth.

[2] From the squatting position (resting merely on the soles of the feet) which is customary in such cases.

[as in vers. 43, 44]. Then he speaks to the bountiful Armaiti (spirit of the earth): O bountiful Armaiti! I commit to thee this progeny (lit. man), mayst thou restore this progeny to me at the triumphant renovation (of creation, at the resurrection)! as one knowing the Gâthas, knowing the Yasna, attending to the discourses,[1] intellectual, experienced, embodying the sacred word. Then thou shouldst announce his name as Fire-produced (*âtare-dâta*), or Fire-offspring (*âtare-chithra*), or Fire-race (*âtare-zañtu*), or Fire-land (*âtare-daqyu*), or any other name of (those) formed with (the word) Fire.[2]

53. The righteous Srosh, with lowered club, asked the Drukhsh: O Drukhsh, inglorious (and) inactive! who is the fourth of these thy paramours?

54, 55. Thereupon, she who is the fiendish Drukhsh answered him: O righteous, handsome Srosh! that, indeed, is the fourth of these my paramours, when a man, after (his) fifteenth year, frequents a courtezan, ungirdled or uncovered,[3] then at the fourth departing step, immediately afterwards, we who are demons, at once we occupy (his) tongue and marrow; afterwards the possessed ones destroy the settlements of righteousness (which are) supplied with creatures, as the spells of sorcerers destroy the settlements of righteousness.

56. The righteous Srosh, &c. [as in ver. 36].

57-59. Thereupon, she who is the fiendish Drukhsh answered him: O righteous, handsome Srosh! there is no extermination whatever of it; when a man, after (his) fifteenth year, &c. [as in vers. 54, 55].

60. Inquire, O just one! &c. [as in ver. 7].

61. Zarathushtra asked, &c. [as in ver. 8, to] righteous one! who offends thee, who art Ahuramazda, with the

---

[1] Or "conversations," referring probably to such conversations between Ahuramazda and Zarathushtra as are common in the Vendidad.

[2] The same kind of names, according to Dastur Hoshangji, ought to be used for still-born children, who must all be named.

[3] That is, without sacred thread-girdle (*kustî*) or sacred shirt (*sadarah*); *anabdâtô* is a contraction of *anaiwi-dâtô*.

greatest offence? [(Zend) who annoys (thee) with the greatest annoyance?]

62. Then said Ahuramazda: Truly the courtezan, O righteous Zarathushtra! who commingles the seed of the pious and impious, of idolaters and non-idolaters, of self-destroying sinners and non-self-destroying sinners (*i.e.*, those whose sins are heinous and mortal and the reverse).

63. With a look, O Zarathushtra! she stagnates one-third of the mighty waters flowing in streams. With a look, O Zarathushtra! she destroys one-third the growth of the up-shooting, flourishing, golden-coloured [1] trees.

64. With a look, O Zarathushtra! she destroys one-third the coverings (crops) of the bountiful Armaiti (spirit of the earth). With a leer, O Zarathushtra! she destroys one-third of the strength, and success, and righteousness of a righteous man of very good thoughts, of very good words, of very good deeds.

65. I tell thee, O Spitama Zarathushtra! these females are also more destructive than darting serpents, or than howling wolves, or than a she-wolf suckling her young [2] (who) rushes into a (sheep-) fold, or than a frog spawning thousands (who) dives into the water.

66. Inquire, O just one! &c. [as in ver. 7].

67, 68. Zarathushtra asked, &c. [as in ver. 8, to] righteous one! whoever, knowingly (and) intentionally cohabits with a menstruous woman (who is) conscious, knowing, and informed (of it), what is his punishment? what is his atonement? what works performed in compensation for this may the culprit execute?

69, 70. Then said Ahuramazda: Whoever, knowingly, &c. [as in ver. 67, to] informed (of it), he shall furnish a thousand young cattle, and he should offer, with perfect rectitude, the fat of the kidneys [3] of all these cattle to the

---

[1] Perhaps "green-coloured, verdant."

[2] This translation of the epithet azrô-daidhîm is only a guess; perhaps "seeing a goat" might also be suggested, but the meaning is very uncertain.

[3] All the old MSS. read asmanivdo (not afsmanivdo), and the Pahlavi translation quotes, as an explanation,

priest for the fire; he should offer (it) to the good waters with (his) arm.

71. He should offer with perfect rectitude a thousand loads[1] of hard firewoods, well-hewn, (and) selected (as dry), for the fire; he should offer, with perfect rectitude, a thousand loads of soft firewoods of the sandal-wood (*urvâsna*), or benzoin (*vohû-gaona*), or aloe-wood (*vohû-kereti*), or pomegranate (*hadhânaêpata*),[2] or any other of the most odoriferous trees, for the fire.

72. He should lop off a thousand loppings[3] for the sacred twigs (Barsom). He should offer, with perfect rectitude, to the good waters, fallen twigs of the shrub which is called pomegranate, for a thousand consecrated waters (*zaothra*) with Homa and milk, (which are) purified, examined (as to purity), purified by a pious man (a priest, and) examined by a pious man.

73. He should kill a thousand serpents gliding on their bellies, (and) two thousand others. He should kill a thousand land-frogs, (and) two thousand water-(frogs). He should kill a thousand ants carrying away corn, (and) two thousand others.

74. He should erect thirty bridges across navigable waters.[4] One should strike (him) a thousand blows with a horse-goad, two thousand with a scourge (*sraoshôcharana*).

75, 76. That is his punishment, that is his atonement, such are the works, performed in compensation for this, the culprit may execute. If he shall execute (them) he shall attain that life which is for the righteous, (but) if he shall

---

the Avesta phrase: *yaḍ añtare veredhka asma reja*, from which it appears that *asman* is connected with *veredhka*, "a kidney."

[1] That is, loads for a man's back.

[2] Such are the traditional explanations of these terms for odoriferous woods.

[3] That is, he should supply the material for the Barsom. The verb *frastairyâḍ* cannot refer to the preparation or final arrangement of the Barsom, which can be performed only by a priest. The same remark applies to all the other offerings here mentioned, which must be brought to a priest for him to offer.

[4] That is, he should form foot-bridges across streams which are not fordable with safety.

not execute (them) he shall attain that life which is for the wicked (and is) gloomy, originating in darkness, (and) dark.[1]

7.—THE NINETEENTH FARGARD.
FRAGMENT OF AN OLD EPIC SONG, vers. 4, 6–9.
(The devil's attempts to frustrate Zarathusthra's doings.)

The verses 1–3 are introductory to the ancient song, and evidently intended as some explanation of the contents of this ancient text. In this introduction is described how Drukhsh, one of the evil spirits in Ahriman's service, came forth from the northern regions at her master's command, to destroy Zarathushtra. The prophet frustrated all such attempts to ruin him by simply repeating the sacred formula *Yathâ-ahû-vairyô*. Drukhsh, having been thus defeated, told the chief of the evil spirits, Angrô-mainyush, that it was impossible to do any mischief to the prophet.

Zarathushtra perceived the snares laid for him, and thought about escaping them. This is described in the verses of the old song, which were undoubtedly current in the mouths of the Iranian people. The song is composed in the heroic metre of the ancient Aryans, the Anushṭubh, which has given rise to the common Shloka.[2]

[1] It is probable that this sentence in this world, as well as in the future refers to rewards and punishments existence.
[2] The original ballad is here subjoined in its metrical form, its translation being given in the text.

(4)
Uschishtad	Zarathushtrô		asaretô	aka	manaṇha
khruzhdya	dbaêshô parshtanãm,		asânô	zasta	druzhimnô.

DEFECTIVE.

(6)
Paiti	ahmâi	adavata		duzhdâmô	Aṇrô	mainyush:
Mâ	mê	dâma	mereñchaṇuha,		ashâum	Zarathushtra!
Tãm	ahi	Pourushaspahê		puthrô	barethryâḍ	hacha
Zâvishi;	apa-stavaṇuha		raṇuhîm	daênãm	mâzdayasnîm,
Viñdâi	yãnem	yatha	vindaḍ		Vadhaghanô	daṅhupaitish.

(7)
Paiti	ahmâi	avashata		yô	Spitâmô	Zarathushtrô:
Nôiḍ	hê	apastavânê		vaṇuhîm	daênãm	mâzdayasnîm.
Nôiḍ	asta	nôiḍ	ushtânem		nôiḍ	baodhascha	urvisyâḍ.

1. From the northern quarter [(Pâz.) from the northern quarters], Angrô-mainyush, the deadly, the demon of demons, rushed forth. Thus spoke the evil-doing Angrô-mainyush, the deadly: Drukhsh (demon of destruction)! rush forth and kill the righteous Zarathushtra. Then the Drukhsh rushed about him, the demon Bûiti, the destroyer intending to kill.

2. Zarathushtra recited the Ahuna-vairya (formula); he invoked the good waters of good qualities, he confessed the Masdayasnian religion. Drukhsh was overthrown by it; the demon Bûiti, the destroyer intending to kill, ran away.

3. Drukhsh then replied: Impostor Angrô-mainyush! I do not think about doing any harm to Spitama Zarathushtra [(Pâz.) the all-glorious, righteous Zarathushtra]. Zarathushtra perceived in his mind that the wicked, evil-doing demons were laying snares for him.

Song.

4. Zarathushtra arose [(Pâz.) Zarathushtra went forward] uninjured by the hostile intentions of the evil spirits, holding a stone (?) in his hand, [(Zend) as large as a cottage]. The righteous Zarathushtra was praying to Ahuramazda the creator: Wherever thou touchest this wide, round, far-extended earth, incline to support Pourushaspa's house.

5. Zarathushtra informed Angrô-mainyush: Evil-doing Angrô-mainyush! I will destroy the creatures produced

(8)
Paiti	ahmâi	adavata	duzhdâmô	Anrô	mainyush:
Kahê	vacha	vandhi ?	kahê	vacha	apayasâhi ?
Kana	zaya	hukeretdonhô	mana	dâma	Anrô mainyush ?

(9)
Paiti	ahmâi	avashata	yô	Spitâmô	Zarathushtrô :
Hâvanacha	tashtacha	haomacha	vacha		mazdô-fraokhta
Mana	zaya	asti	vahishtem;	ana	vacha	vanâni,
Ana	vacha	apa	yasâni,	ana	zaya	hukeretâonhô,
di	duzhda	Anra	mainyô /	dathaḍ	speñtô	mainyush,
Dathaḍ	zruni	akaranê,		fradathen	ameshâo	speñta
Hukhshathrâ	hudhâonhô.				

by the demons, I will destroy death produced by the demons, I will destroy the witch Khnāthaiti[1] for whose (destruction) the triumphant Soshyâns will be born out of the water Kāsoya from the eastern quarter [(Paz.) from the eastern quarters].

6. To him spoke Angrô-mainyush the creator of evils: Do not destroy my creations, O righteous Zarathushtra! Thou art Pourushaspa's son, from birth thou invokest. Curse the good Mazdayasnian religion, (then) thou shalt obtain fortune such as King Vadhaghana obtained.

7. To him replied Spitama Zarathushtra: I will not curse the good Mazdayasnian religion, not (if my) body, not (if my) soul, not (if my) life should part asunder.

8. To him spoke Angrô-mainyush the creator of evils: With whose words wilt thou smite? with whose words wilt thou suppress my creatures (who am) Angrô-mainyush? (and) with what well-made weapons?

9. To him replied Spitama Zarathushtra: The mortar and dish and Homa, and the words pronounced by Mazda are my best weapons; with these words will I smite, with these words will I suppress, with these well-made weapons, O evil-doing Angrô-mainyush! The beneficent spirit made (them), he made (them) in boundless time, the immortal benefactors (Ameshaspentas), the good rulers and good arrangers, co-operated.

(*The fate of the soul after death*, vers. 27–32.)

27. Creator of the settlements supplied with creatures, righteous one! What are the events [(Paz.) what events happen? what events take place? what events are met with?] (when) a man shall give up his soul in this world of existence?

28. Then said Ahuramazda: After a man is dead [(Paz.) after a man has departed, when the running evil-doing demons make destruction (of his life)], at daybreak after the third night, [(Paz.) when aurora is shining], he reaches

---

[1] Probably an idol-worshipper in Kandahar, or thereabouts.

Mithra, rising above the mountains resplendent with their own rightful lustre [(Pâz.) when the sun rises].

29. The demon Vîzaresho by name, O Spitama Zarathushtra! carries the soul bound towards the country of the wicked Deva-worshipping men.[1] It goes on the time-worn paths, which are for the wicked and which are for the righteous, to the Chinvad bridge, created by Mazda, and right, where they ask the consciousness and soul their conduct in the settlements (*i.e.*, world) [(Pâz.) what was achieved in the world of existence].

30. She, the beautiful, well-formed, strong, (and) well-grown, comes with the dog, with the register, with children, with resources, with skilfulness.[2] She dismisses the sinful soul of the wicked into the glooms (hell). She meets the souls of the righteous when crossing the (celestial mountain) Harô-berezaiti (Alborz), and guides them over the Chinvad bridge [(Pâz.) the bridge of the heavenly spirits].

31. Vohu-mano (the archangel Bahman) rises from a golden throne; Vohu-manô exclaims: How hast thou come hither to us, O righteous one! from the perishable life to the imperishable life?

32. The souls of the righteous proceed joyfully to Ahuramazda, to the Ameshaspentas, to the golden throne, to paradise (Garô-nemâna) [(Pâz.) the residence of Ahuramazda, the residence of the Ameshaspentas, and the residence of the other righteous ones.]

(*Fragment not connected with the preceding.*)

33. The righteous man being purified, the demons, the wicked evil-doers, are so frightened at (his) scent, after death, as a sheep encompassed by wolves is frightened by a wolf.

---

[1] The country of the deva-worshippers is India.

[2] The dog is requisite to be looked at by a man at the last gasp, but the meaning of the two following epithets is very uncertain. This passage evidently refers to the maiden who is a personification of one's actions during life, and is said to meet the soul after its third night's separation from the body. Compare the Hâdôkht Nask (Yt. xxii. 9, p. 220).

34. The righteous men assemble, Nairyô-sanha assembles. Say: Ahuramazda's friend is Nairyô-sanha; thyself invoke, O Zarathushtra! this creation of Ahuramazda.

35. Zarathushtra said unto me the words: I praise the rightful creation, formed by Ahuramazda; I praise the earth created by Ahura, the water created by Mazda, the rightful vegetation; I praise the sea Vouru-kasha (*i.e.*, having distant shores); I praise the brightly-shining sky; I praise the eternal luminaries (the fixed stars), the self-created.[1]

36. I praise the best life (paradise) of the righteous, (which is) resplendent (and) all-glorious; I praise the house of song (*garô-nemâna*, equivalent to "paradise"), the residence of Ahuramazda, the residence of the Ameshaspentas, the residence of the other righteous ones; I praise the bridge Chinvad (bridge of the gatherer), created by Mazda, in the self-created intermediate region (between heaven and hell).

37. I praise good fortune, the wide-eyed; I praise the strong guardian-angels (Fravashis) of the righteous, benefiting all creatures; I praise Behram created by Ahura, the bearer of splendour created by Mazda; I praise the shining, glorious star Tishtar (Tîr, Mercury), with the body of a golden-horned ox.

38. I praise the beneficent hymns (the five Gâthas), ruling over the (five) periods (of the day), the righteous ones. I praise the Ahunavaiti Gâtha; I praise the Ushtavaiti Gâtha; I praise the Spentâ-mainyû Gâtha; I praise the Vohu-khshathra Gâtha; I praise the Vahishtôishti Gâtha.

39. I praise the region (*Karshvare*, or Keshvar) Arezahi (and) Savahi; I praise the region Fradadhafshu (and) Vîdadhafshu; I praise the region Vouru-bareshti (and) Vouru-jareshti; I praise the region Qaniratha; I praise the splendid Hêtumat (Hilmand), the shining, the glorious. I praise the good wealth (Ashi); I praise the good science,

[1] Throughout these verses 'I invoke' would be more correct than 'I praise.'

I praise the rightest science. I praise the glory of the Aryan countries; I praise the glory of Yima the king, rich in flocks.

8. THE FARGARDS XX.–XXII.

These last three Fargards of the Vendidad seem to have belonged originally to some medical book. They contain spells for curing diseases, which resemble very much the mantras which are intended for the same purpose in the Atharvaveda. *Thrita* is said to have been the first physician who relieved mankind from the distress and misery caused by diseases. The angel, presiding over the medical art, is called *Airyaman*, to whom even Ahuramazda despatches his messenger *Nairyô-sanha* (Neryosangh).

XV.—BRIEF SURVEY OF AVESTA LITERATURE.

Having described, and illustrated by selected specimens, the various branches of the sacred literature of the Parsis, we may conclude this Essay with a brief summary and survey of the whole.

At the head of this literature undoubtedly stand the FIVE GÂTHAS, which we must regard as the work of Spitama Zarathushtra himself and his disciples, as any one can easily convince himself by a careful perusal of the numerous passages, translated above from these hymns, and by comparing them with those extracted from other parts of the Zend-Avesta. Besides the internal evidence, which is strong and convincing enough, some external reasons may be alleged to corroborate the opinion that these Gâthas contain the undoubted teachings and sayings of the celebrated Zoroaster himself. While the other parts are nowhere said to be the work of Spitama Zarathushtra himself he is distinctly and expressly mentioned, in the Srosh Yasht, as the author of these ancient and sacred songs (see p. 141). Whereas in the other parts of the Zend-Avesta Zarathushtra is spoken of in the third person, and even occasionally invoked as a divine being—in the Gâthas he speaks of himself in the first person, and acts throughout as a man who is commissioned by God to perform a great task. We find him placed among men, surrounded by his friends, Kava Vîshtâspa, Jâmâspa, and Frashaoshtra, preaching to his countrymen a new and purer religion, exhorting them to forsake idolatry and to worship only the living God.

The Gâtha literature was, in ancient times, certainly not confined to the scanty fragments which are now extant. There existed, no doubt, a much larger collection of the hymns and sayings of Spitama Zarathushtra and his disciples, including those of the ancient prophets called *Saoshyañtô*, which are now and then alluded to in the Yasna. Out of this larger collection those verses were selected, which were believed to be most efficacious for putting down the evil influences of the hostile Devas and their priests (the Brahmans), and for increasing the welfare of the Zoroastrians; and these only have been preserved. The collection of the Gâthas, extant now-a-days, may be well compared to the Sâmaveda, which contains detached verses, selected from the Rigveda, intended only for being sung at the celebration of the great Soma sacrifices. While the Brahmans preserved their complete Rigveda, or entire collection of hymns, irrespective of their liturgical application, the ancestors of the Parsis, who were apparently more careless of their sacred literature than their Brahmanical brethren, lost it almost entirely.

Next to the Gâthas in rank stands the YASNA OF SEVEN CHAPTERS (see p. 170). For reasons pointed out above, we cannot regard it as a genuine work of Spitama Zarathushtra himself. It appears to be the work of one of the earliest successors of the prophet, called in ancient times *Zarathushtra* or *Zarathushtrôtema* (see sect. ii. 3, of the fourth Essay), who, deviating somewhat from the high and pure monotheistic principle of Spitama, made some concessions to the adherents of the ante-Zoroastrian religion by addressing prayers to other beings than Ahuramazda.

The first part of the Yasna, styled above the LATER YASNA, is certainly of a far later date than even the "Yasna of Seven Chapters." The high-priests seem to have tried to conciliate the men of the old party (called *paoiryô-ṭkaêshô*, "of the old creed"), who were unwilling to forsake the ancient polytheistic religion, and its time-hallowed rites and ceremonies. The old sacrifices were reformed, and adapted to the more civilised mode of life of the Iranians. The intoxicating Soma beverage was replaced by a more wholesome and invigorating drink, prepared from another plant than the original Soma plant, together with twigs of the pomegranate tree, and without any process of fermentation (water being merely poured over them); but its name in the Iranian form, *Haoma*, remained, and some of the ceremonies also, as we shall see in the fourth Essay; the solemn sacrificial cakes of the Brahmans (*puroḍâsha*) were superseded by the sacred bread called *draonô* (Darûn). New invocations, addressed to those divine beings who occupied the places of the ancient Devas or gods (branded by Spitama Zarathushtra as the originators of all evil and sin), were composed and adapted for the reformed Soma sacrifice (Homa ceremony). These new prayers form the substance of the later Yasna which was to represent the formulas of the Brahmanical Yajurveda.

If we compare this later Yasna with the Gâthas, we find (irrespective of the difference of dialect) such a vast difference in their contents, that it is quite impossible for a conscientious critic to assign them to one author. While in the Gâthas we never find mentioned either Homa, Barsom, or gods like Mithra and Anâhita, or even Amesha-spenta, the general name for the heavenly councillors, we meet with their names in nearly every page of the later Yasna. Here naturally arises the question why the author of the Gâthas, in propounding his new religious doctrines, entirely overlooked the things which were considered in after times as the most indispensable implements of divine service, and why he disregarded those gods and divine beings whom it was afterwards held very sinful to neglect? The only answer is, that he neither believed in them, nor thought them to be an essential part of religion.

In the same rank as the later Yasna may be classed the VISPARAD (see p. 191). It was composed by one of the later high-priests for the celebration of the Gahanbârs.

While the Yasna and Visparad represent the Vedas among the Parsis, their VENDIDAD corresponds exactly to the *Smṛitis*, or collections of customs, observances, laws, penalties, and fines, which form the groundwork of the so-called Dharma-Shâstra. Its different constituent parts have been noticed above (p. 225), and every thinking man can convince himself of the impossibility of ascribing the whole to Spitama Zarathushtra himself. The book only professes to give the conversations, which Zarathushtra is unanimously said (even in the Gâthas) to have held with God himself; and that there was, in very ancient times, a work in existence purporting to contain such conversations, follows undoubtedly from the notice of such a work to be found in the Visparad and Vendidad itself (see p. 142).

If we compare Zarathushtra's conversations with Ahuramazda, as contained in the Gâthas, with those which are reported in the Vendidad, we find a considerable difference between the two. In the Gâthas there is never any allusion made to the numerous ceremonies and observances which were deemed absolutely necessary for a pious Hormazd-worshipper. Thus, for instance, among the questions put by Spitama Zarathushtra to Ahuramazda in Yasna xliv. (see p. 158), about the true religion and its observance, there is not a single one which refers to the treatment of the dead body, one of the most important things in the time of the Vendidad, or to the great purification ceremony (see p. 241), deemed so essential for the welfare of the Iranian community. Very likely Spitama Zarathushtra himself never gave any direct precepts about the customs and usages which already existed in his time. Had he done so we should expect him to allude to them, especially in those verses where he mentions the means of checking the evil influences exercised by the Devas (demons); but all he mentions are the splendour of fire, the mighty words revealed to him by Ahuramazda, the cultivation of the soil, and purity in thought, word, and deed. From his never mentioning the ceremonies enjoined in the Vendidad, it undoubtedly follows that, though he might know them, he did not attach much weight to their observance.

Only on one point we find the laws given in the Vendidad corroborated by the Gâthas. These are those which refer to the sacredness of a promise or contract, called *Mithra*, as one may learn from comparing Vend. iv. (see p. 238) with Yas. xlvi. 5 (see p. 164). These seem to have originated from Spitama Zarathushtra himself, when he called into existence a new religious community, to be founded on the principle of inviolable faith and truth.

From a careful consideration of these and other circumstances which are pointed out above (p. 226), we cannot regard the Vendidad as a work of Spitama Zarathushtra himself, but as the joint work of his successors, the supreme high-priests of the Iranian community. That the chief high-priests, together with the kings, were believed to stand in direct communication with Ahuramazda himself, and to receive from him answers to their questions, we may see distinctly from Visp. i. 9 (quoted above, p. 193). The chief high-priest is there called *Zarathushtrôtemô*, which word literally means "the greatest Zarathushtra, or high-priest" (*tema* being the superlative suffix). His communications are held sacred in this passage, and placed on a level with the Gâthas. From this circumstance we may distinctly gather that the works of the Zarathushtrôtemas were held in ancient times to be about equally sacred with those of Spitama Zarathushtra himself. If we then consider the Vendidad as their joint work, compiled during several successive centuries, it is not to be wondered that we find it so highly revered by the Zoroastrians even to the present day.

Of the three stages which we can discover in the present Vendidad, the AVESTA, no doubt, is very old, and perhaps partially traceable to oral sayings descended from the prophet himself. Even the ZEND, which makes up by far the larger portion of the present Vendidad, belongs to a very early age, and seems to be at least as old as the later Yasna. The PAZAND is comparatively recent, and seems to be more of a literary and learned character than of practical consequence.

In the YASHTS (see p. 194), which correspond partially to the Purâṇic literature of the Brahmans, one may distinguish generally two classes of works, firstly, hymns, and secondly, conversations with Ahuramazda.

The metrical pieces or hymns represent the fragments of the ancient epic poetry of the Iranians, as living in the mouths of their bards, and are not only to be found in the properly so-called Yashts, but are scattered throughout the whole Zend-Avesta (see Yas. ix., x.; Vend. xix.). In their present form the Yashts, together with the shorter prayers, such as Afrîngâns, Gâhs, &c. (see p. 224), are evidently the most modern pieces of the Zend-Avesta, and have not the slightest claim to have been composed by Zarathushtra, or even by his earlier successors. This kind of literature grew up at a time when the Zoroastrian religion had already very much degenerated, and its original monotheism had partially given way to the old gods, who had been stigmatised and banished by Spitama Zarathushtra, but were afterwards transformed into angels. The songs of the bards, which we find introduced into the Yashts, may be old and genuine, but, strictly speaking, they have very little concern with the Zoroastrian religion. The Zoroastrian conversations with Ahuramazda, which we often find in the Yashts, may be the work of the later high-priests, but they seem to be entirely foreign to all that we know of Spitama.

The tendency of the authors of these Yashts was to raise the dignity of the angels, such as Mithra, Tishtrya Anâhita, &c., to that of Ahuramazda, with whom they are said even to have equal rank (see p. 202). Therefore Ahuramazda himself is called, now and then, their worshipper. Zarathushtra is also reported to have paid them great reverence, but not the slightest trace of this can be discovered in his own Gâthas.

This kind of literature has, no doubt, largely contributed towards the deterioration of the religion founded by Spitama Zarathushtra, and has partially re-established what the prophet endeavoured to destroy. As to its age, there is happily a certain historical hint to be found in the Fravardin Yasht, where mention is made of *Gaotema* (Gautama Buddha), the founder of Buddhism (see p. 208). That Buddhism was spread over Bactria, at a very early time, we know from other sources. Buddha entered Nirvâna (died) in B.C. 543; and before his lore could spread in Bactria, at least one or two centuries must have elapsed after the master's death. Thus we arrive at a date, between B.C. 450 and B.C. 350, for the Fravardin Yasht; and there is no difference, in language and ideas, between it and the others. A later date than this cannot be reasonably assigned to the majority of the Yashts, because their language had already begun to die out before the commencement of the Christian era, and most of the Yashts are written in comparatively correct language, without more grammatical errors than abound in some parts of the Vendidad. There is, besides, another reason for attributing the principal Yashts to the fifth century before the Christian era. At that time, as we learn from two inscriptions of King Artaxerxes Mnemon,[1] the worship of Mithra and Anâhita was spreading through all the dominions of

---

[1] See Benfey, "Persische Keilinschriften," p. 67; Norris, "Memoir on the Scythic version of the Behistun Inscription," p. 159.

the Persian Empire, which was not the case at the time of Darius Hystaspes, who never mentions these deities in his numerous inscriptions. This new form of worship called into existence a new appropriate sacred literature, which is partially preserved in the Yashts.

The question as to the age of the other and older parts of the Zend-Avesta is closely connected with the determination of the period at which Spitama Zarathushtra himself lived. As we shall see in the fourth Essay, we cannot place his era at a much later date than B.C. 1200; and if we assign this date to the Gâthas, as the work of Spitama Zarathushtra and his disciples, then we must fix the age of the larger portion of the Vendidad at about B.C. 1000–900, and that of the later Yasna at about B.C. 800–700. The Pâzand portion of the Vendidad is very likely not older than B.C. 500, and at the same time the collection of its different parts may have taken place.

If we date the commencement of the sacred literature of the Parsis from B.C. 1200, and place its close at B.C. 400, we allow a period of about 800 years, which is, in comparison with other sacred literatures, such as those of the Jews and Brahmans, rather too short than too long.

IV.

THE ZOROASTRIAN RELIGION

AS TO ITS

ORIGIN AND DEVELOPMENT.

IV.

THE ZOROASTRIAN RELIGION AS TO ITS ORIGIN AND DEVELOPMENT.

IN this Essay it is intended to give a summary view of the origin of the Zoroastrian religion,[1] its general character and development, so far as they can be ascertained from the original Avesta texts. The reader being furnished, in the preceding Essay, with translations of a good many passages referring particularly to this subject, the conclusions to be drawn from them can be here condensed into comparatively

I.—THE RELATIONSHIP BETWEEN THE BRAHMANICAL
AND ZOROASTRIAN RELIGIONS.

Before we can properly discuss the question of the origin of the Zoroastrian religion, and the time when its founder flourished, certain traces of an originally close connection (which the attentive reader of both the Vedas and Zend-Avesta will readily perceive to exist) must be pointed out between the Brahmanical and Zoroastrian religions, customs, and observances.

1.—NAMES OF DIVINE BEINGS.

The most striking feature, in this respect, is the use which we find made, in both the Vedas and Zend-Avesta, of the names, *deva* and *asura* (*ahura* in the Avesta). *Deva*

[1] This subject has been already briefly treated in the author's "Lecture on the origin of the Parsi religion," delivered on the 1st of March 1861, at Poona; and more fully in the Essay appended to his German work on the Gâthas, vol. ii. pp. 231-259.

is in all the Vedas, and in the whole Brahmanical literature, the name of the divine beings, the gods who are the objects of worship on the part of the Hindus to the present day. In the Zend-Avesta, from its earliest to its latest texts, and even in modern Persian literature, *deva* (Pers. *dîv*) is the general name of an evil spirit, a fiend, demon, or devil, who is inimical to all that comes from God and is good. In the confession of faith, as recited by Parsis to this day, the Zoroastrian religion is distinctly said to be *vî-daêvô*, "against the Devas," or opposed to them (see Yasna xii. 1, p. 173), and one of their most sacred books is called *vî-daêvô-dâta* (now corrupted into *Vendidâd*), i.e., what is given against, or for the removal of, the Devas. The Devas are the originators of all that is bad, of every impurity, of death; and are constantly thinking of causing the destruction of the fields and trees, and of the houses of religious men. The spots most liked by them, according to Zoroastrian notions, are those most filled with dirt and filth, especially cemeteries, which places are, therefore, objects of the greatest abomination to a true Hormazd-worshipper.

Asura is, in the form *Ahura*, the first part of AHURA-MAZDA (Hormazd), the name of God among the Parsis; and the Zoroastrian religion is distinctly called the Ahura religion (see Yasna xii. 9, p. 174), in strict opposition to the Deva religion. But among the Hindus *Asura* has assumed a bad meaning, and is applied to the bitterest enemies of their Devas (gods), with whom the Asuras are constantly waging war, and not always without success, as even Hindu legends acknowledge. This is the case throughout the whole Purâṇic literature, and as far back as the later parts of the Vedas; but in the older parts of the Rigveda Sañhitâ we find the word *Asura* used in as good and elevated a sense as in the Zend-Avesta. The chief gods, such as Indra (Rigveda i. 54, 3),[1] Varuṇa (Rv. i. 24, 14), Agni

[1] In the quotations from the Rigveda, the first number refers to the Maṇḍala ("book," of which there are ten), the second to the hymn, and the third to the verse.

(Rv. iv. 2, 5; vii. 2, 3), Savitṛi (Rv. i. 35, 7), Rudra or Shiva (Rv. v. 42, 11), &c., are honoured with the epithet "Asura," which means "living, spiritual," signifying the divine, in its opposition to human nature. In the plural, it is even used, now and then, as a name for all the gods, as for instance in Rv. i. 108, 6: "This Soma is to be distributed as an offering among the Asuras," by which word the Ṛishi means his own gods whom he was worshipping. We often find one Asura particularly mentioned, who is called "Asura of heaven" (Rv. v. 41, 3; heaven itself is called by this name, Rv. i. 131, 1), "our father, who pours down the waters" (Rv. v. 83, 6); Agni, the fire god, is born out of his womb (Rv. iii. 29, 14); his sons support heaven.

In a bad sense we find Asura only twice in the older parts of the Rigveda (ii. 32, 4; vii. 99, 5), in which passages the defeat of the "sons or men of the Asura" is ordered, or spoken of; but we find the word more frequently in this sense in the last book of the Rigveda, (which is only an appendix to the whole, made in later times), and in the Atharvaveda, where the Ṛishis are said to have frustrated the tricks of the Asuras (iv. 23, 5), and to have the power of putting them down (vi. 7, 2).

In the Brâhmaṇas, or sacrificial books, belonging to each of the Vedas, we find the Devas always fighting with the Asuras.[1] The latter are the constant enemies of the Hindu gods, and always make attacks upon the sacrifices offered by devotees. To defeat them all the craft and cunning of the Devas were required; and the means of checking them was generally found in a new sacrificial rite. Thus the Asuras are said to have given rise to a good many sacrificial customs, and in this way they largely

[1] In the Purâṇas the *Asuras* are fighting not with the Devas, but with the *Suras*. The latter word is a mere fiction of later times, and not to be found in the Vedas. A false etymology has called this new class of gods into existence. The bad sense attached to *Asura* was thought to lie in the negative prefix *a*, and therefore their opponents should appear without it, in the form *Sura*.

contributed towards making the Brahmanical sacrifices so complicated and full of particular rites and ceremonies. To give the reader an idea of the way in which the battles between the Devas and Asuras are said to have been fought, a translation of a passage, taken from the *Aitareya Brâhmaṇa* (i. 23)[1] of the Rigveda, is here given:—

'The Devas and Asuras waged war in these worlds.
'The Asuras made these worlds fortified places (*pur*, i.e.,
'*polis*, town), and made them as strong and impregnable
'as possible; they made the earth of iron, the air of silver,
'and the sky of gold. Thus they transformed these worlds
'into fortified places (castles). The Devas said: These
'Asuras have made these worlds fortified places; let us
'thus build other worlds in opposition to these (now occu-
'pied solely by them). They then made out of her (the
'earth) a seat, out of the air a fire-hearth, and out of the
'sky two repositories for sacrificial food (these are called
'*Havirdhâna*). The Devas said: Let us bring the *Upa-
'sads*;[2] by means of a siege (*upasada*) one may conquer
'a large town. When they performed the first Upasad,
'then they drove them (the Asuras) out from this world
'(the earth); when they performed the second, then they
'drove them out from the air; and when they performed
'the third, then they drove them out from the sky. Thus

---

[1] An edition and translation of the whole work (in two volumes) was published by the author in 1863, giving full information regarding the Brahmanical sacrifices, which were previously little known to European Sanskrit scholars, as it is scarcely possible to obtain a knowledge of them without oral information from professional sacrificial priests. But they are too essential a part of the Vedic religion (now chiefly preserved by the so-called *Agnihotris*) to be overlooked by those who are inquiring into the Brahmanical religion and its history.

[2] This is a particular ceremony which is to take place immediately after the great *Pravargya* ceremony, during which the priests produce for the sacrificer (*yajamâna*) a golden celestial body, with which alone he is permitted by the gods to enter heaven. When in this way the sacrificer is born anew, he is to receive the nourishment appropriate for an infant's body, and this is milk. The chief part of the Upasad ceremony is, that one of the priests (the *Adhvaryu*) presents milk to him in a large wooden spoon, which he must drink. Formerly it had to be drunk from the cow which was to be milked by the Adhvaryu. But this custom has now fallen into disuse.

'they drove them out from these worlds. The Asuras,
'thus driven out of these worlds, repaired to the Ritus
'(seasons). The Devas said: Let us perform Upasad.
'The Upasads being three, they performed each twice
'(that makes six in all, corresponding with the six seasons).
'Then they drove them (the Asuras) out from the Ritus.
'The Asuras repaired now to the months. The Devas
'made twelve Upasads, and drove them out from the
'months. After having been defeated here also, they re-
'paired to the half-months. The Devas performed twenty-
'four Upasads and drove the Asuras out of the half-
'months. After having been defeated again, the Asuras
'repaired to the day and night; the Devas performed the
'Upasads and drove them out. Therefore, the first Upasad
'ceremony is to be performed in the first part of the day
'and the other in the second part of the day. He (the
'sacrificer) leaves thus only so much space to the enemy
'as exists between the conjunction of day and night (that
'is, the time of twilight in the morning and evening).'

That the Asuras of the Brahmanical literature are the supreme beings of the Parsis (Ahuramazda with his archangels) is, according to these statements, hardly to be doubted. But there exists, perhaps, a still more convincing proof. Among the metres, used in the Yajurveda, we find seven which are marked by the epithet *âsurî*, such as *Gâyatrî âsurî, Ushnih âsurî, Pankti âsurî*.[1] These Asura metres, which are foreign to the whole Rigveda, are actually to be found in the Gâtha literature of the Zend-Avesta, which professedly exhibits the doctrines of the Ahura (Asura) religion. The *Gâyatrî âsurî* consists of fifteen syllables, which metre we discover in the Gâtha Ahunavaiti (see p. 144), if we bear in mind that the number of sixteen syllables, of which it generally consists, is often reduced to fifteen (compare, for instance, Yas. xxxi. 6, and the first two lines of xxxi. 4). The *Ushnih âsurî*, consisting of fourteen syllables, is completely extant in the Gâtha

[1] See the "White Yajurveda," edited by A. Weber, vol. i. p. lx.

Vohu-khshathra (Yas. li.), each verse of which comprises fourteen syllables. The *Pankti âsurî* consists of eleven syllables, just as many as we found (p. 144) in the Gâthas Ushtavaiti and Spentâ-mainyû. This coincidence can certainly not be merely accidental, but shows clearly, that the old Gâtha literature of the Zend-Avesta was well known to the Ṛishis who compiled the Yajurveda.

Of great importance, for showing the original close relationship between the Brahmanical and Parsi religions, is the fact that several of the Indian gods are actually mentioned by name in the Zend-Avesta, some as demons, others as angels.

Indra, the chief god of the Brahmans in the Vedic times, the thunderer, the god of light and god of war, for whom pre-eminently the Ṛishis, the ancient founders of Brahmanism, squeezed and drank the intoxicating Soma beverage, is expressly mentioned in the list of the Devas or demons which we find in Vend. xix. 43.[1] He is there second only to *Angrô-mainyush* (Ahriman), the arch-fiend who is sometimes designated *daêvanãm daêvô*, "demon of demons" in the Avesta, but "god of the gods" in Sanskrit.

Next to Indra stands *Sâurva daêva*, whom we discover in one of Shiva's names *Sharva* (see the White Yajurveda, xvi. 28). In *Nâoṇhaithya daêva* we readily recognise the *Nâsatyas* of the Vedic hymns, which name is there given to the two Ashvins, the Dioskuri of the Indian mythology.

Some names of the Vedic Devas are, however, used in a good sense, and are transformed into Yazatas or angels in the Zend-Avesta. The most noticeable is *Mithra*, the Sanskrit form being *Mitra*. In the Vedic hymns he is generally invoked together with *Varuṇa* (identical with the god *Uranos* of the Greeks), the ruler of heaven and master of the universe;[2] but in the Zend-Avesta he was

---

[1] This passage is omitted in two of the oldest manuscripts.

[2] In later times he was believed to preside over the waters only; but in the Vedic hymns he occupied a much higher position. The whole universe is subject to his laws.

everywhere separated from his ancient companion. However, there is one hymn in the Rigveda (iii. 59, *mitró janán yátayati*) in which Mitra alone (as the sun) is addressed in the following way:—

'Mitra calls men to their work; Mitra is preserving 'earth and heaven; Mitra looks upon the nations always 'without shutting his eyes. To Mitra bring the offering 'with ghî!

'O Mitra! that man who troubles himself to keep thy 'order (rule), O son of eternity (*áditya*)! shall have abun-'dance; he, protected by thee, shall neither be slain nor 'defeated; no distress befalls him, neither from near, nor 'from far.'

In comparing these verses with the extracts given above from the Mihir Yasht, one may easily be convinced of the complete identity of the Vedic Mitra and the Persian Mithra.

Another Vedic deity, *Aryaman*, who is generally associated with Mitra and Varuna (Rv. i. 136, 2), is at once recognised in the angel *Airyaman* of the Zend-Avesta. Aryaman has in both scriptures a double meaning, (*a*) "a friend, associate" (in the Gâthas it chiefly means "a client"); (*b*) the name of a deity or spirit who seems particularly to preside over marriages, on which occasions he is invoked both by Brahmans and Parsis (see p. 142). He seems to be either another name of the sun, like Mitra, Savitri, Pûshan, &c., or his constant associate and representative. In the Bhagavad Gita (x. 29) he is mentioned as the head of the *pitaras*, "manes, or ancestral spirits."

Bhaga, another deity of the Vedas, belonging to the same class as Mitra and Aryaman (to the so-called *Adityas*), is to be recognised in the word *bagha* of the Zend-Avesta, which word is, however, not employed there as a name of any particular divine being, but conveys the general sense of "god, destiny"[1] (lit. "portion").

[1] This word is to be found in the Slavonic languages (Russian, Polish, &c.) in the form *bog* as the common name for "God." The ancient Slavonic mythology knew a *biel bog* or white god, and a *czerny bog* or black god.

That the Vedic god *Bhaga* (compare the adjective *baghôbakhta*, "ordained by fate," which is to be found in both the Veda and the Zend-Avesta) was believed to be a deity, presiding over the destiny and fortune of men, may be clearly seen from some passages in the Rigveda, of which Rv. vii. 41, 2, is here quoted: 'Let us invoke the victor 'in the morning (*i.e.*, the sunlight which has defeated the 'darkness of night), the strong Bhaga, the son of Aditi '(imperishableness, eternity), who disposes all things (for 'during the night all seemed to be lost). The poor and 'the sick, as well as the king, pray to him, full of trust, 'saying: Give us our portion.'

Aramati, a female spirit in the Vedas, meaning: (*a*) "devotion, obedience" (Rv. vii. 1, 6; 34, 21), (*b*) "earth" (x. 92, 4, 5), is apparently identical with the archangel *Armaiti*, which name has, as the reader will have learned from the third Essay, exactly the same two meanings in the Zend-Avesta. In the Vedas, however, her name is of rare occurrence, being found in some hymns of the Rigveda only.[1] She is called a virgin who comes with butter offerings in the morning and evening to Agni (Rv. vii. 1, 6), a celestial woman (*gnâ*, see p. 170) who is brought by Agni (Rv. v. 43, 6).

Narâshansa (see Yâska's Nirukta, viii. 6), an epithet of several Vedic gods, such as Agni, Pûshan, and Brahmaṇaspati (but especially of Agni), is identical with *Nairyôsaṇha* (Neryosangh), the name of an angel in the Zend-Avesta, who serves Ahuramazda as a messenger (see Vend. xxii.), in which capacity we find *Agni* and *Pûshan* in the Vedic hymns also. The word means "one praised by men," *i.e.*, renowned.

The Vedic god *Vâyu* (wind, especially the morning wind), "who first drinks the Soma at the morning sacrifice," is to be recognised in the spirit *Vayu* of the Zend-Avesta, who is supposed to be roaming everywhere (see

---

[1] See, about *Aramati* and *Armaiti*, the author's article in the journal of the German Oriental Society, vol. viii. (1854) p. 769-771.

the Râm Yasht above, p. 214). He is the only Vedic deity who is mentioned by name (*vayû*) in the Gâthas (Yas. liii. 6), but, of course, not called a *deva*, which word has always a bad meaning in the Zend-Avesta.

Vritrahâ, "killer of Vritra (a demon)," one of the most frequent epithets of *Indra* in the Vedic books, is to be recognised in the angel Verethraghna (Behrâm, see the Behrâm Yasht above, p. 213). It looks rather strange at the first glance, that we should find one and the same Vedic god, Indra, with his proper name "Indra" entered in the list of demons, and with his epithet "Vritrahâ" worshipped as a very high angel. But the problem is very easily solved if one bears in mind that *Vritrahâ* is applied in the hymns of the Rigveda not exclusively to Indra, but also to another deity, *Trita*, who occupied in the most ancient times the place of Indra as thunderer and killer of the demons of the air (Rv. i. 18, 71). That this Trita is identical with Thraêtaona (Frêdûn) in the Iranian legends, we shall soon see.

A very remarkable coincidence, as to the number of divine beings worshipped, is to be found between the statements of the Vedas and the Zend-Avesta. In the Vedas, especially in the Atharvaveda and the Brâhmaṇas, the gods number thirty-three (*trayas-triñshad devâḥ*) in all. Although the passages do not vary as to the number, they do not throughout agree as to the names of the individual gods by which the number is made up. In the Aitareya Brâhmaṇam (iii. 22, p. 67, of the author's edition) they are enumerated in the following order: eight *Vasavas*, eleven *Rudras*, twelve *Adityas*, one *Prajâpati*, and one *Vashaṭkâra*.[1] Instead of the last two we find *Dyâvâ-Prithivî* (heaven and earth) enumerated in the Shatapatha Brâhmaṇam (forming part of the white Yajurveda), iv. 5, 7, 2. In another passage (xi. 6, 3, 5) of the same work,

[1] This is a personification of the formula Vauṣhaṭ, "may he (Agni) carry it up!" which is pronounced with a very much lengthened sound by the sacrificial priest, when throwing the offering into the fire. When personified, the efficacy of the sacrifice is to be understood.

we find Indra and Prajâpati mentioned as the last two. In the Râmâyana (iii. 2, 15) the two Ashvins are mentioned instead of them.[1] In the Atharvaveda (x. 7, 13, 22, 27), all the thirty-three gods are said to be included in Prajâpati (Brahma) as his limbs.[2]

With these thirty-three Devas of the Vedas we may compare the thirty-three *ratus*, or chiefs, for maintaining the best truths, as they are instituted by Mazda, and promulgated by Zarathushtra (Yas. i. 10). From their not being expressly enumerated according to their several classes, as the thirty-three Devas are in the Vedas, we may gather, with some certainty, that the "thirty-three *ratus*" was only a time-hallowed formula for enumerating the divine existences, the bearing and import of which was no longer understood by the Iranians after their separation from the Brahmans.

2.—NAMES AND LEGENDS OF HEROES.

There is not only a great similarity between, and even identity of, names of divine beings in both the Veda and Zend-Avesta, but a similar close resemblance extends also to the legends of heroic feats related in both scriptures. But, at the very outset, we can discover, notwithstanding this similarity, a striking difference between the Iranian and Brahmanical notions regarding these legends. The Brahmans attribute them generally to gods, the Iranians partly to great heroes and partly to angels. The following are some of the most striking resemblances:—

Yima khshaêta (*Jamshêd*) and *Yama râjâ*. The names

---

[1] The later tradition, as laid down in the Purânas, has increased the Vedic number of thirty-three deities to thirty-three koṭis, or 330 millions. This fact is a striking instance how unscrupulously and ridiculously the statements of the Vedas have been expanded and exaggerated in later times, which has contributed towards bringing Hinduism into the deplorable state in which we find it now.

[2] This tendency towards establishing a kind of monotheism is, now and then, to be discovered in the ancient Vedic hymns. Compare, for instance, the celebrated passage, Rigveda i. 164, 46, where it is said that "the wise men understand by the different gods only one being."

and epithets are the same; *Yima* is identical with *Yama*, and *khshaêta* means "king," the same as *râjâ*. The family name of both is the same: *Vîvaṇhâo* or son of *Vîvanghvat* in the Zend-Avesta (see the second fargard of the Vendidad above, p. 231), and *Vaivasvata* or son of *Vivasvat* in the Veda. In the Zend-Avesta Yima gathers round him men and animals in flocks, and fills the earth with them; and after the evils of winter had come over his territories, he leads a select number of the beings of the good creation to a secluded spot, where they enjoy uninterrupted happiness. According to the hymns of the Rigveda, 'Yama, the king, 'the gatherer of the people, has descried a path for many, 'which leads from the depths to the heights; he first 'found out a resting-place from which nobody can turn 'out the occupants; on the way the forefathers have gone, 'the sons will follow them' (Rigveda x. 14, 1, 2). Yama is here described as the progenitor of mankind; as the first mortal man he first experienced death, and first went up from the low valley of this earth to the heights of heaven, where he gathers round him all his descendants, who must follow in his track by the law of nature, and rules over all who have entered his dominions, which are full of bliss and happiness. This happy ruler of the blessed in paradise has been transformed, in the modern Hindu mythology, into the fearful god of death, the inexorable judge of men's doings, and the punisher of the wicked. In the legends of the Iranians, as extant in the Zend-Avesta and Shâhnâmah, he was the king of the golden age and the happy ruler of the Iranian tribes.

Thrita, Thraétaona (Frêdûn) and *Trita, Traitana.* Thrita, one of the Sâma family (from which the great hero Rustam sprang), is in the Zend-Avesta (see p. 257) the first physician, the curer of the diseases created by Ahriman; an idea which we find also attached to *Trita* in the Vedas. He is said, in the Atharvaveda (vi. 113, 1), to extinguish illness in men, as the gods have extinguished it in him; he must sleep for the gods (xix. 56, 4). He grants a long life (Taittirîya Sañhitâ, Black Yajurveda, i. 8, 10, 2). Any evil thing is to be sent to him to be appeased (Rigveda viii. 47, 13). This circumstance is hinted at in the Zend-Avesta by the surname *Sâma*, which means "appeaser." He is further said to have been once thrown into a well, whence Brihaspati rescued him (Rv. i. 105, 17). The Indian tradition makes him a Rishi, and ascribes several hymns of the Rigveda to him (as for instance Rv. i. 105). There are some traits discoverable in the ancient hymns which make him appear rather like a god than a mortal man. He drinks Soma, like Indra, for obtaining strength to kill the demon Vritra (i. 187, 1), and, like him, he cleaves with his iron club the rocky cave where the cows (the celestial waters) are concealed (i. 52, 5).

Thraêtaona (*Frêdûn*) is easily recognised in the Vedic *Traitana*, who is said to have severed the head of a giant from his shoulders (Rv. i. 158, 3). His father is called *Athwyô*, which corresponds exactly with the frequent surname of *Trita* in the Vedas, viz., *Aptya*. Trita and Traitana seem to have been confounded together in the Veda, whereas originally they were quite distinct from one another. Trita was the name of a celebrated physician, and Traitana that of the conqueror of a giant or tyrant; the first belonged to the family of the *Sâmas*, the latter to the *Aptyas*. In the Zend-Avesta the original form of the legend is better preserved (see about *Thraêtaona*, p. 178).

Kava Us (*Kaîkâûs* in the Shâhnâmah) and *Kâvya Ushanas*. He is one of the great heroes of the Iranians, and believed to have been a ruler over Iran. In the later Indian literature, he is identified with *Shukra*, the planet Venus, and said to have been during his lifetime the Guru (prophet or teacher) of the Daityas or Asuras, the enemies of the gods. But he is not viewed in this light in the ancient Vedic hymns. There he is associated with the god Indra, who calls himself *Kâvya Ushanâ* (Rv. iv. 26, 1), and is invoked by the name *Kavi Ushanâ* (Rv. i. 130, 9).

This Kâvya Ushanâ (meaning "*Ushanâ*, son of *Kavi*") installed Agni as a high-priest for mankind (Rv. viii. 23, 17); he led the heavenly cows (the clouds) to pasturage (Rv. i. 83, 5), and made Indra's iron club, by which the god killed his enemy Vritra. In the Bhagavad Gita (x. 27) he is considered as the first of the poets, wherefore Krishna, who calls himself the first in every particular branch, identifies himself with Ushanas. According to the Mahâbhârata (i. 2544) he has four sons, who offer sacrifice to the Asuras. In the Iranian legend he does not appear as blameless; he is said to have been so proud and self-conceited as to endeavour to fly up to heaven, for which arrogance he was then severely punished.

The name *Dânava* is given, both in the Vedas and Zend-Avesta, to enemies with whom wars are to be waged. Compare Yt. v. 73, and Atharvaveda iv. 24, 2. In the Rigveda it is often a name of the archdemon Vritra, with whom Indra is fighting.

In the legend of Tishtrya (see p. 200) some of the particulars relating to *Indra* and *Brihaspati* in the Vedas may be recognised. Tishtrya cannot bring the rain from the sea Vouru-kasha over the earth, if not assisted by the prayers of men. In the same way Indra cannot release the celestial cows (the clouds) from the rocky cave, whither they have been carried by demons, without the assistance of *Brihaspati*, who is the representative of the prayers sent up by men to the gods, and the personification of their devotion and meditation.

3.—SACRIFICIAL RITES.

Although sacrifices are reduced to a few rites in the Parsi religion now-a-days, we may discover, on comparing them with the sacrificial customs of the Brahmans,[1] a great

---

[1] Most of the Vedic sacrifices are still in use. Those Brahmans, who perform all the sacrifices required for going to heaven, according to the Vedic system, are called *Agnihotris*. Their number was very large at the time of the Peshwas, and is even now considerable in some of the native states, as for instance, in the dominions of the Gaikwar at Baroda.

similarity in the rites of the two religions. Some of the most striking of these resemblances will be here pointed out.

At the very outset the attentive reader of the Vedas and the Zend-Avesta will observe the identity of a good many terms referring to priestly functions. The very name for "priest" in the Zend-Avesta, *âthrava*, is to be recognised in the *atharvan* of the Vedas, by which term a priest of Fire and Soma is meant. The Vedic words *ishṭi* (a series of invocations of several deities, accompanied by the offering of the sacrificial cakes, the so-called Puroḍâsha) and *âhuti* (the invocation of one deity with the offering, within the limits of the *ishṭi*) are to be recognised in the *íshti* and *âzûiti* of the Zend-Avesta, where the original peculiar significations are lost, and only the general meanings "gift" and "invocation or praise" have survived. The particular names of several officiating priests, at the time of performing a solemn ceremony, are the same in both religions. The *Hotâ*, or reciter of the mantras of the Rigveda, is identical with the *Zaota* priest, while the *Adhvaryu* or managing priest, who has to prepare everything for the Hotâ, is the same with the *Rathwi* (now called Raspi), who is only the servant of the Zaota or chief priest. In the *Sraoshâvarcza*, who represents the angel Srosh, the *Pratiprasthâtâ* of the Brahmanical sacrifices may be recognised, because this priest holds in his hand a wooden sword, during the time of sacrifice, to drive away the evil spirits, which weapon is constantly ascribed to Srosh for the same purpose (see p. 190). In the *Atarevakhshô*, who has charge of the vessel in which the

The performance of the manifold sacrifices enjoined to the Agnihotris, or the strict followers of the Vedic religion, entails too much expense upon an individual to be performed by many without public support. The Peshwas used to support them. Among all the Agnihotris (about twelve or fifteen) who presented themselves at the Dakshiṇa meeting at Poona, between the 15th November and 15th December 1861, only one could be found (and he was from Satâra) who had performed all the numerous sacrifices, some of which require from six to twelve days for their performance and an outlay of many thousands of rupis.

fire is, we find the *Agnîdhra* (who holds the fire) of the Brahmans.

The Yajishn or Ijashne ceremony, as performed by the Parsi priests now-a-days (see p. 139), contains all the elements which constitute the different parts (four or seven) of the *Jyotishtoma* cycle of sacrifices, the prototype of all the Soma sacrifices. The Agnishtoma (*i.e.*, praise of Agni, the fire), which is the opening sacrifice of this cycle and indispensable for every Agnihotri to gain the object wished for, viz., heaven, bears a particular resemblance to the performance of Ijashne. Of course, the whole ceremony is much shortened, and the rites changed in accordance with the more enlightened and humane spirit of the Zoroastrian religion. In the Agnishtoma four goats must be killed and their flesh is partly offered to the gods by throwing it into Agni, the fire, who is the mediator between gods and men, and partly eaten by the sacrificer and the priests. During the Ijashne ceremony no animal is killed; only some hair of an ox is placed in a small vessel and shown, together with the other things, to the fire. This is now-a-days the only remnant of animal sacrifice on this occasion, but formerly they used a piece of meat besides. The *Purodâsha* of the Brahmans, or the sacrificial cakes, which must be offered to different deities in a certain order, during the recital of two mantras for each deity, is changed into a flat kind of bread (similar to a very small pancake), called *Darûn*. The fresh milk, required at the time of performing the Upasad ceremony (see p. 270), is to be recognised in the *gâush jîvya* (see p. 139). Ghî, butter, &c., required for less important ceremonies at the time of the Agnishtoma (when making the so-called *Prayâjas* for the six seasons) are represented by the *gâush hudhâo* (see p. 139). The *Zaothra* or consecrated water is required at the commencement of the Brahmanical sacrifices also, where it is called *udaka shânta*.

The most important part of the offerings in both the Jyotishtoma sacrifices and the Ijashne ceremony, is the juice of the Soma plant. In both the twigs of the plant itself (the Brahmans use the stalks of the Pûtika, which is a substitute for the original Soma, and the Parsis use the branches of a particular shrub which grows in Persia) in their natural state are brought to the sacred spot, where the ceremony is to take place, and the juice is there extracted during the recital of prayers. The contrivances used for obtaining the juice, as well as the vessels employed, are somewhat different, but, on closer inquiry, an original identity may be recognised. The Brahmans beat the stalks of the plant, which are placed on a large flat stone, with another smaller stone till they form a single mass; this is then put into a vessel and water is poured over it. After some time this water, which has extracted the greenish juice, is poured through a cloth, which serves as a strainer, into another vessel. The Parsi priests use, instead of stones, a metal mortar with a pestle whereby the twigs of the Homa plant, together with one of the pomegranate tree, are bruised, and they then pour water over them to obtain the juice, which is strained through a metal saucer with nine holes. This juice (Parahaoma) has a yellow colour, and only very little of it is drunk by one of the two priests (the Zaota) who must be present, whereas all the Brahmanical priests (sixteen in number), whose services are required at the Jyotishṭoma, must drink the Soma juice, and some of the chief priests (such as the Adhvaryu and Hotâ) must even take a very large quantity. The Parsi priests never throw any of the juice into the fire, but the Brahmans must first offer a certain quantity of the intoxicating juice to different deities, by throwing it from variously-shaped wooden vessels into the fire, before they are allowed to taste "the sweet liquor." The Parsi priests only show it to the fire, and then drink it. Afterwards the juice is prepared a second time by the chief priest (Zaota) and then thrown into a well. These two preparations of the Homa juice correspond to the morning libation (*prâtaḥ savana*) and mid-day libation (*madhyandina* savana) of the Brahmans; for the third, or evening libation, there was no opportunity in the Parsi ritual, because no sacrificial rites are allowed to be performed in the evening or night time.

The Barsom (*Baresma*), or the bundle of twigs which is indispensable at the time of reciting Ijashne, is to be traced to one of the sacrificial rites at the great Soma sacrifices. It has hitherto been erroneously identified with the *Barhis* or sacred grass (Kusha grass is used) of the Brahmans, which they spread at their sacrifices as a seat for the gods who are expected to come. But the close connection of the Barsom with the Ijashne ceremony, and the circumstances that wood (branches of a particular tree) and not grass is taken, and that these branches are laid on a stand, not spread on the floor, lead to the conclusion that it does not represent the seat for the divine beings, as the Kusha grass does. It refers, in all likelihood, to a peculiar rite at the great Soma sacrifices, which is as yet little known, but about which the author had an opportunity of obtaining oral information. At the time of the Soma libation (called *Savana*), which is to be performed three times on the same day, from 8–12 A.M. (morning libation), 1–5 P.M. (mid-day libation), 6–11 P.M. (evening libation), the three Sâmaveda priests, the Udgâtâ, the Prastotâ, and the Pratihartâ, require a certain number of wooden sticks to be placed in a certain order when chanting the sacred Sâmans (verses of the Sâmaveda). They use for this purpose the wood of the Udumbara tree, and call them *kusha*, which name is generally given to the sacred grass. In the Agnishṭoma fifteen such sticks are required at the morning libation, seventeen at noon, and twenty-one in the evening; in other sacrifices, such as the Aptoryâma, even a much larger number of such sticks is required. The three singers must then chant successively, one by one, in a very solemn manner, the five parts,[1] into which every

---

[1] Such Sâmans are called *panchabhaktika*, *i.e.*, divided into five parts, viz.: *Prastâva* (prelude), *Udgítha* (the principal part, to be chanted by

Sâman or verse adapted for singing is divided at certain sacrifices, while putting some of the sticks into a certain proper order. This ceremony is considered to be most essential, and unless observed and properly performed, all the effect of the Sâmans (which are believed to carry the sacrificer up to heaven, the most important of all being called *Rathantaram*, "carriage") is lost.

At the same time there is another peculiar custom to be observed, which may be traced in the Yasna also. As soon as the singers have chanted their verse, one of the Hotâs must repeat a series of mantras from the Rigveda (not in the usual way of repetition, but in one approaching the recital of the Yajurveda), in order to praise and extol the Sâman, which ceremony is called *Shastram*. At the end of the different Hâs of the Yasna, especially its Gâtha portion, verses of these hymns are often invoked as divine beings, and in Yas. xix. 6 (p. 186) we have seen that it is considered very meritorious to worship the Ahuna-vairya formula after having repeated it.

With regard to the division of the *Sâmans* into five parts, it may be remarked that the Ahuna-vairya formula, which is as important for the Parsis as the Rathantaram Sâman was for the Vedic Brahmans, was also divided into five parts (see p. 188).

In the Afringân ceremony of the Parsis (see p. 224) there may be discovered a trace of the Brahmanical Apri ceremony (see Aitareya Brâhmana, ii. 4, p. 28, of the author's edition), which is preparatory to the killing and offering of the sacrificial goats. The name is the same: *â-prî* in Sanskrit, *â-frî* in the Avesta (the formula used being *âfrînâmi*), which literally means to "invite;" with which invitation the name of the being or beings, in whose honour the ceremony is being performed, must always be mentioned. The Parsis mention the name of a deceased person, or of an angel; the Brahmans insert the names of

the Udgâtâ), *Pratihâra* (response), (great finale), to be chanted by all *Upadrava* (little finale), and *Nidhana* three.

different deities¹ (there are eleven invocations), who are expected to come and enjoy the meal prepared for them. These solemn invitations being accompanied with a blessing, the Parsis understand by this ceremony a benediction, which form it seems to have assumed at a very early time.

The *Darsha pûrnama ishṭi* (new and full moon sacrifice) seems to correspond with the *Darûn* ceremony of the Parsis. Both are very simple; the Brahmans use chiefly the Purodâsha, or sacrificial cakes, the Parsis the sacred bread (Darûn), which corresponds to the Purodâsha.

The *Châturmâsya ishṭi*, or the sacrifice offered every four months or two seasons, corresponds to the Gahanbâr ceremony of the Parsis, which is celebrated six times a year. Sacrificing animals was essential for the proper performance of these ceremonies among the Parsis until recent times; so it is with the Brahmans also. But as to animal sacrifice, there is always a great difference between the Brahmanical and Zoroastrian rites. The Brahmans must throw some parts of the slaughtered animal, such as the *vapâ* (peritoneum), into the fire; while the Parsis simply consecrate the flesh and eat it as a solemn meal, without throwing anything into the fire. On such occasions even the Brahmans now-a-days also eat some of the flesh.

4.—RELIGIOUS OBSERVANCES, DOMESTIC RITES, AND COSMOGRAPHICAL OPINIONS.

Although there are a good many similarities to be discovered in respect to observances, domestic rites, &c., we must confine our remarks to a few of the most striking points of coincidence.

The great purification ceremony (see p. 241), by means of cow's urine (called *gômêz*), as practised by the Parsis to this day, may be compared with a similar observance of the Brahmans. The latter use, in order to remove all

¹ See Yáska's Nirukta, viii. 4-21, and Max Müller's "History of Ancient Sanskrit Literature," pp. 463-467.

inward impurity from the body, the so-called *Puncha-gavyam*, or five products of the most sacred animal, the cow, one of which is her urine. This custom comes from the most ancient times, when this liquid was regarded as a very effective remedy against any disorder of the bodily organs. Such remedies as cow-dung and cow's urine have been used even on the continent of Europe by peasant physicians down to our times.

To the Parsis, as well as to the Brahmans, the investiture with the sacred thread (called *kustî* by the Parsis, *aiwydonhancm* in the Zend-Avesta) is enjoined as a religious duty. As long as this ceremony has not been performed, one is no real member of either the Brahmanical or Zoroastrian community. The time for performing it lasts among the Brahmans from the eighth to the sixteenth year (see Yâjnavalkya, i. 14, 37); the Parsis are invested with the Kustî in their seventh year.

With regard to the funeral rites of both religions some similarities may be pointed out. After the death of a man, Brahmans as well as Parsis must pray to raise the soul of the deceased up to heaven, which is the so-called third-day's ceremony of the Parsis. On the tenth day after the death, the Parsis perform a certain ceremony (Ijashne is read), and the Brahmans use the important ceremony of *Kâkasparsha*, that is, they expose a ball of rice to be taken by a crow.

As to cosmographical opinions the Brahmans divide the whole world into seven *dvîpas*, the Parsis into seven *kêshvars* (*karshvare* in the Avesta), *i.e.*, zones or regions. Both acknowledge a central mountain, which is called by the former *Meru*, by the latter *Alborz* (*Harô berezaiti* in the Avesta).

II.—ORIGIN OF THE ZOROASTRIAN RELIGION.—SPITAMA ZARATHUSHTRA AND HIS PROBABLE AGE.

After having established, in the preceding section, the fact that a close and intimate connection once existed between the religion of the Parsis and that of the Brahmans, we may now proceed to trace the origin of the Zoroastrian religion, and characterise the period at which it must have arisen.

I.—TRACES OF THE ORIGIN TO BE FOUND BOTH IN THE VEDAS AND ZEND-AVESTA.

In the Vedas, as well as in the older portions of the Zend-Avesta (see the Gâthas), there are sufficient traces to be discovered that the Zoroastrian religion arose out of a vital struggle against the form which the Brahmanical religion had assumed at a certain early period. Both creeds are known as diametrically opposed to one another in both their scriptures. One is called the belief of the Asuras (*Ahura* in the Avesta), the other that of the Devas. This circumstance cannot be merely accidental, the less so, as we find the word *Asura* used in the older Vedic hymns (see p. 268) in a perfectly good sense, and as a name of several Devas themselves, which fact clearly shows that there must have been once a vital struggle between the professors of the Deva and those of the Ahura religion, in consequence of which the originally good meaning of Asura was changed to a bad one.

Although it is, therefore, impossible to deny the existence of the original close connection between the Deva and Asura religions, some might still be inclined to doubt whether the adherents of the Deva religion were actually the direct ancestors of the present Brahmans. It is true the word *deva*[1] and the cognate word *dyaus* are found in most of the Aryan languages with the meaning of "heaven," or "divine being," and the Deva-worshippers, combated by the Zoroastrians, might be another kindred tribe of the Aryan stock, different from the Brahmans. But the fact that several of the Brahmanical Devas are mentioned by

---

[1] Best preserved in the Lithuanian *diewas*, "god," and in Latin *deus*. The cognate *dyaus*, "heaven," is extant in the Greek *Zeus*, gen. *Dios*, and the name of an ancient Teutonic god *Tius*, preserved in the word "Tuesday" (in Anglo-Saxon: *Tiws dæg*).

name in the Zend-Avesta, leaves no doubt whatever that the opponents of the Ahura religion actually were the ancient Brahmans; for the names of the Devas, mentioned in the Zend-Avesta, such as Indra, Sharva, Nâsatya, are purely Brahmanical, and unknown to any other nation of the Aryan stock.

We have seen above that the names of the Indian Devas or gods were not all entered in the list of the Zoroastrian Devas or demons, but some of them retained their old dignity by being transformed, in accordance with the new spirit of the Zoroastrian religion, from gods into angels (Yazatas). The names of these are also identical with those of some Vedic deities, such as Aryaman, Mitra, Aramati, &c.

Some of the ancient gods occur with one name in the list of angels, and with another in that of the demons. Thus, for instance, the Zoroastrian demon, *Indra*, has become, under his other name, Verethraghna (Vṛitrahâ), one of the mightiest angels, as has been shown above (p. 275).

These facts throw some light upon the age in which that great religious struggle took place, the consequence of which was the entire separation of the ancient Iranians from the Brahmans, and the foundation of the Zoroastrian religion. It must have occurred at the time when Indra was the chief god of the Brahmans. This was the case at that early period to which we must assign the composition of the majority of the Vedic hymns, before the Brahmans had immigrated into Hindustan Proper. In the post-Vedic period, whose events called into existence the great epic poems Mahâbhârata and Râmâyaṇa, we find Indra's place at the head of the gods occupied by the Trimûrti of Brahma, Vishnu, and Shiva, which idea is utterly foreign to the Vedic hymns. The Trimûrti never being alluded to in the Zend-Avesta, we must assign to the religious struggle a much earlier date.

Before proceeding to fix the probable age of the origin

of the Zoroastrian religion, some facts derived from passages in the Vedas and Gâthas may be adduced, which throw much light upon this difficult subject.

The priests and prophets of the Devas are mentioned by the names *kavi, karapan,* and *usikhsh* in the Gâthas (see Yas. xxxii. 14; xliv. 20; xlvi. 11; xlviii. 10; li. 14). The first is of very frequent occurrence in the Vedic hymns, the third is also occasionally met with there, and the verb (*kalpayati*)[1] and noun (*kalpa*) connected with the second name are very frequently employed. *Kavi,* which means "poet" in the classical Sanskrit, is the name of seers and priests in the Vedic hymns (Rv. i. 128, 8; 142, 8; 188, 1); by drinking the "delicious," but intoxicating, Soma juice, the power of Kavi is attainable (Rv. i. 91, 14); the term is, therefore, applied to the Soma priest (Rv. ix. 37, 6; 72, 6); these Kavis or seers, being believed to be in possession of divine revelation and secret wisdom, were consulted as prophets (Rv. i. 164, 6; vii. 86, 3). The gods themselves, especially Agni, are called by this name (Rv. ii. 23, 1; iii. 14, 1), which circumstance clearly shows that it was a high title, which could be given only to the heads and spiritual guides of the ancient Brahmanical community.

Synonymous with this name is *ushij,* which exactly corresponds to *usikhsh* (nom.) in the Gâthas (Yas. xliv. 20). It means "a wise, intelligent man," as one may see from such passages as Rv. ii. 21, 5; x. 46, 2, and Shânkhâyana's Grihya Sûtra vi. 12, 19, where it changes places with *kavi,* as is the case in Yas. xliv. 20, also.

By the *karapanô,* who are mentioned together with the *kâvayas* in the Gâthas, we must understand specially the sacrificial priests, the performers of the sacrifices, those men who are known nowadays to the Brahmans by the name of Shrotriyas. As to its grammatical formation, this word is derived from a root *karap,* which corresponds exactly with the Sanskrit root *kalp,* "to perform a cere-

[1] The sound *l,* being completely unknown in the Avesta language, is there always represented by *r.*

mony," whence the word *kalpa*, "the ritual, or the doctrine of the ceremonies," is derived. *Karapanô*, therefore, means really "performers of sacrificial rites."

These two names, *kavi* and *karapan*, designate in the fullest sense all the spiritual guides of the professors of the Deva religion, who tried to put down the adherents of the Ahuramazda religion, and we necessarily find, therefore, a bad meaning attached to them in the Gâthas. This appears the more strange, as the word *kavi* itself forms part of the names of highly celebrated personages of Iranian antiquity, such as Kavi Husrava (Kaî Khusro), Kavi Kavâta (Kaî Kabâd), Kavi Vîshtâspa (Kaî Gushtâsp), &c., and has become, in its derived adjectival form " Kayanian," the designation of a whole dynasty of the ancient Bactrian rulers.

Here the question naturally arises, how could a designation, which distinguished the bitterest enemies of the Zoroastrian religion, be applied to kings who were, like Kavi Vîshtâspa, believed to be its staunchest friends and protectors? The only reasonable answer is, that before the outbreak of the schism, when the Iranians and Brahmans lived peacefully together, the Kavis were at the head of both communities; and that, on account of their violent opposition to the religious and social reforms which were adopted by some of the Aryan tribes, such as the Iranians, their very name was branded, and became a word of abomination with the Zoroastrians. But the designation having been already closely connected with their ancient history, and having become the constant epithet of some of their greatest heroes and kings, it was difficult, nay, impossible, to expunge it entirely in its good and high sense from the language. The adversaries of the Kavis, therefore, had to rest satisfied with a slight change of the hateful word when they wished to use it with a good meaning. Thus we actually find this word in the old texts, when forming part of the names of the great Iranian heroes and kings, changed from its only true and original form *Kavi* into *Kavâ*, as, for instance, *Kavâ Vishtâspa*, instead of *Kavi Vishtâspa*.[1]

Now this word *Kavâ* became a party name, denoting the opponents of the Deva religion. And in this sense we find it unmistakeably employed in the ancient Vedic hymns. *Kavâsakha* or *Kavâri* or *Kavatnu*, which all mean "followers of Kavâ or adherents of Kava," are names, given to the enemies of Indra and the despisers of his sacred drink (Soma). In one passage (Rv. v. 34, 3) *Kavâsakha* is even called a *maghavâ*, by which name the disciples and earliest followers of Zarathushtra are denoted in the Gâthas (see p. 169). Indra is there said to turn out the Maghava, who follows the Kava party, from his possession, which refers to the settlements (*gaêthas*) of the Iranians.

That Zarathushtra's attacks were really directed against the Soma sacrifices of the Brahmans, undeniably follows from several passages of the Gâthas (see Yas. xxxii. 3; xlviii. 10). This is not to be wondered at, if we bear in mind that the Indian tribes, as described in the ancient hymns of the Vedas, never engaged themselves in their frequent predatory excursions for stealing cows, horses, sheep, &c., without having previously secured the assistance of Indra by preparing for him a solemn Soma feast. The Karapans dressed it in due manner, and the Kavis composed or applied those verses which were best calculated to induce Indra to accept the invitation. The Kavis were believed to recognise by certain signs the arrival of the god. After he had enjoyed the sweet beverage, the delicious honey, and was supposed to be totally inebriated, then the Kavis promised victory. The inroads were undertaken, headed by those Kavis who had previously intoxicated themselves, and they appear to have been in most cases successful. The Iranian settlers, who had to suffer so much from these attacks (see p. 173), ascribed the success to those Soma sacrifices, which, therefore, must

[1] See further particulars in the author's work on the Gâthas, i. p. 179, 180, and ii. p. 238-41.

have been objects of abomination and horror to them. But the belief in the great efficacy of such a ceremony, as the solemn squeezing and preparing of the Soma juice, being too deeply rooted in the minds of the Iranians, as well as in those of the ancient Indians, the Iranians forsook only the old Aryan fashion of preparing the sacred drink, and invented one of their own, which was more in accordance with the spirit of their new religion (see p. 282). As we have seen, Spitama Zarathushtra himself never mentions this reformed Homa (Soma) ceremony in the Gâthas; it is doubtful, therefore, whether it existed in his time, or, if so, whether he approved of it. It is true, legends were afterwards circulated, to the effect that he himself had given his sanction to this ceremony, as the reader will have learned from the Homa Yasht (see p. 176).

Having established now, beyond any reasonable doubt, the fact that the Zoroastrian religion arose in consequence of a serious conflict of the Iranians with those other Aryan tribes which emigrated into Hindustan Proper, and whose leaders became in later times the founders of Brahmanism, the questions as to the cause of this religious schism, the leader of the seceding party, and the time at which this great event happened, have to be decided.

2.—Causes of the Schism.

The causes, which led to the schism, may be readily learned from the more ancient parts of the Zend-Avesta, especially from the Gâthas. They were of a social and political as well as of a religious nature. The Aryan tribes, after they had left their original home, which was in all likelihood a cold country (see the allusions to it in the first and second Fargards of the Vendidad), led mainly a pastoral life, and cultivated only occasionally some patches of land for their own support. In this state we find the ancient Aryan community throughout the earlier Vedic period, and the Brahmanical tribes were given to this nomadic life as long as they occupied the upper part of the Panjâb, whence they afterwards emigrated into Hindustan Proper. Some of these tribes, whom we may style the Iranians proper, became soon weary of these constant wanderings, and after having reached such places between the Oxus and Yaxartes rivers and the highland of Bactria as were deemed fit for permanent settlements, they forsook the pastoral life of their ancestors and their brother tribes, and became agriculturists. In consequence of this change the Iranians estranged themselves from the other Aryan tribes, which still clung to the ancestoral occupation, and allured by the hope of obtaining booty, regarded those settlements as the most suitable objects for their incursions and skirmishes. How frequent these attacks of the Deva-worshippers upon the property of the Mazda-yasnians must have been, the reader can learn from the formula, by which the Deva-worshippers abjured their religion, and entered the community of the Iranians (see p. 173), and from some verses of the Gâthas (especially Yas. xxxii. and xlvi.).

The success of the attacking Deva-worshippers was, as we have seen, mainly ascribed to spells (mantras) and sacrificial skill. Their religion, therefore, must have become an object of hatred in the eyes of the Iranians, although the latter were well aware that it was closely related to their own, or even to a certain extent identical with it. Their own religion, therefore, had to be totally changed, in order to break up all communication whatever with the devastators of their settlements. The Deva religion was branded as the source of all mischief and wickedness, and instead of it, the Ahura religion of agriculture was instituted, which separated them thenceforth for ever from their Brahmanical brethren.

If we ask who instituted this Ahura religion, we can hardly believe that it was the work of a single man only, though it is not to be denied that the peculiar form which it assumed was mainly due to one great personage, Spitama Zarathushtra.

3.—SPITAMA ZARATHUSHTRA.

In the Gâthas we find Zarathushtra alluding to old revelations (Yas. xlvi. 6), and praising the wisdom of the *Saoshyantô*, "fire-priests" (Yas. xlvi. 3; xlviii. 12). He exhorts his party to respect and revere the *Añgra* (Yas. xliii. 15), *i.e.*, the *Angiras* of the Vedic hymns, who formed one of the most ancient and celebrated priestly families of the ancient Aryans, and who seem to have been more closely connected with the ante-Zoroastrian form of the Parsi religion than any other of the later Brahmanical families. These Angiras are often mentioned together with the Atharvans or fire-priests (which word, in the form *âthrava*, is the general name given to the priest caste in the Zend-Avesta), and both are regarded in the Vedic literature as the authors of the Atharvaveda which is called the Veda of the Atharvângiras, or the Atharvâna, or Angirasa veda, *i.e.*, the Veda of the Atharvans or Angiras.[1] This work was for a long time not acknowledged as a proper Veda by the Brahmans, because its contents, which consist chiefly of spells, charms, curses, mantras for killing enemies, &c., were mostly foreign to the three other Vedas, which alone were originally required for sacrifices. On comparing its contents with some passages in the Yashts and Vendidad, we discover a great similarity.

Although a close connection between the ante-Zoroastrian and the Atharvana and Angirasa religion can hardly be doubted, yet this relationship refers only to the magical part, which was believed by the ancient Greeks to be the very substance and nature of the Zoroastrian religion.

In all likelihood, as the names Atharvana and Angirasa, or fire-priests, indicate, the worship of fire was a characteristic feature of this ancient religion.

The Saoshyantô, or fire-priests, who seem to be identical with the Atharvans, are to be regarded as the real predecessors of Spitama Zarathushtra, who paved the way for

[1] See Max Müller's History of Ancient Sanskrit Literature, p. 448.

the great religious reform carried out by the latter. It is distinctly said (Yas. liii. 2) that the good Ahura religion was revealed to them, and that they professed it in opposition to the Deva religion, like Zarathushtra himself and his disciples (Yas. xii. 7 ; see p. 173). We must, therefore, regard these ancient sages as the founders of the Ahura religion, who first introduced agriculture and made it a religious duty, and commenced war against the Deva religion.

The struggle may have lasted for several centuries before Spitama Zarathushtra appeared in Iran, professedly by divine command, to strike a death-blow at idolatry, and to banish it for ever from his native soil. But however this may have been, the decisive step of completely separating the contending parties from one another, and establishing a new community governed by new laws, was taken by Spitama Zarathushtra. He has, therefore, many claims to be regarded as the founder of the true Mazdayasnian or Parsi religion, which absorbed the old Ahura religion of the ancient fire-priests. He himself was one of the Saoshyantô or fire-priests, because we find him, when standing before the sacred fire, delivering his speeches and receiving answers from Ahuramazda out of the sacred flames.

The events of his life are almost all enshrouded in darkness, to dispel which will be for ever impossible, should no authentic historical records be discovered in Bactria, his home. The reports regarding him, given by the Greeks and Romans (see the first Essay), are as unhistorical and legendary as those found in the majority of the Avesta books themselves. In the Vendidad and the Yashts (see p. 212) he is represented to us not as a historical, but as a dogmatical personalty, stripped of nearly everything that is peculiar to human nature, and vested with a supernatural and wholly divine power, standing next to God himself and being even elevated above the archangels. The temptations of the devil, whose whole empire was threatened by the great prophet, form a favourite subject of the traditional reports and legends. He was the concentration of all wisdom and truth, and the master and head of the whole living creation (see p. 211).

The only source whence we may derive some very scanty historical facts is the older Yasna. In this part of the scriptures only, he appears before our eyes as a real man, acting a great and prominent part in the history of his country, and even in the history of the whole human race in general. He was a member of the Spitama family, which name is given to the *Haêchadaspas* also (Yas. xlvi. 15), who seem, therefore, to have been his nearest relations. His father's name was *Pôurushaspa*, according to the later Yasna and Vendidad. Of his children only his daughter *Paouruchista* (Yas. liii. 3) is mentioned by the two names *Haêchadaspânâ Spitâmî*, which can be interpreted only as "belonging to the Spitama family of the Haêchadaspa lineage." He was distinguished by the surname *Zarathushtra*, which the Greeks corrupted to Zarastrades or Zoroastres, and the Romans to Zoroaster, by which name alone he is known to Europeans, while the Persians and Parsis changed it to Zardosht. Although the original meaning of this name is uncertain,[1] yet it can hardly be doubted that it was not merely the proper name of the founder of the Parsi religion, but denoted a certain high dignity, that of the high-priest of the country. This follows clearly from Yas. xix. (see p. 188), where the Zarathushtra is mentioned as the fifth chief, in those countries where there are four others of an inferior order, and as the fourth, where there are only three others below him; and it is also evident from the title *Zarathushtrôtemô*. This

---

[1] See the author's work on the Gâthas, ii. p. 245-46, note 1, where the different explanations of the name hitherto given are mentioned and refuted. The most probable meaning of "Zarathushtra" is not "the most excellent poet," as the author suggested formerly, but "senior, chief" (in a spiritual sense), and the word may be traced to the Sanskrit *jarat*, which means in compounds "old;" *ushtra* is then equivalent to *uttara*, "superior, excellent."

title must mean, according to grammar (*tema* being the superlative suffix), "the greatest or highest Zarathushtra," which denomination can be understood only if we assume the existence of several contemporaneous Zarathushtras, at whose head he was placed. The name "Zarathushtra" must, therefore, have conveyed in ancient times nearly the same meaning as the word "Dastur" does nowadays: it must have meant the spiritual guide and head of a whole district, or even province. The *Zarathushtrôtemô* is, therefore, to be compared with the Dastur-i-Dasturân or chief high-priest. Even according to the notions of the modern Parsis, a Dastur occupies a very high rank among them; he is a *ratu* or chief in the living creation, and in his praise and honour even ceremonies may be performed.

A clear proof that the word "Zarathushtra" itself was not alone deemed sufficient to distinguish the prophet from other men, is that his family name "Spitama" is generally prefixed [1] when he is spoken of. This circumstance implies distinctly that there were other Zarathushtras besides the one who was distinguished by the name "Spitama," and who alone was regarded as the real founder of the Mazdayasnian religion.

His home seems to have been in Bactria, which is called *Berekhdha ârmaiti* in the Gâthas, and *Bâkhdhi* (a corruption of the former) in the Vendidad. In his own works he calls himself a *mâthran*, "reciter of mantras," a *dûta*, "messenger," sent by Ahuramazda, a speaker (*maretan*); he listens to the oracles given by the spirit of nature (*geush urvâ*), and sacred words are revealed to him by Ahuramazda through the flames.

His doings are best learned from the Gâthas, extracts from which have been given above (see pp. 149–170), so we

---

[1] In a similar manner each of the present Dasturs introduces the title, Dastur, between his own name and that of his father, so that his own name is prefixed to the title, as, for instance, Peshotan Dastur Behramji Sanjana (see the title-page of that learned Dastur's edition of the Dinkard).

may here confine ourselves to a few remarks as to the probable age in which he lived.

4.—THE AGE WHEN SPITAMA ZARATHUSHTRA LIVED.

The accounts given of the time when he is said to have flourished, differ so widely from one another, that it is impossible to fix exactly the era when he was living. The Greeks and Romans make him very ancient. Xanthos of Lydia (B.C. 470), the earliest Greek writer who mentions Zoroaster, says that he lived about 600 years before the Trojan war (about B.C. 1800). Aristotle and Eudoxus place his era as much as 6000 years before Plato, others say 5000 years before the Trojan war (see Pliny, Historia Naturalis, xxx. 1–3). Berosos, the Babylonian historian, makes him a King of the Babylonians, and the founder of a dynasty, which reigned over Babylon between B.C. 2200 and B.C. 2000.

The Parsis believe that their prophet lived at the time of Darius's father, Hystaspes, whom they identify with the *Kava Vishtâspa* of the Zend-Avesta, or Kaî Gushtâsp of the Shâhnâmah, and place his era accordingly about B.C. 550. But the groundlessness of this supposition may be seen on comparing the names of the predecessors of Hystaspes with those of the ancestors of Vishtâspa. The lineage of *Vishtâspa* or Hystaspes, according to the Bisutûn cuneiform inscription of Darius, and the statements of Herodotus, is as follows:—*Hakhâmanish* (Achæmenes), *Chaishpish* (Teispes), *Ariyârâmna* (Ariaramnes), *Arshâma* (Arsames), *Vishtâspa* (Hystaspes), *Dârayavush* (Dareios). But the lineage of *Vishtâspa* or Gushtâsp, according to the Avesta and Shâhnâmah, is as follows:—*Kavi Kavâta* (Kaî-Kabâd), *Kava Usa* (Kaî-Kâûs), *Kava Husrava* (Kaî Khusrô), *Aurvadaspa* (Lahurâsp), *Kava Vîshtâspa* (Kaî Gushtâsp). From these genealogies it will be seen that the names of the ancestors of the Vishtâspa mentioned in the cuneiform inscriptions (called Hystaspes by the Greeks), are totally different from those of the ancestors of the

Vishtâspa celebrated in Zoroastrian tradition (the Gushtâsp of the Shâhnâmah). We must, therefore, conclude that the Vishtâspa of Iranian tradition was a totally distinct person from the Hystaspes of the Greeks, the father of Darius. That the Persians themselves, in the time of the Sasanians, were quite uncertain as to when the former Vishtâspa lived, appears clearly from the testimony of the historian Agathias, quoted in p. 11.

On comparing the accounts of the Greeks about the early era of Zoroaster, with the researches into the original texts of the Parsi scriptures, we must believe their concurrent testimony to be much more trustworthy and reliable than the opinions held by the modern Parsis. There can be no doubt whatever that Spitama Zarathushtra, the founder of the Parsi religion, lived at a very early period, because the great religious movement, of which he was the chief leader, is even alluded to in the earlier portions of the Vedas. Of his high antiquity at least two significant traces may be discovered in the present Zend-Avesta. Firstly, as we have seen in the fifteenth section of the third Essay, his writings stand at the head of the extensive Avesta literature, which required centuries for its growth, and which was already complete about B.C. 400. Secondly, he is expressly called "the famous in *Airyana vaêjô*" (Yas. ix. 14), which means, "the famous in the Aryan home," whence the Iranians and Indians emigrated in times immemorial. This title would certainly not have been given to him had his followers not believed him to have been living at that early time. Under no circumstances can we assign him a later date than B.C. 1000, and one may even find reasons for placing his era much earlier and making him a contemporary of Moses. Pliny, who compares both Moses and Zoroaster, whom he calls inventors of two different kinds of magic rites, goes much further in stating that Zoroaster lived several thousand years before Moses (Historia Naturalis, xxx. 2). The confusion of opinions regarding his age was, no doubt, mainly caused by his appellation " Zarathushtra" or high-priest, which was afterwards taken as the proper name of the prophet. The assertion that he was born at *Ragha* (*Rai* near Teheran) is owing to the circumstance that, according to Yasna xix. (see p. 188), this large town seems to have been governed by the Zarathushtras themselves; it was, therefore, pre-eminently the Zoroastrian country.

III.—SPITAMA ZARATHUSHTRA'S THEOLOGY AND PHILOSOPHY, AND THEIR INFLUENCE ON THE DEVELOPMENT OF THE PARSI RELIGION.

Having shown in the preceding section the historical origin of the Zoroastrian religion, we may proceed next to consider the new ideas, theological and philosophical, which Spitama Zarathushtra introduced into the world, and in consequence of which he may be said to have become the founder of a new religion, and to have exercised a lasting influence on the history of the human mind.

His real doctrines, untouched by the speculations of later ages, can be learned only from the older Yasna, chiefly from the Gâthas. The leading idea of his theology was *Monotheism*, i.e., that there are not many gods, but only one; and the principle of his speculative philosophy was *Dualism*, i.e., the supposition of two primeval causes of the real world and of the intellectual; while his moral philosophy was moving in the *Triad* of thought, word, and deed. Having regard to the early period at which he must have lived, long before the Greeks were acquainted with anything like philosophical speculation, we cannot expect him to have established a complete and developed system of philosophical thoughts, which cannot even be said of Plato; but the few philosophical ideas which may be discovered in his sayings, show that he was a great and deep thinker, who stood far above his contemporaries, and even above the most enlightened men of many subsequent centuries. The great fame he enjoyed, even with the ancient Greeks and Romans who were so proud of their own learning and wisdom, is a sufficient proof of the high and pre-eminent position he must once have occupied in the history of the progress of the human mind.

1.—ZARATHUSHTRA'S MONOTHEISM.

That his theology was mainly based on monotheism, one may easily ascertain from the Gâthas, especially from the second (see pp. 155–166). His predecessors, the Saoshyantô, seem to have worshipped a plurality of good spirits, whom they called *Ahuras*, "the living ones," who were opposed to the Devas. Spitama, not satisfied with this indistinct expression of the Divine Being, reduced this plurality to unity. The new name, by which he called the Supreme Being, was *Ahurô mazdâo*, which means, "the Ahura who is called Mazdâo." *Mazdâo*, which has been compared with the Vedic *medhâs*, "wise" (or when applied to priests, "skilful, able to make everything"), means either "joint creator," or "creator of all."[1] Those Ahuras who were regarded as creative powers might have been already called by the name *mazdâo* (we find the plural, *mazdâonhô*, in Yas. xlv. 1) by the Saoshyantô; but these old fire-priests had no clear conception of the nature and working of this creative power. Although Spitama combined the two names (which were formerly used separately, and not intimately connected with one another) into one appellation, *Ahurô-mazdâo*, yet they were still not considered as a compound, because we find both con-

[1] That *mazdâo* is phonetically identical with Sans. *medhâs*, is not to be denied, but its original meaning is not "wise." Were this the case, we ought to suppose it to be a contraction of *maiti-dhâo*, "producing wisdom;" but *maiti*, "thought, wisdom," (Sans. *mati*) is generally affixed, not prefixed, to another word, as in *tarô-maiti*, "perverse thought, disobedience." But the word *maḍ*, "with," is very frequently prefixed to other words; and if prefixed to *dhâo*, "creating," the compound must be changed, according to phonetical laws, into *mazdâo*. The general meaning of *maḍ* being "together with, all" (see Visp. xiv. 1), the word *mazdâo* must mean either "joint creator," or "creator of all," as may be clearly seen from Yas. xlv. 1.

stituent parts subject to inflection (*e.g.*, *ahurâi mazdâi* in the dative, not *Ahura-mazdâi*); one part, *Mazdâo*, was the chief name; the other, *ahura*, was an adjectival epithet. But in consequence of their being jointly employed to express the name of the Supreme Being, they were afterwards considered a compound, as we may distinctly see from the cuneiform inscriptions of the Achæmenian kings, where the Supreme Being is generally called *Aûramazdâ*, and only the latter part of the word is subject to inflection, except in a few instances where both words are inflected. In the Sasanian times the name was changed to *Aûharmazdî*, and in modern Persian to *Hôrmazd* or *Ormazd*, which forms are used by the Parsis nowadays. In the Gâthas we find the two words frequently separated, and indiscriminately employed to express the name "God," as no difference of meaning is attached to either. In translating them, *Ahura* may best be rendered by "living" or "lord," and *Mazdâo* by "wise" or "creator of the universe."

Spitama Zarathushtra's conception of Ahuramazda as the Supreme Being is perfectly identical with the notion of *Elohîm* (God) or *Jehovah*, which we find in the books of the Old Testament. Ahuramazda is called by him "the Creator of the earthly and spiritual life, the Lord of the whole universe, in whose hands are all the creatures." He is the light and source of light; he is the wisdom and intellect. He is in possession of all good things, spiritual and worldly, such as the good mind (*vohu-manô*), immortality (*ameretâḍ*), health (*haurvatâḍ*), the best truth (*asha vahishta*), devotion and piety (*ârmaiti*), and abundance of every earthly good [1] (*khshathra vairya*). All these gifts he grants to the righteous man, who is upright in thoughts, words, and deeds. As the ruler of the whole universe, he not only rewards the good, but he is a punisher of the wicked at the same time (see Yas. xliii. 5). All that is created, good or evil, fortune or misfortune, is his work

[1] See especially Yas. xlvii. 1 (p. 167).

(Yas. xlviii. 4. p. 167, and li. 6, p. 169). A separate evil spirit of equal power with Ahuramazda, and always opposed to him, is entirely foreign to Zarathushtra's theology; though the existence of such an opinion among the ancient Zoroastrians can be gathered from some of the later writings, such as the Vendidad.

2.—ZARATHUSHTRA'S TWO PRIMEVAL PRINCIPLES.

The opinion, so generally entertained now, that Zarathushtra was preaching a Dualism, that is to say, the idea of two original independent spirits, one good and the other bad, utterly distinct from each other, and one counteracting the creation of the other, is owing to a confusion of his philosophy with his theology. Having arrived at the grand idea of the unity and indivisibility of the Supreme Being, he undertook to solve the great problem which has engaged the attention of so many wise men of antiquity, and even of modern times, viz., how are the imperfections discoverable in the world, the various kinds of evils, wickedness, and baseness, compatible with the goodness, holiness, and justice of God? This great thinker of remote antiquity solved this difficult question *philosophically* by the supposition of two primeval causes, which, though different, were united, and produced the world of material things, as well as that of the spirit; which doctrine may best be learned from Yas. xxx. (see pp. 149–151).

The one, who produced the "reality" (*gaya*), is called *vohu-manô*, "the good mind," the other, through whom the "non-reality" (*ajyâiti*) originated, bears the name *akem manô*, "the evil mind." All good, true, and perfect things, which fall under the category of "reality," are the productions of the "good mind;" while all that is bad and delusive, belongs to the sphere of "non-reality," and is traced to the "evil mind." They are the two moving causes in the universe, united from the beginning, and therefore, called "twins" (*yēmâ*, Sans. *yamau*). They are present everywhere; in Ahuramazda as well as in men.

These two primeval principles, if supposed to be united in Ahuramazda himself, are not called *vohu-manô* and *akem manô*, but *speñtô mainyush*, " the beneficent spirit," and *angrô mainyush*, "the hurtful spirit." That Angrômainyush is no separate being, opposed to Ahuramazda, is to be gathered unmistakeably from Yas. xix. 9 (see p. 187), where Ahuramazda is mentioning his "two spirits," who are inherent in his own nature, and are in other passages (Yas. lvii. 2, see p. 189) distinctly called the "two creators" and "the two masters" (*pâyû*). And, indeed, we never find Angrô-mainyush mentioned as a constant opponent of Ahuramazda in the Gâthas, as is the case in later writings. The evil against which Ahuramazda and all good men are fighting is called *drukhsh*, "destruction, or lie," which is nothing but a personification of the Devas. The same expression for the "evil" spread in the world, we find in the Persian cuneiform inscriptions, where, moreover, no opponent of Ahuramazda, like Angrô-mainyush is ever mentioned. God (*Aûramazdâ*), in the rock records of King Darius, is only one, as Jehovah is in the Old Testament, having no adversary whatsoever.

Spentô-mainyush was regarded as the author of all that is bright and shining, of all that is good and useful in nature; while Angrô-mainyush called into existence all that is dark and apparently noxious. Both are as inseparable as day and night, and though opposed to each other, are indispensable for the preservation of creation. The beneficent spirit appears in the blazing flame, the presence of the hurtful one is marked by the wood converted into charcoal. Spentô-mainyush has created the light of day, and Angrô-mainyush the darkness of night; the former awakens men to their duties, the latter lulls them to sleep. Life is produced by Spentô-mainyush, but extinguished by Angrô-mainyush, whose hands, by releasing the soul from the fetters of the body, enables her to rise into immortality and everlasting life.

3.—DEVELOPMENT OF ZARATHUSHTRA'S DOCTRINES OF THE SUPREME BEING. THE TWO SUPREME COUNCILS; SROSH AND BOUNDLESS TIME.

Such is the original Zoroastrian notion of the two creative spirits, who form only two parts of the Divine Being. But in the course of time, this doctrine of the great founder was changed and corrupted, in consequence of misunderstandings and false interpretations. Spentô-mainyush was taken as a name of Ahuramazda himself, and then, of course, Angrô-mainyush, by becoming entirely separated from Ahuramazda, was regarded as the constant adversary of Ahuramazda; thus the Dualism of God and Devil arose. Each of the two spirits was considered an independent ruler endeavouring to destroy the creation of the other, and thus both waged constant war. This Dualism is best perceived in the first fargard of the Vendidad. After the sovereignty and independence of these two spiritual rulers was once acknowledged by some of the most influential leaders of the congregation founded by Spitama Zarathushtra, each of them was then supposed to have, like terrestrial rulers, his own council and court. The number of councillors was fixed at six, who were regarded as the actual governors of the whole universe, each ruling over a separate province assigned to him by his spiritual ruler. To Ahuramazda, or Spentô-mainyush, no other power was left but to preside over the celestial council. We often find him even included in the number of the celestial councillors, who are then called "the seven Ameshaspentas" (now corrupted to Amshaspends), *i.e.*, immortal benefactors.

The several names, by which we find the Ameshaspentas called, viz., Vohu-manô, Asha-vahishta, Khshathra-vairya, Spenta-Armaiti, Haurvatâd, and Ameretâd, are frequently mentioned in the Gâthas, but they are, as the reader may clearly see from the passages (see Yas. xlvii. 1) as well as from etymology, nothing but abstract nouns and ideas representing all the gifts which Ahuramazda, as the only Lord, grants to those who worship him with a sincere heart, by always speaking truth, and performing good actions. In the eyes of the prophet they were no personages; that idea being imported into the sayings of the great master by some of his successors.

VOHU-MANÔ (Bahman) is regarded as the vital faculty in all living beings of the good creation. Originally, his name was nothing but a term for the good principle, as emanating from Ahuramazda, who is, therefore, called the father of Vohu-manô. He pervades the whole living good creation, and all the good thoughts, words, and deeds of men are wrought by him.

ASHA-VAHISHTA (Ardibahisht) represents the blazing flame of fire, the light in luminaries, and brightness and splendour of any kind whatever, wherever it may exist. The first part of the name, *asha* (plural of *ashem*), has various meanings, such as "rectitude, righteousness, truth," and its epithet *vahishta* means originally "most splendid, beautiful," but was afterwards used in the more general sense of "best." Light being of the nature of Ahuramazda, and being believed to pervade the whole good creation, Asha-vahishta represents the omnipresence of the Divine Being. Light maintaining the vitality of the whole creation, animate and inanimate, and being the cause of all growth, Asha-vahishta is the preserver of all life and all that is good. He represents, in this respect, God's Providence.

KSHATHRA-VAIRYA (Shahrivar) presides over metals and is the giver of wealth. His name means simply "possession, wealth," afterwards it was applied to metal and money. Wealth is considered as a gift from Ahuramazda.

SPENTA-ARMAITI (Spendarmad or Isfendarmad), "the bountiful Armaiti," represents the earth. The original meaning of Armaiti, as we have seen above (see p. 274), however, is "devotion, obedience." She represents the pious and obedient heart of the true worshipper of Ahuramazda, who serves God alone with body and soul. When the name is applied to the earth, it means that she is the servant of men, who, if well treated (*i.e.*, cultivated), will yield abundance of food.

HAURVATAD and AMERETAD (Khordâd and Amardâd) preside over vegetation, and produce all kinds of fruits; but this is very likely not their original meaning. As the names indicate (*Haurvatâd* means "completeness, health," and *Ameretâd*, "immortality"), they represent the preservation of the original uncorrupted state of the good creation, and its remaining in the same condition as that in which it was created by God. They are generally both mentioned together, and express, therefore, a single compound idea.

Quite separate from the celestial council stands SRAOSHA (Srosh), who is, however, regarded as an archangel vested with very high powers. While the Ameshaspentas in Zarathushtra's eyes represented nothing but the qualities and gifts of Ahuramazda, Sraosha seems to have been considered by him as a personality. He is the angel who stands between God and man, the great teacher of the good religion who instructed the prophet in it. He shows the way to heaven and pronounces judgment on human actions after death (for further information see the Srosh Yasht, p. 189). Originally his name meant "hearing" (from the root *sru* to hear), which, taken in a religious sense, means the sacred tradition. In this respect we may best compare the word with the Sanskrit *Shruti*, by which name the Brahmans understand the sacred tradition, as laid down in the various parts of the Vedas, especially in that which treats of sacrificial rites. All that is said of Srosh, in the Srosh Yasht, fully agrees with this meaning of his name. We must, therefore, regard him only as the personification of the whole divine service, including the prayers as well as the sacrificial rites. When he is said to be the guardian of the whole creation, and that without his protection the world would fall a prey to the demons, it is meant that men must offer up prayers to God and worship him; and should they fail to do so, the good mind (*Vohu-manô*) within them becomes powerless, and the bad mind (*Akem-manô*) takes entire possession of them, instigating them to commit sins and crimes, in consequence of which they will become utterly cast away, both in this life and in that to come. Srosh fights chiefly against the Devas. This means, that the Zoroastrian divine service is destined to counterbalance the mischief which the Indian Devas were supposed to be doing to the good creation.

Like Ahuramazda, his adversary Angrô-mainyush was, in later times, supposed to be also surrounded by a council. This idea is completely foreign to the older texts, and is evidently only an imitation of the celestial council. The number of councillors of the infernal kingdom was likewise fixed at six (not in the Avesta texts, but only in the Bundahish), who were called pre-eminently *Devas* and headed by Angrô-mainyush, who, for this reason, was called *Daêvanãm Daêvô*, or archdemon. The first in rank after Angrô-mainyush was AKEM-MANO, which means the "evil mind," and is nothing but Zarathushtra's philosophical term of the second principle, the "non-reality." He produces all bad thoughts in men, and makes them utter bad words and commit sins. His influence is checked by Vohu-manô, the good mind. The second seat in the infernal council is occupied by the King of the Vedic gods, INDRA; the third place is assigned to SAURVA, the Shiva of the Hindus. Fourth in rank is NAONHAITHYA, the collective name of the Indian Ashvins (Dioskuri); the fifth and sixth places are occupied by two personifications, DARKNESS and POISON (see the Bundahish, edited by Westergaard, p. 5).

There are a good many other names of Devas to be found in the Zend-Avesta; but almost all are nothing but personifications of vices and evils. Thus, for instance, *Aêshema* means "rapine, attack," *Driwish* is "poverty," *Daiwish*, "deceit," &c. While the celestial council is always taking measures for promoting life and spreading truth, the infernal councillors are constantly plotting designs for the destruction of life, and endeavouring to spread lies and falsehood everywhere. The Zoroastrian idea of the Devil and the infernal kingdom coincides entirely with the Christian doctrine. The Devil is a murderer and father of lies according to both the Bible and the Zend-Avesta.

In consequence of this entire separation of the two parts of Ahuramazda, and the substitution of two independent rulers governing the universe, the unity of the Supreme Being was lost, and Monotheism was superseded by Dualism. But this deviation from, and entire change of, the prophet's doctrine could not satisfy the minds of all the divines and philosophers in ancient Persia. It was very likely only the innovation of an influential party or sect, probably that which was called *Zendik*, *i.e.*, following the interpretation (Zend), and which was opposed to that of the *Magi* (see p. 14). That Dualism was actually the doctrine of the Zendiks, we best learn from the commencement of the Bundahish, which book purports to expound the lore of this party. The Magi seem still to have clung to the prophet's doctrine of the unity of the Supreme Being. But to refute the heretical opinions of the Zendiks, which were founded on interpretations of passages from the sacred texts, a new and fresh proof of the unity of the Supreme Being was required. This was found in the term *Zarvan akarana*, "boundless time," which we meet with occasionally in the Zend-Avesta. The chief passage, no doubt, was Vend. xix. 9 (see pp. 24 and 254); but the interpretation for proving that *Zarvan akarana* means the Supreme Being, out of whom Ahuramazda and Angrômainyush are said to have sprung, rests on a grammatical misunderstanding, as we have seen above (p. 24). This interpretation, however, must be very old; for all the present Dasturs believe in it as an incontrovertible fact.

That this doctrine of *Zarvan akarana* was commonly believed in Persia, during the times of the Sasanians, may be distinctly seen from the reports quoted above (pp. 12-14). The true meaning of the expression, that "the beneficent Spirit made (them) in boundless time," is that God (Ahuramazda) is from eternity, self-existing, neither born nor created. Only an eternal being can be independent of the bounds of time to which all mortals are subject.

4.—The Two Intellects; Two Lives; Heaven and Hell; Resurrection; and Palingenesis.

In the Gâthas we frequently find "two intellects" (*khratu*) and "two lives" (*ahu*) spoken of. These notions, therefore, formed undoubtedly part of Spitama Zarathushtra's speculation. The two intellects are distinguished as the "first" and "last." From the passages where they are mentioned (Yas. xliv. 19, xlviii. 4), their meaning cannot be ascertained with certainty. But happily we find them mentioned in later Avesta writings (see Yt. ii. 1) by more expressive names; one of the intellects is called *âsnô khratu*, "the original intellect or wisdom," which we can best identify with the "first" in the Gâthas; the other is styled *gaoshô-srûtô khratu*, "the wisdom heard by the ear," which corresponds to the "last." Another name of the "first" is *mainyu khratu* (*mînô khird*), "spiritual or heavenly wisdom." Now we cannot be mistaken as to the meaning of these two intellects. The "first intellect" is not from earth, but from heaven; not human, but divine. The "last intellect" represents what man has heard and learned by experience. The wisdom gained in this way is, of course, inferior to the heavenly wisdom. Only the latter can instruct man in the higher matters of life, as we see from a later book called "Mînôkhird," which is written in Pâzand (see p. 105).

The "two lives" are distinguished as *astvat*, "bodily," or *pardhu*, "prior life," and as *manahya*, "mental," or *daibitya*, "the second" (see Yas. xxviii. 3; xliii. 3; xlv. 1; xlvi. 19). Their meaning is clear enough, and requires no further comment; they express our idea "body and soul."

ZARATHUSHTRA'S THEOLOGY.

To be distinguished from these "two lives," are the "first" and the "last lives," which mean this life and that hereafter. The idea of a future life, and the immortality of the soul, is expressed very distinctly already in the Gâthas, and pervades the whole of the later Avesta literature. The belief in a life to come is one of the chief dogmas of the Zend-Avesta. See the passages about the fate of the soul after death, translated in the third Essay (pp. 220, 254).

Closely connected with this idea is the belief in HEAVEN and HELL, which Spitama Zarathushtra himself clearly pronounced in his Gâthas. The name for Heaven is *Garôdemâna* (*Garotmân* in Persian), "house of hymns," because the angels are believed to sing hymns there (see Yas. xxviii. 10; xxxiv. 2), which description agrees entirely with the Christian idea as founded on Isaiah vi. and the Revelation of St. John. Garô-demâna is the residence of Ahuramazda and the most blessed men (Yas. li. 15). Another more general name for Heaven is *ahu vahishta*, "the best life," afterwards shortened to *vahishta* only, which is still extant in the modern Persian *bahisht*, "paradise."

Hell is called *Drûjô demâna*, "house of destruction," in the Gâthas. It is chiefly the residence of the poets and priests of the Deva religion, the Rishis of the Brahmans (Yas. xlvi. 11). The later name is *Duzhaṇha* (Yasht xix. 44), which is preserved in the modern Persian *Dûzakh*, "hell."

Between Heaven and Hell is CHINVAT PERETU (*Chinvad pûl*), "the bridge of the gatherer," or "the bridge of the judge" (*Chinvat* can have both meanings), which the soul of the pious alone can pass, while the wicked fall from it down into Hell. It is mentioned, as we have seen, already in the Gâthas (Yas. xlvi. 10, 11).

The belief in the RESURRECTION of the body at the time of the last judgment also forms one of the Zoroastrian dogmas, as the reader will have learned from the passage quoted above (p. 217). In consequence of Burnouf's inquiries into the phrase *yavaêcha yavatâtaêcha* (which had been translated by Anquetil "till the resurrection," but which means nothing but "for ever and ever"), the existence of such a doctrine in the Zend-Avesta was lately doubted. But there is not the slightest reason for doubting it, as any one may convince himself from the passage quoted in p. 217, where it is clearly stated that the dead shall rise again. That the resurrection of the dead was a common belief of the Magi, long before the commencement of our era, may be learned from the statement of Theopompos (see pp. 8, 9). Now the question arises, had Spitama Zarathushtra already pronounced this doctrine, which is one of the chief dogmas of Christianity, and of the Jewish and Mohammedan religions, or is it of later, perhaps foreign, origin?

Though in the Gâthas there is no particular statement made of the resurrection of the dead, yet we find a phrase used which was afterwards always applied to signify the time of resurrection, and the restoration of all life that has been lost during the duration of creation. This is the expression *frashem kerenaon ahûm* .(Yas. xxx. 9,[1] see p. 150), "they make the life lasting," *i.e.*, they perpetuate the life. Out of this phrase the substantive *frashô-kereti*, "perpetuation" of life, was formed, by which, in all the later Avesta books, the whole period of resurrection and palingenesis at the end of time is to be understood. The resurrection forms only a part of it. That this event was really included in the term of *frashô-kereti* one may distinctly infer from Vend. xviii. 51, where Spenta-Armaiti (the earth) is invoked to restore "at the triumphant renovation" of creation, the lost progeny, in the form of one "knowing the Gâthas, knowing the Yasna, and attending to the discourses" (see p. 249).

According to these statements, there can be no doubt

[1] A full explanation of it is to be found in the author's work on the Gâthas, vol. i. pp. 109-112.

that this important doctrine is a genuine Zoroastrian dogma, which developed itself naturally from Spitama Zarathushtra's sayings. There is not the slightest trace of its being borrowed from a foreign source. Besides these direct proofs of its forming a genuine and original part of Zoroastrian theology, it agrees completely with the spirit and tendency of the Parsi religion. All life of the good creation, especially that of man, bodily as well as spiritual, is a sacred pawn intrusted by God to man who must keep his body free from impurity, and his soul from sin. If death destroy the body (in the natural course),[1] it is not the fault of man who falls to an inexorable fate; but it is considered as the duty of God, who is the preserver of all life, to restore all life that has fallen a prey to death, to destroy this arch-enemy of human life, and so make life everlasting. This is to be done at the time of the resurrection.

A detailed description of the resurrection and the last judgment is contained in the 31st chapter of the Bundahish (see pp. 70-77 Westerg.), which is, no doubt, founded on original Avesta sources which are now lost. In it an old song is embodied, the purport of which is to show that, though it appears to short-sighted mortals impossible for the body (when once dissolved into its elements, and those elements scattered in every direction) to be restored again, yet nothing is impossible for the hand of the Almighty, who created heaven and earth, endows the trees with sap, gives life to embryos in the womb, &c.

For awakening the dead bodies, restoring all life destroyed by death, and holding the last judgment, the great prophet *Sosyosh* (*Saoshyâs* in the Avesta) will appear by order of Ahuramazda. This idea is already to be found in the Avesta texts, only with the difference, that sometimes several (see p. 217), sometimes only one Soshyâns is men-

[1] Suicide is, according to the Zoroastrian religion, one of the most horrible crimes, belonging to the class of *marg-arzân*, or "deadly" sins. To the same class belongs adultery. The committal of such sins leads straight down to hell, whence no Ijashne can release the soul.

tioned (see p. 254). The later Parsi legends distinguish three great prophets who will appear before the end of the world. These are the men who will perpetuate life (who will produce *frashô-kereti*), men of the same stamp as the ancient prophets and fire-priests, and bearing the same name, viz., Saoshyantô. They will be commissioned to check the influence of the devil, which increases at the time when this world is verging towards its end, by restoring truth and faith and the good Zoroastrian religion. Their names are poetical and imply a simile; the dark period of wretchedness and sin, in which they appear, being compared to night, and the era of eternal bliss, they are endeavouring to bring about, being likened to the brilliant day. The first of these prophets is called *Hukhshathra Mâo* (Hushêdar-mâh), " the moon of happy rule;" the second is *Hukhshathra Bâmya* (Hushêdar-bâmî), "the aurora of happy rule;" and the third and greatest is called *Saoshyâs* (Sosyosh). He is believed to be a son of Spitama Zarathushtra, begotten in a supernatural way. This means, that just as Spitama Zarathushtra was the greatest prophet and priest in ancient times, so will Sosyosh be the greatest of those to come. Therefore, he alone brings with him a new Nask of the Zend-Avesta, which was hitherto unknown, and reveals it to mankind.

APPENDIX.

———♦———

SOME further translations from the Zend-Avesta, prepared at various times by the author, but not hitherto published, together with his notes descriptive of the mode of performing some of the Parsi ceremonies, are here added in the form of an Appendix to the foregoing Essays.

I.—TRANSLATIONS FROM THE AVESTA.

These translations, which were written by the author in German, supply the following additions to the passages already given in the third Essay :—

1.—*Vendidad, Fargard III.* 1-23, *and* 34, 35.

1. Creator of the settlements supplied with creatures, righteous one ! Where is the first most pleasing (spot) of this earth ?[1] Then said Ahuramazda : Wherein, indeed, a righteous man shall pray,[2] O Spitama Zarathushtra ! holding the firewood, holding the Barsom, holding the milk-offering (*gâush jîvya*), holding the Homa-mortar. [(Pâzand) Recite the words containing *âkhshti*[3]

---

[1] Or "Where is the first (spot) most pleasing to this earth," according to the Pahlavi translator.
[2] So understood by the Pahlavi translator, who uses the word *frand-mêd*; compare also Yas. lxii. 1. This Pahlavi word can, however, also be read *fravâmêd*, " goes forth."

[3] This appears to refer to the word *âkhshti* in the Afringân Dahmân (see Yas. lx. 5). The passage containing this word is the most sacred part of the Afringân, during the recital of which some sandal-wood is thrown into the fire, and it must occur in all Afringâns.

with religion; they may invoke both Mithra, ruling over wide fields, and Râma-qâstra].[1]

2, 3. Creator, &c. [as in ver. 1]. Where is the second most pleasing (spot) of this earth? Then said Ahuramazda: Wherein, indeed, a righteous man has built a house provided with fire, with cattle, with a wife, with a son, with plenty. Thenceforward the cattle of this house are in abundance, the righteousness in abundance, the pasture[2] in abundance, the dog in abundance, the wife in abundance, the child in abundance, the fire in abundance, the whole good creation in abundance.

4. Creator, &c. [as in ver. 1]. Where is the third most pleasing (spot) of this earth? Then said Ahuramazda: Wherein, indeed, one cultivates, O Spitama Zarathushtra! the most corn, and pasture, and fruit-bearing trees; either where one provides water for unwatered (land), or where one provides drainage for watery (land).

5. Creator, &c. [as in ver. 1]. Where is the fourth most pleasing (spot) of this earth? Then said Ahuramazda: Wherein, indeed, cattle and draught beasts are born most.

6. Creator, &c. [as in ver. 1]. Where is the fifth most pleasing (spot) of this earth? Then said Ahuramazda: Wherein, indeed, cattle and draught beasts void most urine.[3]

7. Creator, &c. [as in ver. 1]. Where is the first most unpleasing (spot) of this earth? Then said Ahuramazda: What is on the ridge of Arezûra,[4] O Spitama Zarathushtra! on which the demons congregate out of the pit of destruction (hell).

8. Creator, &c. [as in ver. 1]. Where is the second most unpleasing (spot) of this earth? Then said Ahuramazda: Wherein, indeed, both dead dogs and dead men are most lying buried.

9. Creator, &c. [as in ver. 1]. Where is the third most un-

---

[1] This passage is here taken either as a Pâzand interpolation, or as an Avesta quotation in the Pahlavi translation. It has reference to the Dir-Mihir or Agiari, where Mithra and Râma-qâstra (the angel Râm, see p. 214) are supposed to dwell, and where they must be invoked. Some MSS. have "*I* will invoke," in which case the passage may perhaps be taken as an exclamation of the righteous man.

[2] Some MSS. and the Pahlavi translation have "clothing."

[3] The five most pleasing spots on the earth (or most pleasing to the spirit of the earth, if we accept the Pahlavi interpretation) are, therefore, the fire-temple, the house of a pious Zoroastrian, cultivated lands, stables, and pastures.

[4] A mountain said to be situated at the gate of hell.

pleasing (spot) of this earth? Then said Ahuramazda: Wherein, indeed, vaulted tombs[1] are most constructed, in which dead men are deposited.

10. Creator, &c. [as in ver. 1]. Where is the fourth most unpleasing (spot) of this earth? Then said Ahuramazda: Wherein, indeed, there are the most holes (of the creatures) of Angrômainyush.

11. Creator, &c. [as in ver. 1]. Where is the fifth most unpleasing (spot) of this earth? Then said Ahuramazda : Wherein, indeed, O Spitama Zarathushtra! the wife or child of a righteous man shall travel the devious[2] path, (and) he brings forth wailing words coupled with dust and with sand.

12. Creator, &c. [as in ver. 1]. Who first rejoices this earth with the greatest joy? Then said Ahuramazda: When, indeed, he most digs up where both dead dogs and dead men are lying buried.

13. Creator, &c. [as in ver. 1]. Who secondly rejoices this earth with the greatest joy? Then said Ahuramazda: When, indeed, he most demolishes the vaulted tombs in which dead men are deposited.

14. No one is carrying alone what is dead.[3] For if he should carry alone that which is dead, the Nasush would indeed defile (him) from the nose, from the eye, from the tongue, from the chin, from the sexual part, from the anus.[4] This Drukhsh Nasush falls upon them (on such carriers), on their speech,[5] (and) afterwards they are impure for ever and ever.

---

[1] Covered tombs are forbidden to the Zoroastrians, as the corpse must remain exposed to the light of the sun, and not be laid in any closed sepulchre.

[2] The Dasturs understand by *varaithîm pañtãm* the forbidden or perilous path of death, and consider this passage as a direct prohibition of all lamentations and outward signs of mourning for the dead. The Pahlavi commentary is obscure, but appears to describe the path as grievous, but to return upon it as still more gloomy or impracticable.

[3] No corpse can be carried by less than two men, according to the religious laws of the Zoroastrians.

[4] The *drukhsh yâ nasush*, or demon of corruption, issues from the corpse and settles upon the man who is carrying it improperly. It seems likely that the text means to state that the Nasush issues from all the nine openings of the body, but in that case the doubtful word *paitish-qarena* must be "ear" (not "chin" or "jaw"); it is equivalent to a Sanskrit form *pratisravaya*, which would not be an impossible term for an "ear."

[5] This is the traditional explanation, which seems probable enough.

15. Creator, &c. [as in ver. 1]. Where should be the place of this man who is an *iristô-kasha*[1] (single carrier of the dead)? Then said Ahuramazda: Where there may be the most waterless and treeless (spot) of this earth, with the most ground fit for the purification ceremony and the most dry land; and the cattle and draught beasts shall go least forth on the paths, and (there are least) fire of Ahuramazda, and Barsom rightly arranged, and men who are righteous.

16. Creator, &c. [as in ver. 1]. How far from fire, how far from water, how far from the Barsom to be arranged, how far from righteous men?

17. Then said Ahuramazda: Thirty steps from fire, thirty steps from water, thirty steps from the Barsom to be arranged, three steps from righteous men.

18, 19. There the Mazdayasnians should enclose for him an enclosure of this earth. Then for victuals they who are Mazdayasnians shall provide—then for clothes they who are Mazdayasnians shall provide—(some) among the very hardest and foulest. These victuals let him eat, these clothes let him wear, always till when he shall become an aged man, elderly or impotent.[2]

20, 21. Then when he shall become an aged man, elderly or impotent, the Mazdayasnians should afterwards, in the most effectual, most rapid, and most skilful manner, strip the extent of the skin, the support of the hair,[3] off his head. To the most voracious of the beneficent spirit's carnivorous creatures, the birds (and) vultures, one should deliver over the body, speaking thus: These depart with him, all (his) evil thoughts, and evil words, and evil deeds. And if other wicked deeds were perpetrated by him, his atonement is through *patita* (renunciation of sin); moreover, if other wicked deeds were not perpetrated by him, the *patita* of that man is (completed) for ever and ever.

22. Creator, &c. [as in ver. 1]. Who thirdly rejoices this

---

[1] The *iristô-kasha* is one who carries the dead in an improper manner, and must be carefully distinguished from the *nasu-kasha* (Vend. viii. 11, 13), who is the lawful carrier.

[2] According to the Pahlavi translation, and the Farhang-i Oîm-khadûk (p. 5, ed. Hoshangji), the *hanô*, "aged man," is one seventy years old; the *zaururô*, "elderly man," is one of fifty; and the *pairishtâ-khshudrô*, "impotent or decrepit man," is one of ninety years.

[3] The Pahlavi translator says: "He is detained on a summit, on the top of a hill," till they scalp or behead him.

earth with the greatest joy? Then said Ahuramazda: When, indeed, he most destroys the holes of (the creatures) of Angrô-mainyush.

23. Creator, &c. [as in ver. 1]. Who fourthly rejoices this earth with the greatest joy? Then said Ahuramazda: When, indeed, he cultivates, O Spitama Zarathushtra! the most corn, and pasture, and fruit-bearing trees; either where he provides water for unwatered (land), or where he provides drainage for watery (land).

24-33. [See the translation in pp. 235-237.]

34, 35. Creator, &c. [as in ver. 1]. Who fifthly rejoices this earth with the greatest joy? Then said Ahuramazda: When, indeed, O Spitama Zarathushtra! he shall labour on this earth, (and) gives with righteousness and goodness to a righteous man. When, indeed, O Spitama Zarathushtra! he shall labour on this earth, (and) gives not with righteousness and goodness to a righteous man, one should thrust him out of the bountiful earth (Armaiti) into darkness, and distress, and the worst existence, and he must submit to all thorns.

36-42. [Not translated.]

2.—*Vendidad, Fargard IV.* 44-55.

44-46. And[1] when men of the same (Mazdayasnian) religion should come here, either brothers or friends, seeking property, or seeking a wife, or seeking wisdom; if they should come seeking property, they may acquire their property here; if they should come seeking a wife, you may let a woman marry; if they should come seeking wisdom, you may recite the beneficent text[2] both early in the daytime and late, both early in the night-time and late, for the increase in wisdom of the learner[3] for the

---

[1] Ver. 44 has been already translated in p. 240, but it is so closely connected with the following verses that it is necessary to repeat it here.

[2] The Pahlavi translation adds: "That is, its words are to be taught."

[3] The Pahlavi version is: "When it may have increased his wisdom (that is, when it may be made quite easy to him) and he may have repeated (?) it through righteousness (that is, he may have quite understood what is declared by it)." The Avesta word *vîdrvânahê* ("of the learner") occurs nowhere else, and is here explained by *bari darâd* in Pahlavi, which is equally obscure, but the general sense indicated by the Pahlavi is that of "learner or pupil." It may, however, be remarked that if *vîdrvânahê* be traced to *vi-dru* we ob-

sake of righteousness; and with righteousness and reverence he sits at home for increase in wisdom.¹ In the middle of both day and night he may sleep, by day and by night, always till when they should recite those sayings which the Herbads had previously recited.² They (the sayings) are adapted for men (who are) like boiling water (through zeal). Not for meat, not for clothes, (but) unrewarded, must he (the teacher) utter the chapters (Hâs).³

47. And, moreover, I tell thee thus, O Spitama Zarathushtra! verily the priest (*magava*)⁴ must recite from it sooner for the married man than for thee, for him with a house than for him without a house, for him with a son than for him without a son, for him with property than for him without property.

48. And of these two men he shall be more possessed of the good mind (Vohu-manô) who shall promote the growth of meat (or cattle) than he who does not. So he being dead, he is as much as an *asperena*,⁵ he is as much as a young animal, he is as much as a draught beast, he is as much as a man (in weight).⁶

---

tain a meaning ("of the fugitive or refugee") which would also suit the passage, as the men seem to have come as exiles from their own homes. The anomalous Pahlavi word *darâḍ* can also be read *girikht*, which suggests *girîkht*, "fled" (although this is generally written *virîkht*); and the Pahlavi phrase would then mean: "and he may have fled on account of righteousness." The explanatory phrases of the Pahlavi translation, given above in parentheses, are probably later interpolations. The phrase "to make easy" is a Pahlavi and Persian idiom for "to learn by heart."

¹ The Pahlavi version is: "In awe of God and thankfulness towards God that wisdom increases which is made easy to him, (and) he is constant in exertion that he may retain it by labour and the grace of God." That *vaonem* (which is here rendered by Pahl. *ayâjishn*, "exertion") means

"home, place," is plain from the passage, Vend. xxi. 4: *hām yaêtâonhô yaonemcha avi zâmcha, zâmcha avi yaonemcha*, "(the waters) striving towards home and the earth, towards the earth and home (in the sea Vourukasha)."

² The Pahlavi version adds the name of Adarpâd Mâraspendân.

³ The Pahlavi version is: "Thou shouldst not speak of the non-giving of meat nor of clothes which should be thine; always say: No! and afterwards even, at the time, say: A little!"

⁴ The Pahlavi version renders *yatha magavô fravâkhshôiḍ* by: "as (one) who has progressed in the *Maghî* (the Barashnom ceremony), that is, has no wife;" alluding to the fact that a man undergoing that ceremony must live separate from his wife.

⁵ A weight equivalent to a *dirham*.

⁶ Probably referring to the weight of his good works.

49. For this man, on meeting, fights with Astô-vîdhôtu.[1] Whoever fights an arrow shot by himself, whoever fights Zemaka (the Winter demon, and) wears scanty clothing, whoever fights a wicked man, a tyrant, and (strikes him) on the head,[2] whoever fights an unrighteous apostate (and) starvation;[3] (any) of these deeds being performed a first time, is not (to be done) a second time.

50. That such as are in this material world may here understand (the agony) of this exploit there,[4] one should cut away to the bones with iron knives; verily, it is greater than any such (agony) of his mortal body.[5]

51. That such as are in this material world may here understand (the agony) of this exploit there, one should tear away to the bones with iron pincers; verily, it is greater than any such (agony) of his mortal body.

52. That such as are in this material world may here understand (the agony) of this exploit there, one should fall involuntarily into a pit (deep as) a hundred men; verily, it is greater than any such (agony) of his mortal body.

53. That such as are in this material world may here understand (the agony) of this exploit there, one should stand involuntarily on an extreme verge (of a precipice).[6]

---

[1] The demon of death, who is said, in later writings, to cast a halter around the necks of the dead to drag them to hell, but if their good works have exceeded their sins they throw off the noose and go to heaven. Perhaps the grammatical difficulties of this sentence may be best overcome by the following translation :— " For this one, Astô-vîdhôtu, on meeting men, fights."

[2] The Pahlavi version says : " A beheader like Zarhûndâd."

[3] If asha be taken in its primitive sense of "right," this phrase may merely mean : "whoever fights mischievous and unusual hunger." The Pahlavi version, instead of "starvation," has : "a tyrant like Mazdak(-i Bâmdâdân who ate his own liver, and it was given to him in anguish and death);" but the passage in parenthesis is not found in the oldest MSS. In the Pahlavi each clause of the sentence is also wound up by stating that "his fight is with Astô-vîdhôtu," that is, at the risk of death.

[4] That is, of the conflict of the soul with Astô-vîdhôtu in the other world. Possibly aêtadha (here translated "here") may be taken as the missing noun " agonies ; " compare aêithâhu, "through terrors," Yt. xxii. 25, see p. 222.

[5] The translation of this difficult passage has been much revised, so as to correspond more closely with the text without introducing additional words, which are always hazardous suggestions.

[6] The Pahlavi translator misunderstands this verse as referring to sexual enjoyment.

X

54. That such as are in this material world may here understand (the agony) of this exploit there, one knowing a lie should drink up the beneficial, golden, intelligent water with denial of the truth (*Rashnu*) and breach of promise (*Mithra*).[1]

55. Creator, &c. [as in iii. 1]. Whoever knowing a lie should drink up, &c. [as in ver. 54]; what is his punishment? Then said Ahuramazda: One may strike seven hundred blows with a horse-goad, seven hundred with a scourge.[2]

3.—*Vendidad, Fargard V.*

1. A man dies there in the depths of the valleys; thereupon a bird flies aloft from the summits of the hills into the depths of the valleys; it feeds upon the body of the dead man. Then the bird flies aloft from the depths of the valleys to the summits of the hills; it flies on to a tree, either of the hard or of the soft (kinds). It (the *nasush*, "dead matter") is vomited on it, is voided on it, is dropped on it.

2. A man goes forth there from the depths of the valleys to the summits of the hills; he goes up to the tree where that bird was; he wants faggots for the fire; he fells it, he hews it, he splits it,[3] he kindles it in the fire, the offspring of Ahuramazda. What is the punishment for this?

3. Then said Ahuramazda: No dead matter (*nasush*) brought by a dog, none brought by a bird, none brought by a wolf, none brought by the wind, none brought by a fly, pollutes a man.

---

[1] This refers to an ordeal in which a cup of water is drunk after solemnly invoking curses upon one's head if one has not told the truth. The water is prepared with great solemnity, and contains various sacred substances, among them some Homa juice, which is referred to in the Pahlavi version by the epithet *gôkard-hômand* for *saokeñtavaittim*, "beneficial;" and a little gold is added, which accounts for the second epithet in the text. See the Saugand-nâmah.

[2] The Pahlavi version adds: "Whoever performs an ordeal (*var*) his punishment—says a voice—is this."

[3] The additional words, *dâyata dâityâ-pairishta*, "it was kept lawfully inspected," appear to be merely an Avesta quotation in the Pahlavi translation. This inspection is afterwards more fully noticed in the long Pahlavi commentary to ver. 4, where it is stated that firewood must be rejected if contaminated with dead matter, or if decayed, or from a gallows, or mixed with grease, or polluted by a menstruous woman, except in case of death or distress; the burning of such firewood is a *tanâpûhar* sin, but burning greasy wood is a mortal sin.

4. If, indeed, the dead matters which are brought by a dog, and brought by a bird, and brought by a wolf, and brought by the wind, and brought by a fly, are the dead matter (which) would be polluting a man, speedily my whole material world would overthrow (its) essential righteousness (or regularity, and be) distressing the soul (and) ruining the body, through the multitude of these dead matters which have perished upon this earth.

5. Creator, &c. [as in iii. 1]. A man pours water on to a corn-field; he shall go into the water-channel (*vaidhîm*)[1] through it, into (it) a second time, into (it) a third time, and after the fourth time they drag dead matter in, (be they) dog, or fox, or wolf. What is the punishment for this?

6. Then said Ahuramazda, &c. [as in ver. 3].

7. If, indeed, the dead matters, &c. [as in ver. 4].[2]

8. Creator, &c. [as in iii. 1]. Does the water destroy a man? Then said Ahuramazda: The water does not destroy a man. Astô-vîdhôtu binds him; the flying demon (*Vayô*)[3] conveys him bound; the water carries (him) up, the water carries (him) down, the water casts (him) away; the birds (*vayô*) then devour him. There[4] he then proceeds, through fate he then departs.

9. Creator, &c. [as in iii. 1]. Does the fire destroy a man? Then said Ahuramazda: The fire does not destroy a man. Astô-

---

[1] In Pahlavi *jôi*, "a rivulet."

[2] The Pahlavi commentary on this passage states: "It is declared by the Avesta, the dry channel of a rivulet (*jôi khûshk vurû*, Pers. *burû*) is to be inspected for dead matter. *Yêzi rasen Mazdayasna zâm raodhayen* ('If the Mazdayasnians wish they may irrigate the land')." It then proceeds to say that a man before admitting the water must descend three times into the channel and inspect it carefully, to see that it is free from impurity, and after a fourth inspection he may allow the water to enter. Further provisions are made in case of the inspection being impracticable, and as to the merit acquired by diverting the water from any impurity in its way. Most of this commentary is omitted in Spiegel's edition of the Pahlavi text, but will be found in the old MS. at the India Office Library in London, mentioned in p. 95.

[3] *Vyê-i sarîtar*, "the evil Vyê," in the Pahlavi version; this is the Vaê i-vatar of the Mainyô-i-khard (ii. 115), where he is one of the demons who oppose the soul's progress towards heaven.

[4] That is, to the other world. The Pahlavi version has: "When he sets out back from thence (that is, shall come) fate will convey him back (that is, she is in the leading path when he shall come)."

vîdhôtu binds him; the flying demon (*Vayô*)[1] conveys him bound; the fire consumes the bones and vitality. There he then proceeds, through fate he then departs.[2]

10. Creator, &c. [as in iii. 1]. They pass out of summer, then in winter how should they act, they who are Mazdayasnians? Then said Ahuramazda: In every dwelling, in every neighbourhood,[3] they shall erect three Katas for any one when dead.

11. Creator, &c. [as in iii. 1]. How large are these Katas for any one when dead? Then said Ahuramazda: So that he may not strike his head against the upper part,[4] nor the further end with the feet, nor across with the hands; verily, this is a lawful Kata for any one when dead.

[1] The Pahlavi version adds: "That is when, as some say, the good Vâyû will ever receive him." This refers to the Vaê-i-veh of the Mainyô-i-khard (ii. 115), where he is one of the angels who assist the soul's progress to heaven. He is identical with the angel Râm, the *Vayu* of the Râm Yasht, see p. 214.

[2] The Pahlavi commentary on this passage is: "Worldly (benefits are acquired) through fate, spiritual through action; some say that wife, child, wealth, authority, and life are through fate, the rest through action. The happiness which is not destined for a man he never attains to; (this) is evident from the passage (beginning): *gairi-masô anhô aêtahê* ("thou mightest be mountain-sized of this"); that which is destined for him, and which will come before him through exertion, is *anyô aredrô zeñgô qarenô* ("the other persistent glory"), and it was through his sinfulness when trouble happens to him. *Aḍ qarenô frapairyêiti* ("then glory delivers") and the misfortune destined for him he is able to avert by proper exertion; *pouru-qarenanhô ashava Zarathushtra* ("full of glory (he is) O righteous Zarathushtra!"); and his sinfulness ever anew destines it (misfortune) for him. *Aêshâmcha narãm* ("and of these men") one man, when through the destiny of another man it was necessary for him, had died when through the destiny of that dead one it was still improper, but he (the first one) was able to do it so that, through the slaying of that innocent one, justice (*râdth*) should well deal with this quarrel." This commentary is a fair specimen of the mode in which Avesta quotations are used in the Pahlavi version of the Vendidad. In the above quotations the word *qarena*, "glory, brilliance," is probably used for *bakhta*, "fate, destiny," which would obviously be more appropriate in meaning. Both these words would be equivalent to the same Huzvârish logogram, *gadman*, and this fact might lead to the one word being substituted for the other, provided we assume that the Avesta quotations had been, at one time, written in Pahlavi.

[3] The oldest Pahlavi MSS. have merely, *Mân vîs khânak khadûk dast kaḍo*, explaining *mân* by *khânak*, "a house," and *vîs* by *dast-i kaḍo*, "group of huts."

[4] The Pahlavi MS. version has: "So much as, when standing (that is, living) the head strikes not against the limits (*âhân*), nor when the foot is forth (that is, when the foot is extended), nor when the hand is unmoved (that is, his hand is held back)."

12. There shall they deposit his lifeless body for two nights, or three nights, or a month long, until the (time) when the birds shall fly forth, the plants shall shoot out, the descending (floods)[1] shall run off, (and) the wind shall dry up the ground.

13. Then when thus the birds shall fly forth, the plants shall shoot out, the descending (floods) shall run off, (and) the wind shall dry up the ground, the Mazdayasnians should now set his body viewing the sun.

14. If the Mazdayasnians should not set this body viewing the sun for the length of a year, thou shalt order as much punishment as for murdering a righteous man (a Zoroastrian), in order that the corpses (be) attended to, the Dakhmas attended to, the impurities[2] attended to, and the birds gorged.

15. Creator, &c. [as in iii. 1]. Wilt thou, who art Ahuramazda, release the water from the sea Vouru-kasha, together with the wind and clouds?

16. Wilt thou convey (it) to a corpse, thou who art Ahuramazda? Wilt thou convey (it) on to a Dakhma, thou who art Ahuramazda? Wilt thou convey (it) on to impurity, thou who art Ahuramazda? Wilt thou pour (it) forth on a bone, thou who art Ahuramazda? Wilt thou conduct (it) forth unnoticed, thou who art Ahuramazda? With those (impurities) wilt thou conduct (it) forth to the sea Pûitika?

17. Then said Ahuramazda: Verily it is so, O Zarathushtra! as thou sayest, O upright one! I who am Ahuramazda will release the water from the sea Vouru-kasha, together with the wind and clouds.

18. I will convey (it) to a corpse, I who am Ahuramazda; I will convey (it) on to a Dakhma, I who am Ahuramazda; I will convey (it) on to impurity, I who am Ahuramazda; I will pour

---

[1] What are "lying low" or "directed downwards," as implied by the word *nyâoñchô*, must be guessed from the context, and floods, streams, icicles, and snow might be suggested. The Pahlavi equivalent of *nyâoñchô* is ambiguous, even in the best MSS., and may be read either *vashâyingunth*, "a clearing off, an open sky," or *nishâyingunth*, "solidification, congelation;" the latter might be preferred, as the Pahlavi translator adds, "the adversity of winter shall depart;" but these readings are too irregular in form to be relied on.

[2] The term *hikhra*, "impurity," is applied to any bodily refuse or excretion from mankind or dogs, including saliva, skin, hair, nail-parings, &c. In this passage it appears to refer to exudations from a corpse.

(it) forth on a bone, I who am Ahuramazda; I will conduct (it) forth unnoticed, I who am Ahuramazda; with those (impurities) I will conduct (it) forth to the sea Pûitika.

19. There exist streaming currents[1] in the inner part of the sea for purifying, (and) the waters flow from the sea Pûitika to the sea Vouru-kasha,[2] to the tree Hvâpa;[3] here grow all my trees of every kind.[4]

20. I rain these down together,[5] I who am Ahuramazda, both as food for the righteous man and fodder for the well-yielding ox. Man shall eat my corn, and fodder is for the well-yielding ox.

21. This is better, this is more excellent, than thou, upright one! sayest. By this speech the righteous Ahuramazda rejoiced him, the righteous Zarathushtra: Mayst thou purify for man the best (things) for procreation.[6] This which is the Mazdayasnian religion is pure, O Zarathushtra! He who purifies himself by good thoughts and good words and good deeds.[7]

22. Creator, &c. [as in iii. 1]. How much greater, better, and more excellent is this Zarathushtrian Provision against the

---

[1] Or perhaps "splashing waves;" the Pahlavi translation is obscure, but seems to say: "they remain in a water-skin (áv khátk, Pers. khík) and bucket (dûlá) kept full."

[2] The Pahlavi version adds: "Towards the southernmost side, and it (the water) stays behind in mist (pavan hir, or khir), and the blue (karud) body of (the sea) Satavaêsa stays behind around it. Pûitika stands away from the shore of Satavaêsa, this is a fact, but from which shore it stands away is not clear to me. The water comes to Satavaêsa through the bottom (pêkh); some say that it traverses a fissure (káfak)."

[3] The Pahlavi version adds: "Afarg says the root of a tree; Mêdôk-mâh (says) a forest."

[4] Some MSS. add the Avesta: "by hundreds, by thousands, by myriads of myriads;" and the Pahlavi version adds: "among species, chaiti heñti urvaranãm saredha ("how many are the kinds of trees?") that is the prin-

cipal species." Either a list of species is omitted, or chaiti here merely means "many," as the Pahlavi chand often does.

[5] That is, both waters and plants. The Pahlavi commentary ascribes this to Tishtar, according to the later tradition, thus: "he who is Tishtar takes the water (that) they may take it in the wells of waters it comes to."

[6] This is a quotation from the Speñta-mainyû Gâtha (Yas. xlviii. 5) which continues as follows:—"for the ox mayst thou nourish that of those labouring for our food." It forms part of an address to Armaiti, the spirit of the earth. The disconnected phrases which follow are probably also texts quoted from the Scriptures.

[7] The Pahlavi version adds the note that, "aṅhrãm (life, self) and daênãm (intuition, religion, self) are both the same.

Devas[1] above the other traditions in greatness and goodness and excellence.

23. Then said Ahuramazda: Verily, one may consider, O Spitama Zarathushtra! this Zarathushtrian Provision against the Devas above the other traditions in greatness and goodness and excellence, as the sea Vouru-kasha is above the other waters.

24. Verily, one may consider, &c. [as in ver. 23], as the greater water overpowers the lesser waters.[2] Verily, one may consider, &c. [as in ver. 23], as the greater tree overshadows the lesser trees.[3]

25. Verily, one may consider, &c. [as in ver. 23], as it has been both on and around this earth.[4]

Let the judge (*ratu*) be nominated, let the executor of the sentence (*sraoshávareza*) be nominated, on a Draona (consecrated cake) being uplifted or not uplifted, on a Draona being offered or not offered, on a Draona being delivered or not delivered.[5]

26. Afterwards this judge is able to remit for him a third of this punishment. And if other wicked deeds were perpetrated by him, his atonement is through *patita* (renunciation of sin); moreover, if other wicked deeds were not perpetrated by him, the *patita* of that man is (completed) for ever and ever.[6]

---

[1] The Vendidad, which is a corruption of *vîdaêrô-dâtem*, see p. 225.

[2] The Pahlavi version has: "as the great water when it advances upon the little water, bears (it) away when it falls into the *chitha*" (perhaps equivalent to *châh*, "a pit").

[3] The Pahlavi adds an obscure phrase which may perhaps, in the old MSS., be: *sarvân malkâ âb-akhêzak-ac*, "the king of cypresses is one (growing) in a marsh."

[4] The Pahlavi version in old MSS. has: "as it will travel (*barâ bâminêd*) to this earth and over the sky, that is, ever in all (places)." Then follows a commentary which seems to refer to the succeeding sentence, thus: "some say this about Nasush, and that in the eighth (fargard) about decision and judgment, is that in the Hûspârûm (Nask) about the formula (*nîrang*) of worship." There is evidently a change of subject here.

[5] The Pahlavi commentaries on this passage are: "The Dastur considers, (the Sraoshâvareza) accuses of sin." And with reference probably to the offender, the Dastur considers: "what was in his thoughts but not committed, and not in his thoughts but committed; what was promised him was not brought, and not promised was brought; what was his intention but not performed, and unintended but performed." This, however, throws little light into the obscurity of the Avesta text.

[6] This passage has occurred also in iii. 21, and perhaps "his punishment is abandoned" might be substituted for "his atonement is through *patita*," and "acquittal" be read instead of the second "*patita*." The

27. Creator, &c. [as in iii. 1]. When men happen to be in the same place, on a rug together, or on a mat together, and others are on it; there may be two men, or five, or fifty, or a hundred; (and) the same of women;[1] (and) then one of these men shall die; how many among the men does this Drukhsh Nasush (the destroyer, Corruption) reach with impurity and rottenness and filth?

28. Then said Ahuramazda: If he be a priest (who dies), verily, O Spitama Zarathushtra! this Drukhsh Nasush rushes forth; if she reaches the eleventh she pollutes indirectly to the tenth. If, however, he be a warrior, verily, O Spitama Zarathushtra! this Drukhsh Nasush rushes forth; if she reaches the tenth she pollutes indirectly to the ninth. If, however, he be a husbandman, verily, O Spitama Zarathushtra! this Drukhsh Nasush rushes forth; if she reaches the ninth she pollutes indirectly to the eighth.

29. Moreover, if it be a shepherd's dog (*pasush-haurva*), verily, &c. [as in ver. 28]; if she reaches the eighth she pollutes indirectly to the seventh. If, however, it be a house-dog (*vish-haurva*), verily, &c. [as in ver. 28]; if she reaches the seventh she pollutes indirectly to the sixth.

30. If, however, it be a bloodhound (*vohunazga*), verily, &c. [as in ver. 28]; if she reaches the sixth she pollutes indirectly to the fifth. If, however, it be a young (*tauruna*) dog, verily, &c. [as in ver. 28]; if she reaches the fifth she pollutes indirectly to the fourth.

31. If, however, it be a *sukuruna*[2] dog, verily, &c. [as in ver. 28]; if she reaches the fourth she pollutes indirectly to

drift of the sentence being that no offender can be tried or punished for an older offence than the one for which he has been already condemned. The Pahlavi version adds: "that is, when the Dastur considers and deplores the sin, and they shall perform good works uncomplainingly, it will be allowable for the judge (*ratu, i.e.,* Dastur) to remit one-third of the soul's sin; this is declared where the decision is among the judges [as in cases of appeal or joint decisions], not the judges' own; when it shall be the judges' own it will be allowable to remit the whole of it."

[1] The Pahlavi version misinterprets *hām nāirinām* by "in fellowship (and) in contact."

[2] What description of dog or animal is meant by this epithet, or any of the three succeeding, is quite uncertain. The Pahlavi version merely transcribes the Avesta words, and owns that the last three are not intelligible.

the third. If, however, it be a *jazhu* dog, verily, &c. [as in ver. 28]; if she reaches the third she pollutes indirectly to the second.

32. If, however, it be an *aiwizu* dog, verily, &c. [as in ver. 28]; if she reaches the second she pollutes indirectly the first. If, however, it be a *vizu* dog, verily, &c. [as in ver. 28]; if she reaches the first she pollutes indirectly the first.

33. Creator, &c. [as in iii. 1]. If, however, the dog be a fox (*urupi*), how many of the creatures of the beneficent spirit does the dog which is a fox pollute directly? how many does it pollute indirectly?[1]

34. Then said Ahuramazda: This dog, which is a fox, does not pollute directly (any) of the creatures of the beneficent spirit, nor does it pollute indirectly, any other than he that smites and kills (it). To him it adheres for ever and ever.

35. Creator, &c. [as in iii. 1]. Moreover, if he (who dies) be a miscreant, a two-legged unbeliever (*drvâo*),[2] as an unrighteous apostate is, how many of the creatures of the beneficent spirit does he pollute directly? how many does he pollute indirectly?

36. Then said Ahuramazda: Like any toad[3] dried up (and) over a year dead; for living, O Spitama Zarathushtra! a miscreant, a two-legged unbeliever, as an unrighteous apostate is, pollutes directly (any) of the creatures of the beneficent spirit; living he pollutes (them) indirectly.

37. Living it (the toad) spoils the water, living it quenches the fire, living it drives the cattle mad, living it strikes the righteous man a blow depriving of consciousness (and) cutting off life; not so (when) dead.

38. So, living, O Spitama Zarathushtra! a miscreant, a two-legged unbeliever, as an unrighteous apostate is, plunders the

---

[1] *Hâm raêthwayêiti* means that it contaminates or communicates contagion by direct contact, and *paitiraêthwayêiti* means that it infects or spreads infection through an intermediate person or thing.

[2] Or "a two-legged, unbelieving serpent."

[3] Strictly speaking, *vazayhu* is a poisonous lizard.

righteous man of a profusion¹ of food and clothing and wood and carpet² and iron; not so (when) dead.

39. Creator, &c. [as in iii. 1]. When we bring together, O righteous Ahuramazda! in the dwellings in this material world, the fire and Barsom and cups and Homa and mortar, (and) afterwards either a dog or a man of this dwelling shall die, how should they act, they who are Mazdayasnians?

40. Then said Ahuramazda: Off from these dwellings, O Spitama Zarathushtra! they should carry the fire and Barsom and cups and Homa and mortar, off from (them) the dead one. They may think of it as the lawful man (that) is both brought to the lawful (place) and devoured.³

41. Creator, &c. [as in iii. 1]. How should these Mazdayasnians bring the fire back again to this dwelling where the man had died?

42. Then said Ahuramazda: Nine nights should they who are Mazdayasnians hesitate in winter, but in summer a month long; afterwards these Mazdayasnians may bring the fire back again to this dwelling where the man had died.

43. Creator, &c. [as in iii. 1]. And if these Mazdayasnians should bring the fire back again to this dwelling where the man had died within the space of the nine nights, (or) within the space of the month long, what is the punishment for this?

44. Then said Ahuramazda: One may inflict on the vitiated body of such a one two hundred blows with a horse-goad, two hundred with a scourge.

45. Creator, &c. [as in iii. 1]. When in this Mazdayasnian dwelling a woman shall go with child for one month, or two months, or three months, or four months, or five months, or six months, or seven months, or eight months, or nine months, or

---

¹ The word *anhēush*, "of the world," although it would suit the sense well enough, appears to be a corruption since the time of the Pahlavi translation. Some MSS. have *hañhush*, others *hañhčush*, and the Pahlavi version translates the word by *asarîh*, "endlessness" (*sar*, "head," is always applied to the "end" in Pahlavi, *bûn*, "root, origin," being the "beginning"). In Yas. liii. 4, *hañhush* is translated in Pahlavi by *sêrîh*, "repletion," which is an approximation to the meaning of *asarîh*, while neither word can be used for "world."

² In Pahlavi *namad*, Pers. *namad*.

³ Alluding both to the dead body being taken to the Dakhma to be devoured by birds, and also to the Homa juice, considered as a creature to be consumed by a righteous man in the consecrated place.

ten months, and then this woman shall be delivered in childbirth of something lifeless, how should they act, they who are Mazdayasnians?

46-48. Then said Ahuramazda : Where there is in this Mazdayasnian dwelling especially the most ground fit for the purification ceremony, and the most dry land, &c. [as in iii. 15-17].

49. There the Mazdayasnians should enclose for her an enclosure of this earth. Then for victuals they who are Mazdayasnians shall provide, then for clothes they who are Mazdayasnians shall provide.

50. Creator, &c. [as in iii. 1]. What food should this woman first eat?

51. Then said Ahuramazda : Ashes with bull's urine, three draughts, or else six, or else nine ; these she should pour (by drinking)[1] on the receptacle of the dead within the effusing womb.

52. Then, afterwards, (she may swallow some) of the warm milk of mares and cows and sheep and goats, of (the fruits) with rind (and) without rind, and cooked meat undiluted, and true corn undiluted, and honey undiluted.

53. Creator, &c. [as in iii. 1]. How long should they hesitate? how long does she remain in seclusion, eating meat and corn and honey?

54. Then said Ahuramazda : Three nights they should hesitate ; three nights does she remain in seclusion, eating meat and corn and honey. Then, moreover, after the three nights she should wash over (her) body, freed from clothing, with bull's urine and water, on the nine stones (*magha*) ; so they should purify (her).

55. Creator, &c. [as in iii. 1]. How long should they hesitate? how long does she remain in seclusion after the three nights, in a separate place, with separate food, with separate clothing, apart from the other Mazdayasnians?

56. Then said Ahuramazda : Nine nights they should hesitate ; nine nights does she remain in seclusion after the three

---

[1] So understood by the Pahlavi translator and modern Parsis, but the Avesta may perhaps refer here rather to outward purification, preparatory to drinking the milk, than to drinking itself.

nights, in a separate place, with separate food, with separate clothing, apart from the other Mazdayasnians. Then, moreover, after the nine nights she should wash, &c. [as in ver. 54].

57. Creator, &c. [as in iii. 1], Are those clothes, set apart after purifying (and) washing, for the Zaota, or for the Hâvanân, or for the Atarevakhsha, or for the Frabaretar, or for the Abereta, or for the Asnâtar, or for the Raêthwishkara, or for the Sraoshâvareza,[1] or for the priest (who is) a man, or for the warrior, or for the husbandman?

58. Then said Ahuramazda: Those clothes, set apart after purifying (and) washing, are not for the Zaota, &c. [as in ver. 57, but substituting everywhere "not" for "or"].[2]

59. When in this Mazdayasnian dwelling there shall be a menstruous woman, or when there is a place marked by defloration (and) stained by intercourse, here she remains in it, and a rug and mat should cover (her) up, always so that she may frequently put out (her) hands together.

60. For I, (who am) Ahuramazda, allow no defiling of unused clothes, not the size of an *asperena*, not even so much as the infinitesimal quantity[3] this damsel would defile.

---

[1] These appear to be names of eight officiating priests in the ceremonies of ancient times, of whom only two are now employed, the Zaota, who is the chief officiating priest, and his assistant, the Rathwi, who takes the place of the remaining seven. These seven are now considered as spirits who are summoned by the Zaota when beginning to recite Visp. iii. (after finishing Yas. xi.), and the Rathwi answers in the name of each as he stands successively in their proper places. According to a diagram, given in some MSS., the Zaota's station being near the northern end of the *Arvis-gâh*, or ceremonial space, as he looks southwards towards the fire he has one of the spiritual priests facing him from beyond the fire, and a line of three of them stationed along each side of the *Arvis-gâh*. The stations of the eight priests, real and ideal, are as follows: 1, Zaota, on the north side; 2, Hâvanân, at the north-west corner; 3, Atarevakhsha, at the south-west corner; 4, Frabaretar, at the north-east corner; 5, Abereta, at the south-east corner; 6, Asnâtar, on the west side; 7, Raêthwishkara, on the east side; 8, Sraoshâvareza, on the south side. From the word *mashyâi*, "mortal, man," being put in apposition with *athaurunô*, the general term for "priest" which follows the enumeration of the officiating individuals in the text, it may be suspected that these latter were not considered as mortals even at the time this text was written.

[2] The meaning is that such clothes cannot be used by any respectable person, but only by the very lowest classes.

[3] What is immeasurably small, an indivisible atom; the word is *a-vimâm*, not *avi-mâm*. An *asperena* is a *dirham*.

61. And if these Mazdayasnians should cast over the dead one an infinitesimal quantity, such as the infinitesimal quantity this damsel would defile, none (of them) living shall be righteous, none (of them) dead has a share of the best existence (paradise). 62. He shall have that life of the wicked which is gloomy, originating in darkness, and dark. Verily, the wicked, through their own deeds, through their own tradition, shall depart that life for the worst existence (hell).

4.—*Vendidad, Fargard XIX.* 10-26, *and* 40-47.

10.[1] Zarathushtra recited the Ahuna-vairya (formula, thus): As a (heavenly) lord is to be chosen, &c.[2] The righteous Zarathushtra uttered (the hymn): That I shall ask Thee, tell it me right, O Ahura![3]

11, 12. Zarathushtra asked Ahuramazda: O Ahuramazda! most munificent spirit, creator of the settlements supplied with creatures, righteous one! (I am) waiting for (what are) to be fixed on the roof[4] (as protection) for[5] Ahuramazda, for the good well-thought (Vohumanô), for perfect rectitude (Asha-vahishta), for suitable wealth (Khshathra-vairya), for bountiful devotion (Spenta-ârmaiti). How shall I defend them from that Drukhsh, from the evil-doing Angrô-mainyush? How shall I exorcise the direct pollution, how the indirect pollution, how the corruption (*nasush*), from that Mazdayasnian home? How shall I purify the righteous man? How shall I bring the righteous woman purification?

---

[1] For verses 1-9, see pp. 253, 254.
[2] See p. 141, note 2.
[3] Yas. xliv., see pp. 158-161.
[4] This refers to what is mentioned in Zarathushtra's address to Ahuramazda in ver. 4 (see p. 253), which would be better translated as follows:—"Where dost thou keep (any) of this (*asânô?*) on this wide, round, far-compassed earth, to be fixed on the roof of the dwelling of Pourushaspa?" The word *paiti-zbarahi* can only be the locative of *paitizbaranh*, equivalent to Sans. *pratihvaras*, which would mean "a curving towards, a lean-to," a significant term for a roof which is actually used, in the latter form, in English technical language; and in Sanskrit *prati-hvara* (Rv. vii. 66, 14) is a term for the vault of the sky. *Darêjya* has been mistaken for the river *Dâraja* mentioned in the Bundahish (pp. 53, 58, W.) as having the house of Pourushaspa on its bank; but it is evidently only a gerund of the verb *darg*= *darez*, "to fix." Some Dasturs understand by *asânô* (in ver. 4) the *naugirah*, or "nine-jointed" staff used by Zarathushtra as a defence against the demons; they also understand *zbarahi* as the same "weapon" (comp. Pers. *zibar*, a "shield").

[5] Or "Resting-places (are) to be fixed on the roof for," &c.

13. Then said Ahuramazda: Do thou invoke, O Zarathushtra! the good Mazdayasnian religion. Do thou invoke, O Zarathushtra! that the Ameshaspentas may keep guard over the seven-regioned earth. Do thou invoke, O Zarathushtra! (the spirits) of the self-sustained universe, of boundless time, of the upper-working air (*vayu*). Do thou invoke, O Zarathushtra! the mighty wind created by Mazda, (and) the bountiful one (Armaiti), the lovely daughter of Ahuramazda.

14. Do thou invoke, O Zarathushtra! the Spirit (*fravashi*) of me who am Ahuramazda, that which is the greatest and best and most excellent, and strongest and wisest and most beautiful, and most pervaded by righteousness, whose soul is the beneficent text. Do thou thyself invoke this creation of Ahuramazda.

15. Zarathushtra proclaimed my word (thus): I invoke the rightful creation, created by Ahuramazda. I invoke Mithra of the wide cattle-pastures, the well-armed, with most glorious missiles (rays), with most victorious missiles. I invoke Srosh the righteous, the handsome, holding a sword in both hands against the head of the demons.

16. I invoke the beneficent text (*māthrô speñtô*) which is very glorious. I invoke (the spirits) of the self-sustained universe, of boundless time, of the upper-working air. I invoke the mighty wind created by Mazda, (and) the bountiful one (Armaiti), the lovely daughter of Ahuramazda. I invoke the good Mazdayasnian religion, the Zarathushtrian Provision against the Devas (Vendidad).

17. Zarathushtra asked Ahuramazda: O giver of good,[1] Ahuramazda! with what ceremony shall I reverence, with what ceremony shall I propitiate, this creation of Ahuramazda?

18. Then said Ahuramazda: Thou shalt go, O Spitama Zarathushtra! to (one) of the growing trees, a handsome, full-grown, strong (one, and) recite this saying: Reverence (to thee) O good tree, created by Mazda (and) right! righteousness is the best good, &c. [as in p. 141, note 2].

19. One may carry off the Barsom (twigs) from it, a span long, a barley-corn thick. Thou mayst not clip its clipped Bar-

---

[1] The reading *dâtô-vaṇhen* is doubtful; it has been altered to *dâtô aṇhen* in the old MSS., and is rendered in the Pahlavi version by *dâḍâr avâḍ hômanâe*, "Creator, mayst thou be (or may they be) prosperous!"

som, they should be righteous men (priests who do that). (One should be) holding (it) in the left hand, reverencing Ahuramazda, reverencing the Ameshaspentas, and the golden-hued Homa, the exalted,[1] and the handsome (spirits), and the gifts of Vohumanô (saying to the Barsom): O good one, created by Mazda (and) right! (thou art) the best.

20. Zarathushtra asked Ahuramazda: Omniscient Ahuramazda! thou art sleepless, unstupefied, thou who art Ahuramazda! a good-minded man pollutes himself directly, a good-minded man pollutes himself indirectly, from a person who is stricken by a demon, he pollutes himself directly with a demon; may the good-minded man become purified?

21. Then said Ahuramazda: Thou shouldst procure, O Zarathushtra! bull's urine lawfully formed by a young entire bull. Thou shouldst bring out the purified things[2] on the ground created by Ahura. The man who is a purifier (priest) should score around (it) a surrounding furrow.

22. He should mutter a hundred praises of righteousness (thus): Righteousness is the best good, &c. [as in p. 141, note 2]. Twice (as often) he should recite aloud the Ahuna-vairya (thus). As a (heavenly) lord is to be chosen, &c. [as in p. 141, note 2]. With four washings he should wash with bull's urine of (that) supplied by the bull, twice with water of (that) created by Mazda.

23. Purified shall they be, the good-minded man; purified shall they be, the man (who polluted him). The good-minded man shall draw on (his clothes) with the left arm and the right, with the right arm and the left. Then thou shouldst expose the good-minded man to the power-formed luminaries, that (some) of the stars appointed by destiny may shine upon him, always till when his nine nights shall elapse.

24. Then after the nine nights thou shouldst bring consecrated waters (zaothra) to the fire, thou shouldst bring (some) of the hard firewoods to the fire, thou shouldst bring (some) of the benzoin incense to the fire, (and) the good-minded man should have himself fumigated.

---

[1] Perhaps the grammatical irregularities would be diminished by taking this as a verb, and assuming that the priest's speech is addressed to the Homa, and not to the Barsom.

[2] Or, perhaps, "the purifier," if we suppose the nominative to have been substituted for the accusative, which is not an unusual irregularity in this fargard.

25. Purified shall they be, &c. [as in ver. 23, to] and the left. The good-minded man shall exclaim: Reverence to Ahuramazda! reverence to the Ameshaspentas! reverence to the other righteous ones!

26. Zarathushtra asked Ahuramazda: O omniscient Ahuramazda! shall I arouse the righteous man? shall I arouse the righteous woman? shall I arouse the frontier of the turbulent Deva-worshipping men? (that) they may consume the land created by Ahura, (that) they may consume the flowing water, the crops of corn, (and) other of its superfluities? Then said Ahuramazda: Thou mayst arouse them, O righteous Zarathushtra!

27–39. [See the translation in pp. 254–257.]

40. Srosh the righteous, prayed to (and) invoked, is pleased (and) attentive, the handsome, triumphant Srosh, the righteous! Thou shouldst bring consecrated waters (*zaothra*) to the fire, thou shouldst bring (some) of the hard firewoods to the fire, thou shouldst bring (some) of the benzoin incense to the fire. Thou shouldst propitiate the fire Vâzishta, the smiter of the demon Spenjaghra. Thou shouldst bring cooked victuals (and) plenty of sweetmeats.[1]

41. Thou shouldst propitiate Srosh the righteous, (that) Srosh the righteous may destroy the demons Kunda (stupidity?), Banga (drunkenness, and) Vibanga[2] (dead-drunkenness). He attacks the frontier of the wizards, the turbulent Deva-worshipping men, from the nearest[3] country having the purification ceremony. One should persevere in the practice, (and) should cultivate sheep's food (and) food for cattle in the pastures.

42. I invoke the Kara[4] fish (which is) in the water at the

---

[1] Very probably "gravy;" the idea of sweetness is based upon the Pahlavi version, which is not, however, altogether unambiguous.

[2] The Pahlavi version explains *vîbanga* as "drunk without wine," or inherently drunk; *vî* must be used here as an intensive prefix.

[3] From this point to the name Angrô-mainyush in ver. 44, both text and Pahlavi translation are omitted in all MSS. of the Vendidad with Pahlavi, except one or two which seem to have been amended from the Vendidad Sâdah. The word *daêrô*, which occurs in the MSS. before *mazdishtâd*, belongs to the Pahlavi version of the preceding clause.

[4] The chief of the water creatures. Ten of these fish, according to the Bundahish, are constantly employed in guarding the Hom tree, in the midst of the sea Vouru-kasha, from the assaults of a poisonous lizard sent by Angrô-mainyush to injure it.

bottom of deep lakes. I invoke the primeval self-sustained boundary, most resisting the creatures of the two spirits. I invoke the seven illustrious in fame, they are aged men, sons, (and) descendants.

43. He shouted (and) countershouted, he considered (and) reconsidered, (did) the deadly Augrô-mainyush,[1] the demon of demons, (with) Indra[2] the demon, Saurva[2] the demon, Nâonhaithya[2] the demon, Tauru, Zairicha,[3] Aêshma[4] the impetuous rusher, Akatasha the demon [(Pâzand) he causes frost produced by the demons, deadly decay, (and) old age ill-treating the fathers], Bûiti[5] the demon, Driwi[6] the demon, Daiwi[6] the demon, Kasvi[6] the demon, Paitisha the demon, the most demoniacal demon of the demons.[7]

44. Thus shouted he who is the evil-causing Augrômainyush,[8] the deadly: Why do the demons, the turbulent evil-originators, assemble in an assembly on the summit of Arezûra?[9]

45. The demons rushed, they shouted, the turbulent evil-originators; the demons howled, they shouted, the turbulent evil-originators; the demons displayed an evil eye, the turbulent evil-originators: We must assemble in our assembly on the summit of Arezûra.

46. Born, indeed, is he who is the righteous Zarathushtra, at the dwelling of Pourushaspa. How shall we procure his death? he is the smiter of the demons, he is the opponent of the demons, he is the destroyer of destruction (or falsehood); downcast is

[1] This appears to be a fragment of an old hymn in octosyllabic metre, which, with some irregularities, can be traced through the greater part of verses 43-45; it begins as follows:—

Fradavata vîdavata
Framanyatu vîmanyata
Aṇrô mainyush pouru-mahrkô.

[2] See pp. 272 and 308.
[3] The demons of disease and decay, compare Sans. *tura = âtura*, "diseased," and *jaras*, "decay." (See Darmesteter's Haurvatât et Ameretât, pp. 33, 34.)
[4] The demon of Anger or Wrath

(*khashm* in Persian). This *Aêshmô daêvô* appears to be the Asmodeus of the Apocryphal book of Tobit iii. 8.
[5] Compare Sans. *bhûta* and the vernacular *bhût*, the general name for goblins or evil spirits in India.
[6] These three demons are respectively Poverty, Deceit, and Dwarfishness; see Vend. ii. 29, p. 234.
[7] The word *daêvô* is taken as the last of this verse, and not as the first of the next one.
[8] Here ends the omitted passage mentioned in p. 336, note 3.
[9] The mountain said to be situated at the gate of hell.

Y

the Deva-worshipper, (with) the impurity (*nasush*) produced by the demons, lying, (and) falsehood.

47. The demons shouted, they rushed, the turbulent evil-originators, to the bottom of the world of darkness which is the raging hell.

II.—Translations from the Pahlavi Versions.

Excepting the first fargard of the Vendidad, these translations were written by the author in English. In revising them use has been made of collations of Spiegel's edition of the texts with Dastur Jamaspji's old MS. of the Pahlavi Yasna (see p. 96), with the London and Teheran MSS. of the Pahlavi Vendidad (see p. 95), and with Dastur Hoshangji's unpublished edition of the same.

The Pahlavi versions of the Avesta throw but little light upon the obscure passages in the original text, which are generally rendered by a slavishly literal translation, or even transliteration, with some faint attempt at explanation, more or less unfortunate in its result. The chief value of these versions consists in the longer commentaries which are often interpolated, especially in the Vendidad. They also indicate how the original Avesta was understood in the later Sasanian times,[1] and how it is understood by the present Dasturs, who rely almost entirely upon the Pahlavi version.

1.—*Pahlavi Yasna XXVIII.*

Happy was the thought, happy the word, and happy the deed, of the righteous Zarathushtra. [On account of proper thought and word and deed he was estimable in virtue.][2] The Ameshaspends held forth the Gâthas, [that is, they were kept forth in the world by them]. Devotion to you, O righteous Gâthas!

1. (*a*) I beg the reward of him who is Aûharmazd himself, through devotion, when I make intercession (with) God (for) the

---

[1] To which the last thorough revision of the Pahlavi texts may probably be referred, whatever date we may assume for their original composition.

[2] Explanations interpolated by the Pahlavi translators are enclosed in brackets, to distinguish them from the words inserted by the present translator, which are given in parentheses.

good, uplifting the hand (and) the mind also with its own joy. (b) In spirituality Aûharmazd is first, in the Gâtha-lore [1] is the increase of righteousness which (should) be in every action, [that is, actions are all to be performed through the Gâtha-lore]. (c) In that which is His wisdom, in the original wisdom, is the satisfaction of Gôshûrûn,[2] [that is, the care of cattle is to be undertaken with judgment].

2. (a) When I shall attain unto you,[3] O Aûharmazd! through good thought (Vohuman), [that is, perfect in rectitude I shall have come unto your own possession]; (b) give ye to me in both lives, (that) which is material and (that) which is spiritual, the happiness which is here (in this world) and that also which is there (in the other world). (c) Prosperity is owing to the assistance of righteousness, [that is, you give me through rectitude the abundance[4] which you give to that gladdener], and it is necessary to cause glory through joy.

3. (a) When I shall be your own, O Ashavahisht (and) Vohuman, who is first! [that is, I shall remain in your possession]; (b) and I shall be also Aûharmazd's own, through whose unweakened acquisition is their dominion, [that is, his sovereignty over the Ameshaspends is strict]; (c) and of her also who is the giver of increase, Spendarmad, I shall be her own, she comes to me with joy through calling; when I shall call unto you, come on towards me with joy.

4. (a) Whoever gives (his) soul into paradise (garôdmânô, it is) through the assistance of good thought (Vohuman), [that is, every one who gives has given it through the assistance of Vohuman]. (b) And his respect for the doers of deeds who do for him what is proper, is evidenced by that of Aûharmazd and the religion of Aûharmazd. (c) As long as I am a supplicant and wealthy, so long I have learned[5] the requirements of righteousness, duty and good works.

5. (a) O Ashavahisht! When do I see thee through the in-

---

[1] Or "psalmody" or "hymnology," but *pâsânîkîh* can hardly mean Gâtha-chanting here.
[2] The Pazand term for *gêush urvâ*, "the soul of the ox or earth."
[3] Observe that "you" and "thou" are not used indiscriminately in the Gâthas; "ye" or "you" always refers to the whole celestial council of the Ameshaspends, including Aûharmazd.
[4] Reading *padîkhrîh* = Paz. *padîqî*, see Mainyô-i-khard ii. 2, xlix. 6.
[5] Or "taught," or "am taught."

struction of good thought (Vohuman)? this I (would) know, [that is, I see thee at the time when every one is intelligent through rectitude, when will it be?] (*b*) When do I see also the place of Aûharmazd, who is a seeker of worth? that place is known through Srosh, [that is, when they have a Dastur he ought to know what happiness is from that place]. (*c*) That is the greatest text; he whose understanding is confounded by its belief and maintenance, he also whose understanding is confounded by the tongue, for him this one thing is excellent, when they shall form a priestly assembly (*aêrpatistân*).

6. (*a*) Grant the coming of good thought (Vohuman) to the body of others (and) the giving of long life to me, O Ashavahisht! [that is, may he not grant that thing which, in the future existence, they would require again to destroy]! (*b*) Through the true word he has shown thee, O Aûharmazd! to Zaratûsht; it is owing to him who is Thy powerful Vishtâsp that I am Thy delight, [that is, I am carrying Thee forth in goodness to the rulers]. (*c*) And my people (*manîkân*) also, O Aûharmazd! my disciples, are also carrying Thee forth in goodness. The distress of the distressers is when they shall thus take injury, [that is, the distress owing to them becomes inoperative].

7. (*a*) Grant me, O Ashavahisht! the reverence which is in plenteousness of good thought (Vohuman), [that is, may he so grant me reverence which, in the future existence, they shall not require again to destroy]! (*b*) And do thou grant me, O Spendarmad! that which is to be requested from Vishtâsp, the mobadship of the mobads (the high-priesthood); and my people also, my disciples, grant them the mobadship of the mobads. (*c*) And grant me a sovereign praiser, O Aûharmazd! Vishtâsp who when they chant this your text, [that is, they shall speak your tradition (*dîn*)], furnishes the arrangements so that they may make (it) continuous (they may propagate it).

8. (*a*) When thy excellence and thy religion, which is the best of other things, are in the best righteousness (Ashavahisht), let me enjoy it[1] through rectitude. (*b*) Let me obtain by prayer, O Aûharmazd! the man who is Frashôshtar, [that is, give up Frashôshtar into my discipleship]; give Frashôshtar my people also in his discipleship. (*c*) To them also then be liberal

---

[1] Reading *ghal ham-dôshdnê*.

as long as all are in good thought (Vohuman), [that is, ever cause thereby the happiness of Frashôshtar and the disciples of Frashôshtar till the future existence].

9. (*a*) Because of not coming to you, O Aûharmazd! I may not do this, [that is, I shall not come to you]; and Ashavahisht too I trouble not about happiness, I ask not even a single happiness which Ashavahisht deems undesirable. (*b*) Vohuman also, the excellent, I trouble not him, who is he who gives you this your infinitude, the praisers, [that is, he will bring Hûshêdar, Hûshêdar-mâh, and Sôshâns to your conference]. (*c*) You are propitious through the prayer of a beneficial sovereignty, [that is, you will be pleased with a beneficial sovereignty, and will give].

10. (*a*) When thus I shall be acquainted with[1] righteousness, and that also which is the gift of good thought (Vohuman), [that is, I shall have become fully acquainted with truth and rectitude], (*b*) which is proper, O Aûharmazd! may ye fulfil my desire with them! [that is, cause my happiness thereby]. (*c*) When thus, by what is useless to you, food and clothing are obtainable,[2] by that chanting, when it is not useful in your worship, let him obtain food and clothing.

11. (*a*) When I shall guard righteousness by observance, and good thought (Vohuman) also unto everlasting, [that is, I shall cause the protection of truth and rectitude], (*b*) teach Thou forth to me what is Aûharmazd, that is Thyself, in words. (*c*) Spirituality is the Gâtha-lore which is declared from this by Thy mouth, and till it is declared by that Thou wilt speak by Thy mouth, which was the first in the world, [that is, He who was first, His law became the Gâtha-lore].

2.—*Pahlavi Yasna XXIX.*

1. (*a*) To you, O Ameshaspends! Gôshûrûn complained, [some say[3] the lord Bull spoke towards the direction of Aûharmazd],[4] thus: To whom am I allotted as to feeding (and) keep-

---

[1] Reading *akâs hômandnê*.
[2] Reading *vindînidak*, "caused to obtain."
[3] This frequent phrase for introducing alternative interpretations in the Pahlavi version is literally: "there is (one) who thus says."
[4] The oldest reading is *khûdât-gâsh gûft val Aâharmazd rûno*.

ing? For whom am I formed? [that is, for whom am I created?] (*b*) This is he I (have) : Wrath who smites me with anger and is oppressive, [that is, he harasses me utterly], who is torturing, [that is, my immoderate beating disfigures me perpetually], and also a tearer away, [that is, he accomplishes the destruction of my life],[1] and a plunderer too, [that is, he utterly robs me]. (*c*) There is no well-wisher (*vâsnîdâr*) for me besides you, [that is, I know not any one from whom my welfare so (proceeds) as from you], so let one prepare for me what is good pasture.

2. (*a*) So he who is the former of cattle, Aûharmazd, asked thus: O Ashavahisht! who is the master of thy cattle? [that is, how is thy opinion of this as to who is the master of cattle?] (*b*) Who is given this authority to feed (and) to keep? who is it gives them pasture, and is also diligently promoting the cattle creation? [that is, gives it pasture, and thereby indicates its one cattle-guardian who will increase cattle]. (*c*) What is that lordship with goodness which, when they provide no nourishment, feeds it with authority? Who gives this reply to the non-Iranian[2] devastation of wicked Wrath, that they may make him stupefied?

3. (*a*) To him who (has) the guardianship of the bodies of cattle Ashavahisht spoke the reply: (He is) not without distress, for (he is) in distress, [that is, they shall effect his punishment]. (*b*) They are not aware of the peace of Rashn the just, and may they not know what (and) how much punishment they shall inflict upon the soul of a wicked one ! (*c*) Of beings he is the more powerful, [that is, the strength of him is that which is more effectual], who comes into action on calling to him, [that is, when they call him thus: Perform duties and good works! he does (them)].

4. (*a*) Aûharmazd is a computer of words, that he may form an account as to the sin and good works (*b*) which were done by them, demons and men, both formerly and also what they practise hereafter. (*c*) He is the deciding Lord, [that is, he determines action and law], so we are as is His will, [that is, even (what) is wanted by us is what He (wants)].

---

[1] This is the sin of *bôjôk-zêd*, which is defined in modern times as that of selling men or cattle, whether stolen or one's own property, into misery; also the sin of spoiling good clothes or food.

[2] Or "unmanly."

5. (*a*) So (rather) than you, O Ameshaspends! I diligently reverence, with uplifted soul (and) mental uplifting of hands, Him (who is) Aûharmazd, [that is, I reverence one thing more than the Ameshaspends, I reverence the things of Aûharmazd more, and I do (them)];[1] (*b*) that my soul may be with the bull Az, [that is, may I give my soul a reward[2]], (and) may I consult him who is Aûharmazd (about) that which is in doubt! [that is, (about) that of which I may be doubtful may it be possible for me to inquire of Aûharmazd]! (*c*) For the upright liver is no utter ruin, [that is, whoever lives with uprightness, in his soul is no ruin], nor for the increaser,[3] [that is, for the increaser who possesses anything through rectitude it is not so as (aforesaid], except him who is wicked, for to the wicked one it happens.

6. (*a*) Thus with his mouth said Aûharmazd intelligently: Destruction is to be avoided, [that is, wisely was it said by him that there is a remedy for the mischief from the evil spirit]. (*b*) No such lordship is to be admitted, [that is, in that place it is not possible to effect a remedy because they do not even consider the Lord as lord], no mastership whatsoever, for the sake of righteousness, is to be given, [that is, a Dastur even, such as it is necessary to introduce, they do not possess]. (*c*) So for him who is an increaser, who is a tiller, thou art destined and art formed, [that is, for him who is diligent (and) moderate thou art given].

7. (*a*) That which is copiousness in the text Aûharmazd (gives) to that worker who is in friendliness with righteousness, [that is, they give the reward revealed by the text to him who shall perform duties and good works]. (*b*) Aûharmazd makes the cattle grow, [that is, he will increase them], for the eaters, that one may eat in moderation; that which is plentiful Aûharmazd taught (one to eat) by the lapful and armful.[4] (*c*) Who is this good thought (Vohuman) of thine? [that is, this one who leads to thee], who gives the reciters (and) priests a mouth with all the Avesta and Zand?

[1] This explanatory clause appears to be in great confusion in all MSS.
[2] As the Persian *muzd* is both "a reward" and "a he-goat," this may possibly be an attempt to explain *Az*.
[3] Or "cultivator."
[4] Literally: "by the bosom size and arm size."

which resembles a Pahlavi word for "goat."

8. (*a*) This my¹ gift he obtained, [that is, that (which is) so, this one obtained], to that teaching of ours this one is he who was listening : (*b*) Zaratûsht the Spitaman, for him is our will of Aûharmazd and righteousness also, [that is, a desire for complete duty and good works]. (*c*) He chanted also a counterspell,² [that is, he uttered a remedy for the destroyer (*drûj*) in the world], through which saying one gives unto him a good place, [that is, on account of the excellence of the saying he utters they give him there, in heaven, a good place which is excellent].

9. (*a*) So too Gôshûrûn complained thus : It is owing to the non-applicant I am powerless, O Zaratûsht ! unseemly thinking (comes) through what is illiberal giving, when they will not bestow on it copiously, (*b*) owing to the insufficiency of the words even of those men, when the religion is not fully current, whose desire is a demand for our³ sovereignty, [that is, owing to them a mobadship of the mobads is necessary for me]. (*c*) How does that gift ever exist? [that is, does that time ever come?] when it is given to him through the aid of powerful supplication, to him who is Zaratûsht.

10. (*a*) And ye give assistance to them, O Aûharmazd, and Ashavahisht, and Khshatvêr ! that Zaratûsht and the disciples of Zaratûsht may thereby practise virtue. (*b*) So also Vohuman, the good mind which gives him a place of pleasant dwelling there (in the other world) and likewise joy. (*c*) I too am he, O Aûharmazd ! that Zaratûsht, by him something is first to be obtained from Thee, [that is, his virtue is first from Thee].

11. (*a*) Where is the gift, O Ashavahisht, and Vohuman, and Khshatvêr ! which thus ye send to me, the speech of Zaratûsht ? [that is, (in) what place remains that reward?] (*b*) Ye reward me much, O Aûharmazd ! by this arch-Magianship, [that is, they would effect my reward by this pure goodness].⁴ (*c*) O Aûharmazd ! now our desire is (that) what is liberality towards us (shall be) from you; now when I know more of your wondrousness, benefits from you are more desired by me ; [some said that

---

¹ The word "my" is accidentally omitted in the old MSS.
² Literally : "a remedy-making."
³ So apparently in Dastur Jamaspji's MS.

⁴ The *mas-magîh* or arch-Magianship is here explained as "pure goodness," and in the Farhang-i Oim-khadûk (p. 25) *magha* is also explained by *arêjak*, "pure."

now when the religion (has) become quite current, I and the disciples (have) a desire for benefits and reward from Thee].

3.—*Pahlavi Yasna XXX.*

1. (*a*) So both those sayings are to be desired, which are the Avesta and Zand given by Aûharmazd, (by) whomsoever is intelligent, [that is, the priestly studies are to be performed [1] by him (who is) wise]. (*b*) Which (sayings) are the praise of Aûharmazd and the reverence of good thought (Vohuman) revealed by those which are the Avesta and Zand. (*c*) Whoever is a virtuous thinker through righteousness, even he who thinks of virtuous things, his good work is as great as a religious ceremonial (*yazishn*), (he it is) whose happiness (consists) in looking into their light,[2] [that is, when they see their spiritual worship it becomes their joy].

2. (*a*) The listening to what is heard by the ears, [that is, the ear listened to it (and) became glad], they will call the extension of the best, [that is, his performance of priestly study], and whatever is not affording him vision (becomes) what is light through the mind, [that is, the light of the priests is dark to him]. (*b*) Desires are to be discriminated by us who are men (and) women, for our own selves, [that is, proper things are to be discriminated from those which are improper, and those which are improper are not[3] to be accomplished by us]. (*c*) As, besides, in that great performance through the consummation in the future existence they announce a reward for what is our teaching, [that is, on account of our teaching proper things they will provide a reward].

3. (*a*) So both those spirits, Aûharmazd and the Evil one, first proclaimed themselves (as) those who are a pair, [that is, they declared themselves (as) sin and good works]. (*b*) Of what is good, and also of what is bad [4] of the thought, speech, and deed of both, one thinks, speaks, and does that which is good, and one that which is bad.[4] (*c*) From them choose ye

---

[1] Or perhaps "a priestly assembly is to be formed."

[2] Or possibly "into the light of the Yazads (angels)." There is considerable doubt about the proper application of the pronouns in many places.

[3] This negative is omitted by mistake in most MSS.

[4] Literally "worse" or "very bad."

out rightly him who is wise in good, Aûharmazd, not him who is wise in evil, the Evil spirit.

4. (*a*) So also both those spirits have approached together to that which was the first creation, [that is, both spirits have come to Gayomard]. (*b*) Whatever is in life is through this purpose of Aûharmazd, that is: So that I may keep it alive; and whatever is in lifelessness is through this purpose of the Evil spirit, that is: So that I may utterly destroy it; whatever is thus, is so until the last in the world, so that it may occur even to men of another (race). (*c*) The utter depravity of the wicked[1] and the devastation owing to Ahriman and the wicked are fully seen, and so is the righteous perfect thoughtfulness which accompanies Aûharmazd everlastingly.

5. (*a*) Of the two spirits that (one) is liked, by him who is wicked, who is the evil-doing Ahriman, he who was desirous of evil-doing. (*b*) Righteousness likes the spirit of righteousness, the fostering Aûharmazd; by whom[2] also the hard-pot-covered[3] sky likewise is completed around the earth through this purpose, that is, so that righteousness may become current. (*c*) Whoever also satisfies Aûharmazd, and his desire is that of Aûharmazd, is for Aûharmazd through public action, [that is, he should come to Aûharmazd with that desire and action].

6. (*a*) They who are demons do not allow (one) to discriminate rightly in any way, [that is, the demons would not do anything proper], even (one) whom they deceived; they whom the demons have deceived can form no right desire. (*b*) For inquiry they have come on, [that is, there is a consultation of them with the demons], (they) by whom the worse in thought is liked. (*c*) So they (the demons) have run in together with Wrath, and the lives of men are weakened by them, [that is, with Wrath they disfigure men].

---

[1] Of course "the wicked" include all unbelievers in Zoroastrianism as well as the mere transgressors.

[2] As the Avesta word is *yē* it is probable that *amat*, "when," ought to be *mân*, "whom," the substitution of one of these words for the other being a common blunder of transcribers.

[3] Or perhaps "hard-shell-covered."

This epithet is evidently based upon a rather eccentric etymology of the Avesta word *khraozhdishtēñg*, which the Pahlavi translator divides into three parts, namely, *khraozh*, "hard;" *dish* by *dîg*, "a pot" and *tēñg* by *nihûft*, "covered;" reminding one of some European attempts at etymologising the name of Zarathushtra.

7. (*a*) To him[1] comes Khshatvêr, and Vohuman and Ashavahisht also come up to him to work. (*b*) And so Spendarmad gives him a powerful body without lethargy, [that is, whilst it is his he is not stupefied]. (*c*) They are thine, [that is, they come thus to that person], whose coming is such as the first creation, [that is, his desire and action are those of Gayomard].

8. (*a*) So also hatred comes into the creation, in the future existence, to those haters and sinners, [that is, they shall execute their punishment]. (*b*) So, O Aûharmazd! whoever is for thy sovereignty Vohuman will give him the reward. (*c*) Through their teaching of Aûharmazd, in the religion of Aûharmazd, when (given) to him who (has) righteousness, [that is, he is instructed in proper things], the destroyer is given into his hand, and the mischief (*drûj*) of infidelity.

9. (*a*) So also we who are thine, [that is, we are thine own], by us this perpetuation (*frashakard*) is to be made in the world. (*b*) Also the whole congregation of Aûharmazd and likewise the bringing of Ashavahisht, [that is, an assembly about the future existence is always to be formed by them]. (*c*) Whosever thought is endless, [that is, thought in priestly authority (*dastôbarîh*) is the life (or guardian angel) which he possesses], his knowledge is there (in the other world), [that is, he will know the end of things through rectitude], in (his) place.

10. (*a*) So in the creation in the future existence he who is a destroyer, the evil spirit, is in discomfiture, when his things shall stand still for weakness, and (his) army is shattered. (*b*) So they swiftly spring to seize the reward, that which is in the good dwelling of Vohuman, when they have continued in rectitude. (*c*) To Aûharmazd and Ashavahisht too they spring who establish what is good renown, [that is, that person goes to seize the reward who is well-famed].

11. (*a*) Both those benedictions are to be taught which Aûharmazd gave to men, (*b*) and whose heedless[2] teaching is

---

[1] The other, who prefers righteousness.

[2] This is merely a guess. The text in the Copenhagen MS. (as published by Spiegel) is here unintelligible, and the obscurity is only partially removed by Dastur Jamaspji's MS., which runs as follows: *mûnich qin âmûkhtishno zak mindaram*, &c., with *ahinh* written over *qin* either as a gloss or as an addition to that doubtful word. It is possible that instead of Pâzand *qin* we should read the similarly written Pahlavi *arên*, " un-

the thing that should not be during my celebration of worship; whose lasting injury also (arises) from such celebration by the wicked. (c) And (they are) also an advantage of the righteous, [that is, as it is necessary to perform (them) so afterwards they are beneficial], when that advantage (has) become complete.

4.—Pahlavi Yasna XXXI.

1. (a) Both those benedictions which I recite unto you, the Avesta and Zand,[1] we teach him who is no hearer of the infidel,[2] by speaking; in a doubtful matter (*varhômandîh*) he is to be told three times, and one time when (one) knows without doubt (*aîvar*) that he learns. (b) They who, by benediction[3] of the destroyer of righteousness, utterly devastate the world, when they maintain the destroyer by benediction, (c) then even they may be excellent when they shall be causing progress in what is Aûharmazd's, [that is, of even those infidels this one thing may be excellent, when they shall make current the religion of Aûharmazd].

2. (a) Whoever does not believe through observation is in what is to him no doubtfulness when he is not even doubtful or God in anything, [that is, assertion[4] about existence is good when they exhibit it by an estimate of the world]. (b) So all come to you, [that is, every one will come into your possession], when thus they become aware of the mastership of Aûharmazd, [that is, they shall know the miraculousness of Aûharmazd]. (c) From Aûharmazd, from them (the Ameshaspends) it is to come when I live with the aid of righteousness; from the Ameshaspends is this benefit for me, from Aûharmazd, when I live on with the duties and good works which are mine.

---

seeing, heedless," which suits the sense very well; the Pâzand gloss *ahînh* must then be read *awînâ*, which would be very similar in form, and would confirm the meaning "heedless" here adopted.

[1] It is not certain from his language that the Pahlavi translator did not mean the Avesta and Zand of both benedictions.

[2] As the sentence stands in the old MSS. it ought to be translated: "we teach him who is no hearer, the infidel," &c.

[3] Referring probably to the incantations of sorcerers.

[4] Dastur Jamaspji's MS. has *lâ-yazishnîh*, "irreverence, non-worship," instead of *nikîzishnîh*. It cannot be said that this explanatory clause throws much light on the subject.

3. (*a*) What[1] the fire and Ashavahisht gave by spirituality, and was explained by Thee to the disputants, (was) understanding, [that is, the purified and the defiled were made known by Thee]. (*b*) And by Thee, who gave a desire of benediction to the interpreters of numbers (arithmancists), was given the rite of ordeal (*nîrang-i var*); tell it to us intelligibly, O Aûharmazd! wisely, that rite of ordeal. (*c*) Through Thy tongue, in (my) mouth all kinds of living creatures believe, and afterwards it is said of it that I speak.

4. (*a*) When in the creation in the future existence I shall be an invoker of Ashavahisht and Aûharmazd also, [that is, let me have such a virtue that it may be possible for me to invoke Aûharmazd and Ashavahisht]; (*b*) and I shall be an invoker of her also who is the submissive Spendarmad, I pray for excellence, the gift of good thought (Vohuman). (*c*) (May) the authority of my people also, my disciples, be from him who is powerful, [that is, give them sovereignty from Soshâns], through whose bravery, [that is, through his own resources he is able to do it], the destroyer (*drûj*) is beaten, [that is, I know this, that at that time it is possible to make the destroyer confounded].

5. (*a*) Speak decided to me, speak clear, where is that reward? how ought one to make (it) one's own? which (comes) to me through righteousness when duty and good works are performed by me, the good gift, [that is, the giving of that good reward to me]. (*b*) Grant me the gift of understanding through good thought (Vohuman), [that is, talk wisdom through excellence], which is mine through the good judgment (*hû-vârîh*) which is his, [that is, through the excellence of that wisdom it is possible for me to give a reply of good judgment]. (*c*) Aûharmazd speaks that also which does not exist by means of that which exists, [that is, by means of the Gâtha-lore which exists he says where it does not exist].

6. (*a*) He is the best who would speak intelligently to me (what is) manifest and clear, [that is, the priest is better than the disciple], (*b*) the text which is all-progressive, [that is, all creatures by way of the text come back into the possession of Aûharmazd], which when they preserve it with righteousness is working well, (and) one's immortal progress arises therefrom in

---

[1] Assuming that *amat* has been substituted for *mûn*, see p. 346, note 2.

the fifty-seven years.¹ (c) The dominion of Aûharmazd is so long as good thought (Vohuman) grows in one, [that is, his sovereignty in the body of a man is so long as good thought (Vohuman) is a guest in his body].

7. (a) His promise came first who mingled His glory with the light, who is the Aûharmazd who did this, [that is, the goodness which is His here (in this world) is with Him there (in the other world); this thing has happened to Him so that his Gâtha-lore may return to Him]. (b) His are the creatures, [that is, the proper creatures are His own], who possesses righteousness through wisdom and perfect thinking, [that is, he considers with uprightness and propriety]. (c) Both those (creations) Aûharmazd causes to grow through spirituality, [that is, he will increase spiritual and worldly things], (He) who is also now the Lord for ever.²

8. (a) Thus I thought, O Aûharmazd! regarding Thee, that Vohuman might be the first among Thy offspring, and when I saw Vohuman I thought thus, that (he) was Thy child. (b) Art Thou Vohuman's father? Thou art the father of Vohuman when thou art taken in altogether by my whole eyesight, [that is, Thou art seen by both my eyes], so I thought that Thou art the father of Vohuman. (c) Manifest are the creatures of righteousness, (and) clear, [that is, Thy proper creatures are created]; through deeds in the world Thou art Lord, [that is, they shall form an account with sin and good works].

9. (a) Thine is Spendarmad, [that is, Thine own], with Thee is that which is the fashioner of cattle, wisdom. (b) Through spirituality, O Aûharmazd! a path is given to her by Thee, [that is, the path of that place (the other world) is given to her by Thee]. (c) Whoever is in activity comes, [that is, his duty and good works are performed], whoever is no worker is not allowed by Thee.

10. (a) So both the origin and produce are assigned by Thee to that (one) of those men who is a worker (and) acquirer of wealth,³ [that is, the source and produce of cattle are given by

---

¹ In the Bundahish (p. 72) it is also stated: "In fifty-seven years Soshâns (and his companions) prepare all the dead; all men arise, both (those) who are righteous and (those) who are wicked."

² Reading *mûn kevanich hamât khûḍât*.

³ The terms used seem to imply "an agriculturist and cattle-breeder."

Thee to him who is diligent (and) moderate]. (*b*) The lord is righteous whose wealth¹ (comes) through good thought (Vohuman), [that is, they should exercise the ownership of cattle with propriety]. (*c*) Aûharmazd does not allot to him who is an idler, the infidel who is any hypocrite in the sacred recitations. In the good religion it is asserted that even as much reward as they give to the hypocrite they do not give to the infidel.²

11. (*a*) When for us, O Aûharmazd! the world was first formed by Thee, and religion, (they were) given by Thee through this wisdom of Thy mind. (*b*) When life was given by Thee to the possessors of bodies, [that is, life was given by Thee to the body of Gayomard], it, too, was given through this wisdom of Thy mind. (*c*) When work (and) instruction were given by Thee, [that is, work (and) proper instruction were given by Thee], (they), too, were given through this wisdom of Thy mind. And when (there is one) whose desire is for that place (the other world), by Thee his desire was granted, [that is, that which he requires when he shall come to that place, this which is so required by him is given by Thee, in that way he will come to that place], it, too, was granted through this wisdom of Thy mind.

12. (*a*) There the voices are high, that of the teller of lies, the Evil spirit, and that of the teller of truth, Aûharmazd, (*b*) that of the intellectual Aûharmazd and that of the unintellectual Evil spirit, in the solicitation for the heart and mind of Zaratûsht, [that is, while we shall solicit them³], (*c*) who, through complete mindfulness as to what the spirit communicated by the religion of the spirit, (has) his abode there (in the

---

¹ That is, wealth in cattle.

² This appears to refer to a passage in the Spend Nask, which the Shâyast-lâ-shâyast quotes thus: "As in the Spend Nask it was shown to Zaratûsht, concerning a man, that the whole body was in torment and one foot was outside. Zaratûsht asked Aûharmazd about the matter. Aûharmazd said that he was a man Davâns by name; he was ruler over thirty-three provinces, and he never practised any good work, except one time when he conveyed fodder to cattle with that one foot." In the Ardâ-Vîrâf-nâmak (ch. xxxii.) a similar tale is told of "a lazy man whom they called Davânôs," whose right foot is treated with the same exceptional mercy, which is not granted to the infidel or apostate in ch. xlvii. There seems little doubt that this Davâns is a representation of the *draôs* translated "hypocrite" in the text.

³ Literally "it" or "him."

other world), [whoever shall quite mindfully perform priestly studies,[1] his place is there (in the other world)].

13. (a) Whoever converses with what is public must perform public good works, O Aûharmazd! whoever converses with what is secret sin may commit much secret sin. (b) Whoever in what is a small quarrel tries (*aîzmâyêd*) that which is great, for the sake of deliverance, [that is, they would commit a small sin and, afterwards, they would commit a large one, so that it may not be apparent], (c) it is he who would be in both (Thy) eyes, [that is, Thou seest], in that combination Thou art Lord, [in sin which is mingled with good works], over righteousness Thou art also Lord,[2] and Thou seest over everything.

14. (a) Both those I ask of Thee, O Aûharmazd! what has come? (and) what yet comes? (b) Whoever gives a loan of what is from lenders to him who is righteous, (gives) of that which is such as is necessary to give, O Aûharmazd! (c) And whoever (gives) to the wicked is as they are, so the settlement is this, that is; What is the decree? tell me what is the decree?

15. (a) Thus it should be asked him: Would his punishment in that perdition be well inflicted who would provide a dominion for him who is wicked, (b) who is evil-doing,[3] O Aûharmazd! who does not announce life even through a reward? [that is, when they give him a bribe he would not release a man who is yet alive]. (c) He also persecutes the agriculturist who is averting destruction among cattle and men, [that is, even a good man who well preserves mankind and cattle, him he regards with malice].

16. (a) Thus it should be asked him:[4] Would his reward be

---

[1] Or perhaps "form a priestly assembly."

[2] This part of the verse is omitted in Spiegel's edition.

[3] Evidently referring to Ahriman, who is here represented as incorruptible in his adherence to evil. The idea of a being wicked enough to be bribed to betray an evil cause to which he still remains devoted, appears to be a refinement in evil of later date than either Ahriman or the devil.

[4] The forms of some of the verbs in this and the preceding verse are rarely used, such as *pârsî-nâḍ*, *pârsî hâḍ*, "there should be an asking, or it should be asked;" *yehabûnt-hâḍ*, "there would be a giving, or it would be given;" and the form which can be only doubtfully read *vâdânyên-it*, "it would be done or inflicted." This last form looks like the phrase "there is a *vâdânyên*, or there is a they-would-do," a clumsy way of saying "it would be done," if that be the origin of the form.

well given in whose dwelling (*demân*) He who is wise in goodness is Lord ? [that is, Aûharmazd through spirituality is made lord within his body]. (*b*) And in the town which is in His country he who is (engaged) in the propagation of righteousness is no chastiser, [that is, in His world that one is lord who, when they would perform duty and good works, does not chastise]. (*c*) Such are Thine, O Aûharmazd! in whose actions it is even so.

17. (*a*) Which convinces more, the righteous or the wicked? [that is, does he who is righteous (among) people convince more thoroughly, or he who is wicked?]. (*b*) Speak information for him who is intelligent, and become not him who is ignorant thereafter while I shall speak to thee. (*c*) Apprize us, O Aûharmazd! [that is, fully inform us], and mark us out by good thought (Vohuman), [that is, furnish us with a badge through rectitude].

18. (*a*) So no one of you should hear the teaching of the text from that wicked one, [that is, hear not the Avesta and Zand from the infidels]; (*b*) for in the dwelling, village, town, and country he produces evil proceedings and death, he who is an infidel; (*c*) so prepare ye the sword for those infidels.

19. (*a*) The listening in which is discretion (and) righteousness is thus acquainted with both worlds, O Aûharmazd! [that is, he in whom is discretion (and) righteousness understands the working of spiritual and worldly affairs]. (*b*) Rightly spoken speech is that which is authorised, which is fearless in tongue persuasion, [that is, for his speech which is true and proper (one's) wishes are to be renounced]. (*c*) This Thy red fire, O Aûharmazd! will give a decision to disputants, that they may fully make manifest the certain and the undecided (*ayirâid*).[1]

20. (*a*) Whoever comes to the righteous with deceit his lamentation is behind him, [that is, it becomes lamentation in his soul], (*b*) and long is his coming into darkness, [that is, he must be there a long time], and bad feeding, [that is, they give him even poison], and he says (it is) an unjust proceeding, [that is, it has happened to him unjustly]. (*c*) To the world of darkness, ye

[1] This evidently refers to the ordeal by fire, one form of the *nîrang-i rar*.

who are wicked! the deeds which are your own religion[1] lead you, (and) must do (so).

21. (*a*) Aûharmazd gave Horvadad and Amerôdad the perfect to him who is righteous, [him by whom duty and good works are performed]. (*b*) And His own authority (*patih*) is in the domination (*sardârîh*) of him who is lord, [that is, the sovereignty which is His He maintains in the Dastur], (*c*) whose munificence is of the good thought (Vohuman), [that is, the reward which Vohuman gives he also gives], which is for him who is a friend of his own spirit through deeds.

22. (*a*) Manifestly he is well-informed when he gives (and) thinks according to his knowledge, [that is, in thought he minds him who is spiritual lord (*ahû*) of his Dastur].[2] (*b*) Good is the lord who would practise righteousness in word and in deed; (*c*) he whose body is a conveyer of Thee, O Aûharmazd! [that is, Thy lodging in the world is in his body].

5.—*Pahlavi Yasna XXXII.*

1. (*a*) He who is in possession of his life begged what is its productiveness together with submissiveness, [that which is a reward the demons (begged of) Aûharmazd himself in these (words): That we may be productive and submissive to Thee! By them it was begged]. (*b*) They who are his[3] demons are of my (way of) thinking, [that is, our thinking is as excellent as Zaratûsht], he who is Aûharmazd's delight. [By them it was begged]: (*c*) That we may be testifying! [that is: May we become Thy promoters!] we hold those who harass you, [that is, we hold them back from you].

2–16. [Not translated.]

---

[1] Probably referring to the traditional hag who is said to meet the souls of the wicked on the fourth morning after death, and is a personification of their evil religion and deeds (see Ardâ-Vîrâf-nâmak, xvii. 12). The original description of this being in the Hâdokht Nask (Yasht xxii. 27-33) is lost (see p. 223).

[2] So in Dastur Jamaspji's MS., otherwise "he minds those who are his guardian angel and Dastur" would be a preferable reading.

[3] Probably meaning those who are called demons by Zaratûsht; but this verse is by no means free from obscurity.

PAHLAVI VENDIDAD I.

6.—Pahlavi Vendidad I.[1]

1. (1)[2] Aûharmazd said to Spîtâmân Zaratû$_s$ht : (2) I created, O Spîtâmân Zaratûsht ! the creation of delight [3] of a place where no comfort was [4] created ; (a) this is where man is, the place where he is born (and) they bring him up seems good to him, [that is, very excellent and comfortable]; this I created. (3) For if I should not have created, O Spîtâmân Zaratûsht ! the creation of delight of a place where no comfort was created, (4) there would have been an emigration of the whole material world to Aîrân-vêj, (a) that is, it would have remained in the act, while their going would have been 'impossible, for it is not possible to go so far as from region (*kêshvar*) to region, except with the permission of the angels (*yazadân*) ;[5] some say that it is possible to go also with that of the demons.

2. (4) (*b*) *Asô râmô-dâitîm* ("a pleasure-creative place"), *nêid* ("not") *aojô-râmishtâm* ("most pleasing in strength") ;[6]

---

[1] For th Pahlavi text of the first part of the Vendidad we have to rely upon MSS. which are only second-rate in point of age, as has been already noticed in p. 95. This is all the more to be regretted as the first fargard contains many rare words and obscure phrases which one would wish to have, as nearly as possible, in their original form. Fortunately these second-rate MSS. are still 283 years old, and were therefore written before the mania for "improving" old texts set in (some time last century), which has induced some copyists to adapt the text to their own limited knowledge, in preference to raising their knowledge to some comprehension of the text as they found it.

[2] The paragraphs are numbered to correspond with Westergaard s edition of the Avesta text and its translation in pp. 227-230 of these Essays; but the subdivisions of Spiegel's edition, which correspond with those of the Pahlavi MSS., are also numbered in parentheses. For the further indication of the Pahlavi commentaries and their subdivision by the letters (*a*), (*b*), (*c*), &c., the present editor is responsible.

[3] The meaning appears to be, that whatever creates delight in a place was created by Aûharmazd, as more fully detailed in the sequel.

[4] The writer seems to use the usual present form of this verb for the past. See "remained" in (4 *a*).

[5] It is doubtful whether *yazadân* is to be taken in its original sense of "angels," or in its later meaning "God." In the Bundahish (p. 21 W.) we are told, "It is not possible for one to go from region to region ;" and the Mainyô-i-khard (ix. 6) says, "It is not possible to go from region to region otherwise than with the permission of the *yazads* or the permission of the demons," which corresponds closely with the statement in the text.

[6] This seems to be a critical remark on the foregoing Avesta text, and implies that there had been some doubt whether *asô râmô-dâitîm* (the reading adopted) should not have been *aojô-râmishtâm*. It may be noted that the two phrases are more alike when

the effect would be one (the same), the effect would be "the delight of a place;"[1] some say it is also (*zakoîch*) "the delight which (arises) from industry." (*c*) *Paoirîm* ("the first") is *bitîm* ("the second"); this enumeration is that first the work of the law was produced at a place, and the second at that place, till the spirit of the earth arranged the whole in connection,[2] is the work of opposition. The place where he mentions two— one, that in the original creation, and one, that which is after— is *aad ahê paityârem* ("thereupon, as an opposition to it").[3] (*d*) Every one of the following places and districts is the joint production of both; some say that a "place" (*jînâk*) is that place whereon mankind do not dwell, and a "district" (*rûstâk*) is that place whereon mankind dwell. (*e*) *Mashamârava shathâm haitîm* ("he has proclaimed the existing destruction");[4] this is revealed in this fargard, (and) every place is mentioned. Some say *Aît-hômand* ("material") is also a river.[5]

3. (5) The first of places and districts produced perfect by me, me who am Aûharmazd, was (6) Aîrân-vêj, where the good Dâitîh ("organisation") is; (*a*) and its good Dâitîh is this, that the place sends out even our Dâit while they perform work (agriculture?) with the *avaêpaêm* ("stream"); some say that it comes out in a stream unless they perform the work of the

---

written in Pahlavi characters than they are in sound. The remarks which follow, if their meaning has been correctly caught, imply that either phrase would be suitable.

[1] Two other readings of this obscure phrase may be suggested: first, "one thing is 'an army'' (*hênak*), one thing is 'the delight of a place;'" secondly, "the work is of two kinds (*dô aînak*), one work is 'the delight of a place.'" The reading *kolâ dô* for *kâr âe* is a modern guess.

[2] Or "gave up the whole into one hierarchy," according as we read *khadû-kurdakîh*, or *khadûk radakîh*. Most of this latter part of the commentary refers to what follows in the text.

[3] These are the words which introduce each Avesta account of the evils produced by the evil spirit, as detailed in the following verses.

[4] *Mashamârava* is here supposed to be for *mashmûrâva*, which is taken as the perf. third sing. of a root *shmru* = *mru*, "to speak;" compare *mar* = Sans. *smri*. The reading *ash mârava*, "very deadly," has also been proposed, which would be synonymous with *pôuru-mahrkô*, the usual epithet of the evil spirit.

[5] This is evidently a later supplementary comment, and refers to the word *ast-hômand*, "material," in (4); this would be *aît-hômand* in Huzvârish, and has reminded some commentator of the river thus described in the Bundahish (p. 52 W.): "The Aîtômand (Hêtumend) river is in Sîstân, and its sources are from Mount Apârsîn; this is distinct from that which restrained Frâsiyâv." See also p. 229, note 3.

place.[1] (7) And in opposition to that were formed by the evil spirit, who is deadly, (8) both the Rûdik ("river"?) serpent (which) becomes numerous, and the winter, produced by the demons, (which) becomes more severe.

4. (9) Ten months are winter there, and two months summer; (a) and afterwards also *hapta heñti hâminô mâonha, pañcha zayana* ("seven are the summer months, five the winter ") is declared.[2] (10) Those, too, have cold water, cold earth, (and) cold vegetation, those ten months; some say the two months; (11) *adha zimahê maidhîm, adha zimahê zaredhaêm* ("then is midwinter, then is the heart of winter "), (a) in that manner the month Vohûman is the month Shatvêrô, which is the heart of winter, [that is, it would be more severe (compared) even with this that is ever severe; and afterwards also, at that time, it

---

[1] This is the traditional interpretation which describes Dâitih as a river; thus the Bundahish (p. 51 W.) says, "The Dâitik (Dâiti) river is the river which comes out from Aîrân-vêj, and goes on by the mountain of Panjastâ; of all rivers the noxious creatures in it are most, as it is said, the Dâiti river is full of noxious creatures." It may be guessed from the text that the river came from snowy mountains, and therefore flowed most freely in the spring and summer; hence the idea that its flowing was dependent upon the tillage of Aîrân-vêj, which produced either more than the natural drainage or less, according to the view taken by the commentator. Traditionally, *avaêpaêm* is a "subterranean channel or drain," and it can be easily explained as "a stream." Its identification with the Pâzand *arêbîm*, "fearless," is merely a guess of later times, ingenious but hazardous. If it were adopted, and the material river were idealised into "organisation or law," we should have to translate somewhat as follows: "And its good organisation is this, that the place sends out even our organisation (or splendour) while they perform work (or duty), as it were, fearlessly (steadfastly); some say that it comes out, as it were, fearlessly, unless they perform the duty of the place." It is, however, far safer to assume that the Pahlavi commentator takes the most material view of every passage. Many MSS. have *rûd*, "the river," instead of *lanman*, "our;" and it may be noticed that the latter Pahlavi word, when badly written, can be easily read as the former, but the converse mistake is not so easy.

[2] The word *ashkare* is merely the Pahlavi *âshkârak*, "declared, manifest," written with the Pâzand termination -*e* instead of the Pahlavi -*ak*. This commentary on the alteration in the relative lengths of summer and winter agrees with the Bundahish (p. 60 W.), which states that the months from Fravardîn to Mitrô (the first seven months of the year) are summer, and from Avân to Spendarmad (the last five months of the year) are winter. It must be observed that the Persian Parsi calendar has not corresponded with that described in the Bundahish since the eleventh century (say A.Y. 400); but as that book describes the year as always corresponding with the sun, it implies that some mode of intercalation was employed, so that it may have been written at any earlier date.

becomes more severe].[1] (12) Then when the winter falls off, [that is, goes], then is the *frâêstô vôghnê* ("chief disaster"),[2] [that is, the opposition winter ever goes off with it; some say that annihilation enters thereby].

5. (13) The second of places and districts produced perfect by me, me who am Aûharmazd, was (14) Gavâ, which is the Sûrîk dwelling, [that is, the plain of the Sûrîk dwelling-place; the characteristic thereof is no disturbance]. (15) And in opposition to that was formed by the evil spirit, who is deadly, (16) a swarm of locusts (*kûruko mêg*) which even destroys (*yahêd-ich*) the cattle, and is deadly; (*a*) this locust comes forth, (and) corn that is without blade comes up; to tie up the ox is not necessary, (and) it becomes the death even of the sheep.

6. (17) The third of places and districts produced perfect by me, me who am Aûharmazd, was (18) Marûv, of resources combined with the work of the law, and active, [that is, they do much in it]. (19) And in opposition to that were formed by the evil spirit, who is deadly, (20) inquisition (and) privacy (*gôshak*);[3] [inquisition, that is, they would make an inquisition of friends there; and privacy, that is, solitary incontinence is there].

---

[1] The meaning is, that the summer was as cold as winter, and the winter still colder. As the months stand in the text, they would answer very well for the present time, when the *qadîm* month Bahman occurs in June-July, and Shahrivar in January-February; but we find the same months given in MSS. written 283 years ago, when the Parsi months were seventy days later in the year, and we have every reason to believe that they were also given in MSS. written 553 years ago, when the months were 138 days later in our year than they are at present. It seems hazardous to assume that the Parsi months were allowed to retrograde continuously during Sasanian times, otherwise we might suppose that this commentary was written about 1460 years ago, when the months would have been in their present position. But it is more probable that some copyist has reversed the position of the two months in the text, as Vohûman is a winter month, and Shatvêrô a summer one, in the Bundahish (p. 62 W.).

[2] There seems here to be some perception of the disastrous consequences of a sudden thaw in snowy regions. But one of the commentators seems to understand *frâêstô vôghnê* as "gone forth to destroy," misled perhaps by the Persian *firistâd*, "sent."

[3] Modern tradition suggests *dûshak*, "evil;" but as *dûsh*, "evil," is already an adjective, the form *dûshak* is doubtful. If it were adopted the sentence might be thus translated: "Commerce (lit. reckoning) and evil commerce, [that is, the commerce which friends would practise there is evil, that is, unnatural intercourse is there]." This, however, would be taking advantage of an ambiguity in the English word "commerce," which the Pahlavi *âmâr* does not possess.

PAHLAVI VENDIDAD I.

7. (21) The fourth of places and districts produced perfect by me, me who am Aûharmazd, was (22) Bukhâr[1] the handsome in appearance, with uplifted banner, [that is, they keep[2] a banner elevated; some say that they domineer over a multitude, that is, they overwhelm it[3]]. (23) And in opposition to that was formed by the evil spirit, who is deadly, (24) an ant-hill (which) becomes numerous; [some say that a place furrowed by a plough till it springs up will become an ant-hill].[4]

8. (25) The fifth of places and districts produced perfect by me, me who am Aûharmazd, was (26) Nisâi, which would be between Marûv and Bukhâr; [I mention that since there is also the other[5]]. (27) And in opposition to that was formed by the evil spirit, who is deadly, (28) scepticism; [in the concerns of the angels (or God) they are doubtful whether they exist;[6] some

---

[1] Or it may be Bâkhar or Bâhl.
[2] Some MSS. have "come with," others "bring."
[3] Some modern MSS. have " they slaughter the enemy."
[4] This clause presents several difficulties to the translator, and the text is probably corrupted. In all probability the word *nurtu* or *nurutu* (Dastur Hoshangji mentions *nub*), which ends the Avesta version in the printed editions, is really a Pâzand word beginning the Pahlavi version, and the missing equivalent of the Avesta *bravarem*. It might be taken for the Persian *navard*, "combat," but this is *naparto* in Pahlavi. Possibly the *t* is a corruption of *mû* (see p. 357, note 1), and the whole word a blunder for a Pahlavi form, *vurmân* or *barmûr*, "a bee;" but this is a mere guess. The word *gûlchakâd* (one old MS. gives *dûrchakât* as a gloss) is traditionally understood as "an ant which carries off corn," the *môr-i dân-kash* of Vend. xiv. 14 and xviii. 146 Sp.; but how tradition arrived at this conclusion is not obvious. Here *chakâd* is taken in its usual sense of "summit, hill," and *gûl* is assumed to be a corruption of *môr*, "ant" (*m* inverted being *k*, an error which sometimes occurs, and *kôr* being practically equi-valent to *gûl* in writing). The Teheran MS. has *gûlak-chakâd* in one instance, which would lead up to the translation "porcupine mound" were it not that the porcupine or hedgehog is specially an animal of the good creation (because it destroys ants), and could not have been produced by the evil spirit. Darmesteter's suggestion (Revue Critique, No. 33 of 1877, p. 90) of *jûrdh-kâd* for *jârdâk-kâd*, "greedy of corn," is hardly admissible, as no old Pâzand writer would be likely to use *dh* for a final *d*. If we were to throw aside the tradition altogether, and assume that the Pahlavi translator was better acquainted with the meaning of the original Avesta word *usadhas* than the traditionalists were, we might take *gûl-chakâd* as the name of some noxious weed which sprang up all over the country; *gûl* or *gûlak*, "flower," being frequently used as the first member of the name of a plant. The reading adopted for the phrase, "a place furrowed by a plough till it springs up," is *jinâk sûlak-dâd* (or *sûl-kisht*) *rad barâ khambêd*.
[5] Or "since it still exists."
[6] More literally, "that is, if they should not be."

say that they are (so) also in those of the demons whether they exist].

9. (29) The sixth of places and districts produced perfect by me, me who am Aûharmazd, was (30) Harîb (or Harâv) the village-deserting; (a) and its village desertion is this, where we keep the periods of nine nights and a month,[1] they desert the house as evil (*khânak pavan vaḍak*) and go away. (31) And in opposition to that was formed by the evil spirit, who is deadly, (32) the mosquito[2] whose cry of long-continued annoyance (*dêr-sêjakîh*) would be this: I am hungry![3] [some say that they may perform with a drum].

10. (33) The seventh of places and districts produced perfect by me, me who am Aûharmazd, was (34) Kâvûl the evil-shadow-ing,[4] (a) and its (evil) shadowing is this, that the shadow of the trees on the body is bad; some say that of the mountains. (35) And in opposition to that was formed by the evil spirit, who is deadly, (36) a longing for witches, the adoration of idols, with whom Kereshaspô associated, [that is, he practised it, and they also would practise not according to the law].

11. (37) The eighth of places and districts produced perfect by me, me who am Aûharmazd, was (38) Urê full of pasture (and) grandees,[5] (a) and its full pasturage is this, that there is

---

[1] Dastur Hoshangji observes that these periods refer to the time which places once defiled remain unclean, which varies according to the season of the year.

[2] The word *sarchâ* or *sarchakh* is here assumed to mean "a gnat or mosquito," in accordance with the traditional meaning of the phrase. It may, however, be only the Pâzand form *sardha*, "sort, kind," in which case we should have to read a "kind of long-continued annoyance whose cry would be this," &c., referring perhaps to beggars. It is singular that the Pahlavi translator should have missed using the Persian word *sârashk*, "a gnat," for the Avesta *sraskem*; and Dastur Hoshangji observes, very justly, that *sarchâ-î* may be merely a miswriting of *sarchask*, which might well be a copyist's transposition of *sarask-ich*.

[3] Or "a dagger," according as we read *pushnak* or *dashnak*.

[4] It seems singular that a place when made perfect should still have an evil shadow, and no doubt we can read *Kâvûl-î vêh-sâyako* instead of *Kâvûl-i dâsh-sâyako*, and can translate as follows: "Kâvûl the well-shadowing, and its shadowing is this, that the shadow of the trees is on a bad body which is called that of the mountains." But as the Pahlavi translator found *duzhakô* in the Avesta text, he could hardly avoid translating it by *dûsh*, "evil." As the Pahlavi version differs here, in its translation of Av. *shayanem*, from (14) and (42) Dastur Hoshangji suggests *sayanem* as the correct reading.

[5] Or we may read *mêgân*, "fogs," (Pers. *mêgh*); or perhaps *râstar-masân*. "forage-gatherers" (compare Pers. *masîdan*, "to gather").

plenty of corn and pasturage in it. (39) And in opposition to that was formed by the evil spirit, who is deadly, (40) the worst of residences when its grandees dwell on it.

12. (41) The ninth of places and districts produced perfect by me, me who am Aûharmazd, was (42) Khnān, the abode of wolves, [that is, the Khnān river is the habitation of wolves; the characteristic [1] thereof is disturbance]. (43) And in opposition to that was formed by the evil spirit, who is deadly, (44) the vile sin of those who cannot pass the bridge,[2] which is intercourse with men, [that is, sodomy]; (a) this they should not perpetrate according to the law of the angels (or God).

13. (45) The tenth of places and districts produced perfect by me, me who am Aûharmazd, was (46) Harakhmônd the handsome in appearance. (47) And in opposition to that was formed by the evil spirit, who is deadly, (48) the vile sin which cannot pass the bridge, which is burying the dead; (a) this is heathenish (ak-dîn-hômand), and according to their law.

14. (49) The eleventh of places and districts produced perfect by me, me who am Aûharmazd, was (50) Hét-hômand the illustrious (and) glorious; (a) busy and diligent is the spirit which it subdued,[3] some say that of the Vêh river.[4] (51) And in opposition to that was formed by the evil spirit, who is deadly, (52) that which is vile, [that is, sorcery], which is ever evil; (a) some say that of the Frâsâyâvân;[5] they were able to perform that, and were not able to abandon it. (b) Some say that sor-

---

[1] The old MSS. have *dashak*, but compare the end of (14).
For whom the bridge Chinvad, which leads to paradise, is impassable; this is neatly expressed by the single Pahlavi word *anâpûhalakân*, "those not for the bridge," or those whose sins are inexpiable.

[3] Reading *î sikast* (for *î shikast*); or it may be *î kasist*, "the smallest." Some modern MSS. alter the word into Sîstân because the Hêtumand river is in Sîstân, see p. 356, note 5. The whole clause seems doubtful.

[4] The Vêh (or good) river is one of the two chief rivers of the world according to the Bundahish, which states (p. 49 W.) that "these two rivers flow forth from the north part of the eastern Alborz, one towards the west, that is the Arang, (and) one towards the east, that is the Vêh river." The spirits of the two rivers are also mentioned (Bund. p. 50), and further particulars are given, thus (Bund. p. 51): "The Vêh river passes by on the east, goes through the land of Sînd, (and) flows to the sea in Hindûstân, and they call it there the Mehrâ river;" and in p. 53 it is stated that the Vêh river is also called the Kâsak in Sînd.

[5] The descendants of Frâsîyâv the Turanian, the Afrâsiyâb of the Shâhnâmak.

cery is this which although they desire (it) not, yet it happens easily (*narm*), then it is said that (it is) in a way not allowable.[1]

15. (53) This also is the token of its manifestation, which I call the practice of the thing; (54) and this also, its manifestation, is through examination; when they observe it becomes manifest. (55) As wherever they come (there) is evidently an outburst (*jasto*) of sorcery, (56) so also they are most addicted to extreme sorcery; (57) so also they bring up snow and hail, [that is, they would occasion even them]; (*a*) some say that the snow and hail will so arise from them where sinfulness, through them, becomes excessive. (58) Whosoever is sick (*mudak*) and whosoever is again impotent (are so through the deeds of such sorcerers).[2]

16. (59) The twelfth of places and districts produced perfect by me, me who am Aûharmazd, was (60) Râk of the three races of Atarôpâtakân; (*a*) some say Râî; and its triple race is this, that its priest, warrior, and husbandman are virtuous and belong to it. (*b*) Some say Zaratûsht belonged to that place, and it was his government (*patîh*) of all these three which was called Râî;[3] its triple race is this, that his union of these three arose and issued from that place: *vaêdhanhô nôid uzôish* ("of knowledge, not of conjecture"?). (61) And in opposition to that was formed by the evil spirit, who is deadly, (62) the vilest over-scepticism,[4] [that is, they are doubtful themselves, and will also make others doubtful].

17. (63) The thirteenth of places and districts produced perfect by me, me who am Aûharmazd, was (64) Chakhar of resources, the grand doer.[5] (65) And in opposition to that was

---

[1] The author's translation of this fargard ends here.

[2] As already noticed (p. 229, note 4), the whole of this paragraph seems to be translated from an old commentary in the Avesta language. The last sentence is translated here as it stands in the printed text, but it will probably be discovered hereafter that the word *tân* in the Avesta text is part of the Pahlavi translation; and that the final words *lakhvâr atâ* are altogether corrupt.

[3] This seems to be a pun on the name Râî, which can be divided, in Pahlavi, into the two words *li* 3, "my three."

[4] Perhaps "active scepticism" or "rampant unbelief" would express the meaning better, though not the words.

[5] Perhaps *mazân*, taken here as "grand," may be for *mazânâ*, "a balance," or *mazdân*, "selling," or *mazdâr*, "a labourer."

formed by the evil spirit, who is deadly, (66) the vile sin of those who cannot pass the bridge, by whom dead matter was cooked; (a) this is not according to the law of the angels (or God), yet they cook many (things), such as the fox and weasel.[1]

18. (67) The fourteenth of places and districts produced perfect by me, me who am Aûharmazd, was (68) Varen the four-cornered, subduing[2] Mount Padashkhvâr,[3] some say Kirmân; (a) and its quadrangularity is this, that it stands upon four roads; some say that its city has four gates. (69) At which (place) Frêdûn was born for the destruction of Azhi Dahâk. (70) And in opposition to that were formed by the evil spirit, who is deadly, (71) both the unnatural menstruation (which) becomes more violent, and dwelling on non-Aryan territories, (during) the winter of (him) who says Mount Padashkhvâr (and) the autumn of (him) who says Kîrmân.[4]

19. (72) The fifteenth of places and districts produced perfect by me, me who am Aûharmazd, was (73) (that of those) who are the seven Hindus (*Hindûkân*); (a) and its seven-Hinduism is this, that the chief rulers are seven; yet I do not say this, that there are not seven, since (it is) from the Avesta *hacha ushastara Heñdva avi daoshastarem Heñdum* ("from the eastern Hindu to the western Hindu").[5] Some say that there is one to each region (*kêshvar*).[6] (74) And in opposition to that were formed by the evil spirit, who is deadly, (75) the unnatural menstruation which becomes more violent, (and) the unnatural heat which is beyond measure.

20. (76) The sixteenth of places and districts produced perfect by me, me who am Aûharmazd, was (77) on the waters of

---

[1] Probably the ichneumon or Indian mangûs.

[2] The old MSS. have *kîr = gîr*, "seizing;" otherwise we might read *sar*, "the chief," meaning the metropolis or seat of government of Mount Padashkhvâr.

[3] According to the Bundahish (p. 23 W.), "the Padashkhvârgar mountain (or range of Mount Padashkhvâr) is that in Tapristân and that side of Gîlân."

[4] Such appears to be the meaning of the commentator, as Padashkhvârgar being chiefly a cold country, and Kirmân chiefly a hot one, it would be natural for the inhabitants to quit the former in the winter and the latter in the autumn or hottest season. Perhaps we should read *amat*, "when," for *mân*, "who," and translate "when it is the winter of the said Padashkhvârgar, when it is the autumn of the said Kirmân."

[5] The commentator probably means to say that the doubt about there being *seven* Hindus is not his own, but is occasioned by an Avesta text which mentions only *two*.

[6] Of which there are seven.

Arangistân,[1] which is Arûm,[2] (78) whose residences are unwalled (*adîvâr*), so that they soon retreat; (*a*) some say they have no ruler in authority. (79) And in opposition to that was formed by the evil spirit, who is deadly, (80) even the winter, produced by the demons, (which) becomes very severe.[3]

21. (81) There are also those famous places and districts which remain unmentioned, which are handsome in appearance, profound in the work of the law, desirable, [that is, suitable], . . . [4] [that is, they would appoint many as chiefs], splendid, [that is, having fame,[5] some say flourishing[6] as Fârs the pure is splendid].

7.—*Pahlavi Vendîdâd XVIII.*

1. (1) Many are the men—this way spoke Aûharmazd—O righteous Zaratûsht! [that is, the men in the world are many; some say that they who are like these are many] (2) (who) wear the other mouth-veil[7] (though) unversed in religion, [that is, he has not performed its ceremonial; some say that he does not mentally abide by the religion]. (3) Owing to the deceit which he utters to others, the priesthood is his own, [that is, he says: O man! I am a good man]. (4) Don't say of that that

---

[1] That is, the country of the Arang river, one of the two chief rivers of the Iranian world, see p. 361, note 4. It is likewise said in the Bundahish (p. 51 W.): "The Arag (or Arang) river is that of which it is said that it comes out from Alborz in the land of Sûrâk, which they also call (or in which they also call it) Ami, (and) it passes on through the land of Spêtôs which they also call Mesr, and they call it there the Niv."

[2] The eastern empire of the Romans.

[3] The second clause of the Avesta sentence is not translated by the Pahlavi commentator, but that it forms a part of the Avesta text is shown by the enclitic conjunction *cha* occurring in both clauses.

[4] The equivalent of the Avesta word *frashâosrha* seems to be omitted in all old MSS., which give only its explanation. Some modern MSS. have, therefore, altered the text to the following: "inquisitive, [that is, they make much inquiry]," which is simply absurd as an epithet of a place.

[5] Reading *shem-hômand*. The Teheran MS. has *dâm-hômand*, probably for *bâm-hômand*; and modern MSS. improve this into *gadman-hômand*, "glorious."

[6] This word is doubtfully read *vakhsâk*, for *vakhshâk*, "growing." In the Farhang-i Oîm-khadûk (p. 6, ed. Hosh.) we probably have the same word in the phrase *bâmîk chîgûn vêsâk*, where it may perhaps be compared with Pers. *vêshîdah*, "exalted."

[7] See p. 243, note 1. A layman has to veil his mouth and nose when performing the Abân and Atash Nyâyishes, Patit, or any Namâz.

PAHLAVI VENDIDAD XVIII.

(it) is priesthood—this way spoke Aûharmazd—O righteous Zaratûsht! (*a*) The mouth-veil (*padâm*) may be of any stuff, (and) while it keeps back on the mouth it must be two fingers beyond, (as) is clear from the passage, *baê erezu frathaṇhem* ("two fingers' breadth"). (*b*) The two ties (*do-vand*) of a mouth-veil project as ringlets (*pavan gurs*); it should be double (*dô-bâi*) and it should be perfect; some say that one fastening (*dâshtâr*) is behind, [it is said that all there are should be (so)], (and) it should be stronger[1] than that which even the *kûstî* requires. (*c*) With a mouth-veil once (tied) which is single[2] (and) strong,[1] while it is not allowable to pray for the Darûn yet unpresented for tasting,[3] it is allowable to perform the ceremony (*yazishn*).

2. (5) He carries the other vermin-killer [snake-killer] (though) unversed in religion. (6) Owing to the deceit which he utters to others is (his) priesthood.[4] Don't say of him that (he) is a priest—this way spoke Aûharmazd — O righteous Zaratûsht! (*a*) A mouth-veil may be of any stuff, (and) while it comes back on the mouth it must be two fingers beyond, (as) is declared by the passage, *baê erezu âi ashâum Zarathushtra* ("two fingers, O righteous Zarathushtra!").[5] (*b*) The snake-killer[6] may be of anything; a leathern (one) is good, (as) is declared by the passage[7] (beginning with) *Vohû manaṇha janaiti apemchiḍ Aṇrô*

---

[1] Reading *tushkûk*; compare Pers. *tâsh*, "strength."
[2] Reading *padâm* 1-*vîn-î khadâ-vâk*. The whole clause is difficult to translate.
[3] The word *atafdâḍ* (compare Pers. *tavî*, "feast") is probably the same as occurs in the following sentence from the Farhang-i Oîm-khadûk (p. 38, ed. Hosh.): "*Ataft-dâḍ* is that when one keeps food and drink away (from him) in whom is hunger and thirst."
[4] This sentence is omitted in the Pahlavi version of the old MS. in London, which abbreviates many repetitions in the text.
[5] This is evidently clause (4*a*) repeated by mistake, owing to the preceding sentence being the same in both places. It contains, however, some variations from that clause.
[6] The priests used to recite the following formula as often as they performed the meritorious work of killing any creature of the bad creation: *Shkanom, vânom, nizâr kunom kâlbuḍ-i shumâ, dêvân va drûjân va jâdûân va furṇân, pa hôm va baresom va dîn-i râst va durust ke man châshiḍ* ("I break, smite, and make withered the bodies of you demons and demonesses and sorcerers and witches, through the hôm and barsom and the true and correct religion which is taught me"); compare Mainyô-i Khaṛḍ lvii. 28.
[7] This Avesta quotation is evidently incomplete, and probably only the first few words are given, which is the usual Eastern mode of quoting passages.

mainyush ("whatever water Angrô-mainyush shall smite, by Vohumanô," &c.).

3. (7) He carries the other plant [Barsom, some say *kûtîno*[1]] (though) unversed in religion. (8) Owing to the deceit, &c. (as in (3) and (4), which are not repeated here in Pahlavi by the old MS. in London).

4. (9) He uses the goad and the miscreant[2] so that he groans [and some say that he passes away], (though) unversed in religion. (10) Owing to the deceit, &c. (as in (3) and (4), which are not repeated here in Pahlavi by the old MS. in London).

5. (11) Whoever lies[3] ever throughout the night a non-prayer and a non-chanter, [that is, he does not utter the Avesta residing in the chanting of the service], (12) a non-reciter, a non-performer, speechless, and wishing for his mourning in life;[4] (13) owing to the deceit, &c. (as in (3) and (4), which are not repeated here in Pahlavi by the old MS. in London).

6. (14) Say of him that (he is of) the priesthood—this way spoke Aûharmazd—O righteous Zaratûsht! (15) who all through the night consults the wisdom of the righteous, [that is, forms a priestly assembly[5] so that he may learn (or teach) rightful things], (16) which is preservation from difficulty,[6] the expander of the intellect, the giver of good existence on the Chinvad bridge [stout-heartedness on the Chinvad bridge], (17) deserving spiritual lords (*ahûân*), deserving the place of righteousness, and

---

[1] Probably the name of some plant improperly used for the Barsom. It may be an adjectival form meaning "made of *kût* or *kard*."

[2] The reading of the old MS. in London is *ashtar va mar kânad*. The *ashtar*, "goad," is the usual implement mentioned in the Vendidad for the punishment of criminals (see p. 239), and seems to have been specially used by the priests and their assistants.

[3] This is the correct meaning of the Huzvârish verb *shkbhânastan*, which is variously given by different authorities. In Dastur Hoshangji's edition of the Pahlavi-Pâzand Glossary (p. 15, line 11), the Pâzand *vindâdan* should be omitted, and then both *shkbhânastan* and *khelmûntan* would be correctly explained by *khâftan*, "to lie down, to sleep."

[4] According to the old MS. in London, which has *asâkhûn afash val shîvan kâ:nak paran khapú*. The writer of a modern MS., not understanding that the Pahlavi translator meant to express the Av. *chinvad* by *kâmak*, has added the words *makhîtûnêd radûkîh-i Chinvad pâhal*, "destroys the benefit of the Chinvad bridge."

[5] Or perhaps "performs priestly studies."

[6] Reading *î min tangîh*. The ol'. MS. in London has *amûdayîh*, "freedom from ailment," which would suit the sense well enough, but is not a good equivalent of the Av. *âzô*, which is usually translated by *tangîh*.

deserving the paradise of duty and good works, the reward (and) recompense in the better world.

7. (18) Ask[1] again of me, O pure one! [that is, the question was the last, and He hereupon considered whether something might not yet remain] (19) of me who am the Creator, [that is, I created the creatures], the most developing, [that is, from one thing I know[2] many things], the most intelligent, [that is, by calculation I know much], the best replier to questions, [that is, of those from whom they would make inquiry I give the best reply]. (20) For so it is good (for) thee, so mayst thou become prosperous, if thou askest again of me.

8. (21) Zaratûsht inquired of Aûharmazd thus: O Aûharmazd, favouring spirit! creator of the material world, righteous (one)![3] in whom is the secretly-progressing destruction? [that is, in whom is its lodging? and owing to whom is its progress most?]

9, 10. (22) And Aûharmazd said to him thus: In him (who is) the guide of a vile religion, O Spîtâmân Zaratûsht! the infidel who is a deceiver. (23) Whoever does not put on the sacred string-girdle (for) three spring seasons, [that is, does not have a sadarah (and) kûstî[4] (for) three years], (a) some say that who-

---

[1] Here begin a series of dislocations in the text of the old MSS., which is fully described and accounted for in the introduction (p. 4) to Westergaard's edition of the Avesta texts. Some MS. from which the oldest now existing (and through them all later ones) have descended, must have consisted of bundles of ten folios each; but the bundle containing most of the remainder of this fargard had its folios displaced, so that they stood in the following order: 3-8, 2, 9, 1, and folio 10 was lost. In Spiegel's edition this displacement has only so far been rectified as to put the complete sentences right, while any fragment of a sentence with which one folio ended is left (as in the old MSS.) in connection with the fragment of another sentence with which the next misplaced folio began. Thus, in this sentence (18) the old MSS. give the first two words (which Spiegel omits) here, namely, lakhvâr min, but for the next words we have to turn over several pages (equivalent to the eight folios (3-8, 2, 9) to p. 206, line 6, of Spiegel's text, where we find the rest of the sentence, namely, li arêzak pûrs, &c. We must then turn back again to find sentence (19) in its right place.

[2] So all MSS., but a slight alteration in the form of one letter would give us hankhetûnam, "I place or dispose."

[3] This opening sentence is not given in Pahlavi by the old MSS. here, as it has so often occurred in previous fargards.

[4] The muslin shirt and string girdle worn by Parsis of both sexes, except young children, as enjoined by their religion.

ever does not put on the sacred string-girdle (for) those three spring seasons is the third[1] year an outcast, forsaken below and forsaken above;[2] (it is) according to the law of such that it is not necessary to have a *sadarah* (and) *kûstî*. (24) (And whoever) does not chant the Gâthas (and) does not consecrate the good water.[3] (25) Whoever also has taken him, who is my man, into confinement, [that is, has taken him (as above) described (*nipishtak*) into it],[4] (and) delivers him up to liberty, [that is, makes him an exile], (26) does no better by that act than though he had forced[5] the extent of the skin (off) his head, [that is, had cut the head and had made it alive again].

11. (27) For the blessing of one unrighteous, vile infidel is a curse the length of his jaw; (28) of a second, the length of a tongue; of a third,[6] nothing; a fourth progresses himself, [that is, becomes himself].

12. (29) Whoever gives an unrighteous, vile infidel the outsqueezed Hom-juice, and the priesthood (*zôtîh*), (30) (and) then the consecrated feast (*myâzd*) [this is said because with him are the good and worthy of the feast],[7] (31) does no better by that act than though the enemy's army, having a thousand horse [five hundred men with two horses (each) from the professed warriors], should be conveyed by him on to a village of the Mazdayasnians, (and) he[8] should slay the people (and) they[8] should drive away

---

[1] Dastur Hoshangji suggests that the first two letters of this word have changed places, and that we should read *tasûm*, "fourth," instead of the unusual *sitâm*, "third."

[2] Reading *arajâstô frôbujo avarbûjo*, and taking *arajâstô* as a variant of *arajistô*, "most wrong, most erring." The literal meaning is probably "most wrongful, escaping from what is below, and escaping from what is above," that is, from both the world and heaven.

[3] The old MSS. add the Avesta quotation *yaish yazaiti* ("with which he performs ceremonies").

[4] That is, has taken such a one as just described into custody. Most modern MSS. attempt to alter *nipishtak*, as their writers have failed to see

that the word can be taken in its literal meaning.

[5] The old MS. in London has *karḍ hômanâe aîgh rôêshman*, &c.

[6] Here we have the second dislocation of the text, as described in p. 367, note 1; and for the remainder of sentence (28) we have to turn to the end of (98) on p. 205, line 10, of Spiegel's edition. The additional words in the old MS. in London are *lâ mindaram, tasûm nafshman sâtânêd, aîgh nafshman ycherûnêd*. The incoherence in this sentence is due to the Avesta original. See p. 245.

[7] Or "he would say the good and worthy are in his feast."

[8] So in the old MS. in London, but the persons are reversed in Spiegel's edition.

the cattle as plunder.¹ (*a*) That is, when² one gives him the priesthood (*zôtîh*) (it is) a *tanâpûhar*³ (sin), and when² they shall do it frequently (it is) a mortal sin (*margarjân*).

13. (32) Ask again of me, &c. (as in ver. 7 (18–20) above).

14. (33) Zaratûsht inquired, &c. (as in ver. 8 (21) to) righteous (one)! who is he (belonging to) Srosh the righteous, the mighty, the self-subduing, [that is, he keeps (his) body in God's control], the admirably-armed,⁴ the lord (*khûdâ*) of the *brôithrô-taézhem*⁵ ("sharp battle-axe") *frashusaiti Sraoshô ashyô* ("the righteous Srosh goes forth"), (who is he)' the *Srôshavarezô* ? [that is, who is his stimulator of the world]?

15–17. (34) And Aûharmazd said to him thus : The bird whose name is Parôdarsh, O Spîtâmân Zaratûsht ! (*a*) This Parôdarsh would be "prior indication" (*pêsh-dakhshakîh*), and its prior indication is this, that first it flaps (its) pinions, [that is, wings], (and) then utters a cry.⁶ (35) On whom men, in disparagement, bestow the name of fowl, some would say the cock ; (*a*) though (if) they did not say (so) it would be possible for him to do better. (36) That bird raises an outcry during the preparation of dawn,⁷ which arises at midnight,⁸ (37) thus : Rise up ! be men ! praise the righteousness which is perfect ! and overthrown are the demons, [that is, when righteousness is praised by them the demons are overthrown by them] ; (38) for this (one) who has run to you is Bûshâsp the long-talking,⁹ [some say thus : This (one) has run to you, Bûshâsp the long-pawed],⁹ (39) who by prosy chatting (*frâj-gôp-lâyishnîh*) with the whole

---

¹ Or perhaps "in a drove."
² Perhaps *mûn*, "whoever," should be read for *amat*, "when."
³ A sin which prevents the soul from passing over the Chinvaḍ bridge to paradise.
⁴ The author adds here "the ruler in the Arezahi and Savahi (kêshvars)," a gloss taken from a modern MS. Such modern glosses are, however, mere guesses, of no authority.
⁵ Mentioned in the Srosh Yasht (Yas. lvii. 31).
⁶ The same explanation of *parôdarsh* is given in the Pahlavi translation of the fragment in Westergaard's Yasht xxii. 41, as follows : *afash*

Parôkdarshîh aê, aîghash fratûm parân shikâvêḍ, va akhar vâng vâdânêḍ.
⁷ This *aûsh afzâr* is defined in the Farhang-i Oîm-khadûk (p. 42) as the third quarter of the night, in which the Ushahina Gâh begins.
⁸ The third dislocation of the text, as described in p. 367, note 1, occurs after the first Avesta word in clause (37) ; but being in the Avesta text, it has been properly corrected in Spiegel's edition.
⁹ It is doubtful whether these two epithets, *dêrang-gâbo* and *dêrang-gâk*, are not both intended to mean "long-handed" or "long-pawed."

material world, when every one ought to be free from sloth (*bûshâsp*), lulls it off to sleep. (40) This she says: Sleep a long time (*daregînîh*)! be men! for there is nothing which requires you,[1] [that is, your work of the law[2] will not stop]. (41) And let not the three perfections be over yourselves, good thought in the mind, good words in speech, (and) good deeds in action; [(a) some say that the religion asserts that Bûshâsp speaks for this reason, lest the three perfections should be over yourselves, good thought in the mind, good words in speech, (and) good deeds in action]. (42) But let the three turpitudes (*vadtûmîh*) be over yourselves, bad thought in the mind, and bad words in speech, and bad deeds in action.

18, 19. (43) Then the first third of the night my fire, (who am) Aûharmazd, begs the householder of the house[3] for assistance, thus: O householder of the house,[3] rise up! (44) put on (your) clothes! wash (your) hands thoroughly! request that they may bring me firewood! illumine my molester (*patîyârak*)[4] with firewood purified (by) thoroughly-washed hands. (45) For it seemed to me (it was) Az, produced by the demons, with forward-gliding coils, who tore out (my) life.[5]

20, 21. (46) Then in the second third of the night my fire, who am Aûharmazd, begs the husbandman for assistance, always (with) the same phrase (*hamîshak kâr-*1), thus: O husbandman, rise up! (47) (as in (44) and (45), which are not repeated here, in Pahlavi, by the old MS. in London).

22. (48) Then the third third of the night the fire of Aûharmazd begs Srosh the righteous for assistance, thus: O Srosh the righteous, the handsome! (49) then let any firewood of the material world be brought[6] unto me, purified (by) thoroughly-

---

[1] Literally "for (there is) not that which suits you."

[2] The old MS. in London has *kâr ra îtnâ*, "work and religious duty," that is, secular and religious duties. This phrase is generally written *kâr îtnâ*, and it may be doubted whether the conjunction *ra* or the relative *î* is to be understood as connecting the two words.

[3] The old MS. in London has *manô mânpat* in both places.

[4] So in the old MSS., and *padîrak* seems no improvement.

[5] The old MS. in London has here *maman barâ li-î âz-î shêdâân-dâd-î khamîh pêsh-tajishno-î ahâ barâ sedkând medammânast*, but in (50) it has the following variations: *li âz-î shêdâân-dâd mayâ; ahû-î;* and *medammûnêd*.

[6] The old MS. in London has *dedrânyên-yâd*, but modern MSS. of course alter the termination to a form better understood by their writers, without much attention to the meaning.

washed hands. (50) For there seems the water of Az, produced by the demons, flowing forward on me, which is a tearing away of life.[1]

23-25. (51) Then Srosh the righteous upbraided (*frâj-gôp-lâyîd*) the bird whose name is Parôdarsh, O Spîtâmân Zaratûsht! (52) (as in (35) to (42), which are not repeated here, in Pahlavi, by the old MS. in London).

26, 27. (53) Then speaks a friend to his friend, they who shall lie on a bed, (54) thus: Do thou rise up! for I am driven away. (55) Either one who shall rise up beforehand, his progress is towards the best existence (paradise), (a) so that they proclaim that even with a good work of three *srôshô-charanâm*[2] it is possible to attain to the best existence. (56) Either one who (shall have) brought beforehand, up to the fire of Aûharmazd, firewood purified (by) thoroughly-washed hands, (57) him the fire blesses, when pleased, uninjured, (and) satisfied, (58) thus: May the herd of cattle attain (*âkhtâd*) unto thee! [that is, may it be thine!] (59) besides the full continuance of men [much progeny]! (60) May a desire in the mind for the will of thy (heavenly) lord (*ahû*) attain unto thee! [that is, may that something be in thy mind which should be thy (heavenly) lord and high priest!] (61) and may the well-pleased lord (*ahû*) live in (thy) life![3] so that the nights when thou shalt live thou mayst live in joy. (62) This is the blessing which the fire always offers him, [that is, (it is) ever (for) him], who (has) brought to it firewood which is dry (and) inspected according to rule (*rôshanîh*), (63) on account of a wish for rectitude [on account of a desire for duty and good works], (and) which is purified, [that is, pure].

28. (64) Whoever gives that bird of mine, which is Parôdarsh, O Spîtâmân Zaratûsht! female and male together, to a righteous man with perfect rectitude, (65) thinks of it thus: It will produce me a dwelling; (a) when they give him the reward (and) recompense, he considers about it thus: When a dwelling like a

---

[1] Translated here differently from (45), in accordance with the variations in the old MS. in London, but the reading *mayâ*, "water," for *khamîh*, "coiling," is very improbable.

[2] This is not the scourge or compeller of attention, but some very small weight of the same name, by which the value of the most trivial actions is estimated.

[3] The old MS. in London has *ra aûrvakhsht* (or *hâ-ravakh-dâd*) *ahvô pavan khayâ zîvâd*.

palace[1] shall be given to me it may even be large; (66) (with) a hundred columns, a thousand corridors,[2] a myriad large (and) a myriad small (rooms).

29. (67) (Of him) who gives that bird of mine, which is Parôdarsh, small morsels of meat[3] along with *pilâv*,[4] some say cumin seed,[5] [(*a*) some say that he gives out meat in that quantity to a righteous man], (68) of him, the ever-bringing,[6] I who am Aûharmazd would not be an inquirer for his second statement, [(*a*) once I shall ask[7] everybody], (69) for he proceeds onwards to the best existence (paradise).

30. (70) Srosh the righteous asked of the Drûj, of Disgrace,[8] [(*a*) some say that (it is) of Wrath; some, of the evil spirit], (71) without the accompaniment of a club, [that is, he put down his club, (*a*) so that he might intimate that confession (*khâstûkîh*) through fear is not to be considered as confession], (72) thus: O Drûj, who art inglorious, [that is, thou hast no benefit whatever from it[9]], (and) inactive! [that is, thou doest nothing which is proper]! (73) art thou thus conceiving without cohabitation of the whole living creation? [that is, when they do not cohabit with thee dost thou become pregnant?].

31, 32. (74) And she who is the demon Drûj exclaimed (in) reply to him, thus: O Srosh the righteous, the handsome! (75) I do not conceive without cohabitation of the whole living crea-

---

[1] It is assumed here that *gân bará* is a corruption of *gânbad*, "a dome," which is usually written *gâmbad*. The reading *gâr*, "a tomb," is hardly probable.

[2] This is a guess at the meaning of *fras*, compare *frasp*, *frasp*, "a beam or lintel."

[3] This is translated in accordance with the view taken of the Avesta text in p. 247, but a more literal translation of the Pahlavi would be: "(Of him) who gives (away) meat the size of the body of that bird of mine," &c. The Pahlavi translator evidently considered the whole passage as referring to the meritorious work of charity.

[4] The old MS. in London has *pilâî*, a way of writing *pilâv*, an Eastern dish in which boiled mutton or fowl is smothered in rice, and garnished with hard-boiled eggs, onions boiled and fried, raisins, almonds, and spices.

[5] Assuming that *zûrak* means *zîrak*.

[6] Perhaps *akaraz-var* should be corrected into *akaraz*.

[7] Or "they have inquiry made of."

[8] Reading *khâduk* for Pers. *khudâk;* a similar Pahlavi form occurs in Vend. v. 153, where it must be read *khâdak* =Pers. *khâdah*, "truth," as it is the equivalent of Av. *ashem*.

[9] Meaning probably from the divine glory. But the word *ajash* ought perhaps to be omitted, as it is an addition to the text in the old MS. in London, and we should then read "thou hast no goodness whatever."

tion. (76) There are even (for) me too [1] four males. (77) They impregnate me just as any other male, when the semen is in the females it impregnates, [that is, I become pregnant].

33. (78) Srosh the righteous, &c. (as in (70) to (72), which are not repeated here in Pahlavi by the old MSS.): Which is the first of those thy males?

34, 35. (79) And she who is the demon Drûj exclaimed (in) reply to him, thus: O Srosh the righteous, the handsome! (80) even that (*zak-îch*) is the first of those my males, (81) when a man gives not even a trifle of his hoard of wealth, when he lived (*zîst*), [that is, exists], to a righteous man with perfect rectitude. (82) He impregnates me, &c. (as in (77) above).

36. (83) Srosh the righteous, &c. (as in (70) to (72), which are not repeated, in Pahlavi, by the old MSS.): What is a counteraction of the effect of that?

37, 38. (84) And she who is the demon Drûj exclaimed (in) reply to him, thus: O Srosh the righteous, the handsome! (85) it is a counteraction of the effect of that, (86) when the man gives even a trifle of his hoard of wealth, when not alive [2] (*lâ zîst*), to a righteous man with perfect rectitude. (87) He will so destroy my pregnancy as a four-legged wolf when it tears out a son from the womb by tearing. (*a*) This is evident from the Avesta: it happens so when the former (*valman*) is (one) who is impure (*mûn palisht*), and the latter (*va le-denman*) is in want through dissemination of good; when he gives up such wealth to such a man he will destroy the Drûj; even when he gives up the wealth to that man the Drûj is destroyed, although that man also should give up the same wealth lest (*al hat*) it should likewise be contaminated; some say that she is destroyed afterwards.[3]

39. (88) Srosh the righteous, &c. (as in (70) to (72), which are not repeated, in Pahlavi, by the old MSS.): Which is the second of those thy males?

---

[1] The most probable reading is *hômand-îch lî-ch* 4 *gûshan*.

[2] Meaning probably that he arranges by will for a charitable distribution of his property after death, which appears to be a misunderstanding of the language of the Avesta.

[3] This commentary would be hardly intelligible without the corrections supplied by the old MS. in London. The form *le-denman* is occasionally used for *denman*, of which it was probably an almost obsolete form at the time when the commentator wrote.

40, 41. (89) (She) who is the demon Drûj exclaimed (in) reply to him, thus: O Srosh the righteous, the handsome! (90) even that is the second of those my males, (91) when a man, through sinfulness, makes water an instep's length beyond the front of the instep. (92) He impregnates me, &c. (as in (77), which is not repeated here, in Pahlavi, by the old MSS.).

42-44. (93-95) (As in (83-85), which are not repeated, in Pahlavi, by the old MSS.), (96) when the man, after standing up three steps (off), [some say beyond[1] the three steps], (97) having repeated three (praises of) righteousness,[2] and two Humatanâms (Yas. xxxv. 2), and three Hukhshathrôtemâis (Yas. xxxv. 5), recites aloud four Ahunavars (Yas. xxvii. 13, and) prays aloud the Yênhê-hâtâm (Yas. vii. 27), (98) he will so destroy, &c. (as in (87) above). (a) This is evident from the Avesta: it happens so when a man, through sinfulness, makes water an instep's length beyond the front of the instep; for him (it) is the beginning of a tanâpûhar (sin), and he atones for it by the Avesta.[3] When he makes water standing up it is the beginning of a tanâpûhar (sin) for him, and he does not atone for it by the Avesta. It is in front,[4] it is not backwards. It is as to that which proceeds from the body[5] (that) *chrad yad hê kasishtahê erezvô fratemem dbaêshish* ("as much as the extremity of his smallest finger is an offence"); that amount of distance, (when) bent together, is suitable for every foul action.[6] Gôgôshasp[7] said that for the sake of preserving the clothes it is allowable to make water far off. (b) When (one) accomplishes the action lawfully (and) well, when he squats down, one Yathâ-ahû-vairyô is to be uttered by him. Sôshâns[8] said that, in case of

---

[1] It appears in the sequel that *barâ min* must mean "beyond," that is, "more than" the three steps off; but according to its usual meaning it would be "without" taking three steps backwards.

[2] That is, three Ashem-vohû formulas. See p. 141, note 2.

[3] By reciting the Avesta passages above prescribed.

[4] Probably "in front of the toes" is meant. The whole of this commentary is difficult to divide correctly into separate sentences.

[5] The word *tanû* is given by the old MS. in London, but is omitted by Spiegel and most later MSS.

[6] Reading *zak-i dârak âmâr hamkhâl visp khârak ghal kânishn varâz*. There are many difficulties in the sentence, and the traditional explanation is different, but decidedly erroneous.

[7] The name of one of the old commentators who is often quoted in the Pahlavi version of the Vendidad and other works.

[8] The name of another old commentator.

haste (aûshtâp), when he utters (it) on a road it is also allowable. (c) And when he stands up the Avesta is all to be uttered by him within the three steps; some say beyond the three steps, and on his walking[1] apart, the Avesta is ever to be uttered, [this walking is that when he goes on from the three steps], or the Avesta is taken inwardly by him.[2] (d) When he accomplishes the action lawfully (and) well, (but) through sinfulness does not utter the Avesta, it is not clear to me (whether it is) one (or) two[3] srôshô-charanâms of a tanâpûhar (sin). Gôgôshasp said that when he accomplishes the action lawfully (and) well, he also (utters) three Ashem-vohûs.[4]

45. (99) Srosh the righteous, &c. (as in (70) to (72), which are not repeated, in Pahlavi, by the old MSS.): Which is the third of those thy males?

46, 47. (100) And she, &c. (as in (89) above)! even that is the third of those my males, (101) when a man asleep has an emission of semen, [that is, his semen comes out]. (102) He impregnates me, &c. (as in (77), which is not repeated, in Pahlavi, by the old MSS.).

48–50. (103–105) (As in (83–85), which are not repeated, in Pahlavi, by the old MSS.), (106) when the man, after arising from sleep, extols righteousness, [that is, recites three Ashem-vohûs], (107) two Humatanâms, (and) three Hukhshathrôtemâis, and prays aloud four Yathâ-ahû-vairyôs (and) Yênhô-hâtâm,[5] he will so destroy, &c. (as in (87) above).

51. (108) Then this (man) speaks to Spendarmad thus: O Spendarmad! (109) I deliver up to thee this man, and do thou deliver this man back to me, (110) on the production, by skill,

---

[1] Traditionally, chamishn is "making water" (compare Pers. chamîn, "urine"), but here it is otherwise explained by the commentary itself.

[2] That is, it is muttered in a low tone of voice.

[3] So in the old MS. in London. This mode of translation is in accordance with the idea of "the beginning of a tanâpûhar" mentioned in (a), as a tanâpûhar is equivalent to a great number of srôshô-charanâms.

[4] The fourth dislocation of the text, as described in p. 367, note 1, occurs after the words ashem vohû (the last having been the catchword at the end of a folio in the original MS.); the remaining words, vohû vahishtem 3, are found attached to the first word (uschishta) of the Avesta of (37) in MSS., and have been omitted by Spiegel. The last eight Pahlavi words added to (98) really belong to (28), as noticed in p. 368, note 6.

[5] The same prayers as those enjoined in (97).

of the reorganisation in the future existence, (111) knowing the Gâthas and knowing[1]   *   *   *

55. (115) *   * taking (the fourth step), quickly afterwards, we who are demons, at once we injure him by disease of the tongue. (116)[2] *Khshayamna paschaêta mereghentê gaêthâo astvaitîsh ashahê yatha zanda yâtumenta merenchantê gaêthâo ashahê* ("afterwards the possessed ones destroy the settlements of righteousness, supplied with creatures, as the spells of sorcerers destroy the settlements of righteousness"). (a) So that up to the fourth step it is not more (than)[3] three *srôshô-charanâms*, and at his fourth step it amounts to the beginning of a *tanâpûhar*, [some say that (he is) within what is permitted him in going the three (steps)]. When he walks on very many (steps) it is also not more than a tanâpûhar, all that[4] remains over from the beginning.

56-59. (117, 118) (As in (83-85), which are not repeated, in Pahlavi, by the old MSS.), (119) (not given, in Pahlavi, by the old MSS.). (120, 121) (As in (115, 116), which are not repeated, in Pahlavi, by the old MSS.).

60, 61. (122) (As in (18-21), which are not repeated, in Pahlavi, by the old MSS. to) righteous one! (123) Who persecutes thee, thee who art Aûharmazd, with the greatest persecution, and annoys with the greatest annoyance? [that is, (does) all this another time].[5]

62. (124) And Aûharmazd said to him thus: The courtezan,

---

[1] The fifth dislocation of the text, as described in p. 367, note 1, occurs after the words *va âkâs*, where there is a break in the text owing to the loss of a folio in the original MS. This is all the more to be regretted as it is evident, from the small quantity of missing text, that the lost folio must have contained a long commentary. The remaining eighteen Pahlavi words attached to (111) really belong to (18), as noticed in p. 367, note 1; the word *min* being repeated because it was the catchword at the end of a folio.

[2] There seems little doubt of this being merely an Avesta quotation belonging to the commentary, which has been accepted as part of the Avesta text both here and in (121), see p. 249. It is not translated into Pahlavi, and the commentary which follows it belongs to the preceding sentence in the Avesta text.

[3] It is doubtful whether we should not read "not more than (aî) a *srôshô-charanâm*."

[4] Assuming that we may read *mûn* instead of *amat*, see p. 346, note 2. This phrase seems to mean that he only completes the *tanâpûhar*, already begun, by walking beyond the fourth step; but the phrase is obscure.

[5] Or perhaps "does all this at one time."

O righteous Zaratûsht! who mingles together the seed of the pious and impious, the idolaters and non-idolaters, the *tanapûhar*-sinners and also the non-*tanâpûhar*-sinners, (a) and it is not her business; for when cohabitation is three times conceded by her (she is) worthy of death (*marg-arjân*). Gôgôshasp said that this is a courtezan who is within bounds (*vîmand*).[1]

63. (125) Of one-third the waters flowing from the mountains the power is exhausted by her gazing on (them), O Zaratûsht! (126) Of one-third the trees which are growing, graceful, and golden-hued, the growth is exhausted by her gazing on (them), O Zaratûsht!

64. (127) Of one-third of Spendarmad (the earth) the freedom from scarcity (*atangîh*) is carried off by her walking on (it), O Zaratûsht! (128) Of one-third the excellent thoughts, the excellent words, the excellent deeds of a righteous man she abstracts the strength and dignity (*shukûhih*), the success, fame (*khanîdîh*), and even righteousness, through agitation (*levatman nafâmishn*), O Zaratûsht!

65. (129) Concerning such (females) also I say unto thee, O Spîtâmân Zaratûsht! that they are more destructive than a darting serpent (*az*), [some say a darting snake (*mâr*)], (130) than a raving (*shît*)[2] wolf, (131) than a jungle-bred[3] wolf when it rushes into enclosures upon the sheep, (132) than a frog spawning thousands when it plunges into the water,[4] [that is, it drops at once into the water; some say from the male to the female].

66-68. (133) (As in 18-21) which are not repeated, in Pahlavi, by the old MSS. to) righteous one! (134) whoever observantly, [that is, he sees that (she) is menstruous], knowingly, [that is, he knows that (it) is a sin], (and) risking penalty, [that is, he would say thus: I will incur the penalty], cohabits with a woman suffering from any kind of menstruation,[5] with that observation and knowledge and risk of penalty, (135) what is (his)

---

[1] Meaning perhaps "in bondage," but the sense is rather uncertain. The word *âhîd*, which follows in the old MSS., is probably only the Pahlavi *ait*, "is," or *hâd*, "would be," in a Pâzand form, and ought to end this sentence.

[2] Or perhaps *yahêd*, "who destroys."

[3] This epithet is very doubtful; and "jungle" is to be understood in its wide Indian meaning of "wilderness," not in its limited European sense of "forest."

[4] Thereby polluting it.

[5] This is merely a free translation.

penalty in cash (*khrâstak*)? and what is it (at) the bridge[1] with the goad (and) scourge (*srôshô-charanâm*)? How does he remove the penalty for the perpetration of that action? [that is, how should he atone?].

69, 70. (136) And Aûharmazd said to him thus: Whoever observantly, &c. (as in (134) above), (137) he should[2] search out a thousand young (cattle), (138) and of all those cattle, of those which are suitably decorated,[3] and (consecrated) with holy-water, *yaḍ añtare veredhka asma reja*, ("what is in the kidneys, the kidney fat"),[4] he should carry forth for the fire with perfect rectitude; (139) (his) arm should carry (it) forth for the good water.

71. (140) A thousand back-loads of hard firewood, dry and inspected,[5] he should carry forth for the fire with perfect rectitude. (141) A thousand back-loads of soft firewood emitting fragrance, or benzoin, or aloe-wood, or pomegranate,[6] or any other of the most sweet-scented of trees, he should carry forth for the fire with perfect rectitude.

72. (142) He should (have) a thousand Barsoms arranged in (their) arrangement. (143) A thousand consecrated waters, with Hom (and) with flesh, which are purified, [that is, pure], watched, [that is, they are kept by a chief (priest)],[7] purified by a holy man,[8] [that is, prepared by a holy man], and watched by a holy man, [that is, a holy man kept (it) as chief (priest)], in connection[9] with which are those plants which are called

---

[1] At the Chinvaḍ bridge where the soul has to account for its actions in this life.

[2] Grammarians should notice that the conditional in these sentences (137-149) is formed by prefixing (instead of affixing) the auxiliaries *dê*, *ê*, or *hana*, to the indicative present.

[3] Reading *rurâz varâz* = Pers. *burâz barâz*; this is, however, doubtful, as the oldest reading is *gvâ râz nrâz*, all in Pâzand, and may perhaps be some part of an animal.

[4] The words *asma reja* look more like "stone and gravel," but the phrase is traditionally understood as referring to fat smeared on splinters of wood which are thrown into the fire along with pieces of sandal-wood and pomegranate twigs.

[5] To ascertain that it is free from impurity.

[6] The *hadhânaêpata*, being classed here among odoriferous substances, can hardly have been the pomegranate shrub, as assumed by tradition.

[7] The *zaota*, or chief officiating priest at all important ceremonies, must be intended by *sardâr* here.

[8] That is, by a priest, which must be the meaning of *ddhmân* here.

[9] Assuming that *ham-gûmîh* stands for *ham-gûmêjîh*. The oldest reading is *ham-gânamîh*, which might be a miswriting of *ham-gûnakîh*, "the same manner" (an inverted *k* being *m* in Pahlavi).

pomegranate, he should carry (all these) forth for the good water with perfect rectitude.

73. (144) A thousand serpents who are created erect (*lâlâ-dahîshno*)¹ he should destroy, two thousand of those other female snakes (*mâr-bânûk*). (145) A thousand land-frogs he should destroy, and two thousand of those of the water. (146) A thousand ants carrying off corn (*dân-kash*) he should destroy, two thousand of those other venomous ones (*dahîrak*).²

74. (147) He should throw thirty over-bridges across navigable water (and) streams containing water, with arches (*dahan*).³ (148) He is to be beaten with a thousand blows of a horse-goad, (or) two thousand *srôshô-charanâms*.

75. (149) That is his penalty at the bridge;⁴ that is his penalty in cash (*khvâstak*), that is his (penalty at) the bridge, with the goad (and) scourge (*srôshô-charanâm*); and so he should remove the penalty for the perpetration of that action, [that is, he should atone].

76. (150) If he removes (it) he gathers⁵ for the better world of the righteous, [that is, his gathering is made for that place]. (151) If he does not remove (it) he gathers⁵ for the world of the wicked, [that is, his gathering is made for that place], (152) of those deserving gloom, [that is, their desert is for that place], of gloomy origin, [that is, the Drûj who makes a man wicked originates from that place], (and) gloomy, [that is, a dark place].

8.—*Pahlavi Vendîdad XIX.*

1. (1) From the northern direction of the directions, from the northern direction of the place, from the direction of the demons, the evil spirit rushed forth, the deadly demon of the demons; (2) and thus exclaimed he, the evil spirit, the deadly: (3) Rush on, O Drûj! and destroy him, the righteous Zaratûsht. (4) On to him they rushed, the Drûj, the demon Bût, and secret-moving Destruction, the deceiver.

---

¹ That is, who stand partly erect when prepared to strike their prey or enemy, like the cobra and many other snakes.

² Assuming that *dahîrak* (the oldest reading) stands for *zâhirak*, "poisonous."

³ This is merely a guess.

⁴ See p. 378, note 1. This first clause appears to be superfluous, but occurs in the oldest MSS.

⁵ That is, he accumulates a store of good works, or sin, as the case may be. The meaning can hardly be "he is gathered to," although the phrase might perhaps be so translated without doing much violence to grammar.

2. (5) Zaratûsht chanted aloud the Ahuna-vairya (formula), [those two Yathâ-ahû-vairyôs which stand before *hushiti* (Yas. lxviii. 14)], and he consecrated the good water which is of good creation,[1] and the Mazdayasnian religion was professed by him, [that is, he uttered the *fravardnê*, (Yas. i. 23)]. (6) The Drûj was confounded by that; away they rushed, the demon Bût and secret-moving Destruction, the deceiver.

3. (7) The Drûj exclaimed (in) reply to him thus: Thou art a misleader, O evil spirit! this thou art, [that is, anything unlooked for, which it is not possible for thee to do thyself, thou orderest us (to do)]. (8) The ruin of him, who is Spîtâmân Zaratûsht, is not contemplated by us, (9) owing to the full glory [owing to the great diligence] of the righteous Zaratûsht; (*a*) so that they announce that whoever remains in activity, on him less affliction comes. (10) Zaratûsht perceived in (his) mind thus: The wicked demons, astute in evil, consult together about my ruin.

4. (11) Up rose Zaratûsht, forth went Zaratûsht, (12) from the extinction of evil thought (*Akômanô*) [when the evil thought in his body is extinguished] by severely distressing questions, [by those questions, so severe, which are proposed to it]; (*a*) some say that evil thought is extinguished by him when it asks what is severely distressing.[2] (13) And he held a stone (*sag*) in his hand, which was the size of a hut, the righteous Zaratûsht! [the rocky stone,[3] some say, is the spirit of the Yathâ-ahû-vairyô], (14) who thus besought the creator Aûharmazd: (15) Where is that kept on this wide, round, far-traversed (earth, which) is to be fixed on the roof[4] in the dwelling of Pôrûshasp? (*a*) Some say it is kept on this earth, so wide, round, (and) far-traversed, and the place which is kept for it is fixed on the roof in the dwelling of Pôrûshasp.

---

[1] The "good Dâitî" would probably be identified, by the Pahlavi translator, with the river of that name, see p. 357, note 1.

[2] It is not clear whether the Pahlavi translator means to personify Akômanô as a demon existing independent of the mind or not.

[3] Or "the stone of three kinds," if we read *sag-i 3-gûnô* instead of *sag-i saginô*. As *sag* (not *sang*) is the usual word for "stone" in the Pahlavi Vendidad, there seems little doubt that a stone is meant, though tradition prefers to understand the phrase as "the thrice three," applicable to the *naugirah*, or "nine-jointed" staff of Zaratûsht, see p. 333, note 4.

[4] The words *danjîk zbâr*, being merely a transcription of the Avesta, are translated in accordance with the meaning adopted in p. 333, note 4.

5. (16) Zaratûsht proclaimed aloud, [that is, he openly (*patdîd*) conveyed], to the evil spirit, thus : O evil spirit, astute in evil ! (17) I destroy the creatures produced by the demons, I destroy the corruption (*nasush*) produced by the demons, (18) I destroy the desire for witches, [the worship of idols], until the triumphant *Sûḍ-hômand* ("beneficial one") is brought forth by the water of Kashôsâî, [(*a*) both I destroy and my disciples destroy thee ; and after he arrives he will annihilate thee by his own deeds], (19) from the eastern direction of the directions. (*a*) (From) the place where the sun comes up on the longest day to the place where it comes up on the shortest day is the east ; from the place where it comes up on the shortest day to the place where it goes down on the shortest day is the south ; from the place where it goes down on the shortest day to the place where it goes down on the longest day is the west ; and the remainder is the north. Some say that the north is an abyss.[1]

6. (20) (In) reply to him exclaimed the evil spirit, astute in evil, (21) thus : Destroy not these my creatures, O righteous Zaratûsht ! (22) Thou art the son of Pôrûshasp, and thou art from the conception of thy mother's womb, I know thee, [(*a*) some say that I had the worship of thy ancestors, and do thou also worship me]. (23) Curse the good religion of the Mazdayasnians, (and) obtain happiness as Vôghnô, the king, obtained it.

7. (24) (In) reply to him spoke he who is Spîtâmân Zaratûsht, (25) thus : I curse not that which is Aûharmazd's own, the good religion of the Mazdayasnians ; (26) not for love of body nor life, not for much result and not for good result, not on account of the parting of body and soul, [that is, although they cut off my head yet I curse not].

8. (27) (In) reply to him exclaimed the evil spirit, astute in evil : (28) With what words dost thou smite me ? [that is, wouldst thou make me confounded ?] and with what words wilt thou molest me ? [that is, wouldst thou force me apart from the creatures ?] with (what) well-formed implement, (from) these creatures of me who am the evil spirit ?

9. (29) (In) reply to him spoke he who is Spîtâmân Zara-

---

[1] Reading *tih-i*, "a bottom," as hell is supposed to be in the north. But the word may be also read *tâ-i*, "a summit," which might refer to the mountain Arezûra at the gate of hell, see p. 316, note 4, and p. 337, note 9.

tûsht, (30) thus: With the Homa-mortar and dish and Homa, even the words Aûharmazd pronounced, the Avesta, (31) are my best implements. (32) With those words I smite thee, [that is, I would make thee confounded], with those words I molest thee, [that is, I would force thee apart from the creatures], with those well-formed implements, O evil spirit, astute in evil! (33) which were given to me by him, the beneficent spirit, and were given to him in boundless time, [some say thus: which were given to me by him, the beneficent spirit, and were given to me by him in boundless time], (34) and were given over to me by them, the Ameshaspends, the good rulers and good arrangers, [that is, they have been assisting in the giving by them].[1]

10. (35) Zaratûsht chanted aloud the Ahuna-vairya, [that is, the Yathâ-ahû-vairyô]; (36) the righteous Zaratûsht spoke out thus: That which I ask of thee Thou tellest to me right, O Aûharmazd![2] I am firmly of opinion, [some say thus: Right is what Thou tellest to me].

11. (37)[3] Through what is to be fixed on the roof[4] where Aûharmazd (and) the good one [Vohuman] of good estimation are stationed (*ahist*), [this "estimation" (stands) for Vohuman again], (38) (with) Ashavahisht, Shatvêr, (and) Spendarmad.

12. (39) How should I act with them (to defend) from that Drûj who is from the evil spirit, astute in evil? [that is, how should I make her quite confounded?]. (40) How when it has become polluted directly, how when it has become polluted indirectly, how shall I dispossess the corruption (*nasush*) from the residence (*vîs*) of Mazdayasnians? (41) How do I purify a righteous man? How do I bring purification on a righteous woman?

13. (42) And Aûharmazd said to him thus: Thou mayst call, O Zaratûsht! upon the good religion of the Mazdayasnians,

---

[1] These words, "by them," lead one to suspect that the Pahlavi translator considered "boundless time" as much an individual as "the beneficent spirit," and that we ought to read "by boundless time" (the Pahlavi *pavan* being both "by" and "in"). The rare forms *mânamash*, *afamash*, and *afamshân* (for *afamshân*), in these sentences, are of interest to grammarians, as they show that two pronominal suffixes can be added to one particle.

[2] Yas. xliv., see pp. 158–161.

[3] The Pahlavi translator omits the usual opening invocation of the Creator, see the translation of the Avesta text, p. 333.

[4] See p. 380, note 4.

[that is, celebrate a Vendidad]. (43) Thou mayst call, O Zaratûsht! upon the Ameshaspends in invisible concealment on the seven regions of the earth, [that is, although thou seest them not they are to be propitiated]. (44) Thou mayst call, O Zaratûsht! upon the self-sustained universe, [its self-sustainment is this, that through the energy which is within it nothing from without is wanted within it], and boundless time, (and) the upper-working air (*vâi*). (45) Thou mayst call, O Zaratûsht! upon the swift wind created by Aûharmazd, and also call Spendarmad, the graceful daughter of Aûharmazd.

14. (46) Thou mayst call, O Zaratûsht! upon the spirit (*fravashi*) of me who am Aûharmazd, (47) which is (of the creations) of Aûharmazd the greatest in body, the best in worth, the most excellent in appearance, the most formidable [strongest], the most sagacious [wisest], the best-shaped, [that is, the limbs most adapted one for the other], the highest in righteousness, (48) the soul of which is the beneficent text. (49) Thou shouldst thyself, O Zaratûsht! call these creatures of Aûharmazd, [that is, do not surrender (it) from (thy) hand].

15. (50) Zaratûsht considered[1] my words, [that is, he hearkened to them]; (*a*) some say that Zaratûsht considered my words, [that is, he believed about them that it would be necessary to keep (and) hear (them)]; (51) (and said) : I call upon the righteous Aûharmazd, the creator of creatures. (52) I call upon Mitrô of the wide cattle-pastures, the well-armed, glorious with missiles,[2] the most victorious of missiles, [that is, these are good (and) more (than) those of the angel Vâhrâm]. (53) I call upon Srosh the righteous, the handsome, when he holds a sword in (his) hand over the head of the demons, at that time I call him most.

16. (54) I call upon the beneficent text which is very glorious. (55) I call upon the self-sustained universe, boundless time, and the upper-working air. (56) I call upon the swift wind created by Aûharmazd; Spendarmad, the graceful daughter of Aûharmazd, I also call. (57) I call upon the good religion

---

[1] This sentence is corrected by comparing it with (114) further on.
[2] Reading *zâyâno*, " arms, missiles," but the word is ambiguous, and might be read *zahishno*, "emanation, radiation."

of the Mazdayasnians; the law against the demons,[1] the law of Zaratûsht, I also call.

17. (58) Zaratûsht inquired of Aûharmazd thus: Thou art a generous creator,[2] O Aûharmazd! [that is, the benefit from him is much]; (59) with what words do I reverence, with what words do I worship Thee? (and do) my disciples and these creatures of Aûharmazd?

18. (60) And Aûharmazd said to him thus: When thou comest up to a growing tree, O Spîtâmân Zaratûsht! (61) which is fine, well-grown, (and) strong, recite these words: (62) Salutation to the good tree created by Aûharmazd (and) righteous![3] (a) Righteousness is the best prosperity, [a store of these is good, duty and good works]; (b) virtuous is righteousness, virtuous is he who is a right-doer through perfect righteousness, [that is, he performs duty and good works].[4]

19. (63) Thou mayst carry off Barsom for that ceremony a span long, a barley-corn thick. (64) Thou shouldst not cut up the Barsom with over-attention,[5] [that is, thou shouldst leave (it) to][6] men become righteous,[7] and it is held by them in the left hand; (65) and Aûharmazd is prayed to by them, and the Ameshaspends are prayed to by them. (66) Homa, too, the golden-hued, the exalted, and they also who are excellent, Vohuman and good liberality created by Aûharmazd, the righteous (and) best, are prayed to likewise by them.

20. (67) Zaratûsht inquired of Aûharmazd thus: Thou art omniscient, O Aûharmazd! (68) Thou art sleepless, O Aûharmazd! and unintoxicated, thou who art Aûharmazd! (69) A

---

[1] The Vendidad.
[2] Or it may be translated as in p. 334, note 1.
[3] Dastur Hoshangji observes that when a Parsi priest goes nowadays up to a pomegranate tree to cut the urvarâm he does not use these words, but washes his hands and the knife with consecrated water, thrice reciting khshnaothra Ahurahê Mazdâo, ashem vohû, and cuts a twig from the pomegranate tree for the urvarâm, and a leaflet from the date tree for the aiwyâonhana, or girdle of the Barsom. The instructions in the text, however, refer to the cutting of the Barsom itself, which is now hardly ever done, as they generally use metal wires instead of twigs.
[4] This Pahlavi translation of the Ashem-vohû formula is omitted by Spiegel, but is given by the old MSS.
[5] The word avar-nikîrishnîh is not a correct equivalent of the Avesta pairi-keretem, but it is hazardous to alter it into arar-karînishnîh.
[6] Or "thou shouldst break (it) off for," if shikan-âe be read instead of shedkân-âe.
[7] That is, priests.

good-minded man is mingled in direct pollution with him (*val*), a good-minded man is mingled in indirect pollution with him (*val*) whose body is stricken by the demons and defiled, and the demons mingle him with it, [that is, they would make (him) completely defiled]; did the good-minded (one) become purified ?

21. (70) And Aûharmazd said to him thus: Seek for bull's urine, O Zaratûsht! of a young, entire bull, lawfully inaugurated.[1] (71) Thou mayst carry on the purification on the land created by Aûharmazd, [that is, they may perform (it) in a wild spot of *nava vîbâzva drâjô* ("nine fathoms length")]. (72) With a surrounding furrow he should score (it) around, the man who is purifying.

22. (73) One hundred praises of righteousness are to be recited (thus): Ashem vohû, (&c., and) (74) two hundred (Yathâ-ahû-vairyôs).[2] (75) With four times thorough washing he is washed over, (by) the man who is purifying, with bull's urine produced by bulls, twice with water which should be created by Aûharmazd,[3] which should be well-formed.

23. (76) Purified becomes the good-minded man, purified becomes the man who shall come with him.[4] (77) The clothing of the good-minded (one) is to be taken up by the left arm with the right, and by the right arm with the left, with the assistance of one another. (78) Then the good-minded (one) is to be called out[5] in the light produced by skill, that we may brighten his star given by destiny, (79) always till those nine nights shall elapse over the man.

24. (80) After the nine nights thou mayst carry forth consecrated water to the fire, thou mayst carry forth the hard firewood to the fire, thou mayst carry forth sweet-scented incense to the fire, (81) (and he) who is good-minded should fumigate his clothes.

---

[1] The bull whose urine is employed for such purposes has to be once properly consecrated by a certain ceremony, when he becomes *dâityô-keretô*, and can then supply lawful urine for the rest of his life.

[2] The words *yathâ ahû vairyô rad vâstârem*, which have been taken into the Avesta text (see p. 335), belong, no doubt, to the Pahlavi translation.

[3] Probably meaning pure water. In the old MSS. the conditional *dê* occurs twice, as here translated.

[4] Or "who shall come in contact with him."

[5] So all unaltered MSS., but Dastur Hoshangji suggests that *shart tânishn*, "is to be opened or exposed," should be read instead of *karîtânishn*

25. (82) Purified becomes the clothing of the good-minded (one), purified becomes the man who holds the clothing. (83) The clothing, &c. (as in (77) above). (84) The good-minded (one) exclaims thus: Salutation to Aûharmazd! salutation to the Ameshaspends! salutation to those other righteous ones! (*a*) Afarg[1] showed from this passage that he whose hands are not washed should not reverence the sun, and should not engage in silent prayer (*vâj*).

26. (85) Zaratûsht inquired of Aûharmazd thus: Thou art omniscient, O Aûharmazd! (86) Shall I raise the righteous man? shall I raise the righteous woman? shall I raise the wicked and the idolaters, the men who are polluters?[2] (87) The giving up[3] removes away the earth created by Aûharmazd; the giving up removes away the flowing water, the grown corn, and the other wealth. (88) And Aûharmazd said to him thus: Thou mayst raise (them), O righteous Zaratûsht!

27. (89) Creator of the material world, righteous one![4] Where are those events[5] in lodgment? where do those events proceed? [that is, where is the place of their coming and going?] wherewith are those events in connection? where do those events come back to the same place for a man whom they give up to his own soul in the material life of mankind?[6]

28. (90) And Aûharmazd said to him thus: After the passing away of men, after the proceeding forth of men, [that is, when their proceedings in the world are completed], after the tearing away of the life from the former body by the demons, the wicked ones astute in evil, [that is, of everyone they most tear away that from which unseparated (*î abarâ*) he does not die]; (91) on the complete up-lifting of the third night, when the dawn glows, the beaming, (92) on the mountain of the

---

[1] The name of one of the old commentators.

[2] The reading of the old MSS. is certainly *gushno-zahishnân*, a misinterpretation of the Av. *merczujîtim*.

[3] Taking *barâ yehabûntano* (which the old MSS. append to both clauses of the sentence) as the nominative. It might be translated "result," but the passage seems to refer to the resurrection, or to the soul's entrance into its separate spiritual life, as detailed in the following verses.

[4] This opening sentence is abbreviated in the old MSS.

[5] The traditional meaning of *dâsar* is "destiny."

[6] As the meaning is not very clear it is safest to give the literal translation.

glory of righteousness where it[1] arouses Mitrô the well-armed, (93) and the sun rises up there in (its) ascent.

29. (94) The demon Vîzarsh by name, O Spîtâmân Zaratûsht! carries off the soul bound, the wicked (and) the idolaters, the men who are polluters. (*a*) That is, with a halter (*band*) which falls upon the neck of every one when he dies; when righteous it falls off from his neck (*ash min chavarman*), when wicked they will drag him with that same halter to hell. (95) He comes to the time-worn path, whoever is wicked (and) whoever is righteous. [(*a*) Every one will come to that place to behold Aûharmazd (and) Ahriman; he who is righteous to offer prayer, (but) he who is wicked is unable to offer prayer and becomes repentant, and by his repentance they restore the dead again]. (96) (To) the Chinvad bridge created by Aûharmazd, where they clear away (*barâ zadênd*) the worldly portion of the consciousness (and) soul, (97) which was given to them in the material world.

30. (98) She who is graceful in appearance, well-formed, [that is, it is not necessary to do anything to her],[2] strong, [that is, powerful],[3] well-developed, [that is, she has grown in excellence], comes (99) with a dog, [that is, protection is with her], with discrimination, [that is, it is evident who is who and which is which], with replies,[4] [that is, with goodness and crime],[5] willing, [that is, as a man requires], (and) provided with skill. (100)[6] . . . She supports the soul of the righteous across Alborz. (101) They pass across by the Chinvad bridge whose two extremities (2-*sarîh*) are their own heavenly angels; (*a*) one stands at Chakâd-i Dâitih,[7] and one at Alborz.

---

[1] Probably the dawn.
[2] Literally: "it is not necessary to perform an operation upon her."
[3] Assuming that *kîk aîgh tuban*, the reading of the old MSS. in London, stands for *takîk aîgh tâbân*.
[4] The oldest reading is *pasukhohômand*, but Dastur Hoshangji suggests reading *pusân-hômand*, "having sons."
[5] Probably meaning that she has the replies both of the good and the bad. The oldest reading is *rasîh va bajak*, and *rasîh* is very like *rêhîh*;

Dastur Hoshangji suggests reading *vêsh bachak*, "many children."
[6] The old MSS. omit the Pahlavi translation of the first clause of this sentence in the Avesta: "She dismisses the sinful soul of the wicked into the glooms" (see p. 255). This is, no doubt, a blunder, as there is no reason to suppose that this clause is an Avesta quotation introduced by the Pahlavi translator.
[7] The Bundahish (p. 22, W.) states that the mountain "Chakâd-i Dâitih" is that of the middle of the world,

31. (102) Vohuman shall rise up from a throne made of gold, (a) where he transacts the affairs of the dominion of the eternal ones.[1] (103) Vohuman exclaims thus: How hast thou come up here? O righteous one! tasting immortality (*anôshvashtamân*), (104) from that perishable world which is afflicted, unto this imperishable world which is unafflicted?

32. (105) Contented the soul of the righteous goes on from Vohuman (106) up to Aûharmazd and up to the Ameshaspends and up to the throne made of gold, (107) up to Garôdmân, the abode of Aûharmazd, the abode of the Ameshaspends, the abode of those others who are also alike (*hamîch*) righteous ones.

33. (108) Owing to the purified state of that righteous (one), [owing to the protection[2] of purity in the soul], after passing away, the wicked demons, astute in evil, are frightened away by its scent, (109) as a sheep molested by wolves when it is frightened off by the scent of a wolf.

34. (110) The righteous men come together[3] every one; (a) some say Hushêdar, Hushêdar-mâh, and Sôshyâns; (111) and Nêryôsang brings them together. (112) The messenger[4] of Aûharmazd call Nêryôsang; (113) thou shouldst thyself, O Zaratûsht! call upon these creatures of Aûharmazd, [that is, do not surrender (it) from (thy) hand].[5]

35. (114) Zaratûsht considered my words, &c. (as in (50) above); (115) (and said): I call upon Aûharmazd the righteous, the wise.[6] (116) I call upon the earth created by Aûharmazd, the water created by Aûharmazd, and the rightful vegetation. (117) I call upon the sea which is made wide.[7] (118) I call upon the sky, the handsome-formed, [that is, it is formed well-vaulted].[8] (119) I call upon the endless light, the self-sustained,

---

the height of a hundred men, on which the Chinvad bridge stands, and they take account of the soul at that place."

[1] Reading *arîdamânkarâno*, "those acting without time," but this is liable to the objection that *avî* ought to be otherwise written.

[2] The word *pâinakîh* seems to have been written by mistake in the old MS. in London, and to have been corrected by a marginal gloss into *pâkîh*; later copyists give both words in the text, as here translated.

[3] The old MSS. are here, for once, more corrupt than the modern ones.

[4] Traditionally, "the friend."

[5] This is a repetition of (49), and the subject now returns to the point it left when interrupted by the inquiries in (58).

[6] This is a misinterpretation of the Avesta, see p. 256.

[7] A free translation of Vourukasha, which is always Farâkhû-kard in Pahlavi.

[8] So in the old MSS., but "vaulted together" in later ones.

[that is, its self-sustainment is this, that they[1] make every one its own for itself].

36. (120) I call upon the better world of the righteous, of all-glorious light. (121) I call upon Garôdmân, the abode of Aûharmazd, and the abode of the Ameshaspends, and the abode of those other righteous ones. (122) I call upon the constantly advantageous place,[2] the self-sustained, [its constant advantageousness is this, that when it once became (so) all of it became thereby ever-advantageous]; the Chinvad bridge, created by Aûharmazd, I also call.

37. (123) I call upon good-fortune the wishful-eyed, the favouring, the spirit of favour (hû-chashmîh). (124) I call upon the valiant guardian-angels of the righteous, who benefit all creatures. (125) I call upon the victorious angel Verehrân (Behrâm), created by Aûharmazd, who bears the standard of the glory created by Aûharmazd. (126) I call upon the star Tishtar, the brilliant, the glorious; at the time when (it is) in the form of a bull with golden horns I call it most.

38. (127) I call upon the propitious Gâthas, ruling the chiefs (of the creation, and) righteous; [their rulership of the chiefs is this, that it is proper to pray to any of the others through them]. (128) I call upon the Ahunavaiti Gâtha; I call upon the Ushtavaiti Gâtha; I call upon the Spentâ-mainyû Gâtha; I call upon the Vohu-khshathra Gâtha; I call upon the Vahishtôishti Gâtha.

39. (129) I call upon the region (kêshvar) of Arezahi and of Savahi; I call upon the region of Fradadafshu (and of) Vîdadafshu; I call upon the region of Vouru-bareshti and of Vouru-jareshti; I call upon the region of Qaniratha the splendid; (a) this they assert as they are stationed (âhist) in this (one). (130) I call upon Hêt-bômand[3] the illustrious, the glorious. (131) I call upon the good Ashishang.[4] I call upon the most rightful (rajistak), the learned, the good. (132) I call upon the

---

[1] The fixed stars, which produce their own light.
[2] This Hamîshak-sûḍak gâs appears to be the place of the Hamîstakân of the later books, the intermediate place, between heaven and hell, reserved for those souls whose good works exactly counterbalance their sins, and where they remain in a stationary state till the final resurrection.
[3] See Vend. i. (50), p. 361.
[4] See p. 215.

glory of the Iranian countries. I call upon the glory of Jam shêd the rich in flocks.

40. (133) When Srosh is satisfied with the three nights'[1] worship, and (has) recognised, [that is, completed (its) consideration], and accepted (it), Srosh the righteous! the handsome, triumphant Srosh, the righteous! (134) consecrated water is to be carried forth to the fire; thou shouldst carry forth hard firewood to the fire, (and) thou shouldst carry forth sweet-scented incense to the fire. (135) The fire Vâzisht is to be propitiated, which smites the demon Spenjagar. (136) Cooked food is to be carried forth, full of dried sugar-plums.[2]

41. (137) Thou shouldst propitiate Srosh the righteous; (138) Srosh the righteous who destroys the demons, who are stupid, drunk, and causelessly drunk, [that is, drunk without wine]. (139) He hurls them down to the Drûj of Askân,[3] the wicked (and) the idolaters, the men who are polluters, back to Vîzarsh the demon.[4]

. . . . . .

44. (140) (The evil spirit exclaimed) thus: Why do we assemble in an assembly, O wicked demons astute in evil! on the summit of Arezûr?[5] [that is, when we go back what report (srôbâk) do we carry back?]

45. (141) They rushed and they shouted the cries of demons, they became worse about the matter, the demons, the wicked ones astute in evil.[6] . . . (142) (For) this we assemble in an assembly on the summit of Arezûr.

---

[1] Meaning the three nights after a death, during which ceremonies in honour of Srosh are to be performed. After the third day and night ceremonies commence in honour of the Ardâî Fravard or righteous guardian angels. The word meaning "the three nights" is traditionally pronounced sedôsh or sadis (see Mainyô-i-khard xxi. 10; lxiii. 7), and is sometimes confounded with Srosh; but it seems to be nothing but satâîh, "a triplet," (compare Pers. satâ).

[2] The oldest reading looks like barâ khashâṭ shakarpâk, but should probably be read barâ khushkîḍ shakar-rêjâk.

[3] The oldest reading is drûj-i as-kâno, but the meaning is uncertain. It seems to be merely a transcript of the Avesta drujaskanãm.

[4] The word duĉrô (which although in Avesta letters seems to belong to the Pahlavi text) is omitted by Spiegel. A long passage (see pp. 336, 337) is here omitted in the old MSS. with the Pahlavi translation. This omission has evidently been caused by the loss of a folio in some original MS., whence they have all descended.

[5] See p. 337, note 9.

[6] Two clauses of this sentence (see p. 337) are omitted in the old Pahlavi translation.

46. (143) Because the righteous Zaratûsht is born in the dwelling of Pôrûshasp. (144) Where (can) we procure his death? for he is the smiter of the demons, and he is the adversary of the demons. (145) He restrains the destroyer from destroying, [that is, he takes away his oppressiveness], he puts down idolatry, [that is, he makes (it) powerless]. (146) He proclaims avoidance of the corruption (*nasûsh*) produced by the demons; the falsehoods of *Mîtôkht* (the liar) he also makes powerless.

47. (147) The demons shouted, the demons fled, the wicked ones astute in evil, to the bottom of the world of darkness which is the grievous[1] hell, and back to constant smoke.

9.—*Pahlavi Vendidad XX*.

1. (1) Zaratûsht inquired of Aûharmazd, &c. (as in Vend. xviii. (21), p. 367, to) righteous one! Who was the first of the men who are careful ones,[2] [who know well how to take care of the body, such as Spendyâd ;[3] some say that a sword[4] made no effect upon (him)], (2) (who are) accomplished ones, [sages, such as Kâî-Us], (3) (who are) willing ones, [such as Jamshêd], (4) (who are) fortunate ones, [and powerful ones, such as Pâtsrôb],[5] (5) (who are) brilliant ones, [and skilful ones, such as Zaratûsht], (6) (who are) valiant ones, [such as Keresâspa], (7) (who are) those of the early law (*pêshdâdân*), [such as Hôshâng; this early law was this, that he first set going the law of sovereignty], (8) (and) by whom disease was kept[6] to disease, and death was kept to death by him, [that is, they could not escape from his control (*band*)]; (9) he kept (back) the drawn dagger,[7] [that is, it was stopped by him on the way], (10) and the scorching of fire was kept by him away from the bodies of men?

[1] Reading *atrang;* compare Pers. *ârang*. The Dasturs prefer reading *atrôg*, which they translate "stinking."

[2] Said to mean those rendered secure or invulnerable by means of spells.

[3] The Pahlavi form of Isfendyâr, a son of Vishtâsp, who conquered Arjâsp.

[4] Or a battle-axe, according as we compare *tish* with Pers. *tish*, or *tishah*.

[5] Traditionally identified with Kaî-Khûsrô, but this seems only a guess. It is more probable that Pât-khûsrô is meant, who is said to have been a brother of Vishtâsp in the Pahlavi Shâhnâmah.

[6] Reading *dâsht* in all the phrases (as suggested by Dastur Hoshangji) instead of the *ash dâd* of the MSS. ; the Pahlavi letters being the same in both cases.

[7] This is merely a guess.

2. (11) And Aûharmazd said to him thus: Srît[1] was the first, O Spîtâmân Zaratûsht! of the men who are careful ones, &c. (as in (1–10) above). (*a*) That is, Srît of the Sâmâns, not Srît of the Sêrjâns,[2] (at) the place where he had come he was able to act. (*b*) Some say that he was Yim, and his Srîtship was this, that he was the third ruler.[3]

3. (12) He begged (and) obtained a weapon (*vîshchîhar*) from Shahrivar, [(*a*) some say that it was obtained through Shahrivar, so that its top (and) bottom might be bound with gold],[4] (13) for withstanding disease, for withstanding death, for withstanding pain, for withstanding fever, (14)[5] . . . for withstanding *aghish*[6] the putrid, the disfigurer, the malignant eye which the evil spirit formed in the bodies of men; [every one is good as to his own (and) evil as to others].

4. (15) Then I who am Aûharmazd brought forth healing plants; (16) many and many hundreds, and many and many thousands, and many and many myriads; (17) and therewith one Gôkerenô, the Homa which is white.[7]

5. (18) The inviter to work of every kind, the commander (and) Dastur of every kind, the possessor of every kind of blessing, [that is, it provides healthiness of life], for the bodies of men.[8]

. . . . . .

7. (19) Disease! I say unto thee: Flee away! Pain! I say

---

[1] The Avesta Thrita, see pp. 178, 277.

[2] So spelt in the old MS. in London; later MSS. alter it into Sêrzân. The nearest Avesta equivalent appears to be the *sarejâ* of Yas. xxix. 3; but perhaps the allusion is to *Thritô aêvô-saredhô* in Yasht xiii. 125, as *Sêrjân* can also be read *êsarjân*, and the Pahlavi *ch* = *j* is a letter of practically the same form as the Av. *dh*.

[3] This is an attempt to connect the name Thrita with Av. *thritya*, "third," As Hôshâng has already been mentioned as the first sovereign (see (7) above) Yima would be, of course, the third.

[4] Because Shahrivar is the archangel who has special charge of all metals.

[5] The names of eight diseases are here left untranslated by the Pahlavi version.

[6] The name of this disease or evil is written, in Avesta characters, *aghâish* here and in (24), and *âghish* in (20), in the old MS. in London.

[7] This is the tree of life which is said to grow in the sea Vouru-kasha, where it is carefully preserved from the evil spirit, in order that it may furnish immortality at the end of the world. See Bundahish (p. 42, W.).

[8] Verse 6, which is a repetition of (13) and (14), is not translated in the Pahlavi version.

unto thee : Flee away ! and Fever ! I say unto thee : Flee away !
(20)[1] . . . *Aghish!* I say unto thee : Flee away !

8. (21) What is vanquished by the vigour of that Homa is the Drûj, and the vigour of that Drûj is vanquished (by) its resources. (22) What is the strength of its dominion is I who am Aûharmazd.[2]

9. (23)[3] . . . I counteract disease, I counteract death, I counteract pain, I counteract fever, (24)[4] . . . I counteract *aghish* the putrid, the disfigurer, the malignant eye, which the evil spirit formed in the bodies of men, [every one is good as to his own (and) evil as to others].

10. (25) I counteract every disease and death, every sorcerer and witch, and every wicked courtezan.

11. (26) The longing for Aîrmân[5] is for me the arrival of joy, [that is, it is necessary for thee to come with joy], (and) they compel (him) to act for the men and women of Zaratûsht. (27) Vohuman is joyful, [that is, it is necessary for thee also to come, that they may compel thee to act with joy]. He who is desirous of religion becomes worthy, with the reward here (in this world) and that also there (in the other world). (28) The reverent supplication for righteousness is Ashavahisht, [that is, my reverence is through him]; may he become the dignity of Aûharmazd, [the mobadship of the mobads].

12. (29) The longing for Aîrmân destroys every disease and death, every sorcerer and witch, and every wicked courtezan.

III.—Notes Descriptive of some Parsi Ceremonies.

These notes were written by the author in German, merely as memoranda of what he noticed during the performance of the ceremonies, and of such information as the priests communicated. It is to be regretted that the author confined his notes almost entirely to the ceremonies connected with the celebration

---

[1] The exorcism of the eight other diseases is here left untranslated by the Pahlavi version, as in (14).

[2] The Avesta of the latter part of this verse is a paraphrase of Yas. xxxi. 4*c*.

[3] The names of four other diseases or evils are here left untranslated by the Pahlavi version. The concluding verses (9–12, W.) of this fargard occur again as the conclusion of each of the fargards xxi. and xxii.

[4] The names of the eight diseases, omitted in (14) and (20) are here again left untranslated by the Pahlavi version.

[5] The angel Airyaman, see p. 273.

of the Yasna or Ijashne; but he probably relied upon Anquetil's description of the commoner ceremonies being a sufficient memorandum, as he had found his statements quite correct on such matters (see p. 25).

The editor's revision of these notes has been confined to such further explanation as seemed necessary for making the rough memoranda intelligible to the reader. If any Parsi priest should notice errors in these notes, he will confer a favour by pointing them out in a letter to the editor through the publishers.

1.—*The Ceremony preparatory to Ijashne.*

This preparatory ceremony is called *pargannah* or *paragnah*, and commences with the arrangement of the various ceremonial vessels and materials in the *arvîs-gâh* or ceremonial area. This arrangement is shown upon p. 395.

The ceremonial vessels and apparatus are made of metal, generally brass or copper, but more valuable metals can be used. They consist of several round-bottomed cups (about the size of tea-cups) and saucer-like dishes, besides other vessels of a more special character.

The fire burns on a bed of ashes in a vase-like vessel placed on a stone near the southern end of the Arvîs-gâh where the Rathwi (Râspî) or assistant priest is stationed, facing the Zota or chief officiating priest, who sits cross-legged on a low stone platform near the northern end of the Arvîs-gâh, but facing the fire. Both priests wear close-fitting trousers instead of the usual loose pyjamas, so as to avoid touching any of the apparatus with their clothes; they also wear the *penôm* or mouth-veil (see p. 243, note 1).

Some spare *aêsma* or firewood (in the form of chips of sandalwood) and *bôî* or incense (benzoin) are laid alongside the fire to the Râspî's left; and small fire tongs and an incense ladle are similarly laid to his right.

The Zota has a supply of water in a large metal water-vessel to his right, which also contains the pestle and strainer for the Homa; and before him the remaining apparatus is arranged on a low stone platform called the *takht-i âlât*. Besides the cups and saucers mentioned above, the following apparatus (p. 395) stands on this platform.

ARRANGEMENT OF THE ARVIS-GAH.

	SOUTH.		
	Ráspí's station.		
Tongs,	Incense ladle.	Fire in a vase on a stone.	Spare firewood and incense.

EAST.   WEST.

Spare Homa-juice in cup with saucer cover.	Darûn and butter saucer.	Barsom knife.	Homa mortar.	
			Homa and pomegranate twig saucer.	
Homa juice cup.				
			Varas cup with cover.	Large water vessel containing strainer and pestle.
Barsom laid on its stands.	Milk saucer		Zor cup. Zor cup.	

Zota's seat.

NORTH.

The *barsom-dân* or stand for the Barsom, consisting of two separate stands with upright stems and crescent-shaped tops, hence called *mâh-rû*, "moon-faced." The Barsom, when arranged, is laid resting on the two crescents. The *kârd-i barsom-chîn*, or knife for cutting the Barsom, &c., is also laid on the *takht*.

The *hâvanîm* or Homa mortar is generally shaped like a wine-glass, with foot and stem, but much larger; and the pestle or *dastah*, chisel-shaped at one end, is kept till wanted on one side in the large water-vessel. The Homa strainer or *tashta bâ-sûrâkh* is one of the saucers with nine small holes, arranged diamond-fashion about half an inch apart, in its bottom; this also lies on one side in the water-vessel.

The *darûn* (*draona*) or ceremonial wafer-bread is a small, tough, flexible pancake (about the size of the palm of the hand), made of wheaten flour and water, with a little melted butter (*ghî*), and fried. A *frasast* is a similar pancake marked on one side, before frying, with nine superficial cuts (in three rows of three each) made with the finger-nail while repeating the words *humat hûkht huvarsht* thrice, one word to each of the nine cuts. Any Darûn or Frasast that is torn must not be used in any ceremony. A small piece of butter, called *gâush-hudhâo*, generally accompanies the Darûn. Other ceremonial apparatus is sufficiently explained in the following notes.

The *aiwyâonhanem* is the girdle or tie with which the Barsom is to be tied together. It is prepared from a leaflet of the date-palm, which is cut from the tree by the priest after he has poured consecrated water over his hand, the knife, and the leaflet.[1] When brought to the Arvîs-gâh in the water-goblet the leaflet is split longitudinally into thread-like ribbons. Six of these leafy threads are then laid together, three one way and three the other,[2] and are all tied together in a knot at one end. One triplet is then twisted tightly together with a right-handed twist, and the other triplet with a left-handed twist, so that when laid together the two triplets twist together into a single string, by partially untwisting, and they are then secured together by a

---

[1] A twig is cut in the same manner from a pomegranate bush to form the *urvarâm*. And the Barsom twigs were also similarly cut in former times, before metal wires were used.

[2] That is, the ends belonging to the base of the leaflet are at one end of one triplet, and at the other end of the other triplet.

knot at the other end. The Aiwyâoŋhanem is now ready for use, and is laid upon the Barsom-dân.

The *varasa* consists of three, five, or seven hairs from the tail of a white bull, which are tied to a gold[1] ring, as large as a thumb-ring. The ring has a gap in its circumference, as the metal wire of which it is formed does not quite meet. This Varasa, when once prepared, can be used as long as the bull lives, whose hair has been taken. But as often as it is used it must be consecrated by the recital of the 1001 names of God, that is, by ten repetitions of the 101 names, which are all that are now known.

The *zaothra* or Zor is water consecrated in the following manner :—The priest takes two metal cups in his hands, and recites *ashem-vohu* thrice, *fravarânê* (Yas. iii. 24, to) *frasastayaêcha*, *aiwyô vaŋuhibyô* (as in Frag. vii. 1, p. 333, W. to) *frasastayaêcha*, and *yathâ ahû vairyô* (Yas. iii. 25, omitting W.'s second line). Then reciting the words *frâ tê staomaidê* he fills both cups with water, and continues reciting *yathâ ahû vairyô* twice, *yasnemcha vahmemcha aojascha zavarecha âfrînâmi* (Yasht i. 23), and *aiwyô vaŋuhibyô* (as before, to) *tava ahurânê ahurahê*. These last three words must be recited twice, once aloud and once muttered as a *bâj*. The water is now Zor, and the cups are placed on the *takht*, one over the other, with a saucer between them.

The Barsom consists of a number of slender rods or *tâi*, formerly twigs of some particular trees, but now thin metal wires are generally used. The number of these *tâi* depends upon the nature of the ceremony to be celebrated. For Ijashne (*yazishn*) alone 21 *tâi* are required, for Ijashne with Vendidad and Visparad 33 *tâi*, for Yasht-i Rapithwin 13 *tâi*, for Darûn Bâj five *tâi*, or seven when a priest becomes a *herbad*.[2] Besides these *tâi*, which form the actual Barsom, two other *tâi* are required, one to lie across the saucer which contains the milk or *gâush jîrya*, and the other to lie on the projecting feet of the

---

[1] Or silver, copper, or brass.

[2] According to other information the Darûn Bâj requires seven *tâi* of double thickness, or nine if performed in the house of a king or chief high-priest. In the Nirangistân it is stated that the Barsom twigs may be cut from any tree whose trunk is sound, and that they should be from one to three spans in length and a barley-corn in thickness, and their number either 3, 5, 7, 9, 12, 15, 21, 33, 69, or 551, according to the circumstance of the ceremony.

two *mâh-rû* which form the Barsom-dân; the first of these *tâi* is called the *jîvâm*, the other the *frâgâm*. At first the Frâgâm is laid at one end of the bundle of *tâi* forming the Barsom, so that it projects beyond the rest, as the priest takes the bundle in his left hand and the Jîvâm in his right; the Aiwyâonhem being laid upon the two *mâh-rû*. The priest then recites *ashem vohu* thrice, *fravarânê* (Yas. iii. 24, to) *frasastayaêcha, khshathrahê,* &c. (Sîroz. i. 4),[1] *khshnaothra yasnâicha vahmâicha khshnao-thrâicha frasastayaêcha, y. a. v.*[2] (Yas. iii. 25, omitting W.'s second line, to) *mraotû, ashem a. v.,*[3] *y. a. v.* twice, *yasnemcha* (Yt. i. 23, to) *âfrînâmi, khshathrahê,* &c. (Sîroz. i. 4), *a. v.* thrice, and *fravarânê* (Yas. iii. 24, to) *frasastayaêcha*. Then while reciting the words *Ahurahê mazdâo raêvatô qarenanhutô* the priest proceeds to tie the Barsom together with the Aiwyâon-hanem in the following manner:—The Jîvâm being held in his right hand, and the Frâgâm projecting from the Barsom held in his left hand, he prepares to pass the Aiwyâonhanem thrice round the middle of the Barsom and to tie it with knots, in the same way as the *kustî* or sacred thread-girdle is secured round the waist of a Parsi man or woman.[4] But, first, the above formulas, from *khshnaothra* to *mraotû*, must be again recited, and then *ashem a. v.* thrice.[5] Each time the words *ashem ashem vohu* are uttered the Barsom must be dipped in water and again taken out. This water, which is not Zor, and will be used in the Homa ceremony, is called *apem haomyâm*. The Barsom is now tied together with two double knots in the Aiwyâonhem, one above and the other below, while reciting *y. a. v.* twice; and the two

---

[1] Formerly, before wires were used, only the words *Ahurahê mazdâo raêvatô qarenanhutô* were used.

[2] Henceforth *yathâ ahû vairyô* will be contracted into *y. a. v.*, and *ashem vohu* into *a. v.* In all cases the whole formula is to be understood, when it is not otherwise stated.

[3] Wherever *ashem a. v.* is used it indicates that the first word (*ashem*) of the formula is spoken twice.

[4] This is done as follows:—The middle of the string, being taken in the hands, is applied to the waist (outside the *sadarah* or muslin shirt) in front, and the ends passed round the waist by the hands meeting behind, changing ends there, and bringing them round again to the front, so that the string has then twice encircled the waist. The long hanging ends are then tied loosely together in front, first with a right-handed knot and then with a left-handed knot; and the long loose ends are finally passed backwards, the third time round the waist, and tied again behind with a similar double knot.

[5] Formerly, four times.

SOME PARSI CEREMONIES.

projecting ends are cut to an equal length with the knife, each time reciting *y. a. v.*, and a single knot is tied in each end; after these two *y. a. v.* must follow *yasnemcha*, &c. (as before). The priest then says *Ahurahê mazdâo raêvato* aloud, and lays the properly-arranged Barsom on the two Mâh-rû while muttering the same words as a Bâj. After the Barsom is thus laid on the Barsom-dân he takes out the Frâgâm, and lays it upon the projecting feet of the two Mâh-rû.

The Homa twigs must next be purified. These twigs are brought from Iran by traders, and are, therefore, considered impure until they have been purified, laid aside for a year, and again purified. The purification is accomplished by water and formulas. The priest takes the Homa twig (one is sufficient) in his right hand, holding a copper goblet of water in his left, from which he pours water, at intervals, over the twig as he thrice recites *khshnaothra Ahurahê mazdâo*, &c., and *a. v.* He then takes the Jîvâm in his left hand and recites *a. v.* thrice, *fravarânê* (Yas. iii. 24, to) *frasastayaêcha*, *haomahê ashavazanhô* (Yas. x. 1, but only these two words), *khshnaothra*, &c. (as in p. 398, lines 8-10 above, to) *mraotâ*, and *ashem a. v.* thrice, each time dipping the Jîvâm and Homa, which he holds one in each hand, into the water. Then follow *y. a. v.* twice, *yasnemcha* (Yt. i. 23, to) *âfrînâmi*, and *haomahê ashavazanhô*; these last two words must be first spoken aloud, and then repeated in a low voice as a Bâj. The Homa twig is now laid in its place, in a metal saucer on the *takht*.

The priest takes three small pieces of the Homa and one of the Urvarâm (the *hadhânaêpatâm* or pomegranate twig), and lays them on the Hâvanîm or Homa mortar which is placed, upside down, upon the *takht*. When the Varasa is to be laid in its place, in a cup on the *takht*, after being consecrated, it must be held below between the fingers.

The Homa juice is now to be prepared. The priest takes the Varasa and Jîvâm[1] in his hands, and recites *a. v.* thrice, *fravarânê* (to) *frasastayaêcha*, and *Zarathushtrahê Spitâmahê* (to) *mraotâ*. He then dips the Varasa into a cup full of water, utters the word *ashem* twice (once aloud and once in a low voice as a Bâj), and then lays the Varasa in its proper place.

[1] Some call this the Zor *tât*.

The priest then recites Yas. xxiv. 1-9 as far as the words *manaṇhô shkyañti*, but he must omit the clause containing the words *gãm jîvyãm* (in vers. 1 and 6), because the milk is not yet in its place on the *takht*. He must then recite *yâoscha uiti* (Yas. iv. 4-8, to) *râmanô qâstrahê*, and next invoke the angels of the day and the month in which the ceremony is being celebrated; for instance, if the ceremony be performed on the day of Spendarmad in the month of Ardibahisht, he must recite *speñtayâo vaṇhuyâo ârmatôish y. v. kh. f. aaḍ dîsh âvaêdhayamahi*, and then *ashahê vahishtahê sraêshtahê y. v. kh. f. aaḍ dîsh âvaêdhayamahi*. Then follow *tava âthrô* (Yas. iv. 17-22, to) *aaḍ dîsh âvaêdhayamahi*, *Zarathushtrahê* (Yas. iv. 23, to) *aaḍ d. â., ashaonãm* (Yas. iv. 24, to) *aaḍ d. â., vîspaêibyô vaṇhudhâbyô* (Yas. iv. 25, to) *vahishtâḍ*, and Yas. xxv. 1-3 (omitting the clause containing the words *gãm jîvyãm* in ver. 1, as before). While reciting the words *ameshâ speñtâ* (Yas. xxv. 1), the priest knocks the Hâvanîm thrice upon the *takht;* at the words *imem haomem ashaya uzdâtem yazamaidê* he puts the small pieces of the Homa twig into the Hâvanîm, and at the words *imãmchâ urvarãm hadhânaêpatãm* he puts in the small piece of the Urvarãm (the *dirakht-i anâr* or pomegranate twig). He pours a little of the consecrated water from the upper Zor cup into the Hâvanîm while uttering the words *aiwyô vaṇuhibyô imâo zaothrâo* (&c., to) *yaz.;* and also more water (*apem haomyãm*) from the large vessel to his right (which contains the pestle and strainer) while uttering the words *aiwyô vaṇuhibyô apemcha haomyãm yaz*. After Yas. xxv. 3, there follows *Zarathushtrahê* (Yas. xxvi. 5, to) *yaz.*, on the recitation of which the priest bows to the Varasa. He then takes the strainer out of the water in the large vessel to his right, and places it upon a cup (the Homa-juice cup) before him while reciting *iristanãm urvãnô* (Yas. xxvi. 11, to) *fravashayô*, followed by *yêñhê hâtãm* (&c., to) *tâoschâ yaz.*[1] Then, while reciting *athâ ratush ashâḍchîḍ hachâ frâ ashava vîdhvâo mraotû*, he takes the pestle out of the water, holding it so as to touch, with the lower part of its side, the north-eastern part of the rim of the large water-vessel, and

---

[1] When Nirang-dîn (*çômêz*) or Varasa is to be prepared (each of which requires a formal Ijashne with Homa), a small piece of the sandal-wood and incense lying near the fire is now thrown into it. This is not done, however, in the ordinary Ijashne.

SOME PARSI CEREMONIES. 401

passes it all round in contact with the rim (N. W. S. E.) to the same point again. With the pestle in his hand he recites *aêtad* (Yas. xxvii. 1, to) *dazdyâi ahûmcha* (he knocks the lower end of the pestle on the *takht*) *ratûmcha* (he knocks its upper end on the *takht*) *yim Ahurem mazdām* (he bows to the fire). Continuing the recitation of Yas. xxvii. 1, the Devas are beaten by striking sonorous blows with the pestle on the outside of the mortar in the following manner:—With a blow on the eastern side he recites *snathdi Aṇrahê mainyēush drvatô*, with a blow on the southern side he recites *snathdi Aêshmahê khrvîdraosh*, with a blow on the western side he recites *snathdi Māzainyanām daêvanām*, with a blow on the northern side he recites *snathdi vîspanām daêvanām*, with three more blows on the northern side he recites *daêvanām varenyanāmcha drvatām*. The priest then recites in a low voice, as a Bâj, the Pâzand formula *shikasta Ganā-mainyô*, &c.,[1] and *fradathâi ahurahê* (Yas. xxvii. 2, to) *ashaonām* aloud, and then begins to pound the Homa and Urvarām in the mortar while reciting *y. a. v.* four times; during the first three he pounds with the pestle on the bottom of the mortar, but during the fourth he strikes it against the sides, so as to produce a ringing sound. He continues the same practice during four recitations of *mazdā aḍ môi* (Yas. xxxiv. 15, to) *ahûm*, and four recitations of *â Airyēmâ ishyô* (Yas. liv. 1, to) *mazdāo*, pounding on the bottom during the first three, and against the sides, with a ringing sound, during the fourth. He next takes the upper Zor cup in his hand, recites *a. v.* thrice, and pours a little Zor into the mortar each time he utters the word *ashem*. Then, he recites *haoma pairi-hareshyañtê* (Yas. xxvii. 6, 7, to) *vachām* in eleven portions; during the recital of each portion he passes the pestle once round (N. W. S. E.) in contact with the inside of the mortar rim. He then takes the fragments of Homa and Urvarām out of the mortar, and, holding them between his fingers and thumb, he touches with them the Barsom at the word *athâ* (Yas. xxvii. 7), the saucer for the milk at the words *zî nē*, the Homa cup at the word *humâyô*, the Arvîs-gâh at the word *tara*, and throws them back into the mortar at the word *aṇhen*. He next takes the upper Zor cup in

---

[1] Some Mobads repeat the formulas for beating Angrô-mainyush and the Devas without striking blows upon the mortar; but they strike them while reciting the formula *fradathâi*, &c. (Yas. xxvii. 2).

his left hand, and continues to pound the Homa with his right hand, while reciting four *y. a. v.* in the following manner:—During the first *y. a. v.* at the word *athâ* he pours a little Zor into the mortar with his left hand, and continues to pound with his right; at the word *yim* he passes the pestle once round (as before) in contact with the inside of the mortar rim; and at the last word, *vâstârem*, he pours the whole contents of the mortar (Homa, Urvarâm, and water) into the strainer, whence all the liquid portion of the contents runs through into the Homa-juice cup below it (see p. 400, line 30). The solid portion remaining in the strainer is then thrown back into the mortar, and the pounding is resumed while the second *y. a. v.* is recited to the word *ashâd*, when more Zor is poured into the mortar and the after proceedings are similar to those connected with the first *y. a. v.* A similar routine is adopted in connection with the third and fourth *y. a. v.*, the Zor being poured into the mortar at the word *hachâ* in the third, and at the word *dazdâ* in the fourth. By means of these four successive dilutions, poundings, and strainings, all the properties of the Homa juice are supposed to be extracted. The solid remains of the twigs, out of which the liquid has been well squeezed by the fingers in the strainer, are laid aside to dry thoroughly,[1] and the pestle is washed and returned to its place.

The priest then takes the strainer off the Homa-juice cup while reciting *yê sevishtô* (Yas. xxxiii. 11, to) *paitî* thrice, and at the final repetition the last words, *âdâi kahyâichîd paitî*, must be recited thrice. The strainer is now washed and laid upon the mortar; the Varasa is put into the strainer so that the knots in the hairs are upwards, and the priest recites *us môi uzâreshvâ* (Yas. xxxiii. 12–14, to) *khshathremchâ*, followed by *a. v.* twice, once aloud and once in a low voice as a Bâj. He then pours all the Zor which remains in the upper Zor cup into the strainer, through which it runs into the mortar; and the upper Zor cup is then placed near the lower one, instead of over it as heretofore. He next takes the strainer, containing the Varasa, in his right hand, and the Homa-juice cup in his left, and proceeds to recite *humata hûkhta hvarshta* in a low voice, as a Bâj. When

---

[1] When thoroughly dry, they are put into the fire at the time of Atash Nyâyish.

he mutters the word *humata* he pours a few drops of the Homa juice through the strainer on to the Arvîs-gâh; when he mutters the word *hûkhta* he pours a few drops, in a similar manner, into the upper Zor cup, which has just been emptied; when he mutters the word *hvarshta* he pours a few drops, in a similar manner, into the mortar; and he does this thrice. The Homa-juice cup is now put in its proper place, the strainer containing the Varasa is placed upon it, all the liquid in the mortar is poured into the strainer, through which it flows into the Homa-juice cup, and the mortar is put into its proper place. The *gâush-jîvya* or milk-saucer is also put into its proper place near the two Mâh-rû. The priest then takes the Varasa in his left hand and recites *y. a. v.* twice, *yasnemcha* (Yt. i. 23, to) *âjrî-nâmi*, and *Zarathushtrahê Spitâmahê ashaonô fravashêê* twice, once aloud and once in a low voice. He then dips the Varasa into the Zor, and puts it into its proper place. The strainer is also put back into the large water-vessel, and the Jîvâm is laid upon the milk saucer.[1] The priest must now leave the *Arvîs-gâh* and go outside, reciting *a. v.* once, *ahmâi raêshcha* (Yt. i. 33), *hazanrem, jasa mê*, and *kerfe mozda* (Pâz.). He must then perform the Kustî ceremony, and the preparatory ceremonial is complete.

2.—*The Ijashne Ceremony.*

After the Paragnah is completed, the Zota and Râspî go to the *takht* on which all the necessary things (Homa juice, &c.) have been placed, and each of them repeats *a. v.* once; that is, they take the Bâj inwardly in this manner. They then recite *y. a. v.* several times, the number depending upon the nature of the Ijashne. If it be celebrated for Rapithwin, twelve are necessary; if for Hormazd, ten; if for the Frohars, eight; if for Srosh, five; and if for all the Yazads, seven.

The Zota then takes the consecrated water in his hand, and goes to the stone on which the fire-vase stands, where he recites *nemase tê âtarsh* (Atash Nyâyish 4, to) *yazata, a. v.*, and washes the stone, walking round it; he then washes his hands (by pouring the water over them) and returns to his place.

He then mutters *humata hûkhta hvarshta* in a low voice, as a Bâj, and announces for whom the Ijashne is being celebrated by

---

[1] If any incense happens to be at hand, it may now be thrown into the fire.

reciting *iñ khshnûman* (of so-and-so) *bē rasâd* (&c., to) *patit hom*. Then follow *frastuyê* (Yas. xi. 17, 18), *a. v.* thrice, and *fravarânê*, &c.; then the *khshnûman* (according to the Sîrozah) of each of the angels in whose honour the Ijashne is being celebrated; then *y. a. v.* (&c., as in Yas. iii. 25, omitting W.'s second line); and then *a. v.* thrice, and *y. a. v.* four times; the last time the final words, *dadaḍ vâstârem*, must be uttered thrice.

The Zota now takes the Barsom in his hand, and both priests begin to recite *nivaêdhayêmi* (Yas. i. 1, 2, to) *ameshanãm speñtanãm*. The Zota then continues to recite alone Yas. i. 3–23.

Continuing to recite Yas. ii., at the words *zaothra âyêsê*, &c. (ver. 1), the Zota takes the Barsom in both hands and holds it upon the two Mâh-rû; at the words *ahmya zaothrê*, &c. (ver. 2), he lays his hand upon the Mâh-rû, and continues to recite as far as Yas. vii. 25 without further action; but while reciting *y. a. v.* twice (in ver. 25) a little sandal-wood and incense are thrown into the fire by the Râspî.

The Zota continues to recite as far as Yas. viii. 1, and at the word *paiti-jamyâḍ* more sandal-wood and incense are thrown on the fire by the Râspî, who then advances towards the Zota and says *qarata narô* (Yas. viii. 2, to) *frēreticha*. The Zota then continues reciting *amesha speñta* (Yas. viii. 3, 4, to) *jasaiti*, and *a. v.* thrice. He then takes a very small piece of the Darûn and eats it, afterwards washing his mouth with water.

The Zota then recites Yas. viii. 5-7, and both priests continue the recitation of Yas. viii. 8—ix. 1, as far as the word *Zarathushtrem*. The Zota then recites the Homa Yasht to the words *vish apãm* (Yas. x. 1), when he pours water over the Barsom, and continues reciting to Yas. x. 20.

Yas. x. 21—xi. 8 is recited by both priests. The Râspî then pours water over his hand, takes the Homa-juice cup in his hand, and goes to the fire, into which he throws some sandal-wood and incense. He then returns to the Zota and says *yô nô aêvô* (Yas. xi. 9, to) *yaêthma*, handing the Homa-juice cup over to the Zota, who recites *pairi-tê* (Yas. xi. 10, 11, to) *vahishtem astî*, and then drinks the Homa juice, continuing to recite alone as far as *ravascha* (compare Yas. viii. 8), whenceforward both priests recite to the end of Yas. xi. 18.

The recitation is then continued by the Zota alone. From

y. a. v. (four times recited) in Yas. xiii. 7, to the end of *yêṅhê hâtãm* (ver. 8) he sprinkles the Barsom with some of the milk (*gâush jîvya*). At the words *sasticha raṅtâcha* (Yas. xv. 1) he pours half the milk into the cup which he emptied when drinking the Homa juice. And at the words *Ahurem mazdãm* (Yas. xvi. 1) he puts the mortar into the large water-vessel standing to his right.

Both priests recite Yas. xviii. 2, 3 twice, and each time the Zota sprinkles the Barsom with the milk. He then continues the recitation alone, and at the words *ahunem vairîm yaz.* (Yas. xviii. 9) he stretches out his legs (hitherto crossed), lays the right toes upon the left, and sprinkles the Barsom with the milk. While reciting Yas. xxii. 1-3, and 20-27, he again sprinkles the Barsom with the milk.

When the Zota commences Yas. xxiv. he takes the mortar out of the large water-vessel, sets it again upon the *takht* upside down, and at the beginning of Yas. xxv. he knocks it thrice upon the *takht* and turns it right side upwards. At the words *imem haomem* (Yas. xxv. 1) he puts a small piece of the Homa twig into the mortar, and proceeds exactly in the same manner as in the Paragnah ceremony (see p. 400, lines 17-29), except that while reciting the clause containing the words *gãm jîvyãm* (which is omitted in the Paragnah) he pours a little of the milk into the mortar. When he recites Yas. xxvi. 7, he takes the strainer out of the large water-vessel and places it upon the Homa-juice cup on the *takht*. Just before Yas. xxvii. comes *athâ ratush ashâḍchîḍ hachâ frâ ashava vîdhvâo mraotû* (see Yas. vii. 28), when the Zota takes the pestle into his hand, and proceeds with the pounding of the Homa and the recitation of Yas. xxvii. exactly in the same manner as in the Paragnah ceremony (see pp. 400, 401).

The recitation of the Gâthas is now commenced. The first verse *ahyâ yâsâ*, &c. (Yas. xxviii. 1, Sp.), is recited twice by both priests while the Zota sprinkles the Barsom with the milk. And at the end of each Hâ of the Ahunavaiti Gâtha (Yas. xxviii.—xxxiv.) the same verse (*ahyâ yâsâ*, &c.) is again twice recited while the Zota sprinkles the Barsom with the milk. When Yas. xxxi. 5 and 22 are recited the Zota pounds the Homa, also at the words *bûmyâo haptaithê* (Yas. xxxii. 3) and *yē îsh pâḍ* (Yas. xxxii. 13), and at the words *nazdishtăm drujem* (Yas. xxxiii. 4) and *â mâ* (Yas. xxxiii. 7); this pounding is of two kinds, the first time in each Hâ the pestle strikes upon the bottom of the mortar, but the second time it strikes against the sides so as to produce a ringing sound. When Yas. xxxiii. 10 is recited, the contents of the mortar are poured into the strainer, and the liquid runs through it into the Homa-juice cup below. The mortar is then set down, upside down, and the cup with the Homa juice (*parâhôm*) is placed upon it.

In the other four Gâthas the first verse of each Gâtha is recited twice, and again repeated twice at the end of each Hâ the Gâtha contains. And each time these first verses are recited, the Zota sprinkles the Barsom with the milk, as in the first Gâtha.

When Yas. lix. 31 is recited by the Zota, he pours some Zor and milk (*gâush jîvya*) into the milk saucer standing near the two Mâh-rû. After the words *stavas ashâ*, &c. (Yas. lxi. 5), he takes the Barsom from the two Mâh-rû, and, standing up and looking at the fire, he recites Yas. lxii. (the *âtash nyâyish*). At the word *yaozhdâtăm* (Yas. lxii. 10) he sits down again; and at the beginning of each of the three *a. v.* which follow, he pours a little more Zor into the milk saucer. While reciting Yas. lxiii. 1, he sprinkles the Barsom with Zor. After the word *avaṇhê* (Yas. lxiv. 3 = l. 7) he lays down the Barsom, and after the words *vasnâ frashôtemem* (Yas. lxiv. 7) he turns the mortar right side upwards.

At the beginning of Yas. lxv. the Zota pours some Zor into the mortar, at the word *perethû-frâkăm* he pours in the Homa juice, and at the word *baêshazyăm* he pours in some of the milk. He then stands up, turns towards the large water-vessel, and recites the remainder of Yas. lxv. 1–15 (the *âbân nyâyish*). At the words *yênhê mê ashâḍ* (ver. 16) he sits down again, and sprinkles the Barsom with Zor, and continues to do so while reciting Yas. lxvi. and lxvii.

The Zota then takes the Zor cup in his hand and waves it around the mortar during the recitation of Yas. lxviii. 1–19. While reciting ver. 20, he mixes the water in both Zor cups. The words *vaṇuhîm idhâḍ* (ver. 21, to) *apaschâ vâo* are recited thrice, and each time he says *apaschâ vâo* he pours some Zor into the mortar. At the word *jaidhimnâo* he pours the whole of the milk (*gâush jîvya*) into the mortar. At the words *nemô Ahurâi mazdâi* (ver. 22) he stands up and turns towards the east; and the three phrases, *vohû ukhshyâ* (ver. 23, to) *ushtâ-tanûm, imâ raochâo barezishtem barezemanãm*, and *yahmi* (to) *jasô*, are all recited thrice. At the words *nemô vē gâthâo* (ver. 24) the Zota sits down again and sprinkles the Barsom with Zor.

The recitation is then continued to Yas. lxxi. 25, where, at the words *gavê adâish*, the Zota takes the Barsom in his hand and touches the *takht* twice with each end of it. At the words *yē huddo yôi heñtî* (Yas. lxxii.) he gives the Barsom to the Râspî, recites two *y. a. v., yasnemcha*, &c., and so gives up the Bâj. The Râspî lays the Barsom on the two Mâh-rû, and both priests go out of the Arvîs-gâh. They perform the *hamâzôr*,[1] and both give up the Bâj again by reciting *yasnemcha vahmemcha* (to) *âfrînâmi*. They both perform the Kustî ceremony, and the Ijashne is ended.

The Zota goes with the Râspî to a well and pours the Homa juice and milk out of the mortar into the well. When he does this he recites one *y. a. v.* and one *a. v.*

3.—*The Darûn Ceremony.*

Any priest who wishes to perform this ceremony must either undergo the nine nights' purification of the Barashnôm ceremony, or must still retain some of its purifying influence.

The small flat cakes, called Darûn (*draona*) and Frasast (see p. 396) are the chief materials for the ceremony, and are arranged as shown on p. 408.

The two Darûns are placed by the priest upon the left side of the low table before him, the nearer one having a small piece of butter (*gâush hudhâo*) upon it. The two Frasasts are placed upon the right-hand side of the table, the further one having a pomegranate twig (*urvarãm*) upon it, and between this and the further Darûn is placed an egg.

The formulas used in consecrating the Darûns are to be found in the Darûn-yashtan. First, a *dibâja* is recited in Pâzand: *humata hûkhta hvarshta*, &c.; then comes *baresmana paiti-bareta*

---
[1] This is a formula for solemn greetings at festivals, &c., as follows: the greeter (says): *Yazdân panâh bâd!* (the greeted answers): *Dêr-zîvâ shâd bâd!* (both say): *Hamâ zôr hamâ ashô bêd.*

	SOUTII. Fire in a vase on a stone.	Sandal-wood and incense.	
Darûn.	Egg.	Frasast with urvarâm.	
Darûn with butter.		Frasast	Water vessel.
	Priest sitting with Barsom.		

(Yas. iii. 1—viii. 4). Variations are introduced according to the particular object of the ceremony; and the name of him in whose honour the ceremony is performed must be mentioned after the khshnûmainê, whether he be an angel or a deceased person. After the consecration, pieces are broken off the Darûns by the officiating priest, and eaten by himself and those present, beginning with the priests.

4.—*The Afrîngân Ceremony.*

At all the great festivals, and on solemn occasions, the Darûn ceremony is followed by the Afrîngân, but on other occasions the Afrîngân can be celebrated alone. Like the Darûn ceremony, it is performed in honour of some angel or deceased person.

A tray containing wine and fruits is placed before the fire, and flowers are laid to the left of the tray. The ceremony begins with a *dibâja* spoken by the Zota: *pa-nâm-i Izad-i bakhshâyandah*, &c., followed by *y. a. v.* several times repeated; if the ceremony be in honour of Hormazd,[1] the *y. a. v.* must be recited ten times; if in honour of Srosh, five times; and on other occasions in proportion. Then follow *a. v.* thrice,

---

[1] In which case the Afrîngân is recited by both the Zota and Râspî.

and the actual Afrîngân (see Westergaard's Zend-Avesta, pp. 318-324). And the Zota concludes the consecration with the Afrîn: *hama zôr ham ashô bêd*, &c. Afterwards the fruit is eaten and the wine drunk in the same manner as the Darûn is eaten.

When a person eats or drinks the consecrated objects, he recites Yas. xxxvii. 1, followed by *a. v.* thrice. After all is eaten and drunk there are recited *a. v.* four times, *y. a. v.* twice, *a. v.* once, and then *ahmâi raêshcha* (Yas. lxviii. 11).

INDEX.

INDEX.

ABÂLISH, 108
Abân nyâyish, 98, 224, 364, 406
—— yasht, 107, 197
Abereta, 332
Abraham, 16
Abu Jafir Attavari, 123
Achæmenes, 298
Achæmenian, 54, 66, 80, 136, 302
Achæmenians, 67
Adam, 15, 211
Adarbaîjân, 79
Adarfrobag-i Farukhzâdân, 55, 101, 104, 110
Adarpâd-i Adarfrobag-i Farukhzâdân, 55
—— Admîtân, 55
—— Mâraspendân, 101, 110, 111, 320
Adarpâdyâvand, 104
Adhvaryu, 193, 270, 280, 282
Aditi, 274
Adityas, 273, 275
Advice of a certain man, 110
Æschylus, 4
Aêshma, 185, 190, 308, 337
Aêsma, 394
Æthiopic, 31
Ætolians, 69
Afarg, 386
Afghânic, 67
Afrâsiyâb, 361
Afringân, 134, 139, 284, 408, 409
—— dahmân, 98, 142, 315
—— gahanbâr, 98, 225
—— gâtha, 98, 225
—— rapithwin, 225
Afringâns, 224, 225, 262, 315
Afrîn-i dahmân, 99
—— myazd, 98
—— tû pêshgâb-i khudâ, 113
—— Zaratusht, 98, 223
Afsh-chithra, 200
Agathias, 11, 299
Agereptem, 239
Aghish, 392, 393
Agiari, 316
Agni, 145, 268, 269, 274, 275, 279, 281

Agnîdhra, 281
Agnihotri, 281
Agnihotris, 270, 279, 280
Agnishtoma, 281, 283
Ahriman, 8, 24, 53, 129, 133, 134, 252, 277, 346, 352, 387
Ahu, 187, 354, 371
Ahuna-vairya, 141, 144, 179, 185-190, 218, 248, 253, 333, 335, 374, 380, 382
Ahunavaiti. See *Gâtha*
Ahura, 71, 141, 144, 149, 152, 155, 158-164, 166, 168, 172, 173, 179, 188, 197, 199, 211, 212, 256, 267, 268, 271, 287, 288, 293, 295, 302, 333, 335, 336
Ahuramazda, 8, 10, 11, 35, 53, 54, 140, 142, 148-159, 162, 163, 165-174, 185-189, 191-200, 202-211, 214-222, 227-236, 238, 239, 243-247, 249, 250, 253-258, 268, 271, 274, 290, 295, 297, 302-311, 313, 315-319, 322-336
Ahuras, 301
Ahurô mazdâo, 301
Ahûryan, 174, 175, 191, 231
Ahuti, 280
Airân, 78. See *Iran*
Airân-vêj, 355-357
Airmân, 393
Airyaman, 153, 196, 257, 273, 393
Airyana-vaêjô, 179, 227, 232, 233, 299
Airyêmâ ishyô, 142, 196
Aishkata, 203
Aitareya-brâhmanam (quoted), 270, 271, (referred to) 182, 275, 284
Aît-bômand, 356
Aiwisrûthrema gâh, 159
Aiwizu, 329
Aiwyâonhanem, 286, 384, 396-398
Akatasha, 337
Akem manô, 150, 303, 304, 308, 380
Akhtar, 200
Akhtya, 107

INDEX.

Alborz, 5, 190, 197, 203-205, 216, 235, 286, 361, 364, 387
Aldebaran, 182
Alexander the Great, 15, 54, 78, 81, 123-125, 129, 130, 133, 136
Amasis, 7
Amerdâd, 9, 307
Ameretâd, 9, 10, 52, 167, 169, 191, 218, 302, 305, 307
Amerôdad, 354
Ameshâspend, 101, 132
Ameshâspends, 101, 112, 132, 134, 338, 339, 341, 343, 348, 382-384, 386, 388, 389
Ameshaspenta, 259
Ameshaspentas, 9, 53, 167, 169-171, 173, 187, 189, 210, 212, 215, 254-256, 305, 307, 334-336
Ami, 364
Ammianus Marcellinus, 84
Amshaspends, 9, 24, 150, 194, 305
Anâhid, 197
Anâhita, 6, 10, 43, 197-199, 207, 208, 259, 263. See *Ardvi*
Anaitis, 6, 10, 11, 43, 197
Anandates, 10
Andarj-i Adarpâd-i Mâraspendân, 111
—— dânâk mard, 112
—— Hûdâvar-i dânâk, 108
—— Khûsrô-i Kavâdân, 110
Andreas, 88
Angiras, 294
Anglo-Saxon, 287
Angra-mainyu, 53
Angrô-mainyush, 8, 24, 147, 178, 179, 187, 189, 223, 227-230, 234, 252-254, 272, 304, 305, 308, 309, 317, 319, 333, 336, 337, 366, 401
Anquetil Duperron, 17-26, 28, 35, 38, 44, 45, 47, 48, 50, 78, 105, 312, 394
Ante-Zoroastrian, 258, 294
Anushṭubh, 175, 252
Aogemadaêcha, 99, 114
Apâ, 214
Apaoshô, 201
Apârsiu, 356
Apem haomyãm, 398, 400
Aphrodite, 6, 11, 197
Apistân val yazdân, 121
Apri, 284
Aptoryâma, 283
Aptya, 278
Arab, 6, 80, 123
Arabian, 14, 16
Arabic, 19, 20, 31, 34, 80-82, 84, 85, 93, 113, 125, 128, 152, 181
Arabs, 6, 48
Arachosia, 229
Aramati, 274, 288
Araṇa, 181
Arang, 361, 364

Arangistân, 364
Araṇyaka, 181
Ardâî fravard, 390
Ardashîr-i Pâpakân, 86, 88, 90, 91, 111, 125
Ardavân, 78, 91
Ardâ Virâf, 106, 107
—— —— nâmah, 43, 46, 50, 54, 56, 94, 97, 106, 124, 351, 354
Ardibahisht, 9, 148, 195, 196, 225, 306, 400
—— yasht, 196
Ardvi-sûra Anâhita, 193, 194, 197, 199. See *Anâhita*.
Aredush, 239
Areimanios, 8-10
Arezahi, 256, 369, 389
Arezûra, 316, 337, 381, 390
Arhmen, 13, 14
Ariaramnes, 298
Aristotle, 8, 206, 298
Ariyârâmna, 298
Arjâsp, 109, 391
Arktos, 206
Armaiti, 9, 150-152, 155, 156, 158-160, 162, 167, 168, 173, 191, 207, 232, 249, 250, 274, 297, 302, 306, 319, 334
Armenian, 39, 40, 67, 79, 139
—— writers, 12-14
Arrian, 124
Arsacidans, 67, 79, 80
Arsames, 298
Arshâma, 298
Arshtâd, 215
Artaxerxes, 7, 263
Arûm, 364
Arvis-gâh, 332, 394-396, 401, 403, 407
Aryaman, 273, 288
Aryan, 180, 191, 200, 211, 214, 215, 226, 230, 257, 288, 290, 292, 293
Aryans, 242, 252, 294
Aryas, 69
Asha, 148, 151, 171, 185
Asha-vahishta, 9, 141, 302, 305, 306, 333, 339-342, 344, 347, 349, 382, 393
Ashem, 217-219
Ashem vahishtem, 172, 191
Ashem-vohu formula, 97, 98, 174, 212, 217, 246, 248, 374, 375, 384, 385, 397-399, 401-404, 406-409; (translated) 141
Ashi, 215, 256
Ashîrvâd, 113
Ashishang, 215, 389
Ashi-vaṇuhi, 184, 215, 216
Ashi yasht, 215, 216
Ashkâuian, 54
Ashtâd yasht, 215, 216
Ashvins, 272, 276, 308
Asia Minor, 202

Askârum, 133
Asmodeus, 337
Asnâtar, 332
Aspandiârji Frâmji, 58
Aspârum, 133
Asperena, 320, 332
Assyrian, 81, 112, 125
Assyrians, 6, 12
Astarte, 6
Asti, 153
Astô-vîdhôtu, 321, 323
Astvaḍ-ereta, 213
Asura, 53, 71, 267-269, 271. 287
Asuras, 268-271, 278, 279, 287
Asûristân, 101
Atarevakhshô, 280, 332
Atarôpâtakân, 362
Atash-gâh, 11
Atash-i âdarân, 140
—— Behrâm, 140
Atash nyâyish, 98, 224, 364, 402, 403, 406
Atha jamyâd, 224
Atharvan, 280, 294
Atharvaveda, 182, 196, 206, 257, 269, 275-277, 279, 294
Athenokles, 12
Athrava, 182, 212, 280, 294
Athwya, 178, 278
Attic dialect, 75
Aûharmazd, 104, 107, 111-113, 127, 129-132, 134, 338-356, 358-367, 369-372, 376, 378, 380-389, 391-393
—— yasht, 98
Aûharmazdî, 302
Aûramazdâ, 302, 304
Aurvaḍ-aspa, 298
Avaoirishtem, 239
Avân, 357
Avûraoshtra, 213
Avar chim-i drôn, 112
Avesta, *passim;* (defined) 14, 15, 67, 68, 119-121, 226, 239, 262; dictionary, 31, 47, 114; glossary, 49, 99; language, 67-78, 177, 289; manuscripts, 18, 21, 29, 30, 45; (ordinary), 65, 72-75, 142, 147, 174, 191; (passages noted), 227-240; quotations in Pahl. trans., 52, 60, 61, 94, 98-100, 120, 177-179, 227, 229-232, 235, 238, 243, 251, 316, 322, 324, 355-358, 362, 363, 365, 368, 369, 374, 376, 378, 385; studies, 18-42; translations (English) 44, (French) 18, 51, 52, (German) 20, 34, 41, 42, (Gujrati) 58, 60
Avesta and Zend, 119-122, 124, 125, 134, 135, 343, 345, 348, 353
Avesta-Sanskrit glossary, 46
Avîjeh-dîn, 58, 102
Ayâthrema, 192

Az, 343, 370, 371
Azhi-chithra, 196
Azhi-Dahâka, 178, 198, 230, 363
Azi, 246
Azûiti, 280

BABYLON, 298
Babylonia, 3, 4
Babylonians, 6, 12, 197, 298
Bactria, 14, 65, 169, 228, 263, 293, 295, 297
Bactrian, 65, 66, 73, 74, 76, 159, 290
Badakhshân, 66
Bagdad, 15, 108
Bagha, 214, 273
Baghân yasht, 132
Bagh nask, 127
Baghô-bakhta, 274
Bahisht, 311
Bâhl, 359
Bahman, 9, 255, 306, 358
—— yasht, 43, 107, 108, 124
Bâj, 397, 399, 401-403, 407
Bakân-yastô nask, 132
Bâkhar, 359
Bâkhdhi, 228, 297
Bakô nask, 127, 134
Bakht-âfrîḍ, 110
Balkh, 66, 208
Balsâr, 45
Bambo, 107
Banga, 336
Barashnôm, 197, 241, 320, 407
Barhis, 283
Barish nask, 129
Baroda, 279
Barsom, 4, 13, 139, 171, 189, 214, 243, 251, 259, 283, 315, 318, 330, 334, 335, 366, 378, 384, 395-399, 401, 404-408
Barsom-dân, 396-399
Barzû Qiyâmu-d-dîn, 126, 130
Bavaria, 29
Behistun, 66, 263. See *Bisutûn*
Behrâm, 193, 213, 214, 256, 275, 389
—— yasht, 98, 213, 214, 275
Bel, 11, 12
Benfey, 35, 39, 263
Berekhdha ârmaiti, 297
Berezô-hadhaokhdha, 142
Berosos, 12, 298
Bethlehem, 5
Bhaga, 273, 274
Bhagavad-gita, 273, 279
Bhroch, 45, 57, 58, 95, 97
Bible, 5, 15, 207, 309
Birma, 123
Bisutûn, 32, 298. See *Behistun*
Bleeck, 44
Bôdôk-zeḍ, 342

INDEX.

Bog (God), 273
Bôi, 394
Bokhara, 66
Bombay, 17, 21, 31, 32, 44, 47, 50, 56, 58, 59, 61, 95-97, 100, 104, 108, 109, 111; government, 45, 46, 48
Bopp, 29, 31
Bör, 147
Boundless time, 12, 15, 24, 53, 382
Brahma, 147, 192, 276, 288
Brâhmanam, 181
Brâhmanas, 269, 275
Brahmanaspati, 274
Brahmanical, 135, 170, 172, 179, 180, 185, 258, 259, 267, 268, 270-272, 276, 281, 282, 284-289, 292-294
Brahmanism, 206, 272, 292
Brahmans, 15, 21, 22, 39, 44, 69, 73, 76-78, 121, 138, 140, 143, 147, 176, 179-181, 191, 207, 258, 259, 262, 264, 272, 273, 276, 279, 281-291, 294, 307
Brihaspati, 278, 279
British Museum, 87
Brockhaus, 30, 31, 37, 38
Buddha, 208, 263
Buddhism, 22, 23, 208, 263
Buddhist caves, 50
Buddhistic, 211
Buddhists, 15, 123
Bûiti, 253, 337
Bukhâr, 359
Bundahish, 30, 33, 42-44, 46-48, 58, 104, 105, 113, 114, 182, 192, 233, 308, 309, 313, 333, 336, 350, 355-358, 361, 363, 364, 387, 392
Burnouf, 22, 26, 29, 31, 36, 37, 39, 312
Bûshâsp, 369, 370
Bûshyâsta, 245
Bût, 379, 380
Bûtâl, 128

CALENDAR (Parsi), 57
Cambyses, 7
Caucasus, 67
Celtic, 65
Ceylon, 123
Chaishpish, 298
Chakâd-i dâîtîh, 387
Chakhra, 230, 362
Chaldæo-Pahlavi, 82, 83, 86, 87, 89, 90
Chaldaic, 199
Chaldee, 20, 31, 39, 59, 62, 82, 86-88
Changhraghâch-nâmah, 43
Chanranhâch, 192
Chatrang-nâmak, 110
Châturmâsya ishti, 285
Chidak avistâk-i gâsân, 98
Chidrashtô nask, 131
Chinese, 31, 107

Chinvad bridge, 128, 165, 224, 225, 244, 255, 256, 311, 361, 366, 369, 378, 387-389
Christian, 12, 53, 103, 309, 311; era, 67, 73, 137, 263
Christianity, 4, 312
Christians, 12, 15, 104
Churl's wain, 206
Chwolsohn, 14, 15
Cities of the land of Iran, 105
Constantius, 84
Copenhagen, 21, 28-30, 33, 34, 44, 48, 56, 95-99, 104, 105, 108, 109, 111, 127
Cornelius Nepos, 7
Cuneiform inscriptions, 6, 32, 54, 66, 79-81, 169, 206, 298, 302, 304
Curtius, 124
Cyaxares, 15
Cyrus, 4, 136

DÂDAK nask, 130
Dâdâr bin Dâd-dukht, 113
Dâd-gâh, 11, 140, 241
Dâdistân-i dînî, 102, 103
Daênâo, 152
Daêvanâm daêvô, 308
Dahmân âfrîngân, 98, 142, 315
Dahmas, 242
Dahmi vanuhi, 142
Dâîtîh, 356, 357, 380
Daityas, 278
Daiwish, 308, 337
Dakhmas, 240, 325
Dakshina, 280
Damascius, 12
Dâmdâd nask, 127
Dânava, 279
Danish writers, 20, 21, 32-34, 36, 37
Dâraja, 333
Dârayavush, 298
Darî, 66
Darius, 11, 136, 264, 298, 304
Darmesteter, 52, 53, 337, 359
Darsha pûrnama ishti, 285
Dârûk-i khûrsandî, 110
Darûn, 259, 281, 285, 365, 395, 396, 404, 407-409. See *Draonô*.
—— bâj, 397
Dastah, 396
Dastur, 18, 46, 96, 103, 131, 132, 134, 139, 297, 327, 328, 340, 343, 354, 392
—— Aspendiârji Kâmdinji, 58
—— Dârâb, 17, 45
—— Edalji Dârâbji, 25, 58
—— -i dastûrân, 193, 297
—— Hoshangji Jâmâspji, 46, 48-51, 60, 61, 99, 104, 112, 128, 134, 249, 338, 359, 360, 368, 384, 385, 387, 391
—— Jâmâsp Asâ, 57, 95, 99

INDEX. 417

Dastur, Jâmâspji Minochiharji, 34, 56, 61, 96, 97, 109-111, 338, 347, 348, 354
—— Jâmâsp Wilâvati, 56, 57, 99
—— Kai-Khusro Dârâb, 45
—— Minochihar Yûdân-damân, 102
—— Nôshirvânji Jâmâspji, 99, 126, 134
—— Peshotanji Behramji, 58, 59, 100, 102, 108, 110-113, 297
—— Sohrâbji Rustamji, 102
Dasturs, 17, 18, 24-26, 33, 36, 42, 43, 45, 53, 55, 57, 61, 76-78, 104, 112, 113, 126, 129, 131, 139, 147, 176, 197, 215-217, 297, 333, 338, 391
Davâns, 351
Deinon, 7
Delphi, 211
Denmark, 28
Dêva, 201, 267, 268, 275; religion, 149, 174, 211, 268, 287, 290, 291, 293, 295; worshipper, 173, 338; worshippers, 287, 293; worshipping, 255, 336
Dêvas, 150, 152, 153, 161, 168, 172, 173, 184, 185, 190, 204, 205, 217, 227, 230, 258, 259, 261, 268-272, 276, 287-289, 301, 304, 308, 327, 334, 401
Dêvasârm, 110
Dêvî-drukhsh, 190
Devil, 4, 53
Dêvîs, 184
Dharmashâstra, 260
Dibâja, 407, 408
Dimishqi, 15
Dinî vajarkard, 126-134
Dinkard, 54, 55, 59, 60, 97, 99-101, 104, 114, 123, 126, 128, 131, 132
Dinkhard, 104, 105
Dinûr, 66
Din yasht, 215
Dio Chrysostomos, 11
Diodorus, 124
Diogenes of Laerte, 8
Dioskuri, 272, 308
Dirakht-i Asûrik, 110
Dirham, 320, 332
Dir Mihir, 316
Dorians, 69, 70
Draonô, 259, 327, 396, 407. See Darûn
Dreñj, 143
Driwish, 308, 337
Drûj, 349, 372-374, 379, 380, 382, 390, 393
Drûjô-demâna, 311
Drukhsh, 213, 247-249, 252, 253, 304, 333
—— nasush, 241, 317, 328
Drvâspa, 202
Dualism, 53, 300, 303, 305, 309

Dûbâsrûd or Dûbâsrûjd, 132
Dughda, 132
Duncker, 43
Dushmata, 223
Dûta, 297
Dutch, 70
Duzhaka, 228
Duzhanha, 311
Duzhûkhta, 223
Duzhvarshta, 223
Dvâsrûb or Dvâsrûzd, 133
Dvâsrûjad or Dvâsrûnjad, 132
Dvâzdah hâmâst, 127
Dvîpas, 286
Dyaus, 287
Dyâvâ-prithivî, 275

Edda, 147
Elisæus, 13, -4
Elohim, 199, 302
England, 16, 18-21, 32
English, 5, 32, 44, 50, 65, 67; translation, 33, 44, 49, 50, 59, 102, 106, 107, 111, 338
Erlangen, 30
Etymander, 229
Eudemos, 12
Eudoxos, 8, 298
Europe, 16, 18, 23, 29, 30, 32, 44, 49, 77, 114, 135, 196, 213, 286
European, 17, 18, 25, 44, 45, 51, 52, 58, 59, 67, 68, 108, 115, 138, 270, 346, 377; researches, 16-53
Europeans, 17, 21, 45, 115, 119
Ewald, 39
Ezekiel, 4
Eznik, 13, 14

Farâkhû-khard, 388
Fargard, 225, 227, 230, 235, 237, 239-243, 252, 257, 315, 319, 322, 327, 333, 338, 355, 356
Farhang-i oîm-khadûk, 99, 114, 120, 236, 245, 318, 344, 364, 365, 369
Fârs, 78, 80, 102, 364
Farsang, 233
Fârsi, 80, 86
Firdausi, 34, 48, 66, 78, 80, 81, 85, 86
Five dispositions of priests, 110
Form of marriage contract, 110
Forms of letters to kings, 110
Formula for destroying demons, 365
Frabaretar, 332
Frahda, 248
Fradadhafshu, 256, 389
Frâgâm, 398, 399
Frâmji Aspendiârji, 31
Framru, 143
France, 18, 20, 21, 28
Frasast, 396, 407, 408
Frâsâyâvân, 361
Frashakard, 347

2 D

Frashaoshtra, 146, 158, 166, 167, 169, 174, 213, 258
Frashô-kereti, 312, 314
Frashôshtar, 340, 341
Frâsîyâv, 356, 361
Frasrâvay, 143
Fravardîgân days, 129
Fravardîn (month), 225, 357
—— yasht, 44, 206–213, 263
Fravartish, 206
Fravashi, 168, 171, 206, 334, 383
Fravashis, 170, 172, 194, 203, 206, 256
Frêdûn, 178, 198, 202, 223, 230, 275, 277, 278, 363
French, 17-19, 51, 52; translation, 18, 51, 105
Fróhars, 129, 203, 206, 403
Fryâna, 165
Fshûshô-mâthra, 142, 190

GAÊTHAS, 152, 165, 178, 199, 291
Gahanbâr, 58, 128, 129, 285
Gahanbârs, 140, 192, 193, 225, 260
Gâhs, 134, 139, 159, 225, 262
Gaikwar, 279
Ganj-i shâîgân, 111
Gaochithra, 200
Gaotema, 208, 263
Garô-demâna, 203, 311, 339, 388, 389
Garô-nemâna, 255, 256
Gâtha, 41, 137, 140, 141, 143-149, 151, 152, 154, 167, 222, 258, 271, 272, 406; (defined) 143; dialect, 65, 69, 72-75, 140-142, 147, 170, 172; lore, 339, 341, 349, 350; metres, 143-146
—— ahunavaiti, 142, 144, 146-154, 256, 271, 338-354, 389, 405
—— days, 112, 225
Gâthâo, 175
Gâthas, 23, 28, 38, 41, 42, 65, 72-75, 98, 106, 141, 167, 168, 170, 171, 177, 183, 186, 221, 244, 249, 257-261, 263, 264, 267, 273, 275, 287, 289-294, 296, 297, 300-302, 304, 305, 310-312, 338, 368, 376, 389, 405, 406; described and translated, 140, 142-170; (the five) 34, 41, 140, 141, 171, 190, 256, 257
Gâtha speñtâ-mainyû, 142, 145, 167-169, 256, 272, 389
—— ushtavaiti, 142, 144, 145, 154-166, 220, 222, 256, 272, 389
—— vahishtôishti, 142, 170, 256, 389
—— vohû-khshathra, 142, 169, 170, 256, 272, 389
Gâu, 203, 227
Gâush, 173
—— bud̠hâo, 139, 281, 396, 407
—— jîvya, 139, 281, 315, 397, 405-407

Gautama, 208, 263
Gavâ, 358
Gâyatrî, 144
—— âsurî, 271
Gayô-marathan, 211
Gayomard, 15, 101, 211, 346, 347, 351
Genâ, 170
German, 19, 20, 28, 29, 31, 47, 70, 146, 147, 154, 167, 393; translation, 20, 30, 34, 41-44, 47, 105, 106, 108, 315
Germans (ancient), 180
Germany, 20, 21, 23, 28, 29, 31, 46, 48
Gêush tashâ, 147, 151
—— urvâ, 147-149, 165, 168, 202, 297, 339
Ghena, 193
Ghîlân or Gîlân, 230, 363
Gnâ, 274
Gôgôshasp, 374, 375, 377
Gôkerenô, 392
Gômêz, 285, 400
Gôsh, 202; yasht, 201, 202
Gôsht-i Fryânô, 50, 56, 107
Gôshûrûn, 147, 339, 341, 344
Gotama, 208
Gothic, 68
Grantha, 181
Greece, 8, 202
Greek, 5, 12, 16, 21, 40, 65, 68, 69, 86, 87, 123, 124, 143, 148, 188, 194, 206, 211, 287, 298; dialects, 69; (Homeric) 70, 75; writers, 6-12
Greeks, 5, 8, 11, 54, 66, 79, 123, 124, 135-138, 197, 205, 272, 294, 295, 298-301
Gujrât, 32, 33, 45
Gujrâti, 31, 55, 58, 59, 61, 139; translation, 58-60, 93, 102, 111
Guru, 278
Gushtâsp, 108, 130, 298, 299

HÂ, 140, 152, 167, 405, 406. See Hâs
Hades, 8
Hadbânaêpata, 139, 251, 378, 399
Hâdôkht nask, 46, 50, 51, 56, 97, 133, 134, 139, 217-224, 354
Haêchadaspas, 296
Haêtumat, 229
Hâfiz, 197
Hâjîâbâd, 33, 87
—— inscriptions, 87-89
Hakhâmanish, 298
Hakhedhrem, 200
Hamadân, 66, 79
Hamaspathmaêdaya, 192, 210
Hamâzôr, 407
Hamîstakân, 389
Hañdareza, 241

Haṇhaurvat, 213
Haoma, 70, 259
Haoshyaṇha, 198, 202, 214
Haptân yasht, 98, 195
Haptôiriñg, 206
Harakhmônd, 361
Haraqaiti, 229
Harauvati, 229
Harîb, 360
Hariva, 228
Harlez, 51, 61
Haró berezaiti, 5, 190, 203-205, 216, 255, 286
Haróyu, 66, 203. 228
Hâs, 146, 153, 170, 320
Hâthra, 233
Haurvatâd, 9, 52, 167, 169, 191, 196, 197, 218, 302, 305, 307
Hâvanân, 332
Hâvanî gâh, 159, 176
Hâvanîm, 396, 399, 400
Havirdhâna, 270
Hebrew, 4, 5, 31, 80, 175, 199
Hêchadaspa Spitama, 166
Hellenes, 6, 69
Hendva, 201
Heracles, 11
Herat, 66, 203, 228
Herbad, 213, 397
Herbads, 129, 197, 205, 320
Hermann, 39
Hermippos, 7-9, 33, 123, 136
Herodotus, 4-7, 298
Hêt-hômand, 361, 389
Hêtumand, 356, 361
Hêtumat, 256
Hikhra, 325
Hilmand, 229, 256
Hindu, 215, 230, 268, 269, 277, 363
Hinduism, 276
Hindu-kush, 201
Hindus, 70, 205, 268, 363
Hindûstân, 288, 292, 293, 361
Hiñdvô, 205
Hiriwî, 66
Homa, 22, 139, 146, 171, 176-185, 193, 219, 251, 254, 259, 292, 330, 335, 336, 378, 382, 384, 392-396, 399-405; juice, 139, 140, 174, 176, 177, 185, 245, 282, 322, 368, 395, 399, 400, 402-407; mortar, 315, 330, 382, 395, 396, 399, 401-403, 405-407; twigs, 191, 282, 399, 400, 405; yasht, 175-185, 292, 404
Hômâst (herbad), 94
Honovar, 185. See *Ahuna-vairya*
Hormazd, 8, 10, 11, 24, 268, 302, 403, 408; worshipper, 260, 268; yasht, 195
Hormisdas, 12
Horvadad, 354
Hôshang, 198, 202, 391, 392

Hotâ, 193, 280, 282
Hotṛi ritual, 179
Hukhshathrôtemái, 248, 374, 375
Hûkhta, 221
Humata. 221
Humatanâm, 248, 374, 375
Hunus, 213
Hushêdar, 341, 388
—— bâmî, 314
—— mâh, 314, 341, 388
Hushkyaothma, 213
Hûspâram nask, 99, 133, 327
Huvarshta, 221
Huzvârish, 42, 49, 59, 85, 86, 92, 112, 122, 324, 356
Hvâpa, 326
Hvare khshaêta, 199
Hyades, 182
Hyde, 16, 123
Hystaspes, 11, 264, 298

IBN FOZLAN, 15
—— Hauqal, 80
—— Muqaffa, 84, 85
Idhâfat, 89, 90, 94
Ijashne, 139, 140, 174, 281. 283, 286, 313, 394, 397, 400, 403-407
Incense, 335, 336, 385, 394, 403, 404, 408
India, 3, 16-18, 32, 33, 45. 55, 79, 94, 96, 97, 99, 100, 105-110, 112, 114, 205, 230, 255
Indian, 107, 110, 182, 192, 213, 214, 272, 278, 288, 291, 377
Indians, 292, 299
Indo-Iranian, 53
Indra, 145, 213. 268, 272, 275, 276, 278, 279, 288, 291, 308, 337
Indus, 107, 230
Injunctions to bahdins, 110
Ionians, 69, 70
Iran, 65, 76-79, 88, 203, 295, 399; (western) 78
Iranian, *passim*; antiquities, 51; construction, 49, 81-83; dastur, 56; equivalents, 42, 49, 82, 85; languages, 27, 39, 65-67, 73, 77, 206
Iranians, 53, 70, 82, 165, &c.
Iristô-kasha, 318
Isaiah, 4, 311
Isfendarmad, 9, 306
Isfendyâr, 391
Ishti, 280
Ispahân, 66, 79, 104
Istakhar, 66
Istûdgar nask, 126
Izads, 194. See *Yazads*
Izhâ, 170

Jâmâspa, 108, 146, 167, 174, 213, 258

Jâmâspas, 166, 169
Jâmâsp nâmah, 43, 108, 110, 114
Jamshêd, 23, 177, 198, 202, 230, 276, 391
Javîd-dêv-dâd, 133
Javîd-shêdâ-dâd, 133, 225
Jazhu, 329
Jehovah, 302, 304
Jeremiah, 3
Jerusalem, 3, 5
Jesus, 5
Jewish religion, 16, 312
Jews, 4, 5, 15, 78, 103, 104, 135, 136, 264
Jirasht nask, 131
Jivâm, 398, 399, 403
Jones (Sir W.), 19
Jud-dêv-dâd, 133
Jupiter, 53
Justi, 47, 48, 105, 114
Jyotishtoma, 281, 282

KABISAH controversy, 58
Kâbul, 228
Kadmî sect, 102
Kâh-i kashân, 217
Kahrkatâs, 245
Kaî Gushtâsp, 198, 290, 298
—— Kabâd, 290, 298
—— Kâûs, 223, 278, 298
—— Kavus, 198
—— Khusrô, 198, 223, 290, 298, 391
—— Us, 391
Kâkasparsha, 286
Kâmah Bahrah, 126
Kambay, 95, 96
Kambâyat, 56
Kâm nemôi zâm, 222
Kandahâr, 229, 254
Kanheri, 50
Kant, 19
Kapâmajûn, 128
Kara fish, 336
Karapan, 289-291
Kârnâmak-i Ardashir-i Pâpakân, 59, 78, 90, 111
Karshipta, 235
Karshvare, 205, 256, 286
Kâsak, 361
Kashkasîrah, 130
Kashkîsrôbô nask, 130
Kashôsâî, 381
Kasksrôb, 130
Kâsôya, 254
Kasvi, 337
Kata, 324
Kâtyâyana, 76
Kaus, 18
Kava, Kavâ, or Kavi, 289-291
—— Husravn, 198, 290, 298
—— Kavâta, 290, 298
—— Usa, 198, 278, 298

Kava, Kavâ, or Kavi, Vishtâspa, 156, 166, 169, 173, 198, 202, 212, 215, 223, 258, 290, 298
Kavâri, 291
Kavâsnkha, 291
Kâvasjî Edalji Kanga, 60
Kavatnu, 291
Kavis, 216, 290, 291
Kâvûl, 360
Kâvya Ushanas, 278, 279
Kayânian, 80, 290
Kayân race, 107
Kayomars, 211
Kayomarthiyah, 15
Keresâni, 182
Keresâspa, 178, 179, 228, 391
Kereshaspô, 360
Kôsh-i Ibrâhim, 16
Kôshvars, 198, 256, 286, 355, 363, 369, 389
Khasht nask, 130
Khnân, 361
Khnâthaiti, 228, 254
Khneûta, 229
Khordâd, 9, 53, 307
—— yasht, 196
Khorehe vehîjak, 58
Khowaresmia, 203
Khrafstraghna, 243
Khshaotha, 201
Khshathra, 167
—— vairya, 9, 191, 302, 305, 306, 333
Khshatvêr, 344, 347
Khshnûman, 404, 408
Khurdah Avesta, 98
Khurshêdji Rustamji Kâmâ, 60
Khurshêd nyâyish, 98, 224
—— yasht, 98, 199, 217
Khûshkand, 101
Khusrô-i Anôshak-rûbân, 110
—— Kavâdân, 101, 109, 110
—— Nôshirvân, 111
Khûstô nask, 130
Khûzî, Khûzistân, 80
Khvêtûk-das, 103, 133
Kirmân, 97, 100, 102, 103, 114, 230, 363
Kleuker, 20
Krishûnu, 182
Krishna, 279
Krittikâ, 182
Kronos, 11
Ktesias, 7
Kunda, 336
Kusha, 283
Kustî, 244, 249, 286, 367, 368, 398, 403, 407

Lahurâsp, 298
Lakshmi, 215
Lassen, 43

INDEX.

Latin, 21, 40, 41, 65, 68, 69, 71, 154, 287
Leipzig, 30
Letto-Lithuanian, 65
Lithuanian, 27, 152, 287
London, 29, 30, 48, 56, 95, 106, 338
Louvain, 51

Mâdigân-i Gujastak Abalish, 108
—— Gôsht-i Fryânô, 107
—— haft ameshaspend, 112
—— mâh Fravardin rôj-i Horvadad, 112
—— sî rôj, 110-112
—— sî yazadân, 112
Magavas, 166, 169
Magha, 331, 344
Maghava, 14, 291, 320
Magi, 3-8, 10-12, 14-16, 18, 20, 80, 166 169, 309, 312
Magic rites, 11, 299
Magush, 169
Mahâbhârata, 79, 279, 288
Mahâbhâshya, 182
Mahârâshtra, 181
Mâh nyâyish, 224
Mâh-rû, 396, 398, 399, 403, 404, 406, 407
Mâhvandâd Narimahân, 101
Mâh yasht, 98, 200
Maidhyâirya, 192
Maidhyô ishâdha, 213
—— mâonha, 212
—— shema, 192
—— zaremya, 192
Mainyô-i khard, 51, 55, 104, 105, 323, 324, 339, 355, 365, 390
Mâmûn (khalîf), 108
Manes, 207
Manichæans, 104
Manjerj, 18
Mânsarspend, 141
Mantras, 293, 297
Manu, 79, 211
Mar (to recite), 143
Marâthî, 44
Marburg, 47
Mardân-farukh-i Aûharmazd-dâd, 104
Maretan, 297
Marg-arjân, 313, 369, 377
Mârik-nâmak-i Asûrik, 112
Marjpân Frêdûn, 102
Marutas, 180
Marûv, 358, 359
Marv, 66, 203, 228
Masudi, 14
Mâthra, 182, 195-197
Mâthran, 297
Mâthra-spenta, 140, 211, 334
Matthew, 5

Mâzanian dêvas, 190
Mazda, 88, 141, 144, 146, 148, 149, 151-153, 155, 156, 158-162, 164, 166-169, 172, 182, 186-190, 195, 211, 215, 218, 219, 254-256, 276, 334, 335
Mazdak-i Bâmdâdân, 321
Mazdakyahs, 15
Mazdâo, 301, 302
Mazdayasnian, 101, 105, 107, 127, 133, 171, 173, 174, 182, 201, 235-237, 240, 245, 253, 254, 295, 297, 319, 332-334, 380
Mazdayasnianism, 53
Mazdayasnians, 105, 109, 173, 212, 293, 318, 323-325, 330-333, 368, 381, 382, 384
Mazdian, 184
Mâzenderân, 190
Medes, 12
Medhâs, 301
Media, 14, 65
Median, 194
Mêdyômâh, 100
Mebrû, 361
Meiners, 20
Mercury, 200, 256
Meru, 286
Mesr, 364
Metres, 144, 145, 176, 196, 199, 237, 252, 253, 337
Mihirâpân-i Kaî-Khusrô, 56, 94-96, 109, 114
Mihir nyâyish, 224
Mihiryâr-i Mâhmâdân, 104
Mihir yasht, 43, 202-205, 273
Milky-way, 202, 217
Mînôkhird, 43, 310
Mînôk-i khard, 105
Mithra, 7, 177, 193, 194, 202-204, 207, 209, 211, 217, 224, 255, 259, 263, 272, 273, 316, 334; (promise) 164, 202, 238. 261, 322
Mithrô-drukhsh, 7, 202
Mitôkht, 391
Mitra, 6, 272, 273. 288
Mitrô, 357, 383, 387
Mobad, 108, 132
Mobads, 76, 77, 129, 197, 401
Mog, 14
Mohammed, 16
Mohammedan conquest, 54, 55, 81, 94, 107, 124; religion, 312; writers, 14-16, 84
Mohammedans, 12, 14, 16, 57, 124, 125
Monotheism, 149
Monotheists, 53
Mosaic, 4, 135
Moses, 135, 136, 299
Môuru, 203, 228
Mrigashiras, 182

Mujizàt-i Zartosht, 25
Mujmilu-t-tawârikh, 80
Mullà Bahman, 102
—— Fîrûz, 58, 102, 104, 114
Müller (Max), 285, 294
—— (M. J.), 29, 30, 121
Mumbaî, 108
Muncherjee Hormusjee Cama, 44
Munich, 29, 43, 50
Murdâd, 53
Musalmâns, 15, 107
Myâzd, 112, 363
Myazda, 139
Mylitta, 6, 197

Nâdar or Nâdûr nask, 128
Nairyô-sanha, 210, 256, 257, 274
Nakshatras, 182
Namâz, 364
Nâonhaithya, 272, 308, 337
Naráshañsa, 274
Naremanâo, 179
Narîmân Hôshang, 126
Nâsatya, 272, 288
Nask, 97, 125-135, 314, 351
Naskô, 181
Nasks, 54, 100, 101, 106, 121, 125, 135, 137; (contents of) 126-134
Nasupâka, 241
Nasush, 241, 317, 322, 327, 333, 381, 382
Nâwsâri, 45, 46, 57, 95, 99
Nebuchadnezzar, 3
Neryôsangh, 22, 26, 41, 42, 51, 55, 90, 104, 106, 120, 257, 274, 388
New Testament, 5
Nidhana, 284
Nihâvand, 79
Nikâdûm nask, 132
Nikhshâpûr, 106
Nineveh, 81
Nirang, 327; din, 400; i var, 349, 353
Nirangistân, 46, 47, 99, 107, 114, 397
Nirukta, 274, 285
Nirvâṇa, 263
Nisæa, 228
Nisâi, 228, 359
Niv (Nilu?), 364
Niv-Ardashîr, 110
Niyârum, 132
Non-Aryan, 363
—— Iran, 88
—— Zoroastrian, 46
Norris, 263
Nöshirvân, 101, 109-111
Nyâyish, 134, 139, 224

ODHIN, 180
Old Testament, 4-6, 20, 135, 175, 302, 304
Olshausen, 28, 30

Omanes, 10
Onkelos, 199
Ordeal, 322, 349, 353
Orion, 182
Ormasdes, 11
Ormazd, 53, 302
Ormizt, 13, 14
Oromasdes, 8, 9
Ossetic, 67
Oxford, 16, 29, 30, 47
Oxus, 293

PADA, 181
Padâm, 243, 365
Padashkhvâr, 363
Pahlav, 66, 78, 79
Pahlavânî, 66
Pahlavâs, 79
Pahlavi, *passim;* (explained), 20, 49, 78-86; âshîrvâd, 112, 113; characters, 86, 87, 356; commentaries, 355; dictionary, 61; farhang or glossary, 47-50, 59, 60, 112, 366; grammar, 33, 51, 59, 112; inscriptions, 80 (see *Sasanian*); literature, 93-113; manuscripts, 21, 30, 45, 46, 48, 56, 94-114; rare forms, 352, 370, 378, 382; rivâyat, 43, 46, 106; shâhnâmah, 56, 109, 391; suffix -*man*, 87; texts, 42, 43, 46, 47, 50, 55, 59, 60, 97-114; translations, 25, 26, 30, 34-36, 42, 68, 85, 94-98, 100, 113, 119, 120, 178, 179, 318-328, 338-393; Vendidad, 94-96, 99, 107, 113, 114, 338, 355-393; Visparad, 96, 97; Yasna, 96, 114, 338-354
Pairika, 195, 201, 228
Paitiparshtô-sravaṇhem, 142
Paitisha, 337
Paitish-hahya, 192
Pâjak, Pâjan, or Pâji nask, 128
Pâli, 143
Panchagavyam, 286
Pandnâmak-i Adarpâḍ Mâraspend, 47, 110, 111
—— Vajûrg-Mihir, 111
—— Zaratûsht, 111
Pâṇini, 76
Panjâb, 293
Panjastâ, 357
Pankti âsurî, 271, 272
Paoiryô-tkaêshô, 259
Paouruchista, 296
Pâpak, 78, 88, 90, 91, 111
Paradise (*pairi-daêza*), 5
Paraginah, 394, 403, 405
Parahaoma, 139, 191, 282, 406
Paris, 18, 21, 28-30, 108
Pârs, 195. See *Pairika*
Parmenides, 206
Parô-darsh, 245-247, 369, 371, 372

Parsi, *passim;* calendar, 57, 58, 112, 192, 357, 358; libraries, 34, 45, 57, 97, 99, 100, 102, 108, 109, 111, 126, 134; writers, 58-61, 181
Pârsî (language), 33, 34, 40, 66, 86, 93, 147; (grammar of), 33, 106
Parsiism, 167, 169
Parsis, *passim*
Parthava, 203
Parthia, 79, 203
Parthian, 49
Parthians, 54, 79, 80
Parthva, 79
Pashtû, 67
Pasush-haurva, 328
Patanjali, 76, 182
Patit, 364
Patita, 318, 327
Patit-i Adarpâd Mâraspend, 112
—— khûd, 112
Pât-khûsrô, 391
Pâtsrôb, 391
Paurvas, 182
Pausanias, 10, 11
Pâzand, 47, 51, 55, 60, 90, 92, 93, 100, 104-109, 112, 113, 147, 239, 348, 357, 359, 360, 377, 401, 407; (defined) 14, 33, 34, 85, 86, 122, 226, 262, 264; grammar, 51; passages, 182, 186, 231, 232, 235-239, 253-255, 316
Penôm, 11, 243, 394
Pentateuch, 135
Persepolis, 32, 54, 66, 80, 87, 124
Persia, 3, 14, 16, 32, 33, 54-57, 65, 66, 79-81, 90, 94, 95, 99, 102, 104, 106, 109, 114, 122, 176, 202, 282, 309
Persian, *passim;* calendar, 57; customs, 5-16; empire, 19, 66, 123, 135, 138, 175, 264; rivâyats, 106; words in Bible, 5
—— (ancient) 49, 66, 80, 81, 105, 206
Persians, 4-7, 10-15, 79, 80, 83, 84, 124, 136, 296, 299; (ancient) 19, 76, 80, 123, 138, 197
Persis, 80
Peshdâdian, 80
Peshô-tanu, 242
Peshwas, 279, 280
Pèshyôtan Râm Kâmdîn, 97
Photios, 12
Phraortes, 206
Pitaras, 207, 273
Plato, 11, 206, 207, 298, 300
Pleiades, 182
Pliny, 8, 123, 298, 299
Plutarch, 8, 9, 192
Polish, 273
Polytheism, 149
Pomegranate, 139, 251, 282, 378, 379, 384, 396, 399, 400, 407

Poona, 44, 46, 99, 126, 134, 267, 280
Portuguese, 108
Pôurushaspa, 179, 253, 254, 296, 333, 337, 380, 381, 391
Pouruta, 203
Pôryôdkèshân, 101
Prajâpati, 192, 275, 276
Prâkrit, 76
Prastâva, 283
Prastotâ, 283
Pratihâra, 284
Pratiharta, 283
Pratiprasthâtâ, 280
Pravargya, 270
Prayâjas, 281
Pûitika, 325, 326
Purâṇas, 135, 269, 276
Purâṇic, 262, 268
Purodâsha, 259, 281, 285
Pûshan, 273, 274
Pûtika, 282

Qâdaêna, 213
Qadîm reckoning, 57, 358
Qadmî. See *Kadmî*
Qaêtu, 153
Qâirizem, 203
Qandahâr. See *Kandahâr*
Qaniratha, 219, 256, 389
Qanvat, 201
Qarenô, 216
Qaretem, 139
Quatremère, 79

Raêthwishkara, 332
Ragha, 66, 188, 229, 300
Raghuvañsha, 182
Rai, 66, 79, 300, 362
Râk, 362
Râm, 214, 316, 324
Râma-qâstar, 193, 316
Râmâyaṇa, 276, 288
Râm yasht, 214, 275, 324
Rânyô-skereti, 159
Rapithwin, 397, 403
Rapithwina gâh, 159, 232
Rashnu, 204, 205, 207, 210, 322, 342
—— yasht, 205, 206
Rask, 21, 22
Rasmî reckoning, 57
Râspî, 193, 280, 394, 395, 403, 404, 407, 408
Rathantaram, 284
Rathwi, 193, 280, 332, 394
Ratôshtâîtî nask, 129
Ratu, 175, 187, 191, 192, 297, 327, 328
Ratus, 276
Ratushtâî nask, 129
Resurrection, 5, 162, 216, 311
Revelations, 311
Rhode, 20

Ribhus, 148
Richardson, 19
Rigveda, 39, 40, 143, 148, 258, 268-271, 274, 275, 278-280; (quoted) 145, 273, 274, 276, 277; (referred to) 178, 182, 183, 206, 268, 269, 273-275, 278, 279, 289, 291, 333
Riksha, 206
Rishí, 206, 269, 278
Rishis, 269, 272
Ritus, 271
Rivâyat, 100; (Pahlavi) 43, 46, 106
Rivâyats (Persian), 93, 106, 126-134
Rohiṇî, 182
Roman, 16, 79, 81; characters, 31, 41; type, 47, 51
Romans, 8, 79, 135, 137, 207, 295, 298, 301, 364
Rome, 202
Rudra, 269, 275
Rûm, 78
Russian, 273
Rustam, 277
Rustam-i Mihirâpân, 56, 94, 96, 127

SABEANS, 15
Sachau, 51
Sadarah, 25, 249, 367, 368
Sad-dar Bundahish, 43, 113
Sadis, 390
Sajastân, 66, 228. See *Sistân*.
Sakâdûm nask, 133
Sakzi, 66
Salsette, 25
Sâma, 277, 278
Sâman, 284
Sâmans, 283, 284
Samaritan Jews, 135
Samarkand, 203
Sâmas, 178, 278, 392
Sâmaveda, 73, 143, 258, 283
Sandal-wood, 378, 404, 408
Sandes, 11
Sañhitâ, 181
Sanskrit, *passim*; (classical) 22, 68-70, 72, 75, 76, 206, 289; manuscripts, 45; sîrôzah, 46; translation, 22, 26, 38, 41, 42, 46, 51, 55, 93, 100, 106, 120. See *Vedic*
Saoshyâns, 213, 313, 314
Saoshyañtô, 258, 294, 295, 301, 314
Sâsân, 111
Sasanian, 54, 59, 67, 78, 80, 81, 86, 87, 89, 90, 121, 122, 125, 302, 338, 358; characters, 59; inscriptions, 49, 59, 80, 82, 86-89; Pahlavi, 82, 86-90
Sasanians, 12, 15, 25, 33, 125, 299, 309
Satan, 12
Satâra, 280
Saugand-nâmah, 322

Sâurva, 272, 308, 337
Savahi, 256, 369, 389
Savana, 282, 283
Savitri, 269, 273
Sâyaṇa, 69
Scandinavians, 147, 180
Scythic, 79
Sedôsh, 390
Semitic, 5, 42, 49, 59, 81-86, 89, 90, 92; ideograms, 83-85, 90
Sêrjâns, 392
Sfend nask, 131
Shâhanshâhî reckoning, 57
Shâhnâmah, 80, 93, 190, 194, 202, 226, 277, 278, 298, 299, 361
Shahpûhar I., 86-88, 111
—— II., 84
Shahrastani, 15
Shahrivar, 9, 306, 358, 392
Shahryârji Dâdâbhâî, 111
Shânkhâyana grihyasûtra, 289
—— shrautasûtras, 182
Shapurji Edalji (Revd.), 111
Sharva, 272, 288
Shâstras, 135
Shatapatha brâhmaṇa, 206, 275
Shatrôvair, 101
Shatvêr, 357, 358, 382
Shâyast-lâ-shâyast, 56, 106, 351
Shâyast-nashâyast, 43
Shikand-gumânî, 46, 55, 60, 104, 105, 114
Shiva, 269, 272, 288, 308
Shloka, 144, 175, 212, 252
Shrotriyas, 289
Shruti, 307
Shukra, 278
Sîmaêzhi, 213
Simakos, 12
Sîmrâ, 101
Sind, 361
Sindhavas, 205, 230
Sirius, 9
Sîrozah, 10, 46, 98, 134, 139, 225, 404
Sistân, 94, 356, 361. See *Sajastân*.
Slavonian, 65
Slavonic, 273
Smṛitis, 260
Sogdiana, 66, 203
Soma, 22, 70, 168, 176, 180, 182, 185, 258, 259, 269, 272, 278, 280-283, 289, 291, 292
Sôshâns, 101, 341, 349, 350, 374
Sôshyâns, 254, 313, 388
Sôshyañtô, 174, 177, 209, 217
Spendarmad, 306, 339, 340, 347, 349, 350, 357, 375, 377, 382, 383, 400
Spend nask, 131, 351
Spendyâd, 391
Spenjaghra, 336, 390

Spenta ârmaiti, 191, 305, 306, 312, 333
Speñtâ-mainyû. See *Gâtha*
Speñtô mainyush, 24, 179, 187, 189, 304, 305
Spêtos (Gpêtos?), 364
Spiegel, 29-31, 33-38, 41-44, 51, 95-97, 106, 108, 323, 338, 347, 352, 355, 367-369, 375, 384
Spitama, 36, 138, 166, 176, 177, 188, 209, 258, 263, 296, 297, 301
Spitâmân, 355, 367, 369, 371, 377, 380, 381, 384, 387, 392
Spitama Zarathushtra, 35, 136, 138, 141, 146-148, 165, 186, 190, 207, 209, 212, 218, 223, 227, 235, 236, 244-246, 250, 253-255, 257-264, 292-295, 298-300, 302, 305, 310-317, 319, 320, 327-330, 334
Sraosha, 155-160, 184, 189, 193, 204, 205, 210, 307
Sraoshâvareza, 245, 280, 327, 332, 369
Sraoshô-charana, 251
Srâvay, 143
Srît, 392
Srôsh, 141, 174, 189, 191, 195, 200, 245-249, 255, 280, 307, 308, 334, 336, 340, 369-375, 383, 390, 403, 408
—— bâj, 164
—— yasht, 46, 189-191, 200, 257, 307, 369
—— —— hâdôkht, 98, 205
Srôshô-charanâm, 371, 375, 376, 378, 379
Srvara, 178
Stâyishn-î drôn, 111
Strabo, 4, 10
Stûdgar nask, 126
Stûd-yasht nask, 134
Stuttgart, 97, 99, 107
Sûd-hômand, 381
Sûdkar nask, 107, 126
Sughdha, 203, 228
Sughdi, 66
Suicide, 313
Sukuruna, 328
Sura, 269
Surâk, 364
Surat, 17, 45, 48, 57, 59, 100, 102
Sûrîk, 358
Syriac, 31, 80

Taittirîya brâhmana, 182
—— sañhitâ, 278
Takhma urupa, 214
Takht, 394, 397, 399-401, 405
Talmud, 135, 226
Talmudic literature, 136
Tâmûk or Tânak, 109
Tanâpûhar, 322, 369, 374-377

Tanuperethas, 242
Tanûra, 5
Tapristân, 363
Tauru, 52, 337
Tauruna, 328
Teheran, 95, 109, 300, 338, 359, 364
Teispes, 298
Ten admonitions, 110
Teutonic, 52, 65, 148, 287
Thais, 124
Themis, 205
Theodoros, 12
Theopompos, 7, 8, 33, 312
Thomas, 87, 88
Thorah, 135
Thraêtaona, 178, 198, 202, 215, 216, 230, 275, 277, 278
Thrita, 178, 257, 277, 392
Tighrish, 200
Tîr, 256
—— yasht, 200
Tishtar, 9, 256, 389
Tishtrya, 9, 194, 200, 201, 263, 279
Traitana, 277, 278
Trimûrti, 288
Trishtubh, 145
Trita, 275, 277, 278
Trojan war, 298
Turanian, 361
Turkish, 31
Turnour, 123
Tychsen, 20

Udaka shânta, 281
Udgâtâ, 283, 284
Udgîtha, 283
Udra, 242
Udumbara, 283
'Ulamâ-i islâm, 43
Upadrava, 284
Upasad, 270, 271, 281
Uranos, 272
Urô, 360
Ursa major, 206
Urupi, 329
Urvâ, 228
Urvâkhshaya, 178
Urvâuô, 168
Urvarâm, 396, 399-402, 407
Urvâsna, 251
Urvatad-narô, 235
Urvâtas, 151
Usaghanas, 213
Ushahina gâh, 159, 369
Ushâm sûrâm, 245
Ushanas, 278, 279
Ushidarenem, 216
Ushidhâo, 216
Ushnih âsurî, 271
Ushtavaiti. See *Gâtha*
Usikhsh, 289
Uzayêirina gâh, 159

Vâchak aêchand, 110
Vadhaghana, 254
Vaê-i vatar, 323
— veh, 324
Vaćkereta, 228
Vaêtha nask, 46
Vahirâm-i varjâvand, 107, 110
Vahishta, 311
Vahishtem ahûm, 186
Vahisht-mânsrah nask, 127
Vahishtôishti. See *Gâtha*
Vâhrâm, 383
Vaivasvata, 277
Vajarkard-i dînî, 43, 59, 100, 110, 112, 126
Vâjasaneyi saṅhitâ, 182
Vajûrg-mihir, 110, 111
Valkhash, 54
Vâmadeva hymns, 148
Vanant, 217; yasht, 217
Vandîdâd, 133. See *Vendidad*
Vapâ, 285
Varasa, 139, 395, 397, 399, 400, 402, 403
Varâza, 214
Varena, 230, 363
Vareshau, 213
Varshtamânsar nask, 127
Varuna, 53, 268, 272, 273
Vasavas, 275
Vashatkâra, 275
Vashtî nask, 130
Vasishthas, 178
Vayu, 274, 275, 324, 334
Vâyu, 214, 274
Vayush, 214, 215
Vazagha, 329
Vâzishta, 336, 390
Vazra, 205, 217
Veda, 20, 41, 53, 70, 73, 170, 180, 274, 276-278, 294
Vedângas, 181
Vedas, 21, 22, 27, 39, 40, 69-71, 77, 135, 138, 155, 182, 193, 205, 206, 213, 216, 230, 260, 267-269, 273-280, 287, 289, 291, 299, 307
Vedic, 27, 40, 44, 69, 70, 77, 145, 176, 192, 194, 214, 270, 272-276, 278-280, 284, 288, 292, 294, 308; hymns, 28, 137, 143, 206, 272, 274, 276, 278, 287-289, 291, 294; Sanskrit, 40, 68, 70, 72, 75, 147
Vêhijakîk, 58
Veh river, 361
Vehrkâna, 229
Vendidad, 22-24, 28, 30, 34, 35, 37, 38, 43, 46, 50-52, 58, 60, 61, 94-96, 99, 107, 109, 113, 114, 127, 133-135, 137, 139, 141, 142, 199, 211, 225-257, 260-264, 268, 277, 292, 294-297, 303, 305, 315-338, 355, 374, 383, 384, 397; sâdah, 22, 28, 30,

46, 52, 235, 336; (Pahlavi) 46, 56, 61, 127, 336, 338, 355-393; (Sanskrit), 46; xii. (modern Pahl.), 95, 96
Venus, 197, 278
Verchrân, 389
Verethraghna, 213, 275, 288
Verezêna, 153
Vibanga, 336
Vîdadhafshu, 256, 389
Vienna, 34, 95-97
Vîk-dêv-dâd nask, 133
Vîk-shêdâ-dâd, 133
Vish-haurva, 328
Vishṇu, 288
—— purâṇa, 213
Vishtâsp, 101, 109, 130, 340, 391
Vishtâspa, 146, 156, 158, 167, 298, 299
Vishtâspâd, 130
Vishtâsp nask, 139
—— sâstô, 130, 134
—— shâh, 130
—— yasht, 97, 224
Visparad, 22, 30, 36, 38, 41, 43, 51, 96, 97, 134, 135, 139, 141, 142, 191-194, 260, 397; with Pahlavi, 46
Vivanghana, 231-234
Vivanhâo, 177, 277
Vîzareshô, 255, 387, 390
Vizu, 329
Vôghnô, 381
Vohû-gaona, 251
—— kereti, 251
—— khshathra. See *Gâtha*
Vohumanô, 9, 10, 151, 158, 167, 171, 190, 222, 255, 302-306, 308, 320, 333, 335, 339-341, 344, 345, 347, 349-351, 353, 354, 357, 358, 366, 382, 384, 388, 393
Vohunazga, 328
Vohunemaṅh, 213
Vologeses, 54
Vouru-bareshti, 256, 389
—— jareshti, 256, 389
—— kasha, 197, 200, 201, 205, 208, 256, 279, 320, 325-327, 336, 388, 392
Vritra, 275, 278, 279
Vṛitrahâ, 213, 275, 288

WEBER, 271
West, 50, 51, 106
Westergaard, 24, 32-34, 36-39, 44, 47, 51, 60, 77, 87, 97, 105, 114, 139, 140, 194, 217, 223, 308, 355, 367, 369, 409
Western India, 16-18, 33, 44, 55
Wilson (Rev. Dr.), 32, 45
—— (Prof. H. H.), 213
Windischmann, 43, 47, 105
Wodan's heer, 180
Wonders of the land of Sistân, 109

XANTHOS of Lydia, 298
Xenophon, 4
Xerxes, 124

Yâdkâr-i Zarîrân, 109
Yajamâna, 270
Yajishn, 139, 281. See *Yazishn*
Yâjnavalkya, 286
Yajurveda, 143, 206, 259, 271, 272, 275, 278
Yama râjâ, 276, 277
Yasht, 174-177, 185, 189, 194
Yashts, 6, 14, 38, 43, 51, 98, 134, 139, 224, 262-264, 294, 295; (translated) 175-185, 189-191, 194-217; (Pahl. translations) 98
Yâska, 274, 285
Yasna, 22, 23, 26, 27, 30, 31, 34, 36-38, 41, 43, 46, 47, 50, 51, 55, 58, 97-99, 101, 109, 134, 135, 137, 139-143, 146, 171, 174, 175, 177, 190, 191, 249, 258-260, 394; (described) 139-142; haptanhaiti, 140-142, 170-172, 190, 258, 259; (later) 140, 142, 171, 174-191, 259, 260, 262, 264, 296; (older) 73, 140-142, 174, 242, 296, 300; (Pahlavi) 56, 96, 114, 120, 338-354
Yathâ ahû vairyô, 50, 54, 98, 126-134, 174, 252, 374, 375, 380, 382, 385, 397-399, 401-405, 407-409; text, 125; translation, 141
Yaxartes, 293
Yazads, 112, 345, 403
Yazamaidê, 171, 186
Yazatas, 194, 200, 272, 288
Yazd, 114
Yazdah, 14
Yazdân, 194
Yazishn, 345, 365. See *Yajishn*
Yênhê hâtâm, 98, 141, 174, 248, 374, 375
Yima, 23, 177, 202, 214-216, 226, 230-235, 257, 277, 392; khshaêta, 177, 198, 276, 277
Yôishtô yô Fryananãm, 107

Zâbulistân, 66
Zâd-sparam-i Yûdân-damân, 102
Zairicha, 52, 337
Zamyâd yasht, 216
Zand, 85. See *Zend*
Zand-âkâs, 104
Zandîk, 108
Zaota, 193, 280, 282, 332, 378
Zaothra, 139, 189, 214, 251, 281, 335, 336, 397
Zarades, 11
Zaradusht, 14, 16
Zarastrades, 12, 296

Zarathushtra, 24, 35, 36, 41, 53, 74, 101, 121, 122, 138, 146-151, 153, 154, 156, 157, 161, 163, 165-170, 173, 175-177, 179, 185, 188, 189, 195-198, 202, 207-209, 211, 212, 214, 215, 218, 219, 222, 223, 230, 231, 233, 238, 243-246, 249, 250, 252-264, 276, 291, 294-297, 300, 303, 307, 325, 326, 333-338, 346, 365; Spitama, 148, 170, 172, 202, 211
Zarathushtras, 226
Zarathushtrian, 188, 211, 326, 327, 334
Zarathushtrôtemô, 142, 193, 258, 261, 296, 297
Zaratûsht, 101, 107, 111, 112, 127, 130, 132, 338, 344, 351, 354, 355, 362, 364-367, 369, 371, 377, 379-388, 391-393
—— nâmah, 43
Zardosht, 296
Zaremaya, 222
Zarbûndâd, 321
Zarouam, 12
Zarvan, 13
—— akarana, 12, 15, 24, 309
Zâûli, 66
Zavârish, 84, 85
Zemaka, 321
Zend, 19, 21, 47, 50, 52, 124, 125, 134, 135, 177, 239 (see *Avesta*); (defined) 14, 15, 67, 68, 119-122, 226, 262, 309; (original) 174, 177, 227, 229, 235, 362; (passages noted) 207-210, 212, 213, 227-230, 232-238, 250, 253
Zend-Avesta, 18, 36, 68, 119, 120, 123, 194, 195, 224, 257, 262, 264, 267, 268, 271-280, 287, 288, 292, 294, 298, 299, 308-310, 312, 314, 315, 409
Zendik, 14, 15, 309
Zendist, 235
Zend-Pahlavi glossary, 47-49, 99
Zeruan, 13, 14
Zervanites, 15
Zeus, 6, 8, 11, 53, 287
Zohak, 183, 198
Zor, 395, 397, 398, 400-403, 406, 407
Zoroaster, 3, 9, 11, 19, 29, 46, 51, 123, 137, 138, 171, 216, 296; (his age) 15, 298, 299; (his writings) 123, 257
Zoroastrian, *passim*; studies, 43
Zoroastrianism, 44, 103, 346
Zoroastrians, 14, 23, 46, 54, 57, 74, 121, 123, 125, 168, 170, 258, 262, 287, 290, 303
Zota, 394, 395, 403-409
Zvârish, 42

www.ingramcontent.com/pod-product-compliance
Lightning Source LLC
Chambersburg PA
CBHW021417300426
44114CB00010B/539